CLEMENT OF ALEXANDRIA
AND A SECRET GOSPEL OF MARK

CLEMENT OF ALEXANDRIA
AND A
SECRET GOSPEL OF MARK

Morton Smith

HARVARD UNIVERSITY PRESS

CAMBRIDGE, MASSACHUSETTS

1973

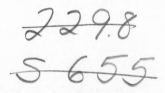

Library of Congress Catalog Card Number 72–148938
SBN 674–13490–7

Printed in the United States of America

This book was written for
Arthur Darby Nock and is
dedicated to his memory

Contents

Preface

The Monastery of Mar Saba is located in the Judean desert, a few miles southeast of Jerusalem. In its tower library there are a number of Greek manuscripts and early printed books containing manuscript supplements. When I visited Jerusalem in the summer of 1958 His Beatitude Benedict, Patriarch of Jerusalem, kindly gave me permission to spend a fortnight at the monastery, study this material, and publish it. Let me begin this book with my sincere thanks to His Beatitude, to Archimandrite Seraphim, the Hegoumenos of Mar Saba, and to the brothers of the monastery. My greatest debt of thanks, to the late Custodian of the Holy Sepulchre, Archimandrite Kyriakos, is one which can no longer be paid.

The manuscripts of Mar Saba proved, on examination, to be mostly modern. This was no surprise, since it was well known that the rich collection of ancient manuscripts, for which the monastery was famous in the early nineteenth century, had been transferred to Jerusalem for safekeeping in the eighteen-sixties. Little seems to have been left behind at that time except scraps and printed books. But in subsequent years there has been a gradual accumulation of other manuscript material, both new and old. During my stay I was able to examine, label, and describe some seventy items. Besides these there were some twenty distinct manuscripts and two large folders full of scraps which I did not have time to study. My notes on the collection have been printed in an article, "Ἑλληνικὰ χειρόγραφα ἐν τῇ Μονῇ τοῦ ἁγίου Σάββα," translated by Archimandrite Constantine Michaelides, in the periodical of the Patriarchate of Jerusalem, *ΝΕΑ ΣΙΩΝ* 52 (1960) 110ff, 245ff. To this article readers must be referred for a description of the manuscript material as a whole.

Among the items examined was one, number 65 in my published notes, of which the manuscript element consisted of two and a half pages of writing at the back of an old printed book. The writing begins with the cross which Greek monastic scribes commonly set down first of all. Then comes a heading, "From the letters of the most holy Clement, the author of the Stromateis; to Theodore." Then comes the text of part of a letter, certainly not complete, since it breaks off in the middle of a sentence. The content of this text is so surprising that if Clement (who wrote at the end of the second century) really was its author the consequences for the history of the early Christian Church and for New Testament criticism are revolutionary.

The present book is an attempt to describe this document and to set forth the major

elements which must be considered in judging it. The first chapter describes the manuscript. The second studies the relation of the letter to the commonly acknowledged works of Clement. The similarities and differences are examined in a word-by-word commentary; then the results thus attained are summed up and other, general, considerations added. This examination leads to the conclusion that the letter is correctly attributed to Clement, and this conclusion is made the point of departure for the third chapter, which studies the letter's quotations from a secret Gospel it attributes to Mark. After considering the external evidence relevant to this Gospel, the study proceeds, by way of a detailed commentary on the quoted texts, to establish, first, their stylistic, then, their structural relations to the canonical Gospels. The fourth chapter deals with the historical value of both letter and Gospel, especially with their importance as evidence concerning the secret side of early Christianity. A final chapter presents what little evidence can be found concerning the history of the text of both Gospel and letter, and indicates some of the hypotheses with which this evidence may plausibly be filled out. Important bodies of evidence, too large for presentation in the text, have been added in a series of appendices. Appendix B, in particular, contains the complete dossier of Carpocrates and his followers, who played an important role in the history of the new Gospel material. For convenience of reference, the photographs of the manuscript, with facing transcriptions and translations, have been placed at the very end of the volume.

My thanks are due to the Columbia University Council for Research in the Social Sciences and to the Department of History of Columbia University for grants which helped me in the preparation of the present work. Mr. Stanley Isser verified the references throughout the first four hundred pages of the manuscript, Mr. Levon Avdoyan gave me much help in the preparation of the indices, and Professor Jacob Neusner of Brown University read the entire text and made many corrections; I sincerely thank them all. Many different scholars have helped me in different aspects of the work; my indebtedness to them is recorded and my thanks are offered at the beginnings of the chapters with which they have been concerned. I thank Mrs. Elisabeth J. Munck, Professor Zeph Stewart, and Mrs. Mailice Wifstrand for permission to publish quotations from the letters of the late Professors Johannes Munck, A. D. Nock, and Albert Wifstrand. I am grateful to the Akademie Verlag, the British Museum, the British and Foreign Bible Society, and Usines Brepols for permissions to reprint sections of their publications. Finally, I am indebted to the Harvard University Press for its consent to publish and care in publishing this difficult manuscript.

I shall of course want to follow the discussion of this text; I therefore hope that scholars who write about it will be so kind as to send copies of their publications to me at the Department of History, Columbia University, N.Y. 10027, U.S.A.

Morton Smith

New York, 1970

CLEMENT OF ALEXANDRIA
AND A SECRET GOSPEL OF MARK

ONE

The Manuscript

The pages on which the text is written are reproduced in actual size on Plates I–III. The book in which they are found is an exemplar of Isaac Voss's edition of the *Epistulae genuinae S. Ignatii Martyris* (Amsterdam: J. Blaeu, 1646). Its front cover and title page have been lost, but Voss's name is given at the end of the dedication; I was able to identify the edition by photographing the first preserved page (p. 2) and the last numbered page (p. 318) and comparing these photographs with the corresponding pages of complete copies. The manuscript was written over both sides of the last page (which was blank) of the original book and over half the recto of a sheet of binder's paper. The binding was of that heavy, white paperboard so often found on books bound in Venice during the seventeenth and eighteenth centuries. From the remains of it, I should guess that it was approximately contemporary with the book itself. Therefore the date of the book, plus about fifteen or twenty years (1660 or 1665), may be taken as the date *after* which the manuscript insertion was probably made.

As for the date *at* which it was probably made, that can be settled only by dating the hand. For assistance in this my thanks are due to A. Angelou and C. Dimaras of the Greek National Foundation, the late A. Delatte of the University of Liège, G. Kournoutos of the Ministry of Education of Greece, M. Manousakas of the Archives of the Academy of Athens, the late A. D. Nock of Harvard University, M. Richard of the Institut de Recherche et d'Histoire des Textes, V. Scouvaras of the Gymnasium of Volos, G. Soulis of the Dumbarton Oaks Library, and P. Topping of the University of Cincinnati. All these scholars were so kind as to examine photographs of the manuscript and give me independent opinions about the date of the hand. Their opinions varied from the late seventeenth or early eighteenth century (Kournoutos and Manousakas) to the late eighteenth or early nineteenth (Delatte, Scouvaras, Topping), but all would agree on an eighteenth-century date as possible. Delatte and Scouvaras, while thinking it possible that the writer may have written in the nineteenth century as an old man, think it certain that the hand was formed in the eighteenth century. Kournoutos and Manousakas think it all but impossible that the writing was done in the nineteenth century. The consensus, therefore, would date the hand about 1750, plus or minus about fifty years.

The hand is generally agreed to be that of an experienced writer and a scholar. The

small size of the letters together with the rapidity at which they were evidently written, the remodeling of the letters to fit the flow of the hand, their unusually even alignment and the tasteful, but economical, placing of the text on the page, all testify to the writer's experience. He shows considerable skill in observance of a right-hand margin and, like many writers of the eighteenth century, fills out his short lines with two dots (:) to keep the margin straight. His tiny writing, too, is an eighteenth-century trait and one closely connected with scholarship. That century produced innumerable manuscripts of classical Greek texts with interlinear translations into modern Greek or with scholia in hands so minute that it is impossible to read them without a glass.

That the writer was a scholar is also shown by his spelling. Although confusion of the various vowels sounded as $\bar{e}$ was common in his time, he has only once fallen into it ($\dot{\epsilon}\xi\alpha\nu\tau\lambda\hat{\eta}\tau\alpha\iota$, for $\dot{\epsilon}\xi\alpha\nu\tau\lambda\epsilon\hat{\iota}\tau\alpha\iota$, II.9,[1] unless $\dot{\epsilon}\xi\acute{\eta}\nu\tau\lambda\eta\tau\alpha\iota$ is to be read). He always writes iota subscript and writes it as subscript. He usually writes the coronis. He frequently distinguishes grave from acute accents, and does so correctly; there is only one misplaced accent in the whole text ($\beta\lambda\alpha\sigma\phi\eta\mu\acute{o}\nu$ for $\beta\lambda\acute{\alpha}\sigma\phi\eta\mu\nu$, II.7), and this is probably due to haste rather than ignorance, as is his use of $\acute{o}$ for $\ddot{o}$ in the preceding line and his omission of the accent of $\kappa\alpha\acute{\iota}$ at the ends of lines (I.2,7 and III.11). That he consistently accentuates $M\acute{\alpha}\rho\kappa o\varsigma$ rather than $M\hat{\alpha}\rho\kappa o\varsigma$ reflects the usage common in the seventeenth and eighteenth centuries. His most frequent fault is one to which modern Greeks are especially liable—failure to notice rough breathings. He has written what are probably smooth breathings in four places where rough breathings should have appeared (I.23,26, II.21,22), and he once has $o\dot{\upsilon}\kappa$ instead of $o\dot{\upsilon}\chi$ before a rough breathing (III.13). These errors do not prove that the manuscript he copied was incorrect in these points; nor does the usual correctness of his spelling prove that it was generally correct. He probably copied by reading the phrases and then repeating them as he wrote them down. Therefore it is not surprising that what he wrote should sometimes reflect either his knowledge or his pronunciation, rather than the reading of the text he wăs copying.

That he was a scholar is shown also by the shapes of his letters. The whole style of the hand shows the influence of the Greek typography of western Europe. I am indebted to A. Angelou for the observation that the shape of the *nu*, in particular, is characteristically western. Western influence, however, is no proof of western origin, and here the basic hand, on which the influence has been exercised, seems to be native Greek. Most of the larger and many of the smaller Greek monasteries stocked their libraries, during the seventeenth and eighteenth centuries, with western editions of the Church fathers, and the type used in these editions perceptibly influenced monastic hands. Professor Scouvaras has produced an eighteenth-century ecclesiastical document in a native Greek hand strikingly similar to that of our manuscript. (See Plate IV.) A number of the *nu*s, in particular, are practically identical. Since Scouvaras' document is an autograph codex of the Oecumenical Patriarch Callinicus III and was written about 1760 in the Phanariot hand which

---

1. References in this form are to the plates at the end of the volume and to the lines of the text as shown on the plates.

had been formed in Constantinople shortly before that time, we may suppose with some probability that the writer of the present letter had been trained in the Patriarchal Academy in Constantinople.

Further proof of the writer's scholarship is his familiarity with many of the older Greek manuscript abbreviations and ligatures. A list of all his abbreviations and a number of his more drastic ligatures will be found in Appendix A; it contains perhaps slightly more of these forms than would normally be found in a manuscript of the mid-eighteenth century. The writer's usage of these special forms is universally correct, though sometimes ambiguous. The use of a flourish to indicate both the smooth breathing and the circumflex reduces both -οῦ and οὐ to ſ or ſ ; the circumflex combined with the rough breathing is sometimes no more florid than without (ᴑᴜ = οῦ or -οῦ). In general, the hand is remarkably cursive.

As the manuscript progresses the cursive character of the hand becomes more marked. The writer was evidently in a hurry. It may be that lack of time forced him to break off, as he did, in the midst of a page and of a sentence; on the other hand, the text he was copying may itself have been a fragment and have broken off at this point. The copyist's haste appears unmistakably in the greater size and sweep of the letters at the end of his text, by comparison with those at the beginning. It is shown also by a number of minor mistakes of writing besides those already mentioned. ταταυτοῦ, probably for τὰ αὐτοῦ, in I.19 may reflect uncertainty rather than haste, and ἀποθνῄσκων written over ἀποθαγῳγ (?) in I.28 may be a deliberate correction of the reading of the manuscript he was copying. But in II.20 τῶν seems to have been omitted by haplography after αὐτῶν (though such omission of the article is not uncommon in later Greek prose), and on III the curious υς ligature at the end of the first word probably results from correction of a minor slip of the pen, immediately after it was made; the π of ἐπί in III.8 shows another slip of the pen, uncorrected, and the ſ of ἔστιν in III.17 shows yet another, caught and corrected at once. For the most part, however, the text is amazingly correct, especially considering the small size and obvious speed of the writing. These characteristics prove it to be a copy of some earlier manuscript. That anyone in the seventeenth or eighteenth centuries should have written such Greek at such speed as an original composition is incredible.

From all these observations taken together it would seem that our text was copied probably in the eighteenth century, by a monk (he began his work with a cross) who pronounced his words in modern Greek fashion but had an excellent knowledge of patristic Greek. His handwriting had been influenced by his study of patristic texts in western editions which were presumably available to him in his monastery and had probably come by way of Venice. He was interested not only in patristics, but also in the beginnings of western critical scholarship, for the book into which he copied our text—Voss's edition of the genuine epistles of Ignatius—was no mere reprint of a standard author, but one of the most advanced works of scholarly criticism of its time.

Since the copyist was a scholar, it is impossible to decide how far his copy owes its amazing orthographic correctness to him. For the same reason it is difficult to

3

say whether the avoidance of hiatus by elision, when it is thus avoided, is due to the copyist or to the original. Admittedly the copyist was in a hurry while he copied, but he might previously have studied the text and inserted minor corrections. For the time being we shall assume that his corrections, if any, were minor. With this assumption we proceed to the primary test for authenticity—examination of the wording.

TWO

The Letter

I. TEXT AND COMMENTARY

The following commentary illustrates the relationship between the style of the letter and that of the generally accepted works of Clement of Alexandria. However, it does not present the parallels to extremely common expressions, which could be paralleled from any good Greek author of the period; these seemed insignificant for the question of authenticity. Similarly, when Clement has provided plentiful parallels, the usage of other authors has not been cited. The discussion of points of content, likewise, has been limited as far as possible to the presentation of evidence relevant

5

to the question of authenticity. The work for this chapter was completed in 1961, at which time I turned from Clement to study the Gospel fragment. Since that time I have made only minor changes in the text and have not attempted to take account of recent publications on Clement, of which I should mention as particularly valuable A. Méhat's *Étude*. I have not been persuaded by P. Nautin's attempt to redate the events of Clement's later life (*Lettres*, 139f) though the traditional dates are certainly dubious (Barnes, *Origen*, 314 f.)

The first draft of the following commentary on the text of the letter was read by E. Bickerman, Columbia University; W. M. Calder III, Columbia; H. Chadwick, Oxford; B. Einarson, Chicago; L. Früchtel, Ansbach; R. Grant, Chicago; M. Hadas, Columbia; W. Jaeger, Harvard; G. Lampe, Cambridge; C. Mondésert, Lyon; J. Munck, Aarhus; A. D. Nock, Harvard; J. Reumann, Lutheran Theological Seminary, Philadelphia; M. Richard, Paris; C. Richardson, Union Theological Seminary, New York; R. Schippers, Amsterdam; W. Völker, Mainz; and A. Wifstrand, Lund. I am indebted not only for their kindness in examining the text and expressing their opinions on its authenticity, but also for a great many corrections and suggestions in matters of detail. I sincerely thank them for the help they have given me. My thanks are due also to a number of scholars who have commented on particular passages and whose help is, at those passages, acknowledged. All substantial comments are included in square brackets and followed by the initials of the commentator; the initials are explained in the list of abbreviations at the end of the volume. Bracketed comments are not exact quotations except when set within quotation marks; I have often taken the liberty to summarize or to translate, the more so because the untimely deaths of a number of the commentators have made it impossible for them to approve small rectifications in the wording of their statements. Moreover, besides the bracketed comments, many minor corrections have been accepted and incorporated in grateful silence.

I.1[1]

+ ἐκ τῶν ἐπιστολῶν

ἐκ τῶν ἐπιστολῶν. Citations from Clement's letters appear in the *Sacra Parallela* attributed, perhaps rightly, to John of Damascus, who worked at Mar Saba from about 715 to 750 (Beck, 477, 482). Among the lemmata to them given by Stählin, III.223f, are Κλήμεντος Στρωματέως ἐκ τῆς κ̄ᾱ ἐπιστολῆς and Κλήμεντος Στρωματέως ἐπιστολή. Ishodad of Merv reportedly refers to a writing, possibly a letter, against heretics who rejected marriage, and such were the Carpocratians; but Stählin, III.lxff, thinks the reference merely an inference based on Eusebius, *HE* III.30, where the passages cited come from the *Stromateis*.

1. Numerals refer to plate and line. The dot between the two numbers is located over the point at which the new line begins.

I.2

τοῦ ἁγιωτάτου Κλήμεντος τοῦ στρωματέως· Θεοδώρῳ. καλῶς ἐποίησας ἐπιστομίσας

τοῦ ἁγιωτάτου. Clement is cited as τοῦ ἁγιωτάτου in collections of patristic material attributed to Maximus the Confessor, fl. 620–650 (Beck, 437); citations, III.219f.[2] For Maximus he is also μακαριώτατος (III.220; cf. Osborn, *Philosophy*, 190, 191 n1); for Anastasius of Sinai, ἱερὸς καὶ ἀποστολικός (*ibid.*); and for the *Chronicon Paschale*, ὁσιώτατος (III.216). Already, in his own lifetime, Alexander of Jerusalem called him μακάριος and ἱερός (Eus., *HE* VI.11.6; 14.9). The use of ἁγιώτατος for ecclesiastical personages appears in Athanasius (Müller, *Lexicon* s.v.) as a development from the earlier Christian usage of the absolute (Williger, 84ff).

τοῦ στρωματέως. See above, on ἐπιστολῶν. Also used by Maximus (III.220.5,12; 224.15), John Moschus (III.196.21), codex Laura 184 B (III.218.15), and Palladius, *HL* 60; also (according to Cedrednus) by Sextus Julius Africanus (about A.D. 225). Africanus, although a friend of Origen, placed Clement's activity in the time of Commodus, 180–192 (Routh, II.307).

Θεοδώρῳ. Unknown? The name was common in Jewish and thence in Christian circles and could easily have been that of a correspondent in Palestine. Clement, before coming to Alexandria, had studied in Palestine under a teacher of Jewish ancestry (II.8.23) whom he listed among those who had received the Christian tradition by straight descent from Peter, James, John, and Paul (Eus., *HE* V.11.5). Clement was also a friend of a subsequent bishop of Jerusalem (Eus., *HE* VI.11.6; 13.3; 14.9), to whom he dedicated a book against Judaizing heretics or Jews (Photius, 111). He may have had other connections in the city.

καλῶς ἐποίησας. As the beginning of a letter, with the following aorist participle, Libanius, *Epistulae* (ed. R. Foerster, Leipzig, 1903–1927, vols. X,XI) 51,679, etc. Baur, I.584, lists 8 instances, including one from Athanasius and two from Basil. [This is, of course, a common formula in papyrus letters of the period. C.H.R.]

ἐπιστομίσας. I.187.8, τοὺς χρωμένους αὐτῇ ⟨αἰσχρολογίᾳ⟩ ἐπιστομιστέον; again I.192.22. This is perhaps a reminiscence of Titus 1.11 where pseudo-Paul declares that Jewish libertine teachers should be shut up (οὓς δεῖ ἐπιστομίζειν). Clement cited Titus 1.10 (II.27.14f), in an attack on libertine heretics, and Titus 1.12 (II.37. 25ff) in an attack on Hellenizers. ἐπιστομίζω normally has for its object a person or an animal—so always in Clement—but it is used with an inanimate object often in Philo, of the passions, and in Josephus, *AJ* XVII.251: τὴν Ἰουδαίων νεωτεροποιίαν ἐπιστο-μιοῦντες.

2. Hereafter, numerals thus given refer to the Stählin edition of Clement by volume, page, and, if a third number is given, line.

I.3

τὰς ἀρρήτους διδασκαλίας τῶν Καρποκρατιανῶν. οὗτοι γὰρ οἱ προφητευθέντες "ἀστέρες πλανῆται,"

ἀρρήτους. I.17.5, of the Eleusinian mysteries, emphasizing their sexual symbolism.
I.17.21, of the worshipers of Dionysus, μόρια ἄρρητα ὡς ἀληθῶς ὑπ᾽ αἰσχύνης ἀναισχύντως
σέβουσιν.

διδασκαλίας. I.47.3, αὗται τῶν συμπορνευόντων ὑμῖν Θεῶν αἱ διδασκαλίαι.

τῶν Καρποκρατιανῶν. Referred to as a sect (αἵρεσις), II.197.27; 200.5. (For Carpocrates and the question whether he or Epiphanes founded the sect, see below, II.3–4;
for testimonia and literature, Appendix B.) The letter agrees with Clement not
only in its general moral judgment of the Carpocratians, but also in identifying them
as the heretics attacked in the Epistle of Jude and in associating them—probably—
with the Nicolaïtans; see the commentary on the following lines. The letter also agrees
with Irenaeus' report (Harvey, I.20.3 = Stieren, I.25.5) that the Carpocratians
claimed to be the possessors of a secret apostolic tradition which justified their libertine
practices, τὸν Ἰησοῦν λέγοντες ἐν μυστηρίῳ τοῖς μαθηταῖς αὐτοῦ καὶ ἀποστόλοις κατ᾽ ἰδίαν
λελαληκέναι, etc. Liboron, 46f, conjectured that this claim was based on Mk. 4.11; the
present letter confirms at least the conjectured relationship of the sect to Mark.

οὗτοι γάρ. II.195.10, οὗτοι, φασίν, εἰσὶν οἱ ἐκ γενετῆς εὐνοῦχοι (initial, as in the letter);
II.178.14, οὗτοι γὰρ οἱ (initial).

οἱ προφητευθέντες. II.135.24, Christ is ὁ ὑπὸ νόμου προφητευθείς; cf. I.249.23.

ἀστέρες πλανῆται. Jude 13. Jude is cited by Clement (I.262.19ff; II.200. 25ff) where it
is said to refer to the Carpocratians, as it does in this letter. A similar interpretation of
this passage of the epistle, referring it to libertine heretics, is probably condensed from
Clement, III.206ff, esp. 208. In a different connection Riedinger, 165, has remarked
on how consistently Clement's exegesis follows a certain line of thought when directed
against certain opponents, and how each line of thought is regularly associated with
certain biblical passages. That Clement used Jude in the *Stromateis* and the *Hypotyposes*
is remarked by Eus., *HE* VI.13f. Clement also compares sinners to planets in I.51.21ff
(believers in astrology) and probably 177.5 (gluttons, lechers, and drunkards);
similarly, Theophilus of Antioch, *To Autolycus* II.15 end. [Cumont, *Egypte* 168 n1,
notes the use of πλανήτης for victims of demoniacal possession. C.H.R. This passage
recalls Plutarch, *De genio Socratis* 591d–f, where stars disappearing into a chasm
represent souls completely plunged into the body. Could ἀστέρες πλανῆται possibly
refer to shooting stars? B.E.]

I.4
οἱ ἀπὸ τῆς στενῆς τῶν ἐντολῶν ὁδοῦ εἰς

ἀπό. Clement does not use ἀπό with πλανᾶσθαι, but he might well have done so in the fashion of this letter, since the usage here is part of a reminiscence of Wisdom 5.6, where the wicked say ἄρα ἐπλανήθημεν ἀπὸ ὁδοῦ ἀληθείας, καὶ τὸ τῆς δικαιοσύνης φῶς οὐκ ἔλαμψεν ἡμῖν. This in turn is based on Dt. 11.28 (LXX). There are reminiscences of Wis. 5.6 in James 5.19 and II Peter 2.15. Clement cites Wis. 5.3–5 in II.287.4–8 and echoes 5.6 in I.145.10: φωτίζει τοῖς πλανωμένοις τὴν ἀλήθειαν. [W.M.C. notes πλανᾶσθαι ἀπὸ τοῦ λόγου; Plato, Politicus 263a.]

τῶν ἐντολῶν. Inserted adjectival genitives are frequent in Clement: e.g., II.423.10f. The road "of the commandments" here is paralleled by that "according to the commandments" in II.346.6, a reminiscence of Dt. 11.28 (see the preceding paragraph) where the road is that of the commandments. [Expressions of this type, a metaphor with an adjective attribute and an explicative genitive, are for the most part Christian. In pre-Christian prose there are no instances save in Philo, where the usage begins. They arise easily out of allegorical exegesis. In the New Testament there are a few—e.g., I Peter 5.4. Clement has them sometimes; e.g., I.5.5: τὸν πρᾶον καὶ φιλάνθρωπον τῆς θεοσεβείας ... ζυγόν, this in connection with a phrase from the Gospels, as above with τῆς στενῆς ... ὁδοῦ; again I.197.1, τῷ σωφροσύνης ἀμβροσίῳ χρίσματι. In later Christian Greek they become more common, and instances appear also in the later neoplatonists. A.W.]

ὁδοῦ. The στενὴ ὁδός comes from Mt. 7.13f. The simile was a favorite with Clement; see Stählin's Citatenregister to Mt. 7.13f and index s.v. ὁδός. In III.67.6 heretics are particularly condemned for having left the right (ὀρθή) road, which is, for Clement, the road of the commandments—he is particularly hostile to antinomians (Buri, Clemens 36). The broad road of carnal sins and pride appears in II. 263.12ff; 346.6. The letter may also have been intended to recall Prov. 2.13–14 (LXX), ὦ οἱ ἐγκαταλείποντες ὁδοὺς εὐθείας τοῦ πορεύεσθαι ἐν ὁδοῖς σκότους, οἱ εὐφραινόμενοι ἐπὶ κακοῖς καὶ χαίροντες ἐπὶ διαστροφῇ κακῇ. Proverbs was one of Clement's favorite Old Testament books; he cited it more often than any others save Psalms and perhaps Genesis. He cites 2.3–7 in II.17.20ff, and 2.21f in II.169.6ff.

εἰς. Clement's regular usage; Mossbacher, 56. With πλανᾶσθαι: πεπλανημένα ... εἰς τὴν δεῦρο γένεσιν, II.239.12.

ἀπέρατον ἄβυσσον πλανώμενοι τῶν σαρκικῶν καὶ ἐνσωμάτων ἁμαρτιῶν.
I.5
πεφυσιωμένοι γὰρ εἰς γνῶσιν,

ἀπέρατον.   Dubious whether ἀπέρᾱτος, "*impassable*," or ἀπέρᾰτος, "*limitless*." The latter appears in the scholion on Aristophanes *Nubes* 3, and in perhaps two passages of Philo, *De fuga* 57 and *Quis rerum* 212. [But see the note of F. Colson and G. Whitaker on the latter passage, where they would read ἀπέραντος, in their edition of Philo (Loeb Library) IV.572. A.D.N.] Philo greatly influenced Clement. Clement uses ἀπέραντος of God (II.380.14); but in III.137.15 he explains Dan. 3.55 (LXX), Εὐλογημένος εἶ ὁ βλέπων ἀβύσσους, καθήμενος ἐπὶ Χερουβίμ, with the words ὁ Δανιὴλ λέγει, ὁμοδοξῶν τῷ Ἐνὼχ τῷ εἰρηκότι "καὶ εἶδον τὰς ὕλας πάσας," ἄβυσσος γὰρ τὸ ἀπεράτωτον κατὰ τὴν ἰδίαν ὑπόστασιν, περαιούμενον δὲ τῇ δυνάμει τοῦ Θεοῦ. αἱ τοίνυν οὐσίαι ὑλικαί, ἀφ' ὧν τὰ ἐπὶ μέρους γένη καὶ τὰ τούτων εἴδη γίνεται, ἄβυσσοι εἴρηνται. Here ἀπεράτωτον almost certainly means "quite without limit" (as it does in Plutarch and Damascius, *LSJ* s.v.) and περαιούμενον means "being limited" or "bounded," the process of limitation being that by which particular genera are separated from undifferentiated matter. For this meaning of περαιόω see *LSJ* s.v., II. [In the letter the meaning "limitless" seems indicated by the contrast with στενή. B.E. In any event, the two senses are very close in Clement, Philo, and elsewhere, as in this text, where they are almost equivalent. C.M.]

ἄβυσσον.   The abyss into which the errant stars are cast for punishment appears in *Enoch* 21.2; cf. the use of *Enoch* in the preceding paragraph. *Enoch* is referred to in Jude 14, and Jude 13 has been quoted just above. Clement by implication compares drunkenness to an abyss in I.206.21, but this is hardly a parallel.

πλανώμενοι.   Many instances of metaphorical use in connection with sensual indulgence, IV.649–650. See below, on τὸν ζόφον τοῦ σκότους.

σαρκικῶν καὶ ἐνσωμάτων.   II.318.17f, τῆς ἁμαρτίας καὶ ἀπειθείας σαρκικῆς τε οὔσης καὶ ἐνσωμάτου καὶ νεκρᾶς καὶ διὰ τοῦτο βδελυκτῆς.

πεφυσιωμένοι.   I.104.28, οἱ εἰς γνῶσιν πεφυσιωμένοι; cf. I.121.9f, σφᾶς τελείους τινὲς τολμῶσι καλεῖν καὶ γνωστικούς ... φυσιούμενοί τε καὶ φρυαττόμενοι. All three passages come from I Cor. 8.1, ἡ γνῶσις φυσιοῖ. For the type of sentence incipit (nominative participle + γάρ + dependents of participle + verb), see, e.g., II.204.9ff; this was a structure Clement favored.

I.6

ὡς λέγουσιν, "τῶν βαθέων τοῦ Σατανᾶ," λανθάνουσιν εἰς "τὸν ζόφον τοῦ σκότους,"

ὡς . . . Σατανᾶ. Apoc. 2.24, ἔγνωσαν τὰ βαθέα τοῦ Σατανᾶ, ὡς λέγουσιν, of heretics whose doctrines lead them to commit adultery and eat things sacrificed to idols. These are the followers of a prophetess whom the author of the Apocalypse calls Jezebel (2.20). He elsewhere attacks a party called the Nicolaïtans and accuses them of teaching the same practices (2.14f). Therefore the Nicolaïtans and the followers of Jezebel have often been identified. Clement knows the Nicolaïtans, attributes to them similar practices, and therefore associates them, as this letter probably did, with the Carpocratians, whom he accuses of practicing community of wives (II.177. 2ff; 207.17–208.9). His attempt to rescue the reputation of Nicholas is probably a sign of embarrassment that his opponents should be able to cite an authority so near the apostles. Clement knows the Apocalypse and quotes it often; Stählin, *Citatenregister* s.v. The claim to know the deep things of Satan is akin to Paul's claim to know the deep things of God, I Cor. 2.10, which is taken up by Clement (II.116. 25f; 517.26f), probably in deliberate contrast to gnostic claims (cf. below, II.14, the conclusion of the note on ἀποκρίνου and the note on πρός). Perhaps the contrast was not so great as the terminology suggests [τοῦ Σατανᾶ was presumably an abusive comment by the Christian author—A.D.N.]. And in II.363.1–12 Clement warns that τὸ βάθος τῆς γνώσεως is not to be revealed to those whom it might scandalize (a theme which recurs in II.495.21f; evidently this secret doctrine was likely to be misunderstood). Hippolytus, *Philosophumena* V.6, says the name "gnostics" was taken by those φάσκοντες μόνοι τὰ βάθη γινώσκειν; and Irenaeus (Harvey II.32.6 = Stieren, II.22.1) attacks the Valentinians for their claim "adinvenisse profunda Bythi" (cf. Tertullian, *Adversus Valentinianos* I.4). The Nicolaïtans who appear in the Middle Ages—I.333.30, scholion on I.224.27—are probably irrelevant to the present discussion.

λανθάνουσι. I.195.25; 251.16; etc., with participle as here.

εἰς. See below, on ἀπορρίπτοντες.

τὸν ζόφον τοῦ σκότους. Continues the quotation of Jude 13; see above, on ἀστέρες πλανῆται. The combination of πλανῆται and σκότος made appropriate the intervening reminiscence of Wis. 5.6; see above, on ἀπό. The metaphor was a favorite with Clement: e.g., I.63.17f, τοῦ σκότους . . . τοὺς πεπλανημένους διανίστησιν. "ἔγειρε" φησίν, "ὁ καθεύδων . . . καὶ ἐπιφαύσει σοι ὁ Χριστός," and especially the conclusion to Book III of the *Stromateis*—the book which deals particularly with libertine heretics and notably the Carpocratians: "μὴ πλανᾶσθαι" φησίν, "οὔτε πόρνοι οὔτε εἰδωλολάτραι οὔτε μοιχοὶ οὔτε μαλακοὶ οὔτε ἀρσενοκοῖται . . . βασιλείαν Θεοῦ οὐ κληρονομήσουσιν," καὶ "ἡμεῖς" μὲν "ἀπελουσάμεθα" . . . οἱ δέ, εἰς ταύτην ἀπολούοντες τὴν ἀσέλγειαν, ἐκ σωφροσύνης εἰς πορνείαν βαπτίζουσι . . . ψευδωνύμου γνώσεως προσηγορίᾳ τὴν εἰς τὸ ἐξώτερον σκότος ὁδοιπορίαν ἐπανῃρημένοι (II. 246–247); cf. III.65.21ff.

I.7

τοῦ ψεύδους, ἑαυτοὺς ἀπορρίπτοντες· καὶ καυχώμενοι ἐλευθέρους εἶναι,

τοῦ ψεύδους. This looks like a gloss, but may possibly be original. There is a similar instance of abrubt explanation in Clement's *Paedagogus* I.129.11ff: καθυλομανεῖ γὰρ μὴ κλαδευομένη ἡ ἄμπελος, οὕτως δὲ καὶ ὁ ἄνθρωπος. καθαίρει δὲ αὐτοῦ τὰς ἐξυβριζούσας παραφυάδας ὁ λόγος, ἡ μάχαιρα, καρποφορεῖν . . . ἀναγκάσας. The equation of darkness with falsity is a commonplace and is therefore common in Clement's works: I.4.11; 20.24f (with πλανᾶσθε, from the *Sibylline Oracles*); 81.20; 106.22; etc. [Perhaps τοῦ ψεύδους is not an appositive explanation of τοῦ σκότους, put in the same case and to be included in commas. It could be an explicative genitive to the metaphor σκότους, so that here τὸ σκότος τοῦ ψεύδους is put in the genitive through the connection with τὸν ζόφον. Cf. τὸ τῆς ἀγνοίας σκότος, I.206.12. For two genitives in succession, the one dependent on the other, cf. Blass-Debrunner, no. 168; also Dio Cassius, L.12.7, πρὸ τοῦ στόματος τοῦ κόλπου τοῦ Ἀμπρακικοῦ. For a single word, like τοῦ ψεύδους here, adhering to a quotation as an explanation and grammatically connected with the words of the quotation, cf. Clement, I.57.20, μητραγύρτης. A.W. However, the two genitives ζόφον τοῦ σκότους τοῦ ψεύδους sound too clumsy for this elaborate style. If not a gloss, τοῦ ψεύδους may perhaps be a variant to σκότους. Either gloss or variant seems likely. W.J. On the other hand, τοῦ ψεύδους seems necessary to provide a contrast to γνῶσιν. B.E.]

ἑαυτοὺς ἀπορρίπτοντες. II.454.9f, οἱ ἐν Ἅιδου καταταγέντες καὶ εἰς ἀπώλειαν ἑαυτοὺς ἐκδεδωκότες καθάπερ ἔκ τινος νεὼς εἰς θάλασσαν ἑκόντες ἀπορρίψαντες.

καυχώμενοι. II.218.25, as here, the participle with a dependent infinitive. Used of heretics who deny marriage. Clement rather favored the word for abusing heretics (IV.508, eight references). This is a Pauline trait.

ἐλευθέρους. I.269.31, etc. [The accusative in this construction is frequent in Greek of this period; see Radermacher, 181, and Schmid, II.57; III.81; IV.83,620. ἑαυτούς may be supplied. A.D.N. Nevertheless, the construction in this letter is difficult. The parallels in Radermacher and Schmid have for the most part expressed subjects of the infinitives and are not so hard as this instance, where the nominative participle is immediately followed by the accusative. Similarly Thucydides, I.12.1 and IV.84.2, where predicate adjectives of the infinitive are put into the accusative, are easier than that of this letter. If the text here is right, I can understand it only as influenced by the ἑαυτούς of the preceding line. A.W.] Cf. Apoc. 3.9: τῶν λεγόντων ἑαυτοὺς Ἰουδαίους εἶναι. In the preceding phrase, the writer had been thinking of Apoc. 2.24. [If the text is corrupt, a possible emendation would be ἐλευθεροῦσθαι. C.H.R.] The content of the letter here is paralleled in II.216.24, where gnostic libertines are described as λεγόντων ἐλευθερίαν τὴν ὑπὸ ἡδονῆς δουλείαν.

I.8

δοῦλοι γεγόνασιν ἀνδραποδώδων ἐπιθυμιῶν. τούτοις οὖν ἀντιστατέον
πάντῃ τε καὶ πάντως, εἰ γὰρ καί τι ἀληθὲς

δοῦλοι. Slaves of the passions (also with the perfect of γίγνομαι), I.26.12; cf. II.216.24
in the preceding paragraph. II.14.20, of the Greeks who seek after wisdom. Frequent;
see Tsermoulas, 58.

γεγόνασιν. γεγόναμεν, III.15.10.

ἐλευθέρους εἶναι, δοῦλοι γεγόνασιν. [The style is antithetic throughout, but not in
the naive, early rhetorical way of Attic prose. The antitheses are calculated to
contrast words and reality, or different meanings of a word, apparent and real
meaning, and so on. E.g., I.8f: he contrasts ἀληθέα with ἀλήθεια in a deeper sense
and summarizes the contrast by saying (I.9) οὐ γὰρ πάντα τἀληθῆ ἀλήθεια. We might
compare the truth of certain facts of science with that of which the Christian gospel
says, "I *am* the truth." And going even beyond that, he can contrast the *seeming truth*
of human δόξαι and the *true truth* (ἀληθὴς ἀλήθεια) which is based on faith. This
sophisticated rhetoric should therefore not surprise us by its repetition of the same
word, which indeed is not Clement's usual manner, but should be valued as a genuine play on the various meanings of one and the same word (ἀληθής–ἀλήθεια). W.J.]

ἀνδραποδώδων. I.176.21 (of belchings).

ἐπιθυμιῶν. II.237.27, ἐπιθυμίαις δεδουλωμένους. Frequent.

τούτοις οὖν. Initial, I.27.1, etc. Again below, II.10.

ἀντιστατέον. Frequent (II.212.19; 213.17; 240.18) in argument with the gnostics.
The form does not appear in Stählin's index, but Clement was fond of these verbal
adjectives (see below, on προκριτέον in I.10). Here the use of the verb is perhaps a
reminiscence of I Pet. 5.9, (τῷ διαβόλῳ) ἀντίστητε. Clement quotes I Peter often,
5.7 in II.52.16 and 5.10 in III.206.16. The directive to oppose the Carpocratians
with might and main is repeated below, II.10; it appears also in Epiphanius' attack
on the sect, *Panarion* XXVII.7, δεῖ τοίνυν τούτους ἀνατρέπειν παντὶ σθένει. Evidently
it was a rule accepted in the Church.

πάντῃ τε καὶ πάντως. Verbatim, II.511.24.

εἰ γὰρ καί . . . οὐκ ἄν. Both with optatives, as here, in a "future less vivid" construction, II.420.20f. εἰ γὰρ καί concessive and initial, with indicative, I.48.22; 49.24;
57.8; etc.

τι ἀληθές. ἀληθές τι, III.89.21; τι followed by an adjective, I.254.2 (τι βέλτιον);
τὸ ἀληθές is frequent in Clement, though not indexed by Stählin. The way the letter
in the following lines harps on ἀληθές and its cognates is unlike Clement's usual
concern for variation of terms (Tengblad, 4ff), but Clement sometimes uses repetition
for emphasis (Tengblad, 4,22ff). Cf. the note on ἀλήθεια in the following line and
Jaeger's note on ἐλευθέρους εἶναι, δοῦλοι γεγόνασιν, above.

I.9
λέγοιεν οὐδ'οὕτω συμφωνοίη ἄν αὐτοῖς ὁ τῆς ἀληθείας ἐραστής. οὐδὲ γὰρ
I.10
πάντα τἀληθῆ ἀλήθεια. οὐδὲ τὴν κατὰ

λέγοιεν. Clement uses λέγω in the present active optative nine times, according to Scham, 13. The use of the optative here in a "future less vivid" conditional clause is classically correct and is paralleled in II.30.13. This is a general consideration. When the text comes to the particular case, in lines 12–13 below, it will use the indicative, περιέχει.

οὐδ'οὕτω. Neither οὐδέ nor οὕτω is fully indexed by Stählin, Ast, or Leisegang, but the combination with this sense is classical (Thuc. II.76.3; Lysias, I.14).

συμφωνοίη ἄν. With the dative, II.233.20. The use of ἄν is normal. (Clement's use of ἄν is studied in Hort and Mayor in their Appendix B.)

ὁ τῆς ἀληθείας ἐραστής. III.67.3, τῷ τῆς ἀληθείας ἐραστῇ, in polemic against those who force Scripture to suit their own ends, without being orthodox. [The phrase is an echo of Plato, *Republic* VI.501d. W.M.C.] The notion that ὁ γνωστικὸς δὲ ἀληθείας ἐρᾷ (II.252.8f) is fundamental to Clement's thought and is developed at length in the *Stromateis*, especially in Book IV.

οὐδὲ γάρ . . . οὐδέ. Neither . . . nor, I.45.11f (initial, as here), etc.

τἀληθῆ. II.517.14; III.162.11, with crasis; II.465.14; III.66.5, without crasis; these irregularities in the use of crasis are probably scribal, but Stählin notes them also in the other MSS of Clement, IV.223 s.v. ἀλλά. Ἀληθῆ without the article, as a substantive, III.39.14, where Clement explains that the true Christian will sometimes lie, as might a doctor, for therapeutic purposes—a principle he justifies by appeal to the example of St. Paul (Acts 16.3; I Cor. 9.19f). [Cf. Philo, *Questions . . . on Genesis* IV.204. J.R.] It is characteristic of Clement to talk most of truth when recommending falsity.

ἀλήθεια. For the contrast, τἀληθῆ ἀλήθεια, cf. II.509.22ff, οὔκουν ποτὲ τὰς ἐπὶ μέρους ἀληθείας, καθ'ὧν ἡ ἀλήθεια κατηγορεῖται, αὐτὴν δὲ τὴν ἀλήθειαν πολυπραγμονητέον: that is to say, one should study theology and not the subordinate sciences. This sort of play on words is a favorite of Clement's; Tengblad, 80, goes so far as to restore it by analogy when it is lacking; cf. Jaeger's note on ἐλευθέρους εἶναι, above in I.7. (On the various meanings of ἀλήθεια in early Christian usage, Bultmann, ἀλήθεια, 242ff. The contrast here is evidently between his meanings [3] "wirkliche Tatbestand" and [5] "die rechte Lehre, der rechte Glaube" or [6] "göttliche Wirklichkeit, Offenbarung.")

κατά. Mossbacher, 66: numerous examples of this use.

I.11

τὰς ἀνθρωπίνας δόξας φαινομένην ἀλήθειαν προκριτέον τῆς ἀληθοῦς ἀληθείας τῆς κατὰ τὴν πίστιν. τῶν τοίνυν

ἀνθρωπίνας δόξας. II.365.15, to describe the secret doctrines of the mystery cults. (As these are hidden from the ignorant, how much more should the holy science of Christianity be hidden!) III.69.15, heretics who have not learned the mysteries of Christian gnosis, and are not able to grasp the greatness τῆς ἀληθείας, are motivated by ἀνθρωπίναις δόξαις (cf. 67.13ff, αἱρέσεων ἀνθρωπίνων). Δόξα opposed to ἀλήθεια, III.46.31. [CH, Extr. IIA.7—the whole of Extr. IIA illustrates this contrast between truth and human opinion. A.D.N.]

κατὰ τὰς ἀνθρωπίνας δόξας. [The same phrase, but in the singular, Plato, Sophista 229a. This is skillful irony. Plato contrasted doxa with philosophia; Clement now identifies Plato's philosophia as doxa. W.M.C.]

φαινομένην ἀλήθειαν. II.473.15, μερικῆς οὖν τυγχανούσης τῆς κατὰ τὴν Ἑλληνικὴν φιλοσοφίαν ἐμφαινομένης ἀληθείας, ἥ τῷ ὄντι ἀλήθεια (differs from it). Cf. II.63.2, χωρίζεται δὲ ἡ Ἑλληνικὴ ἀλήθεια τῆς καθ' ἡμᾶς, and ours, of course, is truer. III.64.27ff, one must distinguish τὴν τῷ ὄντι ἀλήθειαν from the teaching of the heretics as true from wax fruit, and as τὸ ἀληθὲς ἀπὸ τοῦ φαινομένου. φαινόμενος meaning "seeming," i.e. "false," is frequent in Clement; contrast classical usage, where δοκεῖν is usually "seem and be not," φαίνομαι usually "appear to be and be." [In II.473.15 there is truth in the ἐμφαινομένη ἀλήθεια; its fault lies in being particular. Here, however, φαινομένη is "apparent" as opposed to "real." Clement perhaps did not here say δοκοῦσαν because that might have introduced a certain cacophony—δόξας δοκοῦσαν. But the very word δόξας seems to have suggested to him the opposition of apparent to real. B.E.]

προκριτέον. Clement is fond of these verbal adjectives in -τέος and -τέον, e.g., II.3.1ff; III.64.25ff (7 in 13 lines). This particular verb in this form, with genitive and accusative, as here, occurs in I.223.19. [For the ablative genitive, cf. Plato, Apology 35b, and Kühner-Gerth, I.393. W.M.C.]

τῆς ἀληθοῦς ἀληθείας. The play on words is reminiscent of Plato, Theaetetus 162a, 171c. See above, on ἀλήθεια. Clement cites Plato more often than any other author outside Scripture; of his citations, those which stand nearest Theaetetus 162–171 are 155e in II.348.4ff; 173c in II.391.7ff.

τῆς κατὰ τὴν πίστιν. II.64.3, ἡ κατὰ τὴν πίστιν ἀλήθεια is contrasted to the inferior truth attained by Greek philosophy.

τῶν. Initial τῶν with participle followed by τὰ μέν . . . τὰ δέ, III.94.21ff; cf. 24f; 95.4f,18ff,27f. Further examples in Tengblad, 47.

τοίνυν. Thus in I.9.24; 10.20; etc. Frequent.

I.12

θρυλουμένων περὶ τοῦ θεοπνεύστου κατὰ Μᾶρκον εὐαγγελίου,

θρυλουμένων. Frequently contemptuous, as here; e.g., II.13.5, τὰ θρυλούμενα πρός τινων ἀμαθῶς ψοφοδεῶν, 213.28, etc.

περί. Mossbacher, 69: many examples. περί with the genitive is used thus with θρυλεῖν in Epicurus (H. Usener, Epicurea frag. 423). Aristotle, Historiae animalium I.36, 620b.10f (τὰ . . . θρυλούμενα περὶ τὸν βάτραχον . . . ἐστιν ἀληθῆ) is interesting as proof that our author sometimes did not use accusatives for which there were precedents.

θεοπνεύστου. III.73.5ff, an attack on those who τὰ προσφυῆ τοῖς θεοπνεύστοις λόγοις ὑπὸ τῶν μακαρίων ἀποστόλων τε καὶ διδασκάλων παραδιδόμενα ἑκόντες εἶναι σοφίζονται δι' ἑτέρων παρεγχειρήσεων, ἀνθρωπείαις διδασκαλίαις ἐνιστάμενοι θείᾳ παραδόσει ὑπὲρ τοῦ τὴν αἵρεσιν συστήσασθαι. Explicitly of Scripture, with quotation of II Tim. 3.16f, in I.65.7f. Again, III.71.23.

κατὰ Μᾶρκον εὐαγγελίου. Verbatim, III.163.13. Nothing is said in the recognized works of Clement, or anywhere else in the heresiologists, about special use by the Carpocratians of a peculiar Gospel attributed to Mark. Hippolytus, Philosophumena VII.30.1, speaks of refuting Marcionites by pointing out that the Gospel according to Mark does not contain material they had evidently claimed to find in it—but probably had found by exegesis. The material was hostile to the demiurge ἐκ τῆς ἀντιπαραθέσεως ἀγαθοῦ καὶ καλοῦ. This phrase might conceivably reflect material from the Carpocratian tradition quoted below (II.3–4, at the end of the note on Carpocrates), "opposing" things truly good to things commonly believed to be so; but it might equally well reflect Marcionite doctrine, more or less misunderstood (especially if κακοῦ be read for καλοῦ). Irenaeus (Harvey, III.11.10 = Stieren, III.12.7) speaks of those qui autem Iesum separant a Christo, et impassibilem perseverasse Christum, passum vero Iesum dicunt, id quod secundum Marcum est praeferentes evangelium. This could have come from canonical Mark, 1.10 + 15.34 [but it is not likely that Irenaeus read Mark in this way—A.D.N.]. Irenaeus could have had the Carpocratians in mind, but he adds cum amore veritatis legentes illud, corrigi possunt, and this is not like the things he said elsewhere about the Carpocratians; see Irenaeus (Harvey, I.20.2 = Stieren, I.25.3), ad velamen malitiae ipsorum nomine abutuntur. On the other hand, Irenaeus is not always consistent. It is interesting that Harvey, in his note on this passage, was led to postulate the existence in Egypt of a secret Gospel according to Mark—a conjecture which the present text confirms. But, although no special connection with the Carpocratians is reported, the Gospel according to Mark was the most popular of the canonical Gospels with the gnostics in general (which may account for its comparative neglect by the orthodox). Swete, xxxi, remarks on this and cites evidence of its use by Heracleon and other Valentinians, certain docetists, the Gospel of Peter, and the Clementine Homilies, esp. XIX.20.1: εἶπεν ἡμῖν "τὰ μυστήρια ἐμοὶ καὶ τοῖς υἱοῖς τοῦ οἴκου μου φυλάξατε." διὸ καὶ "τοῖς αὐτοῦ μαθηταῖς κατ' ἰδίαν ἐπέλυε" τῆς τῶν οὐρανῶν βασιλείας τὰ μυστήρια. This probably uses Mk. 4.11

I.13

τὰ μὲν ψεύδεται παντελῶς, τὰ δέ, εἰ καὶ ἀληθῆ τινα περιέχει, οὐδ' οὕτως ἀληθῶς παραδίδοται,

and 4.34 as proof of secret teaching by Jesus (Sanday, *Gospels* 179f), and it quotes the preceding agraphon as if it came from the same Gospel. Now Clement of Alexandria quotes, from some unknown author, a quotation of the same agraphon (in the form μυστήριον ἐμὸν ἐμοὶ καὶ τοῖς υἱοῖς τοῦ οἴκου μου) as written ἔν τινι εὐαγγελίῳ (II.368.27. Ropes, *Sprüche* 94f, is mistaken in thinking the quotation continued from the preceding sentence, which comes from *Barnabas* 6.10. His attempt to explain τοῖς υἱοῖς τοῦ οἴκου μου as derived from a mistranslation of אוי לי is ludicrous.) Resch[1] correctly noted the Semitism, which suggests translation from a Hebrew original (167ff). Taken over from Clement or the *Clementina* (?) and hellenized— τοῖς ἐμοῖς—the agraphon spread through Christian tradition, is preserved in Hilary Jerome, Chrysostom, Theodoret, and John of Damascus and in a contamination of some MSS of Symmachus and Theodotion on Is. 24.16—where a literal mistranslation of the Hebrew had yielded τὸ μυστήριόν μου ἐμοί; Field, II.470 n24; Resch[1], 167ff, 103f, 282.

ψεύδεται.   Clement uses the verb in III.40.6, as here; I.22.25; etc. The usage is classical, *LSJ* s.v. A. II.

παντελῶς.   Final, following verb, as here, I.274.16; II.31.6.

εἰ καί.   In a concessive, inserted clause, with the indicative, as here, II.201.7. In both instances what is conceded is probably no more than the facts of the particular case. εἰ γάρ . . . οὐ δή, both with indicative, I.221.9–12.

ἀληθῆ τινα.   II.55.10, ἐν δὲ τοῖς ψεύδεσιν καὶ ἀληθῆ τινα ἔλεγον οἱ ψευδοπροφῆται.

περιέχει.   Of books, II.13.1; 70.7; 71.23; 235.23; etc.

οὐδ' οὕτως.   With the indicative following εἰ καί, II.305.31–306.1; classical examples plentiful, *LSJ* s.v. οὕτως.

ἀληθῶς.   III.43.29, etc. Frequent. The use here was determined by the concern to play on ἀλήθεια.

παραδίδοται.   The same form of the verb, III.41.11. Clement uses the verb for traditions he believes true, but he must have been aware that the heretics also handed down their teachings. Like θρυλουμένων, which is also used for the doctrines of a sect, the word here suggests not commonly known, but specifically sectarian, tradition.

I.14
συγκεκραμένα γὰρ τἀληθῆ τοῖς πλάσμασι παραχαράσσεται ὥστε—τοῦτο
I.15
δὴ τὸ λεγόμενον—'' καὶ τὸ ἄλας μωρανθῆναι.''

συγκεκραμένα. The perfect middle participle (singular), III.125.12 (*Extracts from Theodotus*). For the structure, see above, I.5, πεφυσιωμένοι γάρ.

πλάσμασι. Cf. Clement's usage, III.70.7, where the gnostics πάμπολλα συγκαττύουσι ψεύσματα καὶ πλάσματα, which are evidently synonymous. In the present instance the choice of πλάσμασι was probably determined by the desire not to repeat too often forms cognate with ψεύδομαι. Tengblad, 4ff, collects examples of Clement's use of such deliberate variation. [Further, the word πλάσματα had been used for religious fictions throughout pagan Greek theological language. Xenophanes of Colophon (Diels, frag. 1.22) calls impious myths about the immorality of the Homeric and Hesiodic gods πλάσματα τῶν προτέρων. For the way in which Critias imagined such πλάσματα to have been introduced into religious thought, see the great fragments taken from his satyr play, *Sisyphus* (Diels, frag. 25), and the comments in Jaeger, *Theology* 186ff. W.J.]

παραχαράσσεται. II.208.19ff, καὶ τῶν τοῦ κυρίου φωνῶν διαψεύδονται οἱ τῆς ἀσελγείας κοινωνοί, οἱ τῆς λαγνείας ἀδελφοί, ὄνειδος οὐ φιλοσοφίας μόνον, ἀλλὰ καὶ παντὸς τοῦ βίου, οἱ παραχαράσσοντες τὴν ἀλήθειαν μᾶλλον δὲ κατασκάπτοντες ὡς οἷόν τε αὐτοῖς· οἱ γὰρ τρισάθλιοι τὴν ⟨τε⟩ σαρκικὴν καὶ ⟨τὴν⟩ συνουσιαστικὴν κοινωνίαν ἱεροφαντοῦσι καὶ ταύτην οἴονται εἰς τὴν βασιλείαν αὐτοὺς ἀνάγειν τοῦ Θεοῦ. Both the metaphor expressed by παραχαράσσεται and this verb to express it were favorites with Clement. Stählin cites nine uses of the verb (*Register*, s.v.).

ὥστε. Stählin (IV.827 s.v.) remarks Clement's frequent use of ὥστε with a following infinitive.

τοῦτο δὴ τὸ λεγόμενον. Verbatim. Interjected, as here, to introduce a following conventional expression, I.8.9; 51.13.

καὶ τὸ ἄλας μωρανθῆναι. Mt. 5.13, ἐὰν δὲ τὸ ἄλας μωρανθῇ, ἐν τίνι ἁλισθήσεται; = Lk. 14.34. The text here is closer to Lk., which differs from Mt. by beginning ἐὰν δὲ καί. Behind the choice of this proverb probably lies not only recollection of the context of these Gospel passages (and Mk. 9.50), which declare corrupted Christians fit only to be cast out, but also recollection of Jeremiah 28.17 (LXX) (= 10.14 Heb.) ἐμωράνθη πᾶς ἄνθρωπος ἀπὸ γνώσεως . . . ὅτι ψευδῆ ἐχώνευσαν, οὐκ ἔστιν πνεῦμα ἐν αὐτοῖς (and ff), which made the verse particularly appropriate for use against gnostics who had corrupted the Scriptures. This sort of multiple biblical allusion

ὁ γοῦν Μᾶρκος

is typical of Clement and would be very difficult for a forger to imitate. In III.183.23ff Clement identifies as "the salt of the earth" those "more elect than the elect," "who hide away, in the depth of thought, the mysteries not to be uttered." The passage is clearly a description of orthodox gnostics, and the application to the Carpocratians of the saying about corruption of the salt suggests that Clement saw the Carpocratian secret society as a perverted parallel of similar secret groups within the Church. The same suggestion is brought to mind by I.281.25ff, where Clement argues that "we are the salt of the earth" (see below, II.17, "we are the children of light") and therefore should not follow the libertines in their abuse of the Christian liberty of kissing. In quoting the phrase from the NT, Clement, like this letter, uses ἅλας, elsewhere ἅλς. Greek proverbs frequently begin with καί; e.g. Strömberg, *Proverbs* 38, 60, 67, 73; Leutsch-Schneidewin, *Corpus* I.505; II.809–810. It is possible that the Gospel saying reflected a popular proverb. *Talmud Babli* (hereinafter *B*), *Bekorot* 8b, has, in a trial of wits, the question

מילחא כי סריא במאי מלחי לה, אמר לתו בסילתא דכודניתא,
ומי איכא סילתא לכודנתא, ומילחא מי סרי.

"⟨They asked R. Joshua ben Hananya, ca. A.D. 90:⟩ 'When salt has lost its savor, with what can it be salted?' He said to them, 'With the after-birth of a female mule.' ⟨They said,⟩ 'But does any female mule have an after-birth?' ⟨He said⟩ 'And does salt lose its savor?'" Billerbeck, on Mt. 5.13b, saw a slur on the story of the virgin birth in the reference to a she-mule's giving birth (a possibility which is also dismissed as absurd in the sentence just preceding the quotation). This may be correct, but even so the exchanges quoted may reflect either the popular saying, or polemic against the Christian one, or both. (The literature in Bauer, *Wb.* s.v. ἅλας, to which add Bauer, *Sal*, and Nauck, *Salt*, does not suffice to decide the question.) Note the five successive long syllables in the clausula; Clement often uses this ending, as it is used here, for emphasis.

ὁ γοῦν. Initial, I.201.19; II.188.27; 190.23; III.165.15. Clement often used it thus for introducing proof.

Μᾶρκος. We have three reports that Clement gave this account of the origin of the second Gospel. Two come from Eusebius (*HE* II.15 and VI.14.5–7), and one from the Latin *Adumbrationes Clementis Alexandrini in Epistolas Canonicas*, a translation and adaptation of parts of Clement's *Hypotyposes*, made in the early sixth century (III.XL). These three are arranged on the two following pages in parallel columns with Eusebius' report of the same account as given by Papias of Hierapolis in Asia Minor in the early second century.

Adumbrationes Clementis Alexandrini in Epistolas Canonicas (III.206.17ff)

Eus., *HE* II.15

Marcus, Petri sectator praedicante Petro evangelium palam Romae coram quibusdam Caesareanis equitibus, et multa Christi testimonia proferente, petitus ab eis, ut possent quae dicebantur memoriae commendare,

scripsit ex his, quae a Petro dicta sunt,

evangelium quod secundum Marcum vocitatur;
sicut Lucas quoque Actus

Apostolorum stilo exsecutus agnoscitur,

et Pauli ad Hebraeos interpretatus epistolam.

Οὕτω δὴ οὖν ἐπιδημήσαντος αὐτοῖς τοῦ θείου λόγου ἡ μὲν τοῦ Σίμωνος ἀπέσβη καὶ παραχρῆμα σὺν καὶ τῷ ἀνδρὶ κατελέλυτο δύναμις. Τοσοῦτον δ᾽ ἐπέλαμψεν ταῖς τῶν ἀκροατῶν τοῦ Πέτρου διανοίαις εὐσεβείας φέγγος, ὡς μὴ τῇ εἰς ἅπαξ ἱκανῶς ἔχειν ἀρκεῖσθαι ἀκοῇ, μηδὲ τῇ ἀγράφῳ τοῦ θείου κηρύγματος διδασκαλίᾳ, παρακλήσεσιν δὲ παντοίαις Μάρκον, οὗ τὸ εὐαγγέλιον φέρεται, ἀκόλουθον ὄντα Πέτρου, λιπαρῆσαι ὡς ἂν καὶ διὰ γραφῆς ὑπόμνημα τῆς διὰ λόγου παραδοθείσης αὐτοῖς καταλείψοι διδασκαλίας, μὴ πρότερόν τε ἀνεῖναι ἢ κατεργάσασθαι τὸν ἄνδρα, καὶ ταύτῃ αἰτίους γενέσθαι τῆς τοῦ λεγομένου κατὰ Μάρκον εὐαγγελίου γραφῆς. γνόντα δὲ τὸ πραχθέν φασι τὸν ἀπόστολον ἀποκαλύψαντος αὐτῷ τοῦ πνεύματος, ἡσθῆναι τῇ τῶν ἀνδρῶν προθυμίᾳ κυρῶσαί τε τὴν γραφὴν εἰς ἔντευξιν τῆς ἐκκλησίας. Κλήμης ἐν ἕκτῳ τῶν Ὑποτυπώσεων παρατέθειται τὴν ἱστορίαν, συνεπιμαρτυρεῖ δὲ αὐτῷ καὶ ὁ Ἱεραπολίτης ἐπίσκοπος ὀνόματι Παπίας. τοῦ δὲ Μάρκου μνημονεύειν τὸν Πέτρον ἐν τῇ προτέρᾳ ἐπιστολῇ, ἣν καὶ συντάξαι φασὶν ἐπ᾽ αὐτῆς Ῥώμης, σημαίνειν τε τοῦτ᾽ αὐτόν, τὴν πόλιν τροπικώτερον Βαβυλῶνα προσειπόντα διὰ τούτων. ἀσπάζεται ὑμᾶς ἡ ἐν Βαβυλῶνι συνεκλεκτὴ καὶ Μάρκος ὁ υἱός μου.

Eus., *HE* VI.14.5–7

Αὖθις ... περὶ τῆς τάξεως τῶν εὐαγγελίων
παράδοσιν τῶν ἀνέκαθεν πρεσβυτέρων τέθειται,
τοῦτον ἔχουσαν τὸν τρόπον. προγεγράφθαι
ἔλεγεν τῶν εὐαγγελίων τὰ περιέχοντα τὰς
γενεαλογίας. τὸ δὲ κατὰ Μάρκον ταύτην
ἐσχηκέναι τὴν οἰκονομίαν. Τοῦ Πέτρου δημοσίᾳ
ἐν Ῥώμῃ κηρύξαντος τὸν λόγον καὶ πνεύματι
τὸ εὐαγγέλιον ἐξειπόντος, τοὺς παρόντας,
πολλοὺς ὄντας, παρακαλέσαι
τὸν Μάρκον, ὡς
ἂν ἀκολουθήσαντα αὐτῷ πόρρωθεν καὶ
μεμνημένον τῶν λεχθέντων, ἀναγράψαι τὰ
εἰρημένα. ποιήσαντα δέ, τὸ εὐαγγέλιον

μεταδοῦναι τοῖς δεομένοις αὐτοῦ. ὅπερ ἐπιγνόντα
τὸν Πέτρον προτρεπτικῶς μήτε κωλῦσαι μήτε
προτρέψασθαι.

Eus., *HE* III.39.15 (Papias)

καὶ τοῦτο ὁ πρεσβύτερος ἔλεγε·

Μάρκος μὲν
ἑρμηνευτὴς Πέτρου γενόμενος, ὅσα
ἐμνημόνευσεν ἀκριβῶς ἔγραψεν οὐ μέντοι
τάξει, τὰ ὑπὸ τοῦ Χριστοῦ ἢ λεχθέντα ἢ
πραχθέντα. οὔτε γὰρ ἤκουσε τοῦ κυρίου, οὔτε
παρηκολούθησεν αὐτῷ, ὕστερον δέ, ὡς ἔφην,
Πέτρῳ, ὃς πρὸς τὰς χρείας ἐποιεῖτο τὰς
διδασκαλίας ἀλλ' οὐχ ὥσπερ σύνταξιν τῶν
κυριακῶν ποιούμενος λογίων. ὥστε οὐδὲν
ἥμαρτε Μάρκος οὕτως ἔνια γράψας ὡς
ἀπεμνημόνευσεν. ἑνὸς γὰρ ἐποιήσατο πρόνοιαν,
τοῦ μηδὲν ὧν ἤκουσε παραλιπεῖν ἢ ψεύσασθαί
τι ἐν αὐτοῖς. Ταῦτα μὲν οὖν ἱστόρηται τῷ
Παπίᾳ περὶ τοῦ Μάρκου. Περὶ δὲ τοῦ Ματθαίου
ταῦτ' εἴρηται. Ματθαῖος μὲν οὖν Ἑβραΐδι
διαλέκτῳ τὰ λόγια συνεγράψατο, ἡρμήνευσε
δ' αὐτὰ ὡς ἦν δυνατὸς ἕκαστος. Κέχρηται δ'
αὐτὸς μαρτυρίαις ἀπὸ τῆς Ἰωάννου προτέρας
ἐπιστολῆς καὶ ἀπὸ τῆς Πέτρου ὁμοίως.

Eusebius remarked the similarity of Clement's account to that of Papias. The parallels between the passages make it seem that Clement relied on Papias for his statement about Mark and for the proof of it from I Pet. 5.13, which may have been the source of the whole story (though Papias attributed it to one John of Ephesus, a presbyter and a "disciple of the Lord," albeit not an apostle; Eus., *HE* III.39.4,15). But Clement had other sources, which he preferred to Papias, for his statements about Matthew and Luke, Acts and Hebrews. Moreover, even in respect to Mark he did not follow Papias closely. Papias wanted to defend Mark from charges of confusion, *misrepresentation*, and *omission* (charges which become significant in the light of the present letter). Clement wants to excuse him from writing down oral tradition and so making it potentially public—a charge against which he had to defend himself too; *Stromateis* I.1–17. He therefore develops the basic story, given by Papias, in his own fashion. His account has been further rewritten by Eusebius, especially in II.15 (note the rhetorical larding and the contradiction of the report of Peter's reaction given in VI.14.7). Harnack, it is true, denied that Eusebius' account in *HE* II.15 came mostly from Clement and Papias. He maintained that the repeated φασίν in the text there must refer to a secondary tradition. The one solid piece of evidence in his argument was the statement (*Pseudopapianisches* 160 n2): "For Clement, *Babylon* means the real Babylon." For this statement, however, I can find no justification. On the contrary, the passage from the *Adumbrationes* cited above (III.206.17ff) is a comment on I Pet. 5.13 and clearly supposes that the "Babylon" mentioned in that text is Rome. This disposes of Harnack's denial that the repeated φασίν in Eusebius (*HE* II.15f) refers to Clement and Papias. It is not, of course, necessary to suppose that both witnesses said everything there reported; Eusebius is writing a summary based on both their reports. ["In comparison with the older descriptions of the importance of Peter for the Gospel of Mark, the letter stresses what *Mark* has done . . . Here nothing is said of Peter as the source of the Gospel of Mark. After Peter's death Mark goes to Alexandria with his own and Peter's *hypomnemata*—a remarkable change in the situation of the *hermeneutes* of Peter—and there he composes his second, more spiritual, Gospel; cf. the Canon Muratori, *quibus tamen interfuit et ita posuit*, if these words are to be understood as meaning that Mark had been an eyewitness to some of the doings of the Lord. In this way Mark is connected with Alexandria, and Mark, not Peter, is the authority behind his Gospel. As the general trend of patristic thought is to stress the part of Peter in the composition of the Gospel according to Mark, this letter seems to be an Alexandrian statement." J.M.] See below, Chapter Five, section I.

I.16

κατὰ τὴν τοῦ Πέτρου ἐν Ῥώμῃ διατριβὴν, ἀνέγραψε τὰς πράξεις τοῦ Κυρίου,

κατά.   For synchronism, I.42.15; 107.3; etc.; Mossbacher, 65.

τοῦ Πέτρου ἐν Ῥώμῃ.   III.197.21 in Eusebius' summary of Clement's account, *HE* VI.14.6. Use of ἐν, I.35.23, etc.; Mossbacher, 60.

διατριβήν.   In this sense, I.242.11.

ἀνέγραψε.   In Eusebius' summary, *HE* VI.14.6, the Christians of Rome beseech Mark ἀναγράψαι τὰ εἰρημένα. Clement uses the verb often, IV.232–233. See further the comment by J.M. on πνευματικώτερον εὐαγγέλιον below, in I.21–22.

πράξεις.   Perhaps by analogy from τὰς πράξεις τῶν ἀποστόλων, which Clement often cites by title, IV.668 s.v. πρᾶξις end. However, the usage here may reflect the influence of Papias, whose account of the origin of Mark's Gospel, we saw, probably influenced Clement. [Papias said Mark wrote τὰ ὑπὸ τοῦ Χριστοῦ λεχθέντα ἢ πραχθέντα (Eus., *HE* III.39.15), with which compare Acts 1.1, τὸν μὲν πρῶτον λόγον ἐποιησάμην περὶ πάντων ... ὧν ἤρξατο ὁ Ἰησοῦς ποιεῖν τε καὶ διδάσκειν. A.D.N.] Another source of influence may have been Roman imperial usage. The *Res gestae divi Augusti*, for instance, became in translation πράξεις ... Σεβαστοῦ θεοῦ; Bauer, *Wb*. s.v. [πράξεις were an established literary form, which the author of our πράξεις ἀποστόλων followed as his example. In retrospect, referring to both pagan and early Christian πράξεις, the author of this letter here calls the Gospel πράξεις, and perhaps he is right in assuming that the Christian Gospel form developed under the influence of such earlier types of writing. W.J.]

τοῦ Κυρίου.   Κύριος for Jesus; Stählin has over six columns of references to particular instances, IV.529–533, nos. 3, 6, 10, 11.

I.17

οὐ μέντοι πάσας ἐξαγγέλλων, οὐδὲ μὴν τὰς μυστικὰς

οὐ μέντοι πάσας ἐξαγγέλλων. ["Origen in his commentary on Mt. ⟨GCS, Origenes, vol 10, I.2, p. 441⟩ by his treatment of the parable, Mt. 20.1–16, showed himself convinced that Matthew knew the secrets (or mysteries) of this parable as well as those of the parables of the sower and of the tares, but kept silent about them. He did not make known everything which was revealed because he was aware of the danger." J.M., comparing Origen's defense of Matthew to the praise of Mark in this letter.]

οὐ μέντοι. "Not, however," I.208.28; see also II.329.28.

ἐξαγγέλλων. Clement uses this only once, II.43.9, for a prophet's declaring the decree of the goddess Lachesis (Fate), Plato, Republic 617d. The use here is probably determined by the word's connotation, "betray a secret" (LSJ s.v.). It is used elsewhere with this sense concerning the mystery cults; e.g., Epictetus (Arrian), III.21.16, where, having assimilated the teachings of philosophy to the secrets of the Eleusinian mysteries, the philosopher complains, σὺ δ' ἐξαγγέλλεις αὐτὰ καὶ ἐξορχῇ παρὰ καιρόν, παρὰ τόπον, ἄνευ θυμάτων, ἄνευ ἁγνείας· οὐκ ἐσθῆτα ἔχεις ἣν δεῖ τὸν ἱεροφάντην, etc.

οὐδὲ μήν. "Nor yet." Frequent. Following οὐ, I.45.6; 50.21ff; 206.5; etc. οὐ μέντοι . . . οὐδὲ μήν I have not found in Clement.

μυστικάς. Clement uses this often, both in the sense of "secret" and in that of "pertaining to the mysteries"; it is impossible to prove which is intended here. Clement uses it in II.496.17 of Jesus' teaching: The Holy Spirit spoke obscurely through the prophets in order to prove that all gentile sages ignored τὴν ἐσομένην τοῦ κυρίου παρουσίαν καὶ τὴν ὑπ' αὐτοῦ παραδοθησομένην μυστικὴν διδασκαλίαν. But this probably refers to all his teaching, as hidden from former ages, while the reference in the letter is to certain actions as symbolic or secret or connected with a mystery, by contrast with others which were not. [Most likely, as having symbolic meaning, but the use with πράξεις is surprising. A.D.N. C.M. also thinks that the sense of μυστικάς is "having symbolic meaning"; Clement considers the person and the actions of Jesus himself as being par excellence the μυστήριον ἐμφανές.]

[If the letter is by Clement, it may be that an original τὲ καὶ λέξεις following πράξεις—as in Acts 1.1—has dropped out. A.D.N.] The combination of πράξεις καὶ λέξεις not only is found in Acts and Papias (who was ignorant of Luke-Acts), but also is adumbrated in Mk. 6.2,30. Cadbury (Making 50) thinks it may be older than Lk. Although Clement does not use μυστική with the general term πρᾶξις he does use it with terms indicating particular actions, things, or rituals: μυστικὸν φίλημα, I.281.9; τὸ μυστικὸν τοῦ ἄρτου, I.117.29. Julius Pollux lists as usual usage ἔργων μυστικῶν (I.17) and τέλη μυστικά (I.36).

I.18

ὑποσημαίνων ἀλλ’ ἐκλεγόμενος ἃς χρησιμωτάτας ἐνόμισε πρὸς αὔξησιν

ὑποσημαίνων. Clement uses the verb to mean "indicate," with no connotation of obscurity, II.250.1—τοῖς ὁδὸν ἀπιοῦσιν ἣν οὔκ ἴσασιν ἀρκεῖ τὴν φέρουσαν ὑποσημῆναι μόνον. (Here the context shows the meaning is "merely indicate," as opposed to "describe in detail.") III.162.5, ⟨ἡ⟩ ἐσχάτη σάλπιγξ ὑποσημήνῃ ... τῆς ἐντεῦθεν ἐξόδου; I.101.8f, τοῦτό τοι ⟨an extremely dubious significance of νήπιος⟩ σαφέστατα ὁ μακάριος Παῦλος ὑπεσημήνατο εἰπών ⟨I Thess. 2.7⟩. In spite of the σαφέστατα Paul did not say it explicitly, but perhaps implied it. The *implicit* contrast with ἐξαγγέλλων in the preceding phrase of the letter probably determines the meaning here as the classical one, "indicate obscurely" or "hint at"; so *LSJ*. Clement also uses ὑποση-μείωσις—although in a different sense—in a context where the general thought and vocabulary are so close to this letter as to deserve quotation at length (II.9.4ff): Ἀλλ’ οἱ μὲν τὴν ἀληθῆ τῆς μακαρίας σῴζοντες διδασκαλίας παράδοσιν εὐθὺς ἀπὸ Πέτρου ... ἧκον δὴ σὺν Θεῷ καὶ εἰς ἡμᾶς τὰ προγονικὰ ἐκεῖνα καὶ ἀποστολικὰ καταθησόμενοι σπέρματα· καὶ εὖ οἶδ’ ὅτι ἀγαλλιάσονται, οὐχὶ τῇ ἐκφράσει ἡσθέντες ... μόνῃ δὲ τῇ κατὰ τὴν ὑποσημείωσιν τηρήσει. ποθούσης γὰρ οἶμαι ψυχῆς τὴν μακαρίαν παράδοσιν ἀδιάδραστον φυλάττειν ... ᾗ καὶ οὐ κεκώλυκεν ὁ κύριος ἀπὸ ἀγαθοῦ σαββατίζειν, μεταδιδόναι δὲ τῶν θείων μυστηρίων καὶ τοῦ φωτὸς ἐκείνου τοῦ ἁγίου τοῖς χωρεῖν δυναμένοις συγκεχώρηκεν· αὐτίκα οὐ πολλοῖς ἀπεκάλυψεν ἃ μὴ πολλῶν ἦν, ὀλίγοις δέ, οἷς προσήκειν ἠπίστατο ... τὰ δὲ ἀπόρρητα, καθάπερ ὁ Θεός, λόγῳ πιστεύεται, οὐ γράμματι ... τὰ μυστήρια μυστικῶς παραδίδοται ... Ἡ μὲν οὖν τῶνδέ μοι τῶν ὑπομνημάτων γραφή ... ἐπαγγέλλεται ... οὐχ ὥστε ἑρμηνεῦσαι τὰ ἀπόρρητα ἱκανῶς, πολλοῦ γε καὶ δεῖ, μόνον δὲ τὸ ὑπομνῆσαι. [It should be noted that in the letter the *explicit* contrast is between *both* ἐξαγγέλλων and ὑποσημαίνων on the one hand and ἐκλεγόμενος on the other. A.D.N.]

ἀλλ’. For emphasis after a string of negatives, II.117.18f; 241.20; 465.13ff; etc.

ἐκλεγόμενος. Frequent in middle with accusative, IV.373. With χρήσιμον, II.114.29, τὸ ἐξ ἁπάσης παιδείας χρήσιμον ἐκλεγομένους ἡμᾶς ἔχειν; see II.21.7.

χρησιμωτάτας. The superlative, II.113.15; with πρός, I.264.21; II.17.32; Mossbacher, 73–74.

ἐνόμισε. Judge to be, consider, I.17.25; II.12.20.

αὔξησιν. Frequent in Clement. With πίστις, II.327.8ff, φαίνεται οὖν ὁ ἀπόστολος διττὴν καταγγέλλων πίστιν, μᾶλλον δὲ μίαν, αὔξησιν καὶ τελείωσιν ἐπιδεχομένην. The context declares, as does the text here, that faith can be increased by learning.

τῆς τῶν κατηχουμένων πίστεως. τοῦ δὲ Πέτρου μαρτυρήσαντος,

κατηχουμένων. Used thus as a technical term for persons receiving instruction preparatory to admission to the sacraments, II.13.25; 476.19. The motivation ascribed
to Mark here, by the letter, is strikingly similar to that Clement claims for himself,
II.476.18f, τῷ δ'ἀπανθιζομένῳ τὸ χρειῶδες εἰς ὠφέλειαν τῶν κατηχουμένων. In II.494.
11f Clement, arguing from the example of St. Paul, implies, as does this letter, that
catechumens may be left without full information—not to say misinformed—in
order to protect their faith: αὐτίκα ὁ Παῦλος τὸν Τιμόθεον περιέτεμεν διὰ τοὺς ἐξ
Ἰουδαίων πιστεύοντας, ἵνα μή, καταλύοντος αὐτοῦ τὰ ἐκ τοῦ νόμου σαρκικώτερον προειλημ-
μένα, ἀποστῶσι τῆς πίστεως οἱ ἐκ νόμου κατηχούμενοι, εἰδὼς ἀκριβῶς ὅτι περιτομὴ οὐ
δικαιοῖ· τοῖς πᾶσι γὰρ πάντα γίγνεσθαι ὡμολόγει, κατὰ συμπεριφορὰν σῴζων τὰ κύρια
τῶν δογμάτων, ἵνα πάντας κερδήσῃ. (Cf. Acts 16.3; Gal. 5.2ff; I Cor. 9.19–22.) [The
sense of κατηχούμενοι in II.494.11ff seems, however, to be general rather than
technical, and it is the general sense which the term in the letter probably has, if
the letter is by Clement. A.D.N. So, too, C.M. On the other hand, W.J. wrote, in
substance: It is interesting to see how Clement's classification of early Christian
literature takes for granted, as a criterion, the suitability of each book for the classes
of Alexandrian religious instruction, κατηχούμενοι and τελειούμενοι (inf., l. 22). Such
classification perhaps produced the concept of a secret Gospel, which Mark did
not disclose to the *simpliciores*. This concept, in turn, may have caused imaginative
people to interpolate the canonical Gospel of Mark and add to it their particular
kind of gnosis, like that of the Carpocratians. Clement himself believes in a secret
Gospel; he objects only to the Carpocratian "mixture" by interpolation. Such
Christian fictions of secret or esoteric versions of their accepted holy books seem to
follow the trend of Greek philosophers in Hellenistic times, to distinguish an exoteric
from an esoteric kind of Pythagoreanism and Platonism, and, finally, to forge such
a pseudoliterature as we still have under allegedly ancient Pythagorean names. Also,
the misinterpretation of Aristotle's λόγοι ἐξωτερικοί (dialogues)—as opposed to the
esoteric writings (treatises) which were "hypomnemata"—must be understood as
a consequence of this later trend.]

τοῦ δὲ Πέτρου. With the article, I.116.11; 277.5; 283.5; etc. τοῦ Πέτρου in genitive
absolute, beginning a sentence, III.197.21 (Eusebius' summary of Clement). Genitive
absolute in the beginning of a narrative to indicate the time after which the events
occurred, III.188.3,12. The repetition of proper names, found here and again below
(ὁ Μᾶρκος) is a marked characteristic of both the Eusebian summaries (above, I.15).

μαρτυρήσαντος. The only reference to Peter's death in Clement's recognized works
has κοιμάω, III.106.24, but the context there would make a reference to the martyrdom intrusive. Clement regularly uses μαρτυρεῖν as a technical term with the sense
it has here—to undergo martyrdom, II.254.27; 285.14; etc. [The earliest use in

I.19
παρῆλθεν εἰς ᾿Αλεξάνδρειαν ὁ Μᾶρκος, κομίζων καὶ τὰ [τ] αὐτοῦ καὶ

this technical sense seems to be not in the NT, but in Clement of Rome, *First Epistle to the Corinthians* 5.4; therefore this appearance in Clement of Alexandria is interesting. W.J.] Swete, xxv, remarks that Clement of Alexandria differs from the Asiatic tradition about Mk. (Irenaeus—Harvey, III.1.2 = Stieren, III.1.1, etc.) by representing the Gospel as composed before Peter's death. The present letter shares this Clementine peculiarity. [This is an important argument for authenticity. E.B.]

παρῆλθεν. II.96.13; cf. *LSJ* s.v. III, "pass on and come to a place," which is the sense here.

εἰς. Regularly used with παρέρχομαι; see the passages cited in the preceding paragraphs and Mossbacher, 55.

᾿Αλεξάνδρειαν. Without the article after εἰς, I.37.17; after ἐν, II.86.8; 92.12.

Μᾶρκος. The tradition that Mark came to Alexandria does not appear in the preserved works of Clement, but Clement and Papias were probably the sources from which it was drawn by Eusebius (*HE* II.16). The φασίν which now stands in the first sentence of II.16, if not used impersonally, should refer to Clement and Papias, who were named as the sources of information in the preceding sentence. [C.M. thinks this suggestion concerning the subject of φασίν plausible. J.M., however, argued that because, "we have no tradition . . . about Mark's connection with Alexandria before Eusebius (*HE* II.16)," therefore this letter depends on Eusebius.]

κομίζων. In Clement this verb usually means "provide"; but the sense it has here, "carry away so as to preserve, carry, convey, bring" (*LSJ* s.v. II), is common in classical authors and perhaps appears in metaphor in II.29.16f, ὁ δὲ πρὸς τὸν βίον ἀναφέρων ἕκαστα τὸν ὀρθόν, ἔκ τε τῶν ῾Ελληνικῶν καὶ τῶν βαρβαρικῶν ὑποδείγματα κομίζων, πολύπειρος οὗτος τῆς ἀληθείας ἰχνευτής; cf. II.256.9f, σοφίσματα εἰς μέσον κομίζοντες. [The verb is often used of introducing and, in that sense, "bringing" a doctrine; Bonitz, *Index* 402ᵇ23ff. Here it seems to mean simply "bring" from one place to another, but the extension of this meaning to the former is well illustrated by the passage. W.J.] Jerome, *De viris inlustribus* 8, writes of Mark, "adsumpto itaque evangelio quod ipse confecerat perrexit Aegyptum." Swete, xix n1, thinks this an inference from Eus., *HE* II.16.

καί . . . τ᾿ . . . καί. [If one reads καὶ τά τ᾿ αὐτοῦ καὶ τὰ τοῦ Πέτρου, which I find preferable to τὰ ἑαυτοῦ, the καί . . . καί cannot mean "both . . . and," because a τέ cannot be combined with a καί in this manner, but the last καί must be connected with the τέ and the first καί is connected closely with κομίζων and stands for "also." He carried with himself also his own and Peter's hypomnemata. A.W.]

I.20
τὰ τοῦ Πέτρου ὑπομνήματα

τὰ αὐτοῦ. MS, ταταυτοῦ. [A.D.N. would read τά τ' αὐτοῦ, on the supposition that the copyist did not understand the letters he found in his MS and so reproduced them *en bloc*.] This would suggest that he may have had before him a MS without accents and breathings. [But had that been the case, there would have been many more instances of omitted accents and of false divisions. I suspect that an ancestor had τὰ αὐτοῦ, which became ταυτοῦ. This can represent either τὰ αὐτοῦ, or τοῦ αὐτοῦ. To show that it represented τὰ αὐτοῦ someone superscribed τὰ—hence ταταυτοῦ. καὶ τά τ' αὐτοῦ καί is odd Greek; I should expect καὶ τὰ αὐτοῦ or (omitting καί) τά τε αὐτοῦ. B.E.] Stählin, I.XXXVIf, remarks on the frequency with which his manuscript used αὐτοῦ, etc., after articles, in place of the reflexive forms, and omitted the coronis in crasis. However, I think the error here must be given an explanation which will accord with the amazing correctness of the rest of the MS. I should suppose, therefore, that the writer found a folio of an uncial MS with few or no explanatory signs or word divisions. Therefore he studied it carefully, correcting the spelling, marking the divisions, adding accents, breathings, and the like. Along with his other changes he indicated by a superscribed τά, as B.E. suggests, that *TAYTOY*, which stood in his text, was to be understood as τὰ αὐτοῦ. Then he copied his corrected text into his book. He was pressed for time when he copied, and therefore made a number of minor mistakes, of which ταταυτοῦ was one.

ὑπομνήματα. Clement uses this often for his own writings, occasionally for those of others; e.g., II.73.25. He apparently uses it to mean "notes" or "papers," as it probably does here [and this is the regular usage—W.J.]. Eusebius, in his summary of Clement, *HE* II.15, describes the cononical Gospel according to Mark as a ὑπόμνημα. [The word is normally used in the singular to mean simply "book." W.J. J.M. thought it derived from Eusebius; see his comment on πνευματικώτερον εὐαγγέλιον below, I.21–22.] For the customary use of ὑπομνήματα to describe either private notebooks or works composed without attention to arrangement of material, or not in finished form, Lazzati, 24; Lieberman, *Hellenism* 87; Munck, *Untersuchungen* 39; Jaeger, *Studien* 135; Hyldahl, 75ff. The term could also mean, generally, "documents"; e.g., Eus., *HE* VI.12.1. Justin Martyr knew ἀπομνημονεύματα "of Peter," *Dialogue* 106.3 [and "of the apostles," *First Apology* 67.3—W.V.] and quoted from them material now to be found only in Mk. 3.16f. Clement quotes as statements of Peter material from Mt., Mk., Acts, I Tim. (! I.233.10ff), I Pet., the *Preaching of Peter*, and the *Apocalypse of Peter*; but he also had a good deal of information about Peter from a source or sources now lost, and he seems to have made use of this information in those of his own works which have also been lost—or suppressed: I.220.15; 453.11ff;[3] III.46.1ff; 196.12(?); 22ff; 197.17ff; 32ff; 198.20ff; 199.21ff

3. Probably not from the *Preaching*; it differs in type of content from the *Preaching* material which precedes it in this passage of Clement, and it circulated separately (Eus., *HE* V.18.14, where it is reported as ὡς ἐκ παραδόσεως).

ἐξ ὧν μεταφέρων

(cf. II.466.9); 206.17ff; 230.2ff(?). Of these 11 passages, the last 8 come from works of Clement now lost, and at least 1 is of typically gnostic content—III.199.21f, from Eus., *HE* II.1.4f, which reports that Clement said Ἰακώβῳ τῷ δικαίῳ καὶ Ἰωάννῃ καὶ Πέτρῳ μετὰ τὴν ἀνάστασιν παρέδωκεν τὴν γνῶσιν ὁ κύριος. It is precisely from these apostles and Paul that Clement claims his teachers had received, evidently by private tradition, and handed on to him the essential teachings of the Lord. Thus II.9.4ff: Οἱ μὲν τὴν ἀληθῆ τῆς μακαρίας σῴζοντες διδασκαλίας παράδοσιν εὐθὺς ἀπὸ Πέτρου τε καὶ Ἰακώβου, Ἰωάννου τε καὶ Παύλου τῶν ἁγίων ἀποστόλων παῖς παρὰ πατρὸς ἐκδεχόμενος . . . ἧκον δὴ σὺν Θεῷ καὶ εἰς ἡμᾶς τὰ προγονικὰ ἐκεῖνα καὶ ἀποστολικὰ καταθησόμενοι σπέρματα. This is not merely the public Christian tradition. See the context of the passage (it has been quoted above, on ὑποσημαίνων, I.17). It definitely refers to a body of secret doctrine. Other gnostics also claimed to have secret traditions derived from Peter; Clement mentions particularly the followers of Basilides, whose teacher, Glaucias, had been Peter's "interpreter" (III.75.16), and those of Valentinus, whose teacher had been Theodas, an acquaintance of Paul's. The books accepted as authoritative by Clement and his friends—those books of which some eventually became "The New Testament"—seem to have said nothing of Glaucias and Theodas, but some books accepted as authoritative by Basilides and his friends similarly said nothing of Peter's "interpreter," Mark (Eus., *HE* III.39.15) or of Paul's acquaintance, Luke (unknown even to Papias), from whom the party Clement represents claimed to have gotten their traditions. And Basilides (fl. ca. 135) was considerably earlier than Clement (fl. 175–200). The claim to have apostolic traditions was common in the ancient church and, since new apostolic traditions were discovered to settle new disputes as they arose, it must have been believed that the traditions had been secret before the times of their fortunate discovery. Therefore, this common method of doctrinal argument presupposes a general belief in a considerable body of secret apostolic traditions to which privileged members of the clergy [and perhaps other privileged persons—J.R.] had access. For example, see the material quoted from Eusebius by Holl, 175, on the claim of a secret tradition about the date of the Pascha [and cf. Eus., *HE* V.25—A.D.N.]. The system by which the dates of the festivals were set was a most important element of the secret doctrine of the Samaritans, and probably also of the Qumran sect (Bowman, *Calendar* 24,27), as of rabbinic Judaism. On the public tradition about secret traditions, see A. D. Nock in *Gnomon* 29 (1957) 527–528.

ἐξ ὧν μεταφέρων. Ἐκ is used to refer to taking material from a book or books, in II.435.3; again, with μεταφέρειν, as here (II.442.20f) Ἀριστοφάνης . . . ἐν ταῖς πρώταις Θεσμοφοριαζούσαις τὰ ἐκ τῶν Κρατίνου Ἐμπιπραμένων μετήνεγκεν ἔπη. The context is concerned with examples of plagiarism, so the verb almost certainly means "took over," not "remodeled"; cf. line 10 of the same page, Εὔροις δ' ἂν . . . Ὅμηρον . . . κατὰ λέξιν μετενηνοχότα παρ' Ὀρφέως ἐκ τοῦ Διονύσου ἀφανισμοῦ.

I.21

εἰς τὸ πρῶτον αὐτοῦ βιβλίον τὰ τοῖς προκόπτουσι περὶ τὴν γνῶσιν

εἰς. Clement uses with μεταφέρειν, but metaphorically, III.171.31. The literal use is, of course, well established; e.g., Plato, *Timaeus* 73e.

πρῶτον. For πρότερον; so II.442.20ff, quoted above; also III.118.4; noted by Stählin, IV.691. [Cf. Acts 1.1. W.M.C.]

βιβλίον. Frequent in this sense in Clement; II.51.3, etc.

προκόπτουσι περί. II.473.9ff, οὐκ ἀπολειφθήσεται τοίνυν ⟨ὁ γνωστικὸς⟩ τῶν προκοπτόντων περὶ τὰς μαθήσεις τὰς ἐγκυκλίους καὶ τὴν Ἑλληνικὴν φιλοσοφίαν. Parallels to the use of περί, Mossbacher, 70f. [That προκόπτουσι is to be understood here in accord with this usage of Clement's, as meaning "whatever things make for headway" rather than "the persons advancing" toward gnosis, is proved by the concluding phrase of the sentence, where τῶν τελειουμένων makes the antithesis to τῶν κατηχουμένων above. Were not the sense of προκόπτουσι that indicated by the Clementine parallel, the antithesis would be spoiled by its intrusion and the last phrase would be tautologous. Parallels are found in Thuc., IV.60.2, and Sextus Emp., *Pyrroneion Hypotyposeon* II.240. A.D.N. C.H.R. comments, "προκόπτω appears with τὰ ἔργα as its subject in a third century papyrus quoted in F. Preisigke, *Papyruswörterbuch*; but I find it very hard to take it here otherwise than in a personal sense." A.W. is of the opinion that τοῖς προκόπτουσι "*must*" stand for "the persons advancing." He observes that the προκοπτόντων in Thuc. IV.60.2 has a personal subject, while in Sextus Emp. *Pyr. Hyp.* II.240 the subject is τὸν λόγον. W.V. is of the same opinion, remarking that if τοῖς προκόπτουσι refers to the persons we have an orderly progression, τῶν κατηχουμένων—τοῖς προκόπτουσι—τῶν τελειουμένων, in which this second term is a necessary connective between the first and the third.] But if so, how are we to explain that by adding to his text things suitable for τοῖς προκόπτουσι he produced a gospel for the use of τῶν τελειουμένων? This difficulty seems to me to require either the unlikely equation of τοῖς προκόπτουσι with τῶν τελειουμένων or the translation proposed by A.D.N. and confirmed by the striking parallel in Clement. [But why, then, κατάλληλα? Wouldn't τὰ προκόπτοντα περὶ τὴν γνῶσιν be enough? B.E.] No, the meaning is not the same. Clement's point is that Mark did not write down the essentials of the secret doctrine, but merely things suitable to lead the initiates toward these essentials. It would seem, therefore, that Clement's wording here is precise (and precisely answers the objection that the letter cannot be by him because he thought the gnostic tradition unwritten; see below, on συνέταξε).

γνῶσιν. III.36.29; 142.3, ἐκ πίστεως καὶ φόβου προκόψας εἰς γνῶσιν ἄνθρωπος. This phrase expresses those conceptions of faith as inferior to knowledge, and of the believer's advance from faith to knowledge, which are also implied by the letter and by many other passages in Clement's works: e.g., III.41–42; II.187.33f.

κατάλληλα συνέταξε

κατάλληλα. Frequent with the dative, and of spiritual suitability: e.g., I.149.25; 268.2; etc.

συνέταξε. Clement regularly uses this for the composition of books, IV.734 (13 instances). A tradition that Mark wrote in Egypt is preserved by Chrysostom and certain NT MSS; Swete. xxxix. [In this account of Mark's writing a second, "more spiritual," Gospel W.V. finds the principal theological motive of the letter and the conclusive proof that it is not by Clement. Clement knows a gnostic tradition within the Church, but for him the characteristic of this tradition is that it is unwritten; cf. Völker, 363f. Gnosis is that κατὰ διαδοχὰς εἰς ὀλίγους ἐκ τῶν ἀποστόλων ἀγράφως παραδοθεῖσα (II.462.28f). Accordingly, Clement says explicitly οὐκ ἔγραφον δὲ οἱ πρεσβύτεροι (III.144.26), and only this fact explains why the Stromateis begin with Clement's self-defense for having broken with this custom and written down the tradition. Consequently III.145.5-15 cannot mean that the gnostics within the Church had secret books; the reference must be merely to written confirmatory evidence of the oral tradition, in the sense of Stromateis I.1 (= II.1.1ff). Consequently, too, the present letter is not by Clement. Further evidence for this conclusion is found in the fact that the letter reflects a Church more highly institutionalized than that known to Clement—one which inherits property and of which presbyters are ecclesiastical officials rather than spiritual teachers (see below, on I.28 and II.5). The date of the letter is to be determined by two considerations: on the one hand, the gnostic controversy is still a living issue; on the other hand, the ecclesiastical organization has become fixed and established in the ways mentioned.] However, it must be pointed out that: (1) This letter does not say that Mark, in his second Gospel, wrote down the gnostic tradition. On the contrary, it is careful to deny that he did so (I.22-24). He merely added to his former Gospel material he knew would serve as points of departure to those instructed more fully (see above, end of the paragraph on τοῖς προκόπτουσι). (2) Mark was not a presbyter, and there is no doubt that Clement thought Mark *did* write, so Clement's statement that the presbyters did not write is no evidence as to what Clement thought Mark wrote. (3) Stromateis I.1 is not an apology for breaking with the tradition that instruction should be oral only. Clement never in this chapter mentions any such tradition; on the contrary, he repeatedly takes for granted that Christian instruction is already both oral and written (II.4.24f; 6.12; 8.3). He could hardly do otherwise, since he goes on in the Stromateis to quote a great deal of written Christian literature. Moreover, Harnack agreed with Mercati that even some of the passages Clement reports as "traditions" were before him in written form (*Fragment* 903). Whether or not Clement thought any *secret* Christian material was in writing he does not explicitly say in this chapter; but his concession that it is impossible that secret material, if written down, should not fall into the wrong hands (II.11.4f) would be more understandable if he had known of some material which had done so—for instance, Mark's second Gospel, which the Carpocratians had got hold of. Further, Clement

I.22
πνευματικώτερον εὐαγγέλιον

does not, in *Stromateis* I.1, defend himself for writing down the gnostic tradition. Instead, he is at pains to say that he did *not* write down this tradition, and he says so in words strikingly similar to those used in this letter to say the same thing about Mark (compare Clement II.10.17–11.11 with the letter I.22–24 and 27). Clement's defense in *Stromateis* I.1 is against the charge of presumption, which might be brought for his writing at all, the charge of indiscretion, for making the truth available to the wrong people, and the charge of frivolity, for decking out Christian doctrine with philosophic argumentation. Völker's misunderstanding is admittedly the *communis opinio* (recently repeated by Osborn, *Teaching* 340); but I can find nothing in the text to justify it, nothing which says or even implies that Clement's undertaking was a radically new departure or that there were *no* previous Christian writings of the same sort. (Since there certainly were, and Clement knew them and had made excerpts from them, it is not surprising that he does not deny their existence.) (4) III.144.26–145.15 deserves quotation at length: Οὐκ ἔγραφον δὲ οἱ πρεσβύτεροι μήτε ἀπασχολεῖν βουλόμενοι τὴν διδασκαλικὴν τῆς παραδόσεως φροντίδα ... μηδὲ μὴν τὸν ... καιρὸν καταναλίσκοντες εἰς γραφήν. τάχα δὲ οὐδὲ τῆς αὐτῆς φύσεως κατόρθωμα τὸ συντακτικὸν καὶ διδασκαλικὸν εἶδος εἶναι πεπεισμένοι τοῖς εἰς τοῦτο πεφυκόσι συνεχώρουν. τὸ μὲν γὰρ ἀκωλύτως καὶ μετὰ ῥύμης φέρεται ῥεῦμα τοῦ λέγοντος ... τὸ δὲ ὑπὸ τῶν ἐντυγχανόντων ἑκάστοτε βασανιζόμενον, ἀκριβοῦς τῆς ἐξετάσεως τυγχάνον, ἄκρας καὶ τῆς ἐπιμελείας ἀξιοῦται, καὶ ἔστιν οἷον εἰπεῖν ἔγγραφος διδασκαλίας βεβαίωσις, καὶ εἰς τοὺς ὀψιγόνους οὕτως διὰ τῆς συντάξεως παραπεμπομένης τῆς φωνῆς. ἡ γὰρ τῶν πρεσβυτέρων παρακαταθήκη διὰ τῆς γραφῆς λαλοῦσα ὑπουργῷ χρῆται τῷ γράφοντι πρὸς τὴν παράδοσιν ⟨εἰς σωτηρίαν⟩ τῶν ἐντευξομένων ... φθόνος δὲ ἀπείη γνωστικοῦ. διὰ τοῦτο γὰρ καὶ ζητεῖ πότερον χεῖρον, ἀναξίῳ δοῦναι ἢ ἀξίῳ μὴ παραδοῦναι, καὶ κινδυνεύει ὑπὸ πολλῆς τῆς ἀγάπης οὐ μόνον παντὶ τῷ προσήκοντι, ἀλλ' ἔσθ' ὅτε καὶ ἀναξίῳ λιπαρῶς δεομένῳ κοινωνήσειν, οὐ διὰ τὴν δέησιν ... ἀλλὰ διὰ τὴν ἐπιμονὴν τοῦ δεομένου μελετῶντος εἰς πίστιν διὰ πολλῆς τῆς δεήσεως. This seems to me reasonably plain and complete justification for my statement below (II.5) that Clement thought the teaching of the presbyters "had been oral, but now, written down, formed *part* of the body of secret Christian tradition—and was sometimes indiscretely communicated to the unworthy." How Völker knows that this can not mean that the gnostics in the Church possessed secret books, I do not understand. Accordingly, his basic reason for supposing the letter not by Clement fails to convince me. On the other considerations—the Church's inheritance of property, the use of "presbyter" to refer to a church official—see below, on I.28 (κατέλιπε) and II.5 (πρεσβύτερον).

πνευματικώτερον εὐαγγέλιον. III.197.27ff, τὸν μέντοι Ἰωάννην ἔσχατον ... πνεύματι θεοφορηθέντα πνευματικὸν ποιῆσαι εὐαγγέλιον. This is Eusebius' report (*HE* VI.14.7) of what Clement said in the lost *Hypotyposes*; it is confirmed by the Latin version of Clement's *Adumbrationes* on I John (III.209.25f), *Consequenter evangelio secundum Iohannem*

εἰς τὴν τῶν τελειουμένων χρῆσιν

et convenienter etiam haec epistola principium spiritale continet. Clement uses the comparative form of the adjective in II.465.34ff: στοιχειωτική τίς ἐστιν ἡ μερικὴ αὕτη φιλοσοφία, τῆς τελείας ὄντως ἐπιστήμης ἐπέκεινα κόσμου περὶ τὰ νοητὰ καὶ ἔτι τούτων τὰ πνευματικώτερα ἀναστρεφομένης. πνευματικώτερον as an adverb, to describe an understanding of the hidden sense of Christian teachings, II.370.18f. Here it is used to describe Mark's second Gospel as "more spiritual" than his first because it contained or indicated more of the hidden sense of Jesus' teachings and actions. [Contrast, however, the opinion of J.M.: "The central feature of the letter . . . is the importance ascribed to . . . Mark in Alexandria and his authority as a writer of gospel literature . . . We have no tradition, as far as I know, about his connection with Alexandria before Eusebius (*HE* II.16). Some details could be used to argue in favor of the dependence of the author of the letter on Eusebius: When Eusebius tells about the spiritual Gospel of John (*HE* VI.14.5–7 . . .) after speaking of the Gospel of Mark, a later author identifying Mark with John ('John, called Mark,' Acts 12.25; 15.37) could understand this text as meaning that Mark, after writing his canonical Gospel, had composed another more spiritual Gospel. As smaller items I should like to mention the use of ἀναγράφω in *HE* VI.14.6 and in the letter I.16, and Eusebius' use of the word ὑπόμνημα about the Gospel of Mark (*HE* II.15.1) and the use of the word in the plural in the letter I.19f. It is possible that the letter tries to combine the two traditions about Mark—that he wrote his Gospel before the death of Peter (Clement) and after it (Irenaeus)—by stating that Mark wrote one Gospel before and another one after the death of Peter (both opinions are mentioned by Eusebius).''']

εἰς . . . χρῆσιν. III.36.2, εἰς τὴν τούτων χρῆσιν . . . τὰ πάντα γέγονεν. Clement regularly uses εἰς to indicate objectives; Mossbacher, 56f.

τῶν τελειουμένων. These might be baptized persons, as opposed to the catechumens above. Thus I.105.20ff lists the immediate consequences of baptism: βαπτιζόμενοι φωτιζόμεθα, φωτιζόμενοι υἱοποιούμεθα, υἱοποιούμενοι τελειούμεθα, τελειούμενοι ἀπαθανατιζόμεθα. [But if τελειουμένων referred to baptism it would mean either persons in the process of being baptized or those on the road to it, who would be identical with the catechumens. A.D.N. But C.F.D.M. suggests that the participles in this passage are "frequentative"; κατηχουμένων = "any who (from time to time) become catechumens"; προκόπτουσι = "any who (at any given time) are advancing," and so τελειουμένων and μυουμένους, cf. Gal 6.13.] Richardson's discovery that Mk. 10.13–45 was probably a lection for a baptismal service makes it not unlikely that τελειουμένων here means "persons in the process of being baptized" and that Clement thought the additions were made to adapt the Gospel for catechetic and liturgical use in the Christian initiation. However, the questions raised by Richardson's discovery require more discussion than can be undertaken in this commentary; they will be dealt with in section III of Chapter Three. Here it is enough to say that Clement's notion of τελείωσις is very hard to define and certainly

makes possible the interpretation of τελειουμένων as referring *either* to baptism *or* to some initiatory ceremony other than baptism *or* to a long process of perfection in gnosis. The last of these possibilities is clearly indicated by the discussion in I.105–121, following the passage quoted above. There Clement explains that the consequences he has listed are present only potentially (106.30f, οὐδέπω ... ἀπείληφεν τὴν τελείαν δωρεάν) and that even Paul had to say (121.10ff) "οὐχ ὅτι ἤδη ἔλαβον ἢ ἤδη τετελείωμαι, διώκω δὲ εἰ καὶ καταλάβω" ... καὶ τέλειον μὲν ἑαυτὸν ἡγεῖται, ὅτι ἀπήλλακται τοῦ προτέρου βίου, ἔχεται δὲ τοῦ κρείττονος, οὐχ ὡς ἐν γνώσει τέλειος, ἀλλ' ὡς τοῦ τελείου ἐφιέμενος. Developing the thought of this passage, Clement conceives of τελείωσις as a process which may affect only one or another aspect of a Christian's life—one may be perfected in piety or endurance or prophecy, and so on (II.305.19ff; 307.18ff)—but when he writes of "perfection" without further specification he means perfection in gnosis (Völker, 301f). He sharply distinguishes the gnostic from the mere believer (II.298.23ff and often, esp. 485, 487; III.37.1ff; 42.8; 60.2; etc.) and thinks of the gnostic's being perfected as a process normally continuing throughout the Christian's earthly life (cf. Völker, 151, esp. n2). E.g., II.307.4ff, σπευστέον ἀπανδροῦσθαι γνωστικῶς καὶ τελειοῦσθαι ὡς ὅτι μάλιστα ἔτι ἐν σαρκὶ καταμένοντας, ἐκ τῆς τελείας ἐνθένδε ὁμοφροσύνης μελετήσαντας συνδραμεῖν τῷ θελήματι τοῦ Θεοῦ εἰς τὴν ἀποκατάστασιν τῆς τῷ ὄντι τελείας εὐγενείας τε καὶ συγγενείας εἰς τὸ πλήρωμα τοῦ Χριστοῦ. But he thinks its goal can be anticipated by the gnostic already in this life, III.30.30ff, ὁ γνωστικὸς παρὰ ὅλον εὔχεται τὸν βίον, δι'εὐχῆς συνεῖναι μὲν σπεύδων Θεῷ, καταλελοιπέναι δέ, συνελόντι εἰπεῖν, πάντα ὅσα μὴ χρησιμεύει γενομένῳ ἐκεῖ, ὡς ἂν ἐνθένδε ἤδη τὴν τελείωσιν ἀπειληφὼς τοῦ κατὰ ἀγάπην ⟨ἣν⟩δρωμένου (accepting the emendations of Tengblad, 96, and of Stählin, against Lazzati, 92). The achievement is never absolutely complete on earth (II.330.13), but is made almost complete (II.467.15ff; 468–469; 485ff) by the gift of gnosis. Both Clement and this letter conceive the gift of gnosis as a process of instruction in elements of the Christian tradition, including the Lord's teaching (III.42.5)—instruction given only to chosen candidates after considerable probation and leading eventually to deification (II. 367.3; 460.20; 462.24). So, esp., III.40.21ff–41.25: Ἔστιν γὰρ ... ἡ γνῶσις τελείωσίς τις ἀνθρώπου ὡς ἀνθρώπου, διὰ τῆς τῶν θείων ἐπιστήμης συμπληρουμένη κατά τε τὸν τρόπον καὶ τὸν βίον καὶ τὸν λόγον, σύμφωνος καὶ ὁμόλογος ἑαυτῇ τε καὶ τῷ θείῳ λόγῳ. διὰ ταύτης γὰρ τελειοῦται ἡ πίστις ... καὶ τὰ μὲν ἄκρα οὐ διδάσκεται, ἥ τε ἀρχὴ καὶ τὸ τέλος; πίστις λέγω καὶ ἡ ἀγάπη, ἡ γνῶσις δὲ ἐκ παραδόσεως διαδιδομένη κατὰ χάριν Θεοῦ τοῖς ἀξίοις σφᾶς αὐτοὺς τῆς διδασκαλίας παρεχομένοις οἷον παρακαταθήκη ἐγχειρίζεται ... ὅθεν ἐπὶ τέλει ἡ γνῶσις παραδίδοται τοῖς εἰς τοῦτο ἐπιτηδείοις καὶ ἐγκρίτοις διὰ τὸ πλείονος παρασκευῆς καὶ προγυμνασίας δεῖσθαι καὶ πρὸς τὸ ἀκούειν τῶν λεγομένων καὶ εἰς καταστολὴν βίου καὶ εἰς τὸ ἐπὶ πλέον τῆς κατὰ νόμον δικαιοσύνης κατ' ἐπίτασιν προεληλυθέναι· αὕτη πρὸς τέλος ἄγει τὸ ἀτελεύτητον καὶ τέλειον, προδιδάσκουσα τὴν ἐσομένην ἡμῖν κατὰ τὸν Θεὸν μετὰ Θεῶν δίαιταν ... Θεοὶ τὴν προσηγορίαν κέκληνται, οἱ σύνθρονοι τῶν ἄλλων Θεῶν, τῶν ὑπὸ τῷ σωτῆρι πρώτων τεταγμένων, γενησόμενοι. For further discussion of the problem see, besides Völker, especially the articles of Butterworth, Lebreton, Moingt, and Wytzes. Particularly important is Méhat, *Ordres*, which shows that Clement distinguished three classes of "philosophical," that is, Christian, material: the protreptic, for complete outsiders; the pedagogic

οὐδέπω

(paraenetic), for catechumens *and* ordinary Christians; the didascalic, for the advanced students, the gnostics. Méhat concludes that this classification of philosophical material reflects the system of instruction used in Clement's church. He comments, p. 357: "It is surprising to see that (within this system) the catechumenate does not constitute a peculiar phase. On the other hand, the distinction between the neophytes, still subject to elementary instruction, and the more advanced Christians who are initiated into the true doctrine, ought to be given more attention than it has hitherto received. For my part, I think the origin of this distinction lies in a common practice of the Church, established long before Clement's time, and going much further back than is generally supposed."

οὐδέπω. Initial, II.385.21; meaning "not yet," i.e., "he did not go so far as to," II.460.29; 469.23; 483.19. [So A.W. and B.E. C.F.D.M. here observed: "It seems to me that a case can be made (though I could not make it with deep conviction) for Clement's intending three documents: (1) τὸ πρῶτον βιβλίον (i.e. canonical Mk.) compiled at Rome during Peter's lifetime and containing select praxeis; (2) the πνευματικώτερον εὐαγγέλιον, an enlarged edition of (1) amplified by such material from Peter's and Mark's *hypomnemata* as Mark thought appropriate for any who made progress in knowledge and were initiates, or candidates for initiation; (3) a mystic gospel, an enlargement of (2) by additional praxeis and logia of a mystical sort. The arguments that might be used for distinguishing (3) are as follows: (a) οὐδέπω ὅμως seems naturally to imply not less than two preceding stages, 'yet, not even now' . . .; (b) my no. 2 is called πνευματικώτερον and related to οἱ τελειούμενοι, whereas there are other and more 'mystic' terms which only begin to appear at my stage (3), viz. τὰ ἀπόρρητα, ἡ ἱεροφαντικὴ διδασκαλία, μυσταγωγεῖν (and the whole of that phrase), αὐτοὶ μόνοι οἱ μυούμενοι τὰ μεγάλα μυστήρια, τὸ μυστικὸν εὐαγγέλιον; (c) to achieve a reference to only two, one has to make several rather difficult assumptions, viz. (1) οὐδέπω means 'not yet (and indeed never)'; (2) the ἀλλά clause which follows (including the ἔτι phrase in it) has to be taken in a 'but only' sense and treated as a mere amplification of what has already been described in rather different terms—terms relating only to οἱ τελειούμενοι and to praxeis without logia; (3) since, by assumption no. 1, αὐτὰ τὰ ἀπόρρητα never were written down by Mark and τὸ αὐτοῦ σύγγραμμα does not represent them, the rest of the Clement fragment must be about something less than the most esoteric material." This interpretation, however, Moule abandoned after discussion with Maurice Wiles, who argued to the contrary that in Clement's view τὰ ἀπόρρητα ought not to be written down (*Stromateis* I.13.2; VI.61.3), that Clement's mention of them was intended to assure Theodore that although the Carpocratians had got hold of the secret Gospel they had not learned the highest secrets, and that the use of οὐδέπω rather than οὐδέποτε, although surprising, was not a serious objection.] To the best of my recollection, only one other reader of the letter, Richardson, thought it might possibly refer to three versions of the Gospel, and he also gave up the notion.

I.23

ὅμως αὐτὰ τὰ ἀπόρρητα ἐξωρχήσατο, οὐδὲ κατέγραψε

ὅμως. Postpositive, with the sense it has here, I.283.21, where, as here, it follows a vowel.

τὰ ἀπόρρητα. Τὰ δὲ ἀπόρρητα ... λόγῳ πιστεύεται, οὐ γράμματι (this of Jesus' teaching). II.10.3; 10.17ff, ἡ μὲν οὖν τῶνδέ μοι τῶν ὑπομνημάτων γραφή ... ἐπαγγέλλεται ... οὐχ ὥστε ἑρμηνεῦσαι τὰ ἀπόρρητα ἱκανῶς, πολλοῦ γε καὶ δεῖ, μόνον δὲ τὸ ὑπομνῆσαι. This use of τὰ ἀπόρρητα for the mysteries of Christian teaching is frequent in Clement.

ἐξωρχήσατο. II.14.13ff, μέγας ὁ κίνδυνος τὸν ἀπόρρητον ὡς ἀληθῶς τῆς ὄντως φιλοσο-φίας λόγον ἐξορχήσασθαι. This was a common word for revealing the rites of mystery cults (Lucian, De saltatione 15), and Clement uses it of them as well as of Christian mysteries, I.11.10. [See Nilsson, I².656. A.D.N. For the content, see Origen's state-ment on Mt. 20.1–16 that Matthew knew, but withheld, the secret interpretations of the parables, GCS, Origenes, vol. 10, I.2, p. 441. J.M.]

κατέγραψε. In this sense, II.302.15; used of formally written records, Plato, Laws 741c. Clement believed that in Christian tradition ἦν γάρ τινα ἀγράφως παραδιδόμενα, II.368.2; and he insisted that it was this unwritten tradition which was most important for the instruction of the gnostic, II.462.24ff; 498.15ff. In this the letter and Clement agree. Clement's claim to a secret tradition has been emphasized by Lebreton, 493ff, and is recognized even by Lazzati, 69; Bardy, Origènes 73; and Mondésert, Clément 47–62, 110 and Symbolisme 161, 176–180; etc. The most penetrating study of the problem is that of Mondésert, who begins (51–55) by pointing out that many supposed instances of this claim are really examples of propaedeutic method or reflections of the Platonic tradition and of the allegorical theory of exegesis; but he goes on to recognize that beside these explanations one must admit that Clement claimed there was a secret body of doctrine, revealed by Christ to Peter, James, and John, and handed down orally to Clement's own time (56–57). This secret doctrine is not the ordinary ecclesiastical tradition (110), but is linked with a special Christian initiation by which it is communicated, not to all Christians, but to a chosen few. It thus constitutes a "second gnosis," distinct from the philosophical gnosis of which Clement usually wrote (161, 176, 180). Mondésert points out that this notion is contradictory not only to the philosophical system, but also "to the profound thought and even to the mentality of Clement"—his sympathy for all men, his belief in God's universal self-revelation, etc. (57). Mondésert also remarks that this notion is absolutely contrary to the Christian concept of tradition as the living magistracy of the entire Church (58), a concept beginning to prevail in the Alexandrian Christianity of Clement's time (though it may not have been so impor-tant earlier). These observations are acute and from them it follows that Clement did not himself invent this secret doctrine and its claims; nor did he derive it from

the contemporary tendencies of the church of Alexandria. Whence, then, did he get it? And why did he feel that he had to accept it in spite of its contradiction of his own temperament and theories? Presumably it was there and he believed its claims. Mondésert's suppositions that it was merely pretense, "an esoteric attitude," or that Clement thought he had a secret doctrine although he actually did not (61) are implausible in the face of his own observation of the fact: in Clement's theory the secret doctrine is an alien and intrusive element. This fact can be understood in the light of the present letter. [Commenting on this paragraph, C.M. wrote: "Je suis d'accord avec tout votre commentaire dans son ensemble et même pour votre re-marque sur la page 61 de mon livre." See also W.J.'s remarks in the following paragraph. J.M., on the other hand, wrote: "The most important objection against ascribing the letter to Clement is that he knew only the apostolic writings, e.g., the Gospel of Mark, and the oral tradition from the apostles which he had obtained through his teachers, the presbyters (*Stromateis* I.11.1ff). Every link in this transmis-sion of the tradition was, in his words, 'a son receiving it from his father.' The great change in the transmission is effected by Clement himself by his writings where he publishes the tradition from the apostles which his teachers had given him. I find it impossible to believe that Clement could write that Peter and Mark left ὑπομνήματα. In that case his words on the transmission of the apostolic tradition in the *Stromateis* would be completely un-understandable. The author of the letter has divided the Christian tradition into three parts, the first being represented by the Gospel of Mark where some of the acts (πράξεις) of the Lord have been written down, not all, and not the mystical acts, but those which were most useful to help the faith of the catechumens. The second way of expressing the Christian tradition is found in the mystical Gospel of Mark. Here Mark introduced material from his own and Peter's 'notes' . . . and in this way he brought together a more spiritual gospel to be used for those who are being initiated . . . The third kind of tradition is characterized by the subjects which Mark did not include in his more spiritual gospel (I.23). I do not think Clement would consent to a threefold division of the Christian tradition by which the oral tradition was divided up in an already written tradition from those who had been eyewitnesses to the acts of the Lord (Peter and Mark) and then the tradition which was transmitted only orally. But this threefold division might be more natural at a later time in the history of the Church."] When? After Clement the determination of the canon goes forward steadily. Consequently Clement, of all early Christian writers who can pretend to orthodoxy, is the one most receptive of "noncanonical" writings claiming apostolic authorship. About Peter he undoubt-edly believed that, besides his canonical Epistle, the apostle had left his *Apocalypse*, his *Preaching*, and considerable other material, some of which he thought preserved in written form; see above, I.19–20, on ὑπομνήματα. Consequently I see no justifica-tion for Munck's confidence that Clement cannot have believed that Peter left "papers" and that material drawn from these was incorporated into a second edition of Mark's Gospel. As for the common misunderstanding of the beginning of the *Stromateis*, see item (3) of my comments on Völker's remarks, in the paragraph on συνέταξε above, I.21.

τὴν ἱεροφαντικὴν διδασκαλίαν

ἱεροφαντικήν. I.16.3, of pagan mysteries; cf. I.84.25, ἱεροφαντεῖ δὲ ὁ κύριος, of Christian mysteries. [On this W.J. wrote, in substance: The letter seems to contradict those who have a tendency to interpret away or attenuate the existence in Clement of a theory of an esoteric Christian doctrine, because they feel that it is not consistent with his belief in the Christian religion as a universal message to all. I would not dare to expect in Clement anything like logical or philosophical consistency; and Christianity would remain a message to all, by the way, even if it had room for some kind of esoteric knowledge. The truth, as all the fathers of the Church believed, is not communicable to all men in the same way and by the same means, and the capacity of the human mind to understand these things is very limited at best. Whoever assumes different levels of interpretation must differentiate also between those who can see only the literal meaning and others who can penetrate deeper. We should refrain from letting our modern ideas or preferences influence our historical judgment. There was a strong tendency at Clement's time, and in him most of all, to construe Christianity as a philosophy; and, as I have said before, contemporary philosophical schools insisted on finding an esoteric and an exoteric form of teaching in almost every system. This must have influenced the way Christians looked for their own "philosophy" from the beginning, and every new, private interpretation given by individual Christians or gnostics could be justified only by saying that it was not to be found in the previous tradition of the Church because it had been kept secret. The letter makes clear that Clement does believe in an esoteric Christian tradition and thinks that the gnostics have something to do with it, but have got their knowledge of it in an illegal way and have corrupted its content. Most striking is the consistent use throughout the letter of terminology derived from the mysteries; this is found in Clement's other works as well, but is more concentrated in this letter than elsewhere because the letter deals with this *question*, and the words are not merely a stylistic device. I have always felt and taught that Clement's polemic against pagan religion is most violent when he impugns the mystery religions. It is obvious that they were to him the only serious competition for Christianity, since they were still living religion, involving a personal relation of the individual believer to God. But this letter proves that the competition of Christianity with the mysteries has influenced the form of the Christian religion itself most strongly, so that a Gregory of Nyssa could say that in the Christian religion the mystery is far more important than the dogma. He saw it in the Christian worship, which he interpreted always in this sense. So he solved the problem of the "few" and the "many." In Clement they were still sharply divided.] See also Jaeger's published remarks, *Christianity* 56f and n22.

διδασκαλίαν. This is Clement's favorite word for "teaching"; he rarely uses διδαχή, the common early Christian term. He often uses διδασκαλία with τοῦ Κυρίου, IV.340 (10 references).

I.24

τοῦ Κυρίου, ἀλλὰ ταῖς προγεγραμμέναις πράξεσιν ἐπιθεὶς καὶ ἄλλας, ἔτι

I.25

προσεπήγαγε λόγιά τινα ὧν ἠπίστατο

ἀλλά. A favorite conjunction of Clement's, used probably, on an average, more than once a page; so I.3.15; 4.4 and 18; 5.3 and 19; 7.10 and 14; 8.1; 9.4; etc.

προγεγραμμέναις. Not in Clement's preserved works, but twice in Eusebius' reports of his lost statements, III.197.19; 201.22. [C.H.R. observes that προγεγραμμένος, equivalent to the English "aforesaid," is so common from the fourth century onward in documents of all kinds that he would lay no weight on its occurrence here. W.M.C. remarks on the frequency of forms of the perfect tense in this letter, by contrast with their comparative rarity in classical Greek, for which see Cloud.] This frequency is paralleled in the recognized works of Clement. It is probably an atticizing trait; see Kilpatrick, *Atticism* 136. The letter, apart from the quotations from the secret Gospel, has 12 perfects in about 560 words (or 13, if ἐξήντληται is read in II.9); the first two pages sampled in Stählin—II.64–65—yielded 11 perfects in approximately 450 words.

πράξεσιν. Cf. above, on I.16.

ἐπιθείς. The same form is used, as here, of literary addition, with the dative and accusative, II.305.6. [However, in II.305.6 the ἐπιθείς occurs as part of the set phrase ἐπιθεῖναι τὸν κολοφῶνα. Apart from this phrase, ἐπιθεῖναί τι τοῖς προγεγραμμένοις is not very common in Clement's time; the ordinary word would be προσθεῖναι; but cf. Apoc. 22.18. A.W.]

ἄλλας. "Others of same kind," e.g., I.3.6 and 8, etc.

ἔτι. The sentence structure (participle, ἔτι, main verb), III.169.17 (also in negative form, II.233.21f).

προσεπήγαγε. The same form, as here, of literary addition, I.265.10.

λόγια. Clement has τὰ λόγια τοῦ κυρίου in III.161.14 and probably I.225.4f. Here he might have felt the specifying genitive was adequately replaced by the context; he evidently did so in I.289.27, where τὰ λόγια are the sayings of Jesus.

ὧν. The relative pronoun in the genitive as a connective, I.256.21 (also with ἐπίσταμαι and infinitive).

ἠπίστατο. The same form, also with infinitive, in a strikingly similar context, II.10.1f, αὐτίκα οὐ πολλοῖς ἀπεκάλυψεν ⟨ὁ Ἰησοῦς⟩ ἃ μὴ πολλῶν ἦν, ὀλίγοις δέ, οἷς προσήκειν ἠπίστατο, τοῖς οἵοις τε ἐκδέξασθαι καὶ τυπωθῆναι πρὸς αὐτά.

I.26

τὴν ἐξήγησιν μυσταγωγήσειν τοὺς ἀκροατὰς εἰς τὸ ἄδυτον τῆς ἑπτάκις

ἐξήγησιν. Of τὰ λόγια τοῦ κυρίου, III.161.14.

μυσταγωγήσειν. Also in III.161.18 where, as here, it refers to advanced instruction evidently effected by "exegesis" of "the Lord's sayings." Again, with the same sense, in II.320.7, where the mystery imagery is further developed with emphasis on the ἄρρητα. Gnostic teachers are described as μυσταγωγοί in III.75.7. That Clement conceived of documents, especially the books of Scripture, and their interpretation as means of gnostic initiation is shown by Völker, 354ff. The method which the letter ascribes to Mark is that followed in the earliest period of rabbinic mystical speculation but already being abandoned in the time of Clement. Scholem writes, *Gnosticism* 31: "Tannaïtic tradition has it that a pupil who is found worthy to begin a study of mystical lore is given . . . only . . . 'beginnings of chapters,' whose function is only to point to the subject matter to be dealt with and leaves to the student the task of proving his understanding." For this Scholem finds evidence in the *Talmud Yerushalmi* (hereinafter *J.*) *Hagigah* II.1(77a), and he concludes that texts giving full accounts of secret doctrine are post-Tannaïtic (third century or later) "even though much of the material itself may belong to the Tannaïtic period—which, of course, was, at the same time, the flowering season of Gnosticism."

ἀκροατάς. Frequent (and, as here, without technical sense), IV.219.

εἰς. Not used with μυσταγωγεῖν in Clement's preserved works, but the usage was probably standard. Photius (*Lexicon* s.v.) gives as a meaning of μυσταγωγεῖ, "εἰς μυστήρια ἄγει."

τὸ ἄδυτον. Clement was fond of ἄδυτα, IV.207 (9 references). The same complex of ideas—τὸ ἄδυτον τῆς ἀληθείας with the veil(s) concealing it from most, even, of the chosen people—is found in II.338.27ff, τῆς ἐπικρύψεως τὸν τρόπον, θεῖον ὄντα ὡς ἀληθῶς καὶ ἀναγκαιότατον ἡμῖν ⟨διὰ τὸν⟩ ἐν τῷ ἀδύτῳ τῆς ἀληθείας ἀποκείμενον ἱερὸν ἀτεχνῶς λόγον, Αἰγύπτιοι μὲν διὰ τῶν παρ' αὐτοῖς ἀδύτων καλουμένων, Ἑβραῖοι δὲ διὰ τοῦ παραπετάσματος ᾐνίξαντο, ⟨δι' οὗ⟩ μόνοις ἐξῆν ἐπιβαίνειν αὐτῶν τοῖς ἱερωμένοις.

ἑπτάκις. II.505.2. According to *B. Ketubot* 106a, inf., there were seven veils at the seven gates of the Temple in Jerusalem. Goodenough has seen a reference to them in the seven walls of the Temple represented in the Dura synagogue (panel WB3, *Jewish Symbols* XI pl. XI), and these were probably the seven περίβολοι of the Temple which Clement knew from Jewish tradition and interpreted as symbolic of the ways in which the truth at the heart of Scripture is concealed: II.347.3ff, αὐτίκα ὁμολογεῖ τὴν ἐπίκρυψιν ἡ περὶ τὸν νεὼν τὸν παλαιὸν τῶν ἑπτὰ περιβόλων πρός τι ἀναφορὰ παρ' Ἑβραίοις ἱστορουμένη. (This passage is part of a long list of examples, assembled from pagan and Jewish tradition, to prove that wise men always keep their essential

I.27

κεκαλυμμένης ἀληθείας. οὕτως οὖν προπαρεσκεύασεν, οὐ φθονερῶς οὐδ'

teachings secret; the list began with the passage cited in the preceding paragraph, II.338.27ff.) [With ἑπτάκις compare Apoc. 5.1f—the book sealed with seven seals—and also Clement, II.349.13. C.M.]

κεκαλυμμένης ἀληθείας. Clement uses κάλυμμα for the outer veil of the Temple's adyton in II.347.7, the immediate sequel of the passage referred to above. In II.347.19 and 348.13f he explains the veil as a means of keeping the unworthy from knowledge of the divine secrets (κάλυμμα κώλυμα λαϊκῆς ἀπιστίας). In II.340.28 the style of Greek poetry (?—ποιητικὴ ψυχαγωγία) is a curtain which concealed the theology of the poets from the vulgar. In II.13.26f the manuscript of the *Stromateis* reads ἀξιόπιστος . . . ἡ τοιαύτη ψυχαγωγία, δι᾽ ἧς κακουμένην οἱ φιλομαθεῖς παραδέχονται τὴν ἀλήθειαν. Wilamowitz emended κακουμένην to κεκαλυμμένην; Stählin and Mondésert, *Stromateis* I, accepted the emendation; it is now confirmed by the reading of the new text.

οὕτως οὖν. Initial, II.237.26; 282.2.

προπαρεσκεύασεν. II.422.17. Since *LSJ* s.v. reports the absolute use only of the middle forms of the verb, some object ("the text"? "matters"?) is probably to be understood here. [An object is similarly understood in Aristotle, *Historia animalium* 613a4. Cf. the use with ὅπως and a verb in the future, Plato, *Gorgias* 503a, 510d. A.D.N.]

οὐ . . . οὐδέ. With adverbs, II.289.31; with participles, II.244.25.

φθονερῶς. Clement also defends from the accusation of envy his own practice of teaching only in part, II.10.32–11.3: ταῦτα δὲ ἀναζωπυρῶν ὑπομνήμασι, τὰ μὲν ἑκὼν παραπέμπομαι ἐκλέγων ἐπιστημόνως, φοβούμενος γράφειν ἃ καὶ λέγειν ἐφυλαξάμην, οὐ τί που φθονῶν (οὐ γὰρ θέμις), δεδιὼς δὲ ἄρα περὶ τῶν ἐντυγχανόντων, μή πῃ ἑτέρως σφαλεῖεν, etc. [And in the same connection he lays down the principle φθόνος δὲ ἀπείη γνωστικοῦ. διὰ τοῦτο γὰρ καὶ ζητεῖ πότερον χεῖρον, ἀναξίῳ δοῦναι ἢ ἀξίῳ μὴ παραδοῦναι. III.145.10f. A.D.N.]. He also quotes *Barnabas* to the same purpose, in defense of the secret teaching of Jesus: Ἀλλὰ καὶ Βαρνάβας . . . ἤδη σαφέστερον γνωστικῆς παραδόσεως ἴχνος παρατιθέμενος λέγει . . . "εὐλογητὸς (ὁ) κύριος ἡμῶν, ἀδελφοί, ὁ σοφίαν καὶ νοῦν θέμενος ἐν ἡμῖν τῶν κρυφίων αὐτοῦ. λέγει γὰρ ὁ προφήτης 'παραβολὴν κυρίου τίς νοήσει, εἰ μὴ σοφός' . . ." ἐπεὶ ὀλίγων ἐστὶ ταῦτα χωρῆσαι. "οὐ γὰρ φθονῶν," φησί, "παρήγγειλεν ὁ κύριος" ἔν τινι εὐαγγελίῳ, "μυστήριον ἐμὸν ἐμοὶ καὶ τοῖς υἱοῖς τοῦ οἴκου μου" (II.368.12–28). Clement has the adjective φθονερός (in similar context, II.116.29) but not the adverb φθονερῶς, which, however, appears in Plato (*Phaedrus* 243c) and other classical authors (*LSJ* s.v.). The tradition goes back to *Odyssey* XI.380f. By contrast, Clement accuses the gnostics of secretive jealousy; Osborn, *Teaching* 336.

I.28

ἀπροφυλάκτως, ὡς ἐγὼ οἶμαι. καὶ ἀποθνῄσκων κατέλιπε τὸ αὐτοῦ

II.1

σύγγραμμα τῇ ἐκκλησίᾳ τῇ ἐν Ἀλεξανδρείᾳ ὅπου εἰσέτι νῦν

ἀπροφυλάκτως. Not in Clement. LSJ cites Dio Cassius, XXXVIII.41, and Achilles Tatius, VIII.1. In the latter it has the same meaning as here, "incautiously."

ὡς ἐγὼ οἶμαι. Verbatim, I.26.10; etc., but the simple οἶμαι, inserted without reference to the construction, is much more frequent in Clement's works (IV.592).

ἀποθνῄσκων. Frequent. Stählin, IV.262, cites 11 examples and marks his entry as incomplete. Here the writer of the MS seems to have written first ἀποθανων and then, over ανων, νῄσκ. The form ἀποθνῄσκων, therefore, may represent a deliberate correction by the writer of what he found in his text.

κατέλιπε. II.3.5, πότερον δ' οὐδ'ὅλως ἤ τισι καταλειπτέον συγγράμματα; with the dative as here. [κατέλιπε in the letter is an unmistakable claim to legitimate, testatory inheritance, no doubt by implicit contrast to the gnostics. A.D.N. That a particular church at this time should be heir to such a secret document, and should entrust its presbyters—in the sense of church officials—with the custody of it, is altogether contradictory to the practices of the period and, at about the year 200, quite unthinkable. W.V.] Völker gives no evidence to support his comment, and I do not know of any. Long before Clement's time, the letters of Paul had been sent to particular churches and presumably preserved by them (Goodspeed, *Introduction* 215ff, who remarks that the practice of Paul in directing letters to individual churches was followed by Ignatius and the author of the Apocalypse).

σύγγραμμα. The singular, meaning "composition," "work," II.59.22; 404.8. The συγγράμματα of the apostles, II.307.28. Cf. below, II.4, on Καρποκράτης.

ἐκκλησίᾳ. For single communities, IV.371, sec. 2b. The five passages referred to by Stählin all refer to churches, in the plural, but the usage here is exactly paralleled by many passages in the NT, e.g. I Cor. 1.2; II Cor. 1.1; Col. 4.16; I Thess. 1.1.

τῇ ἐν Ἀλεξανδρείᾳ. II.92.12, τὴν ἐν Ἀλεξανδρείᾳ . . . βιβλιοθήκην.

ὅπου. IV.600. Frequent.

εἰσέτι νῦν. I.8.4; 10.3; 15.26—postpositive and used with the present, as here. This claim on behalf of the church of Alexandria is not unparalleled: the church of Ephesus claimed to have the original manuscript of the canonical Gospel according to John (*Chronicon Paschale*, Migne, *PG* 92.77C, μέχρι τοῦ νῦν πεφύλακται). Sometime in the

42

II.2

ἀσφαλῶς εὖ μάλα τηρεῖται, ἀναγινωσκόμενον πρὸς αὐτοὺς μόνους τοὺς μυουμένους

480s the body of the apostle Barnabas was found in Cyprus, with a copy of the Gospel according to Matthew which Barnabas himself had made; this copy was taken to Constantinople (Lipsius, *Apostelgeschichten* II.2.292). Cf. also Tertullian, *De praescriptione haereticorum* XXXVI.1. As late as the end of the eighteenth century a library in Prague claimed to possess a fragment of Mark's original MS (actually a good sixth- or seventh-century copy of the Vulgate; Metzger, *Survey* 4); the history of this fragment is given in *Acta Sanctorum Aprilis* III.348f.

ἀσφαλῶς. Only (according to Stählin) in II.30.5, where it means "inerrantly." Clement uses ἀσφάλεια and ἀσφαλής in the senses of "security" and "safe" (I.269.23; II.100.29), and he could have found ἀσφαλῶς in the corresponding sense—"securely" —in Mk. 14.44; Acts 16.23; or Tobit 6.4. [Or in many classical authors, e.g., Sophocles, *Oedipus tyrannus* 613. W.M.C.]

εὖ μάλα. Frequent. To strengthen an adverb, as here, I.280.34; II.105.8; III.46.3.

τηρεῖται. Of keeping secrets safe, II.332.20; I.123.32; etc.; objects, I.83.29; 178.2. That the orthodox Christian "gnostics" of Alexandria had certain books which they were supposed to keep secret from the unworthy, and that sometimes one or another, yielding to entreaties, "leaked" one of these books to some unworthy person, is indicated by Clement in his *Eclogae propheticae* 27 (III.145.6–15), quoted above, at the end of the paragraph on συνέταξε, I.21.

ἀναγινωσκόμενον. IV.231 (12 references, and the entry is incomplete). The present passive participle used of reading Scripture, III.145.20.

πρός. Regular usage with verbs of speaking, saying, etc.; see Mossbacher, 73. With ἀναγινώσκειν, I Esdr. 9.48; Jer. 3.12; Aristophanes, *Ranae* 53.

μόνους. Frequent. Declined, e.g. II.455.20, where, as here, it means "alone."

τοὺς μυουμένους. II.497.16ff, τῷ δὲ μὴ πάντων εἶναι τὴν ἀλήθειαν ἐπικρύπτεται ⟨ἡ προφητεία⟩ πολυτρόπως, μόνοις τοῖς εἰς γνῶσιν μεμυημένοις, τοῖς δι'ἀγάπην ζητοῦσι τὴν ἀλήθειαν, τὸ φῶς ἀνατέλλουσα. Cf. I.84.23ff, ὦ τῶν ἁγίων ὡς ἀληθῶς μυστηρίων ... ἅγιος γίνομαι μυούμενος, ἱεροφαντεῖ δὲ ὁ κύριος. It need not be supposed that the participle μυουμένους refers to a very short period of time. Compare the provisions in Hippolytus, *Apostolic Tradition* XX: at unspecified dates, persons who have made sufficient progress in the catechumenate are chosen and set apart to receive baptism. At this time their behavior while catechumens is to be examined. If it proves to have

43

τὰ μεγάλα μυστήρια.

been morally satisfactory, "*then* let them hear the Gospel" (XX.2, my italics). What Gospel it was that the catechumens might not hear before this time neither Dix nor Botte declares. After hearing the Gospel they were exorcised and hands were laid on them daily for at least a week before baptism. During all this time they were presumably μνούμενοι.

τὰ μεγάλα μυστήρια. II.249.8, τὰ μικρὰ πρὸ τῶν μεγάλων μυηθέντες μυστηρίων (of instruction by degrees in the secrets of Christian doctrine; a reminiscence of Plato, *Gorgias* 497c). Clement's use of μυστήριον has been studied by Marsh, who concludes (66) that for Clement "there were two types of Christian μυστήρια, the one reserved" for the true gnostics, "the other revealed" to all believers. This seems to Marsh clear from II.367.19ff, and by means of this he explains (68) the passages in which Clement distinguishes between μικρά and μεγάλα μυστήρια, e.g. that cited above and especially II.373.23–374.4, οὐκ ἀπεικότως ἄρα καὶ τῶν μυστηρίων τῶν παρ' Ἕλλησιν ἄρχει μὲν τὰ καθάρσια, καθάπερ καὶ ⟨τῶν παρὰ⟩ τοῖς βαρβάροις ⟨i.e., the Christians⟩ τὸ λουτρόν. μετὰ ταῦτα δ'ἐστὶ τὰ μικρὰ μυστήρια διδασκαλίας τινὰ ὑπόθεσιν ἔχοντα καὶ προπαρασκευῆς τῶν μελλόντων, τὰ δὲ μεγάλα περὶ τῶν συμπάντων οὗ μανθάνειν ⟨οὐκ⟩έτι ὑπολείπεται, ἐποπτεύειν δὲ καὶ περινοεῖν τήν τε φύσιν καὶ τὰ πράγματα. This distinction seems to Marsh (69) to explain the fact that while Clement usually "emphasizes . . . that the μυστήρια are to be concealed from all save the privileged few, even among the members of the Christian Church itself," he nevertheless in the *Protrepticus* "seems to invite his heathen hearers to a revelation of the μυστήρια," without indicating that some might still be hidden from those who had passed through the Christian initiatory rites. The explanation is that Clement took for granted among the heathen the expectation of a series of graded initiations and, further, that he concealed from "those without" even the existence of the higher "mysteries." Marsh then concludes (80), "there is nothing to suggest that in Clement's works the term ⟨μυστήριον⟩ was ever applied to either Baptism or the Eucharist as a description peculiar to them and distinct from the other uses of μυστήριον." In this connection the passage quoted above is particularly valuable since it clearly shows baptism (τὸ λουτρόν) interpreted as part of a series of "mysteries," but as the preparatory cleansing rather than itself one of the initiations [cf. the preliminary rites at Eleusis—A.D.N.]. Belief in and practice of mysteries allegedly greater than baptism and the eucharist were, of course, frequent in gnostic circles; see *Pistis Sophia, passim* (especially chs. 141–142) and, for a survey, Fendt. Discussion of the mystery terminology in Clement and Philo has too often begun from the presupposition that *either* this terminology refers to a series of secret rites *or* it is merely allegorical description of the stages of philosophical instruction. Therefore it has been taken for granted that if the philosophical significance could be demonstrated, the possibility of the series of rites would be eliminated. But the alternative is not justified: philosophical instruction and secret rites could be combined. Philo has described such a combination in his treatise *On the Contemplative Life.*

II.3

τῶν δὲ μιαρῶν δαιμόνων ὄλεθρον τῷ τῶν ἀνθρώπων γένει πάντοτε μηχανώντων,

Clement hints at something similar in the passage quoted above, and something of the sort seems to be supposed by the text of our letter. [C.M. agrees with this note in general, and in particular with the above conclusion, but adds that one should speak not only of "philosophical instruction" but also and especially of "*religious*"—his italics—"and theological instruction."] A brief and brilliant survey of pagan, Jewish, and Christian usage of mystery terminology is given in Nock, *Mysteries*. Unfortunately, the conclusions Nock reaches are open to a number of objections, one of which is particularly relevant here: even if the authenticity of this letter be denied, the parallels between it and the recognized works of Clement suffice to show that Clement's adoption (or inheritance) of mystery terminology to describe Christianity had been considerably more than "slight" (Nock, *Mysteries* 202). With Nock's conclusions contrast the remarks of Jaeger, above, on I.23.

τῶν ... μηχανώντων. Initial genitive absolute indicating cause or prior condition ("since"), I.90.2f. Genitive absolutes are rare in Clement, but occasionally he uses a number in quick succession, e.g. II.212.29–213.4 (5 in 8 lines). They appear in his narrative style, as here, in III.188.3 and 12ff.

μιαρῶν δαιμόνων. I.30.16, εἰ γὰρ οὖν δαίμονες, λίχνοι τε καὶ μιαροί. Clement often refers to demons (IV.382, almost a full column of references) and, though he nowhere says explicitly that they always plot the destruction of men, he describes them as hostile to men (I.31.17, μισάνθρωποι; so 33.3, etc.), destructive (ὀλεθρίους), and plotting (*ibid*). Presumably he was familiar with this theory, which had been the leitmotif of Justin's *First Apology*, e.g., ch. 26, where the demons were represented as having instigated Simon Magnus, Menander, and Marcion, as they do here Carpocrates. For further parallels in the apologists see Wey.

ὄλεθρον. I.253.19, etc. Always without article, as here.

τῷ τῶν ἀνθρώπων γένει. Verbatim, II.277.4. Clement often spoke of "the race of men": IV.307 s.v. γένος, 11 references, listing not complete.

πάντοτε. Meaning "at every moment," I.255.28.

μχηανώντων. Clement uses the middle in I.261.25, with dative (ἡμῖν understood) and accusative, as here. The active appears only in poetry, ἀτάσθαλα μηχανόωντας (*Odyssey* XVIII.143), which was echoed by Apollonius Rhodius, III.583, and of which the phrasing of the letter may be reminiscent. [Cf. the echo of Sophocles, below, II.14–15; the active of μηχανάω appears also in Sophocles, *Inachus* 21 (*SP*

II.4
ὁ Καρποκράτης

III.24) and *Ajax* 1037. On the latter passage Kamerbeek, *Ajax*, remarks, "It would seem that the rare active use here raises the verb above the all-too-human sphere . . . Note also the sinister associations of ambush and guile inherent in the verb μηχανᾶν." The uses of the passive in Sophocles, *Trachiniae* 586 and elsewhere, also imply the existence of an active. W.M.C.] Clement frequently quoted and paraphrased Homer (IV.41f, four columns of references, including a quotation of *Odyssey* XVIII.130 in II.202.7), and his prose contains many words described in *LSJ* as primarily poetical and appearing in prose only in the work of "late" writers, that is, writers of about Clement's time. Besides these words, Clement uses in prose a considerable number of words cited in *LSJ* only from poetry. Of these latter, inspection of Stählin's index from α–αμ alone has yielded ἀεικίζω, I.40.6; ἀθυρόγλωσσος, I.253.13, etc.; ἀλετρίβανος, I.155.20; and ἀμβρόσιος, I.197.1. Therefore this use of a poetical form is not atypical of Clements' style. [On this point I am particularly happy to record the agreement of C.M., who has had so much experience in edition and translation of Clement's Greek.]

ὁ Καρποκράτης. II.197.16 and 19; 199.29 (with article, as here); 200.15; 207.18; 221.6. (For testimonia and literature, see ch. 4, sec. XIII.) In the first three of these references (pp. 197–199) Clement agrees with the present letter to the extent of representing Carpocrates as an Alexandrian (citizen?)—the letter shows him working in Alexandria—from whom the sect of the Carpocratians derived at least its name; further, he describes the Carpocratian doctrine of free love as expounded by Epiphanes, the son of Carpocrates, and he declares that Epiphanes was the founder of the sect (197.26f, καθηγήσατο δὲ τῆς μοναδικῆς γνώσεως, ἀφ'οὗ καὶ ἡ τῶν Καρποκρατιανῶν αἵρεσις) or at least the cofounder (197.16, οἱ δὲ ἀπὸ Καρποκράτους καὶ Ἐπιφάνους ἀναγόμενοι). In the later references (pp. 200–221) he says nothing of Epiphanes and speaks of Carpocrates as the founder and lawgiver of the sect (200.15, νομοθετεῖν . . . ἔδει implies that he did give other laws, as do, also, κατὰ Καρποκράτην, 207.18, and ἡ δὲ Καρποκράτους δικαιοσύνη, 221.6). Since Clement says Epiphanes died at seventeen, it would be plausible to explain this contradiction by supposing that the father and son cooperated in founding the sect and, after the son's death, the father carried it on so long and conspicuously that it came to be known by his name. At all events, the letter says nothing of Epiphanes, and the recognized works of Clement say nothing of Carpocrates' use of a secret Gospel by Mark. (Given the embarrassment which the author of the letter felt in writing privately on this subject—below, II.10-19—it is hardly to be expected that he would mention it in his published works.) Irenaeus, however (Harvey, I.20.3 = Stieren, I.25.5), speaks of Carpocratian documents representing τὸν Ἰησοῦν . . . ἐν μυστηρίῳ τοῖς μαθηταῖς αὐτοῦ καὶ ἀποστόλοις κατ'ἰδίαν λελαληκέναι, καὶ αὐτοὺς ἀξιῶσαι τοῖς ἀξίοις καὶ τοῖς πειθομένοις ταῦτα παραδιδόναι. διὰ πίστεως . . . καὶ ἀγάπης σώζεσθαι. τὰ δὲ λοιπὰ ἀδιάφορα ὄντα. κατὰ τὴν

II.5

ὑπ' αὐτῶν διδαχθεὶς καὶ ἀπατηλοῖς τέχναις χρησάμενος, οὕτω πρεσβύτερόν

δόξαν τῶν ἀνθρώπων, πῆ μὲν ἀγαθά, πῆ δὲ κακὰ νομίζεσθαι, οὐδενὸς φύσει κακοῦ ὑπάρχοντος. On Clement's thoughts about heretics in general, see Rüther, *Kirche*.

["The description of the Carpocratians in the letter is completely different from what Clement writes about them in *Stromateis* III. It is possible with de Faye (*Gnostiques* 414f) to doubt that Carpocrates and his son Epiphanes had anything to do with the Carpocratians known through other sources. The only thing in Clement . . . of interest for the letter is that Carpocrates was an Alexandrian (II.197.20). In the letter the expressions used about the Carpocratians are vague and uncharacteristic. Anybody could be 'corrupted by the Devil' (cf. Eus., *HE* IV.7.10), could get a copy of a secret gospel through an 'enslaved' presbyter and have a 'blasphemous' doctrine (*ibid.*) and so on. I have taken some parallels from Eusebius' description of the Carpocratians, but I do not find the expressions so characteristic ⟨as to suggest⟩ that the author of the letter must have known Eusebius. Anybody could use language of that kind about the heretics." J.M.]

ὑπ' αὐτῶν διδαχθείς. The aorist passive participle, I.261.8; *sensu malo*, I.248.35–249.1; the passive with ὑπό, II.222.24; 363.1; etc.; elision of the ο of ὑπό, Mossbacher, 46. Demons lead men astray, I.33.10; 48.27ff. That magical arts in particular were taught by demons is explained in *Enoch* 8f, and the theory was adopted by Clement, II.332.16ff (and extended to include philosophy, II.53.5ff).

ἀπατηλοῖς τέχναις. I.47.28, ἀπατηλὸν τέχνην, of art used to make images. Here too the adjective is of the second declension. In the letter it probably refers to magical practices [though A.D.N. thinks this reference not certain]. Clement uses it with this reference in I.4.23, etc. The Carpocratians were widely accused of magical practices, Irenaeus (Harvey, I.20.2 = Stieren, I.25.3); Hippolytus, *Philosophumena* VII.32; Epiphanius, *Panarion* XXVII.3; etc. Clement in his recognized works does not mention the accusation, but he had no occasion to do so.

χρησάμενος. Frequent in Clement, IV.812 (about 60 references).

οὕτω . . . ὥστε. III.168.14f, with both verbs in the indicative, as here.

πρεσβύτερον. II.485.10, πρεσβύτερος . . . τῆς ἐκκλησίας. In this passage Clement allegorizes the title, but the fact that he does so proves that he knew it as a title, as it is used here. He often refers to presbyters as ecclesiastical officials (IV.669c, 9 references). He also speaks of presbyters in a more general sense as elder leaders of the Church, particularly those of earlier generations, whose teaching had been oral, but now, written down, formed part of the body of secret Christian tradition—and was sometimes indiscreetly communicated to the unworthy, III.144.26–145.15. It is

II.6

τινα τῆς ἐν Ἀλεξανδρείᾳ ἐκκλησίας κατεδούλωσεν ὥστε παρ' αὐτοῦ ἐκόμισεν

not surprising that the official presbyters should have been, as the letter represents them, custodians of the books in which the traditions of the earlier presbyters were recorded. The term πρεσβύτεροι is found frequently in second-century papyri, regularly as a title of pagan priests—particularly those in charge of financial matters, who often furnished to the Roman authorities lists of personnel and of temple property evidently under their supervision (Hauschildt, 237, 239; cf. 241). According to Eus., *HE* VI.13.9, Clement in his published works referred to presbyters especially as custodians of oral traditions; see below, II.19, on οὐκ ὀκνήσω end, and III.139.20; 144.26ff (Harnack, *Geschichte* I.291ff). Irenaeus similarly quoted presbyters as sources of unpublished apostolic traditions (Harvey, IV.42.2; 49.1 = Stieren, IV.27.1; 32.1). Papias similarly specifies presbyters, evidently in some technical sense, as the source of his oral traditions about Jesus; Eus., *HE* III.39.3ff (on which see Munck, *Presbyters*). The role of presbyters in Clement's works as bearers of secret tradition is noted by Lazzati, 34f; Zahn, 158; Lebreton, 495; etc. Hornschuh's denial of it (*Anfänge* 359ff) is based on implausible arguments from silence. On the evidence of II.485.10ff it has sometimes been supposed (e.g. by Wytzes, 230) that Clement's gnostic group had its own presbyters, as opposed to those of the main church of Alexandria. Some presbyters, probably of a church in Alexandria, showed Celsus βιβλία βάρβαρα δαιμόνων ὀνόματα ἔχοντα καὶ τερατείας, Origen, *Contra Celsum* VI.40; this about A.D. 175.

τῆς ἐν Ἀλεξανδρείᾳ ἐκκλησίας. II.92.12, τὴν ἐν Ἀλεξανδρείᾳ ... βιβλιοθήκην. On ἐκκλησία see above, I.28. The repeated specification of Alexandria (instead of the use of "here") is perhaps for solemnity. Or perhaps the letter was not written from that city; cf. ὅπου, above, II.1. It may date from the period following Clement's flight (ca. 202?).

κατεδούλωσεν. Twice, in the middle, of evil spirits enslaving men, I.8.3; III.5.14. The active (II Cor. 11.20; Gal. 2.4) is classical (*LSJ* s.v.); more important, it is used in *PGM* IX, line 4, as here, for enslaving the soul by magical means. A presbyter "deceived" (not "enslaved") by a demon acting through a would-be heresiarch appears in Cyprian, *Epistulae* LXXV.10.

παρ'. Use, construction, and elision are all paralleled in Clement; Mossbacher, 45f, 67f. With κομίζειν, III.141.7f.

ἐκόμιζεν. Meaning "get," II.29.17; of writings—as it happens, those of Epiphanes, the son of Carpocrates—II.197.18f, where it means "be in circulation, be preserved." A similar story (without the magical motif) seems to lie behind the textual confusion of the Πράξεις Παύλου καὶ Θέκλης, I. Against Vouaux, 147 n7, the Latin versions are to

ἀπόγραφον τοῦ μυστικοῦ εὐαγγελίου, ὃ καὶ

be preferred: Paul did not suspect the hypocrisy of Demas and Hermogenes which made them unworthy of his secret doctrine (as opposed to his public preaching). Therefore he taught them things they should not have been permitted to learn.

[W.V. objects that the gnostics had their own chains of tradition and therefore did not need to borrow from the Church.] However, that in Clement's time some gnostics did claim the same apostolic authorities as the "orthodox" is proved by Clement's grudging report of Basilidean appeal to Peter, and Valentinian to Paul, III.75.15ff. The Carpocratians known to Irenaeus (Harvey, I.20.2 = Stieren, I.25.4) would seem to have used Mt. 5.25f or Lk. 12.58f. Moreover, even if we suppose the letter to be by Clement, we need not suppose its statements about Carpocrates entirely true. Clement was faced with the problem which now faces us: How did the Carpocratians come by a Gospel strikingly similar to a secret Gospel accepted by the church in Alexandria and by it attributed to Mark? Clement's statement tells us only the answer his party gave when forced to give an answer.

ἀπόγραφον. Not in Clement—who has, however, ἀπογράφεσθαι, meaning "to copy," II.471.7. ἀπόγραφον meaning "copy" or "imitation" is used by Cicero, Ad Atticum XII.52 end (overlooked by Oksala, 158); ἀπόγραφος with the same meaning appears in Dionysius Hal., Usener-Raderm., Isaeus 11. In Diogenes Laertius, VI.84, ἀπόγραφος is taken by R. Hicks, in the Loeb translation, to mean "an imitator" [but more likely it means "a copy"—B.E.]. ἀπόγραφον is, in the preserved literature, a rare word; one can hardly believe that an imitator would have chosen it instead of the common ἀντίγραφον. [But the rarity of ἀπόγραφον is no argument against Clement's possible use of it. A great many words which must have been common in ancient everyday usage are extremely rare in the preserved literature; see the numerous examples in the vocabulary of Krauss, Lehnwörter. A.D.N. Moreover, ἀπόγραφον (-ος) has a contemptuous sense not found in ἀντίγραφον. Thus in Cicero, Diogenes, and perhaps Dionysius ἀπόγραφον is dyslogistic. B.E. With this opinion, however, A.D.N. disagrees, contending that Cicero was only "apologizing whimsically for his philosophical works," and that "when you speak of a man as being a copy, you imply inferiority; it is not so with a book."] But the usage in this letter seems to support the opinion of B.E.

μυστικοῦ. Above, I.17.

εὐαγγελίου. Above, I.12, 21–22.

ὃ καί. This stringing together of sentences by relative pronouns is not uncommon in Clement, e.g. II.7.24f, ἧς οὐδέ . . . ἀλλά; 17.24, ἥν; 20.12; 21.2; 27.13; etc.

II.7   II.8
ἐξηγήσατο κατὰ τὴν βλάσφημον καὶ σαρκικὴν αὐτοῦ δόξαν, ἔτι δὲ καὶ
                                    II.9
ἐμίανε, ταῖς ἀχράντοις καὶ ἁγίαις λέξεσιν ἀναμιγνὺς ἀναιδέστατα

ἐξηγήσατο. Frequent with the sense "interpret," IV.397, over 20 examples, listing incomplete. Aorist, II.232.18, etc.; reference to a specific document, II.308.4; 280.10; 168.3; etc. Irenaeus (Harvey, I.20.3 = Stieren, I.25.5) speaks of the Carpocratian doctrine concerning the secret teaching of Jesus as something which ἐν τοῖς συγγράμμασιν αὐτῶν οὕτως ἀναγέγραπται καὶ αὐτοὶ οὕτως ἐξηγοῦνται.

κατά. Usage regular; Mossbacher, 66. Used as here to indicate the principle of interpretation, II.495.4.

βλάσφημον. II.113.23; III.72.29 (of the utterances of libertine heretics); etc.

σαρκικήν. Frequent, IV.697, 30 references. Not used directly of teachings, but cf. II.151.11f, σαρκικῶς νοοῦντες τὰς γραφάς.

δόξαν. Frequent of heretical or false philosophical teachings, IV.350f (20 examples, listing incomplete). The ψευδεῖς δόξας of libertine heretics, who misrepresent the Scriptures to make them accord with their own desires and doctrines, are attacked in III.72.28–73.8.

καὶ ... ἔτι δὲ καί. II.189.17–18, etc.

ἐμίανε. IV.568, 6 times (4 refer to defilement of holy things). None in the aorist active, but the identical form appears in Philo, De virtutibus 199 end.

ἀχράντοις καὶ ἁγίαις. I.44.3f, τὸ ἄχραντον ἐκεῖνο καὶ τὸ ἅγιον (these are divine attributes). Elsewhere ἄχραντος is used of Jesus, the soul, marriage, etc., and ἅγιος of Scripture, as here (I.289.19, ταῖς βίβλοις ταῖς ἁγίαις). The sayings in the sermon on the mount are ἅγιοι λόγοι, I.77.20; cf. 289.24.

λέξεσιν. Of Scripture, I.125.22; II.385.15 (meaning "saying"); 498.29 (probably meaning "words"); III.3.11 and 16.

ἀναμιγνύς. I.278.7, ἀναμίγνυσθαι (sic). LSJ s.v. gives ἀναμίγνυμι as the prevailing later form (see under ἀναμείγνυμι). Clement uses the active in I.37.52; he uses the verb of literary composition in II.13.1, περιέξουσι δὲ οἱ Στρωματεῖς ἀναμεμιγμένην τὴν ἀλήθειαν τοῖς φιλοσοφίας δόγμασι. He also complains of heretical interpolations in Christian material; see above on θεοπνεύστου, I.11.

ἀναιδέστατα. 5 uses of ἀναιδής in the absolute and 2 in the comparative, IV.234. The superlative was used by Plato, Laws 729C.

II.10

ψεύσματα. τοῦ δὲ κράματος τούτου ἐξαντλεῖται τὸ τῶν Καρποκρατιανῶν
δόγμα. τούτοις οὖν, καθὼς καὶ προείρηκα, οὐδέποτε

ψεύσματα.   III.70.7, of heretics who make up false stories in order to reject the
prophecies: ἀμέλει πάμπολλα συγκαττύουσι ψεύσματα καὶ πλάσματα.

κράματος.   IV.520 (7 references). Genitive singular, I.177.24. Of literary or doctrinal mixture, as here, I.174.3f, τὸ κρᾶμα τοῦ νόμου τοῦ παλαιοῦ καὶ τοῦ λόγου τοῦ νέου.

τούτου.   Similar use of a postpositive demonstrative at the beginning of a sentence,
to express contempt, II.197.18, Ἐπιφάνης οὗτος (referring to the son of Carpocrates).
For this function, the position after the noun is customary; Palm, *Funktion* 12f.
Similar sentence structure, II.493.6, etc.

ἐξαντλεῖται.   The MS reads ἐξαντλῆται, or perhaps ἐξηντλῆται. The latter is paleo-
graphically much less likely, but if it should be the correct reading then ἐξήντληται
could be read by mere change of accent. And Clement's fondness for perfects is an
argument for ἐξήντληται, see above, I.24, on προγεγραμμέναις. But I prefer to follow
the more likely reading. Clement uses the verb in II.9.12, τὰ φρέατα ἐξαντλούμενα
διειδέστερον ὕδωρ ἀναδίδωσι. This fits the meaning "drain, draw off" given by *LSJ*
and suggested by the pejorative context of the letter, where the verb may be a
sarcastic reminiscence of Jn. 2.8, ἀντλήσατε νῦν, in the miracle of Cana. [The letter's
metaphoric use of ἐξαντλέω is rare, but cf. Gregory of Nyssa, *In Canticum Canticorum* p.
457, line 7, Langerbeck (col. 1108 Migne). A. W. Also Cicero, *Academicorum* II.34
(108). W.M.C.]

Καρποκρατιανῶν.   Above, I.2.

δόγμα.   IV.349, 16 times with reference to teachings of philosophers, 6 times to
teachings of the Church, 17 times to teachings of heretics, as here. The singular is
used, as in the letter, to refer to the whole dogmatic system of a heretical school, in
III.68.34f.

τούτοις οὖν.   Above, 1.7.

καθὼς καὶ προείρηκα.   I.110.24, καθὼς προειρήκαμεν; the letter's use of the singular
is less formal. For the addition of καί, I.237.3, καθὼς καὶ ὁ Παῦλος μαρτυρεῖ. With or
without καί, καθώς is a regular form of cross-refernce in Clement, II.75.24; 79.1;
91.6 (all three without); 241.1 (with); etc.

οὐδέποτε.   II.516.12; III.52.26; etc.

II.11
εἰκτέον, οὐδὲ προτείνουσιν αὐτοῖς τὰ κατεψευσμένα συγχωρητέον τοῦ
II.12
Μάρκου εἶναι τὸ μυστικὸν

εἰκτέον. IV.365 lists 5 usages of εἴκω, none of this verbal adjective, but—as re-marked above (I.10, on προκριτέον)—Clement was very fond of the form.

οὐδέποτε . . . οὐδέ. This I have not found in Clement. [But it is perfectly good Greek and Clement might well have used it. A.D.N.]

προτείνουσιν. Meaning "allege," II.329.5 (cf. 130.29). The form προτείνουσι II.173.27f.

κατεψευσμένα. Clement uses the verb once, I.267.6, in the present participle. The perfect participle, used by the letter, is frequent in Philo (13 references in Leisegang s.v.). The meaning common to Philo and Clement—something false, an imitation—has here been extended to include something falsified; or perhaps the reference is especially to the passages peculiar to the Carpocratian Gospel, and the writer wished to indicate that those were imitations of the true text. [One should consider the possibility of τὰ κατεψευσμένα belonging, as sometimes happens in Greek, both to προτείνουσιν and to the infinitive clause dependent on συγχωρητέον. If it does so, one should perhaps translate as follows: "à ces gens-là, il ne faut donc, comme je l'ai déjà dit, jamais céder ni, quand ils présentent eux-mêmes leurs falsifications, ac-corder que c'est là l' 'Evangile mystique' de Marc: au contraire, il faut même le nier avec serment." This is followed by a string of scriptural texts which recall the ideas of spiritual pedagogy so dear to Clement and which are cited, in Clement's way, without introduction or words of transition. The reason for the above translation is the text's report that Mark made, at Alexandria, a second, more "spiritual," re-daction of his Gospel; and that, besides these two *redactions*, there was also the secret *oral* tradition. C.M. See also the comment of C.R., below, on μεθ' ὅρκου.]

συγχωρητέον. Meaning "concede," II.173.20; III.90.24; III.72.31 (sarcastically). In II.173.20 it has, as here, the indirect object αὐτοῖς and the direct εἶναι without τό. The form found in the letter appears in I.204.9.

Μάρκου. Above, I.15.

εἶναι. With genitive, of a work's being "by" its author, II.81.2, Ὀνομάκριτος . . . οὗ τὰ εἰς Ὀρφέα φερόμενα ποιήματα λέγεται εἶναι.

μυστικόν. Above, I.17.

εὐαγγέλιον, ἀλλὰ καὶ μεθ' ὅρκου

εὐαγγέλιον.   Above, I.21–22.

ἀλλὰ καί.   "But moreover," I.121.24; II.197.4; etc.

μεθ' ὅρκου.   This I have not found in Clement. μετὰ πολλῶν ὅρκων occurs in Plato, *Phaedrus* 240e; μεθ' ὅρκων in II Macc. 4.34 and 14.32; μεθ' ὅρκου in Mt. 14.7. [Preisigke, *Papyruswörterbuch*, notes an instance in an official document of the third century B.C. C.H.R.] Clement's use of μετά is normal; Mossbacher, 67. Linguistically, therefore, the phrase presents no difficulty. But in III.37.19–38.27 Clement says the true gnostic will never (or hardly ever) swear, and certainly never swear falsely. In I.279.26–27 he forbids the ordinary Christian to use oaths in buying, selling, and similar transactions; and in II.391.19–392.6 he finds the Judeo-Christian tradition to be the source from which Plato derived his prohibition of oaths. On the other hand, Christians, of course, did swear (see Nock, *Sacramentum*), and in III.190.12 Clement represents the apostle John as swearing; in II.494.11ff he approves deception practiced for a good purpose (citing Paul's claim to have been all things to all men); and in III.39.12–40.10 (the sequel of the first passage cited above) he modifies his previous statements to the extent of teaching that the true gnostic will tell the truth "except sometimes, when it is a matter of helping ⟨someone⟩, he may, as does a doctor . . . lie, or, ⟨to distinguish⟩ as the sophists ⟨do⟩, 'say what is false.'" This exception he again justifies by the same example of Paul, and finally he insists that the true gnostic always tells the truth. (See further the paragraphs on the following quotations). This ambiguous attitude toward truth becomes even more ambiguous when we recall that the true gnostic is partially an ideal figure, and the account of his achievements in the *Stromateis* describes a perfection which Clement himself probably did not hope to realize fully in this life. Accordingly, the contradiction between Clement's principles as expressed in his published works and the practical advice given in this evidently private letter should not be exaggerated, especially since the practical advice was in accord with much philosophical teaching (Düring, *Chion* 20). Compare the reports concerning the Essenes, that there is no swearing among them (Josephus, *BJ* II.135; Hippolytus, *Philosophumena* IV.22) and that they bind their initiates with hair-raising oaths (*BJ* II.139–143; *Philosophumena* IV.23–24). ["Tout à fait d'accord avec votre conclusion: il ne faut pas exagérer la portée de certaines contradictions chez Clément." C.M. "Surely, however, Clement is too devious to advocate unnecessary and downright perjury. One could legitimately (as the Sophists say!) take an oath to the effect that *precisely* what the Carpocratians have is not *Mark's* secret gospel. I find it hard to suppose that Clement's oath is a denial that *Mark's* is the Church's secret gospel, with the consequent admission that the Church *has* a secret gospel, but it is by someone else." C.R.; compare the similar suggestion by C.M., above, on κατεψευσμένα.] I think the denial is intended to give the impression that Mark did not write any secret Gospel, and that consequently the one which the Carpocratians have is a fake. The one the Church has should not be mentioned,

II.13
ἀρνητέον. "οὐ γὰρ ἄπασι πάντα ἀληθῆ λεκτέον."

since the Church has kept its existence a secret even from the lower grades of Christians; thus Theodore did not know of it heretofore. However, I agree that Clement would have wished to avoid perjury. Therefore I think the suggestions of C.M. and C.R. correct in pointing out the deliberate ambiguity of the Greek. [J.R. comments: "I assume the oath to be an example of the 'economic behavior' (κατ' οἰκονομίαν) emerging in the Alexandrian fathers as an ethical stance, developing in part from pagan backgrounds." See his article Οἰκονομία, 370ff.]

ἀρνητέον. Meaning "deny," IV.275 (13 references, listing incomplete). The piling up of forms in τέον here (εἰκτέον, συγχωρητέον, ἀρνητέον, λεκτέον) is typical of Clement; see above, on προκριτέον, I.10, and the passages cited there.

οὐ γάρ. A favorite formula of Clement's for beginning sentences, e.g., II.221.26; 222.24,29; 223.1; 224.12.

οὐ γάρ ... λεκτέον. This saying appeared in Philo, Questions ... on Genesis IV.67, from which it was quoted by Procopius in his commentary on Genesis in the form οὐ πάντα ἀληθῆ λεκτέον ἄπασιν. Philo's text, according to the preserved Armenian translation, went on to elaborate the principle and to teach (in IV.69) that "the wise man requires a versatile art from which he may profit in imitating those mockers who say one thing and do another in order to save whom they can" (my italics). This text strikingly parallels Paul's claim in I Cor. 9.22, "I became all things to all men that I might by all means save some." Since influence of Philo on Paul or of Paul on Philo is almost out of the question, it would seem likely that these two passages derive from a single source. The common-sense idea behind them had long been familiar in ancient philosophy. Diogenes Laertius, VIII.15, quotes from Aristoxenus, as a saying of certain Pythagoreans, μὴ εἶναι πρὸς πάντας πάντα ῥητά; for further examples see Reumann, Οἰκονομία. From philosophy and common sense alike it was taken over by early Christianity, where the example of the Apostles—and especially that of Paul—is often cited to justify the use of deception for good ends (Bauer, Rechtgläubigkeit, 41f; cf. above, on μέθ' ὅρκου). Clement, as remarked above, shared this early Christian belief, which he summed up with the words τῷ μὴ πάντων εἶναι τὴν ἀλήθειαν (II.497.16) and understood as a principle even of divine revelation; cf. Sibylline Oracles XII(X).290f, τὸ δ' οὐχ ἅμα πάντες ἴσασιν. οὐ γὰρ πάντων πάντα. Clement was deeply indebted to Philo (IV.47ff, 7 columns of citations—more than any other non-Christian author except Plato, who has 10). Both his similarity to Philo and his borrowing from him have resulted in considerable confusion in medieval MSS, where many passages now found only in Philo are attributed to Clement (III.LXXI–LXXXII). Among these are at least two from Questions ... on Genesis (III.LXXIV, no. 511.15; LXXX, no. 339). Moreover, Clement himself appropriated

II.14

διὰ τοῦτο ἡ σοφία τοῦ Θεοῦ διὰ Σολομῶντος παραγγέλλει, "ἀποκρίνου τῷ μωρῷ ἐκ τῆς μωρίας αὐτοῦ"

without acknowledgment two considerable sections of *Questions ... on Genesis* (II.474.1–20; 474.23–475.11). Therefore this saying may have come into the letter from Philo; cf. Reumann's note on τἀληθῆ above, on I.10. On the other hand, it may have been a popular proverb (though it does not appear in the *Corpus paroemiographorum*). For further parallels to the idea see Nock, review of Goodenough V–VI, 527ff and, for the relation of Paul to Philo, Chadwick, *St. Paul* and *Philo*. On 297f Chadwick discusses the question of veracity; he has an additional parallel to the present passage (*Cherubim* 15).

διὰ τοῦτο ... παραγγέλλει. I.146.9f (also following a quotation), διὰ τοῦτο φυλάττεσθαι τοῖς νηπίοις διὰ Σολομῶντος παραγγέλλει followed by Prov. 1.10ff as here by Prov. 26.5; cf. also Lk. 11.49, quoted in the following paragraph. For the structure of this whole sentence (διὰ τοῦτο ... διδάσκουσα) see below, on δεῖν ... διδάσκουσα.

ἡ σοφία τοῦ θεοῦ. I.172.13f, ἡ θεία σοφία ... παραγγέλλει, followed as here by a quotation from Prov. (23.20f); cf. II.294.5, ἡ θεία σοφία ... λέγει, followed by Wis. 3.2ff. ἡ σοφία τοῦ θεοῦ probably comes from Lk. 11.49, διὰ τοῦτο καὶ ἡ σοφία τοῦ θεοῦ εἶπεν, followed by a quotation from some lost sacred book. [The Christians of Clement's time often quote Proverbs as "Wisdom" and also share Clement's fondness for Psalms; see my remarks on "*Traditio*," *AJP* 67 (1946) 365ff. A.D.N.]

διὰ Σολομῶντος παραγγέλλει. See the two preceding paragraphs and I.138.4, ταύτῃ τοι καὶ διὰ Σολομῶντος παραγγέλλεται, followed by Prov. 23.14 in a form differing considerably from LXX. Again I.142.28, προτροπῇ ὁ παιδαγωγὸς διὰ Σολομῶντος, with Prov. 8.4,6, also in a variant form. The διὰ Σολομῶντος formula is frequent— especially, as here, to introduce quotations from Proverbs.

ἀποκρίνου ... αὐτοῦ. Prov. 26.5. Clement was particularly fond of Proverbs (IV.6f, three and a half columns of citations, which ties it with Genesis for second place among the books of the OT; Psalms comes first with over 4 columns, and Isaiah third with 3). In II.338.8f Clement quotes this same verse (26.5) in this same form, which differs widely from that of LXX (ἀποκρίνου ἄφρονι κατὰ τὴν ἀφροσύνην αὐτοῦ). [This is of capital importance. An imitator would be likely to know Proverbs and unlikely to give Clement's form of the text. E.B.] In II.338.8f the exegesis is also basically the same as in the letter—like is to be given to like; this implies deception of the wicked, and again the justification, besides this verse of Proverbs, is the example of Paul who was all things to all men. See the preceding paragraphs on μεθ' ὅρκου and οὐ γάρ ...

II.15
πρὸς τοὺς τυφλοὺς τὸν νοῦν

λεκτέον for Clement's other uses of I Cor. 9.22b to excuse deception. In II.338.8f, however, the other consequences of the same principle are the more fully developed. Since like is to be given to like, truth is to be presented to those who desire it in whatever form their training and tradition make most acceptable. But there can be no question that toward hostile or heretical outsiders Clement advocated the same policy of secrecy as does this letter. He makes that plain in another passage which leads to a quotation from Proverbs: II.116. 25ff, οἱ μὲν τὸ ἅγιον πνεῦμα κεκτημένοι ἐρευνῶσι "τὰ βάθη τοῦ Θεοῦ" ⟨cf. above, I.5⟩ τουτέστι τῆς περὶ τὰς προφητείας ἐπικρύψεως ἐπήβολοι γίνονται. τῶν δὲ ἁγίων μεταδιδόναι τοῖς κυσὶν ἀπαγορεύεται, ἔστ'ἂν μένῃ θηρία. οὐ γάρ ποτε ἐγκιρνάναι προσήκει φθονεροῖς καὶ τεταραγμένοις, ἀπίστοις τε ἔτι ἤθεσιν, εἰς ὑλακὴν ζητήσεως ἀναιδέσι, τοῦ θείου καὶ καθαροῦ νάματος, τοῦ ζῶντος ὕδατος. "μὴ δὴ ὑπερεκχείσθω σοι ὕδατα ἔξω πηγῆς σου, εἰς δὲ σὰς πλατείας διαπορευέσθω σὰ ὕδατα." Prov. 5.16. Even in his dealings with fellow Christians Clement advocated and claimed to have followed the policy of concealing certain aspects of Christian doctrine or practice. He declares in the *Stromateis* that he has no intention of writing what he would hesitate even to say (II.11.1f), and in his major justification of the practice of secrecy in religious teaching (*Stromateis* V.IV–X = II.338–370) he makes clear that one of the reasons for secrecy *within* Christianity is the difference between "common faith" and "gnostic perfection," II.342.2ff. The latter is not for every believer, II.367.24; 370.10–16; indeed, ignorant believers may be deceived by the gnostic for their own good, II.494.11–16. Hort and Mayor, lvi–lvii, remark that this attitude flourished especially in Alexandria. (See above II.2, on μυστήρια.)

πρός. With ἐπικρύπτεσθαι, of concealing truth from the unworthy, II.363.5. The passage is an exegesis of Ex. 21.33f: "If any man open a pit . . . and do not cover it, and an ox or donkey fall into it, the owner of the pit shall pay." ἵνα οὖν μή τις τούτων ⟨those without understanding⟩ εἰς τὴν ὑπὸ σοῦ διδασκομένην γνῶσιν ἀκρ⟨ο?⟩ατὴς γενόμενος τῆς ἀληθείας, παρακούσῃ τε καὶ παραπέσῃ, ἀσφαλής, φησί, περὶ τὴν χρῆσιν τοῦ λόγου γίνου, καὶ πρὸς μὲν τοὺς ἀλόγως προσιόντας ἀπόκλειε τὴν ζῶσαν ἐν βάθει πηγήν, ποτὸν δὲ ὄρεγε τοῖς τῆς ἀληθείας δεδιψηκόσιν. ἐπικρυπτόμενος δ'οὖν πρὸς τοὺς οὐχ οἵους τε ὄντας παραδέξασθαι τὸ "βάθος τῆς γνώσεως" ⟨see above, I.5⟩ κατακάλυπτε τὸν λάκκον. (ἀκροατής for ἀκρατής is Heyse's emendation, accepted by Stählin but not by Früchtel.) The connections with the passage quoted in the preceding paragraph are striking.

τοὺς τυφλοὺς τὸν νοῦν. I.75.12, τυφλοὶ μὲν τὸν νοῦν, κωφοὶ δὲ τὴν σύνεσιν of idolaters, just previously called Sodomites. The metaphor of mental blindness was one Clement often used: I.67.16; 164.10; III.70.4; 182.20; etc. [Here it may be a reminiscence of Sophocles, *Oedipus tyrannus* 371; such reminiscences of classical authors are frequent in Clement. W.M.C.]

II.16

τὸ φῶς τῆς ἀληθείας δεῖν ἐπικρύπτεσθαι διδάσκουσα, αὐτίκα φησί, "τοῦ δὲ μὴ ἔχοντος ἀρθήσεται,"

τὸ φῶς τῆς ἀληθείας. Verbatim, II.502.4; III.70.2, ἡ ψυχὴ τοῖς παρὰ φύσιν θολωθεῖσα δόγμασιν οὐχ οἷά τε τὸ φῶς τῆς ἀληθείας διιδεῖν ἀκριβῶς, etc. The frequency of the metaphor in Clement's works is noted by Tsermoulas, 29f.

δεῖν ... διδάσκουσα. II.189.8ff, a sentence of almost exactly the same structure as that in the letter: ὅθεν ὁ Ἀβραάμ ... φησίν ... ⟨Gen. 20.12⟩ ... τὰς ὁμομητρίους μὴ δεῖν ἄγεσθαι πρὸς γάμον διδάσκων. Another sentence of the same type, and also similar in content to that of the letter, is found in II.490.15ff, αὐτίκα ὁ Δαβίδ ... γράφει ⟨Ps. 17.12f⟩ ... ἐπικεκρυμμένους τοὺς ἁγίους λόγους εἶναι διδάσκων. Both δεῖν and διδάσκειν are, of course, frequent in Clement's vocabulary.

ἐπικρύπτεσθαι. A favorite verb of Clement's, IV.411 (17 references, listing incomplete; all but 2 in middle or passive). Some of the passages in which it is used fit the teaching of this letter exactly, e.g. II.35.15 ἐπεὶ δὲ μὴ κοινὴ ἡ παράδοσις καὶ πάνδημος ... ἐπικρυπτέον οὖν "τὴν ἐν μυστηρίῳ λαλουμένην σοφίαν" ἣν ἐδίδαξεν ὁ υἱὸς τοῦ Θεοῦ. II. 497.17, τῷ δὲ μὴ πάντων εἶναι τὴν ἀλήθειαν ἐπικρύπτεται πολυτρόπως, μόνοις τοῖς εἰς γνῶσιν μεμυημένοις, τοῖς δι'ἀγάπην ζητοῦσι τὴν ἀλήθειαν, τὸ φῶς ἀνατέλλουσα.

αὐτίκα φησί. Verbatim and, as here, intial, to introduce a Gospel saying, II.138.28. The phrase is used thus very often, and Clement's use of αὐτίκα both with and without φησί is so frequent and so peculiar that it was discussed by Mayor in appendix A (361ff) of his edition of Stromateis VII. Of the peculiarly Clementine uses of αὐτίκα distinguished there, this is evidently that which should be translated "further" or "again" (363–364).

τοῦ ... ἀρθήσεται. Mt. 25.29 ‖Lk. 19.26. The text is considerably shorter than that now found in the Gospels. This might be the result of deliberate abbreviation. However, Clement's text of this verse probably differed in much the same way from that preserved. He quotes the first half twice (II.10.21 and III.41.7), both times in the form τῷ ἔχοντι προστεθήσεται, which differs from the preserved forms of the first half as the text of the letter does from those of the second. Moreover, Clement's text and that of the letter, put together, yield a simple, epigrammatic, rythmically balanced version of the verse; the Matthaean and Lucan forms are unbalanced and cluttered. This does not prove the simple form the original form. [Simplicity is often the result of revision—A.D.N.] But it strongly suggests that the letter, since it contains the second half of the simple form, comes from Clement, in whose works we find the (parallel) first half of the simple form. (II.100.1ff and 263.25, which Stählin took as references to this passage, are probably from an extracanonical logion, combined in 263.25 with Mt. 6.33 ‖ Lk. 12.31. The tradition of the saying is extremely complex; see Lindeskog. Logiastudien.)

II.17

καὶ "ὁ μωρὸς ἐν σκότει πορευέσθω." ἡμεῖς δὲ

καὶ. As sole connection of two quotations from different sources, II.10.21; 125.1; 221.16,20; etc. But *καὶ πάλιν* is much more common.

The use of a group of quotations, after a long stretch relatively free of them, is typical of Clement; for example, *Stromateis* II:

Ch. I, 3 quotations

Ch. II, 25 quotations　　　　　　　　　Ch. VI, lines 1–6, 3 quotations

Ch. III, no quotations　　　　　　　　Ch. VI, lines 7–64, 2 quotations

Ch. IV, lines 1–50, 8 quotations　　　Ch. VI, lines 65–87, 8 quotations

Ch. IV, lines 51–80, 1 quotation　　　Ch. VI, lines 88–117, 1 quotation

Ch. IV, lines 81–120, 9 quotations　　Ch. VII, lines 1–34, 3 quotations

Ch. V, 23 quotations　　　　　　　　　Ch. VII, lines 35–55, 10 quotations

These figures are approximate.

ὁ μωρός ... πορευέσθω. Ecclesiastes 2.14. Clement quotes Eccles. in II.37.3ff (1.16ff) and 8f (7.12), and in II.385.18ff (1.2), each time in texts almost identical with LXX. The text in the letter differs from LXX by substituting *μωρός* for *ἄφρων* (as did the above quotation from Prov. 26.5) and *πορευέσθω* for *πορεύεται*. The Hebrew text has *holek* (*πορεύεται*) and no variants are noted, so this latter difference may be interpretive. [It may also have been motivated at least in part by stylistic considerations. The imperative is more vigorous Greek. A writer with atticizing traits, like Clement, would prefer it. Similarly, *De sublimitate* IX.9 has *γενέσθω φῶς ... γενέσθω γῆ*, where LXX has *γενηθήτω*. W.M.C.] Clement's willingness to alter scriptural quotations to suit his purposes is noted by Kutter, 22; Tollington, II.178; and others. [It may well have been subconscious, since he quoted from memory. A.D.N.] His use of an OT quotation, as here, to follow and clinch a NT one, is found in II.131.20–29 (the "NT" one is from *Barnabas*) ;135.23–31; 141.22–24; etc.

ἡμεῖς δέ. In Christian self-congratulation, as here, to contrast a preceding unfavorable OT quotation with a following favorable NT one, I.112.12ff, "*μὴ καυχάσθω ὁ σοφὸς ἐν τῇ σοφίᾳ αὐτοῦ*" ⟨etc., Jer. 9.22f⟩ *ἡμεῖς δὲ* "*θεοδίδακτοι*" ⟨I Thess. 4.9⟩. With slightly different form, contrasting two verses of Paul, II.246.23ff, "*μὴ πλανᾶσθε ... οὔτε πόρνοι ... βασιλείαν θεοῦ οὐ κληρονομήσουσιν*" ⟨I Cor. 6.9–10⟩ *καὶ ἡμεῖς μὲν* "*ἀπελουσάμεθα*" ⟨I Cor. 6.11⟩. This comes at the conclusion of *Stromateis* III, Clement's major attack on libertine gnostics, in which he gives most attention to the Carpocratians. There may be an echo of this letter in *Apostolic Constitutions* VI.10 end–11, where the author concludes a list of the abominable teachings of the heretics with an unmistakable reference to those of the Carpocratians, then declares, *οὗτοι δὲ πάντες τοῦ διαβόλου ὄργανα τυγχάνουσι καὶ υἱοὶ ὀργῆς. ἡμεῖς δὲ τέκνα θεοῦ καὶ υἱοὶ εἰρήνης ὄντες, τὸν ἱερὸν καὶ εὐθῆ λόγον κηρύσσοντες ...* and follows this up with a declaration of the mysteries of Christian doctrine which is really an expanded baptismal creed.

"υἱοὶ φωτός" ἐσμεν, πεφωτισμένοι τῇ ἐξ ὕψους ἀνατολῇ τοῦ πνεύματος
II.18
τοῦ Κυρίου.

υἱοὶ φωτός. This, with the preceding ἡμεῖς and the following ἐσμέν, is an adaptation of I. Thess. 5.5, ὑμεῖς υἱοὶ φωτός ἐστε (in contrast to the sinners of the preceding verses, cf. the preceding note). I Thess. 5.5 is quoted by Clement, I.206.13. He uses the metaphor υἱοὶ φωτός again, I.206.24f, deriving it from Jn. 12.36, and he also uses τέκνα φωτός from Eph. 5.8 (I.68.13). The quotation there is introduced exactly as here, without any reference or identification either before or after it. Kutter, 35, comments on this manner of quotation as typical of Clement. The metaphor was commonplace in the early Church; e.g., the fragments of Hippolytus' work against Gaius argue that believers are "children of light" who do not "walk in darkness" and should therefore not be treated as unbelievers (Harnack, *Gwynn'schen* 122). However, it seems to have been particularly popular in semignostic circles in Egypt; *Sophia JC*, 126; *Epistula Apostolorum* 28(39); 39(50); etc. Hornschuh, *Anfänge* 87, 238ff, suggests an Essene background. [So does J.R.]

πεφωτισμένοι. I.206.6, in the context of Clement's quotation of I Thess. 5.5 (above), ὁ πεφωτισμένος describes the initiated Christian gnostic. Clement uses the verb often (IV.806, 26 references). For the thought and the connection with sonship, I.105.20f, βαπτιζόμενοι φωτιζόμεθα, φωτιζόμενοι υἱοποιούμεθα, cf. above, on τελειουμένων in I.22. Illumination by the spirit, as here, II.295.23; 502.5; etc.

τῇ ἐξ ὕψους ἀνατολῇ. The same metaphor, II.36.11f, φωτὸς δ', οἶμαι, ἀνατολῇ πάντα φωτίζεται, of the Logos as the source of all wisdom. Here it is reminiscent of Lk. 1.78, which Clement echoes in I.80.16ff and refers to in II.84.20f. Clement's fondness for metaphors using the sun and light is noted by Tsermoulas, 29f. Christ as illuminator is compared to the rising sun in I.63.17ff; 78.19ff; 81.21ff; etc.

τοῦ πνεύματος τοῦ Κυρίου. This interprets Lk. 1.78 as a prophecy of illumination by the gift of the spirit, normally in baptism, for which see above, on πεφωτισμένοι. ἐξ ὕψους was no doubt justified by Mk. 1.10 and parallels (τὸ πνεῦμα . . . καταβαῖνον sc. ἐξ οὐρανῶν), and Acts 2.2ff (ἐκ τοῦ οὐρανοῦ ἦχος . . . πνεύματος ἁγίου); cf. Acts 8.16; 10.44; 11.15 (ἐπέπεσεν τό πνεῦμα); etc. Clement regularly interpreted Lk. 1.78 as a prophecy of the illumination of Christians (see the passages listed in the previous paragraph), and he regularly conceived of the spirit as illuminating and as coming from without and from above (Frangoulis, 16, citing I.106.22ff). Clement uses πνεῦμα κυρίου in II.502.4f, τὸ γὰρ φῶς τῆς ἀληθείας φῶς ἀληθές, ἄσκιον, ἀμερῶς μεριζόμενον πνεῦμα κυρίου. In II.295.22 he quotes Prov. 20.27 as reading πνεῦμα κυρίου λύχνος, and develops the idea, but it was one for which he evidently had no special fondness. Its use here is dictated by the following quotation of II Cor. 3.17, of which the first half (not quoted) identifies the Lord with the spirit (ὁ δὲ Κύριος τὸ πνεῦμά ἐστιν). This makes it possible to reconstruct the sequence of the writer's

59

"οὗ δὲ τὸ πνεῦμα τοῦ Κυρίου," φησίν "ἐκεῖ ἐλευθερία," "πάντα" γὰρ
II.19
"καθαρὰ τοῖς καθαροῖς."

thought: Dangerous facts should be concealed from the heretics—let the fool walk in darkness—but we are children of light—illuminated by the dayspring (from on high)—the dayspring is Jesus—Jesus is the Lord—the Lord is the spirit (from on high)—therefore we are illuminated by the dayspring of the spirit—but where the spirit is, (there) is liberty. This sort of exegetic stringing together of texts is typical of Clement. The close relation, approaching interchangeability, of πνεῦμα and λόγος in the thought of Clement is noted by Frangoulis, 14f.

οὗ δὲ ... ἐλευθερία. II Cor. 3.17b. ἐκεῖ is read by the koine, G and most Greek manuscripts, the Vulgate and some Old Latin texts, and the Heraclean Syriac. Here it may be a sign of affinity with the "western" text or a "correction" by the copyist. The (unsupported?) τοῦ is probably a copyist's blunder. Clement often quotes II Cor., but never this particular verse. [H.C. comments: Its use here, like that of the following Titus 1.15, is a piece of self-justification for revealing the secret. When a secret gospel has been corrupted by heretics, the true gnostic, being enlightened by supernatural gifts, is able to distinguish the authentic from the false and, in virtue of the ἐλευθερία conferred by his pneumatic state, can be freer with such dangerous material than a Christian of inferior status, to whom the apocryphon would be impure and a pollution to read. The like opinion is found in Origen, *Commentariorum Series in Matt.* 28, middle, and *Prologus in Canticum*, end, and something similar persists even to the time of Isidore of Seville (cf. Chadwick, *Sextus* 123). Therefore in describing Clement's motivation here it is not enough merely to emphasize his concern to justify concealment of truth from the nonelect. This may be too simple an account of his implied reasoning. Of course he believed in reserve in the communication of religious knowledge, and it is a short step from keeping silence on certain topics to saying what one does not oneself wholly believe because it is pastorally expedient for the audience addressed. But he is also seeking to justify his own status as a true gnostic who is therefore free to handle the secret gospel, and besides this he wants to make clear to his correspondent, Theodore, that he too must regard the ensuing quotations as confidential matter. H.C. also calls attention to III.183.16ff: πάντες οὖν οἱ πιστοὶ καλοὶ καὶ θεοπρεπεῖς ... οὐ μὴν ἀλλ' εἰσὶν ἤδη τινὲς καὶ τῶν ἐκλεκτῶν ἐκλεκτότεροι. All the faithful are elect, but some are more elect than others.]

φησίν. This use, interrupting a quotation, is frequent in Clement, e.g., II.115.24; 116.16; 121.28; 124.20; etc.

πάντα ... καθαροῖς. This stringing together of quotations without connectives appears often in Clement's works, e.g., I.206.3–17; II.108.16ff; 150.26–151.6; 216.4ff; 382.20; etc. Here the quotation is Titus 1.15, quoted by Clement in II.246.20

II.20

σοὶ τοίνυν οὐκ ὀκνήσω τὰ ἠρωτημένα ἀποκρίνασθαι, δι' αὐτῶν ⟨τῶν⟩

where it is used as here, in polemic against libertine gnostics, including the Carpocratians. The same purpose as here—to justify concealment of truth from the nonelect and revelation of it to the chosen few—is served by a similar scriptural quotation in II.495.2f, "ἅπαντα ὀρθὰ ἐνώπιον τῶν συνιέντων" φησὶν ἡ γραφή (Prov. 8.9). This justifies Jesus' teaching outsiders only in parables, which he explained to his disciples.

σοί. Sentences beginning with σοί in epistolary style, e.g., Epistolographi Graeci, Alciphron, I.39, Anacharsis, 6; Libanius, Epistulae, 570, 668, 988.

τοίνυν. Thus used in I.10.20; 59.7; 95.26; 119.8; etc.

οὐκ ὀκνήσω. Another epistolary cliché; Libanius, Epistulae 56,251, etc. Frequent also in Clement, IV.593, fifteen references. The future with a dependent aorsit infinitive, as here, II.11.22; Libanius, Epistulae 251. An exact parallel in content to the present passage appears in Epistula Apostolorum 8(19), "Behold, therefore"—because of the false teachings of Simon Magus and Cerinthus—"we have not scrupled to write you concerning the testimony of our saviour, Christ, that which he did." This also leads to the revelation of allegedly secret tradition. The same form was used in a similar connection by Papias, as quoted by Eus., HE III.39.3, οὐκ ὀκνήσω δέ σοι καὶ ὅσα ποτὲ παρὰ τῶν πρεσβυτέρων καλῶς ἔμαθον ... συντάξαι ταῖς ἑρμηνείαις, διαβεβαιούμενος ὑπὲρ αὐτῶν ἀλήθειαν. οὐ γὰρ τοῖς τὰ πολλὰ λέγουσιν ἔχαιρον ... ἀλλὰ τοῖς τἀληθῆ διδάσκουσιν, etc. Further, Eusebius (HE VI.13.9) reports that Clement used a similar form, καὶ ἐν τῷ λόγῳ δὲ αὐτοῦ τῷ περὶ τοῦ πάσχα ἐκβιασθῆναι ὁμολογεῖ πρὸς τῶν ἑταίρων ἃς ἔτυχε παρὰ τῶν ἀρχαίων πρεσβυτέρων ἀκηκοὼς παραδόσεις γραφῇ τοῖς μετὰ ταῦτα παραδοῦναι. The general tradition (with φθονέω instead of ὀκνέω) goes back to Odyssey XI.380f; see the use of φθονερῶς above, I.27.

τὰ ἠρωτημένα. Clement uses the verb often (Stählin does not index it fully) and has the perfect middle passive in III.163.32. The perfect participle meaning, as here, "the questions which have been asked" is found in Plato, Laws 662e.

ἀποκρίνασθαι. Thus used in II.32.11. Frequent in Clement; not indexed by Stählin. The question to be answered is regularly indicated by the accusative, Plato, I Alcibiades 114d (τὰ ἐρωτώμενα), etc.

δι' αὐτῶν ... ἐλέγχων. Strikingly paralleled by II.248.25–249.3, πολλαὶ δὲ ἡμᾶς αἱ πρὸς τοὺς ἑτεροδόξους ἀντιρρήσεις ἐκδέχονται πειρωμένους τά τε ὑπ' αὐτῶν προκομιζόμενα ἐγγράφως διαλύεσθαι, πείθειν τε αὐτοὺς καὶ ἄκοντας, δι' αὐτῶν ἐλέγχοντας τῶν γραφῶν.

⟨τῶν⟩. Possibly omitted by the copyist through homoioteleuton; cf. II.495.4. [A.W. thinks its insertion necessary, especially if one thinks the letter written by Clement. B.E. also suggests it. A.D.N. disagrees.]

61

II.21

τοῦ εὐαγγελίου λέξεων τὰ κατεψευσμένα ἐλέγχων. ἀμέλει μετὰ τό, ΄΄ἦσαν

II.22

δὲ ἐν τῇ ὁδῷ ἀναβαίνοντες εἰς ῾Ιεροσόλυμα,΄΄ καὶ τὰ ἑξῆς ἕως, ΄΄μετὰ τρεῖς ἡμέρας ἀναστήσεται,΄΄ ὧδε

τοῦ εὐαγγελίου. Above, I.21–22.

λέξεων. Above, II.8.

τὰ κατεψευσμένα. Above, II.11.

ἐλέγχων. Above, on δι᾽αὐτῶν. Clement uses the verb often, IV.379 (40 references, listing incomplete). The present active participle, I.141.22; 240.13; etc.; with accusative, ibid. and often (IV.379); with διά and genitive, see above.

ἀμέλει. Meaning "for instance." Clement uses it frequently in this sense, often to introduce quotations, e.g. I.191.24; 455.22; II.39.1(?); 150.18. A closely related meaning, which it often has in Clement and which is also possible here, is "thus" or "similarly," e.g. I.6.23; 99.18; 115.3; 194.6.

μετά ... ἐπιφέρει. II.332.7; 408.20; 497.2; etc.

τό. Before citations, as here, I.110.19; 120.22; II.461.10; 463.26; etc. The accentuation before quotations (whether τὸ or τό) is dubious here and in III.11 and 14; I have followed the appearances, but they may be deceptive.

ἦσαν ... ῾Ιεροσόλυμα. Mk. 10.32. Identical with Nestle's text, which records no variants for these words. [R.S. remarks that the only variants recorded by von Soden are omission by K 1038.] Clement quotes 10.31 in III.176.27. ἀναβαίνειν εἰς, III. 36.16.

καὶ τὰ ἑξῆς ἕως. Verbatim and frequent, II.115.12; 119.14; 135.14; 150.5; etc. Mondésert, 68, mentions this sort of citation with this formula as characteristic of Clement.

μετά ... ἀναστήσεται. Mk. 10.34 end. μετὰ τρεῖς ἡμέρας is read by the principal representatives of both the "western" and the "Alexandrian" texts; the koine has τῇ τρίτῃ ἡμέρᾳ.

ὧδε. Frequent for the introduction of quotations. ὧδε ἔχει κατὰ λέξιν to introduce one from the NT, II.263.17. Other examples: II.43.12; 65.7; 331.13; 359.4; 366.15;

ἐπιφέρει κατὰ λέξιν, II.23–III.11 *Quotation from the secret Gospel*
[III.11 continued] III.12
ἐπὶ μὲν τούτοις ἔπεται τὸ, ''καὶ προσπορεύονται αὐτῷ 'Ιάκωβος καὶ
III.13
'Ιωάννης,'' καὶ πᾶσα ἡ περικοπή. τὸ δὲ

405.14; etc. With ἐπιφέρει, II.303.25f. II.199.31 is all but verbatim, ὧδέ πως ἐπιφέρει κατὰ λέξιν, and introduces a quotation from the works of Epiphanes, the son of Carpocrates.

ἐπιφέρει and κατὰ λέξιν. See above, on ὧδε. Both are very frequent, IV.421, 539. The κατὰ λέξιν formula or an equivalent was used by Clement particularly when quoting heretics; with the passage in the preceding note compare his quotations of Isidore, the son of Basilides, and of Valentinus, II.174.23 (κατὰ λέξιν); 174.30 (αὐταῖς λέξεσι), and again of Isidore, 196.1 (κατὰ λέξιν), and again of Epiphanes, 199.10 (ταῦτα εἰπὼν κατὰ λέξιν, πάλιν ὁμοίως αὐταῖς ταῖς λέξεσιν ἐπιφέρει); Cassianus, 238.10f (κατὰ λέξιν); Valentinus, 458.12 (κατὰ λέξιν); and again Isidore, 458.20.

ἐπί . . . τούτοις. Of literary sequence and, as here, initial, II.248.15, ἐπὶ τούτοις . . . ἐξιστορητέον. The phrase is fairly common in the terminal expression, καὶ τὰ ἐπὶ τούτοις, I.26.29; 61.4; 143.23; 277.8; etc.

μέν . . . δέ. Frequent, II.251.16f; 255.30–256.5 (loosely connected, as here); 236.16 (the δέ never appears); 264.6; etc.

ἔπεται. Frequent (IV.422, 36 references). Of literary sequence, II.119.20, τὰ τούτοις ἑπόμενα (i.e., the rest of the passage). Regularly with ἐπί, LSJ s.v.

τό. Above, II.21.

καὶ προσπορεύονται . . . 'Ιωάννης. Mk. 10.35. No variants.

καὶ πᾶσα ἡ περικοπή. Verbatim and used in exactly the same way, II.154.8–9. Stählin cites 8 other uses of περικοπή (IV.639).

τό. Above, II.21.

δέ. Above, III.11.

"γυμνὸς γυμνῷ"

γυμνὸς γυμνῷ. Aelian, *De natura animalium* 16.28, in *FGrHist*, no. 564F3, Καλλίας ἐν τῷ δεκάτῳ τῶν Περὶ τὸν Συρακούσιον Ἀγαθοκλέα λόγων φησὶ τοὺς κεράστας ὄφεις δεινοὺς εἶναι τὸ δῆγμα. ἀναιρεῖν γὰρ καὶ ζῷα ἄλογα καὶ ἀνθρώπους, εἰ μὴ παρείη Λίβυς ἀνήρ, Ψύλλος ὢν τὸ γένος. οὗτος γοῦν ἐάν τε κλητὸς ἀφίκηται ἐάν τε καὶ παρῇ κατὰ τύχην καὶ θεάσηται πράως ἔτι ἀλγοῦντα, τὴν πληγὴν (ἢ τὸ δῆγμα) μόνον προσπτύσας, εἶτα μέντοι τὴν ὀδύνην ἐπράυνε, καὶ κατεγοήτευσε τὸ δεινὸν τῷ σιάλῳ. ἐὰν δὲ εὕρῃ δυσανασχετοῦντα καὶ ἀτλήτως φέροντα, ὕδωρ ἀθρόον σπάσας εἴσω τῶν ὀδόντων καὶ χρησάμενος αὐτῷ τοῦ στόματος κλύσματι, εἶτα τοῦτο ἐς κύλικα ἐμβαλὼν δίδωσι ῥοφῆσαι τῷ τρωθέντι· ἐὰν δὲ περαιτέρω καὶ τοῦδε τοῦ φαρμάκου κατισχύῃ τὸ κακόν, ὁ δὲ τῷ νοσοῦντι παρακλίνεται γυμνῷ γυμνός, καὶ τοῦ χρωτὸς οἱ τοῦ ἰδίου προσανατρίψας τὴν ἰσχὺν τὴν συμφυῆ, εἶτα μέντοι τοῦ κακοῦ πεποίηκε τὸν ἄνθρωπον ἐξάντη. The practice is attested also by some verses of Nicander's, which Aelian goes on to quote. See Kings I.17.21; II.4.34f; Lucian, *De syria dea* 55; Sulpicius Severus, *Vita s. Martini* (*CSEL* I) 7.3; 8.2; *Vita secunda s. Samsonis* (*AnBoll* VI.97) 16ff, and Daiches, 492f. This type of miracle has been discussed by Bieler, esp. 237–243, and by Weinreich. The above references, except that to Lucian, appear in Bieler. Weinreich, 247ff, adds that the method is implied in Plutarch, *De Iside* 17 (357D), and the underlying idea in Plato, *Symposium* 175c–e: τὸν οὖν Ἀγάθωνα—τυγχάνειν γὰρ ἔσχατον κατακείμενον μόνον—Δεῦρ', ἔφη φάναι, Σώκρατες, παρ' ἐμὲ κατάκεισο, ἵνα καὶ τοῦ σοφοῦ ἀπτόμενός σου ἀπολαύσω, ὅ σοι προσέστη ἐν τοῖς προθύροις. δῆλον γὰρ ὅτι ηὗρες αὐτὸ καὶ ἔχεις· οὐ γὰρ ἂν προαπέστης. Καὶ τὸν Σωκράτη καθίζεσθαι καὶ εἰπεῖν ὅτι Εὖ ἂν ἔχοι, φάναι, ὦ Ἀγάθων, εἰ τοιοῦτον εἴη ἡ σοφία ὥστ' ἐκ τοῦ πληρεστέρου εἰς τὸ κενώτερον ῥεῖν ἡμῶν, ἐὰν ἁπτώμεθα ἀλλήλων, ὥσπερ τὸ ἐν ταῖς κύλιξιν ὕδωρ τὸ διὰ τοῦ ἐρίου ῥέον ἐκ τῆς πληρεστέρας εἰς τὴν κενωτέραν. εἰ γὰρ οὕτως ἔχει καὶ ἡ σοφία, πολλοῦ τιμῶμαι τὴν παρὰ σοὶ κατάκλισιν· οἶμαι γάρ με παρὰ σοῦ πολλῆς καὶ καλῆς σοφίας πληρωθήσεσθαι. Plutarch, *De Iside* 17 (357D) and 19 (358E), reflects the story that Isis, after recovering the body of Osiris, lay upon it and revived it to such an extent that she conceived from it the child Harpocrates. The story is related to a number of magical and erotic passages, e.g.: *PGM* vol. I, p. 71, n7; also no. IV, lines 119ff, 400ff; no. XXXVI, lines 288ff; *DMP*, col. XV, lines 14–20; *Anthologia Palatina* V.128; *Anthologia Latina* 430 (Riese); Kerényi, 39ff. All this material accords with what was said about the Carpocratians, both by Clement (II.197.16–200.15) and by Irenaeus (Harvey, I.20.2 = Stieren, I.25.3–4). And the Carpocratians are said to have interpreted resurrection allegorically as initiation into their sect, Irenaeus, (Harvey, II.48.2 = Stieren, II.31.2). It is not unlikely, therefore, that the Carpocratian text here had an account of a resurrection effected by Elisha's somewhat indiscreet method, but used to justify liturgical or extraliturgical practices of their own. [H.C. refers to the attempt to strip a dead body in a tomb, reported in *Acta Ioannis* 70–80.] This is an account of an attempted assault prompted by necrophilia, but it stands in contrast to the subsequent raising of the body by the apostle; and the raising follows the model in this letter, not that in John—the apostle enters the tomb and takes the hand of the dead. It is possible, therefore, that the story of the assault may be polemic against the

III.14

καὶ τἆλλα περὶ ὧν ἔγραψας οὐχ εὑρίσκεται, μετὰ δὲ τό, "καὶ ἔρχεται εἰς Ἱεριχώ,"

Carpocratians and their ritual. And since *De Iside* 17 reports the occasion of the conception of Harpocrates, was it merely by a scribal error that Origen made Celsus refer to the sect of the "Harpocratians" (*Contra Celsum* V.62)—or was this polemic? Clement often uses γυμνός metaphorically of the state in which the soul must approach God, IV.321 (some 15 references); he also uses it in its liturgical sense, I.255.15, etc. [The metaphorical use is often part of the theme of the restoration of the original condition of humanity in paradise, as is the notion of the disappearance of the difference of the sexes. A.D.N.] The metaphorical use is relevant to the requirement of actual nudity in Christian and Jewish proselyte baptism (Hippolytus, *Apostolic Tradition* XXI.5 and 11, ed. Dix; Werblowsky, *Rite* 99f). The same conjunction of metaphorical and literal meaning appears in the Egyptian youth's account of his joining the gymnosophists, Philostratus, *Vita Apollonii* VI.16: μειράκιον γενόμενος τὰ μὲν πατρῷα τοῖς βουλομένοις ἀφῆκα, γυμνὸς δὲ Γυμνοῖς ἐπεφοίτησα τούτοις, ὡς μαθησόμενος (*sc.* their secret doctrine). In this respect Carpocratian practice seems to have been similar to that of Hippolytus' church, which required that *both* the initiate and the baptizing presbyter be nude (XXI.11). See below, pp. 175–177, and the discussions of Mk. 14.51f and of Clement, *Excerpta* 66 referred to in the Index of Passages Discussed.

τἆλλα. For Clement's usage (or that of the copyists of his works) as regards contractions, see above, I.9, on τἀληθῆ.

περὶ ὧν ἔγραψας. I Cor. 7.1a, which, however, has ἐγράψατε. No variants. (7.1b is quoted by Clement, II.240.12f.) ἔγραψας is an epistolary commonplace; Weichert, 8f. περί τινος γράφειν, in Clement II.222.6f; 341.10f; 402.7; etc.

οὐχ. The copyist wrote οὐκ.

εὑρίσκεται. εὕροις ἄν of finding in Scripture is rather frequent in Clement, II.187.20; 442.8; 448.19 (εὕροιμεν δ'ἄν); etc. The form εὑρίσκεται is used, not of Scripture, in II.316.8 and 466.14; it is used of things being found written ἐν τῇ ἐκκλησίᾳ τοῦ θεοῦ, which here practically means "in Scripture," in a quotation from Valentinus, II.458.14. [Both εὑρίσκεται and οὐχ εὑρίσκεται with this meaning are common in grammarians and scholiasts. A.W.]

μετὰ δὲ τό. Above, II.20–21. Initial, II.507.23 (without τό). μετὰ with ἐπάγειν in citation, II.406.5f.

καὶ ... Ἱεριχώ. Mk. 10.46. ἔρχεται is read by the "western" text (D, Sinaitic Syriac [R.S. adds 788—of the Ferrar group—and some Old Latin: *a b ff² r² i*]);

ἐπάγει μόνον, III.14–III.16: *quotation from the secret Gospel*
III.17
   τὰ δὲ ἄλλα τὰ πολλὰ ἃ ἔγραψας ψεύσματα καὶ φαίνεται καὶ ἔστιν.
III.18
   ἡ μὲν οὖν ἀληθὴς καὶ κατὰ τὴν ἀληθῆ φιλοσοφίαν ἐξήγησις

ἔρχονται, by the rest of the tradition. Clement quotes 10.45 in I.139.30ff and 10.48 (perhaps) in II.498.33.

ἐπάγει. Very frequent in citations, IV.401 (28 references).

μόνον. Frequent, IV.571, not fully indexed.

τὰ δὲ ἄλλα. Not found as the beginning of a sentence in *Stromateis* IV–VI inclusive. καὶ τὰ μὲν ἄλλα, II.281.3; τὰ μὲν οὖν ἄλλα, 303.12; τὰ δ' ὅμοια (following citations, to indicate further literary material), 333.5; 339.3; 409.4 (no δέ); τὰ δ' ἑξῆς, 384.15. All these are beginnings of sentences. The absence of elision is noteworthy; cf. the earlier usage of the letter (I.8,9,27; II.4,6,12; etc.). Does this indicate that the earlier cases were due to the manuscript, not the copyist?

ἔγραψας. Above, III.13; further examples, I.22.22, etc.

ψεύσατα. Above, II.9.

καὶ φαίνεται καὶ ἔστιν. For the contrast, III.64.32ff, διακριτέον δέ . . . τὸ ἀληθὲς ἀπὸ τοῦ φαινομένου. See above, I.10. The expression here might be an ironic reminiscence of Plato, *Hippias Major* 294a–c, esp. c, καὶ εἶναι καὶ φαίνεσθαι. [However, φαίνεται καὶ ἔστιν is so common that it need not have come from the *Hippias*. Could its usage here be due to this: Clement's correspondent had said, "These seem (φαίνεται) to be falsifications," and Clement now answers, "They not only *seem* to be so, they *are*"? B.E.]

ἡ . . . ἐξήγησις. II.249.11, ἡ γοῦν κατὰ τὸν τῆς ἀληθείας κανόνα γνωστικῆς παραδόσεως φυσιολογία (also the beginning of a sentence).

μὲν οὖν. At the beginning of a sentence, following an article, II.347.18, etc.

ἀληθής. Above, I.9.

κατὰ τὴν ἀληθῆ φιλοσοφίαν. Verbatim, II.3.2; 112.5; 247.15; 421.15f; 422.3f. Clement's standard description of his own theories.

ἐξήγησις. II.495.5 (with κατά); 498.12 (τῶν γραφῶν—and so the preceding instance); 361.1 (of profane writings); 9 other references, IV.397.

II. Synthesis of Findings

Of the scholars to whom the preceding commentary was submitted, most concluded that the manuscript's attribution of the text to Clement was probably correct—so Bickerman, Calder, Chadwick, Einarson, Früchtel, Grant, Hadas, Jaeger, Lampe, Mondésert, Reumann, Richard, Richardson, Schippers, and Wifstrand. Nock was inclined to deny this attribution, though basing his opinion only on "instinct," and Munck and Völker denied it emphatically, for the reasons discussed in the commentary. To me, the evidence in the commentary seems, if judged by the standards customarily used in questions of literary authenticity, to justify attribution to Clement. Moreover, there is further evidence which points in the same direction.

A. *Linguistic and Stylistic Data*

The similarity of the letter to the recognized works of Clement in many details of language and style has been illustrated frequently in the commentary. These details must now be summarized and general considerations added.

I. VOCABULARY

Index I lists the words of the text and indicates whether or not they occur in the works of Clement and of Athanasius. (A comparison with Philo was attempted, but Leisegang's index omits too many words.) The "letter" (that is, everything except the heading and the quotations from the secret Gospel) has a vocabulary of 258 different words, of which 7 are not in Clement, 28 not in Athanasius; by contrast, the quotations from the secret Gospel have a vocabulary of only 82 different words, but of these 4 are not in Clement and only 3 not in Athanasius.[4] It appears, therefore, that the vocabulary of the letter is somewhat closer to Clement than is that of the secret Gospel, and is much closer to Clement than it is to Athanasius. This is shown by the following table (see next page).

---

4. The different figures given in the preliminary report were based on a different division of the material.

	Not in Clement			*Not in Athanasius*	
Heading	*Letter*	*Secret Gospel*	*Heading*	*Letter*	*Secret Gospl*
——	ἀναιδέστατος	ἀποκυλίω	Κλήμης	ἀναιδέστατος	ἀποκυλίω
	ἀπέρατος	Βηθανία	στρωματεύς	ἀναμίγνυμι	ὀψία
	ἀπόγραφον	ἐμβλέπω		ἀνδραποδώδης	Σαλώμη
	ἀπροφυλάκτως	ὀψία		ἀπατηλός	
	μηχανάω (act.)			ἀπέρατος	
	προσπορεύομαι			ἀπόγραφον	
	φθονερῶς			ἀπροφυλάκτως	
				ἐξαντλέω	
				ἐξήγησις	
				ἑπτάκις	
				ἐραστής	
				ζόφος	
				ἱεροφαντικός	
				Καρποκρατιανός	
				καταδουλόω	
				κρᾶμα	
				μηχανάω (act.)	
				μυέω	
				παραχαράσσω	
				πλανήτης	
				πνευματικώτερος	
				προπαρασκευάζω	
				προσεπάγω	
				προσπορεύομαι	
				ὑποσημαίνω	
				φθονερῶς	
				φιλοσοφία	
				χρησιμώτατος	

The results above are confirmed by consideration of the words in the text which occur less than five times in either Clement or Athanasius. Here it seems worthwhile to report also those usages recorded in the index to Philo. This has yielded the table on the opposite page, where P, C, and A stand for Philo, Clement, and Athanasius. The plus signs indicate incomplete entries in Stählin's index.

In sum, the letter, of its 258 words, has 63 (a quarter) which are rare in either Clement or Athanasius. But of these words 680+ uses are recorded in Clement, 376 in Leisegang's incomplete index to Philo, and only 142 in Athanasius. By contrast,

From the letter

	P	C	A		P	C	A
ἄβυσσος	3	6	3	Καρποκρατιανός	–	2	–
ἄδυτον	28	9	2	καταγράφω	–	2	2
ἅλας	–	2	2	καταδουλόω	3	3	–
ἀναιδέστατος	–	–	–	καταψεύδομαι	19	1	21
ἀναμίγνυμι	–	4	–	κρᾶμα	11	7	–
ἀνδραποδώδης	–	1	–	μηχανάω (act.)	–	–	–
ἀπατηλός	4	10	–	μυέω	14	13	–
ἀπέρατος	3	–	–	μυσταγωγέω	3	4	2
ἀπόγραφον	–	–	–	μωραίνω	1	4	1
ἀπόρρητος	17	15	1	μωρία	3	1	5
ἀπορρίπτω	–	15	4	ὄλεθρος	31	3	8
ἀπροφυλάκτως	–	–	–	πάντη	–	15+	3
ἀσφαλῶς	–	1	5	πάντοτε	–	6+	3
αὐτίκα	–	100	2	παραχαράσσω	4	9	–
διατριβή	9	7	3	πλανήτης	–	7	–
εἴκω	–	5	4	πνευματικώτερος	–	1	–
εἰσέτι	–	6	1	προγράφω	–	2	5
ἐκλέγω	–	37	4	προπαρασκευάζω	–	5	–
ἐνσώματος	1	1	2	προσεπάγω	–	1	–
ἐξαγγέλλω	–	1	2	προσπορεύομαι	–	–	–
ἐξαντλέω	–	1	–	Σατανᾶς	–	1	7
ἐξήγησις	1	12	–	στενός	–	1	10
ἐξορχέομαι	–	3	2	συγκεράννυμι	6	2	3
ἐπιστομίζω	15	3	1	συμφωνέω	3	3	8
ἑπτάκις	1	1	–	ὑποσημαίνω	7	3	–
ἐραστής	47	12	–	ὕψος	23	6+	3
ζόφος	7	2	–	φθονερῶς	–	–	–
θεόπνευστος	–	4	13	φιλοσοφία	c.100	c.300	–
Ἰεριχώ	–	1	1	φυσιόω	–	3	1
Ἱεροσόλυμα	7	6	4	χρησιμώτατος	2	1	–
ἱεροφαντικός	–	1	–	ψεῦσμα	3	2	2
Καρποκράτης	–	6	2		376	680+	142

From the secret Gospel

	P	C	A		P	C	A
ἀπέρχομαι	–	2	60	κῆπος	–	1	2
ἀποκυλίω	–	–	–	μνημεῖον	12	2	11
Βηθανία	–	–	1	νεανίσκος	1	4	2
ἐμβλέπω	5	–	1	ὀψία	–	–	–
ἐπιτάσσω	–	1+	2	Σαλώμη	–	6	–
ἐπιτιμάω	5	4	10	σινδών	–	1	1
					23	21+	90

the secret Gospel, of its 82 words, has 12 (only a seventh) which are rare in either Clement or Athanasius, and of these words there are only 21 + uses in Clement and 23 in Philo, but 90 in Athanasius. This shows that the letter is much closer to the peculiar language of Clement and Philo than it is to the later Alexandrian tradition as represented by Athanasius. (Indeed, from the above figures the letter would seem closer to Clement than to Philo, but the figures for Philo cannot be pressed.) It further appears that the quotations from the secret Gospel use a vocabulary of which the affiliations are quite different from those of the letter. This suggests that the different vocabularies came from different authors, but it is not conclusive, for the difference of vocabulary might be explained as a result of content and of imitation of Mark.

The rare words in the letter have been discussed in the commentary; the more significant cases may be recalled here. ἀπέρατος meaning "boundless" (I.4) probably appears in Philo, whose influence on Clement is well known; the superlative ἀπεράτωτον seems to be used in the same sense by Clement. ἀπόγραφον meaning "copy" (II.6) and ἀπροφυλάκτως (I.27) are rare in the preserved literature and not found in Clement's preserved works; they would probably not have been used by an imitator anxious to avoid questionable traits, but they are evidenced by contemporary usage and Clement himself could well have used them. αὐτίκα (II.15) appears in one of the senses distinguished by Mayor as peculiar to Clement, who was abnormally fond of this word. μηχανάω in the active (II.3) is extremely rare (in prose otherwise unknown?); that it should have been used by an imitator is almost incredible, but Clement himself might have used it as a deliberate echo of Homer—he was very fond of Homer and often uses poetic verb forms in his prose. The three remaining words not in Clement, Philo, or Athanasius are προσπορεύομαι (III.12) quoted from Mk. 10.35, and ἀναιδέστατος (II.8) and φθονερῶς (I.27), both in Plato, who was the chief pagan influence on Clement. The words in the letter and Clement, but not in Philo or Athanasius, are ἀναμίγνυμι (II.8), ἀνδραποδώδης (I.7), ἐξαντλεω (II.9), and προπαρασκευάζω (I.27), all in Plato; ἱεροφαντικός (I.23) in Iamblichus; προσεπάγω (I.24) in Polybius; and Καρποκρατιανός (I.2) and πνευματικώτερος (I.21) from the Christian vocabulary. πλανήτης, Philo πλάνητες, scarcely belongs in the list, especially since the letter uses it in a quotation from Jude. By contrast, the words peculiar to the secret Gospel, ἀποκυλίω (III.1) and ὀψία (III.7), are both in LXX; but neither is in Plato. There is only one word shared by the secret Gospel and Clement, but not listed for Philo or Athanasius: the name Σαλώμη (III.16)—a name particularly important in the gnostic side of Egyptian Christianity with which Clement was involved. It will be discussed below in the commentary on the secret Gospel.

[J.R. here remarks: "Though I find myself convinced by the *cumulative* arguments for the authenticity of the letter ... I fear the statistics here might only point to a date for the document in the centuries between Philo and Athanasius. A comparison with Origen, if an *index verborum* existed, would be more significant."] With this I agree, but, as things are, the comparisons with Philo and Athanasius seemed the most relevant that could easily be made.

2. VERBAL ASSOCIATION

Not only do the letter and Clement use the same words, but they associate them in the same ways:

σαρκικῶν καὶ ἐνσωμάτων, of sins (I.4)
πεφυσιωμένοι εἰς γνῶσιν (I.5)
καυχάομαι, of libertines who boast of their freedom (I.6)
πάντῃ τε καὶ πάντως (I.8)
ὁ τῆς ἀληθείας ἐραστής (I.9)
ἀνθρωπίνας δόξας and φαινομένην ἀλήθειαν (I.10) as opposed to τῇ ἀληθείᾳ τῇ κατὰ
  τὴν πίστιν (I.11)
αὔξησις πίστεως (I.17-18)
τὰ προκόπτοντα περί (τινα) = those things which make for (I.20f)
πνευματικ⟨ώτερ⟩ον εὐαγγέλιον (I.21f)
αὐτοὺς μόνους τοὺς μυουμένους τὰ μεγάλα μυστήρια (II.2)
μιαρός, of demons (II.2-3)
ἀπατηλός, of the black art (II.4)
τῷ τῶν ἀνθρώπων γένει (II.3)
ἄχραντος καὶ ἅγιος (II.8)
κατὰ τὴν ἀληθῆ φιλοσοφίαν, as a description of the writer's opinions (III.18)

Associations of words similar to all of these, but not usually identical and usually in different contexts, are to be found in Clement and are cited in the commentary. This letter has, also, many of Clement's stock phrases—ὡς ἐγὼ οἶμαι (I.27), εἴσετι νῦν (II.1), εὖ μάλα (II.1), etc.—which belong rather to vocabulary than to verbal association. Against these similarities, I have found in Clement no parallels for the following associations in the letter: παραδιδόναι, of the traditions of heretics (I.13); ἐξαγγέλλειν, of an evangelist's publication of Jesus' teachings (I.16); μυστικάς, of Jesus' πράξεις (I.16-17); ἐπιτίθημι, of addition to a literary work (I.24). It is to be expected that any work of any author will show some peculiar traits, and these seem within the range of Clement's possible usage.

3. COMPARISONS AND METAPHORS

The following are found both in the letter and in Clement's preserved works:

sinners to planets (I.3)
the road of the commandments (I.3, a favorite of Clement's)
wandering into sensual indulgence (I.4)
depths of knowledge (I.5)
casting oneself into damnation (I.6)
the darkness of falsity (I.6)
slaves of the passions (I.7)
counterfeiting the truth (I.14)
salt, as a symbol of goodness (I.15, NT)
dancing out mysteries which are not to be spoken (I.23)
Jesus a hierophant (I.23)

instruction acts as a mystagogue (I.25)
the veiled adyton of the truth (I.26; confirming Wilamowitz' conjecture)
unbelief is mental blindness (II.14f, a favorite of Clement's)
the light of the truth (II.15, another favorite; Tsermoulas, 29f)
the evil walk in darkness (II.16, OT)
right believers are children of light (II.17, NT)
the coming of the spirit of Christ is sunrise (II.17f)
moral purity (II.18f, NT)

Clement's works do not speak of drawing off a doctrine from a book (letter, II.9), nor (clearly) of the abyss of sin (letter, I.4). That men are enslaved by magic or by evil spirits (letter, II.5; Clement, I.8.3; III.5.14) may not be metaphorical. The frequency with which the letter uses metaphors and similes and its failure to develop them—the way they are merely suggested by a word or two and then abandoned—have both been remarked as typical of Clement's style (Tsermoulas, 108; Murphy, xif). Along with metaphor may be mentioned two other characteristics of Clement's style: his fondness for plays on words, conspicuously illustrated in the letter by the play on ἀλήθεια (I.7–13, see the note on I.9), and his deliberate variation of nouns when referring repeatedly to the same thing, illustrated in the letter by the change from ψεῦδος to πλάσμα (I.12–14).

4. FORMS OF REFERENCE

The following forms used in the letter are either closely or exactly paralleled in Clement:

οὗτοι γὰρ οἱ προφητευθέντες, identifying figures of Clement's world as those referred to by a cryptic phase of Scripture (I.3)
τὸ κατὰ Μᾶρκον εὐαγγέλιον (I.12)
τοῦτο δὴ τὸ λεγόμενον, as an interjection to introduce a conventional expression (I.14)
τοῦ . . . τούτου, for contemptuous reference to an object previously indicated (II.9)
καθὼς καὶ προείρηκα (II.10)
ἡ σοφία τοῦ Θεοῦ . . . παραγγέλλει, to introduce a quotation from Proverbs (II.13)
διὰ τοῦτο . . . διὰ Σολομῶντος παραγγέλλει, to introduce a quotation from Proverbs (II.13)
αὐτίκα φησί, to introduce a quotation from a Gospel (II.15)
φησίν interrupting a quotation of Scripture (II.18, very frequent in Clement)
δι᾽ αὐτῶν ⟨τῶν γραφῶν⟩ λέξεων . . . ἐλέγχων, introducing scriptural quotations to refute heretics (II.20)
μετὰ τὸ . . . ὧδε ἐπιφέρει (II.21–22)
καὶ τὰ ἑξῆς ἕως (II.21f)
κατὰ λέξιν (II.22)
ἐπὶ τούτοις and ἕπεται (III.11)
καὶ πᾶσα ἡ περικοπή (III.12)
τὸ δέ (III.13)
μετὰ δὲ τό and ἐπάγει (III.14)

Besides these there are 4 instances in the letter (I.6 and II.16,17,18) in which Scripture is quoted without any introduction, or with only καί or γάρ to connect it to what precedes; this way of quoting Scripture is frequent in Clement's works (see II.18). Like Clement, the letter quotes Philo without mentioning him (II.12). The letter's only form of reference not paralleled in Clement is the epistolary common-place περὶ ὧν ἔγραψας (III.13).

5. FORMULAS BEGINNING SENTENCES

Of 26 such formulas, 17 are found verbatim in Clement:

οὗτοι γὰρ οἱ (I.3)	οὐ γάρ (II.12)
τούτοις οὖν (I.7; II.10)	διὰ τοῦτο (II.13)
εἰ γὰρ καὶ, c.opt. (I.8)	αὐτίκα φησί (II.15)
οὐδὲ γάρ (I.9)	ἡμεῖς δέ (II.16–17)
ὁ γοῦν (I.15)	ἀμέλει (II.20–21)
οὐδέπω ⟨ὅμως⟩ (I.22)	ἐπὶ ⟨μὲν⟩ τούτοις (III.11)
οὕτως οὖν (I.26)	μετὰ δέ (III.14)
τοῦ δὲ . . . τούτου (II.9)	ἡ / τὸ μὲν οὖν (III.17–18)

Of the remaining 9, 5 are exactly paralleled in structure, though the words used are different; these are beginnings with initial participles or with nouns in the genitive, I.5,11,13,18; II.2. Two are epistolary clichés not found in Clement's preserved works (which contain only brief fragments of two letters) but frequent in the imperial epistolography (καλῶς ἐποίησας, I.2; σοὶ τοίνυν, II.19). One is a quotation of II Cor. 3.17 (in II.18). The one unaccounted for is τὰ δὲ ἄλλα (III.17). Of those found in Clement, ἀμέλει and αὐτίκα φησί are so often used by him as to be characteristics of his style.

6. PREPOSITIONS

The uses of prepositions are customarily classified by cases and meanings; by those criteria, all the uses found in the letter are found also in Clement. Of the 25 uses of prepositions with verbs—I.3,4,5bis,10,11,19,20bis,21,26; II.2,4,6,7,14bis,16,20 21(μετά),21(εἰς); III.11,13,14bis—Clement has, for at least the 17 italicized, the same preposition in the same sense with the same verb. The rest are all to be found either in LXX and NT or in standard Hellenistic and classical authors. The preposi-tional phrases in I.15,22, II.12,13,21(ἐν),22bis were excluded from the above list because they are standard adverbial constructions, practically independent of the verbs with which they are used. Of these constructions, those in I.15,22, II.13 and κατὰ λέξιν in II.22 are all found in Clement, while ἐν τῇ ὁδῷ (II.21) and μετὰ τρεῖς ἡμέρας (II.22) are quoted from the NT; only μεθ᾽ ὅρκου (II.12) remains, and it is found in Mt. Thus the individual uses of prepositions in the letter are always in accord with Clement's general usage and often exactly paralleled in his works. But the situation is complicated by the question of the relative frequency with which particular prepositions and cases are used. This was studied for Clement's works by

Mossbacher, who listed 18 prepositions in order of frequency, with estimated totals for the uses of each (p. 7). The first 12 items of his list appear in column *M*, below; column *L* lists the prepositions used in the letter (excluding the heading and the secret Gospel) and column *C* the prepositions in a sample passage from Clement, of approximately the same length as the letter (II.243–246). In the *L* and *C* columns the totals are broken down to indicate the number of uses with each case, the cases being indicated by the initals A (accusative), D (dative), and G (genitive).

L				*M*			*C*		
εἰς	9A			κατά	1995		διά	13A	1G
κατά	7A			διά	1956		ἐν	7D	
ἐν	5D	————		ἐν	1743		ἐπί	3A	2D
μετά	3A	1G		εἰς	1589		κατά	4A	
διά	2G	1A		ἐπί	1239		εἰς	4A	
πρός	3A	————		πρός	1059	————	πρός	2A	
ἐκ	3G	————		ἐκ	933		ἀπό	1G	
περί	2G	1A	————	περί	730		ὑπό	1G	
παρά	1G	————		παρά	565		ἀντί	1G	
ἀπό	1G	————		ἀπό	447		ἄνευ	1G	
ἐπί	1D			μετά	404				
ὑπό	1G	————		ὑπό	402		5G	9D	26A

11G 6D 24A

It will be seen that the 12 prepositions which occur in the letter are precisely the same as the 12 Mossbacher found Clement used most often, and that the relative frequency of their uses in the letter is roughly in accord with Mossbacher's report of their relative frequency throughout Clement's works. In both these respects the letter agrees with Mossbacher's table much better than does the passage of Clement chosen for comparison–an atypical passage chosen deliberately to show that the letter is well inside the range of variations from which Mossbacher's averages were compiled. On the other hand, according to Mossbacher (p. 9) the average frequency of cases throughout Clement's works, is 1.8 genitives and 2.7 accusatives for every 1 dative. The letter has 1.8+ genitives and 4 accusatives for every dative, and Clement, II.243–246, has .55 of a genitive and almost 2.9 accusatives for every dative. Since the use of the accusative increased sharply in the centuries after Clement's work, and that of the dative declined even more sharply, the high relative frequency of accusatives in the letter would be a trait almost certain to be found in a later imitation; it seems to me the chief ground for doubting the letter's authenticity. On the other hand, the uses of εἰς, κατά, and μετά which account for this are almost all determined by content and individually paralleled from Clement's undoubted works, and isolated passages of Clement would be expected to show considerable deviation from averages based on the whole. In particular one might expect to find a private letter

somewhat further along the line of linguistic change than its author's published works. It is also possible that some of the letter's accusatives were introduced by medieval copying; see below, on τὸν Ἰησοῦν, in II.24.

7. SYNTAX

The sentence structures of the letter can all be paralleled from Clement and, generally, from many Greek writers of the imperial period; so can the letter's use of moods and tenses. For the most part these present nothing extraordinary. The exact parallel in Clement—with quite different words and context—to the rather odd sentence form in II.13–15 (διὰ τοῦτο ... παραγγέλλει ... δεῖν ... διδάσκουσα) deserves notice. So does the grammatical slip, καυχώμενοι ἐλευθέρους εἶναι, in I.6–7, which could hardly have been made by a careful imitator capable of writing the rest of the text, but is more understandable in a private letter. Besides these details, the most conspicuous grammatical characteristics of the letter are the fondness for the perfect (I.24) and for verbal adjectives in -τέος and -τέον (I.10), both characteristics of Clement.

8. EUPHONY

The letter's practices are common to Clement and to later Greek generally, but may be due to the copyists rather than the writer. Thus, although the letter agrees with Clement (Mossbacher, 45–47) in neglecting hiatus before prepositions and avoiding it after them (II.4,6,12,20), no importance can be attributed to this; so does the secret Gospel (II.26; III.5,6).

9. CLAUSULAE

Appendix C shows the results of a study of the quantitative rhythms at the ends of the sentences of the letter and of *Stromateis* III (chosen because it is closest in content to the letter). Quotations, sentences introducing quotations, rhetorical questions of less than four syllables, and passages textually corrupt have been excluded. Of the remaining 314 sentences of *Stromateis* III, the quantities of the last five syllables have been tabulated. Five syllables can display only 32 patterns of longs and shorts. If these 32 patterns occurred at random in the 314 sentence endings, each pattern should occur about 9 or 10 times. Actually, however, there are 6 patterns which account for more than a third of the endings, and 9 patterns which together make up only a ninth. This looks like the result of deliberate preference and avoidance. Now the letter contains 21 indubitable sentence endings (apart from those in quotations or introducing quotations) and to these may be added, for the sake of completeness, the endings διδασκαλίαν τοῦ κυρίου (I.23f) and οὐδέποτε εἰκτέον (II.10), which may perhaps conclude sentences, and ἀληθῆ λεκτέον (II.13), the end of an unacknowledged quotation from Philo which this author has probably rephrased. Of the resultant 24 units, 10 come from Clement's 6 favored patterns, 11 from Clement's 17 neutral patterns, and only 3 from Clement's 9 avoided patterns. All his favored

patterns are represented in the letter, but only two of his avoided patterns appear there. The 6 favored patterns account for slightly more than four-twelfths of the endings in *Stromateis* III and five-twelfths of those in the letter, while the 9 avoided ones make up only a ninth of the endings in *Stromateis* III and an eighth of those in the letter. Thus the clausulae of the letter are those we should expect in a composition written by the author of *Stromateis* III.

B. *Conclusions from the linguistic and stylistic data*

When taken together, the above similarities between the letter and the works of Clement virtually prove that the letter is either genuine or a deliberate and careful imitation. There can be no question here of accidental misattribution to Clement of a nameless document which some scribe assigned to a familiar author by a plausible guess. For that, the similarities are too great. Nor is there any evidence to justify the notion that we have here a genuine letter expanded by interpolation: the text is uniform and closely knit throughout. So the letter is *either* entirely genuine *or* a deliberate imitation of Clement's style. But if it be an imitation, its freedom is no less amazing than its accuracy. There is no passage of Clement's extant works from which it could have been derived by adaptation. Nor could it have been made up as a cento by putting together snippets of sentences taken from Clement. Except for a few fixed phrases and a considerable number of syntactic expressions which Clement used over and over, it almost never uses Clement's exact words, though it constantly uses his vocabulary, his phraseology, and his metaphors.

Thus the relation of the letter to the undoubted works of Clement is one of close similarity *without* either quotation or paraphrase. Now this is quite different from the relation of the letter's passages of the secret Gospel to the text of the canonical Gospel according to Mark. The secret Gospel passages are largely made up of phrases which coincide almost word for word with phrases of Mk. If an imitation, it is an imitation of the simplest and most childish sort.

But this difference of relation is the opposite of what we should expect. Mk. is written in simple Greek with many striking peculiarities; it should be easy to imitate freely. On the other hand, Clement's style is often difficult, but has few striking peculiarities which an imitator could exploit. Without profound study it could not be imitated with assurance of accuracy except by taking whole phrases and piecing them together or by taking a whole section and making minor changes in it. So if one imitator had written the whole document, we should expect his imitation of Clement to be a cento or an adaptation, and we should not be surprised if his imitation of Mark were considerably freer. That we find the reverse of this means that *if the letter is an imitation, then the letter and the Gospel fragments were not composed by the same man.* No man who could write such a free and skillful imitation of so difficult an author as Clement would then write such a slavish imitation of so easy an author as Mark.

But what if the letter should be genuine? Then, too, it would follow that the letter and the Gospel fragments were by different hands. For Clement's works make clear that he would never have invented these Gospel quotations. No doubt he was of less than perfect honesty—see above, on II.12—but neither his conscience nor his feeling for Greek style would have permitted him to forge fragments of the sacred Scriptures. Therefore *if the letter is genuine, the letter and the Gospel fragments were not composed by the same man.*

Now as remarked above, we must suppose *either* that the letter is genuine *or* that it is an imitation. Since both these suppositions have led to the conclusion that the letter and the Gospel fragments are not by the same man, we are justified in discussing them as separate compositions. We can therefore deal here with the letter by itself and reserve consideration of the secret Gospel for the following chapter.

Returning to the question of the letter's authenticity, we first remark its title: "From the letters of the most holy Clement, the author of the *Stromateis*, to Theodore." If the letter is not genuine, this title must be the result either of deliberate falsification or of a mistaken guess—some copyist found an unidentified letter "to Theodore" and attributed it to Clement on the grounds of content and style. But it has already been shown that the mistaken-guess theory is unlikely because the style of the letter is so close to Clement's that the work must either be his or a deliberate imitation, and if it were an imitation the imitator would have provided the title. Moreover, the words "from the letters" suggest (but do not absolutely require) that the letter at some time came from a collection of letters by Clement, and a collection is less likely to have been misattributed than a short, isolated text. On the other hand, "to Theodore" argues against falsification, for no Theodore is known to have been associated with Clement; nor was there any eminent Theodore who lived about his time and with whom he might plausibly be supposed to have corresponded. The name, especially because of its acceptability to Christians of Jewish background, fits very well with the content and finding-place of the letter; but a forger would probably have attempted something more spectacular—would have made Clement instruct his reported pupil Origen or his undoubted friend Alexander, Bishop of Jerusalem. Of Theodore one can say, as Lebon said of Dositheus (*Fragments* 17 n58), "This name is neither rare nor illustrious at this period; there is nothing about it which would have tempted a forger."

C. *Content*

I. KNOWLEDGE AND USE OF SCRIPTURE

The letter refers to the canonical Gospels as θεόπνευστοι (I.11) and ἅγια (II.8); so did Clement. It uses, besides the four Gospels, the Pauline epistles, the Pastorals, I Peter, Jude, and the Apocalypse.[5] All these were accepted by Clement. Among the letter's quotations of the NT are a number Clement also used (I.3,5; II.16,

---

5. See Index II for the quotations and reminiscences in the letter.

17*bis*,19), and its quotations show points of contact with the western text (II.18,22; III.14), as did Clement's (Barnard).[6] Its quotation of Mt. 25.29 ‖ Lk. 19.26 suggests that its author had the same peculiar form for the first half of the verse as did Clement (II.16). Of the NT, it uses Mk. 4 times; I and II Cor. together 3; Lk. 3; Mt., Titus, and Jude 2 each; Jn., I Thess., I Pet., and Apoc. 1 each. The prominence of Mark and Jude in this list is determined by the subject matter with which the author had to deal. Clement's order of preference (by columns of references in Stählin's index) is: Mt. 9 cols.; I and II Cor. together 7; Lk. 5.5; Jn. and Rom. 4 each; Mk. 2.5. (Stählin's index is not always accurate in its assignment of material to the various biblical books—cf. Appendix D.)

Of the OT (and Apocrypha) the letter uses Prov. three times and Jer., Wis., and Eccles. once each. Clement's favorites were Pss., 4.5 cols.; Prov. and Gen., 3.5 each; Is., 3; but there is more than a column of Jer., and Wis. and Eccles. are both represented. The letter quotes Prov. 26.5 in a form in which it is quoted by no writer save Clement, and interprets it as Clement did (II.14). It has what may be a reminiscence of one passage of *Enoch*; the particular detail recalled is one for which Clement explicitly referred to *Enoch* (I.4).

Besides *Enoch*, the letter accepts as Scripture the secret Gospel; Clement is outstanding among Christian writers for his acceptance of OT and NT pseudepigrapha. Zahn wrote of him, "His amazingly uncritical attitude to apocryphal literature exceeds anything to be found in other Church fathers" (*Forschungen* III.156). This judgment is documented involuntarily even by the minimizing and incomplete studies of Kutter, 50ff, and Ruwet, *Clément* 406f (neither of whom noticed, for example, that Clement reportedly said Luke composed the *Dialogue of Jason and Papiscus*: so Maximus the Confessor on Dionysius Areopagites, Μυστικῆς Θεολογίας 1 end). Of all important early Christian writers, Clement was the one most likely to have accepted a secret Gospel. His objection to a saying used by the heretic Cassianus, Πρῶτον μὲν οὖν ἐν τοῖς παραδεδομένοις ἡμῖν τέτταρσιν εὐαγγελίοις οὐχ ἔχομεν τὸ ῥητόν, ἀλλ᾽ ἐν τῷ κατ᾽ Αἰγυπτίους (II.238.27f), does not preclude his acceptance of a further, secret document to which he would not refer in public dispute. Compare his statement that the story of the rich young ruler is found in *all* the recognized (ἀνωμολογημένοις) Gospels, which would exclude Jn. (III.163.13ff; cf. Mondésert, *Clément* 118 n2). The attitude shown by the author of the letter is credible of Clement; it would be incredible of Athanasius, a century and a half later.

The letter not only has the same sacred literature as Clement, but also uses it in the same connections, for the same purposes (see the passages cited above, esp.

6. Barnard's conclusions must now be modified by the findings of Swanson, *Text*, who has argued that in the *Stromateis* Clement's use of a text of western type is demonstrable only in his quotations from Lk. In quoting Mt. and Jn. he demonstrably used a text closest to the Egyptian type (represented best by ‫א‬). His quotations from Mk. have points of contact with the western text, but are not sufficient to permit determination of the type of text used. The long quotation of Mk. in *QDS* seems to have come from a mixed text (pp. 97–102, 167ff). These, at least, are the conclusions set forth by Swanson. I have not attempted to check his work in detail, but a number of its aspects—especially the choice of evidence (see the notes to Appendix D)—do not incline me to be confident that these conclusions are conclusive. Nevertheless, my thanks are due to Professor Metzger for calling my attention to Swanson's work.

II.14 and 18), and interprets it in the same ways. Its peculiar interpretation of Prov. 26.5 has been mentioned. It also shares with Clement the habit of using an OT quotation to follow and clinch one from the NT (II.16). Further, it agrees with Clement in interpreting Jude as referring to the Carpocratians (I.3ff) and in associating the Carpocratians with Nicolaïtans of the Apocalypse (I.5). The beginning of its peculiar tradition about Mark agrees with that which Eusebius found in Papias and Clement; moreover, in making Mark write during Peter's lifetime it agrees with Clement against Papias (I.15).

It is in Clement, also (III.162.19–163.12), that we find the quotation of a long, uninterrupted section of Mk., like the letter's quotation of the secret Gospel. Moreover, the section of Mk. (10.17–31) quoted by Clement is adjacent to 10.34 and 46, where the letter locates in Mark the pericopae it quotes from the secret Gospel. And yet more: This was the one part of Mark in which Clement, for some reason, was especially interested. Stählin's list of Clement's quotations from Mark is not reliable; it includes passages probably quoted from the other synoptics or from extracanonical sources. A revision of it will be found in Appendix D. The revised list shows no *certain* quotation of any verse prior to 8.38 (the last verse of ch. 8). The certain quotations are of 8.38; 9.7; 9.29 (?); 10.17–31 and 14.61f. Of the *possible* quotations listed by Stählin there are 13 prior to 8.38, 25 from chs. 9 and 10, and 14 from 11.1 to the end. Allowing for the fact that 11 of the 25 occur in the exegesis of 10.17–31 in *QDS*, it remains clear that Clement was extraordinarily interested in Mk. 9–10, particularly in 10, the chapter from which this letter quotes the additions in the secret Gospel. (The reason for this interest in Mk. 9–10 will be discussed later.)

Both the letter and Clement are much fonder of allusions and reminiscences than of direct quotations, and even when they quote directly they often do not specify the source. Stählin recognized 79 quotations of Mk. as against 100 reminiscences (and about 25 of his "quotations" belong in the reminiscence category—see Appendix D). Of his 79 quotations only 2 carry with them explicit references to Mk. The letter has 18 quotations as against 19 reminiscences, and only one of the quotations is accompanied by a reference to the author (though, of course, the 4 quotations of Mk. used to locate the sections of the secret Gospel are themselves specific references). The reason for the higher percentage of quotation and specific reference in the letter is its polemic content; in polemic passages Clement, too, makes more use of specific reference and allegedly precise quotation (I.22). The less precise practice of reminiscence had an advantage which recommended it both to Clement and to the author of the letter: it made possible their favorite practice of multiple reference, of combining a number of OT and NT passages so as to suggest that each should be interpreted in the light of the rest and that all should be applied as the writer applied them (I.3f,6,14–15; II.13–19; further examples and comment in Ruwet, *Clément* 253).

2. KNOWLEDGE OF THE CLASSICS

Besides scriptural learning, the letter shows considerable knowledge of the classics; for this Clement was praised by Eusebius, Jerome, Cyril, Socrates, Anastasius of

Sinai, and Photius (Stählin, I.IX–XVI). The letter has three or four reminiscences of Plato (see Index II), one or two of Philo (I.2,4; II.11,12–13), and one each of Homer and Sophocles. Clement's favorite authors were Plato (10 columns of references in Stählin), Philo (7), Plutarch (5.5), Chrysippus (5), and Aristotle and Homer (4 each), but Sophocles has more than half a column. As already remarked, Clement usually quotes Philo as the letter does—without acknowledgment. Of all the works to which the letter probably refers, there is only one (apart from the secret Gospel) to which Clement does not refer: Plato's *Hippias Major*.

Because they were learned in classical as well as Christian literature, both Clement and the author of this letter had to face the problem of contradictions between faith and worldly knowledge (Marrou, *Humanisme*), and both met it by distinguishing two kinds of truth—the inferior being that recognized by human opinion, the superior "the truth according to the faith," a phrase they both use (I.9–11; cf. Osborn, *Philosophy* 113). As possessors of this higher truth the Christians are a privileged group, illuminated, as both writers say, by the spirit (II.17). Both writers call themselves and their fellow Christians "children of light" and like to follow unfavorable comments on outsiders with favorable ones on Christians introduced by the complacent words, "But we . . ." (II.16f).

3. KNOWLEDGE, FAITH, AND GNOSIS

Even within the Christian community, however, both writers distinguish higher and lower degrees. Both speak of Jesus as a "hierophant," a teacher of mysteries (I.23), and the Christianity of both has not only mysteries but "great mysteries," probably by contrast with the preliminary ones (II.2). Both connect admission to the great mysteries with progress in "gnosis" (I.21; II.2; Stählin, II.249.8ff; 367.19ff; 373–374). Both, moreover, think that progress in this gnosis is effected by instruction, inter alia instruction as to Christian tradition, having as its point of departure exegesis of stories about Jesus (I.25). This μυσταγωγία, as both call such exegesis, is not given to all Christians, but only to suitable candidates (I.22; II.2).

[Jacob Taubes remarks that one striking similarity between Clement and the author of the letter is the ambivalence of their attitude toward gnosticism; both combine violent abuse of gnostics with claims to enjoy the true gnosis and possess the true secret doctrine; among the fathers of the Church this ambivalent attitude is most typical of Clement and is better suited to Clement's time than to any later period.] Clement himself was almost certainly attacked, in his day, as a gnostic, and not without some reason (Buri, *Clemens* 16, 106ff). For the letter's use of γνῶσις in both good and bad contexts, compare I.5 and I.21; for Clement's, the citations there and II.247.12, etc. H.C. suggests that the author's purpose in his catena of texts (II.17–19) was partly to make clear that he, as a true gnostic, was free to handle the secret Gospel. Clement's *demi-vierge* position in the gnostic controversy can be seen by comparing his private excerpts from Theodotus with his attacks on the Valentinians in the *Stromateis*; see also the remarks of Photius (in Stählin I.XIVf, on which Casey, *Clement*, and the suspicious scholion I.317.36f) and such passages as

III.183.24, where Clement adopts the Valentinian concept, σπέρμα (further examples in Buri, *Clemens* 33, 39f, 61, 73, etc.). Such ambiguities became rare after the work of Irenaeus, Tertullian, and Hippolytus. After the middle of the third century, moreover, this whole complex of concerns—the inner circle of higher initiates, the secret apostolic tradition, the opposition of gnosis to mere faith, and so on—is overshadowed by questions of church discipline and organization. Later still it almost disappears as interest turns to the trinitarian controversy. The letter's conception of Christianity and its main concerns are more like those of Clement than of any other Christian writer I know.

4. THE SECRET TRADITION

In the battle over gnosticism which raged throughout the second century and reached its climax at Clement's time, private letters played an important role. Many were written; a few are preserved. References to the preserved examples are collected in Bauer, *Rechtgläubigkeit* 177ff. This was also, as remarked above, the great age of secret Gospels (Bauer, 181ff). So the literary forms no less than the content of these documents are appropriate to the time to which the heading attributes them.

Neither Clement nor the author of the letter identifies the true gnosis (*sc.* his) with a purely philosophic position. This was already demonstrated for Clement by Daehne (60–67), who also pointed out what has since been generally recognized: that Clement claimed as the source of his gnosis a secret, oral tradition derived from Jesus through the principle apostles (II.9.4ff; 462.28ff; III.199.21ff; further passages collected in Camelot, *Foi* 90ff). Exactly such a tradition is supposed by this letter (I.22). As pointed out in the commentary (I.23), Mondésert saw this claim was alien to Clement's inclinations and to the structure of his thought. Therefore the claim cannot be explained as Clement's invention; he must have accepted it because he found it established in the church in Alexandria. The letter implies that it was. Both the letter and Clement think this secret oral tradition contains the highest truth, which can be revealed only to the gnostic (see the passages cited above and I.26). Both agree that this tradition and other important elements of Christianity should be hidden, not only from outsiders, but even from catechumens and unworthy Christians: it is a Christian's duty to conceal the truth (I.18,22,27; II.2,13–15). Clement makes clear that he has no intention of writing down the innermost secrets (II.11.1ff) and in his published works will exercise such discretion that only the careful student will be able to make out the significance even of what he does say—a promise he kept too well (II.11.9f). This policy he describes and defends in words strikingly similar to the letter's description and defense of Mark's actions (I.16–18).

However, both from Clement's writings and from the letter it appears that some works containing at least important hints about this secret doctrine *had* been written, and some of these written works had fallen into the hands of the unworthy (I.21; II.6). The least worthy are the heretics, the worst heretics are the gnostics, and the worst gnostics are the libertines—on these points Clement is explicit (*Stromateis*

III), and the same judgments are implied by the letter in its initial sentences. The letter agrees with Clement that the knowledge claimed by these gnostics is false and their alleged freedom is slavery to the passions (I.5ff). Both the letter and Clement accuse the gnostics of corrupting the Christian tradition by interpretation and by interpolations (I.11 and 14; Buri, *Clemens* 21–23), and both profess to refute the gnostics by quoting the exact words of genuine documents (II.20 and 22).

5. ATTITUDE TOWARD THE CARPOCRATIANS

Of all libertine gnostics, the particular sect of most concern to the letter and to Clement, but to *no* other known Christian writer, are the Carpocratians. Clement, in his major attack on all gnostics in *Stromateis* III, took the Carpocratian sect as the outstanding example of libertine gnosticism (cf. Buri, *Clemens* 19). It is therefore plausible to suppose that they are referred to by many of his slurs elsewhere at unspecified libertines; sometimes they certainly are (III.143.20). In the works of Irenaeus they are less important than the Valentinians. In Tertullian and later heresiologists they are of quite minor importance. In Alexandria itself they seem to have been almost annihilated by the great persecution which drove Clement from the city (about 202?). Origen, a generation later than Clement, said he had never been able to meet a Carpocratian in spite of his efforts (*Contra Celsum* V.62). The letter is entirely concerned with them. Clement and the author of the letter are at one in referring to them the abusive passages of Jude (I.3), in associating them with the Nicolaïtans attacked in the Apocalypse (I.5), and in declaring that they have cast themselves into darkness (I.6). It appears from both Clement and the letter that Carpocrates worked in Alexandria and the sect arose thence (II.3).

6. DIFFERENCES, REAL OR APPARENT

So far we have seen that the letter has Clement's knowledge both of the Scriptures (including the pseudepigrapha) and of the classics, uses them as Clement does, and adjusts them to each other as Clement does. It also has Clement's notion that within Christianity there is a secret tradition reserved for the few true gnostics (among whom the author, like Clement, includes himself), and it consequently shares Clement's hostility to the competing gnostic groups, particularly the Carpocratians. Now we must consider the differences to be found between it and Clement's works.

Of course there is much material found in Clement but not in the letter; a document of three pages is not likely to reflect all the content of a corpus of three volumes.

Of the material found in the letter and not in Clement, the most surprising part is the information about Mark's secret Gospel and the Carpocratian's corruption of it. The letter presents this as confidential and even directs that Markan authorship of the secret Gospel (or, at least, of the Carpocratian secret Gospel) is to be denied on oath (II.12; see also the comments on κατεψευσμένα, II.11). Therefore, if Clement *were* the author of the letter we should *not* find this information in his published works. To maintain that because it is not in his published works it could not have

been in his private letters, one would have to maintain that Clement was extra-ordinarily outspoken and veracious. But we have seen that he was not (commentary on II.12). On the contrary, he thought the concealment of truth to be part of his Christian duty—a part he said he intended to perform (Stählin, II.11). Among the texts Clement used to justify this opinion were some which the author of this letter used for the same purpose—I.18,22,27; II.2,13–15. Accordingly, it is consistent with Clement's character that we should find in one of his private letters material at which his published works barely hint.

Moreover, the material found in the letter sometimes does seem to be hinted at by passages which are, or once were, in Clement's published works, and on other occasions it is supported by historical facts and by statements in the heresiologists. (This does not imply that the heresiologists ever saw the letter, but does show that the letter's information about the Carpocratians has some claim to reliability, as Clement's certainly would—Chadwick, *Alexandrian Christianity* 26ff). In the first place, there is reason for thinking the *Hypotyposes* contained the letter's statement that Mark went from Rome to Alexandria (I.19). That Peter died a martyr would be common "knowledge." That the canonical Gospel according to Mark was designed for the use of catechumens (I.17–18) looks like good tradition (Weiss, *Christianity* 690). That canonical Mk. omits or barely hints at important elements of Christian teaching, which Christians attributed to Jesus even before it was written, is clear from a comparison of Mk. with Paul and Q (this question will be discussed in the following chapters). That a secret Gospel according to Mark was circulating in Egypt, and that the Carpocratians appealed to Mk. for their claim to have the secret teaching of Jesus, were conjectures made by Harvey and Liboron from the statements of Irenaeus (I.2 and 12). These conjectures are now confirmed. That the Carpocratians practiced magic is asserted by Irenaeus and others (II.4). Clement says that *most* of those who appealed to Jesus for help addressed him as "son of David" (II.498. 32ff); this form of address is rare in the preserved Gospels, but the portion of the secret Gospel quoted in the letter adds another case. Clement says οὐ γὰρ φθονῶν (compare I.27) φησί, παρήγγειλεν ὁ κύριος ἔν τινι εὐαγγελίῳ, μυστήριον ἐμὸν ἐμοὶ καὶ τοῖς υἱοῖς τοῦ οἴκου μου (see above, on I.12) and the *Clementine Homilies* quote the logion together with material from Mk. (19.20.1). Clement speaks of the rich young ruler as ὑπὸ τοῦ κυρίου συντελειούμενος and says ἐδιδάσκετο δι' ἀγάπην μεταδιδόναι (II.221.27); the secret Gospel represents him as loving Jesus, receiving him in his house, and then being initiated by him. Trying to prove the Catholic Church older than the heresies, Clement says that, *after* Marcion, Simon Magus was for a short while an auditor of Peter's (III.75.18–76.1). Since this is clearly false the passage has to be emended, and a number of scholars have conjectured that Μαρκίων should be corrected to Μάρκος; cf. Stählin, *ad loc.*, who rejects this emendation but marks the text as corrupt. It may be that a phrase has fallen out after συνεγένετο. Perhaps Μάρκος δὲ τῷ Πέτρῳ καὶ τῷ Παύλῳ ὡς νεώτερος συνεγένετο. The letter goes to confirm a conjecture of this sort: it shows why Clement, when the secret, "gnostic" tradition of the Church was in question, appealed to the authority of Mark—not Matthew or even John. Finally, the Carpocratian version of the secret Gospel had an account

of Jesus' teaching a favored disciple the mystery of the kingdom of God privately and γυμνὸς γυμνῷ. Clement, though he wrote to Theodore that this phrase did not stand in the true text of the secret Gospel, nevertheless chose to note down, when he was reading the gnostic Theodotus, the statement Ὁ σωτὴρ τοὺς ἀποστόλους ἐδίδασκεν, τὰ μὲν πρῶτα τυπικῶς καὶ μυστικῶς, τὰ δὲ ὕστερα παραβολικῶς καὶ ᾐνιγμένως, τὰ δὲ τρίτα σαφῶς καὶ γυμνῶς κατὰ μόνας (III.128.24ff). Did he note with approval? As remarked above (on III.13), his usage of γυμνός was usually metaphorical. These are trivialities to none of which, taken alone, one would attach importance. But given the document which confronts us, and taken together, they may be thought significant.

More significant are the obvious differences which at first sight look like contradictions between statements in the letter and statements in Clement's published works. Clement says the true Christian will never swear; the letter recommends use of an oath to deceive. But we have seen that Clement's statement is so hedged by modifications as to be compatible with the letter's recommendation (II.12). Clement says the founder of the Carpocratian sect was Carpocrates' son Epiphanes, who died at the age of seventeen after having written a blasphemous book from which the Carpocratians derived their doctrine (II.197.26ff). The letter says the doctrines of the Carpocratians are derived from the secret Gospel of Mark, which Carpocrates got from a presbyter of the church in Alexandria and corrupted by his own interpolations (II.3–10); there is no mention of Epiphanes. Obviously the account in the letter admits that the position of the Carpocratians is considerably stronger than it would appear from the account in the published work.[7] Their teachings come not from the philosophizings of an adolescent, but from that same secret Gospel reserved by the church of Alexandria for those being initiated into its "great mysteries." Of course the Carpocratians are said to have corrupted this Gospel; but even so the admission is obviously embarrassing. We should need no explanation of its nonappearance in the published work, even if the letter did not order that it be kept secret (an order which, as we have seen, is in accord with Clement's character and teaching). Moreover, as shown in the commentary (II.3), it appears from Irenaeus that the Carpocratians did claim to derive at least some of their doctrines from secret apostolic teaching. Why did not Clement discuss this claim in his published work? Was he ignorant of it? Or was it too embarrassing? We also saw that Clement, after disposing of Epiphanes, spoke of Carpocrates as the lawgiver, if not the founder, of the sect. It should be remembered that Photius said the *Hypotyposes* contradicted the *Stromateis* in many points (Stählin, I.XV inf.; cf. Casey, *Clement*). The letter supposes Carpocrates had doctrines of his own by which he interpreted and corrupted the Gospel to produce the mixture from which it then says the Carpocratian doctrines are drawn (II.9); it cannot be carefully worded. So the statements in the letter and the statements in the *Stromateis* could have come from the same man.

The most important thing about the apparent contradictions between the letter and the *Stromateis* is that they are apparent—at first glance they would cause a reader

7. The *Stromateis* was not an esoteric document—Molland, 9; Völker, 31; to the contrary, Lazzati, 35.

familiar with the *Stromateis* to doubt the attribution of the letter to Clement. Therefore no imitator who intended to pass his letter off as Clement's would have included these contradictions unless he were ignorant of what the *Stromateis* said on these subjects, or unless the points made by the contradictory elements were his main concern. But the letter is so close to Clement in style and content that ignorance cannot be supposed (especially since it is closest of all to *Stromateis* III, where the material on Epiphanes and Carpocrates is found). And the contradictions are partly on what seem to be side issues. An imitator could have substituted Epiphanes for Carpocrates or could have avoided the apparent recommendation of perjury without altering the main import of the text.[8] Therefore it seems most likely that the letter is not an imitation: it resembles Clement's work in many trivial details which an imitator might neglect; it differs in conspicuous points of content which an imitator would never have neglected; and all of its differences can easily be explained—if it is genuine—by its private character and stated purpose, but they would be difficult to explain as consequences of any purposes which could plausibly be attributed to an imitator. Who could such an imitator have been? And why would such an imitation have been produced? Munck's suggestion, that the text was produced to glorify the church of Alexandria as possessor of the true secret Gospel written by its founder Mark (commentary on I.15), would be credible only if the church of Alexandria ever had claimed to possess such a Gospel. (Otherwise the church would have been faced with the charge of having lost this invaluable document.) But so far as I know, the church of Alexandria never made any such claim. Therefore, given the absence of any plausible explanation as to why this document would have been forged, and the absence of any strong evidence in the document itself to indicate forgery, and the many strong reasons reviewed above for thinking it genuine, we can proceed on the assumption that the manuscript's attribution of the letter to Clement is correct.[9]

8. Contrast, in this respect and in the matter of obvious contradictions, the forgeries of Pfaff (Harnack, *Pfaff'schen*). Learned forgery was not rare in the eighteenth century, but was customarily edifying and tendentious; this text is neither.

9. This conclusion is further supported by the character of the Gospel fragment which the letter quotes. To this I have not referred above because a reference would have anticipated the argument of the following chapter. However, I quote here the comments of Stendahl, to whom I submitted only the chapter on the Gospel fragment: "Not having seen your part on the Clement problem as such, let me volunteer the impression that I cannot imagine a late forgery (of the Clement letter) containing this type of Gospel text. Nor could such a text originate in a time when Mark was definitely canonized. So, indirectly, all I have seen strengthens my trust in the letter. If this material be related to baptism it may well be an Alexandrian piece which was so related and believed by Clement to be properly Markan. Whether Mark had been in Alexandria is another question to reconsider."

THREE

The Secret Gospel

During the academic year 1962–1963 this chapter was discussed in several meetings of the Columbia University Seminar for the Study of the NT; my thanks are due to the members of the Seminar for their consideration of the material and for helpful suggestions. Professors Pierson Parker, Cyril Richardson, and John Reumann were especially generous in giving my work close study; it has been much improved by their advice. A. D. Nock read the first section of the chapter; the whole was read by Professors H. J. Cadbury, W. M. Calder III, H. Koester, C. Moule, R. Schippers, and K. Stendahl, and by Dr. T. Baarda. I thank them not only for the major observations hereinafter bracketed and initialed, but also for many small corrections.

I. DATE, FORM, AND AFFILIATIONS

The assumption that the letter was written by Clement entails the consequence, remarked upon above (commentary on I.23), that the secret Gospel was not written by Clement,[1] but was accepted by him—rather against his personal inclinations—

1. In his last long letter to me, dated September 20, 1962, A. D. Nock wrote: "I don't think that anyone could suggest that Clement had written the secret Gospel. The alternatives are either your view or the hypothesis of a later person's writing the whole thing. If that is the case, I am inclined to think that it might be a job done with no specific tendency, but mystification for the sake of mystification. A curious instance is *P. Oxy.* 412, where the learned Julius was either duped or faking for faking's sake. ... Another possible point of comparison is the work of the people responsible for the *Clementine Homilies* and *Recognitions.* I think that they had no tendency, like the author or authors of the Grundschrift, and at the same time they were not seeking personal fame like Euhemerus."

P. Oxy. 412 contains the conclusion of the eighteenth book of the *Kestoi* of Julius Africanus, including a quotation of *Odyssey* XI.34–43 and 48–51 expanded by insertion of a transitional passage and a magical incantation; the incantation is re-edited with commentary as *PGM* XXIII. Julius says the whole of the inserted material (29 verses) was to be found in MSS in Jerusalem (Aelia Capitolina) and at Nysa in Caria, and the first 13 verses of it in a MS in Rome, in the library at the Pantheon. Such a brief interpolation in the text of Homer is obviously something quite different from the sophisticated composition which confronts us if the letter and its quotations are taken as the work of a single forger. The *Clementine Homilies* afford a better comparison, but the comparison tells against the argument, for they make no effort to imitate the style of the genuine *Epistle of Clement*; nor do they set their pretendedly early material in a speciously later frame. The most serious objection, however, against any such argument is that it is unnecessary. Almost any work of ancient literature can be supposed a forgery (cf. L. Wiener, *Tacitus' Germania and Other Forgeries* [Philadelphia, 1920], a work of great learning, or the attacks on Aristotle's *Constitution of Athens* referred to by von Fritz and Knapp, p. 4, to say nothing of the

because he found it already accepted by that church in Alexandria to which he attached himself when he came to the city, probably about the year 175. (Julius Africanus said that Clement was already a prominent figure in Alexandria during the reign of Commodus, 180–192; Routh, II.307. Clement's canon was contrasted with that of the Alexandrian church by Harnack, *Origin* 110.) It would seem likely that the church's acceptance of the secret Gospel antedated Clement's arrival by some considerable time; the composition of the secret Gospel of course antedated its acceptance. To allow twenty-five years for these two intervals and so put the composition back to 150 would not be implausible.

But Clement's letter indicates an earlier date. It says the secret Gospel was first written by Mark, then stolen and corrupted by Carpocrates.

Christians of Clement's party were always accusing their opponents of corrupting and misinterpreting the Scriptures (Williams, *Alterations* 31; Bauer, *Rechtgläubigkeit* 186). Presumably their opponents brought the same charges against them, and the charges of both sides were occasionally justified: all parties among the early Christians revised the texts of their Scriptures to meet their doctrinal needs—omitting embarrassing details and inserting words they thought desirable—and imposed on these texts interpretations which were often false (against Bludau, *Schriftfälschungen*, see Williams, *Alterations* 25–53; Bauer, *Leben* 492–504 and *passim*; for Clement's own practice, Buri, *Clemens* 108ff). Consequently, there is no reason to doubt Clement's statement that Carpocrates "corrupted" the text of the secret Gospel. Nor is there any reason to doubt that Clement's own text of the Gospels had been—in the jargon of modern criticism—"adapted to the needs of the growing Church."

We saw above that the letter contradicts the published writings of Clement by admitting that the Carpocratians derived their doctrines from the secret Gospel. This is a damaging concession by the writer and therefore most likely true. The specious contradiction between the letter's two statements, that Carpocrates misinterpreted the Gospel according to his doctrine and that the Carpocratians drew their doctrine from the Gospel, is merely a consequence of Clement's shifting from his own account of what happened to a sarcastic paraphrase of the Carpocratians' claims. His account was that Carpocrates corrupted and misinterpreted the Gospel according to his own doctrine. The Carpocratians' claim was: "Our doctrine is derived from this source." Clement paraphrases the claim, without bothering to deny it, because he has just declared the source polluted. That the Carpocratians did claim to derive their doctrine from the secret Mark is suggested by Celsus' reference to "the Harpocratians who follow Salome" (Origen, *Contra Celsum* V.62, with Chadwick's note, *ad loc.*). "The Harpocratians" are pretty certainly the Carpocratians (the

---

assault on the Dead Sea documents by which S. Zeitlin has more recently made himself more ridiculous). But the supposition of forgery must be justified by demonstration either that the style or content of the work contains elements not likely to have come from the alleged author, or that some known historical circumstances would have furnished a likely occasion for the forgery. In the case of the letter, no such demonstration seems possible, and the supposition therefore rests on nothing more than the feeling that this just cannot be genuine. That feeling may be correct—given Nock's knowledge of Greek and his amazing intuition, one hesitates even to doubt it—but it is not, by itself, conclusive.

god Harpocrates also appears as "Carpocrates"; Nock, review of Harder 221) and Mark is the only one of the canonical Gospels in which Salome appears. She appears again in the fragments of the secret Gospel quoted by Clement, and the Carpocratian text seems to have given her a considerably larger role than Clement's did (III.14–17). However, she also appeared in the *Gospel according to the Egyptians*, and Celsus may have been referring to Carpocratian use of that text or some other now unknown to us.

On the other hand, the story of how Carpocrates got the secret Gospel (inspired by demons and using magic, he so enslaved a presbyter of the church in Alexandria, etc.) is evidently of the cock-and-bull species. No doubt the Carpocratians were elsewhere accused of practicing magic (commentary on II.4) and did practice it—the practice and the accusation seem to have been almost equally common in ancient Christian circles. But the story reports that the magic was efficacious. And if this be excused as Clement's notion of what had happened, yet the basic facts reported are polemic: Carpocrates got the secret Gospel from a presbyter "of the church," i.e., of Clement's party. This claim is intended to prove Clement's party the original possessor. Therefore, though not incredible, it is suspect, being so strongly motivated that, even if it cannot be proved false, it cannot be accepted as true without further confirmation. Nevertheless, it is important because of what it does *not* say.

It does not say that the secret Gospel was introduced into the Carpocratian sect at some recent date. This is a charge Clement would have been happy to make had he known any excuse for it and might have made without excuse had he thought it would be believed. But his words in II.7 ($\dot{\epsilon}\xi\eta\gamma\acute{\eta}\sigma\alpha\tau o$) suggest there was a commentary supposedly by Carpocrates on the secret Gospel, which would be further evidence that the sect had possessed it ever since Carpocrates' time. (In Irenaeus' time the Carpocratians did have an interpretation of writings which reported secret teachings of Jesus [Harvey, I.20.3 = Stieren, I.25.5, $\dot{\epsilon}\xi\eta\gamma o\hat{\nu}\nu\tau\alpha\iota$]. Basilides, whom Eusebius thought a contemporary of Carpocrates, wrote twenty-four books of $\dot{\epsilon}\xi\eta\gamma\eta\tau\iota\kappa\acute{\alpha}$ "on the Gospel"; and Papias, probably an older contemporary, wrote five books of $\dot{\epsilon}\xi\eta\gamma\acute{\eta}\sigma\epsilon\iota s$ of "dominical sayings": Eus. *HE* III.39.1; IV.7.7 and 9; Stählin II.284.5, etc.) At all events, the important fact is Clement's admission that the Carpocratians have had the secret Gospel ever since the time of Carpocrates himself.

The date of Carpocrates will be discussed below in Chapter Four. He evidently worked in or before the time of Hadrian (117–138). Moreover, if he adapted the secret Gospel to his own purposes and represented it as the basis for his teachings, which Clement indicates he did, he must have got hold of it at an early stage in his career—at the latest, one would guess, before 125. Moreover, unless we suppose Clement's church took its secret Gospel, for use in its "great mysteries," from the Carpocratians, we must suppose either that Carpocrates got it from Clement's church—as Clement says he did—or that both Carpocrates and Clement's church got it from some common source. In either event we shall have to suppose the secret Gospel somewhat older than Carpocrates' adoption of it. Thus acceptance of the letter as Clement's entails admission of a probability that the secret Gospel described by the letter was in existence well before 125.

Besides indicating this *terminus ante quem* for the secret Gospel, the letter gives us some notion of what this Gospel was like. First, it was a Gospel "according to Mark" —this was the claim of both the Carpocratians (I.11f) and of Clement (I.21ff). It certainly included at least parts of the present canonical Gospel according to Mark: to such parts Clement gives precise references (II.21,22; III.11f,14). It probably contained all of canonical Mk.—Clement says it was composed by additions to the canonical Gospel, but says nothing of omissions (I.20f,24ff). The additions, Clement says, were made by Mark himself, of material from his "notes" (ὑπομνήματα, I.19f) and those of Peter. The new material did not exhaust these notes, but was chosen from them. It consisted of "things suitable to those studies which make for progress toward knowledge" (τὰ τοῖς προκόπτουσι περὶ τὴν γνῶσιν κατάλληλα, I.20f), both of stories (πράξεις, I.24) like those in the canonical Gospel and sayings (λόγιά τινα, I.25) of which the exegesis would lead the hearers to the hidden truth (I.26). It did not contain τὰ ἀπόρρητα (I.22f), nor "the hierophantic teaching of the Lord" (I.23–24, probably identical with τὰ ἀπόρρητα). The expanded text constituted a "more spiritual Gospel" (πνευματικώτερον εὐαγγέλιον, I.21f), which was intended to be useful to those who were being "perfected" or "initiated" (τελειούμενοι, I.22).

This text was kept secret by Clement's church in Alexandria and read only "to those being initiated (μυούμενοι) into the great mysteries" (II.2). It was in the custody of the presbyters of the church, or they had had access to it, so that one of them had been able to secure an inferior(?) copy (ἀπόγραφον) for Carpocrates (II.5–6). Clement himself either had a copy or knew the text by heart or had access to it; he could quote it verbatim to Theodore.

The Carpocratians also had a text, but it differed from that of Clement's church. Clement perhaps ascribed some of the differences to errors of the original copy (this may be implied by pejorative connotations of ἀπόγραφον, II.6), but his words give the impression that he thought the more important differences due to additions he described as "most shameless lies" (ἀναιδέστατα ψεύσματα, II.8–9). The adjective may be intended to characterize them as obviously false, or obscene, or both; γυμνὸς γυμνῷ in III.13 suggests obscenity, but the obscenity may have originated in Clement's interpretation. What would a hostile interpreter have made of the rubric in Hippolytus, *Apostolic Tradition* (XXI.11): "And let them (the initiate and the presbyter who is baptizing him) stand in the water naked"? [A.D.N. thought "false" was right, not "obscene."] At any rate, the Carpocratian text was longer than Clement's in at least two instances (III.13 and 17) and in the latter of these two it contained a good deal of additional material (τὰ δὲ ἄλλα τὰ πολλά, III.17—unless this refers to a number of unspecified citations, which is unlikely in view of the parallel to III.13 where τἆλλα refers to additional material in the passage discussed).

I mentioned above Irenaeus' report that the Carpocratians had writings allegedly containing the secret teachings of Jesus, which they interpreted (Harvey, I.20.3 = Stieren, I.25.5). Irenaeus says nothing of these works' being secret and writes as if he had seen them. However, he seems to have seen a good many "secret" books of his adversaries, so his knowledge of these does not disprove their secrecy, which, given his description of the Carpocratian sect, is a priori likely. How it happened that some

Carpocratians used their Gospel according to Mark in their argument with Theodore we do not know. Compare Clement's accusation εἰσὶ δ'οἳ λέγοντες εἶναι γνωστικοὶ τοῖς οἰκείοις φθονοῦσι μᾶλλον ἢ τοῖς ἐκτός (III.145.16f). This use of φθονεῖν for those who keep things secret appears also in the letter, I.27. Irenaeus (Harvey, I.20.4 = Stieren, I.25.6), followed by Epiphanius (*Panarion* XXVII.6), identifies those who call themselves "gnostics" as the Carpocratians, but elsewhere other identifications are given [A.D.N. suggests that this passage in Clement may refer to "people who say they are gnostic in Clement's ideal sense"].

Most important in the information afforded by the letter is the fact that the Carpocratian text of the secret Gospel and the text of it used by Clement's church were basically the same. This was the most embarrassing fact the letter had to explain; therefore it is the least dubitable of the data. Moreover, Clement's admission is confirmed—the two texts differed from canonical Mk. at the same places and about the same things. Therefore, in spite of their differences, the two must have had —as Clement said they had—a common original. Accordingly, the question of their differences from this common original and of its differences from the text of canonical Mk. is a question of the history of the text of the NT. The letter's evidence shows that in Clement's time there were at least three forms of the text of Mk.: a short form (preserved in our canonical text) and at least two longer forms (one the possession of Clement's church, another, of the Carpocratians). The longer forms differed considerably from each other, but were both developments of a single, original, longer text which itself had differed considerably from the short one. There is reason to think that this longer text was in existence well before 125. How, then, did it come into existence and what was its relation to the short text which has survived? Was the longer text produced by expansion, or was the short text an abbreviation, or were both derived by different changes from some common original?

These questions Clement has answered in his letter. He says the longer text was an expansion, produced in Alexandria, of the short text which had first been written in Rome. Both the expansion and the short text were the work of Mark, and so on, as stated above. The incredible element in this story is the claim that both texts were written by Mark. This claim is almost certainly false for the short text—i.e., the canonical Gospel—therefore it can hardly be true for the long one (Bultmann, *Geschichte* 1–4, 362–376; against Taylor cf. my *Comments* and Nineham, *Eyewitness*). Clement's credulity about apostolic authorship has already been noticed (above, I.19 etc.). The statements that Mark came to Alexandria and wrote the longer text there may be guesses to explain why the longer text was preserved (or, known to Clement) only in Alexandria. However, Mark's journey to Alexandria may have been reported by Papias (above, on I.15). The statement that the longer text was produced by Mark's expansion of the short one may, again, be a guess; or it may reflect local tradition, which merely imposed a famous name on an essentially correct report.

Apart from the reference to Mark, the story is not implausible. All Christian Scriptures at this time seem to have been kept secret from non-Christians (Tertullian, *De testimonio animae* I.4), and the moment in the training of the catechumens when

they were first (?) permitted to hear the Gospel was evidently an impressive one (Hippolytus, *Apostolic Tradition* XX.2). Therefore if Clement's church had further "great mysteries" beyond the primary initiation (I.22; II.2; cf. Origen, *Contra Celsum* III.59) it might have developed a special Gospel to be used in them. And Mk. would have lent itself to such development because of its well-known esoteric traits (Wrede, *Messiasgeheimnis* 146ff; cf. Wikgren, *APXH*).

Accordingly, there is nothing improbable in Clement's report that the longer text of Mk. originated in Alexandria, by addition of material hinting at secret doctrines, and that Carpocrates then got hold of it and adapted it to his own purposes. But there is nothing improbable, either, in the notion that Clement's church should have made up the story of Markan expansion to cover its ignorance of the actual origin of the longer text, just as the story of Markan authorship was made up to cover ignorance of the actual origin of the short text. We have already noted the polemic motivation for the story that Carpocrates got his Gospel from Clement's church. Invention of such stories is usually observant of probabilities; therefore only the credulous will find in these probable stories more than a possibility of truth. To one who looks for objective evidence the preservation of the longer text in Alexandria will seem an argument for its Alexandrian origin, but the weight given this argument will depend on a study of the relation of the longer text to the short one.

This relation is not unique. Of OT books, Jeremiah, Esther, Daniel, and Ezra-Nehemiah; of uncanonical pseudepigrapha, the *Testaments of the Twelve Patriarchs* and *II Enoch;* of early Christian literature, the Ignatian epistles and the *Didascalia Apostolorum*: these are only a few of the many texts which have survived in several redactions. Even more are proved by internal evidence to be either abbreviations or expansions of texts now lost. The literary procedures which produced these phenomena are admirably analyzed in Bickerman's *Esther*.

Of NT books, the text of Acts is preserved in two forms so different that many critics have thought one a deliberate revision of the other (Hatch, *Text* 10ff). On the analogy of Acts, Blass suggested that the differences between the "Alexandrian" and the "western" texts of Mk. might indicate that there had been two editions of Mk. (*Acta* 33). Other scholars have come to the same conclusion from study of the synoptic problem (recently Brown, *Revision*). But even if this conclusion were accepted it would not be directly relevant to the problem facing us, for the differences between the two editions thus postulated would be small, while the differences between the two texts of Mk. known to Clement were so great that his church treated the longer text as a different Gospel. The two texts must, therefore, have differed at least as much as would the two editions of John, for which evidence has been found in the preserved Gospel (Parker, *Two Editions*).

During the past century it was often thought that the present text of Mk. had been produced by extensive expansion of a shorter Gospel. The most famous presentation of this theory was probably Wendling's *Ur-Marcus*; the most recent known to me is Trocmé's *Formation* (169ff). Trocmé's book appeared in 1963, when this chapter of the present work had been substantially completed; the agreements observable hereinafter are the results of independent consideration of the evidence and

as such may have some evidential value. Fortunately, however, we need not rely on analysis of the present text of Mk. for evidence that the Gospel texts were often extensively revised. Two longer texts of Mk., generally believed to have been produced by expansion of the canonical text but differing so greatly that they are commonly treated as different Gospels, have been preserved—they are the canonical Gospels according to Matthew and Luke. These are generally supposed to date from the last quarter of the first century or the opening years of the second (Leipoldt, *Geschichte* I.108; Jülicher-Fascher, 286–319). It is a likely guess that they owed their preservation primarily to their acceptance by particular churches—Lk. perhaps in Greece, Mt. in Syria (Harnack, *Origin* 68ff). The longer text of Mk. produced in Alexandria was not preserved, no doubt because of its intimate connection with the esoteric interpretation of Christianity which seems to have dominated the churches of Egypt during most of the second century (Bauer, *Rechtgläubigkeit* 51ff; cf. Hornschuh, *Anfänge* 320ff). Esoteric practice limited this longer text to an inner circle and so prevented its attaining even in Egypt the sort of regional pre-eminence to which Mt. and Lk. may have owed their ultimate acceptance by the whole Church.

Since Mt. and Lk. are generally supposed to have been produced by an expansion of canonical Mk., Clement's account of the origin of the longer Alexandrian text is supported by analogy, and further analogies might be found in the yet further expanded texts produced by Tatian and Theophilus of Antioch. The process had not stopped in Clement's day; he knew some "who alter the Gospels" and quoted with approval some of their alterations, which were expansions (II.266.25ff). Moreover, the same process has been thought to have produced canonical Mk. itself, which Dodd, *Framework*, has represented as the expansion of a primitive outline by addition of various pericopae—a theory still plausible in spite of the attacks on it by Nineham, *Order*; Robinson, *Quest* 48ff; and Trocmé, *Formation* 23ff. But analogy is not conclusive evidence. In textual history abbreviations are no less common than expansions. The Ignatian epistles, for instance, underwent both. So did the text of Mk.: even the expanded forms produced by Matthew and Luke show abbreviation; Matthew often condenses the Markan stories and omits some; Luke omits a large section of the text (Mk. 6.44–8.26). The expanded form produced by Luke was abridged by Marcion and the abridgment was represented as the original text—a claim which still finds occasional defenders (Knox, *Marcion*). The expanded form produced by Matthew seems to have been abbreviated by the Ebionites (Hennecke-Schneemelcher, 100). Another abbreviation is probably represented by the so-called "Fayyum fragment" (ibid., 74). The canonical text of Mk. itself is often supposed to have been abbreviated at the end, if not elsewhere (Williams, *Alterations* 44f; Taylor, 610). Dionysius of Corinth, about 170, complained that his own letters in his own lifetime had suffered both deletion and interpolation; hence, he said, there was no reason to wonder that even the Scriptures of the Lord had been tampered with (Eus., *HE* IV.23.12). Accordingly, the question whether the longer, Alexandrian text was an expansion, or the shorter, now canonical, text an abbreviation, will have to be considered carefully. At this point all to be said is that Clement's account of an expansion (except for its claim of Markan authorship) is consistent with the probabilities of the situation

in Alexandria, with the history of early Christian literature in general, and in particular with the history of the canonical Markan text as indicated by the other synoptics.

Additional evidence in support of Clement's account could be brought from the fragments of the apocryphal Gospels, of which some show further modifications of the basic texts of the synoptics, although others may be (like the canonical Gospel according to John?) wholly or partially independent compilations from cognate oral traditions (Mayeda, *Leben-Jesu-Fragment*, in spite of Benoit's review; Dodd, *Historical Tradition* 328 n2; Hornschuh, *Anfänge* 17ff; Hennecke-Schneemelcher, 34, 47ff, 57ff, 104). Fortunately, however, there is no need to rely on this material of which the interpretation is so uncertain. The Gospel described by Clement's letter was unquestionably a variant form of Mk. In structure its closest analogues would seem to have been the other synoptic Gospels. By vocabulary, style, and content it is obviously connected with the synoptics rather than the apocryphal Gospels. Accordingly, the importance of the apocryphal Gospels to the following discussion is chiefly as evidence that from 75 to 125 the production of Gospels was not limited to the canonical four, and traditional material about Jesus was not limited to the many Gospels produced. On the contrary, all the Gospels, canonical and apocryphal alike, are but partial representatives of an oral tradition which still outranked them in the time of Papias (ca. 125; Eus, *HE* III.39.4) and lived on at least in isolated figures to the end of the second century. (Irenaeus, in Eus., *HE* V.20.5–7, was still "chewing" this "cud." See also Klijn, *Survey* 164–165.)

This background of oral tradition is reflected not only by the apocryphal Gospels, but also by the agrapha in the apostolic fathers, of which Köster's study has led him to the conclusion that: "The source of the synoptic tradition . . . is . . . the community, which from its practical needs not only hands down and uses the synoptic material, but also recasts, transforms, and increases the material already available. Actually, moreover, this whole development is still far from completion at the time when our Gospels are composed, i.e., toward the end of the first century. It continues, indeed, not only on the basis of the now developed Gospel texts, but also alongside them" (*Überlieferung* 257). Acceptance of this thesis by reviewers so different as Moule and Martin is significant. Substantially the same thesis was advanced by Dodd as an explanation of Johannine parallels to the synoptics (*Herrnworte* 75). The same conclusion was reached by Duplacy, from his survey of recent work on the history of the NT text: "More and more, today, the redaction of the Gospels and of Acts appears as one stage, albeit essential, of written fixation in the course of a tradition partly written, partly oral, which preceded these works, contained more than they, and did not disappear after their redaction. The same tradition which moulded the sources of these works, and impregnated the minds of their authors, continued to act on the transmission of their text; the sources themselves did not disappear overnight, and they, too, can have influenced the text" (*Où en est* II.274). See also the remarks of Robinson, *ΛΟΓΟΙ ΣΟΦΩΝ* 88f, on the multiplicity of sources available to the apostolic fathers.

This background, then, of oral—and in part, as Duplacy observes, written—tradition is of fundamental importance for the following study. In the first place, it prohibits

hasty conclusions as to literary relation on the basis of occasional identities in wording. Verbal reminiscences of the sort which in classical literature are indications of sources may here be evidence of nothing more than the common tradition of the community or the contamination of the manuscript. In the second place, as Köster pointed out in his crushing critique of Jeremias (*Herrenworte* 222f), the question of priority is reduced to comparative unimportance. Once it is admitted that all Gospels alike are abstracts from the traditions of the early churches, then the fact that one was written down ten or fifteen years before or after another does not make much difference; the later document can easily contain the more important tradition—as Clement said the later text of Mark did. So we have two questions before us, the literary and the historical. They are at least partially independent. We now turn to the former.

Postscript, 1965: The above argument, written in 1962, can now be strengthened by the authority of Dodd and by his demonstration in *Historical Tradition* that the fourth Gospel is not directly dependent on the synoptics, but derives from another, similar, body of material. Particularly important are his remarks on oral tradition (pp. 7ff): "It is important to realize that we are not dealing with a primitive period of oral tradition superseded at a given date by a second period of literary authorship, but that oral tradition continued to be an important factor right through the New Testament period and beyond. Papias, in the first half of the second century, still preferred oral tradition, where it was available, and Irenaeus, towards the close of that century, could cite with great respect that which he had 'heard from a certain presbyter who had heard it from those who had seen the apostles'. . . . The early Church was not such a bookish community as it has been represented. It did its business primarily through the medium of the living voice, in worship, teaching and missionary preaching, and out of these three forms of activity—liturgy, *didache*, *kerygma*—a tradition was built up, and this tradition lies behind all literary production of the early period, including our written gospels. The presumption, therefore, which lay behind much of the earlier criticism—that similarity of form and content between two documents points to the dependence of the later of these documents on the earlier —no longer holds good, since there is an alternative explanation of many such similarities, and one which corresponds to the conditions under which gospel writing began, so far as we can learn them: namely, the influence of a common tradition. To establish literary dependence something more is needed—some striking similarity in the use of words (especially if the words are somewhat unusual) extending over more than a phrase or two, or an unexpected and unexplained identity of sequence, or the like."

Also of great importance for what will follow here is the argument Dodd uses again and again: "It is impossible to treat any one of the Synoptics as the primary source of the Johannine version . . . since he (*sic*) is sometimes closer to one and sometimes to another of the three . . . The hypothesis of literary conflation of documentary sources seems less probable than that of variation within an oral tradition" (p. 79).

Of greater importance for the present work than for Dodd's own are his passing remarks on the probability that elements from floating oral tradition entered the established Gospel texts as interpolations (e.g., p. 355 n2, with reference to the insertions at Lk. 6.5 and 9.56, though the great example is, of course, Jn. 7.53–8.11). Further points, on particular questions, will be noted hereinafter.

The extent of agreement between Dodd's and my own estimates of the history of the composition of the Gospels is not only a source of gratification to me, but also, since the estimates were independent, a piece of historical evidence. Consequently, I have in general left the present text just as it was before my reading of Dodd's book, changing it only by insertion of references to his work and by correction of a few errors. The reader will see that in spite of the large agreement there is considerable difference. In particular, the new material seems to me to indicate literary relation as well as dependence on similar oral traditions. How far my conclusions should be modified in the light of Dodd's study of the Johannine evidence, or Dodd's in the light of the new material, are questions for others to discuss.

II. Stylistic comparison with the canonical gospels

A. *Text and commentary*

The literary problem before us is: To determine the relation of the shorter, now canonical, text of Mk. to the longer text which Clement referred to as "the secret Gospel" and of which Clement's church and the Carpocratians possessed somewhat different forms. This question cannot be stated as one of "authenticity." Contrast the previous question about the letter. To ask whether or not the letter is "authentic" is to ask whether or not it was written by a known individual, Clement, from whom we have a large body of original compositions which provide criteria for authenticity and make the term "authentic" meaningful when used of works attributed to him. But "Mark," the hypothecated writer of the canonical text of the second Gospel, is not a known individual, we have no work of his save this one text, and this text is far from a wholly original composition. It combines many different kinds of material written in considerably different styles (Wohleb, *Beobachtungen*; Guy, *Sayings*; etc.). The combination probably arose by stages (Bultmann, *Geschichte, passim*; Guy, *Origin* 122ff; Schille, *Formgeschichte* 11f); and the present text may be thought as much the work of a "school" (a preaching or teaching tradition) as of an individual editor— Stendahl, *School*, has shown that even the comparatively well-ordered Mt. has such a tradition behind it. Perhaps the strongest argument for this estimate of Mk. is afforded by recent efforts to maintain the contrary: Marxsen, *Evangelist*, Farrer, *St. Mt.*, Carrington, *Mark*, are principally interesting as examples of the extravagance of exegetic fantasy needed to transform "Mark" from an editor—or a series of editors —to an author. Therefore (as indicated in the conclusion of the preceding chapter) the question before us is not to decide the "authenticity" of the new material, but

97

to determine its relationship to the evidently long process of writing and editing which produced the present text of the second Gospel.

Let us begin by comparing the vocabulary and style of canonical Mk. with those of the letter's quotations from the longer text. Data for the comparison are collected in Appendix E, of which the figures are based on Moulton-Geden and Yoder and have been checked, when possible, against Morgenthaler. In the event of differences (which were frequent) Morgenthaler's figures were preferred. It is my impression that the differences are not sufficient to affect the substance of the conclusions. I hope this will be true also of the errors which, in spite of checking, have doubtless crept in. Collection of statistics about common phrases is difficult not only because of its monotony, which induces error, but also because of the frequency with which such phrases have been introduced into some MSS by scribal corruption. In the following pages and in Appendix E the notes on textual variants are from Nestle-Kilpatrick and (somewhat abridged) from Legg's editions of Mt. and Mk. I was not ignorant of the crticisms made of Legg's editions—e.g., Massaux, *Etat* 704f—but had nothing better to use. I was ignorant of the criticisms of the Nestle-Kilpatrick, but those I have heard to date do not seem to justify such reworking of the following figures as would be required by the change of a basic text. The data collected in Appendix E are discussed seriatim in the following commentary. They include material for comparisons with Mt. and Lk. as well as Mk. Since the style of the longer text of Mk. is very close to that of the synoptics, but has only tangential connections with that of Jn., data on Johannine usage are not included in Appendix E but are given in the following commentary when they deserve notice.

Before proceeding, one observation must be made: *we know the longer text only in an eighteenth-century copy of Clement's quotations of it*. Now one of the commonest phenomena in MSS of the Gospels is harmonization of the text of one Gospel with that of the others (Williams, *Alterations* 1ff; Dodd, *Historical Tradition* 77 n4, 165f, etc.; Trocmé, *Formation* 169 n1); and the peculiar readings of Mk., because Mk. was the least familiar of the Gospels, suffered particularly from harmonization (cf. Hills, *Caesarean Text*). Further, when Clement quoted Mk. he usually contaminated his quotations with reminiscences of Mt. and Lk. This is shown clearly by the notes in Appendix D on Clement's quotations from Mk., and even more clearly by the comparison in Appendix F between Clement's text of Mk. 10.17–31 (III.162.19–163.12) and Nestle-Kilpatrick's. It is also interesting to see how in III.162ff, after having quoted the Markan text correctly in his main quotation, Clement carelessly slips into the Matthaean text when he comments phrase by phrase (see especially III.166.24). Accordingly—in spite of the κατὰ λέξιν in II.22—we should expect Clement's quotation of the longer text to show signs of similar contamination deriving from Clement himself, and we should expect our single MS of Clement's quotations to show traces of the harmonizations of the longer text of Mk. to more familiar texts, not only of Mk., but also of the more familiar Gospels. And, last of all, it must be remembered that even the text of Clement's *Stromateis* rests almost entirely on one eleventh-century MS; therefore, as Swanson observed, "it is impossible . . . to determine . . . to what extent the New Testament passages cited by our author have been altered, accidentally or intentionally, by the copyists" (*Text* 2).

II.23

καὶ ἔρχονται εἰς Βηθανίαν, καὶ ἦν ἐκεῖ μία

καὶ ἔρχονται εἰς. Mk. has καὶ ἔρχονται 4 times (2 at the beginning of a pericope—3.31 and 12.18) and καὶ ἔρχονται εἰς 6 or 7 times (5 or 6 times at the beginning of a pericope). Neither Mt. nor Lk. uses the expression at all. This Markan formula cannot be taken as proof of borrowing from any particular passage (cf. Turner, *Usage* 26.225ff). That the subject (Jesus and the people following him) must be understood from the general pattern of Gospel stories and not from the immediate context is typical of Mk. (cf. Doudna, *Greek* 5ff). Another example occurs below in III.6, ἦλθον.

Βηθανίαν. Nesbitt, *Bethany*, has not succeeded in showing that the Bethany stories in the Gospels are based on a special body of traditions, but the notion is not certainly false. Mk. uses the name 4 times, Mt. 2, Lk. 2. Both of the Matthaean and one of the Lucan usages are in parallels to Mk. It would seem that the name was more prominent in the Markan material. Jn. has it 3 times in connection with Lazarus (11.1,18; 12.1; perhaps 1.28—the text is dubious). Besides these usages, D and it.—major witnesses to the "western text"—at Mk. 8.22 have καὶ ἔρχονται εἰς Βηθανίαν, the phrase found in the longer text. But the reading of D and it. is wrong; the place name, as given by all other witnesses, should be Beth Saïda. Yet there is nothing at 8.22 to suggest Bethany. Why, then, did the scribe of the archetype of D and it. make such a blunder? Was it because he knew the longer text? D is characterized by contamination of texts from similar passages (Hatch, *Text* 12; Williams, *Alterations* 1).

καὶ ἦν ἐκεῖ. Verbatim in Mk. 3.1, as the beginning of the second sentence of a story following an initial statement of place, as here. The same words, but with a different meaning ("and he stayed there") occur in Mt. 2.15. More relevant is the occurrence in all three synoptics of ἦν/ἦσαν δὲ ἐκεῖ as a narrative formula: Mt. 27.55,61; Mk. 5.11 ‖ Lk. 8.32. Matthew has introduced the formula where Mk. did not have it. It is a formula, not a sign of literary dependence. [W.M.C. questions this conclusion, remarking that Mk. 3.1 also has the same sentence structure as this phrase of the longer text: copula, verb, adverb, subject, attribute.] But substantially the same sentence structure is also found in Mt. 27.55,61 and Lk. 8.32. Evidently it went with the formula.

μία. Mk. has this adjectival use of εἷς for τὶς in 12.42, ἐλθοῦσα μία χήρα πτωχή, but it is more common in Mt. (4 instances, with a fifth in the western text, D d e Sy.^[c.s.] Arm.). Hawkins (*Horae* 4, 30f) lists it as a Matthaean trait, but it is probably a Semitism (no instances in Lk.), not a sign of literary dependence. (There are occasional occurrences in classical Greek—cf. Aristophanes, *Aves* 1292, and van Leeuwen's note—but the Semitic usage was so common that its influence is probably to be supposed.) εἷς for τὶς in other constructions (εἷς τῶν προφητῶν, εἷς ἐκ τοῦ ὄχλου, etc.) is common in all the Gospels, as in the papyri. Since the decision as to the number of instances depends on the subjective judgment, whether or not the author

γυνὴ ἧς ὁ ἀδελφὸς αὐτῆς

intended to emphasize the singleness of the object referred to, there will be differences of opinion about the lists in Appendix E, which give 14 or 15 instances in Mk., 14 or 18 in Mt. and 13 or 15 in Lk. Cf. Moule, *Idiom-Book* 125 and 176; Blass-Debrunner-Funk, no. 247.2; Doudna, *Greek* 33f.

γυνή. Women *come* to Jesus in Mk. 5.27 (the woman with an issue); 7.25 (the Syrophoenician); 14.3 (the anointing in Bethany); 16.2 (the resurrection). To these Mt. adds 20.20 (the mother of James and John); Lk. adds 7.37f (the Lucan anointing —that the woman came is implied if not stated); 10.40 (Martha's complaint); 23.27 (the women of Jerusalem); Jn.: 11.20 (Martha, in the raising of Lazarus); 11.32 (Mary, in the same); 20.1 (the Johannine resurrection). Besides these the adulteress *is brought* to Jesus (Jn. 8.3) and there are a number of meetings with women or mentions of them in Jesus' entourage. Evidently they played a large part in early Christian tradition. The multiplicity of these stories makes it impossible to be sure that the story in the longer text of Mk. was drawn from any one of them.

ἧς . . . αὐτῆς. Redundant αὐτός following ὅς in the oblique cases is found twice in Mk., once in Mt., and twice in Lk. (one Markan), always in the genitive. ἧς . . . αὐτῆς appears only in Mk. 7.25. The same construction appears again in III.15, below, in the accusative. It is probably a Semitism rather than a sign of literary dependence; there are 10 instances, in all three oblique cases, in Apoc. (These figures do not include the peculiar readings of codex Bezae; Yoder's concordance has not indicated the peculiar usages of αὐτός.) Both the instances in the longer text, and all those in canonical Mk., have in common a trait which Doudna was not able to find in the papyri, "namely, the fact that the redundant possessive pronoun follows its noun immediately" (*Greek*, 38). See also the note on III.15, ὃν ἠγάπα αὐτόν.

γυνὴ ἧς . . . αὐτῆς . . . ἐλθοῦσα. This verbal sequence appears also in Mk. 7.25 (the Syrophoenician). However, it would be hasty to conclude that either passage is dependent on the other, because: (1) γυνή . . . ἐλθοῦσα appears again in Mk. 5.25f; (2) ἐλθοῦσα in our text is not part of the same sentence as γυνὴ ἧς . . . αὐτῆς but is part of the formula ἐλθοῦσα προσεκύνησεν, of which there are 7 variants in Mt. (see below); (3) αὐτῆς in Mk. 7.25 is omitted by ℵDWΔΘ Pap. 45, *fam.*1, *fam.*13(*exc.*124), 28.225.237.253.475**.565.569.700.*al.pauc.it.*vg.Cop.^sa.bo.Geo. (so Legg). Now if we suppose the longer text of Mk. to have been compiled from texts of the types known to us, we should suppose the compiler to have used a text akin to the archetype of D and *it.*, since only from such a text could he have gotten καὶ ἔρχονται εἰς βηθανίαν (above). But the archetype of D and *it.* evidently did not have the redundant αὐτῆς in Mk. 7.25. So there is some difficulty in supposing that *both* similarities resulted from imitation.

II.24

ἀπέθανεν· καὶ ἐλθοῦσα προσεκύνησε

ἀπέθανεν. The form: 2 in Mt., 6 in Mk., 5 in Lk. This perfective meaning for the aorist ("had died" or "was dead") appears in Lk. 8.53 and possibly in Mk. 9.26 and 15.44 (in spite of the fine distinction made by Swete and accepted by Taylor; the emendations—τέθνηκεν WΘ 472.1342 and τεθνήκει D,*l*253—show how the copyists understood the Greek). It is regular in LXX: Ex. 16.3; Num. 14.2; 20.3; Judges 8.33b; 9.55(?); II Sam. 13.39; etc. The sentence structure here, with the verb at the end, is thought typically Markan by Turner, *Usage* 29.352ff.

καί + participle of ἔρχομαι in the nominative + finite verb: 5 in Mk., 12 in Mt. (only one Markan) and 5 in Lk. (none Markan). These figures would be larger if account were taken of the instances with δέ instead of καί or with compounds of ἔρχομαι (εἰς-, προσ-, ἐξ-). This standard construction cannot be taken as evidence of dependence on any particular passage. For the same construction with other verbs see below, on καὶ ὀργισθείς (II.25). The use of redundant participles, especially ἐλθών and ἀναστάς (III.10), is studied by Doudna (*Greek*, 55ff and 117ff) as characteristic of Mk.'s style.

προσεκύνησε καὶ λέγει. [W.M.C. notes the connection—by καί—of an aorist with a historical present and remarks that, though unusual, it does appear in Thuc., VI.4.1.] In Mk. it is common, particularly so with λέγει (1.37,41,43f, etc.), as here in the longer text. In III.7, below, it recurs with ἔρχεται, as in Mk. 6.1. [For a study of earlier examples W.M.C. refers to von Fritz, *Present* esp. 195f.]

προσεκύνησε. προσκυνεῖν after ἔρχομαι: 7 or 8 in Mt., never in Mk. or Lk. In 5 of the 7 instances it follows a participle. One instance (15.25) is particularly close to the above: ἡ δὲ ἐλθοῦσα προσεκύνει αὐτῷ (προσεκύνησε LKXΔΦ 0119ᵇ 157.565.*al. pler.it.pc.*vg.*pler.*Sy.Cop.ᵇᵒ·Aeth.Or.; αὐτόν Δ174.1515). This again is the story of the Syrophoenician woman. If the longer text of Mk. was compiled from the canonical texts, the compiler took his first sentence from Mk. 7.25 and his second from Mt. 15.25, which he revised by substitution of initial καί for δέ—not a likely procedure. Matthew's interest in proskynesis is remarkable; but the verb cannot be taken as proof of dependence on Mt., especially since it here governs the accusative, which it never does in Mt. except when he is quoting the OT. Mark also represents suppliants as approaching Jesus with proskynesis (5.6, governing the accusative) and might have used the καὶ ἐλθών formula to introduce them [R.S. calls attention to Mt. 20.20, τότε προσῆλθεν αὐτῷ ἡ μήτηρ τῶν υἱῶν Ζεβεδαίου μετὰ τῶν υἱῶν αὐτῆς προσκυνοῦσα καὶ αἰτοῦσά τι. This introduces a proskynesis by a woman into the story (= Mk. 10.35–45) which, according to Clement, immediately followed the present quotation from the longer text. Moreover, the woman introduced—the mother of the sons of Zebedee—replaces Salome in Mt.'s parallel to Mk.'s list of the women who witnessed the crucifixion (Mt. 27.56 ‖ Mk. 15.40). Her request, in Mt. 20.20, was

τὸν ᾿Ιησοῦν

refused. Salome is one of the women who appears in the next section of the longer text (immediately following the pericope introduced by Mt. 20.20); there she comes to see Jesus and is refused.] This suggests that Matthew incorporated in 20.20 traces of the preceding and following stories of the longer text of Mk. His introduction of the mother of the sons of Zebedee is commonly explained as a consequence of reverence for the apostles: where Mk. reported their ambition and rebuke, Matthew reported their mother's ambition on their behalf (so, for example, McNeile). But Matthew associated the sons with their mother's request, and the rebuke is still addressed to them (Mt. 20.22ff). And it is Matthew's way, when abbreviating Mk., to use the introduction of an omitted story at the beginning of the next story; for example, he retains Mk. 5.18a (= Mt. 9.1a), omits 5.18b–20, and uses 5.18a to introduce Mk. 2.1 (= Mt. 9. 1b). He also takes details from omitted episodes and uses them elsewhere: thus Mk. 1.21–22 in Mt. 7.28b(f); Mk. 1.24, ἦλθες, in Mt. 8.29; Mk. 1.28 in Mt. 4.24a; etc. Therefore it is noteworthy that, besides introducing in 20.20 his substitute for Salome—making proskynesis—he has also introduced into the story of the Syrophoenician woman the appeal not found there in Mk.: ἐλέησόν με, κύριε, υἱὸς Δαυείδ (Mt. 15.22). The story of the Syrophoenician was that of which the beginning most closely resembled that of the story in the longer text where the appeal is found. These two pieces of evidence (20.20 and 15.22) fit together and suggest that Matthew knew the longer text of Mk. Somewhat similar conclusions have been reached on other grounds by several scholars (Parker, *Gospel*; Vaganay, *Absence*; etc.). Further evidence suggesting that Matthew may have known the longer text of Mk. appears below, on ἀπεκύλισε (III.1f).

τὸν ᾿Ιησοῦν. The accusative after προσκυνεῖν was the classical Greek construction (Blass-Debrunner-Funk, no. 151.2) and appears in Mk. 5.6, where, however, there is minority support for the dative. In Mt. and Lk. it is found only in quotation of Dt. 6.13 (Mt. 4.10 = Lk. 4.8, κύριον τὸν θεόν σου προσκυνήσεις). However, besides the variants noted in Appendix E, most relevant passages have one or two minuscule variants replacing the dative by the accusative; this was the tendency of later Greek. In studying the letter we saw that its chief difference from Clement's usage lay in the preponderance of accusatives after prepositions. If some accusatives there and the one here were introduced by a medieval copyist, they would hardly have been eliminated by a later corrector. [T.B. remarks that "in Mk. 5.6 it is especially the Alexandrian group that testifies for the accusative: BCLΔΨ 892,1241. Beside these MSS we find additional testimony in the I-group of von Soden: A,047,179,230,273, 482,495,544,659,700,1346,1574,1588,1606, of which A, at least, testifies to the Alexandrian reading. This would be an indication for the Alexandrian source of the secret gospel."] Or of classicism in the Alexandrian revision? But see below, on καὶ εὐθύς (III.1), where the agreement with the Alexandrians is in a detail contrary to classical usage.

II.25

καὶ λέγει αὐτῷ υἱὲ Δαβὶδ ἐλέησόν με. οἱ δὲ μαθηταὶ

καὶ λέγει αὐτῷ. 8 in Mk.; in Mt. 6 or 7 (only 2 Markan); never in Lk. Not evidence of dependence on any specific passage. λέγω is often used in the Synoptics to introduce ἐλέησον (but almost always with some other verb of utterance, usually κράζειν—a fact to which my attention was called by T.B.). In Mt. 17.15, however, it stands alone, as here. The parallelism probably results, not from dependence, but from the presence in both instances of another verb form (indicating motion). Three verbs together are cumbersome.

υἱὲ . . . με. This form of appeal is found in Mk. 10.47,48 ‖ Lk. 18.38,39. In Mt. 9.27; 15.22; 20.30,31 (although 20.30,31 are Markan and 9.27 may be) the wording has been changed, probably under the influence of the liturgical use of κύριε ἐλέησον (also used in appeals to pagan deities, Epictetus, *Dissertationes* II.7.12). On 15.22 see above, s.v. προσεκύνησε end. Clement, II.498.32ff, arguing that gnosis is not to be made available to everyone, says, ἀμέλει καὶ τῶν ἐπιβοωμένων τὸν κύριον αὐτὸν οἱ μὲν πολλοὶ "υἱὲ Δαβίδ, ἐλέησόν με" ἔλεγον, ὀλίγοι δὲ υἱὸν ἐγίγνωσκον τοῦ θεοῦ, καθάπερ ὁ Πέτρος, ὃν καὶ ἐμακάρισεν. This is surprising because the canonical Gospels contain many instances of Jesus' being recognized as son of God (Mk. 3.11; 5.7 and parallels; 15.39 and parallels; Lk. 4.41; Mt. 14.33; etc.), while the appeal to the son of David appears only in Mk. 10.47f and parallels, Mt. 9.27 and 15.22. Perhaps Clement may have had in mind also Mt. 21.9 and 15—see his vague exegesis in I.97.10–13. Nevertheless, his mistake is surprising in one who knew the Gospels so well. Surprising, too, is his choice of the Markan form of the appeal rather than the more frequent form in Mt., his favorite Gospel. Are both these surprising details to be explained by his knowledge of additional Markan material, including the selection quoted in the letter, in which other speakers beside Bartimaeus appealed to Jesus as "son of David"? [W.M.C.: The omission of ὦ before the vocative would, in classical Greek, have been impolite and indeed insulting.] In the Gospels ὦ with the vocative has become a sign of emotion (Blass-Debrunner-Funk, no. 146). In Mk. it appears only in ὦ γενεὰ ἄπιστος, 9.19. None of the eight canonical appeals to the son of David (listed above) has ὦ.

οἱ δὲ μαθηταί. Initial, with an immediately following verb, in Mk. 10.13 and 24. Mark has a habit of using the same construction several times in quick succession: see the distribution of εὐθύς in his text. If the quotations from the longer text stood where the letter says they did, their usage of οἱ δὲ μαθηταί would form a third member of the above group. Mt. 19.13 is Markan, but Mt. has the construction independently in 12.1 (whence it has been taken into Mk. 2.23 by a few MSS) and in 28.16 (+ ἕνδεκα) and, modified, in 14.26. DΘit. have it in Mk. 14.4, where it may be original—censorship (altering passages discreditable to the Holy Apostles) would explain the common text. Never in Lk.; in Mt. and Mk. evidently a standard locution.

ἐπετίμησαν αὐτῇ· καὶ ὀργισθείς

ἐπετίμησαν. The verb, 9 times in Mk., 6 or 7 in Mt. (all Markan), and 12 in Lk. (5 non-Markan). In Mk. and Mt. rebukes are connected with the danger of revealing secrets. The demons are rebuked that they should not make him known, Mk. 3.12 and parallels; the disciples are rebuked that they should not declare what Peter has said, Mk. 8.30 and parallels; Peter rebukes Jesus for teaching openly that the Son of Man must die, Mk. 8.32 and parallels (note the reading in *c* and *k*, *ne cui haec/illa diceret*); Ebeling, *Messiasgeheimnis* 136f, thinks the followers of Jesus rebuked Bartimaeus for declaring Jesus the son of David, Mk. 10.48 and parallels. That the disciples should have rebuked Lazarus' sister for blurting out the same title is therefore in accordance with Markan practice.

οἱ δὲ μαθηταὶ ἐπετίμησαν. Verbatim in Mt. 19.13 and many MSS of Mk. 10.13—combination of a common verb with a standard locution for a customary purpose.

καί + nominative participle + finite verb. One of the most common sentence structures in the Gospels. Matthew was fond of it with participles of ἔρχομαι (see above, on καὶ ἐλθοῦσα, II.24), but a check of occurrences with all verbs—in Mk. 1–3 and 10, Mt. 4, 8, 9, 19, and 20, and Lk. 4, 5, 6.1–11, and 18—suggests that it is most common in Mk. In these chapters Mk. has 33 instances, against 22 in Mt. (10 Markan) and 20 in Lk. (8 Markan). καί, participle, ὁ ᾽Ιησοῦς, verb, without interruption, occurs in these chapters 3 or 4 times in Mk., 2 in Mt., and 2 in Lk.; but both Lucan instances are the cliché καὶ ἀποκριθεὶς ὁ ᾽Ιησοῦς εἶπεν.

ὀργισθείς. [Mark did not eliminate emotions of Jesus, as the other evangelists did: cf. Mk. 1.41,43; 7.34; 8.12; 10.14,16,21 with the parallels. R.S.] Hawkins, *Horae* 119, notes that except for the western reading in Mk. 1.41, ὀργή is nowhere in the Gospels ascribed to Jesus save in Mk. 3.5. Therefore, although Mt. uses the verb ὀργίζω 3 times and Lk. 2, their usage is probably irrelevant to the use here in connection with Jesus. The aorist passive participle occurs in Mt. 18.34 (καὶ ὀργισθεὶς ὁ κύριος αὐτοῦ παρέδωκεν) and in Lk. 14.21 in a similar construction: τότε ὀργισθεὶς ὁ οἰκοδεσπότης εἶπεν. It is used of Jesus in the D text of Mk. 1.41: καὶ ὀργισθεὶς ἐκτείνας τὴν χεῖρα αὐτοῦ ἥψατο αὐτοῦ, with support from *it.*, Tatian, and Ephraem. However, ὀργισθείς in Mk. 1.41 is hard to explain (Eitrem, *Demonology* 42), whereas σπλαγχνισθείς, the reading of all other MSS, fits the context (which contains no trace of opposition). In the letter's longer text of Mk., however, ὀργισθείς is easily explicable: Jesus could have been angered either by the use of his secret title or by the disciples' rebuke of the suppliant (cf. Mk. 10.13f). καὶ προσέφερον αὐτῷ παιδία ἵνα αὐτῶν ἅψηται· οἱ δὲ μαθηταὶ ἐπετίμησαν αὐτοῖς. ἰδὼν δὲ ὁ ᾽Ιησοῦς ἠγανάκτησεν. If the story in the longer text is of the raising of Lazarus, its ὀργισθείς corresponds to ἐνεβριμήσατο in Jn. 11.33. And ἐμβριμησάμενος occurs in Mk. 1.43. Perhaps the archetype of D*it.* introduced ὀργισθείς into Mk. 1.41 inadvertently, by reminiscence of the longer text

II.26

ὁ Ἰησοῦς ἀπῆλθεν μετ᾽αὐτῆς εἰς τὸν κῆπον ὅπον ἦν τὸ μνημεῖον.

and anticipation of ἐμβριμησάμενος. The reminiscence would be facilitated by the fact that the following words in Mk.—ἐκτείνας τὴν χεῖρα αὐτοῦ ἥψατο αὐτοῦ—are soon paralleled in the longer text: ἐξέτεινεν τὴν χεῖρα καὶ ἤγειρεν αὐτόν. Βηθανίαν in II.23 suggested that the archetype of D*it.* in Mk. 8.22 was corrupted by a reminiscnece of the longer text. Since D*it.* are representatives of the western text, which was used by Clement, and since Clement knew the longer text, these suppositions are not unlikely. It is interesting that Westcott and Hort, II.appendix.23, supposed ὀργισθείς in Mk. 1.41 "perhaps suggested by verse 43, perhaps derived from an extraneous source." Can it be that we now have the source? [C.F.D.M. thinks more likely a suggestion he heard from W. Howard: that ὀργισθείς in Mk. 1.41 originated as a marginal gloss on ἐμβριμησάμενος.]

ἀπῆλθεν. This form, 9 in Mk., 7 in Mt. (2 Markan), and 6 in Lk. (2 Markan). It is followed by μετά with the genitive only in Mk. 5.24. There, as here, Jesus goes off with a suppliant (Jaïrus) to raise a dead relative. However, the construction is normal and can hardly be taken as evidence of literary dependence. LXX: II Sam. 16.17; To. 14.12; Siracides 14.19. Ἀπελθεῖν εἰς is common.

κῆπος. In the synoptics only in Lk. 13.19, ὁμοία ἐστὶν ⟨ἡ βασιλεία τοῦ θεοῦ⟩ κόκκῳ σινάπεως, ὃν λαβὼν ἄνθρωπος ἔβαλεν εἰς κῆπον ἑαυτοῦ. This may be an adaptation of the mustard-seed parable to the story of Jesus' burial in and resurrection from a κῆπος, Jn. 19.41ff. ἦν δὲ ἐν τῷ τόπῳ ὅπου ἐσταυρώθη κῆπος, καὶ ἐν τῷ κήπῳ μνημεῖον καινόν, κ.τ.λ. Interpretation of the Lazarus story as foreshadowing Jesus' resurrection may have led to the location of Lazarus' tomb, too, in a κῆπος. Tombs in gardens near Jerusalem are mentioned in Josephus, *AJ* IX.227 and X.46. [Burial in gardens was common in the Greco-Roman world and was reflected by the Greek words, κηποτάφιον and κηπόταφος or κηπόταφον, and the Latin *cepotaphium, LSJ* s.vv. A.D.N.]

ὅπου ἦν. ὅπου, 15 times in Mk., 13 in Mt., 5 in Lk. ὅπου ἦν occurs in Mk. 5.40 (as here, of Jesus' going to raise the dead), in Mk. 2.4, and twice in the D text of Lk. (4.16 and 5.19—the second Markan). 6 uses in Jn. One is in the Lazarus story (11.32), one in a reference to Bethany ὅπου ἦν Λάζαρος (12.1), and one in a reference to the κῆπος where Jesus was arrested (18.1). It is difficult to be confident that the expression in the longer text of Mk. was taken from any one of these possibly relevant passages.

τὸ μνημεῖον. 6 in Mk., 7 in Mt., and 7 in Lk. (Morgenthaler); Yoder adds 3 in Mk. and 3 in Lk., from D. The only reference to Jesus' having raised a dead man from a tomb is in the Lazarus story, where μνημεῖον occurs 3 times (Jn. 11.17,31,38) and is subsequently mentioned in the popular report of the miracle (12.17).

III.1
καὶ εὐθὺς ἠκούσθη ἐκ τοῦ μνημείου

καὶ εὐθύς. As the beginning of a sentence or independent clause, 25 in Mk., 2 in Mt. (both instances Markan), never in the best supported text of Lk. Of the instances in Mk., D has only 1.30, 4.5, and 11.3. D omits both the well supported instances in Mt., but is unique (?) in reading καὶ εὐθύς in Mt. 13.5 (also Markan) and almost unique in reading it in Lk. 5.6. Otherwise it consistently substitutes εὐθέως, or omits. The longer text's repeated use of εὐθύς, therefore, links it not only with Mk., but with a small MS tradition of the Markan text—once again that of the Alexandrian MSS. See Appendix E, and T.B.'s remark on τὸν Ἰησοῦν above, on II.24. Since the longer text is right, against D, in this characteristic, it seems more likely that the corruptions of the D text noted above (Βηθανίαν and ὀργισθείς, cf. II.23 and 25) were derived from the influence of the longer text, than that the latter derived these details (which, in it, do not seem to be corruptions) from the archetype of D, to which they were peculiar. καὶ εὐθύς immediately followed by a finite verb, 1 in Mt., 9 in Mk. The entry in Moulton-Geden for Mk. 7.35 is contradicted by the readings in Legg. In the present usage in the longer text, εὐθύς seems to be a connective rather than an adverb of time; so it is in Mk. (Kilpatrick, Notes 4f).

ἠκούσθη. The form occurs in Mk. 2.1 and in Mt. 2.18, where the subject is, as here φωνή—(φωνὴ ἐν Ῥαμὰ ἠκούσθη, LXX Jer. 38.15)—probably coincidental. [T.B remarks that in some "western" texts ἠκούσθη is added where the normal Greek texts read only φωνή: so Mt. 3.17 (Sy.ˢ·); 17.5 (Sy.ᶜ·); Mk. 1.11 (θ.pauc.); Lk. 3.21 (Sy.ˢ·).] Influence? ἀκούω follows εὐθύς in Mk. 7.25, ἀλλ' εὐθὺς ἀκούσασα γυνὴ περὶ αὐτοῦ (אBLΔ 33.579.892; εὐθέως Dit.; ἀκούσασα γάρ rell.), in the story of the Syrophoenician woman, which paralleled the letter's Gospel above in II.23–24. However, given the difference of the constructions and the frequency of both εὐθύς and ἀκούω in Mk., this similarity, too, is probably coincidental.

καὶ εὐθὺς ἠκούσθη. The following story shows many traits in common with resurrection stories—voice, youth, stone, etc. On these see the comment below on ὁ νεανίσκος, III.3.

ἐκ τοῦ μνημείου. The local sense of ἐκ after ἀκούω does not occur in the Gospels. (Cf., however, Jn. 12.34.) But the construction is common: Apoc. 10.4.8; 11.12; etc. On μνημεῖον see above, on II.26. ἐκ τοῦ μνημείου does not appear in the synoptics (though Mt. and Mk. have ἐκ τῶν μνημείων), but is used 3 times in Jn. Note Jn. 12.17, τὸν Λάζαρον ἐφώνησεν ἐκ τοῦ μνημείου, and 5.28f, πάντες οἱ ἐν τοῖς μνημείοις ἀκούσουσιν τῆς φωνῆς αὐτοῦ καὶ ἐκπορεύσονται. These verses reflect the Johannine version of the story, in which Jesus cries out; in the longer text of Mk. the voice comes from the tomb. This contentual relationship will be discussed later.

III.2

φωνῇ μεγάλῃ. καὶ προσελθὼν ὁ Ἰησοῦς ἀπεκύλισε τὸν λίθον

φωνῇ μεγάλῃ. 4 in Mk., 2 or 3 in Mt., 6 in Lk. (one is omitted by D, but another is added). Of the 3 Matthaean usages, the 2 certain ones are Markan; of the 5 certain Lucan usages, 3 are Markan. All the uses in the synoptics are in oblique cases. The phrase is used in Jn. only once, in 11.43: *φωνῇ μεγάλῃ ἐκραύγασεν ⟨ὁ Ἰησοῦς⟩, Λάζαρε, δεῦρο ἔξω.* Since the phrase was not a common element in John's vocabulary but was in Mark's, John is more likely to have derived it from a Markan story of the raising of Lazarus than Mark from a Johannine one. (The rarity of the phrase in Jn. is the more remarkable because of his fondness for *φωνή* in other constructions, noted by Dodd, *Historical Tradition* 282.)

καὶ προσελθών. Initial, 1 or perhaps 2 in Mk., in Mt. 5 or 6 + 1 in D, in Lk. 2. Of these instances the dubious one in Mk. corresponds to the dubious one in Mt.; the rest are independent—evidently the locution was standard. In Lk. 7.14 (the young man of Nain) the actor is Jesus and the following action is a raising from the dead, as here; but there is no other contentual similarity, so these are probably irrelevant. In Mk. 1.31 the following words are *ἤγειρεν αὐτήν* (Peter's wife's mother), but she was raised only from a sickbed. By requiring exact parallel in form and position, the above figures obscure Matthew's characteristic preference for *προσέρ-χομαι.* Moulton-Geden list 52 uses in Mt., 6 in Mk., and 11 in Lk.; Morgenthaler lists 52 uses, 5 and 10, respectively.

καὶ προσελθὼν ὁ Ἰησοῦς. Verbatim, as the beginning of a sentence, in Mt. 28.18. Followed by the charge to make converts of all nations. Here also we have *καὶ προσελθών* + explicit subject + verb, without interruption, as in Mt. 4.3 and 8.19 and the longer text of Mk.

καὶ προσελθὼν ἀπεκύλισε τὸν λίθον. Found in the middle of a verse, in Mt. 28.2 (the angel at the resurrection). *καί* is omitted by many MSS, including D. One form or another of *ἀποκυλίειν* + *τὸν λίθον* appears once or twice in both Mk. and Lk., the usages in Lk. being Markan. The *λίθος* closing the entrance of the *μνημεῖον* appears also in Jn.'s raising of Lazarus (11.38ff) and there, too, is removed. Mt. 28.2 is not a parallel to Mk., but may be an attempt to explain what Mk. reports.

Mt.'s angel of the Lord coming to raise Jesus is much like Jesus coming to raise Lazarus. Where did Matthew get the idea? Not from the Markan resurrection of Jesus; nor from the Johannine story of Lazarus. Perhaps from the longer text of Mk.? That he did not copy thence *ἀπὸ τῆς θύρας τοῦ μνημείου* is not surprising. He did not copy it from Mk. 16.3, either; his way was to abbreviate. The details of the style in the longer text suggest Mk., *ἀπεκύλισε . . . ἀπό, μνημεῖον . . . μνημεῖον . . . μνημεῖον.* Compare the examples at the end of the note on *κρατήσας τῆς χειρός,* below, on III.3–4.

III.3

ἀπὸ τῆς θύρας τοῦ μνημείου καὶ εἰσελθὼν εὐθὺς ὅπου ἦν

ἀπὸ τῆς θύρας τοῦ μνημείου. Verbatim, Mk. 16.3 CDWΘΨ *fam.*13(*exc.*124).543.157* (*cor.***).14.472.517.Eus.^{dem.}Greg.Nyss., with *ab, it.vg.*; ἐκ ℵABLXΓΔΠΣⓎ *minusc. pler.* The reading ἀπό, native to Mk., crept by contamination into Mt. 28.2. The contaminated reading is exactly that of the longer text with ἀπό, not ἐκ. The stages of the contamination are shown in Appendix E. When complete it produced καὶ προσελθὼν ἀπεκύλισε τὸν λίθον ἀπὸ τῆς θύρας τοῦ μνημείου, word for word parallel to the longer text, except for the absence of ὁ Ἰησοῦς. But this complete form appears only in the later versions and uncials, and in minuscules. Therefore—unless it be one of the rare examples of early readings found only in late MSS (Williams, *Alterations* 32)—it cannot have influenced the longer text, already known to Clement, nor can it reflect the influence of the longer text, almost unknown after Clement's time. Thus one of the most striking parallels between the longer text and a canonical Gospel cannot be explained by direct dependence on either side. Among the many possible explanations are (1) that the author of canonical Mk. also wrote the longer text and repeated himself—as he often did in canonical Mk.; (2) that the longer text was produced by the same process of conflation which later produced the contaminated text of Mt.; (3) that the longer text was conformed to that of Mt. by some medieval copyist. [H.K. remarks that Lk. 24.2 also has ἀπὸ τοῦ μνημείου.] Therefore, it is likely that Mt. and Lk. reflect a text of Mk. which had ἀπό rather than ἐκ, but the phrase is so commonplace that no secure conclusion is possible.

καὶ εἰσελθών/οῦσα (etc.). Initial, 5 or 6 in Mk. + 1 in D and Sy.^{s.}; 1 in Mt.; 4 in Lk. (1 Markan) + 1 in D. A standard introductory phrase most favored by Mark; hardly useful as a sign of authorship and not evidence of borrowing from any particular passage. This conclusion is confirmed by the frequency of εἰσέρχομαι in all forms: Mt. 36, Mk. 30, Lk. 50 (Morgenthaler). καὶ εἰσελθοῦσα εὐθύς, initial, appears in Mk. 6.25, but the passage (Salome's approach to Herod) has no contentual similarity to the text here. Therefore, given the frequency of both εἰσέρχομαι and εὐθύς, the coincidence is probably accidental. εἰσελθών, without καί and not initial, introduces in Mt. 9.18 the raising of Jaïrus' daughter—which has a number of verbal parallels to the present passage, probably because of similarity of content. See below, on κρατήσας.

ὅπου ἦν. See above, on II.26. Mk. 2.4 and 5.40. The second occurs in the raising of Jaïrus' daughter, where it follows εἰσπορεύεται and precedes, as here, κρατήσας τῆς χειρός. The conjunction of these conventional phrases in the same sequence is explained by the common content of the passages. [W.M.C. remarks that in εἰσελθών . . . ὅπου the εἰς is pleonastic. ἐλθών would suffice.] However, as already stated, Mk. 5.40 has the same construction with εἰσπορεύεται; and similar pleonastic constructions with εἰσπορεύομαι and εἰσέρχομαι preceded by ὅπου occur in Mk. 6.10,56, and 14.14 but not in the other Gospels. This seems to be a Markan trait.

III.4

ὁ νεανίσκος ἐξέτεινεν τὴν χεῖρα καὶ ἤγειρεν αὐτόν, κρατήσας τῆς χειρός.

ὁ νεανίσκος. 2 in Mk., 2 in Mt., 1 in Lk. All of these νεανίσκοι have traits which relate them to the present story. The one in Mk. 14.51, wearing a sheet over his naked body, was (almost) caught with Jesus late at night; the one in Mk. 16.5, wearing a white garment, was found in Jesus' tomb and announced his resurrection; the one in Mt. 19.20ff was loved by Jesus (Mk. 10.21, ἐμβλέψας αὐτῷ ἠγάπησεν αὐτόν) and was rich (Lk. 18.23, ἦν γὰρ πλούσιος); the one in Lk. 7.14 was raised from the dead, and the story contains the verbal sequence καὶ προσελθὼν ἥψατο . . . νεανίσκε . . . ἐγέρθητι (but this is probably mere chance). Another νεανίσκος was raised or saved from death in the D text of Acts 20.12. Yet none appears in a story so close to the present one as the story of Lazarus, and in the canonical Gospels Lazarus is not called a νεανίσκος. This multiplicity of partial parallels suggests narration in traditional patterns with traditional vocabulary, rather than compilation from written sources. [H.K. agrees, remarking that a similar variety of parallels— voice, youth, stone, etc.—appears also in the earliest apocryphal Gospels, especially Peter, and probably for this same reason. For a study of these parallels he refers to L. Brun, *Die Auferstehung Christi* (1925), which I have not seen.]

ἐξέτεινεν τὴν χεῖρα. ἐκτείνειν + χείρ, 3 or 4 in Mk. (one with χεῖρα merely implicit), 6 in Mt. (3 Markan, χεῖρα once implicit), and 5 in Lk. (2 Markan, 2 from D). The exact combination ἐξέτεινεν τὴν χεῖρα seems to have stood in the achetype of Sy. and some MSS of *it.* at Mt. 12.13. The story there (the man with the withered arm) has no similarity to the present one, so the identity of wording was probably coincidental. More striking are the western variants to Mk. 1.31, the only place where ἐκτείνω precedes ἐγείρω. On these see below, on κρατήσας. Taking the hand and raising the dead is frequent in *Acta Ioannis*: 11, 47, 79, 83, 112. There are many pagan parallels (emperors raising the afflicted, gods welcoming the deified dead, etc.); see Schrade, *Ikonographie* 109ff.

ἤγειρεν. ἐγείρω Mk. 19; Mt. 36; Lk. 18. ἤγειρεν appears only in an OT reminiscence in Lk. 1.69 and in Mk. 1.31 and 9.27 (ἤγειρεν αὐτόν); on these see the following note. καὶ προσελθόντες ἤγειραν αὐτόν in Mt. 8.25 (stilling the storm) is a coincidence, as is κρατήσει αὐτὸ καὶ ἐγερεῖ in Mt. 12.11 (the man with the withered arm) and νεανίσκε, σοι λέγω, ἐγέρθητι in Lk. 7.14 (the young man of Nain).

κρατήσας τῆς χειρός. Verbatim, 2 or 3 in Mk., 1 in Lk. (Markan). κρατέω, Mk. 15, Mt. 12, Lk. 2. χείρ as an instrument of supernatural help, 10 or 11 in Mk. (+ 1 in the long ending), 7 in Mt. (5 Markan), 5 in Lk. (2 Markan + 1 in D*it.*). ἅπτω in the same use, Mk. 11, Mt. 9, Lk. 10. Neither χείρ nor ἅπτω ever has this use in Jn. The exact phrase κρατήσας τῆς χειρός is always used in the Gospels in connection with ἐγείρω:

Mk. 1.31 (Peter's mother-in-law) || *Mt. 8.15; Lk. not similar.*

אBL **καὶ προσελθὼν ἤγειρεν** αὐτὴν **κρατήσας τῆς χειρός.**

D **καὶ προσελθὼν** ἐκτείνας **τὴν χεῖρα κρατήσας ἤγειρεν** αὐτήν.

W **καὶ προσελθὼν** ἐκτίνας (sic) **τὴν χεῖρα καὶ** ἐπιλαβόμενος **ἤγειρεν** αὐτήν.

bq ille autem venit et extendens manum adprehendit eam et levavit.

r¹ et veniens extensa manu adpraehensam elevavit eam.

Mt. 8.15 **καὶ** ἐλθών . . . ἤψατο **τῆς χειρὸς** αὐτῆς . . . **καὶ ἠγέρθη.**

Mk. 5.40f (Jaïrus' daughter) || *Mt. 9.25* || *Lk. 8.54.*

אB, etc. **καὶ εἰσπορεύεται ὅπου ἦν τὸ παιδίον καὶ κρατήσας τῆς χειρὸς**
τοῦ παιδίου λέγει . . . ἔγειρε.

Dit. **καὶ** εἰσπορεύετο **ὅπου ἦν τὸ παιδίον καὶ κρατήσας τὴν χεῖρα**
τοῦ παιδίου (eius, it.) λέγει . . . ἔγειρε.

Mt. 9.25 אB, etc. **εἰσελθὼν** ἐκράτησεν **τῆς χειρὸς** αὐτῆς καὶ ἠγέρθη τὸ κοράσιον.

D ἐλθὼν ἐκράτησεν **τὴν χεῖρα** αὐτῆς καὶ ἠγέρθη τὸ κοράσιον.

it.vg. intravit et tenuit manum eius et dixit puella surge.

Lk. 8.54 αὐτὸς δὲ **κρατήσας τῆς χειρὸς** αὐτῆς ἐφώνησεν λέγων, ἡ παῖς, ἔγειρε.

Mk. 9.27 (the demoniac boy). Mt. and Lk. not similar.

אBDLΔΘΨ *fam.1.fam.*13(*exc.*124).28.53.543.565.892.*it.vg.*Sy.[hier.] Cop.[sa.bo.]Geor.
Arm. ὁ δὲ Ἰησοῦς **κρατήσας τῆς χειρὸς** αὐτοῦ **ἤγειρεν** αὐτόν.

ΑCΝΧΥΓΠΣΦϚ 22.124.33.157.579.700.1071.*al.pler.*Sy.[s.pesh.hl.] Aeth. ὁ δὲ Ἰησοῦς
κρατήσας αὐτὸν **τῆς χειρὸς** (+ αὐτοῦ C*Sy.[s.etc.]Aeth.) **ἤγειρεν αὐτόν.**

(On Mk. 1.31 see Couchoud, *L'Evangile* 174. Pernot, *Prétendu* 50, supposes D influenced by Mk. 1.41, but this is unlikely: the verses are not sufficiently similar. Couchoud's reply, *Marc latin* 294.)

Here the words in boldface type appear in the same forms in the longer text of Mk. To attribute this fact to deliberate compilation from the multiplicity of written texts is implausible. Evidently the similarity of the longer to the shorter text of Mk., like the similarity of the different passages of the shorter text to one another, is the product of free composition in a standard form and with a standard vocabulary. It is hard to believe that any compiler would have produced the awkward repetition χεῖρα . . . χειρός. The D*it.* text of Mk. 1.31 might be a deliberate revision of this, and the W text a further revision of D. Can it be that here, again, memory of the longer text contaminated the archetype of D and produced a text reading ἐκτείνας τὴν χεῖρα κρατήσας τῆς χειρὸς ἤγειρεν αὐτήν, of which various corrections now appear in DW*it*? Pleonasm is a well known trait of Markan style (Hawkins, *Horae* 139ff); so is verbal repetition (above, on μνημεῖον, in III.2). Both the later synoptists and the later MS tradition tended to eliminate these traits by choosing one or the other half of Mark's redundant expressions. For example:

Mk. 1.22   διδαχῇ . . . διδάσκων, *om.* διδάσκων, Lk.

1.26   φωνῆσαν φωνῇ, *om.* Lk.; κράξαν/ας ΑCDΓΔΘΠΣΦϚ *fam.1.al.pler.*

1.29   ἐκ . . . ἐξελθόντες, *om.* Mt. Lk.; ἐλθόντες 73.

1.34   δαιμόνια . . . δαιμόνια, *om. second* δαιμόνια Lk.Θ*Dit.vg.*Sy.[s.]Aeth.

ὁ δὲ νεανίσκος ἐμβλέψας αὐτῷ ἠγάπησεν αὐτόν

1.35 ἐξῆλθεν καὶ ἀπῆλθεν, om. ἀπῆλθεν Lk.B28*al.; om. ἐξῆλθεν καὶ Wit.vg.

1.43 αὐτῷ ... αὐτόν, om. Mt., Lk., Wb.c; om. αὐτῷ 349.517a.e.vg.; om. αὐτόν 255Sy.s.

2.9–12 ἆρον/ἄρας τὸν κράββατον ter, om. first Mt., Lk., W 544.692.it.; om. third Mt.

2.15 πολλοὶ ... ἦσαν γὰρ πολλοί, om. ἦσαν γὰρ πολλοί Mt., Lk.

2.15–16 τελῶναι καὶ ἁμαρτωλοί ter, om. second Mt., Lk., W; τελωνῶν tant. 69al.

2.18–19 νηστεύοντες ... νηστεύουσιν ... νηστεύουσιν ... νηστεύειν ...νηστεύειν, om. νηστεύοντες Mt., Lk.; om. second νηστεύουσιν Lk. 543 it. pauc.; om. first νηστεύειν Mt.; om. second νηστεύειν Mt., Lk. DUW fam.1(exc. 131)33.700.it.vg.Sy.pesh.Geor.[2]

Further examples in Hawkins, Horae 139ff. For the tendency of the later synoptists and the MS tradition to make the same or similar corrections of Mk., see Turner, Usage, passim.

ὁ δέ. Morgenthaler counts 160 instances of δέ in Mk., 1078 of καί. In the quotations from the longer text there are 3 uses of δέ and 18 of καί. Thus the proportions of δέ to καί are 1:6.7 in canonical Mk. and 1:6 in the longer text. This coincidence in proportion can scarcely be considered significant, since the quotations of the longer text are so short. However, its καί ... καί ... καί, with an occasional δέ thrown in, is paralleled in many Markan stories: for example, that of Bartimaeus (Mk. 10.46–52), which, according to Clement, immediately followed the second quotation. (See Hawkins, Horae 150ff. on Mk.'s characteristic preference of καί to δέ.)

νεανίσκος. See above, on III.3. Mark was fond of diminutives (Turner, Usage 29.349).

ἐμβλέψας αὐτῷ ἠγάπησεν αὐτόν. ἐμβλέψας/α at the beginning of a sentence, with a following finite verb: 3 in Mk., 3 in Mt. (1 Markan), and 1 Lk. In Mk. the sequence is twice ἐμβλέψας/α + verb. Two of the Markan usages (10.21,27) come close together, immediately before the place where the letter locates this usage (following 10.34). This accords with Mark's habit of using the same construction several times in quick sequence. (See above, on κρατήσας τῆς χειρός, and, in Appendix E, the distribution of καὶ εὐθύς. [But other writers also have this habit, notably Paul and Luke. H.J.C.] ἀγαπάω is frequent in the Gospels, Mk. 5 (+ 1D), Mt. 8 (2 Markan), Lk. 13 (none Markan, 2 omitted by Dit.). Therefore, on stylistic grounds the fact that the clause ἐμβλέψας αὐτῷ ἠγάπησεν αὐτόν occurs in Mk. 10.21 is no reason to deny that Mark might have repeated it after 10.34. The question of the significance of the repetition must be postponed to the discussion of the content of the quotations from the longer text.

III.5
καὶ ἤρξατο παρακαλεῖν αὐτὸν ἵνα μετ’ αὐτοῦ ᾖ

ἤρξατο/ἤρξαντο. With following infinitive: 26 in Mk. (D*it.* omit 3 but add 3 others), 9 in Mt. (6 Markan), 19 in Lk. (2 or 3 Markan) + 4 (2 Markan) in the D text of Lk. Turner (*Usage* 28.352ff) and Hunkin (ἄρχομαι) remark that the use of ἤρξατο/ντο with the present infinitive as a substitute for the imperfect is typically Markan. καὶ ἤρξατο as the beginning of a sentence is particularly so: 10 in Mk., 3 in Lk., never in Mt. or Jn. (For comparisons with classical Greek and LXX see Doudna, *Greek* 51ff and 111ff.)

παρακαλεῖν. Meaning "entreat," 9 in Mk., 6 in Mt. (4 Markan) + 1 D*it.*, 5 in Lk. (3 Markan) of which 1 is omitted by אD*al.*, but D*it.* also add an instance. παρακαλεῖν regularly governs the accusative. Followed by a ἵνα clause and the subjunctive: 5 or 6 in Mk., 1 in Mt. (Markan), 2 in Lk. (both Markan). *LSJ* cites the construction from Aristeas, Arrian, and others; in the Gospels it seems a Markan trait. Turner thought Mk. characterized by fondness for ἵνα and use of it with other than "its proper sense of purpose"; he included the uses after παρακαλεῖν in his long list of examples (*Usage* 29.356).

αὐτόν ... αὐτοῦ. The repetition is particularly noticeable since it follows αὐτῷ ... αὐτόν in the preceding line. Doudna, *Greek* 36, remarks: "One of the outstanding features of the Greek of the gospels is the frequency of the oblique cases of the personal pronouns; Mark shares this to a slight degree"—and so, as he shows, do the papyri. Kilpatrick, *Atticism* 136, takes the frequency of αὐτός as one sign of a well-preserved, primitive text.

ἵνα μετ’ αὐτοῦ ᾖ. Mk. regularly speaks of Jesus as acting μετὰ τῶν μαθητῶν/τῶν δώδεκα (3.7; 8.10; 11.11; 14.14,17). But there seem traces of a tradition which spoke of the disciples as οἱ μετ’ αὐτοῦ. Thus the twelve are "made" ἵνα ὦσιν μετ’ αὐτοῦ (3.14); the Gerasene demoniac beseeches Jesus ἵνα μετ’ αὐτοῦ ᾖ (5.18); when Jesus goes in to raise Jaïrus’ daughter he takes with him only her parents and τοὺς μετ’ αὐτοῦ (5.40); when he leaves Capernaum he is pursued by Simon and οἱ μετ’ αὐτοῦ (1.36, although, as H.J.C. notes, the reference here is not certain; Lohmeyer, *ad loc.*, plausibly compares 16.7, τοῖς μαθηταῖς αὐτοῦ καὶ Πέτρῳ). Cf. also 2.19; 9.38; 14.67. [Of the preceding passages, in 1.36; 3.14; 5.18; 5.40; 8.10, and 11.11, Mk.'s μετά is not paralleled in Mt. or Lk. R.S. is therefore justified in seeing here a Markan trait.] The phrase μετ’ αὐτοῦ with this sense appears also in Mk. 16.10 and Jn. 9.40 (cf. 6.66) and perhaps Lk. 22.59 (cf. Jn. 18.26). Further traces of the same usage may perhaps be seen in Mt. 12.30 and parallels; 26.51,69,71; 28.20(?); Lk. 22.21,28,33; 23.43; Jn. 13.8,33; 14.9; 15.27; 16.4; 17.12,24. Therefore, that ἵνα μετ’ αὐτοῦ ᾖ should appear both in Mk. 5.18 and in the longer text is not surprising. Moreover, we have here another near-coincidence with a false reading of D and its allies. In Mk. 5.17f the great majority of texts read καὶ ἤρξαντο (*sc.* the Gerasenes)

III.6

καὶ ἐξελθόντες ἐκ τοῦ μνημείου ἦλθον εἰς τὴν οἰκίαν τοῦ νεανίσκου·

παρακαλεῖν αὐτὸν ἀπελθεῖν . . . καὶ . . . παρεκάλει αὐτὸν ὁ δαιμονισθεὶς ἵνα μετ' αὐτοῦ ᾖ. But D (with considerable support) reads παρεκάλουν αὐτὸν ἵνα ἀπέλθῃ . . . καὶ . . . ἤρξατο παρακαλεῖν αὐτὸν ὁ δαιμονισθεὶς ἵνα ᾖ μετ' αὐτοῦ. This shift in the position of the ἤρξα(ν)το construction could hardly have been motivated by considerations of style or meaning; it may reflect a memory of the longer text. Many D variants indicate that the D text of Mt. and Lk. was corrupted by the scribe's memories of canonical Mk. (e.g., those at Lk. 5.14 and 6.1; cf. below, on καὶ ἐξελθόντες, III.5; μεθ' ἡμέρας, III.6–7; etc.); similar corruption by memories of the longer text is therefore possible. [H.J.C., however, comments: "Memories of short Mk. affected scribes of Mt. and Lk., yes, but perhaps oftener memories of Mt. and Lk. affected scribes of short Mk."]

καὶ ἐξελθόντες. Initial, with a following finite verb: 7 or 8 in Mk. (in 3 D*it.* have δέ); 7 in Mt. + 1 in D, 1 in ℵBCLΘ, etc. Both these additional instances are Markan, but only one of the 7 secure readings is so; more contamination—see the preceding note. Only 2 in Lk., and of these 22.62 may be a gloss taken from Mt. Of the 8 in Mk., 3 are followed by ἐκ and 2 of these by ἔρχομαι. Of the certain instances in Mt., 3 (and in B*al.* a fourth) are followed by ἐκ or its compounds, and one by εἰσέρχομαι. Lk. has ἔξω after ἐξελθών in 22.62.

καὶ ἐξελθόντες ἐκ τοῦ μνημείου ἦλθον. Not found verbatim in the Gospels, but in Mt. 28.8 all uncials except ℵBCLΘ, and most minuscules, have καὶ ἐξελθοῦσαι ἀπὸ τοῦ μνημείου; and Mk. 16.8 has καὶ ἐξελθοῦσαι ἔφυγον ἀπὸ τοῦ μνημείου (of the women after their Easter morning visit), while Mt. 27.53 has καὶ ἐξελθόντες ἐκ τῶν μνημείων . . . εἰσῆλθον (of the dead raised along with Jesus). [P.B. compares also Mk. 1.29, where—after the cure of a demoniac—the text goes on, καὶ εὐθὺς ἐκ τῆς συναγωγῆς ἐξελθόντες ἦλθον εἰς τὴν οἰκίαν Σίμωνος.] In view of these multiple parallels it seems plausible to explain the text as free composition in conventional style rather than direct borrowing from any one passage, or word-by-word compilation from several. [T.B. points out that the western text of Mt. 27.53, especially in the Syriac, is very close to the longer text of Mk. Sy.ᵖᵃˡ· omits μετὰ τὴν ἔγερσιν αὐτοῦ, DSy.ᵖᵃˡˢ·Lat. (*partim*) have ἦλθον instead of εἰσῆλθον, and the Syriac ܟܝܣܐ ܕܘܟ ܘ canbe understood as a singular. Perhaps the western variants may reflect some recollection of the longer text.] On ἐξελθόντες . . . ἦλθον as a Markan usage see Turner, *Commentary* 155. On the subject of ἦλθον, see above, on II.23, καὶ ἔρχονται.

εἰς τὴν οἰκίαν. οἰκία, Mk. 18, Mt. 25, Lk. 25. οἶκος, Mk. 12, Mt. 10, Lk. 33. Again the longer text goes with Mt. and Mk. against Lk. References to particular houses which might be called "historical" (by contrast to those in parables or sayings) with οἰκία: 6 in Mk. (+ 2 in D), 9 or 10 in Mt. (only 3 Markan), 9 or 10 in Lk.

ἦν γὰρ πλούσιος.

(+ 1 in D; only 2 Markan). Often these follow forms of (εἰς)ἔρχομαι with εἰς: 2 in Mk. + 2 in D, 5 in Mt. (1 Markan), 3 in Lk. (1 Markan.) This reference to going into a house often connects two scenes, as it does here: Mk. 1.29; 2.15; 9.33; Mt. 9.23; 9.28; 13.36; 17.25. There is no reason to suppose this transition borrowed from any one of its many parallels. Kilpatrick, Notes 5ff, kindly put at my disposal an unpublished study in which he concludes that in Mk. οἶκος corresponds to "home," οἰκία to "house." He observes, however, that the two are sometimes interchangeable, as "home" and "house" in English. This would seem to be the case here.

ἦν γὰρ πλούσιος. ἦν/ἦσαν γάρ, as introduction of an appended explanation; 9 or 10 in Mk. (1 omitted by Dit., etc., 1 by אB, etc.), 5 in Mt. (all Markan), 4 in Lk. (+ 1 in D, only 1 Markan). It is a Markan trait (Turner, Usage 26.145ff; Zerwick, Untersuchungen 130ff; Bird, γάρ) and Mk. might have used it with πλούσιος as a predicate adjective. The canonical text of Mk. uses πλούσιος twice (a third use appears in a variant). However, πλούσιος is typical of Lk. (11 uses, against 2 in Mk. and 3 in Mt.), and ἦν γὰρ πλούσιος σφόδρα [Sy.ᶜ· omits σφόδρα—R.S.] appears in Lk. 18.23, where Mk. and Mt. have ἦν γὰρ ἔχων κτήματα πολλά. This is the young man in Mk. 10.22 of whom Mk. uses the phrase ἐμβλέψας αὐτῷ ἠγάπησεν αὐτόν, also found in the longer text, above. Mk. 10.22 preceded by little the present passage of the longer text, which stood after 10.34. Given Mark's habit of repeating himself after short intervals, he probably would have repeated ἔχων κτήματα πολλά, rather than have summarized it with πλούσιος. The longer text here may have been corrupted by a copyist's memory of Lk. or by a gloss. Perhaps the latter is more likely, since the rest of the text shows no knowledge of Lk. (except in the concluding clause of the second quotation, which is probably spurious; see below, on III.16). Yet another possibility is that Clement misquoted; for the contamination of his quotations of Mk. by his memories of Mt. and Lk., see Appendix F. On the other hand, the dangling phrase is in Mark's manner and makes sense: They went to the young man's house, for he was wealthy (and therefore able to receive the company which traveled with Jesus). Cf. Zacchaeus, Lk. 19.1ff. [W.M.C. remarks that the subjects of ἐξελθόντες ... ἦλθον εἰς τὴν οἰκίαν are, strictly, only Jesus and the youth.] However, as Turner noted (Usage 26.231), Markan reports of the movements of Jesus, even when the verb is in the singular, are normally to be understood as implying that his followers went with him. See the note on καὶ ἔρχονται, in II.23, above. The notion that πλούσιος is a copyist's corruption can be supported by the fact that a similar corruption has introduced πλούσιος into Mk. 10.17 in AKMWΘΠ, many minuscules, and some MSS of the Old Latin, Syriac, Coptic, Armenian, and Georgian translations. [My attention was called to the variant by R.S.] Turner, Readings 6, thought the κτήματα in Mk. 10.22 a corruption introduced from Mt. 19.22 and maintained that the correct reading was χρήματα, preserved by the western text and Clement and repeated—as usual—by Mk. (in the following verse, 10.23).

III.7

καὶ μεθ᾽ ἡμέρας ἓξ ἐπέταξεν αὐτῷ ὁ Ἰησοῦς· καὶ ὀψίας γενομένης ἔρχεται

καὶ μεθ᾽ ἡμέρας ἓξ. Mk. is characterized by its separation of events from eath other by precise numbers of days, intervals it indicates by μετά with the accusative: 5 instances. Mt. has only 3 (2 Markan and 27.63—probably an echo of Mk.); Lk. has only 2 (and 9.28 seems a deliberate correction of Mk.). Dit. have 2 more instances in Mt. and one more in Lk. (another example of the corruption of their archetype by the influence of Mk.; see above, on μετ᾽ αὐτοῦ). Per contra, the Matthaean usage (with the dative) has corrupted the later uncials of Mk. If Lk. 9.28 is a deliberate correction of Mk. 9.2 (so Rengstorf on Lk. *ad loc.*), there was some tradition about these intervals and some importance attached to them. Therefore the specification of the interval may be a datum of tradition, not an echo of Mk. 9.2, where the same words occur. On Mark's fondness for giving specific numbers, Turner, *Usage* 26.337ff.

ἐπέταξεν. The verb: 4 in Mk., never in Mt., 4 in Lk. (1 Markan) + 1 in D. The person commanded is always in the dative. The form ἐπέταξεν occurs twice in Mk. and in the D variant to Lk. (8.55). ἐπέταξεν ὁ Ἰησοῦς αὐτοῖς is found in Dit. to Mk. 6.39 (where other witnesses lack ὁ Ἰησοῦς). These parallels demonstrate merely that the word was used normally by Mk. and Lk. The peculiarity here is the failure to specify the content of Jesus' command; that is understood from the context, as in Mk. 1.27; Lk. 4.36; 8.25. [C.F.D.M., however, remarks that ἐπέταξεν αὐτῷ without direct object is odd, and the parallels adduced here are not quite similar for in all of them the content of the verb is perfectly clear. Moreover, why did the young man have to come to Jesus and stay with him, if Jesus was at *his* house?] The direct object may have been part of the secret oral teaching. It will be argued later that the young man came to Jesus to receive baptism, conceived as a magically efficacious rite. If so, he had to come to Jesus becaues Jesus had to prepare (purify? exorcise?) the area and the materials for the rite. The story suggests a large house, perhaps a villa. The young man was rich. Jesus and his followers may have been given a wing for themselves.

καὶ ὀψίας γενομένης. ὀψίας γενομένης as a genitive absolute at the beginning of a sentence: 4 in Mk. (3 introduced by καί), 6 or 7 in Mt. (6 with δέ, never with καί), never in Lk. or Jn. It is followed by ἔρχεται in Mk. 14.17 (the introduction to the last supper—a secret ceremony, like the one here, but this may be chance), by ἦλθεν in Mt. 27.57 (Joseph of Arimathea), ἐλθών in Mk. 15.42f (also Joseph of Arimathea), and προσῆλθον in Mt. 14.15 (the introduction to the feeding of the five thousand). By contrast with these stylistic affiliations, the content of this story resembles Jn. 3: Nicodemus ἦλθεν πρὸς αὐτὸν νυκτός and received instruction on baptism as necessary for those who would enter the Kingdom of God.

ἔρχεται. As a historical present: 10 in Mk. (+ 1 in ℵ*A, etc., and 2 in Dit., etc.), 4 in Mt. (2 Markan), 1 in Lk. ‖ ἔρχονται, historical present, in Mk.). Recognized as a distinctively Markan trait by Hawkins (*Horae* 143). It is so frequent that its conjunction with the also frequent καὶ ὀψίας γενομένης is no evidence for dependence on Mk. 14.17.

III.8　　　　　　　　　　　　　　　　　　　　　　　　　III.9

ὁ νεανίσκος πρὸς αὐτὸν περιβεβλημένος σινδόνα ἐπὶ γυμνοῦ καὶ ἔμεινε σὺν αὐτῷ τὴν νύκτα

ὁ νεανίσκος. See above, on III.3. This is the fourth occurrence of the word in 6 lines. More Markan repetition.

πρὸς αὐτόν. πρός after ἔρχομαι: 12 in Mk. (+ 1 in DΘit.); 12 in Mt. (+ 1 dubious); 9 in Lk. Only 2 of the Matthaean and 2 of the Lucan constructions are Markan. Therefore it would at first sight seem pure chance that πρὸς αὐτόν after ἔρχομαι occurs 7 or 8 times in Mk., once in Lk., and never in Mt. But προσέρχομαι was used 52 times by Mt., 5 by Mk., and 10 by Lk.

περιβεβλημένος σινδόνα ἐπὶ γυμνοῦ. Verbatim in Mk. 14.51 (except that W fam. 1.c.k.Sy.ˢ·Cop.ˢᵃ· have discreetly omitted ἐπὶ γυμνοῦ, while Θ fam.13[exc.124].543, 565.Sy.ᵖ·Eth. have accidentally replaced it by the γυμνός of the following verse). In 14.51, too, the subject is νεανίσκος τις—the young man in a sheet who was with Jesus at the time of his arrest and who, on being seized, fled naked (an episode both Mt. and Lk. chose to omit). All the words in the phrase (except ἐπί) are comparatively rare in the synoptics: περιβάλλειν, Mk. 2, Mt. 5, Lk. 2; σινδών, Mk. 4, Mt. 1, Lk. 1; γυμνός, Mk. 2, Mt. 4, Lk. 0. Consequently, the occurrence of the phrase both in the longer and in the canonical texts of Mk. can hardly be explained as an accident of free composition. Either the phrase was a fixed formula in the life of some early church (a baptismal rubric?) or its presence in both texts is evidence of some historical connection.

ἔμεινε. 2 in Mk., 3 in Mt., 7 in Lk., 40 in Jn. Of the 3 in Mt., 2 are Markan; of the 7 in Lk., 1. ἔμεινεν δὲ .. σὺν αὐτῇ ὡς μῆνας τρεῖς, in Lk. 1.56 (the visitation), καὶ παρ' αὐτῷ ἔμειναν τὴν ἡμέραν ἐκείνην, in Jn. 1.39 (the first disciples), καὶ ἔμεινεν ἐκεῖ δύο ἡμέρας, in Jn. 4.40 (Jesus in Samaria; cf. 10.40; 11.6), and κἀκεῖ ἔμεινεν μετὰ τῶν μαθητῶν in Jn. 11.54 (after the raising of Lazarus) testify to common usage rather than literary dependence. (Some historical fact of Jesus' practice may underlie the similarity with the story of the first disciples; or the basis may be some early church usage, or mere chance.) μένω was affected by Jn. because of its theological connotations (e.g., 15.4ff), which probably had some connection with baptism and might be relevant here; but the word is too common to justify speculation.

σύν. To indicate the person accompanying or accompanied: 5 in Mk., 2 in Mt., 23 in Lk. Cf. πρὸς αὐτόν in the preceding line. Another instance of Mt.'s preference for compound verbs.

νύκτα. 4 in Mk., 9 in Mt., 7 in Lk. + 1 Dit. (11.30). In the accusative of extent of time: 3 in Mt. and Lk. 11.30. Cf. also the adverbial accusatives νύκτα καὶ ἡμέραν

III,10

ἐκείνην. ἐδίδασκε γὰρ αὐτὸν ὁ Ἰησοῦς τὸ μυστήριον τῆς βασιλείας τοῦ θεοῦ.

in Mk. 4.27 and Lk. 2.37, and τὰς δὲ νύκτας in Lk. 21.37. These parallels are insignificant; the longer text probably derived its phrase from common usage, not from a literary source.

ἐκείνην. The position after the noun is normal in Mk., as shown by Kilpatrick, ἐκεῖνος.

ἐδίδασκε γὰρ αὐτόν. διδάσκειν: Mk. 17, Mt. 14, Lk. 17. The form ἐδίδασκεν used of Jesus: 6 in Mk., 2 in Mt. (neither Markan), 2 (+ 1 D) in Lk. (none Markan). In Mk. 9.31 it is followed by γάρ and refers to the secret teaching of the passion. This follows the stories of the transfiguration and the raising of the demoniac boy, both of which have similarities to the story in the letter's Gospel. Note especially the sequence 9.27 ὁ δὲ Ἰησοῦς κρατήσας τῆς χειρὸς αὐτοῦ ἤγειρεν αὐτόν ... (30), κἀκεῖθεν ἐξελθόντες ... οὐκ ἤθελεν ἵνα τις γνοῖ (31), ἐδίδασκεν γὰρ τοὺς μαθητὰς αὐτοῦ, etc. Mk. 9.27–31 precedes by little the place (10.34) where the letter locates its Gospel fragment, and the recurrence of similar constructions after short intervals is typical of Markan style. As to content, on the other hand, the synoptics never represent Jesus as teaching a single person; but accounts of his having done so are prominent in Jn. (3, Nicodemus; 4, the woman of Samaria; etc.). Kilpatrick, *Mission* 149ff, points out that Mk. frequently uses verbs to begin sentences. [W.M.C. here finds "the interlaced word order (verb—outer object—subject—inner object) ... contrived."] It is not precisely paralleled in Mk. in sentences of which Jesus is the subject, but Mk. often has the similar order: verb—indirect object—subject—direct object—1.25; 2.19; 6.4; 12.24; 14.27,30. In all these, as in the longer text, the verbs imply speaking, the first object is the person spoken to, Jesus is the speaker, and the second object is the thing said.

τὸ μυστήριον τῆς βασιλείας τοῦ θεοῦ. μυστήριον is used only once in each of the synoptics, and in both Mt. and Lk. its use is a parallel to Mk. 4.11, ὑμῖν τὸ μυστήριον δέδοται τῆς βασιλείας τοῦ θεοῦ (+ γνῶναι, C²DΔΘΣΦϷ[*exc.* K] *fam.*1.22.*fam.*13.543. 28.33.157.565.597.700.1071.*al.pler.it.vg.*Sy.^pesh.hl.Cop.^bo.aliq.Geo.Aeth.Arm.; τὰ μυστήρια, GΣΦ *fam.*1.67.106.115.201.235.258.517.569.Sy.^hl.Arm.). Cf. Mt. 13.11, ὑμῖν δέδοται γνῶναι τὰ μυστήρια τῆς βασιλείας τῶν οὐρανῶν (mysterium *a.c.d.f.ff²*.*g¹*.*l.q.aur.vg.* [3 MSS.]Sy.^c.t.pesh.Geo.Aug.^serm.165; *sacramentum k*); Lk. 8.10, ὑμῖν δέδοται γνῶναι τὰ μυστήρια τῆς βασιλείας τοῦ θεοῦ (γνῶναι transp. *post* θεοῦ D, om. a; τὸ μυστήριον Cit.vg. Sy.Clem.Iren.). The uses of τὸ μυστήριον in MSS of Mt. are further examples of the early corruption of the western text by reminiscences of Mk. Matthew's interpretation of the Markan phrase, by changing τὸ μυστήριον to τὰ μυστήρια and adding γνῶναι,

III.11

ἐκεῖθεν δὲ ἀναστὰς ἐπέστρεψεν εἰς τὸ πέραν τοῦ Ἰορδάνου.

got into Lk. (where the secondary character of γνῶναι is indicated by the difference as to its position) and almost got into Mk. The use of τὸ μυστήριον in the longer text of Mk. is either a Markan trait or evidence that τὸ μυστήριον τῆς βασιλείας τοῦ θεοῦ was a fixed phrase in some circles of early Christianity. Its significance will be discussed below, in the section on content. [W.M.C. remarks that we never hear what happened to the youth's sister.] Such disappearance of minor characters is typical of Markan narratives: so Simon, Andrew, James, and John in 1.40ff; the men who brought the paralytic in 2.3ff; Levi in 2.15ff; etc.

ἐκεῖθεν. 5 in Mk. (and κἀκεῖθεν, in 9.30), 12 in Mt., 3 in Lk. (and κἀκεῖθεν, in 11.53). With a participle, as the beginning of a sentence, 3 in Mk. (+ 2 more in D), 5 in Mt. (only 1 Markan), 1 in Lk. In Mt. the participle always precedes and is never ἀναστάς. In two of the well attested uses in Mk. (7.24 and 10.1) the participle is ἀναστάς and follows ἐκεῖθεν, as διαπεράσαντες in the western text (Dit.) of Mk. 6.53, and ἐξελθόντες after κἀκεῖθεν in 9.30. The usage here is characteristically Markan. The exact phrase ἐκεῖθεν δὲ ἀναστάς appears in Mk. 7.24; 10.1 has καὶ ἐκεῖθεν ἀναστάς [and R.S. remarks that it is followed by ἔρχεται εἰς . . . πέραν τοῦ Ἰορδάνου].

ἀναστάς. The participle used pleonastically, imitating the LXX translation of קוּם, with a following finite verb (Blass-Debrunner-Funk, no. 419.2); 4 or 6 in Mk., 2 in Mt. (both Markan), 11 or 12 in Lk. (only 1 Markan). Certainly not a Matthaean usage. See above, on II.24, καί + participle.

ἐπέστρεψεν. The verb: 4 in Mk. (1 with εἰς, 13.16), 4 in Mt. + 2 D, 7 in Lk. + 1 D (with εἰς, 2.39; 17.31 ‖ Mk. 13.16). The usage is normal.

εἰς τὸ πέραν τοῦ Ἰορδάνου. Not found in the synoptics. Mk. 5.1 has εἰς τὸ πέραν τῆς θαλάσσης; Lk. 8.22, εἰς τὸ πέραν τῆς λίμνης; the Alexandrian text of Mk. 10.1, διὰ τοῦ πέραν τοῦ Ἰορδάνου. Otherwise the usage is either τὸ πέραν with no following genitive (Mk. 4.35; 5.21; 6.45; 8.13 and parallels), or πέραν τοῦ Ἰορδάνου without the article (Mk. 3.8; 10.1—see variants in Appendix E). These seem to represent the normal Markan usage, and the expression is predominantly Markan: Lk. has it only once, where he takes it from Mk. and modifies it; Mt. has 7 uses, all Markan except 4.15, a quotation from LXX Is. 8.23. Accordingly it might be argued that the words τοῦ Ἰορδάνου in the letter's Gospel are an epexegetic gloss. But all the Markan uses of τὸ πέραν alone refer to the opposite side of the Sea of Galilee and are explained by the context, while in the letter's Gospel the determinant τοῦ Ἰορδάνου is required by the context. Mk. 5.1 is a parallel case.

With the above words the first of the letter's quotations from the secret Gospel concludes. There follow the comments: ἐπὶ μὲν τούτοις ἕπεται τό, "καὶ προσπορεύονται αὐτῷ Ἰάκωβος καὶ Ἰωάννης," ⟨Mk. 10.35⟩ καὶ πᾶσα ἡ περικοπή, τὸ δὲ "γυμνὸς γυμνῷ" καὶ τἆλλα περὶ ὧν ἔγραψας οὐχ εὑρίσκεται· μετὰ δὲ τό, "καὶ ἔρχεται εἰς Ἱεριχώ" ⟨Mk. 10.46a⟩ ἐπάγει μόνον (III.11–14). These have been discussed in the commentary on the letter in Chapter Two, above. The letter's second quotation from the secret Gospel reads as follows:

III.15
καὶ ἦσαν ἐκεῖ ἡ ἀδελφὴ τοῦ νεανίσκου ὃν ἠγάπα αὐτὸν ὁ Ἰησοῦς

καὶ ἦσαν ἐκεῖ. See above, on καὶ ἦν ἐκεῖ, in II.23. For the plural the closest parallels are Mk. 2.6, ἦσαν δέ τινες τῶν γραμματέων ἐκεῖ, where Sy.[pesh.hl.] perhaps read ἐκεῖ before τινες, and Mt. 27.55 ἦσαν δὲ ἐκεῖ γυναῖκες where Sy.[s.]Aeth.Geor.[1] put the conjunction at the beginning. Such phrases are narrative clichés and can hardly serve as evidence of dependence. [T.B. queries: Is it coincidence that in Mt. 27.55 the phrase also introduces a group of women, and that this group also—to judge from the parallel in Mk. 15.40—once contained Salome?] It is not impossible that Matthew may have used the longer text of Mk. Cf. the remarks on προσεκύνησε, above, II.24.

ἡ ἀδελφὴ τοῦ νεανίσκου. Unparalleled. Sisters of a specific brother (other than Jesus) appear only in Jn. 11—the Lazarus story—and νεανίσκος only in the synoptics; see above.

ὃν ἠγάπα αὐτὸν ὁ Ἰησοῦς. See above, on ἐμβλέψας, in III.4. Although all the Gospels use ἀγαπάω frequently, the synoptics only once speak of Jesus' loving anybody—the man who questioned him in Mk. 10.21: ὁ δὲ Ἰησοῦς ἐμβλέψας αὐτῷ ἠγάπησεν αὐτόν. Jn. says Jesus loved (ἠγάπα) Martha and her sister and Lazarus (11.5) and his disciples (13.1,34; 15.9,12) and the Father (14.31) and an unnamed disciple ὃν ἠγάπα ὁ Ἰησοῦς, thus referred to 4 times: 13.23 (in the last supper); 19.26 (at the cross); 21.7,20 (the resurrection appearances at the Sea of Galilee). Cf. the ἄλλος μαθητής of 18.15f and 20.2ff. It has often been argued from Johannine evidence that the unnamed "beloved disciple" was Lazarus (e.g., recently, Eckhardt, *Tod* 11–20). The longer text strengthens the argument by first telling a version of the Lazarus story in which the dead youth's sister plays an important role and the youth is said to have loved Jesus, and then locating shortly after this a reference to the disciple whom Jesus loved *and his sister*. So the Markan and the Johannine traditions here, as often, are remotely similar. Therefore it is not surprising that the same traditional formulas should occur in both. ὃν ἠγάπα ὁ Ἰησοῦς is a fixed periphrasis in Jn. and the reader will immediately suppose that the longer text got it from Jn. But then the reader will have to explain why the longer text shows no other trace of John's peculiar *phraseology*. Matters of plot are not in question here; they will be dealt with in the

III.16
καὶ ἡ μήτηρ αὐτοῦ καὶ Σαλώμη, καὶ οὐκ ἀπεδέξατο αὐτὰς ὁ Ἰησοῦς.

next chapter. The present question is: When an isolated Johannine phrase occurs in a text which otherwise shows no important traces of Johannine phraseology, is the isolated phrase to be taken as proof of dependence, or is the absence of other traits to be taken as proof of independence? Are we to prove the dependence of Q on Jn. by Mt. 11.25f ‖ Lk. 10.21f? [H.J.C. compares also the Johannine οὐδὲ ὁ υἱός, εἰ μὴ ὁ πατήρ, in Mk. 13.32 and the parallel between Jn. 3.3–5 and Justin, *First Apology* 61.4–5.] Notice also the similarities to John in the phraseology of the Dead Sea documents (Brown, *Schrolls*), and the phrases of canonical Mk. which appear in section IV of Appendix G with parallels only from Jn. Evidently, a number of phrases best known to us as "Johannine" were taken by John from his Christian and Jewish environment. One of these phrases seems to have been the periphrasis ὃν ἠγάπα ὁ Ἰησοῦς, which apparently was a fixed formula in at least two strains of early Christian tradition, like (ὁ) εἷς τῶν δώδεκα as a designation of Judas: Mk. 14.10,20,43; Mt. 26.14,47; Lk. 22.47; Jn. 6.71 (+ ἐκ; cf., however, 20.24, where the same formula refers to Thomas). An early date for the periphrasis is suggested by its anonymity. (Cf. Bultmann, *Geschichte* 72, 256f, etc. Turner's argument to the contrary—*Usage* 26.338—from the practice of rhetoricians is irrelevant. The Gospels were not written by rhetoricians and their content shows the authors did multiply names.) Further evidence that the longer text did not get its formula from Jn. appears in the pleonastic αὐτόν, to which the uses in Jn. afford no parallel, and which a writer familiar with Greek would hardly have added; it is probably a Semitism—cf. ἧς . . . αὐτῆς in II.23, above, and the note there. [P.B. would distinguish the examples of this construction in the longer text and in Mt., where he thinks them Semitisms, from those in canonical Mk., where he thinks them emphatic, and would find in this distinction evidence that the letter's Gospel is not by Mark.] The distinction seems to me so fine as to be subjective; it escaped Moule, *Idiom-Book* 176, and Blass-Debrunner-Funk no. 297.

ἡ μήτηρ αὐτοῦ. Verbatim in Mk. 3.31; Mt. 13.35; Lk. 1.60; 2.48,51; 8.19 (אDit.Sy.); Jn. 2.5,12; 19.25. The phrase is standard and cannot be referred with confidence to any single source.

Σαλώμη. Salome appears in the NT only in Mk. 15.40 and 16.1, in both as the final figure in a list of female witnesses of an important occasion (15.40, the crucifixion; 16.1, the discovery of the empty tomb). In 15.40: Μαρία ἡ Μαγδαληνὴ καὶ Μαρία ἡ Ἰακώβου τοῦ μικροῦ καὶ Ἰωσῆτος μήτηρ καὶ Σαλώμη. In 16.1: Μαρία ἡ Μαγδαληνὴ καὶ Μαρία ἡ Ἰακώβου καὶ Σαλώμη. (There is considerable difference between MSS as to the spelling of the second Mary's name and her connection with James and Joses.) The list in the longer text of Mk. is of the same type as the other two, and may be of the same women. Luke (23.55; 24.1) has omitted both the lists preserved in canonical Mk.; Matthew has deleted the name of Salome from the first list

(27.56) and deleted her altogether from the second (27.61; 28.1); John (19.25) has replaced her by "the sister of his (Jesus') mother" (or?) "Mary of Klopas." [R.S. remarks that *if* we suppose the lists to be of the same women, and *if* we suppose the beloved νεανίσκος here to be the same as the loving νεανίσκος in the former fragment, and *if* we therefore suppose him to be Lazarus, then his sister here would be the Mary Magdalene of the other Markan lists. And since Mary, Lazarus' sister, anointed Jesus in Bethany in Jn. 12.1ff (cf. Mk. 14.3; Mt. 26.27), and a woman who was a sinner anointed Jesus in Lk. 7.36, it would follow that Mary Magdalene, Lazarus' sister, was the sinner ⟨from whom also seven devils were driven out, Lk. 8.2—she had an eventful life.⟩ Again, Mary, the mother of James and Joses, of the other Markan lists, would be "his mother" in the list in the longer text, and "his" would be Jesus', since James and Joses were his brothers: Mk. 6.3, οὐχ οὗτός ἐστιν ὁ τέκτων ὁ υἱὸς τῆς Μαρίας καὶ ἀδελφὸς Ἰακώβου καὶ Ἰωσῆτος καὶ Ἰούδα καὶ Σίμωνος.] If this latter identification be not accepted, Mk. did not mention the mother of Jesus among those who witnessed his passion and burial and discovered his resurrection. On the other hand, by similar reasoning Salome would be both "the mother of the sons of Zebedee," who replaces her in Mt. 27.56, and "the sister of (Jesus') mother" (or?) "Mary of Klopas," who replaces her in Jn. 19.25. [In favor of at least the former of these identifications, R.S. points out that "the mother of the sons of Zebedee" appears in Mt. 20.20, where she may again be a Matthaean substitute for Salome, who played a similar role in the following story of the longer Markan text. See above, on II.24.] The role of Salome in early Christian polemics will be discussed later in this chapter (section III. D.4, "EVIDENCE FOR ABBREVIATION AT MK. 10.46").

ἀπεδέξατο. In the NT, ἀποδέχομαι is found only in Lk.-Acts. Lk. 8.40 (ἀπεδέξατο), of the crowd's giving a good reception to Jesus; 9.11, of Jesus' receiving the crowd kindly. 5 uses in Acts, of which 3 (18.27; 21.17; 28.30) have the same sense (receive a person kindly) and the same construction (an immediately following accusative of the person received). [With the whole phrase here, C.F.D.M. compares Lk. 9.53, καὶ οὐκ ἐδέξαντο αὐτόν, of the Samaritans' refusal to receive Jesus.] This clearly Lucan trait contrasts as such with the preceding text, which is almost entirely free of Lucan traits (the only very probable one being πλούσιος, above, III.6). Clement uses the verb often in the cognate sense, "approve of" a person—that is, of what he says or does—I.178.27; 186.8; 223.10; 265.3; II.3.8; 4.13; 235.25; 237.21. A number of these citations, particularly the last two, show the disciplinary connotation—almost "accept as communicants"—which the word has in Clement's usage. It is this connotation which the word is meant to carry in the above text of the letter's quotation, and which is necessary to give force to the otherwise trivial ending. The story, as Clement quotes it, is quite unlike any other NT story because it has no apparently significant content. There is no miracle, no saying, nothing but Jesus' refusal to receive, on one occasion, three women. Therefore the story, as it stands, can have been invented and preserved only as polemic against these women or their followers or persons who appealed to their authority (as the Carpocratians did to that of Salome: Origen, *Contra Celsum* V.62). But that such a bare polemic notice was what

originally stood in the longer text is almost incredible: it is too little like the patterns of Gospel stories. The original text must have gone on to report some action or saying of Jesus. Accordingly, this final phrase with its sudden change of vocabulary and its anachronistic church discipline is to be attributed to Clement or some editor of almost Clement's time and vocabulary who deleted the original ending of the story as it stood in the longer text of Mk. and substituted this Lucan phrase (with its second-century meaning) for what he had deleted. What he had deleted we can only guess from the preceding context and from the following—and last preserved— sentence of the letter: τὰ δὲ ἄλλα τὰ πολλὰ ἃ ἔγραψας ψεύσματα καὶ φαίνεται καὶ ἔστιν. Most likely it was a conversation with Salome (again see below, in section III).

B. Synthesis of findings

I. INFLUENCE ON THE WESTERN TEXT

Perhaps the most surprising of the facts revealed by the above commentary is the evidence for the influence of the longer text of Mk. on the western text of the canonical Gospels (or, in Klijn's terminology—*Survey*, 4—the "western readings" of the fathers and the Gospel MSS). The relationship of the two texts was independently discovered by Prof. R. Schippers and myself. There are three cases in which an apparently wrong reading in the western text affords the closest parallel to an apparently correct reading in the longer text of Mk: καὶ ἔρχονται εἰς Βηθανίαν II.23; καὶ ὀργισθείς II.25; and καὶ ἤρξατο παρακαλεῖν αὐτὸν ἵνα μετ᾽ αὐτοῦ ᾖ III.4–5. Yet other cases appear in III.4 ἐξέτεινεν τὴν χεῖρα καὶ ἤγειρεν αὐτὸν and III.7 ἐπέταξεν αὐτῷ ὁ Ἰησοῦς, but in III.4 the parallels are so loose and in III.7 the wording is so banal that neither constitutes evidence. By contrast, the error of Βηθανίαν in Mk. 8.22 and the difficulty of ὀργισθείς in 1.41 demand explanation, while the extent of the paralleled phrase in III.4–5 makes the supposition of influence not-unlikely (but does not prove it; see above on III.1–2). The conjunction of the three—not to say five—cases is impressive. As to the question, Which influenced which?—it is surely more probable that the bad readings of the western text were produced by contamination from the longer text, than that the good readings of the longer text were produced by a selection of the errors peculiar to the western. As already remarked, contamination is characteristic of the western text (Williams, *Alterations* 1f; Glasson, *Mt.* 180f), and contamination of MSS of the canonical Gospels by uncanonical material has often been demonstrated (Black, *Aramaic* 204 and 214; Williams, *Alterations* 7, 12ff, 23). Quispel (*Thomas* 198; *Hebräerevangelium* 142), has argued that the western text was influenced by the *Gospel according to the Hebrews*; a fortiori, it might have been influenced by the longer text of Mk. Further, the longer text shows a number of readings which are nonwestern: γυνὴ ἧς ... αὐτῆς ... ἐλθοῦσα (II.23), ἤγειρεν αὐτὸν κρατήσας τῆς χειρός (III.3–4), καὶ εὐθύς (II.26–III.1; III.2). If the longer text be supposed to derive from the western, these nonwestern readings can hardly be accounted for. Therefore the more probable explanation of the facts would seem to be that the

archetype of the western text was contaminated by the scribe's recollections of the longer one. [But the influence may have been more contemporary than "recollections" implies. H.J.C.] This explanation accords with the fact that Clement both quoted the longer text and used the western (Barnard; Klijn, *P. Bodmer II*, 327, 332, 334). [Moreover, as Pierson Parker pointed out to me, if Clement did not use the western text of Mk.—a possibility which Swanson, *Text* 102, leaves open—then the western readings in the longer text cannot be corruptions due to Clement, but must come from an earlier tradition.] The theory that the western text was shaped by the longer text of Mk. also accords with the date reached above for the longer text (before 125) and with the current dating of the western text, which is now thought to have originated in Egypt about A.D. 150 (Duplacy, *Où en est* I.430f). It also suggests both that the scribe who produced the archetype of the western text regarded the longer text of Mk. much as he did the canonical Gospels, of which he also conflated the readings, and that the sections of the longer text quoted by Clement had some important role in the life of the scribe's church, since so many recollections of them turn up in his text. The importance of the sections quoted by Clement might have been inferred also from the facts that they played a leading part in the argument between Theodore and the Carpocratians and that Clement chose to reassure Theodore particularly about them. To the question of what their importance was we shall return later.

Postscript: Further evidence for these conclusions is now afforded by the addition to the Latin translation of Origen's commentary on Mt., to which Klijn, *Question*, has called attention. It quotes from a *Gospel according to the Hebrews* a text closely related to Mt. 19.16ff but deviating from it in details which agree with or approximate the western text (Sy. and *Diatessaron*). Klijn (154f) thinks these details would indicate its priority to the *Diatessaron*, but he then rejects this conclusion as "inconceivable." Now Mt. 19.16ff is the synoptic parallel to Mk. 10.17ff—the story of the "rich young ruler" which stood shortly before Clement's quotation from the longer text and was closely connected with it, as will be shown below. It is just possible, therefore, that this fragment may be another scrap (more or less rewritten) of the longer text. The close relation to Mt. and the attribution to the *Gospel according to the Hebrews* both fit.

2. VOCABULARY, PHRASEOLOGY, AND GRAMMAR

This establishment of the dependence of the western text on the longer text of Mk. enables us to rule out further consideration of the parallels peculiar to the western text. Turning now to the relation between the longer text of Mk. and the Nestle-Kilpatrick text of the canonical Gospels, we observe that the parallels pointed out in the above commentary are of two sorts:

On the one hand there are many brief parallels of words or phrases, like καὶ ἔρχονται εἰς, καὶ ἦν ἐκεῖ, and so on, which are most frequent in one or another of the synoptics—usually Mk., occasionally Mt., very rarely Lk. or Jn.—but which are so commonplace that they cannot be used as evidence of dependence on any particular

passage. Perhaps it is not strictly impossible that a compiler should have picked them out from remote parts of different Gospels and pieced them together in a mosaic (where, nevertheless, there are no abnormal joints, no irrelevant words, no clear signs of mosaic composition!). But it is more plausible to suppose them the result of free composition by an author to whom the formulas of Markan style came as easily as they did to "Mark" himself. (Cf. the similar judgments of Dodd, *Historical Tradition, passim.*)

On the other hand there are several exact parallels of considerable phrases. Conspicuous examples are υἱὲ Δαβὶδ ἐλέησόν με, περιβεβλημένος σινδόνα ἐπὶ γυμνοῦ. These cannot be explained as accidental results of free composition in a vocabulary full of fixed formulas. Either they must be evidence of literary relationship to the passages where they stand in the canonical Gospels, or they must come from the technical terminology and fixed tradition of early Christianity. In either case they have some special theological significance. Consequently, their relation to their parallels in the canonical Gospels must be thought meaningful. (Contrast the clichés like καὶ ἔρχονται εἰς, of which the use in one or another story is a mere matter of chance, signifying nothing.)

Unfortunately, the dividing line between these two groups is not clear. ἐμβλέψας αὐτῷ ἠγάπησεν αὐτόν almost certainly belongs to the latter. ἀπεκύλισεν τὸν λίθον and ἀπὸ τῆς θύρας τοῦ μνημείου doubtless result from assimilation of the Lazarus story to the Easter story, or vice versa, but just when the assimilation took place is hard to say. ἦν γὰρ πλούσιος may be anything from ancient accident to medieval corruption. The γυνὴ ἧς . . . αὐτῆς . . . ἐλθοῦσα προσεκύνησε sequence is probably a mere collection of clichés of which the arrangement was determined by content. And other cases suggest yet other relationships.

Consequently, we shall first collect the evidence afforded by the vocabulary, the phraseology, and those grammatical traits which have been picked out as characteristic of one or another of the evangelists. This sort of evidence is the most objective, it will include the shorter parallels, and it may yield some results which will be helpful in the more difficult questions raised by the longer parallels.

The bulk of the vocabulary is made up of common words, and the different numbers of their occurrences in the several Gospels usually reflect the different sizes of the Gospels. The fragments of the longer text are so short that arguments from the numbers of times it uses words are mostly worthless (εὐθύς and perhaps καί and δέ may be exceptions: see above, on III.1 and 4). The distribution of νεανίσκος is remarkable but accords with Mark's habit of rapid repetition; cf. the distribution of διαστέλλομαι (4 from Mk. 7.36–9.1, 1 in Mk. 5.43, 1 in Mt., none in Lk. or Jn.), κεντυρίων (3 from Mk. 15.39–45, none elsewhere), κράββατος (4 in Mk. 2.4–12, 1 in Mk. 6.55, none in Mt. or Lk., 4 in Jn.), and so on.

That 12 words from the longer text are not in Jn., as against 3 not in Mk., 4 not in Mt. and 3 not in Lk., is further evidence of the remoteness of the longer text from Jn. Mk. 10.26b–34 (which, henceforth, we shall call CS—*canonical sample*) has 4 not found elsewhere in Mk. (ἀδύνατος, ἑκατονταπλασίων, μαστιγόω, and συμβαίνω), 3 not in Mt., 3 not in Lk., and 14 not in Jn.; the similarity of these two sets of figures

a. Vocabulary*

	SG	Mk.	Mt.	Lk.	Jn.		SG	Mk.	Mt.	Lk.	Jn.
ἀγαπάω	2	5	8	13	36	εὐθύς adv.	2	42	7	1	3
ἀδελφή	1	5	3	3	6	ἡμέρα	1	27	45	83	31
ἀδελφός	1	20	39	24	14	Θεός	1	48	51	122	83
ἀκούω	1	44	63	65	58	θύρα	1	6	4	4	7
ἀνίστημι	1	17	4	26	8	Ἰησοῦς	7	81	150	89	237
ἀπέρχομαι	1	23	35	19	21	ἵνα	1	65	41	46	147
ἀπό	1	47	113	127	40	Ἰορδάνης	1	4	6	2	3
ἀποδέχομαι	1	–	–	2	–	καί	18	1078	1169	1455	818
ἀποθνήσκω	1	9	5	10	28	κῆπος	1	–	–	1	4
ἀποκυλίω	1	1	1	1	–	κρατέω	1	15	12	2	2
ἄρχω	1	27	13	31	1	λέγω	1	202	289	217	266
αὐτός	16	758	906	1074	750	λίθος	1	8	11	14	6
βασιλεία	1	20	55	46	5	μαθητής	1	46	73	37	78
Βηθανία	1	4	2	2	4	μέγας	1	15	20	26	5
γάρ	2	64	124	97	64	μένω	1	2	3	7	40
γίγνομαι	1	55	75	129	51	μετά	3	55	70	63	55
γυμνός	1†	2	4	–	1	μήτηρ	1	17	27	17	11
γυνή	1	16	29	41	17	μνημεῖον	4	6	7	7	16
Δαβίδ	1	7	17	13	2	μυστήριον	1	1	1	1	–
δέ	3	160	491	548	196	νεανίσκος	5	2	2	1	–
διδάσκω	1	17	14	17	9	νύξ	1	4	9	7	6
ἐγείρω	1	19	36	18	13	ὁ, ἡ, τό	32	1504	2777	2629	2144
ἐγώ	1	104	210	215	465	οἰκία	1	18	25	25	5
εἰμί	6	192	288	361	442	ὅπου	2	15	13	5	30
εἰς	4	167	216	223	182	ὀργίζω	1	–	3	2	–
εἷς, μία, ἕν	1	37	66	44	39	ὅς, ἥ, ὅ	2	85	122	182	152
εἰσέρχομαι	1	30	36	50	15	οὐ	1	117	204	174	286
ἐκ	2	67	82	87	165	ὀψία	1	5	7	–	2
ἐκεῖ	2	11	28	16	22	παρακαλέω	1	9	9	7	–
ἐκεῖθεν	1	5	12	3	2	πέραν	1	7	7	1	8
ἐκεῖνος	1	23	54	33	70	περιβάλλω	1	2	5	2	1
ἐκτείνω	1	3	6	3	1	πλούσιος	1	2	3	11	–
ἐλεέω	1	3	8	4	–	πρός	1	63	41	165	101
ἐμβλέπω	1	4	2	2	2	προσέρχομαι	1	5	52	10	1
ἕξ	1	1	1	2	3	προσκυνέω	1	2	13	2	11
ἐξέρχομαι	1	39	43	44	29	Σαλώμη	1	2	–	–	–
ἐπί	1	73	120	160	33	σινδών	1	4	1	1	–
ἐπιστρέφω	1	4	4	7	1	σύν	1	6	4	23	3
ἐπιτάσσω	1	4	–	4	–	υἱός	1	34	89	77	55
ἐπιτιμάω	1	9	6	12	–	φωνή	1	7	7	14	15
ἔρχομαι	4	86	111	100	156	χείρ	2	25	24	26	15

* Figures from canonical Gospels from Morgenthaler; for longer text of Mk. see Index I, s.v. *Secret Gospel* (*SG*).

† Two more uses of γυμνός appeared in the Carpocratian version (γυμνὸς γυμνῷ).

Vocabulary (figures from Morgenthaler) of the 175 words of canonical Mk. preceding the first quotation from the longer text (i.e., Mk. 10.26b–34).

	Mk.	Mt.	Lk.	Jn.
ἀγρός 2†	9	16	9	–
ἀδελφή 2	5	3	3	6
ἀδελφός 2	20	39	24	14
ἀδύνατος 1	1	1	1	–
αἰών 1	4	8	7	13
αἰώνιος 1	3	6	4	17
ἀκολουθέω 2	18	25	17	19
ἀλλά 1	43	37	35	101
ἀμήν 1	13	31	6	50
ἀναβαίνω 2	9	9	9	16
ἄνθρωπος 2	56	112	95	60
ἀνίστημι 1	17	4	26	8
ἀποκτείνω 1	11	13	12	12
ἀρχιερεύς 1	22	25	15	21
ἄρχω 2	27	13	31	1
αὐτός 10	758	906	1074	750
ἀφίημι 2	34	47	31	14
γάρ 1	64	124	97	64
γραμματεύς 1	21	22	14	–
δέ 3	160	491	548	196
διωγμός 1	2	1	–	–
δύναμαι 1	33	27	26	36
δυνατός 1	5	3	4	–
δώδεκα 1	15	13	12	6
ἐάν 1	35	66	29	59
ἐγώ 1	104	210	215	465
ἔθνος 1	6	15	13	5
εἰμί 4	192	288	361	442
εἰς 2	167	216	223	182
ἑκατονταπλασίων 1	1	–	1	—
ἐμβλέπω 1	4	2	2	2
ἐμπαίζω 1	3	5	5	–
ἐμπτύω 1	3	2	1	–
ἐν 3	137	291	354	220
ἔνεκα (ἔνεκεν) 2	5	7	5	–
ἔρχομαι 1	86	111	100	156
ἔσχατος 2	5	10	6	7
εὐαγγέλιον 1	8	4	–	–
ζωή 1	4	7	5	36
ἤ 6	33	67	45	12
ἡμεῖς 1	24	49	69	48
ἡμέρα 1	27	45	83	31
θαμβέω 1	3	–	–	–
θάνατος 1	6	7	7	8
θεός 2	48	51	122	83
ἰδού 2	7	62	57	4
Ἱεροσόλυμα 2	10	11	4	12
Ἰησοῦς 3	81	150	89	237
καί 22	1078	1169	1455	818
καιρός 1	5	10	13	3
κατακρίνω 1	3	4	2	–
λαμβάνω 1	20	53	22	46
λέγω 4	202	289	217	266
μαστιγόω 1	1	3	1	1
μέλλω 1	2	10	12	12
μετά 2	55	70	63	55
μή 1	79	129	142	117
μήτηρ 2	17	27	17	11
νῦν 1	3	4	14	28
ὁ, ἡ, τό 19	1504	2777	2629	2144
ὁδός 1	16	22	20	4
οἰκία 2	18	25	25	5
ὅς, ἥ, ὅ 1	85	122	182	152
ὅτι 1	101	141	173	271
οὐ/οὐκ 1	117	204	174	286
οὐδείς 1	26	19	33	52
οὗτος 1	78	147	230	237
πάλιν 1	28	17	3	43
παρά 3	16	18	29	33
παραδίδομι 2	21	31	17	15
παραλαμβάνω 1	6	16	6	3
πᾶς, πᾶσα, πᾶν 2	67	128	152	63
πατήρ 1	18	64	56	137
Πέτρος 1	19	23	18	34
πολύς 1	57	50	51	36
προάγω 1	5	6	1	–
πρῶτος 2	10	15	10	5
σύ 1	89	207	224	151
συμβαίνω 1	1	–	1	–
σῴζω 1	15	15	17	6
τέκνον 2	9	14	14	3
τίς 1	71	90	114	79
τρεῖς 1	7	12	10	4
υἱός 1	34	89	77	55
ὑμεῖς 1	75	247	220	255
φημί 1	6	17	8	3
φοβέομαι 1	12	18	23	5

† The numerals following each word indicate the number of its occurrences in Mk.10.26b–34.

is striking. The occurrence in the longer text of a good number of John's favorite words should not be made an argument for relationship. John is notorious for the frequency with which he uses his favorite words, of which the longer text of Mk. contains. ἀγαπάω, ἀποθνήσκω, ἐγώ, εἰμί, ἐκ, ἐκεῖνος, ἔρχομαι, Ἰησοῦς, ἵνα, μαθητής, μένω, μνημεῖον, ὅπου, <u>οὐ</u>, and προσκυνέω. It would be absurd to suppose that the uses of these common words in the other Gospels were signs of Johannine influence. CS has the 5 underlined above, plus αἰώνιος, ἀλλά, ἀμήν, ζωή, λαμβάνω, νῦν, ὅτι, οὐδείς, πάλιν, πατήρ, and Πέτρος. Similar collections can be made for Lk. (Longer text, γίγνομαι, ἡμέρα, θεός, ὅς, πλούσιος, πρός, σύν, φωνή; CS, ἡμεῖς, ἡμέρα, θεός, νῦν, ὅς, οὗτος) and Mt. (Longer text, γάρ, ἐγείρω, ἐκεῖθεν, ἐκεῖνος, Ἰησοῦς, προσέρχομαι, προσκυνεῖν; CS, ἀμήν, γάρ, ἤ, Ἰησοῦς, λαμβάνω, παραλαμβάνω, φημί) and are equally insignificant.

Of Mk.'s favorite words (as listed by Morgenthaler, 181, on grounds of frequency only) the longer text contains εὐθύς, ἵνα, κρατέω, and ὅπου; CS, ἀλλά, δύναμαι, δώδεκα, πάλιν, and πολύς. The brevity of these lists, by comparison with those from the other Gospels, is explained by the small number of "favorite words" to be found in Mk. Mk. has the largest vocabulary in proportion to its size of any of the Gospels: 1,345 words in 11,200. Mt. has 1,691 in 18,300, Lk. has 2,055 in 19,400, and Jn. has only 1,011 in 15,400: (Morgenthaler, 164). Therefore Mk. uses most words least often, Jn. least words most often. Accordingly, the list of Jn.'s favorite words contains 75 items, and any NT text is sure to show a substantial "Johannine" vocabulary. Lk. has 62 favorites, Mt. 37, and Mk. only 18 (so Morgenthaler, 181f). Thus the 15 "Johannine" words in the longer text (or the 16 in CS) are a fifth of the 75; the 8 "Lucan" words are about an eighth of the 62 (the 6 in CS are a tenth); the 7 "Matthaean" (7 also in CS) are about a fifth of the 37, and the 4 "Markan" (5 in CS) are about a quarter of the 18. Here again, the similarity between the figures for the longer text and those for CS is obvious; and the longer text, like CS, contains a slightly higher percentage of the list of Mk.'s favorite words than it does of the list of any other Gospel's. This, however, may be no more significant than the other data concerning these frequencies.

Morgenthaler's 18 Markan favorites occur 444 times in Mk., that is, about once every 25.22 words. Of the longer text we have just 175 words (181 less the final interpolation καὶ οὐκ ἀπεδέξατο αὐτὰς ὁ Ἰησοῦς, on which see the commentary). An average 175 words of canonical Mk. should contain 6 or 7 uses of Mk.'s favorite terms. The 175 words of the longer text contain 6 (2 of εὐθύς, 1 of ἵνα, 1 of κρατέω, and 2 of ὅπου); the 175 words of CS contain 5 (one each of ἀλλά, δύναμαι, δώδεκα, πάλιν, and πολύς). This, again, is perhaps insignificant, not only because of the banal character of most of the "favorites," but also because so small a sample might be expected to diverge widely from the average. Consequently, its agreement with the average may also be mere chance.

Parker, Gospel, has made a careful study of the vocabulary characteristic of both Mk. and Mt. and has condensed the results into four tables (pp. 41, 245–250) listing with considerable duplication some 119 expressions. Of these, 11 appear in the longer text (ἀπέρχομαι, ἐκεῖθεν, ἐκτείνω, ἐπιτιμάω, εὐθύς/-έως, Ἰορδάνης, κρατέω, ὀψία, παρακαλέω, πέραν, and υἱὲ Δαβίδ), while only 8 appear in CS (ἀγρός, ἀρχιερεύς, ἄρχω,

γραμματεύς, ἐμπαίζω, ἐν τῇ ὁδῷ, εὐαγγέλιον, and προάγω). Thus the longer text, with only a sixty-fourth of Mk.'s 11,200 words, contains about a tenth of the Matthaean-Markan expressions in Parker's list, while CS contains only a fifteenth. This may possibly be significant in view of the evidence seen above (on προσεκύνησε, in II.24) for supposing that Mt. knew the longer text. Again, however, the commonplace character of most of the words and the brevity of the quotations from the longer text make it impossible to build on these data.

The studies of Hawkins (*Horae*) and Turner (*Usage*) have been most valuable because they take into account not only relative frequencies of usage, but also the ways in which words were used—questions of syntax and style. For the same reason, however, their data are more difficult to classify, since some belong properly in the sections on phraseology and grammar. Nevertheless, since Hawkins' classification of his material was primarily lexical, his results may be stated here. He listed 95 "words and phrases characteristic of" Mt. (pp. 4–8). Of these, 5 (γυμνός, εἷς for τις, ἐκεῖθεν in narrative, προσέρχομαι, and προσκυνέω) appear in the longer text of Mk. (none appears in CS). Among these, Hawkins thought προσέρχομαι a "most distinctive and important" trait (p. 7—he did not explain how it happened to occur 10 times in Lk.) and γυμνός "less important than the rest, because mainly or entirely accounted for by the subject matter" (p. 4). For Mk. he listed 41 characteristics, of which 3 (ἔρχεται/-ονται historic present, εὐθύς, and κρατέω) appear in the longer text, 4 in CS (ἐν τῇ ὁδῷ, εὐαγγέλιον, θαμβέω, and πάλιν). He thought εὐθύς and ἔρχεται "most distinctive," κρατέω "less important." Five is one-nineteenth of 95, 3 one-fourteenth (and 4, one-tenth) of 41; so these figures show CS markedly, and the longer text slightly, more Markan than Matthaean. The 41 Markan characteristics appeared in Mk. 357 times, about once every 31.5 words. In both the longer text and CS they should therefore have appeared between 5 and 6 times. They actually appear 5 times in the longer text (2 ἔρχομαι in historical present, 2 εὐθύς, 1 κρατέω), 4 in CS (one each of the traits listed above). Hawkins listed 151 characteristics of Lk. (pp. 16–23); of these only 3 (redundant ἀναστάς, πλούσιος, and σύν) appear in the longer text of Mk. and only 1 (νῦν) in CS. This seems to go beyond chance and to indicate clearly that, like CS, the longer text has little or no connection with Lk. Besides his lists, Hawkins devoted a chapter to minor Markan peculiarities. One of these (p. 119) is the fact that ὀργή is attributed to Jesus nowhere in the Gospels save Mk. 3.5 and the western reading in 1.41. The latter now seems to have been derived from the longer text. Another peculiarity Hawkins noted was Mark's preference for καί as against δέ at the beginnings of sentences. It was shown above (on ὁ δέ, in III.4) that the proportion of καί to δέ in the longer text is almost the same as in canonical Mk.

Turner, *Usage*, concerned himself chiefly with grammar, but included a number of lexical observations; he noted Mark's fondness for numerals (26.337), his use of ἤρξατο/-ντο as a substitute for the imperfect (28.352), his preference for ἐκ as against ἀπό (Matthew and Luke prefer the latter, 29.281), his use of ἐκ after ἐξέρχομαι (*ibid.*), his fondness for diminutives (29.349ff—cf. νεανίσκος), and his fondness for ἵνα and "improper" use of it after παρακαλέω (29.356). All these are found in the longer text of Mk.

To these observations a few may be added. ἀγαπάω, of Jesus' loving another man, is found in the synoptics only in Mk. ἀποκυλίω is a rather rare word which Matthew and Luke seem to have derived from Mk. Βηθανία, as noted in the commentary, was more prominent in Mk. than in the later synoptics. Mk. uses ἐμβλέπω twice as often as any other evangelist, and 3 out of 4 times in the ἐμβλέψας αὐτῷ/-οῖς construction used in the longer text. μυστήριον is another word which Mt. and Lk. use only when they parallel Mk.; in the longer text the use of the singular is specifically Markan. Σαλώμη is peculiar to Mk., the later synoptists chose to omit her name. σινδών is 4 times as frequent in Mk. as in Mt. or Lk. (Moulton-Geden omits the first instance in 15.46). Whenever Mark mentions the word he repeats it; in any other author this would be thought emphatic. χείρ as an instrument of supernatural help is typical of Mk.: 10 or 11 times, 7 in Mt. (5 Markan), 4 in Lk. (2 Markan).

Combining the above observations with the lists of Morgenthaler, Parker, Hawkins, and Turner, we have:

ἀγαπάω (of Jesus)	*'Ιορδάνης
*ἀπέρχομαι	καί (initial, vs. δέ)
ἀποκυλίω	*κρατέω
ἄρχω (for imperfect)	μυστήριον
Βηθανία	νεανίσκος (qua diminutive)
ἐκ (vs. ἀπό)	ὅπου
*ἐκεῖθεν	ὀργίζω (of Jesus)
*ἐκτείνω	*ὀψία
ἐμβλέψας (αὐτῷ)	*παρακαλέω
ἔξ (qua numeral)	*πέραν (τό)
ἐξέρχομαι ἐκ	Σαλώμη
*ἐπιτιμάω	σινδών
ἔρχεται/-ονται (historic present)	*υἱὲ Δαβίδ
εὐθύς	χείρ (with supernatural power)
ἵνα	

* Listed by Parker as characteristic of both Mk. and Mt.

In all, 29 of the 82 words listed can claim to be, at least in one construction or another, characteristically Markan. Here it may be objected that to consider special constructions confuses the data on vocabulary with those on phraseology and grammar, and has resulted in some overlapping of the above list with those in the preceding and following sections. The objection is justified. However, it seemed impossible to exclude consideration of special constructions from an account of the vocabulary, since vocabularies differ not only by the words used, but also by the special meanings given them. If this be granted, it follows that the vocabulary of the longer text is preponderantly Markan.

Indeed, it is so preponderantly Markan that it must be explained as the result either of the same stream of tradition which produced Mk., or of deliberate imitation

b. Phraseology*

	Mk.	Mt.	Lk.	Jn.
καὶ ἔρχονται εἰς	6/7†	–	–	–
καὶ ἦν ἐκεῖ	1	(1‡)	–	–
(ἦν/ἦσαν δὲ ἐκεῖ§	1	2	1)	–
καὶ + participle of ἔρχομαι + verb	5	12	5	–
ἔρχομαι + προσκυνεῖν	–	7/8	–	–
καὶ λέγει αὐτῷ	8	6/7	–	–
οἱ δὲ μαθηταί initial + verb	2/3	3/4	–	–
ὅπου ἦν	2	–	2	6
καὶ εὐθύς initial	25	2	–	–
ἐκ τοῦ μνημείου	–	–	–	3
φωνῇ μεγάλῃ	4	2/3	6	1
καὶ προσελθών initial	1/2	4/6	2	–
καὶ εἰσελθών initial	6/8	1	4	–
εἰσέρχομαι/-πορεύομαι ὅπου	4	–	–	–
ἐκτείνειν τὴν χεῖρα	3/4	6	5	–
κρατήσας τῆς χειρός	2/3	–	1	–
ἐμβλέψας + verb	3	1	1	–
ἤρξατο/-αντο + infinitive	26	9	19/23	–
καὶ ἤρξατο/-αντο initial	10	–	3	–
μετ' αὐτοῦ, of Jesus' followers	4	–	1(?)	1/2
καὶ ἐξελθόντες initial	7/8	7/9	2	–
ἦν/ἦσαν γάρ explicative	9/10	5	4/5	–
(καὶ) μετὰ ... ἡμέρας + numeral	5	3	1	–
ὀψίας γενομένης initial	4	6/7	–	–
καὶ ὀψίας γενομένης initial	3	–	–	–
ἔρχομαι + πρός	12/13	11/12	9	–
ἔρχομαι + πρὸς αὐτόν	7/8	–	1	–
(προσέρχομαι	5	52	10)	–
μένειν σύν	–	–	2	–
(μένειν παρά	–	–	–	4)
(μένειν μετά	–	–	1	1)
ἐδίδασκεν, of Jesus	6	2	2/3	1
ἡ βασιλεία τοῦ Θεοῦ	14	4	32	2
ἐκεῖθεν + participle, initial	3/5	5	1	–

(In Mt. the participle always precedes, in Mk. and in the longer text it follows.)

τὸ πέραν	5	4	1	–
πέραν τοῦ Ἰορδάνου	2	3	–	–
ἡ μήτηρ αὐτοῦ	1	1	3/4	–

* For details see Appendix E.
† 6/7 means "6 or 7," and so hereafter. The uncertainty reflects textual variants.
‡ In a different sense.
§ The indented expressions in this list are not found in the longer text of Mk.

of Mk. (Composition as a cento seems unlikely; the parallels come from too many places, are combined and modified too freely, and fit together too well.) If imitation, it was imitation of a very simple sort. The imitator must have known Mk. almost by heart and deliberately told his story as much as possible in the words and phrases of the original. Therefore we should expect his work to show almost no other words or phrases. On the other hand, if the longer text were a free product of the same stream of tradition, we should expect it to differ from canonical Mk. at least as far as canonical Mk., in its various parts, differs from itself. Now the quotations from the longer text contain only 3 words not in Mk., and of these three ἀποδέχομαι was picked out in the commentary on III.16 as part of a later addition. κῆπος and ὀργίζω remain. But Mk. uses some 634 words once only (Morgenthaler, 166)—approximately one word in every 17.8. The quotations from the longer text (excluding the addition containing ἀποδέχομαι) have 175 words and should therefore have about 10 not found in Mk. That they actually have only 2 non-Markan words suggests that they were produced by imitation of canonical Mk., not by independent composition. But this evidence, again, is not conclusive: CS has only 4 words not found elsewhere in Mk. The percentile originality of Mk.'s vocabulary would probably decline as the amount of material increased; the contentual similarity of the main story in the longer text to the other stories of cures and resurrections would make for the use of many of the same words; and, above all, the distribution of hapax legomena is uneven and the quotations from the longer text are so short that their variation from the average might be mere chance. Compare Jn., of which Parker states that "the number of words occurring in only one chapter . . . ranges from 2 in chap. 17 to 47 in chap. 19" (*Two Editions* 306 n9).

The evidence yielded by this list is clear, especially since Mk. contains only about 11,200 words, Mt. about 18,300, Lk. about 19,400 (Morgenthaler, 164), and the figures for Mt. and Lk. should therefore normally exceed those for Mk. by 7/11 and 8/11 respectively. In the above list, of the 33 entries which represent usages found in the longer text of Mk. there are 18 in which the number of parallels from canonical Mk. is greater than that from either Mt. or Lk., and 9 more in which it runs so close to the largest number from either Mt. or Lk. that the difference is insignificant: οἱ δὲ μαθηταί, ὅπου ἦν, ἐκ τοῦ μνημείου, φωνὴ μεγάλη, ἐκτείνειν τὴν χεῖρα, καὶ ἐξελθόντες, ὀψίας γενομένης, ἐκεῖθεν + participle, and πέραν τοῦ Ἰορδάνου.

Of the 6 remaining, 3 are most frequent in Lk.: μένειν σύν, ἡ βασιλεία τοῦ θεοῦ, and ἡ μήτηρ αὐτοῦ. The differences in frequency of these are determined by content, not style, and are insignificant for the question of the written sources of the longer text of Mk.—which should not be supposed to have derived its references to ἡ βασιλεία τοῦ θεοῦ or ἡ μήτηρ αὐτοῦ from Lk. simply because Lk. uses these phrases most often. μένειν σύν, too, is ordinary Greek and need not be thought to have been derived from Lk. The list clearly shows the distance of Lk. from the style of the longer text of Mk. Of the 33 items, 11 are not represented at all in Lk., 6 others appear in Lk. less often than in either Mk. or Mt., and for 2 others Lk. is tied with the lower of its competitors.

Mt. is much closer than Lk. to the longer text of Mk. (as it is to canonical Mk., Parker, *Gospel* 32–43). And the traits to which most parallels appear in Mt. are usually

traits of style, not content (καὶ + participle of ἔρχομαι + verb, καὶ προσελθών initial, καὶ ἐξελθόντες initial, ὀψίας γενομένης initial, ἐκεῖθεν + participle, initial). To a number of these data Parker called attention in his preliminary report to the Society of Biblical Literature and Exegesis at its New York meeting in December, 1960—an unpublished report to which this study is often indebted. However, in comparison with the full list, the Matthaean traits are insignificant. Mt. leads in only 9 out of 33 instances. In 6 of these 9 (οἱ δὲ μαθηταί, ἐκτείνειν τὴν χεῖρα, καὶ ἐξελθόντες, ὀψίας γενομένης, ἐκεῖθεν + participle, πέραν τοῦ Ἰορδάνου) there are so many Markan instances that the trait cannot be considered typically Matthaean. In two, indeed, there are minor peculiarities which distinguish the Markan from the Matthaean usage, and the longer text has Markan form (καὶ ὀψίας, not ὀψίας δέ; ἐκεῖθεν before the participle). Therefore, as truly Matthaean traits we have only the sentence structure καὶ + participle of ἔρχομαι + verb, ἔρχομαι followed by προσκυνεῖν, and initial καὶ προσελθών. Of these, however, canonical Mk. uses the first 5 times and the last 1 or 2, so they are not alien to Markan style. The only Matthaean trait found in the longer text, but not in canonical Mk., is the use of ἔρχομαι to introduce προσκυνεῖν. Since Mk. 5 times uses ἔρχομαι to introduce other verbs, and once uses προσκυνεῖν of a petitioner coming to Jesus, it is not improbable that a Markan text should have combined these constructions. That the longer text is Markan rather than Matthaean even in this detail is suggested by the fact that in it προσκυνεῖν governs the accusative, as it does in Mk. 5.6, but never in Mt.'s 13 uses except once, when he is quoting the OT. This argument is not conclusive, because the accusative in the longer text, and also in Mk. 5.6, may be corrupt. However, against the one Matthaean trait of ἔρχομαι + προσκυνεῖν must be set the list of non-Matthaean traits (καὶ ἔρχονται εἰς, καὶ εὐθύς, καὶ εἰσελθών, εἰσέρχομαι ὅπου, κρατήσας τῆς χειρός, ἤρξατο + inf., καὶ ἤρξατο initial, οἱ μετ' αὐτοῦ of Jesus' followers, βασιλεία τοῦ θεοῦ), most of which are typically Markan. In Hawkins' list of expressions characteristic of Mt. (*Horae* 4ff) there are 27 of which one example each appears in canonical Mk.; it should be expected, therefore, that a longer text of Mk. would contain additional examples of such isolated Markan usages of expressions common in Mt.

The letter's occasional contacts with John are clearly insignificant for the question of its style (as opposed to content). ἐκ τοῦ μνημείου and ἡ μήτηρ αὐτοῦ are determined by content and have no stylistic peculiarity; ὅπου ἦν, while more frequent in Jn., is also found in canonical Mk. and is ordinary Greek. Those who would see in such occasional parallels proofs of dependence should look at section IV of Appendix G, where it appears that πέραν τῆς θαλάσσης of Mk. 5.1 has 3 parallels in Jn., none elsewhere; so does ὑπήντησεν αὐτῷ of Mk. 5.2; οὐδεὶς ἐδύνατο in Mk. 5.3 has 5 parallels in Jn., 1 in Mt., and none elsewhere; τί ἐμοὶ καὶ σοί in Mk. 5.7 has a verbatim parallel only in Jn. 2.4. Yet no one would take these as proof that Mark used Jn. or John, Mk. See also the Johannine parallels to the material from Mt. 9, in section V of Appendix G, and the remarks above in the commentary on III.15.

Finally, it has not seemed worthwhile to undertake a detailed comparison between the quotations from the longer text and the "apocryphal" Gospels. Of the latter, *Thomas*, being in Coptic, does not admit of close verbal comparison. The earliest

material in Greek—the fragments of *Thomas*, the pericope *De adultera*, *P. Egerton 2*, the *Gospel of Peter*, etc.—are obviously much more remote from canonical Mk. than is the longer text. Therefore close comparison of their vocabularies and phraseology is unnecessary.

c. *Grammar*

Many of the grammatical peculiarities of the text have already been mentioned: under phraseology, several types of sentence structure; under vocabulary, the use of ἤρξατο with the present infinitive as a substitute for the imperfect, the pleonasms (ἐξέρχομαι ἐκ, cf. ἀποκυλίω ἀπό), the use of the historical present (ἔρχεται, λέγει), of ἵνα with the subjunctive after παρακαλέω, and of initial καί. To these can be added the use of the accusative after προσκυνεῖν (unless it be a later corruption of the dative used by the other evangelists—see the commentary, II.24). All these have been noted as Markan traits.

In his preliminary report, Parker used the relative rarity of historical presents as an argument against assigning the longer text to the Markan tradition. Disregarding verbs in subordinate clauses and quotations, the text has 3 historical presents (all in formulas, καὶ ἔρχονται, καὶ λέγει αὐτῷ, ἔρχεται), 3 imperfects, and 16 aorists. Again disregarding verbs in subordinate clauses and quotations, the story of the rich young ruler, with which the longer text is closely linked by location and content, has 3 historical presents (all λέγει), 3 imperfects, and 7 aorists; the prophecy of the passion, which followed it and immediately preceded the first quotation from the longer text, has no present, 4 imperfects and 1 aorist; the story of the sons of Zebedee, which stood between the two quotations, has 2 presents (προσπορεύονται and λέγει) and 6 aorists; Mk. 10.46a, which introduced the second quotation, has a historical present (καὶ ἔρχονται); the story of Bartimaeus, which followed the second quotation, has 1 historical present (φωνοῦσιν), 4 imperfects, and 7 aorists. It appears that in this section of his Gospel Mark was using historical presents almost exclusively in formulas (λέγει, ἔρχονται, etc.) and using the imperfect and aorist "correctly" in the body of his narratives. That is just what we find in the quotations from the longer text and is also characteristic of most passages of Mk.; see the study of Zerwick, *Untersuchungen* 49ff. It may be, however, that the small number of historical presents argues against the supposition that the longer text was a deliberate imitation of Mk., for the frequency of historical presents in many sections of Mk. is just the sort of thing—at once obvious and easy—which an imitator would affect. That in this respect the quotations should accord with the sections of Mk. adjacent to them, and not with the popular notion of Mk.'s style, suggests they were not imitations but products of the same tradition.

As other grammatical peculiarites of the longer text may be mentioned three Semitisms: the use of μία for τις in II.23, found in Mk., but most frequent in Mt. and reckoned by Hawkins (*Horae* 5 and 30) as a Matthaean trait; redundant αὐτός in II.23 and III.15, almost evenly distributed through the synoptics; redundant ἀναστάς in III.10, which Hawkins (16) considered a Lucan trait, though there are 5 or 6

instances in Mk. On all these see the commentary, *ad locc*. This frequency of Semitisms in the longer text might be a sign either of early material or of late imitation— Semitisms catch the eye and are easy to copy.

Less conspicuous are a number of grammatical details noted by Turner, *Usage*, as Markan traits: (1) The frequency of parenthetical explanatory clauses, especially of γάρ clauses like those in the longer text, III.6 ἦν γὰρ πλούσιος and III.9f ἐδίδασκεν γὰρ αὐτὸν ὁ Ἰησοῦς, etc. (26.145). (2) The use of the plural, usually of ἔρχομαι, to denote the movements of Jesus with his disciples and the crowd (26.225). (The later synoptists and MS tradition, concentrating on the Master, regularly replace this with the singular.) There are 3 examples in the longer text, II.23 καὶ ἔρχονται, III.5 καὶ ἐξελθόντες, III.6 ἦλθον. (3) The use of the singular, referring to movements of Jesus, immediately followed by a reference to the disciples or the crowd (the reference is usually eliminated by the later tradition—26.231). Of this the longer text as it stands does not provide an example, but the conclusion of the first quotation, III.11 καὶ ἀναστὰς ἐπέστρεψεν, was immediately followed by καὶ προσπορεύονται αὐτῷ Ἰάκωβος καὶ Ἰωάννης; this is paralleled by Turner's examples from Mk. 1.35f; 2.23; 6.1. (4) Location of the verb at the end of the sentence (29.352). In the longer text, II.23 ἧς ὁ ἀδελφὸς αὐτῆς ἀπέθανεν. On this Turner's comments: "It is not suggested that these instances are typical of Mark in the sense that this order of words is his normal usage: but they are not inconsiderable in number" (29.355). Kilpatrick, *Mission* 149f, found that "for Mk. 13, the normal position for the verb is the initial one," but he reports a count of verbs in five pages of Mk. which yielded 40 initial, 66 medial, 24 terminal. In Mk. 10.17–52—the immediate context of the quotations from the longer text—52 verbs in independent clauses are preceded by expressed subjects or objects, 18 have no expressed subject or object, and 23 are followed by expressed subjects or objects (these figures do not include the OT quotation in verse 19). Evidently Mk.'s usage in this respect differs greatly from one pericope to another. See further Zerwick, *Untersuchungen* 75ff, whose careful critique of Turner leads him to conclude that in this question it is not possible to determine any characteristically Markan practice.

This concludes our survey of the evidence from vocabulary, phraseology, and grammar. I think it has shown that the longer text is related to canonical Mk. not only by a few conspicuous parallels, but also by a multitude of small details which are more like the details of Mk. than of any other evangelist. The vocabulary shows a distribution of Markan and non-Markan words almost identical with that in an adjacent section of equal length from canonical Mk. More than a third of the words listed are themselves characteristically Markan or appear in characteristically Markan constructions. The phraseology is yet more clearly Markan: 18 items most frequent in Mk., 9 in Mt., 4 in Lk., and 2 in Jn.—and these gross figures require modifications which incline the balance even further to the Markan side. The grammar throughout accords with Markan usage and shows half a dozen typically Markan constructions. Above all, there is nothing in the text (except the terminal interpolation) which *on stylistic grounds* requires us to suppose knowledge of any Gospel save Mk. The text

could not have been written by anyone who was not familiar with the tradition represented in Mk., but someone familiar with the Markan tradition could have written it—*so far as the style is concerned*—without knowing Mt., Lk., or Jn. This, I think, is as far as the stylistic evidence will take us. Accordingly, we now turn to the major parallels.

3. THE MAJOR PARALLELS TO THE CANONICAL GOSPELS

The major parallels differ from those already discussed either by size, being so long that it is difficult to explain them as chance collections of clichés, or by peculiarity of content, containing some unusual element which requires explanation. Since these distinctions are matters of degree, there will be differences of opinion as to which parallels should be discussed here.

To begin with, there are those parallels to the western text which seemed evidence for its dependence on the longer text of Mk.: καὶ ἔρχονται εἰς Βηθανίαν (II.23), καὶ ὀργισθείς (II.25), καὶ ἤρξατο παρακαλεῖν αὐτὸν ἵνα μετ' αὐτοῦ ᾖ (III.4–5), and possibly ἐξέτεινεν τὴν χεῖρα καὶ ἤγειρεν αὐτὸν κρατήσας τῆς χειρός (III.4) and ἐπέταξεν αὐτῷ ὁ 'Ιησοῦς (III.7). If these are evidence of the influence of the longer text of Mk., they throw no light on its origin, save to locate it before that of the western text (in other words, before 150?) and probably in the same area where the western text arose (Egypt?).

Next there are the similar (but reverse) cases where the present text of Clement's quotations seems to have been corrupted by the influence of the texts of the canonical Gospels: ἦν γὰρ πλούσιος in III.6 is the most likely example. καὶ προσελθών . . . ἀπεκύλισε τὸν λίθον ἀπὸ τῆς θύρας τοῦ μνημείου in III.1–2 may be another, but καὶ προσελθών is a cliché and the rest of the parallel is so fixed by content (and appears so late and so sparsely in the history of the canonical text) that no confidence as to the origin of the parallelism can be justified. In any event, such corruptions from the texts of the canonical Gospels are similar to those found in Clement's quotations from canonical Mk., as shown in Appendix F, and therefore yield no evidence as to the origin of the longer text, into which they were probably introduced by Clement himself or some later copyist (see above, section II.A, end).

Elimination of these leaves the following:

II.25   υἱὲ Δαβὶδ ἐλέησόν με (2 in Mk., 2 in Lk., 4 in Mt.)
III.4   ἐμβλέψας αὐτῷ ἠγάπησεν αὐτόν (Mk. 10.21)
III.5–6 καὶ μεθ' ἡμέρας ἕξ (Mk. 9.2)
III.8   περιβεβλημένος σινδόνα ἐπὶ γυμνοῦ (Mk. 14.51)
III.10   τὸ μυστήριον τῆς βασιλείας τοῦ θεοῦ (Mk. 4.11)
III.15   ὃν ἠγάπα αὐτὸν ὁ 'Ιησοῦς (4 in Jn.)

To these might be added III.3–4 καὶ ἤγειρεν αὐτὸν κρατήσας τῆς χειρός (Mk. 1.31) and καὶ ἐξελθόντες ἐκ τοῦ μνημείου (Mk. 16.8), but the parallels to these are only approximate, that to the former is found only in part of the textual tradition (אBL,

etc.), and all the elements of both are clichés, except for ἤγειρεν αὐτόν and τοῦ μνημείου, which are determined by content; accordingly these are not of the same class as the six listed above. Of those six, υἱὲ Δαυὶδ ἐλέησόν με, τὸ μυστήριον τῆς βασιλείας τοῦ θεοῦ, and ὃν ἠγάπα αὐτὸν ὁ ᾿Ιησοῦς probably were fixed phrases of early Christian tradition. (That the third did not come from John is indicated both by the general absence of Johannine traits from the longer text and by the fact that the form in the longer text preserves a Semitism, αὐτόν, which the Johannine form has eliminated.) The appearance of these fixed phrases in the longer text is no more evidence of imitation than it is of originality. But the other three, ἐμβλέψας αὐτῷ ἠγάπησεν αὐτόν, καὶ μεθ᾿ ἡμέρας ἕξ, and περιβεβλημένος σινδόνα ἐπὶ γυμνοῦ, are phrases of Markan narrative and their recurrence requires special explanations.

Explanations are suggested both by Mark's practice of self-repetition and by repetitions of Markan material in the earliest of the expanded texts of Mk. which are still preserved (that is, in Mt. and Lk.). As shown above, Mark frequently repeats individual words, narrative phrases, and basic sentence patterns. He also tells stories so much alike that they are generally thought different accounts of the same event (the feedings, the prophecies of the passion), but in these different accounts he does not usually duplicate exactly much of the wording. He often tells several stories of the same type and when he does so he is apt to use the same phrases for similar situations (see above, on ἐξέτεινεν τὴν χεῖρα and κρατήσας τῆς χειρός). Within individual stories he is fond of repeating phrases or even clauses (2.5,9,11,12,15,16, etc.; note in Appendix G, section IV, the parallels to Mk. 5 from Mk. 5 and 6). Finally, in different stories he will repeat striking phrases or entire sayings to indicate some connection between the different events: Mk. 1.11 ‖ 9.7 φωνὴ ἐγένετο . . . ὁ υἱός μου ὁ ἀγαπητός at baptism and transfiguration; 1.24 ‖ 5.7 τί ἡμῖν καὶ σοί, ᾿Ιησοῦ, the demons' confession; 4.9 ‖ 4.23 ‖ 7.16 ὃς ἔχει ὦτα ἀκούειν, ἀκουέτω, to indicate that something has been withheld; 5.31 ‖ 10.52 ἡ πίστις σου σέσωκέν σε; 5.43 ‖ 8.36 καὶ διεστείλατο αὐτοῖς . . . ἵνα μηδείς/μηδενί; 6.15 ‖ 8.28 ᾿Ιωάννης ὁ βαπτίζων . . . ἄλλοι . . . ᾿Ηλείας . . . ἄλλοι δέ . . . εἷς τῶν προφητῶν; 9.2 ‖ 14.33 παραλαμβάνει . . . τὸν Πέτρον καὶ τὸν ᾿Ιάκωβον καὶ τὸν ᾿Ιωάννην (cf. 5.37); 9.35 ‖ 10.44 εἴ τις θέλει πρῶτος εἶναι ἔσται πάντων . . . διάκονος. In most of these the MS tradition shows a tendency to eliminate differences between the parallels. A similar tendency may be supposed to have been at work in the transmission of the letter's quotations from the longer text. [However, as H.K. observes, the longer text was not copied so often as the canonical text and was not subject to the same theological, liturgical, and political pressures. It was therefore less exposed to contamination.]

Of these sorts of Markan repetition, the last is closest to what appears in ἐμβλέψας αὐτῷ ἠγάπησεν αὐτόν and περιβεβλημένος σινδόνα ἐπὶ γυμνοῦ. Particularly close to the latter is Mark's repetition of an OT formula in order to identify the Baptist as Elijah without stating the identification directly: Mk. 1.6 ἐνδεδυμένος . . . ζώνην δερματίνην περὶ τὴν ὀσφὺν αὐτοῦ; II Kgs. 1.8 ζώνην δερματίνην περιεζωσμένος περὶ τὴν ὀσφὺν αὐτοῦ.[2] If the περιβεβλημένος phrase be a formula connected with baptism (a question to

2. The omission of the Markan phrase by D*it*. does not seem to me to warrant the conclusion that it is an interpolation.

be discussed hereafter, in the section on content), then this method of identifying the two youths by their clothing as *baptizandi*, without stating the fact directly, is in Mark's manner. So would be the repetition of the temporal specification μεθ' ἡμέρας ἕξ, to equate the secret revelation given by the transfiguration with the teaching of the mystery of the kingdom of God (Mk. 9.2ff ‖ III.7–10); but here the parallelism may be due to some sabbatarian interest. Such repetitions both presuppose and expect exegesis of the sort known in the Hellenistic world as σύγκρισις πρὸς ἴσον and in the midrashim as *gezerah shawah* (on which see Lieberman, *Hellenism* 58ff), a technique which takes even minor identites of wording as indications of relations between the content of the passages concerned. Such use of repetition in Mk. is therefore important as an indication that the Gospel was expected to be a text for teaching and that (as Clement said in his letter, I.25) some things—in this case, the significance of the repetitions—were deliberately left to be explained by the teacher.

On the other hand, the repetition of ἐμβλέψας αὐτῷ ἠγάπησεν αὐτόν remains somewhat peculiar, because the action is attributed in Mk. 10.21 to Jesus and in the longer text to the youth in the tomb, whereas, of the above examples of Markan self-repetition, all are attributed to the same person except that in 6.15 (to the people) ‖ 8.28 (to the disciples—who, however, are reporting what the people say). Here the relation between Mk. and the longer text is more like that between Mk. and the later synoptics, from which Hawkins made a large collection of such "words differently applied" (*Horae* 67ff; cf. Dodd, *Historical Tradition* 331) which he considered evidence for oral, as against written, tradition. Of his examples, the closest is the parallel of Mk. 10.21, where Jesus says to the rich man (whom he loved) ἕν σε ὑστερεῖ, with Mt. 19.20, where the same man asks Jesus τί ἔτι ὑστερῶ; (though here the change is probably due to deliberate correction rather than oral tradition). In Acts we find stories, already told about Jesus in the Gospels, retold about Peter (Acts 9.33ff ‖ Mk. 2.3ff; 9.36ff ‖ Mk. 5.21ff), and even one of Jesus' miraculous commands put in the mouth of Peter (ταλιθα κουμι Mk. 5.41 ‖ Ταβειθα ἀνάστηθι Acts 9.40). Thus the change of speaker in the repetition of ἐμβλέψας αὐτῷ ἠγάπησεν αὐτόν suggests a relation between Mk. and the longer text similar to that between Mk. and Mt. or Acts. On the other hand, the use of ἠγάπησεν αὐτόν recalls John, for in Jn. Jesus' love of individuals and theirs of him is often mentioned; but in the synoptics, although ἀγαπάω is common, only 4 of its 27 uses refer to specific persons and only 2 of these may refer to Jesus (Mk. 10.21 and perhaps Lk. 7.47). However, neither the parallel to Jn. nor that to the relationship between Mk. and the later synoptics and Acts can be considered decisive. We must leave the problem open for the present, remarking only that, since ἀγαπάω *is* used of Jesus' personal relations in the synoptics, the usage cannot confidently be attributed to Johannine influence. Moreover, as remarked above, the ἐμβλέψας formula is a common Markan introduction. How much theory can safely be built on its recurrence with the two words ἠγάπησεν αὐτόν?

In sum, then, the major parallels between the longer text and canonical Mk. seem mostly due to textual contamination, either of the western text of Mk. by the influence of the longer text (5 possible instances) or of the longer text by the influence of Lk. and perhaps Mt. (2 possible instances). Of the 6 remaining major parallels,

4 (υἱὲ Δαβὶδ ἐλέησόν με, τὸ μυστήριον τῆς βασιλείας τοῦ θεοῦ, ὃν ἠγάπα αὐτὸν ὁ Ἰησοῦς, and περιβεβλημένος σινδόνα ἐπὶ γυμνοῦ) are probably phrases fixed in the usage of certain early Christian circles. Their repetition by the original author is no less likely than their use by an imitator; indeed, it can fairly be said that the repetition of such fixed phrases is a Markan trait. On the other hand, μεθ' ἡμέρας ἕξ is probably derived from a recurrent theological pattern and ἐμβλέψας αὐτῷ ἠγάπησεν αὐτόν remains a problem. Thus the evidence from the major parallels confirms that from the minor stylistic traits: it points almost always to Mk. as the source of the material, shows no strong reason to suppose knowledge of any other Gospel, and leaves the alternatives still open—either a free composition by the same school of tradition which produced canonical Mk., or an early imitation of material now found in the canonical Gospel. Again, too, the evidence slightly—but not decisively—inclines to the side of early imitation.

4. THE FREQUENCY OF PARALLELS TO THE CANONICAL GOSPELS

It remains to consider the frequency of parallels and their distribution in the material. This is an important question, for one of the commonest results of imitation is a product too much like the genuine article. Thus, among the strongest reasons for thinking the Epistle to the Ephesians a forgery are the facts that it parallels Colossians far more closely and in different places than any undoubtedly Pauline epistle parallels any other. Cognate questions are raised by the other cases of NT parallelism: the relationship of Jude to II Peter, of the transfiguration in II Peter and the last supper in I Cor. to those in the Gospels, and so on. These, together with the synoptics and their parallelism to Jn. have provided evidence for many different hypotheses. The hypothesis of deliberate imitation can appeal to the example of Ephesians and the clumsier Pastorals; Mt. and Lk. show several more or less faithful sorts of copying combined with omission of occasional passages and addition of material apparently from other traditions (though Parker, *Gospel*, has made a strong case for a close relationship of some of the Matthaean material to the tradition which produced Mk.); Jn. was variously interpreted as reworking of synoptic material or independent development of cognate traditions until Dodd, *Historical Tradition*, practically settled the question in favor of independent development. Reworking is seen again in II Peter's use of Jude, and independent development in the various stories of the transfiguration and last supper.

To choose between these hypotheses—and others also possible—it is necessary to determine the frequency, type, and distribution of the parallels between the longer text of Mk. and the canonical Gospels, and to compare these with the frequency, type, and distribution of the parallels between a similar passage of canonical Mk. and the canonical Gospels. Evidence on these points is given in Appendix G.

Unfortunately, Mk. does not afford an exact parallel even for the miracle story

in the longer text. Markan miracle stories are of several kinds, but none, in point of style, is exactly similar. Miracles told in connection with stories of legal arguments or of sayings are obviously irrelevant here, as are miracles of which Jesus is himself the subject (baptism, transfiguration) and miracles told only generally, in summary accounts of Jesus' work. The rest—the true miracle stories—fall into two groups distinguished by their style. Those of the one group are told verbosely, with much realistic detail, repetition of phrases, and so on; those of the other, briefly, almost in outline, with little more than the necessary data–occasion, parties concerned, trouble, and means of relief (Dibelius, *Structure* 158–163; Dodd, *Appearances* 9–10).

Of the first of these two groups, the story of the Gerasene demoniac has been chosen for comparison with the longer text because of the many similarities between the two—similarities pointed out in Parker's preliminary report. Of the second group the story of Peter's wife's mother has been chosen, also because of its parallels: ἐκ . . . ἐξελθόντες ἦλθον εἰς τὴν οἰκίαν . . . καὶ εὐθύς . . . καὶ προσελθὼν ἤγειρεν αὐτὴν κρατήσας τῆς χειρός.

Comparison of the ways in which these two stories are paralleled by the rest of the material in the Gospels with the ways in which the longer text is so paralleled reveals: (1) There are more parallels to the longer text than to the canonical texts. (2) Conversely, the longer text has less of the peculiar details which individualize the canonical stories. (3) The elements paralleled in the longer text are usually longer and more significant; many of the parallels to the canonical text are little more than elements of vocabulary (διὰ τό with infinitive, ὑπ' αὐτοῦ, διὰ παντός, etc.), while in the longer text whole phrases are paralleled. (4) In the canonical texts the parallels are chiefly to transitional formulas, elements of framework at the beginnings and ends, technical phrases (πνεῦμα ἀκάθαρτον, the formula for exorcism, etc.), and an occasional fixed saying like τί ἐμοὶ καὶ σοί, 'Ιησοῦ, which evidently circulated in the tradition since variants of it turn up in various stories. In the longer text not only the transitional formulas and framework, but also the main narrative elements are mostly paralleled; the parallels continue throughout the stories, and the number and individual length of the paralleled technical expressions and fixed sayings is conspicuously higher.

These differences must not be exaggerated. Canonical Mk. sometimes does, briefly, parallel itself very closely. Consider, for instance, Mk. 8.22–24: καὶ φέρουσιν αὐτῷ τυφλὸν καὶ παρακαλοῦσιν αὐτὸν ἵνα αὐτοῦ ἅψηται καὶ ἐπιλαβόμενος τῆς χειρὸς τοῦ τυφλοῦ ἐξήνεγκεν αὐτὸν ἔξω τῆς κώμης καὶ πτύσας εἰς τὰ ὄμματα αὐτοῦ, ἐπιθεὶς τὰς χεῖρας αὐτῷ, ἐπηρώτα αὐτόν, εἴ τι βλέπεις; καὶ ἀναβλέψας ἔλεγεν. Here the underlined words are paralleled (solid, verbatim; dotted, approximately) in Mk. 7.32–34, the cure of the deaf mute. Nevertheless, even in these stories there are peculiar details— the men as trees walking, the use of ἐφφαθα—which individualize the episode, as the cure of Peter's wife's mother is individualized by the specification of the parties concerned. In the more verbose Markan stories, like that of the Gerasene demoniac, such peculiar material is conspicuous. (Therefore only the first sixteen verses of that story have been presented in Appendix G; they suffice to show the difference.)

The lifelike details and realistic verbosity of Markan narrative are commonly supposed to be primitive traits, and primitive they certainly are vis-à-vis Mt. and Lk., who frequently eliminated them. It is not sure, however, that they were primitive in relation to oral tradition. Their realistic details can no longer be taken as evidence of eyewitness tradition and are suspiciously like the developments in later apocryphal Gospels (Nineham, *Eyewitness* 22). Dibelius, *Structure* 161, 165f, has maintained on literary grounds that the full Markan miracle stories are secondary expansions of earlier, brief ones. [In this he may be mistaken, H.K. remarks; it is possible that the full and the schematic stories represent equally old traditions from different circles of narrators.] However, if Dibelius were right, we should expect that the formulas of the earlier, schematic accounts would turn up again and again in the framework of the later expansions. Now, as already noted, it is the framework of the Markan stories for which there is a plethora of parallels, like that found for the longer text. Accordingly, the multiple parallels to the longer text can be explained in at least two ways: either this is material earlier than canonical Mk., simpler and more schematic—perhaps a text connected with some important ritual and therefore widely echoed; or this is later than canonical Mk. and shows the Markan phraseology still being used, but in formulaic fashion, as we find it especially in Mt.—the fixed formulas are preserved and the story is told almost entirely in these, the individualistic details having disappeared.

Of these two explanations the first is supported by Clement's statement that the longer text was used in "the great mysteries," and also by the evidence that it has frequently influenced the western text. However, the second explanation is supported by Clement's statement that the longer text was produced by expansion of canonical Mk., and also by the analogy of the existing synoptic Gospels which were so produced.

The analogy is particularly close for certain sections of Mt., which show the same sort of formulaic narration, and have the same plethora of parallels, as does the longer text of Mk. Most conspicuous of these Matthaean passages is 9.27–34, presented in section V of Appendix G, which shows all the secondary traits pointed out above as characteristic of the longer text: It has almost no individualizing details, the elements paralleled are often of considerable length, the parallels are not limited to transitional elements, but continue throughout, and they contain not a few fixed sayings like ἐλέησον ἡμᾶς, υἱὸς Δαυίδ. Nevertheless, Dodd has made a strong case (in *Historical Tradition* 170f) for supposing 9.27–31 an original composition, independent of its Markan parallels and based on a variant form of oral tradition. Other passages in Mt. which present similar problems are 12.22–24 and 21.14–16. Richardson points out the sending of the seventy in Lk. 10.1–20—a striking example, but one not included in Appendix G because it draws principally on material from the sayings tradition, whereas Clement's quotations from the longer text are entirely narrative (though he says that the longer text also contained sayings—λόγιά τινα, I.25).

Given this similarity of type between Mt. 9.27–34 and the longer text of Mk., it is important to notice that most of the parallels to the Mt. passage are found in Mt., most of the parallels to the longer text are found in Mk. The figures are as follows:

To Mt. 9.27–34:   Mt. 74,   Mk. 25,   Lk. 21,   Jn. 38.
To the longer text:[3]   Mt. 84,   Mk. 143,   Lk. 68,   Jn. 33.

This evidence is even more impressive when the different sizes of the Gospels are recalled (Mt. 18,300 words; Mk. 11,200; Lk. 19,400; Jn. 15,400). Given these figures there can be no doubt of the peculiarly close relation of the longer text to the Markan tradition.

The longer text, without the final interpolation (to which, by the way, there are *no* verbatim Gospel parallels), contains 175 words, for which Appendix G shows 328 parallels. Mt. 9.27–34 contains 112 words, for which there are 158 parallels. Thus the extent of parallelism to the longer text is substantially higher. This may be in-significant, since 99 of the parallels to the longer text are afforded by the three phrases καὶ εὐθύς (27), καὶ ἐλθοῦσα (22), and τῆς βασιλείας τοῦ θεοῦ (50), whereas Mt. 9.27–34 has only one phrase for which the figure is above the teens (λέγει αὐτοῖς ὁ Ἰησοῦς, 42).

The high frequency of parallels in the longer text affords support for a special theory of imitation which has been suggested independently by P. Benoit and R. Grant, viz.: The longer text is a cento produced from the texts of the canonical Gospels. Grant supports this theory by reference to Irenaeus (Harvey, I.1.15–20 = Stieren, I.8.1–9.5). Irenaeus is there attacking the Valentinians. He says that, since they have a theory which neither the prophets proclaimed nor the Lord taught nor the apostles handed down, but which they read out of ἄγραφα (that is, uncanonical works, Harvey), they try to twist dominical, prophetic, or apostolic sayings to fit their teach-ings, so as to have some evidence for what they say, and to this end they neglect the order and context of the scriptural passages they use and also distort them. He com-pares their treatment of Scripture to the breaking up of a mosaic in order to make a different picture with the same tessarae. The examples he gives to illustrate this, however, are examples of allegorical or esoteric exegesis of individual sayings or passages of the canonical Scriptures and afford no evidence for the composition of new, pseudo-Scriptural centos. However, he goes on to say (Harvey, I.1.20, middle = Stieren, I.9.4): "Then, collecting scattered expressions and terms, they transfer them, as we said, from the ⟨sense they have⟩ in reality to an unreal ⟨sense⟩ much as do those who set themselves any handy themes and then try to treat them in lines from the Homeric poems, so that less experienced readers might think Homer had com-posed the verses about the themes treated *ex tempore*." This he illustrates by an ex-ample of a Homeric cento, excusing himself by saying, "There is no reason not to cite even such verses, since both ⟨the composer of the cento and the Valentinians⟩ are attempting a similar and, indeed, identical feat." And he concludes that, as the man acquainted with Homer will recognize the verses, but not the theme, and by referring the verses to their proper contexts will show the theme to be spurious, thus

---

3. When alternate numbers of parallels to phrases in the longer text are given in Appendix G, the lower ones have been counted, since the higher reflect readings with weaker MS support and these are not commonly reported by Moulton-Geden, from which the numbers of parallels to the Matthaean passage have been derived for comparison.

the true Christian "will recognize the terms from the scriptures and the expressions and the parables, but will not recognize this blasphemous theme." He will acknowledge the tessarae, but not the picture which has been made of them, "and, referring each of the things said to its proper place and fitting it into the body of the truth, he will expose their fiction and show it to be unsubstantial."

On the strength of this passage, Grant has suggested that the longer text may be a gnostic work of the sort attacked by Irenaeus. However, the longer text has no connection with the Valentinians, and though it was used by the Carpocratians it was also used by Clement's church, which is commonly supposed to have been orthodox. Clement expressly asserts that the Carpocratians got it from the orthodox (that is, from his church), and nothing in the text is clearly gnostic. Therefore there is no reason to associate the text with the Valentinian centos, unless it can be shown to be a cento, which is the point in question. Further, the text of Irenaeus does not precisely say that the Valentinians made centos. Irenaeus may have intended to give that impression. [But in the opinion of E.B. he actually had in mind compositions like the Qumran hymns, which are full of OT echoes but are not true centos. He introduced the bit of cento merely to give his Greek readers the best example he could of the sort of thing he had in mind.] At all events he does not explicitly state that the Valentinians made centos, and—what is most important—he does not produce and demolish any Valentinian cento. This suggests that *either* he had no such document and was merely using the comparison as a reductio ad absurdum of their neglect of context in exegesis, *or* he had a Valentinian Gospel which paralleled the canonical Gospels in many places and which he wished to discredit, so he charged that it was a cento but did not give an example from it for fear of discrediting his charge.

On the other hand Irenaeus (Harvey I.20.2 = Stieren, I.25.4) quotes a Carpocratian version of the counsel to be reconciled quickly with one's adversary, which alternately parallels Mt. 5.25 and Lk. 12.58 in a way that can be interpreted as deliberate choice of elements suited for Carpocratian exegesis (Grant-Freedman, 95). And Dodd, *New Gospel* 24ff, has practically proved that the text on fragment 1 verso of *P. Egerton 2* is a cento of Jn. 5.39,45 and 9.29. The cento form goes back in Greek tradition at least to Aristophanes, *Pax* 1090–1094, and appears in the OT with the psalms in Chronicles and Jonah. So the possibility that the longer text was produced as a cento is undeniable. And there is no necessity of connecting the cento form with the gnostics: Paul used it in Rom. 3.11–18; Tatian's *Diatessaron*, the most famous example of the form, was not a gnostic work; and even Mt. and Lk. could be considered, loosely, as centos compiled from Mk., Q, and other sources. So the question of form and method of composition need not be confused by introducing the question of doctrinal affiliation.

In favor of the cento theory is the high frequency of parallelism and particularly the frequency of the long parallels discussed above. Against it, however, are the following facts: (1) Some elements of the longer text are not paralleled from the canonical Gospels, which would be impossible were it a true cento of the canonical texts. (2) The great majority of the parallels are brief formulas, most of them used

many times in the canonical Gospels and more likely to have been put together freely by an imitator than to have been picked out laboriously from here and there by the compiler of a cento. (3) The text cannot be made up by drawing elements from only two or three stories; to suppose it a cento, one must also suppose that the author derived his scraps from practically every chapter of Mk., to say nothing of the other Gospels—not a likely procedure, especially in antiquity, when most writers, even in citing explicitly, cited from memory.[4] (4) Many details in the text do not look as if they had been produced by the compiler of a cento; see, for examples, the notes on προσεκύνησε in II.24; νεανίσκος, III.3; κρατήσας τῆς χειρός, III.3–4, and καὶ ἐξελθόντες ἐκ τοῦ μνημείου, III.6. (5) The text is too well constructed and economical to be a cento: there are no irrelevant details, every word comes naturally in its place, the narration moves without delays or jumps. Possibly some leisured litterateur might have succeeded in piecing together such a text from the phrases available in the canonical Gospels, but the easier explanation is to suppose it a free composition. (6) The hypothesis that the text is a cento requires the supposition that someone went to great pains to imitate the style of Mk. as closely as possible, since making a cento is the most laborious, but the closest, kind of imitation. But the longer text is datable, by external evidence, before 125 (see above, section I of this chapter) and at this date Mk.'s prestige was not high enough to motivate this sort of imitation. Matthew and Luke, in their expansions of Mk., made no attempt to imitate his style. Jn. and the earlier apocryphal gospels (Hebrews, Thomas, Egyptians, Peter) show no considerable effort to imitate synoptic style. [E.B. remarks that almost none of the early apocryphal Gospels are even attributed to canonical authors.] So to suppose the longer text a cento would be to suppose it a work unparalleled and unlikely in its time. (7) Finally, it is worth recalling the considerations which led Dodd (New Gospel 35ff), after he had proved that one fragment of P. Egerton 2 was a cento, to conclude that the rest was not (a conclusion he has now reasserted more strongly in Historical Tradition 328 n2). He observed that the attempt to explain all variations of early Christian traditions as editorial rehandling of written sources had been discredited by form criticism, which had demonstrated the oral prehistory of the written material and the possibility that variations might have arisen in the oral period. He found evidence of the realization of this possibility in the story of the centurion's servant in Mt. and Lk. and the nobleman's son in Jn.—undoubtedly the same story, yet in forms so different that literary dependence seemed to him unlikely. In the unparalleled elements of P. Egerton 2 he found evidence that the author was using sources other than the canonical Gospels; he therefore concluded that the divergent forms of canonical

---

4. Compare the remarks of J. Pouilloux in Fondation Hardt, Entretiens sur l'antiquité classique, X, Archiloque, Vandoeuvres-Genève, 1963, 172f, on the use of Homeric formulas by Archilochus and the imitation of Homer by Apollonius Rhodius. Apollonius never draws on the whole of the Homeric poems at once, but imitates one passage at a time, whereas the poems of Archilochus are made up almost entirely of Homeric formulas and variations of Homeric formulas, but the formulas come from all parts of the poems and no one passage is imitated. Archilochus was composing freely in the Homeric tradition, as D. Page showed in the paper (Archilochus and the Oral Tradition, 119ff) which Pouilloux was discussing. The longer text is related to Mk. as Archilochus to Homer, not as Apollonius.

stories which *P. Egerton 2* contained were probably also derived from noncanonical sources. And he remarked in conclusion that "as the number of apocryphal Gospel documents increases, it becomes less and less plausible to suppose that they all originated in expansions of material derived from the canonical Gospels" (p. 48). These arguments Dodd has now, in *Historical Tradition*, greatly developed and applied at length to the study of the Johannine problem. Much of his reasoning therein is applicable, mutatis mutandis, to the present case.

If, for the reasons just given, we reject the cento theory, we are left with the alternative previously proposed between free imitation and independent composition in style fixed by the Markan tradition—that tradition of which, by this hypothesis, different elements would appear in the stories of both the canonical and the longer texts. Perhaps, however, the alternative between "imitation" and "composition in traditional style" is false. As remarked above, at this early date "imitation" can hardly have been deliberate faking—Mk.'s prestige was not yet so high as to motivate a forger. "Imitation," therefore, would have been a conscious effort to perpetuate the style of the Markan tradition to which the writer was evidently attached, to express in the traditional phraseology the material now being written down, and to attach it to already written stories by the established Markan technique of repeating phrases as cross references. But this would be practically the same thing as "composition in traditional style."

A similar problem is posed by the remains of early Greek oral poetry which, like the synoptics, was largely written in fixed formulas. The relations of poetic compositions of this sort and the history of their gradual reduction to writing have been elucidated by Parry (*Studies*), Lord (*Singer*), and Notopoulos (*Homer*; *Hymns*). Parry's formulaic analysis of the beginning of the *Iliad* is given at the end of Appendix G; its similarity to the preceding analyses of Gospel material is obvious. Notopoulos, *Hymns* 343–347, is particularly interesting for the question of transition from free development to exact memorization and written preservation.

5. CONCLUSIONS FROM THE STYLISTIC EVIDENCE

With the phenomena of oral literature in mind, we can see the literary problem before us as that of placing the longer text in relation to the other remains of a tradition which was only gradually being fixed in writing. For this purpose, let us review the evidence presented by the preceding stylistic study: (1) The longer text contains nothing which Mark could not have written—nothing incompatible with the canonical Gospel or without analogy there—except for the final clause of the second quotation, a clause which seems a later addition. (2) Its vocabulary is largely neutral—made up of words used by all the evangelists—but insofar as it inclines toward the vocabulary of any of the Gospels it is Markan (29 words in a list of 82). (3) Its phraseology is predominantly Markan (18 items out of a list of 33, in which 9 of the remaining 15 are neutral). (4) Its grammatical peculiarities, in relation to Gospel usage, are few and mostly Markan. (5) It is connected with the canonical text of Mk. by 6 major parallels, of which 4 are peculiar to Mk. On the contrary, of the major parallels which might seem to connect it with other Gospels, none affords convincing evidence. (6)

It has far more parallels to Mk. than to any other Gospel. (7) It contains nothing which necessitates a supposition that the author knew any canonical Gospel other than Mk. On the other hand: (8) It uses only 3 non-Markan words, whereas an equally long section of canonical Mk. might be expected to use 10 (though the section actually tested used only 4). (9) It contains more Markan clauses found in other sections of Mk. than would an equally long section of canonical Mk. (10) Besides these long clauses, it has many more minor parallels to phrases of the canonical Gospels than would an equal section of canonical Mk., and these parallels are individually longer and are distributed more evenly throughout the text than they would be in a section of canonical Mk. (11) In these last three characteristics (8, 9, and 10) it resembles Mt., and particularly Mt. 9.27–34. (12) But there are a few small pieces of evidence (commentary on προσεκύνησεν, II.24, on καὶ προσελθὼν ἀπεκύλισε, III.1 and on καὶ ἦσαν ἐκεῖ, III.15) which suggest—but do not suffice to prove—that it was known to Mt.

Of the points above, 8–11 all are aspects of one essential fact, the plethora of parallelism. This has been said to admit of two explanations—either that the piece was early and widely imitated, or that it was late and highly imitative. Point 11, the similarity to Mt., is prima facie evidence for a late date; point 12, the evidence suggesting it was known to Mt., for an early one. Both possibilities remain open, though the later date has the strong support of the tradition reported by Clement— that the longer text was an expansion—and the analogy to the other synoptics. The longer text would then be an expansion of Mk. by addition of further material from the Markan tradition, as Mt. and Lk. were expansions of Mk. by addition of further material from the Q tradition and other traditions accessible to their respective editors.

As for the date of the longer text: there seems to be no stylistic evidence indicating any date later than that of Mt. A date somewhere between canonical Mk. and Mt. is suggested not only by the evidence for Mt.'s use of it, but also by the consideration that an expansion of Mk. with material from the Markan tradition might be expected to have preceded expansions with alien material. But this consideration has little more than rhetorical plausibility to recommend it. A much stronger reason for an early date is the absence of any clear evidence of knowledge of any Gospel save Mk. Mt. and Lk. seem to have eclipsed Mk. early (to judge from the *indices locorum* of the apostolic fathers and the apologists), so it is unlikely that an author writing long after their composition should have drawn chiefly on Mk., and it is almost incredible that, had he known Mt. and Lk., he should not have left in his phraseology many unmistakable traces of his knowledge. But the only strong argument for supposing knowledge of Lk. (apart from the terminal interpolation) is ἦν γὰρ πλούσιος, and its isolation makes it easier to explain as a corruption of the text than as an original element. (If original, why isolated?) There is no strong argument for supposing knowledge of Mt. Nor is there any valid stylistic evidence to indicate knowledge of Jn. (and it will be shown below that the similarities of content do not indicate such knowledge).

Finally, to this stylistic study of the longer text must be added the statement that the above conclusions are by no means conclusive. The quoted fragments are so

short that it would be foolhardy to take them as fairly representative of the lost material, or to build on the stylistic data which they afford any considerable theory. Metzger, *Reconsideration*, and Cadbury, *Dilemma*, have argued that the evidence afforded by the Pauline corpus is inadequate to settle the problem of the authenticity of Ephesians. A fortiori . . .. Perhaps even more in point is the case of the *pericope adulterae*, of which Cadbury's discussion (*Case*) leads to results so pertinent for the present investigation that I summarize the article here: Lk. "has the most distinctive vocabulary of any New Testament writer, and a style so individual as to be recognizable in nearly every verse." And in the *pericope adulterae* "there are a few unquestioned words that are really characteristic of Luke," as ἀπὸ τοῦ νῦν, ἄρχομαι ἀπό, ἐπιμένω, εἶπεν δέ, ὡς (= when). And besides these there are a number of Lucan expressions attested by some, but not all, MSS, and of expressions thought to be Lucan, but perhaps limited to Luke-Acts by mere accident. Ergo, "it can safely be affirmed that the passage in its oldest form contained as much distinctively Lucan language as the average passage of equal brevity and simplicity in Luke's acknowledged works." However, the best MSS omit the passage altogether, and when it is found it is almost always located in Jn. 8 or at the end of Jn. The Ferrar group alone places it after Lk. 21.38. Therefore: "Either (1) the *pericope adulterae* is an original part of Luke's Gospel and was omitted without leaving any appreciable trace in the MS tradition of that Gospel, or (2) it is written by another than the third evangelist in a style that completely matches his own . . . If the first solution is the correct one, then we must believe that in spite of their age, multiplicity and agreement, our authorities for the New Testament text do not preclude such radical divergence from the autographs as the complete omission of a considerable section from one of the four Gospels . . . Here, . . . we should have a flagrant case of primitive tampering, for the omission could only be intentional . . . If, on the other hand, the passage is not from the pen of the *auctor ad Theophilum*, then some one . . . wrote a style that is indistinguishable from the most distinctive of New Testament styles. In this case style proves to be a most unreliable criterion, and all critical arguments drawn from identity of style—such as the common authorship of John and I John, of Luke and Acts, of the Pauline letters, and even of the separate parts of a single work—lose some of their weight."

Since stylistic arguments are thus inconclusive, we turn to questions of content.

III. Structural relations to sections of the canonical gospels

A. *Other miracle stories of the same type*

In discussing the verbal parallels to the longer text we have already mentioned its similarity in content to the stories of the Gerasene demoniac and of Peter's wife's mother. Parker, in his preliminary report, called particular attention to the former and pointed out a series of details in which it resembled the story in the longer text.

To estimate the significance of these similarities, we must consider the extent to which the stories in the canonical Gospels are also similar to each other. Fortunately, not all of the stories need be considered, since the resurrection reported in the longer text belongs to a readily recognizable class—that of miracles performed in response to intercession.

One of the historical traits of the Gospels is their account of the revelation of divine power in Jesus as spatially limited; later legend may represent it as bursting on distant strangers (the shepherds, the magi) or producing a general resurrection of the deserving dead (Mt. 27.52); but in the stories which approach historicity, miracles happen when the patients are somehow brought to Jesus' attention or touch his person. Therefore either the patient must bring himself to Jesus' person or attention, or an intercessor must act on his behalf. Accordingly, most of the miracle stories fall into these two classes (the chief exceptions being miracles in which Jesus himself is the patient—the baptism, transfiguration, resurrection, etc.). The class of miracles in response to intercession comprises the following stories and their parallels: Mk. 1.30ff (Peter's wife's mother); 4.35ff (stilling the storm); 5.22ff (Jaïrus' daughter); 7.25ff (the Syrophoenician's daughter); 9.14ff (the demoniac boy); Lk. 7.2ff (the centurion's slave); Jn. 2.1ff (the miracle at Cana); 4.46ff (the nobleman's son); 11.1ff (Lazarus). The intercession may be more or less explicit: Jn. 2.1ff is a borderline case; also marginal are Lk. 7.18ff; Mk. 6.35ff—contrast 8.1ff and Jn. 6.5ff—and Mk. 9.1ff. All these stories necessarily follow a single basic pattern: situation, intercession, response, miracle. The pattern is found elsewhere, too—with Mk. 7.25ff and 9.14ff cf. Philostratus, *Vita Apollonii* III.38. It is obviously useful for resurrections of the dead, though not necessary—one corpse came to meet Jesus (Lk. 7.11ff) as another met Apollonius (IV.45). Accordingly, among the nine stories listed above there are two resurrections (Jaïrus' daughter, Lazarus) and two hairbreadth escapes (the centurion's slave, the nobleman's son). Most of these stories begin with the intercessor's coming to Jesus, and in three of them the intercessor is a woman (the Syrophoenician, the miracle at Cana, Lazarus). Often, moreover, the similarities go far beyond these basic structural elements. For instance, consider the parallels between the Markan story of Jaïrus' daughter and the Johannine story of Lazarus:

The patient is not dead, at first, but only sick.
The intercessors arrive and beseech Jesus.
Jesus' coming is delayed; the patient meanwhile dies.
Jesus declares the dead asleep but is misunderstood.
He reassures the relatives and demands that they believe.
The intercessor falls at his feet.
He sees the mourners weeping and *is angry* or puts them out.
The mourners do not believe he will be able to raise the dead.
He then goes to the body.
He calls the dead by name or title and orders him or her to arise or come forth.
In response to his command the dead arises and walks.
Jesus gives directions for further treatment.

Of all these parallels between the Lazarus story and that of Jaïrus' daughter, only the ones underlined are also found clearly stated in the longer text of Mk. By way of contrast with these it is worthwhile to list the similarities of the resurrection story in the longer text of Mk. to the stories of the Gerasene demoniac and Jaïrus' daughter:

Gerasene demoniac	Jaïrus' daughter
Jesus arrives	intercessor
is met	falls at his feet
man from the tomb	beseeches him
προσκυνεῖν with accusative	ἀπῆλθεν μετ' αὐτοῦ
φωνῇ μεγάλῃ	trouble with disciples
nudity (?), clothing	Jesus comes to house
return to house	is angered (?)
παρεκάλει αὐτὸν	goes in to corpse
ἵνα μετ' αὐτοῦ ᾖ	κρατῆσας τῆς χειρός
	raises the dead

Neither of these lists of parallels is so full as the list of those between the raising of Jaïrus' daughter and the Lazarus story. Consequently there is no need to think that the story in the longer text has any closer relation to that of the Gerasene demoniac or of Jaïrus' daughter than the latter does to the Lazarus story. Since *all* these stories (and the others of the same type, listed above) so often parallel both the longer text and each other, it is both unnecessary and unlikely to suppose the longer text modeled on any *one* of them. They are all examples of a familiar type of ancient miracle story and their similarities of content and structure (and sometimes even of phrasing) are to be explained as consequences of their common type, not as traces of literary dependence.

B. *The Lazarus story*

However, within this type, the resurrection story in the longer text is particularly close to that of Lazarus. Admittedly there are important differences between them, as Parker pointed out in his report: one sister instead of two, nameless characters, the cry from the tomb, Jesus' rolling away the stone and himself raising the youth. But similar differences are to be found, for instance, even between such synoptic parallels as the healing of blind Bartimaeus in Mk. 10.46 and the healings of two nameless blind men in Mt. 9.27ff and 20.29ff. And besides synoptic parallels, the Gospels are remarkable for the frequency with which the stories they contain seem to be different versions of the same story. First there are the unmistakable Johannine parallels to synoptic accounts—the cleansing of the temple, the feeding of the multitude, the walking on the waves, the anointing and the passion story. Whether these result from literary dependence or from common tradition is a matter of well-known

and unending dispute, but literary dependence has come to seem the less likely explanation (Haenchen, *Probleme*, and now Dodd, *Historical Tradition*). Next, there are many more remote, but unmistakable, parallels which can best be explained as divergent forms of the same tradition: the call of the first four disciples in Lk. and that in Mk.-Mt.; the miraculous draft of fishes in Lk. and in Jn.; the rejection at Nazareth in Lk. and in Mk.-Mt.; the centurion's slave in Mt.-Lk. and the nobleman's son in Jn.; the anointing in Lk. and in Mk.-Mt.; Peter's confession in Jn. and the synoptics; the parables of the pounds and talents in Mt. and Lk.; the feedings of the multitude in Mk. (where two different versions are found in a single Gospel); the sendings of the twelve and the seventy (here the two different versions are both in Lk.); the gift of the power to bind and loose, in Jn. and Mt. (here two versions in Mt.); the demand for a sign and the Beelzebub charge (also two versions in Mt.); the passion stories in Lk. and in Mk.-Mt. How far this variation may go, it is hard to say. Richardson, for instance, thinks the ten lepers of Lk. 17.11ff a gentile development of that story of which an earlier version appears in Mk. 1.40ff. The transfiguration has often been thought a version of some resurrection story (recently by Carlston, *Transfiguration*, but cf. Burkill, *Revelation* 160f and n117; Dodd, *Appearances* 25 and *Close, passim*; Bultmann, *Geschichte* 65; etc.; an interesting classification of the material is found in Strömsholm, *Examination* 255f). Even more—and yet more remote—examples will be found in Dodd, *Historical Tradition*, especially in part II, ch. 1, pp. 315–334.

We shall come back later to the question of more remote relations, when we consider the parallels between the Lazarus story and the stories of Jesus' resurrection. Here it is enough to have established that this sort of relation is typical of Gospel material and is found within each of the synoptics, and between any two of the synoptics, and between each of the synoptics and Jn. Indeed, related stories are so numerous that a more cautious and convincing type of form criticism might have resulted from the study, not of types of stories, but of these cases, in which comparison might make it possible to determine rather precisely the developments. See, for example, how the following analysis of the Johannine Lazarus story, as indicated by the longer text, differs from the analyses proposed by Bultmann, *Johannes, ad loc.*, and by Wilkens, *Erweckung*.

Comparison of the Lazarus story in Jn. with that in the longer text of Mk. must begin with the observation already made by Parker, that both occur at the same place in Jesus' career. Jesus has gone up from Galilee to Judea, and thence to Transjordan. Therefore it is worthwhile to begin with the parallel between Jn. 10.40 and canonical Mk. 10.1 and go on from this to the Lazarus story:

MARK

10.1 καὶ ἐκεῖθεν ἀναστὰς ἔρχεται εἰς τὰ ὅρια τῆς Ἰουδαίας καὶ πέραν τοῦ Ἰορδάνου, καὶ συνπορεύονται πάλιν ὄχλοι πρὸς αὐτόν, καὶ ὡς εἰώθει πάλιν ἐδίδασκεν αὐτούς.

JOHN *10.40–11.54*

40 Καὶ ἀπῆλθεν πάλιν πέραν τοῦ Ἰορδάνου εἰς τὸν τόπον ὅπου ἦν Ἰωάννης τὸ πρῶτον βαπτίζων, 41 καὶ ἔμενεν ἐκεῖ. καὶ πολλοὶ ἦλθον πρὸς αὐτὸν καὶ ἔλεγον ὅτι Ἰωάννης μὲν σημεῖον ἐποίησεν οὐδέν, πάντα δὲ ὅσα εἶπεν Ἰωάννης περὶ τούτου

40. πρωτον] προτερον p⁴⁵ℵΘ f13 al it

.2–12 dispute on divorce
.13–16 blessing children
.17–23 the rich young ruler
.24–31 sayings on rewards

.32 ἦσαν δὲ ἐν τῇ ὁδῷ ἀναβαίνοντες εἰς Ἱεροσόλυμα, καὶ ἦν προάγων αὐτοὺς ὁ Ἰησοῦς,
καὶ ἐθαμβοῦντο, οἱ δὲ ἀκολουθοῦντες ἐφοβοῦντο. καὶ παραλαβὼν πάλιν τοὺς δώδεκα
ἤρξατο αὐτοῖς λέγειν τὰ μέλλοντα αὐτῷ
.33 συμβαίνειν, ὅτι Ἰδοὺ ἀναβαίνομεν εἰς Ἱεροσόλυμα, καὶ ὁ υἱὸς τοῦ ἀνθρώπου παραδο-
θήσεται τοῖς ἀρχιερεῦσιν καὶ τοῖς γραμματεῦ-
σιν, καὶ κατακρινοῦσιν αὐτὸν θανάτῳ καὶ
παραδώσουσιν αὐτὸν τοῖς ἔθνεσιν καὶ ἐμ-
.34 παίξουσιν αὐτῷ καὶ ἐμπτύσουσιν αὐτῷ καὶ
μαστιγώσουσιν αὐτὸν

καὶ ἀποκτενοῦσιν,
καὶ μετὰ τρεῖς ἡμέρας ἀναστήσεται

42 ἀληθῆ ἦν. καὶ πολλοὶ ἐπίστευσαν εἰς αὐτὸν ἐκ

11 Ἦν δέ τις ἀσθενῶν, Λάζαρος ἀπὸ Βηθανία
ἐκ τῆς κώμης Μαρίας καὶ Μάρθας τῆς ἀδελφ
2 αὐτῆς. ἦν δὲ Μαριαμ ἡ ἀλείψασα τὸν Κύρ
μύρῳ καὶ ἐκμάξασα τοὺς πόδας αὐτοῦ ταῖς θρι
3 αὐτῆς, ἧς ὁ ἀδελφὸς Λάζαρος ἠσθένει. ἀπέστ
λαν οὖν αἱ ἀδελφαὶ πρὸς αὐτὸν λέγουσαι, Κύρ
4 ἴδε ὃν φιλεῖς ἀσθενεῖ. ἀκούσας δὲ ὁ Ἰησο
εἶπεν, Αὕτη ἡ ἀσθένεια οὐκ ἔστιν πρὸς θάνατ
ἀλλ' ὑπὲρ τῆς δόξης τοῦ Θεοῦ, ἵνα δοξασθῇ
5 Υἱὸς τοῦ Θεοῦ δι' αὐτῆς. ἠγάπα δὲ ὁ Ἰησοῦς τ
Μάρθαν καὶ τὴν ἀδελφὴν αὐτῆς καὶ τὸν Λάζαρ
6 ὡς οὖν ἤκουσεν ὅτι ἀσθενεῖ, τότε μὲν ἔμεινεν
7 ᾧ ἦν τόπῳ δύο ἡμέρας· ἔπειτα μετὰ τοῦτο λέ
τοῖς μαθηταῖς, Ἄγωμεν εἰς τὴν Ἰουδαίαν πάλ
8 λέγουσιν αὐτῷ οἱ μαθηταί, Ῥαββεί, νῦν ἐζήτο
σε λιθάσαι οἱ Ἰουδαῖοι, καὶ πάλιν ὑπάγεις ἐκε
9 ἀπεκρίθη Ἰησοῦς, Οὐχὶ δώδεκα ὧραί εἰσιν τ
ἡμέρας; ἐάν τις περιπατῇ ἐν τῇ ἡμέρᾳ, οὐ προ
κόπτει, ὅτι τὸ φῶς τοῦ κόσμου τούτου βλέπ
10 ἐὰν δέ τις περιπατῇ ἐν τῇ νυκτί, προσκόπτει, ὅ
τὸ φῶς οὐκ ἔστιν ἐν αὐτῷ.

11 ταῦτα εἶπεν, καὶ μετὰ
τοῦτο λέγει αὐτοῖς, Λάζαρος ὁ φίλος ἡμῶν κεκο
μηται· ἀλλὰ πορεύομαι ἵνα ἐξυπνίσω αὐτό
12 εἶπαν οὖν οἱ μαθηταὶ αὐτῷ, Κύριε, εἰ κεκοίμητα
13 σωθήσεται. εἰρήκει δὲ ὁ Ἰησοῦς περὶ τοῦ θαν
του αὐτοῦ· ἐκεῖνοι δὲ ἔδοξαν ὅτι περὶ τῆς κοιμ
14 σεως τοῦ ὕπνου λέγει. τότε οὖν εἶπεν αὐτοῖς
15 Ἰησοῦς παρρησίᾳ, Λάζαρος ἀπέθανεν, / κ
χαίρω δι' ὑμᾶς, ἵνα πιστεύσητε, ὅτι οὐκ ἤμ
16 ἐκεῖ· ἀλλὰ ἄγωμεν πρὸς αὐτόν. εἶπεν οὖν Θωμ
ὁ λεγόμενος Δίδυμος τοῖς συμμαθηταῖς, Ἄγωμ

42 εκει] om p45 118 pc lat sy ac2 bopc   11. 2 δ
add αυτη X e: add αυτη η p45   6 εν ω ην] επι τω p45
7 επειτα] ειτα p45vid,66D 435 | τοις μαθ.] om p45vid,66* e
11 κεκοιμηται] κοιμαται D lat, item vs. 12 D latt

THE LONGER TEXT

II.23 καὶ ἔρχονται
εἰς Βηθανίαν καὶ ἦν ἐκεῖ

μία γυνὴ ἧς
ὁ ἀδελφὸς αὐτῆς

.24 ἀπέθανεν

17 καὶ ἡμεῖς ἵνα ἀποθάνωμεν μετ᾽ αὐτοῦ. Ἐλθὼν οὖν ὁ Ἰησοῦς εὗρεν αὐτὸν τέσσαρας ἤδη
18 ἡμέρας ἔχοντα ἐν τῷ μνημείῳ. ἦν δὲ Βηθανία
ἐγγὺς τῶν Ἱεροσολύμων ὡς ἀπὸ σταδίων δεκα-
19 πέντε. πολλοὶ δὲ ἐκ τῶν Ἰουδαίων ἐληλύθεισαν
πρὸς τὴν Μάρθαν καὶ Μαριαμ, ἵνα παραμυθή-
20 σωνται αὐτὰς περὶ τοῦ ἀδελφοῦ. ἡ οὖν Μάρθα
ὡς ἤκουσεν ὅτι Ἰησοῦς ἔρχεται, ὑπήντησεν αὐτῷ·
21 Μαριαμ δὲ ἐν τῷ οἴκῳ ἐκαθέζετο. εἶπεν οὖν ἡ
Μάρθα πρὸς Ἰησοῦν, Κύριε, εἰ ἦς ὧδε, οὐκ ἂν
22 ἀπέθανεν ὁ ἀδελφός μου. καὶ νῦν οἶδα ὅτι ὅσα ἂν
23 αἰτήσῃ τὸν Θεὸν δώσει σοι ὁ Θεός. λέγει αὐτῇ
24 ὁ Ἰησοῦς, Ἀναστήσεται ὁ ἀδελφός σου. λέγει
αὐτῷ ἡ Μάρθα, Οἶδα ὅτι ἀναστήσεται ἐν τῇ ἀνα-
25 στάσει ἐν τῇ ἐσχάτῃ ἡμέρᾳ. εἶπεν αὐτῇ ὁ Ἰησοῦς,
Ἐγώ εἰμι ἡ ἀνάστασις καὶ ἡ ζωή· ὁ πιστεύων εἰς
26 ἐμὲ κἂν ἀποθάνῃ ζήσεται, καὶ πᾶς ὁ ζῶν καὶ
πιστεύων εἰς ἐμὲ οὐ μὴ ἀποθάνῃ εἰς τὸν αἰῶνα·
27 πιστεύεις τοῦτο; λέγει αὐτῷ, Ναί, Κύριε· ἐγὼ
πεπίστευκα ὅτι σὺ εἶ ὁ Χριστὸς ὁ Υἱὸς τοῦ Θεοῦ
28 ὁ εἰς τὸν κόσμον ἐρχόμενος. καὶ τοῦτο εἰποῦσα
ἀπῆλθεν καὶ ἐφώνησεν Μαριαμ τὴν ἀδελφὴν
αὐτῆς λάθρα εἰποῦσα, Ὁ Διδάσκαλος πάρεστιν
29 καὶ φωνεῖ σε. ἐκείνη δὲ ὡς ἤκουσεν, ἐγείρεται
30 ταχὺ καὶ ἤρχετο πρὸς αὐτόν· οὔπω δὲ ἐληλύθει
ὁ Ἰησοῦς εἰς τὴν κώμην, ἀλλ᾽ ἦν ἔτι ἐν τῷ τόπῳ
31 ὅπου ὑπήντησεν αὐτῷ ἡ Μάρθα. οἱ οὖν Ἰουδαῖοι
οἱ ὄντες μετ᾽ αὐτῆς ἐν τῇ οἰκίᾳ καὶ παραμυθού-
μενοι αὐτήν, ἰδόντες τὴν Μαριαμ ὅτι ταχέως
ἀνέστη καὶ ἐξῆλθεν. ἠκολούθησαν αὐτῇ, δόξαντες
32 ὅτι ὑπάγει εἰς τὸ μνημεῖον ἵνα κλαύσῃ ἐκεῖ. ἡ οὖν
Μαριαμ ὡς ἦλθεν ὅπου ἦν Ἰησοῦς, ἰδοῦσα αὐτὸν
ἔπεσεν αὐτοῦ πρὸς τοὺς πόδας, λέγουσα αὐτῷ,
Κύριε, εἰ ἦς ὧδε, οὐκ ἄν μου ἀπέθανεν ὁ ἀδελφός.

καὶ ἐλθοῦσα
προσεκύνησε τὸν Ἰησοῦν καὶ λέγει
.25 αὐτῷ· υἱὲ Δαβὶδ ἐλέησόν με. οἱ δὲ μαθηταὶ
ἐπετίμησαν αὐτῇ. καὶ
.26 ὀργισθεὶς ὁ Ἰησοῦς

33 Ἰησοῦς οὖν ὡς εἶδεν αὐτὴν κλαίουσαν καὶ τοὺς
συνελθόντας αὐτῇ Ἰουδαίους κλαίοντας, ἐνεβρι-

17 Ιησους] add εις Βηθανιαν D f13 33 pm bo^pc   19 την
p^66 𝕏BW al; R] τας περι p^45AΘ f1 f13 pm s: om D (lat)
21 Κυριε] om B sy^s
25 και η ζωη] om p^45 a l* sy^s Cypr Or^pt   28 λαθρα
(, s], λαθρα)] σιωπη D lat sy^s   29 εγειρεται p^45,66AΘ
f1 f13 pm vg^cl,w s] ηγερθη 𝕏BDW al it vg^s co; R | ηρχετο
𝕏BW pc it co; R] ερχεται p^45,66ADΘ f1 f13 pl lat s
33 ενεβριμ... εαυτον] (13. 21) εταραχθη τω πν. ως
εμβριμουμενος p^45,66cD(Θ) f1 d p sa ac ac^2

34 μήσατο τῷ πνεύματι καὶ ἐτάραξεν ἑαυτόν, κα|

35 εἶπεν, Ποῦ τεθείκατε αὐτόν; λέγουσιν αὐτῷ

36 Κύριε, ἔρχου καὶ ἴδε. ἐδάκρυσεν ὁ Ἰησοῦς. ἐλε|

37 γον οὖν οἱ Ἰουδαῖοι, Ἴδε πῶς ἐφίλει αὐτόν. τινὲ|
δὲ ἐξ αὐτῶν εἶπαν, Οὐκ ἐδύνατο οὗτος ὁ ἀνοίξα|
τοὺς ὀφθαλμοὺς τοῦ τυφλοῦ ποιῆσαι ἵνα κα|

ἀπῆλθεν μετ' αὐτῆς εἰς τὸν κῆπον ὅπου ἦν
τὸ μνημεῖον

38 οὗτος μὴ ἀποθάνη; Ἰησοῦς οὖν πάλιν ἐμβριμώ|
μενος ἐν ἑαυτῷ ἔρχεται εἰς τὸ μνημεῖον· ἦν δ|

III.1 καὶ εὐθὺς ἠκούσθη ἐκ τοῦ μνημείου φωνὴ
μεγάλη· καὶ προσελθὼν ὁ Ἰησοῦς

39 σπήλαιον, καὶ λίθος ἐπέκειτο ἐπ' αὐτῷ. λέγει
Ἰησοῦς, Ἄρατε τὸν λίθον. λέγει αὐτῷ ἡ ἀδελφ|
τοῦ τετελευτηκότος Μάρθα, Κύριε, ἤδη ὄζε|

40 τεταρταῖος γάρ ἐστιν. λέγει αὐτῇ ὁ Ἰησοῦς, Οὐ|
εἶπόν σοι ὅτι ἐὰν πιστεύσῃς ὄψῃ τὴν δόξαν το|

.2 ἀπεκύλισε τὸν λίθον ἀπὸ τῆς θύρας τοῦ
μνημείου· καὶ εἰσελθὼν εὐθὺς ὅπου ἦν ὁ

41 Θεοῦ; / ἦραν οὖν τὸν λίθον. ὁ δὲ Ἰησοῦς ἦρε
τοὺς ὀφθαλμοὺς ἄνω καὶ εἶπεν, Πάτερ, εὐχαριστ|

.3 νεανίσκος ἐξέτεινεν τὴν χεῖρα καὶ ἤγειρεν

42 σοι ὅτι ἤκουσάς μου. ἐγὼ δὲ ᾔδειν ὅτι πάντοτ|

.4 αὐτόν· κρατήσας τῆς χειρός· ὁ δὲ νεανίσκος
ἐμβλέψας αὐτῷ ἠγάπησεν αὐτὸν καὶ ἤρξατο
μου ἀκούεις· ἀλλὰ διὰ τὸν ὄχλον τὸν περιεστῶτ|
εἶπον, ἵνα πιστεύσωσιν ὅτι σύ με ἀπέστειλας

.5 παρακαλεῖν αὐτὸν ἵνα μετ' αὐτοῦ ᾖ. καὶ

43 καὶ ταῦτα εἰπὼν φωνῇ μεγάλῃ ἐκραύγασε|

.6 ἐξελθόντες ἐκ τοῦ μνημείου ἦλθον εἰς τὴν
οἰκίαν τοῦ νεανίσκου· ἦν γὰρ πλούσιος.

44 Λάζαρε, δεῦρο ἔξω. ἐξῆλθεν ὁ τεθνηκὼς δεδε|
μένος τοὺς πόδας καὶ τὰς χεῖρας κειρίαις, καὶ |
ὄψις αὐτοῦ σουδαρίῳ περιεδέδετο. λέγει αὐτοῖς |
Ἰησοῦς, Λύσατε αὐτὸν καὶ ἄφετε αὐτὸν ὑπάγειν|

.7–10 the nocturnal initiation

45–53 the Jews' reactions and plot.

54 Ὁ οὖν Ἰησοῦς οὐκέτι παρρησίᾳ περιεπάτει ἐ|
τοῖς Ἰουδαίοις, ἀλλὰ ἀπῆλθεν ἐκεῖθεν εἰς τὴ|
χώραν ἐγγὺς τῆς ἐρήμου, εἰς Ἐφράϊμ λεγομένη|
πόλιν, κἀκεῖ ἔμεινεν μετὰ τῶν μαθητῶν.

.10 ἐκεῖθεν δὲ ἀναστὰς
.11 ἐπέστρεψεν εἰς τὸ πέραν τοῦ Ἰορδάνου.

39 η αδ. τ. τετελ.] trsp post Μαρθα D vg syᵖˑʰ sa bo
om Θ it sy^s ac²   41 λιθον p⁶⁶אBDW al lat; R] add o|
ην A f1 579 al f: add ου ην ο τεθνηκως κειμενος f13 pr|
s: add οπου εκειτο 56   44 περιεδεδετο] εδεδετο p⁴
54 εκειθεν] om p⁴⁵D 579 pc lat sy^s ac² | χωραν] ad|
Σαμφουρειν D | εμεινεν אBW pc; R] διετριβεν p⁴⁵,⁶⁶ADϹ|
f13 pm latt co s

Comparison of these two texts shows that the story in the longer text of Mk. is of more primitive form than that in Jn. The majority of the contentual differences between the two are the results of Johannine[5] additions, to wit:

Jn. 11.1–2: The preface, naming the hero, relating him to Mary and Martha of the same village, and identifying Mary as the woman who performed the anointing in the same village. The basis of this was probably the common name of the village—Bethany. The naming of unknown characters and the attempt to relate the characters

5. "Johannine" here means "in style and/or content typical of the present Gospel according to John."

152

of stories located in the same place are well-known secondary traits (Bultmann, *Geschichte* 70ff, and note in *Ergänzungsheft* to p. 72; also 256f, 338, and *Johannes* 301 n4 end, 302 n1; etc.; Barrett, 324 on verse 1 end; Bauer, *Leben* 516f). That the naming of Lazarus is secondary even in the Johannine story is persuasively argued by Eckhardt, *Tod* 22ff. The doubling of the sister is paralleled by the doubling of the blind men in the Matthaean retellings of Mk.'s Bartimaeus story, Lk.'s doubling of the angel in the resurrection, etc. (more examples in Bultmann, *Geschichte* 345; see further below, on 11.28–31).

11.3: The sisters send word to Jesus. This may be from the story which was known to John, but is probably an attempt to provide motivation for Jesus' return to Jerusalem. John was in the habit of inventing historical explanations: 4.1,45; 5.16,18; 6.2,14f, 22ff; 7.1,5,30; 8.20; 11.45f, 53f, etc.

11.4–15: The Johannine explanation of Lazarus' sickness and of why Jesus let him die—to make possible the miracle, to reveal the glory of God, and to confirm the disciples' faith (cf. 9.3).[6] John's use of the passion prophecy will be discussed later. Here the thing to be noted is that his substitute for it, 11.9f (as against Mk. 10.33f) is typically Johannine (= 9.4f) and obviously intrusive (Bultmann, *Johannes* 304 n1; Dodd, *Historical Tradition* 373ff). The misunderstanding of a metaphor as an excuse for Jesus' explanation (verses 11–15) is a standard Johannine device for introducing secondary material (3.4; 4.11,33; 6.34,52; 8.22,33,39; etc.; Barrett, 173–174. Bultmann's distinction of different types of misunderstanding—*Johannes* 304 n6—is unimportant; this author was not so choosy.) Here Jesus' explanation is intended to prevent any discrediting of the miracle, which might result if κεκοίμηται were taken literally and Lazarus supposed to have been merely cataleptic. Compare the addition of εἰδότες ὅτι ἀπέθανεν in Lk. 8.53 to prevent literal misunderstanding of the similar saying in 8.52 (= Mk. 5.39), and see below, on 11.17.

11.16: The report of Thomas' devotion is an edifying addition (Barrett, 327 on verse 16; Bultmann, *Johannes* 305 n4).

11.17: The specification that the body had been four days in the tomb is added to magnify the miracle and to refute any claim that Lazarus was merely asleep (see below, on 11.39b and 44; also Barrett, 335 on verse 39; Bultmann, *Johannes* 305 n6— cf. n9). John likewise insisted that the blind man whom Jesus cured was born blind and that such a cure was therefore unheard of (9.1f, 20,32, contrast Mk. 8.22f). John also made the centurion's slave into the son of a royal official (4.46, cf. Mt. 8.5; Lk. 7.2), made Jesus identify himself after the resurrection by showing his wounds (20.27), etc. These stories have grown with time.

11.18: The precise specification of the distance from Jerusalem to Bethany is another pseudohistorical explanation (it explains why the Jews came—they were so nearby; so Barrett, and Bultmann, *Johannes*, *ad loc.*). Thus it is probably late, rather than early, material, especially since it happens to be incorrect (Dalman, *Orte* 266).

11.19: The "chorus" of Jewish mourners (so Dodd, *Fourth Gospel* 363) is introduced to provide additional witnesses to the miracle (Bultmann, *Johannes* 306) as well as

---

6. Against Barrett, 325 on verse 6, see Lightfoot, *Jn.* 219 n1, to say nothing of the text, ἀσθενεῖ, verse 3.

the standard Johannine foil to Jesus. The mixed reactions of the Jews—skepticism, conversion, and talebearing (verses 37 and 45)—are also standard in Jn. (chs. 5–10 *passim*).

11.20–27: The homiletic conversation with Martha leading to the formal confession of faith is completely Johannine, though the confession is presumably that current in John's church (Bultmann, *Johannes* 308 n8; 309 n2).

11.28–31: More "historical" explanation, to get the second sister and the chorus into the act (Bultmann, *Johannes* 309 n2; 311 n3). With Mary's arrival (verse 32) John returned to the story as it lay before him, that is, to the saying κύριε, εἰ ἦς ὧδε κ.τ.λ. from which he had departed (verse 21) to introduce the intervening sermonette. (Cf. the similar case below, verse 34–37, and the note on 11.38. Mark does the same thing, 2.5b and 10b, evidently it was customary.) The parallelism with the longer text, which broke off at verse 21, now resumes. This indicates that the doubling of the sisters was John's work and was not in his source. He probably did it to make room for both Mary and Martha, whom he knew as a pair located in Bethany. The appeal κύριε, εἰ ἦς ὧδε does not necessarily imply that messengers had been sent; it may be a typical expression of faith, later "explained" by the story of the sending (11.3).

11.33: ἐνεβριμήσατο τῷ πνεύματι καὶ ἐτάραξεν ἑαυτόν. The difficulty of explaining this behavior as a consequence of the weeping of Mary and the Jews is indicated by Barrett's contortions (*ad loc.*). But καὶ ὀργισθείς in the longer text is easily explicable as a consequence either of the woman's use of the messianic title or the disciples' rebuke of her. The disappearance of the appeal to the son of David (a title Jn. never uses) entailed the disappearance of the rebuke and left the anger unexplained. John (or his source) therefore substituted the vague and portentous καὶ ἐνεβριμήσατο κ.τ.λ., which seemed suitable as an introduction to the miracle because of the words' magical overtones (Bonner, *Technique* 177ff; Lieberman, *Tosefta* Part V, p. 1363). Jn. regularly differs from the synoptics by its use of more pretentious language, with suggestions of something miraculous, mystical, or royal, e.g.: Mt. 8.5 ‖ Jn. 4.46; Mk. 6.45ff ‖ Jn. 6.14f; Mk. 6.53 ‖ Jn. 6.21; Mk. 8.29 ‖ Jn. 6.69; Mt. 18.3 ‖ Jn. 3.3; Mk. 11.8 ‖ Jn. 12.13; Mk. 14.43ff ‖ Jn. 18.3ff; Mk. 15.37 ‖ Jn. 19.29f.

11.36f: ἴδε πῶς ἐφίλει αὐτόν is perhaps intended to show how the Jews twisted Jesus' innocent sorrow into evidence for a charge of homosexuality. οὐκ ἐδύνατο οὗτος ὁ ἀνοίξας τοὺς ὀφθαλμοὺς τοῦ τυφλοῦ ποιῆσαι ἵνα καὶ οὗτος μὴ ἀποθάνῃ; continues the theme by applying to Jesus a commonplace of Judeo-Christian polemic against pagan divinities and thus attempting to discredit his miracles; cf. Chrysostom, *In Joannem homiliae, ad loc.*; Aristides, *Apologia* 11.3: *Si igitur Aphrodite dea est et amatorem suum in morte eius adiuvare non poterat, qui alios adiuvare potest? Et ut audiatur naturam divinam in lacrimas* ⟨cf. Jn. 11.36⟩ . . . *venire fieri non potest.* (Again 11.5, on Rhea, and 6, on Kore.) The theme long continued popular; Wetstein on Jn. 11.37 quotes Ausonius on Zeus and Sarpedon. That it was applied to Jesus appears also from its use in the crucifixion scene, Mk. 15.31 ‖ Mt. 27.42, ἄλλους ἔσωσεν, ἑαυτὸν οὐ δύναται σῶσαι, and in *Midrash Tannaïm* on Dt. 3.23: "Before a man put his trust in flesh and blood ⟨i.e., in another man⟩ and ask him to save him, *let him* ⟨the proposed saviour⟩ *save*

himself from death first." The italicized words appear exactly in the Lucan parallel to Mk. 15.31 (Lk. 23.35). John's purpose in reporting the taunt here is the same as Mark's in the crucifixion scene—dramatic irony to emphasize (1) the coming resurrection, (2) the contrast between Jesus and the pagan divinities, and (3) the error of the Jews.

11.38: John again returns to his source by repeating the word at which he left it: ἐνεβριμήσατο verse 33, πάλιν ἐμβριμώμενος verse 38 (cf. above, on 11.28–31). Again the parallelism to the longer text of Mk. stops with the first occurrence of the repeated word and resumes with the second. This all but demonstrates that the material between the two occurrences was added by John and was unknown to the author of the longer text of Mk. (Cf. Jn. 18.18 and 25, where the repeated words evidently came from a text like Mk. 14.54. The evidence of the longer text thus supports Bultmann's supposition of an interpolation between Jn. 18.18 and 25—*Johannes, ad loc.*—against Dodd, *Historical Tradition* 82 n1.)

11.39b–40: Another Johannine addition to magnify the miracle and explain its purpose; see above, on 11.4–15 and 17, and Bultmann, *Johannes* 311 nn4,6.

11.41b–42: This stage whisper to God—addressed as "Father"—(Barrett, *ad loc.*) is clearly an interruption in the story and completely Johannine; cf. 5.36; 6.57; 7.29; 9.31; 12.28; 17.1; etc; and Bultmann, *Johannes* 311 n6. Bultmann thought it obvious ("selbstverständlich," *ibid.* 312) that the words of the prayer were not to be heard by the crowd, but Chrysostom was almost certainly right in treating them as public instruction (*De Christi precibus contra anomoeos* IX end).

11.44: The grave clothes are another means of emphasizing that Lazarus had really been dead; see above, on 11.4–15, 17, and 38. It is not likely that John thought Lazarus' moving, though bound, an additional miracle; the evangelist would not have been averse to throwing in a miracle, but did not visualize his scenes with sufficient clarity to realize the difficulty. (Contra, Bultmann, *Johannes* 312.)

11.45–46: The Jews' reactions—unmistakably secondary in relation to the structure of the story, and typical of John, cf. 2.23; 7.31ff; 12.10f, 42, etc.; Barrett, 337.

11.47–54a: An independent tradition, developed by independent invention. Its use in relation to the larger structure of the Gospel is obvious (Barrett, 337); it is inserted at this point to provide John's regular explanation for a withdrawal by Jesus, since a withdrawal was reported by his source (11.54b ‖ the longer text) and had to be "explained." Cf. Jn. 7.1; 8.59; 10.39; etc.

This completes the list of material in Jn. which is unparalleled in the longer text of Mk. Every bit of it is obviously secondary and obviously Johannine. With the above analysis that of Dodd, *Historical Tradition* 228ff, can now be compared. Without knowing the longer text, Dodd concluded that the Johannine account was a reworking of an earlier story of synoptic type, which, however, he thought it impossible to dissect. He remarked—228 n2—"as Johannine traits . . . the identification of individual characters, the measurement of time and space (two days, four days, fifteen stades), the use of the term οἱ 'Ιουδαῖοι. Locutions with a Johannine ring are ὑπὲρ τῆς δόξης τοῦ θεοῦ, ἵνα δοξασθῇ ὁ υἱὸς τοῦ θεοῦ, παρρησία, χαίρω δι' ὑμᾶς ἵνα πιστεύσητε, ὅσα ἂν αἰτήσῃ τὸν θεὸν δώσει σοι (cf. 16.23), ἐγώ εἰμι, εἰς τὸν αἰῶνα (twelves times in

John, twice in Mark, once each in Matthew and Luke), ὁ εἰς τὸν κόσμον ἐρχόμενος, ὄψῃ τὴν δόξαν τοῦ θεοῦ, ἵνα πιστεύσωσιν ὅτι σύ με ἀπέστειλας.'' The agreement of this list with the results of the above anslysis is clear. Accordingly there can be no question that the story in the longer text of Mk. is more primitive in form than the story of Lazarus in Jn. Further, it is impossible to suppose that the author of the longer text of Mk. used, or even knew, the Johannine Lazarus story. Had he known it, his text would certainly have shown at least some of the secondary Johannine traits listed above. Since it has none of them, it must be completely independent of Jn.

These facts make it possible to distinguish, in the Johannine Lazarus story, the source John used. It is often recognizable by its parallels to the longer text. But in the material paralleled there are important differences: (1) The sisters are represented as sending word to Jesus (above, on 11.3 and 32). (2) The sister appeals to Jesus with the cry κύριε εἰ ἦς ὧδε κ.τ.λ., rather than υἱὲ Δαβίδ, ἐλέησόν με (on 11.28–31). (3) ὀργίζομαι is replaced by ἐμβριμάομαι (on 11.33). (4) No φωνὴ μεγάλη is heard from the tomb on Jesus' approach. (5) The stone is removed by persons unspecified, not by Jesus himself. (6) Jesus calls Lazarus forth from the tomb (φωνῇ μεγάλῃ) instead of going in and raising him by hand. (7) The Johannine story concludes with reference to Lazarus' grave wrappings and Jesus' order to untie him (on 11.44), whereas the story used by the longer text said nothing of these, but concluded with the raising. (ἐμβλέψας αὐτῷ ἠγάπησεν αὐτόν κ.τ.λ. probably comes from the editor, and καὶ ἐξελθόντες κ.τ.λ. is an editorial transition to the next episode.)

Not all of these differences can confidently be attributed to John's source. As indicated above, the sisters' sending to Jesus probably was John's work; likewise the replacement of ὀργίζομαι by ἐμβριμάομαι. The same probability can be established for the change in the use of φωνὴ μεγάλη (4 and 6, above). The cry from the tomb would have led many ancient readers to question the miracle. Had the man who was raised really been dead? Stories of persons who were thought to have died but came back to life were frequent in antiquity (Plato, *Republic* 614b; Proclus, *In Platonis rem publicam*, ed. Kroll, II.113; Kerényi, *passim*; Philostratus, *Vita Apollonii* IV.45, Eus., *Against the Life of Apollonius* 26 and 31), and the notion that the persons "raised" by Jesus had not been really dead was a frequent embarrassment to Christian apologists (Origen, *Contra Celsum* II.48; GCS, *Origenes*, vol. 12.III.1, frags. 185–186; Ephraem, *Commentaire* VII.27 p. 77; Cramer, I.321 on Mk. 5.43; Chrysostom, *In Matthaeum homiliae* 31 on Mt. 9.18ff). We have seen above that this embarrassment was already felt by John and that (as Chrysostom remarked) John emphasized the four days' entombment and the smell, and so on, "that they should not have any ground to disbelieve that the man whom ⟨Jesus⟩ raised had been dead." Given this apologetic concern, it is understandable that either John or his source should have suppressed the voice from the tomb and transferred the φωνὴ μεγάλη to Jesus—in spite of the fact that it is somewhat out of character, as Cyril of Alexandria remarked (*In Johannem, ad loc.*).

The original significance of the cry from the tomb is probably indicated by the use of φωνὴ μεγάλη in Mk., where it occurs often at crises in the relations between

spirits and men—see the commentary on III.1, above. In 1.26 the demon φωνῆσαν φωνῇ μεγάλη ἐξῆλθεν; in 5.7 the legion of demons κράξας φωνῇ μεγάλη respond with a counter spell to Jesus' command that they leave their victim; in Mk. 15.34 Jesus himself ἐβόησεν . . . φωνῇ μεγάλη Ελωι Ελωι λαμα σαβαχθανει, and in 15.37 ἀφεὶς φωνὴν μεγάλην ἐξέπνευσεν (cf. Fenton, *Destruction* 57). In the longer text, accordingly, the φωνὴ μεγάλη is probably the cry of Death, departing from its prey: cf. Mk. 1.42; Lk. 4.39; I Cor. 15.26; Apoc. 6.8; 20.13f; Brandon, *Personification* 330f. Death or Hades releasing the soul of Lazarus appears in figured representations of the miracle from the fifth century on, Millet, *Recherches* 233. Réau, *Iconographie* II.ii.338, calls this "the first version of the miracle properly so-called." For these two references I am indebted to Meyer Schapiro. [Substantially this same interpretation was proposed independently by R.S., who also, with T.B., suggests that there may be a connection between the longer text of Mk. and Jn. 12.17, where the crowd accompanying Jesus into Jerusalem celebrates his miracles by declaring τὸν Λάζαρον ἐφώνησεν ἐκ τοῦ μνημείου καὶ ἤγειρεν αὐτὸν ἐκ νεκρῶν. This could have been derived from the longer text by substitution of τὸν Λάζαρον for ὁ Λάζαρος either deliberately or by misreading. The possibility of misreading, especially of an Aramaic text, can be seen from the Peshitta, where Jn. 12.17 reads ܟܕܘ ܕܝ ܝ ܡܣܘܟܘ : ܟܢܣܐ ܝ ܕܠܠܙܪ ܟܢܐ. Were it not for the doubling of the first ܠ this might represent ὁ Λάζαρος ἐφώνησεν ἐκ τοῦ μνημείου, καὶ ⟨ὁ Ἰησοῦς⟩ ἤγειρεν αὐτὸν ἐκ νεκρῶν, where the sequence of events and the underlined words are paralleled exactly—albeit with interruption—in the longer text.] Such a misreading (substitution of τὸν Λάζαρον for ὁ Λάζαρος) would be psychologically likely, since Lazarus was dead and therefore not expected to call out. And the demonological parallels given above argue that the story of the raising in the longer text of Mk. is primitive. The fact that it contains a difficulty, which the story in Jn. does not, also argues that it is older than the Johannine form: *difficilior lectio*. Accordingly, I think John knew the story in a form similar to that of the longer text, and the transference of the φωνή to Jesus should be attributed to him rather than to his source. We saw above that it accords with his apologetic concerns. (The possibility that John's source was written in Aramaic will be of some importance hereinafter.)

Thus a number of the peculiarities of the Johannine story are to be referred to John, along with the obviously Johannine interpolations previously listed. However, there is at least one difference which can more confidently be referred to John's source—the appeal κύριε, εἰ ἦς ὧδε, κ.τ.λ., which John repeated as a catchword in verse 32 when he came back to his source after his homiletic and explanatory excursion in verses 23–31 (see above, on 11.28–31 and 38). Similarly, the differences as to who moved the stone (no. 6, above) and how the youth was raised (no. 7) are probably due to John's source; at least, neither of them is directly accounted for by John's peculiar interests or style.

These differences which can be referred to John's source afford reason to believe that even the source was later in form than the story in the longer text.

In the first place, the appeal κύριε, εἰ ἦς ὧδε, οὐκ ἂν ἀπέθανεν ὁ ἀδελφός μου, is a cry of grief from the Church after Jesus' departure and an expression of hope in a future resurrection, whereas υἱὲ Δαβίδ, ἐλέησόν με expresses the primitive Palestinian

hope for immediate action by a present, Davidic Messiah (and was therefore dropped when Christianity moved away from its Palestinian Jewish origins).

In the second place, that Jesus himself should move the stone is more likely to be primitive than that others should do it for him. So far as I can recall, Jesus is never reported in the Gospels to have done any hard manual labor—except for Jn.'s emphatic "himself carrying his cross" (19.17), which is the last humiliation before crucifixion. This lack of reference to Jesus' doing any manual labor is presumably an attempt to make him respectable, like Matthew's alteration and Luke's omission of Mk.'s ὁ τέκτων (Mk. 6.3 ‖ Mt. 13.55; Lk. 4.22). The quite casual and nondogmatic way (contrast Jn. 19.17) with which the longer text refers to Jesus' removing the stone makes it seem that we have here early material.

Finally, it might be argued on similar grounds that a story which reports the direct, physical method of taking the hand and literally raising the dead is probably more primitive than one which reports a raising by remote command. It was remarked above (commentary on III.4) that references to χείρ as an instrument of supernatural help are substantially more frequent in Mk. than in the later synoptics and Jn. (10 or 11 in Mk., 7 in Mt., 5 in Lk., o in Jn.) Notice also the disappearance from Mt. and Lk. of Markan miracles worked by physical means (7.32–37; 8.22–26) and the continuation of this tendency in later Christian apologetics (Fridrichsen, *Problème* 61). Is it possible that the Johannine story was also influenced by considerations of purity, to eliminate the reference to Jesus' touching a corpse?

Having thus established grounds for belief that John's source was later than the resurrection story in the longer text of Mk. and differed from it substantially, we can conclude that Jn. was independent of the longer text no less than it of Jn.

C. The order of events in Mk. and Jn.

This conclusion gives particular importance to the parallelism in order of events which appears between the latter halves of Mk. and Jn. once the longer text is put in its place in Mk. This parallelism can best be demonstrated by an abbreviated synopsis:

Mk. 6.32 καὶ ἀπῆλθον ἐν τῷ πλοίῳ εἰς ἔρημον τόπον κατ' ἰδίαν.	*Jn.* 6.1 μετὰ ταῦτα ἀπῆλθεν ὁ Ἰησοῦς πέραν τῆς θαλάσσης τῆς Γαλιλαίας τῆς Τιβεριάδος.
The feeding of the five thousand	= The feeding of the five thousand
6.45 καὶ εὐθὺς ἠνάγκασεν τοὺς μαθητὰς αὐτοῦ ἐμβῆναι εἰς τὸ πλοῖον καὶ προάγειν εἰς τὸ πέραν πρὸς Βηθσαϊδάν, ἕως αὐτὸς ἀπολύει τὸν ὄχλον.	6.16–17a ὡς δὲ ὀψία ἐγένετο, κατέβησαν οἱ μαθηταὶ αὐτοῦ ἐπὶ τὴν θάλασσαν, καὶ ἐμβάντες εἰς πλοῖον ἤρχοντο πέραν τῆς θαλάσσης εἰς Καφαρναουμ.

Omitted by Luke

6.46 καὶ ἀποταξάμενος αὐτοῖς ἀπῆλθεν εἰς τὸ ὄρος προσεύξασθαι.

The walking on the sea

6.54–55a καὶ ἐξελθόντων αὐτῶν ἐκ τοῦ πλοίου εὐθὺς ἐπιγνόντες αὐτὸν περιέδραμον ὅλην τὴν χώραν.

Summary: Jesus' miracles of healing
The dispute on handwashing
Trip to the territory of Tyre
The Syrophoenician
Return to Galilee
The dumb man (εφφαθα)
The feeding of the four thousand
The demand for a sign
The saying on the leaven of the Pharisees
The blind man of Bethsaida

8.27–30 Peter's confession (in Caesarea Philippi)
Peter is Satan
The sayings on self-sacrifice
The transfiguration
The demoniac boy

9.30–31 κἀκεῖθεν ἐξελθόντες παρεπορεύοντο διὰ τῆς Γαλιλαίας, καὶ οὐκ ἤθελεν ἵνα τις γνοῖ· ἐδίδασκεν γὰρ τοὺς μαθητὰς αὐτοῦ, καὶ ἔλεγεν αὐτοῖς ὅτι ὁ υἱὸς τοῦ ἀνθρώπου παραδίδοται εἰς χεῖρας ἀνθρώπων καὶ ἀποκτενοῦσιν αὐτόν . . .

The dispute on precedence
The stranger who exorcized
The sayings on scandals

10.1a καὶ ἐκεῖθεν ἀναστὰς ἔρχεται εἰς τὰ ὅρια τῆς Ἰουδαίας

10.1b καὶ πέραν τοῦ Ἰορδάνου, καὶ συνπορεύονται πάλιν ὄχλοι πρὸς αὐτόν, καὶ ὡς εἰώθει πάλιν ἐδίδασκεν αὐτούς.

(6.15 Ἰησοῦς οὖν γνοὺς ὅτι μέλλουσιν ἔρχεσθαι καὶ ἁρπάζειν αὐτὸν ἵνα ποιήσωσιν βασιλέα, ἀνεχώρησεν πάλιν εἰς τὸ ὄρος αὐτὸς μόνος.)

= The walking on the sea

6.24–25a ὅτε οὖν εἶδεν ὁ ὄχλος ὅτι Ἰησοῦς οὐκ ἔστιν ἐκεῖ οὐδὲ οἱ μαθηταὶ αὐτοῦ, ἐνέβησαν αὐτοὶ εἰς τὰ πλοιάρια καὶ ἦλθον εἰς Καφαρναουμ ζητοῦντες τὸν Ἰησοῦν. καὶ εὑρόντες αὐτόν . . .

=? Discussion: Jesus is the bread of life

= 6.66–69 Peter's confession (in Capernaum?)
= Judas is a devil

7.1 καὶ μετὰ ταῦτα περιεπάτει ὁ Ἰησοῦς ἐν τῇ Γαλιλαίᾳ· οὐ γὰρ ἤθελεν ἐν τῇ Ἰουδαίᾳ περιπατεῖν, ὅτι ἐζήτουν αὐτὸν οἱ Ἰουδαῖοι ἀποκτεῖναι.

Jesus' brothers taunt him

7.10 ὡς δὲ ἀνέβησαν οἱ ἀδελφοὶ αὐτοῦ εἰς τὴν ἑορτήν, τότε καὶ αὐτὸς ἀνέβη . . .
The disputes in Jerusalem
The man born blind
The sayings on the door to the sheep
The appeal to the witness of his works

10.40–41a καὶ ἀπῆλθεν πάλιν πέραν τοῦ Ἰορδάνου εἰς τὸν τόπον ὅπου ἦν Ἰωάννης τὸ πρῶτον βαπτίζων, καὶ ἔμενεν ἐκεῖ, καὶ πολλοὶ ἦλθον πρὸς αὐτόν.

The question on divorce
The blessing on children
The rich young ruler
The sayings on scandals

                                             The preface to the Lazarus story

10.32 ἦσαν δὲ ἐν τῇ ὁδῷ ἀναβαίνοντες εἰς   11.7–8 ἔπειτα μετὰ τοῦτο λέγει τοῖς μαθηταῖς,
'Ιεροσόλυμα, καὶ ἦν προάγων αὐτοὺς ὁ   ἄγωμεν εἰς τὴν 'Ιουδαίαν πάλιν. λέγουσιν
'Ιησοῦς, καὶ ἐθαμβοῦντο, οἱ δὲ ἀκολουθοῦντες   αὐτῷ οἱ μαθηταί, Ραββει, νῦν ἐζήτουν σε
ἐφοβοῦντο.   λιθάσαι οἱ 'Ιουδαῖοι, καὶ πάλιν ὑπάγεις ἐκεῖ;

Jesus' prophecy of his own passion and   = Jesus' announcement of Lazarus' death
  resurrection   and prophecy of his resurrection
Longer text: The Lazarus story   = The Lazarus story
  The nocturnal initiation
  (The Jews' plot, Mk. 14.1–2, *infra*)   = The Jews' reaction and plot
III.10–11 ἐκεῖθεν δὲ ἀναστὰς ἐπέστρεψεν εἰς   11.54 ὁ οὖν 'Ιησοῦς οὐκέτι παρρησίᾳ περιε-
τὸ πέραν τοῦ 'Ιορδάνου.   πάτει ἐν τοῖς 'Ιουδαίοις, ἀλλὰ ἀπῆλθεν
                                   ἐκεῖθεν εἰς τὴν χώραν ἐγγὺς τῆς ἐρήμου, εἰς
                                   'Εφραιμ λεγομένην πόλιν, κἀκεῖ ἔμεινεν
                                   μετὰ τῶν μαθητῶν.

Mk. The question of James and John
Longer text: The events in Jericho
Mk. Bartimaeus
  The entry of Jerusalem   = (The entry of Jerusalem, Jn. 12.12–19,
  The cursing of the fig tree   *infra*)
  The cleansing of the Temple   = (The cleansing of the Temple, Jn. 2.13–
  The fig tree found withered   17)
  The question as to Jesus' authority   = (The question as to Jesus' authority, Jn.
  The parable of the rented vineyards   2.18)
  Questions by Herodians, Sadducees and
    a scribe
  The question as to the son of David
  The widow's mite
  The prophecy of the destruction of the   = (The prophecy of the destruction of the
    Temple   Temple, Jn. 2.19–22)
  The prophecy of the end
  The Jews' plot   = (The Jews' reaction and plot, Jn. 11.47–
                                   54, *supra*)

  The anointing in Bethany   = The anointing in Bethany
  (The entry of Jerusalem, Mk. 11.1–10,   = The entry of Jerusalem
    supra)   The request of the Greeks
                                   The Evanglist's comments on the Jews
                                 Jesus' declaration of his mission

The preparation for the last supper

                                   The footwashing
The last supper   = The last supper
The passion story   = The passion story

In this synopsis the things which require explanation are the continued parallelism of the geographical framework (shown by the verses quoted in Greek) and the near-identity in *order* of those larger elements which the two Gospels have in common. Of these elements (indicated by the equal sign) three—the cleansing of the Temple, the question as to Jesus' authority, and the prophecy of the Temple's destruction— are not properly in question, since they appear in Jn. 2. (However, it is interesting to note: [1] that in Jn. 2 they appear in the same order as they do in Mk. 11–13; [2] that the *Streitgespräche*, with which they are closely connected, are in Mk. divided between 2.1–3.6 and 11.27–12.37. These facts suggest that their material derives in part from an independent block of tradition which had some connection with an early stage in Jesus' career—a suggestion to which we shall return later.) Of the other 12 major elements listed as common to Mk. (including the longer text) and Jn., all occur in the same order, save that Jn. has the entry of Jerusalem after the Jews' plot and the anointing, and Mk. has it before them.

This coincidence in order of so many events can hardly be accidental. Yet, it seems unlikely that John used Mk. or Mark, Jn. (Haenchen, *Probleme*; numerous studies of detail by Buse; more recently Smith, *Jn. 12.12*; and above all Dodd, *Historical Tradition*). And we have already seen evidence that the longer text and Jn. were independent developments of a common source, possibly in Aramaic, from which Jn. was separated by at least two removes (since his immediate source was later in form than the story in the longer text). Evidence for the independence of Jn. and canonical Mk. is to be found in the great differences of form between some of the elements common to them: Peter's confession, the curse on Peter ("Simon") or Judas ("the son of Simon"), the anointing, the last supper, and the passion story. Most of these were mentioned above as "remote, but unmistakable parallels, which can best be explained as divergent forms of the same tradition."

The same relation seems to hold between the elements of the geographical frame. They are undeniably parallel, and in outline their accounts of Jesus' movements are substantially identical.[7] But the verbal coincidences between them are trivial ($\dot{a}\pi\hat{\eta}\lambda\theta o\nu$, $\tau o\dot{\upsilon}\varsigma$ $\mu a\theta\eta\tau\dot{a}\varsigma$ $a\dot{\upsilon}\tau o\hat{\upsilon}$, $\dot{\epsilon}\mu\beta\hat{\eta}\nu a\iota$ $\epsilon\dot{\iota}\varsigma$ $\pi\lambda o\hat{\iota}o\nu$, $\pi\acute{\epsilon}\rho a\nu$, $\epsilon\dot{\iota}\varsigma$ $\tau\dot{o}$ $\ddot{o}\rho o\varsigma$, $\tau\hat{\eta}\varsigma$ $\Gamma a\lambda\iota\lambda a\acute{\iota}a\varsigma$, $o\dot{\upsilon}\kappa$ $\ddot{\eta}\theta\epsilon\lambda\epsilon\nu$, $\dot{a}\pi o\kappa\tau\epsilon\nu o\hat{\upsilon}\sigma\iota\nu$, etc.) and the differences, not only of wording, but also of content, are so substantial that it would be implausible to suppose either author got them from the other (especially since material of this sort is for the most part theologically unimportant and therefore not likely to suffer deliberate changes). Therefore their continual parallelism and substantial differences must be explained by supposition of a common source of which both authors used different developments.

7. Mk. 10.1, $\kappa a\dot{\iota}$ $\dot{\epsilon}\kappa\epsilon\hat{\iota}\theta\epsilon\nu$ $\dot{a}\nu a\sigma\tau\dot{a}\varsigma$ $\ddot{\epsilon}\rho\chi\epsilon\tau a\iota$ $\epsilon\dot{\iota}\varsigma$ $\tau\dot{a}$ $\ddot{o}\rho\iota a$ $\tau\hat{\eta}\varsigma$ $\dot{\prime}$Ι$o\upsilon\delta a\acute{\iota}a\varsigma$ $\kappa a\dot{\iota}$ $\pi\acute{\epsilon}\rho a\nu$ $\tau o\hat{\upsilon}$ $\dot{\prime}$Ι$o\rho\delta\acute{a}\nu o\upsilon$, has often been thought corrupt, or "explained" as meaning the reverse of what it says. However, neither treatment is necessary, and the plain sense of the verse as it stands (he went first to Judea and then to Transjordan) is supported not only by the parallels in Jn., but also by the independent tradition in Lk. 9.51ff and 17.11. See the discussion in Taylor, *ad loc*. [C.R. suggests that the text of Mk. 10.1 as given above may have been produced by abbreviation, that is, by omission of the stories of what happened in Judea. He compares Mk. 7.31, where the strange geography (from Tyre through Sidon to the Sea of Galilee in the midst of the Decapolis) is possibly the result of amalgamation of parts of a number of introductory notices.]

The same conclusion is indicated again by the fact that in both Gospels the parallel episodes stand in the same relation to the parallel framework; that is, the same events occur not only in the same order, but also in the same places in the parallel frames, and are thus for the most part located in the same geographic places. Here again there are discrepancies sufficient to make it unlikely that either author used the other, but insufficient to obscure the basic identity of the outlines.

Finally, the similarities demonstrated by the above synopsis would be increased yet further if we were to accept the theory of Dodd (*Close*) and Huffmann (*Sources* 128) that Mk. 8.1–26 and Mk. 6.30–7.37 are variant forms of the same body of tradition. This theory yields for Jn. 6.1–65 a double set of Markan parallels which cannot plausibly be explained as accidental coincidence of editorial constructions, especially because the coincidence lies less in matters of wording (which might be editorial formulas) than in the order of events which are not obviously identical but turn out, one after another, to be basically similar. Discussion of Dodd's theory would be irrelevant for our present purpose, but his evidence strengthens materially the already strong case to be made from the synopsis printed above. Incidentally, although when he wrote *Close* Dodd was of the opinion that his data were evidence of John's use of Mk. (p. 288), he has since changed his mind and treated them as evidence of the dependence of both Gospels on common tradition (*Fourth Gospel* 448ff; *Herrnworte* and *Historical Tradition, passim*).

It seems unlikely, however, that oral tradition should account for so extended an agreement in *order*—particularly since the events and, even more, the geographical references reported do not seem to be connected by any coherent plot which would fix their order in the narrator's memory. If we therefore suppose a common written source, how can we account for the differences between the Gospels, and especially for the differences between the material they have in common (which probably came from the source)? The source may have been in Aramaic and the differences may result in part from different translations. Into these different translations both Mark and John would then have inserted, chiefly from other sources, the additional material peculiar to their own Gospels. These suggestions obviously resemble those of Dodd, *Framework*, on which there have been many attacks—for example, Nineham, *Order*, Robinson, *Quest* 48ff, and Trocmé, *Formation* 23ff. See Dodd's reply to Nineham in *Historical Tradition* 233 n2. In the same book, 235ff, Dodd picked out of Jn. a number of transitional passages which he thought derived from material akin to that of the synoptics. Of these, three (Jn. 7.1–2; 10.40–42; 11.54) occur after 6.1, where the parallelism which we have observed begins. All three of these can now be seen to be paralleled in Mk. (11.54 in the longer text). Clearly, this does not settle the matter. But the new evidence is strong prima facie support for Dodd. And the question is important. If a good part of the content of a common source can be discovered by comparison of Mk. and Jn., we shall have not only some notion of an extremely early Gospel, but also good indications of the peculiar elements of the Markan and the Johannine traditions, as evidenced by their additions to this source.

That some of the Markan insertions were made late in the development of Mk. is suggested by the coincidence of Jn. with Lk. in most of Lk.'s "great omission" of

Mk. 6.46–8.26. We need not, however, suppose that either John or Mark copied his source whole. Each may have omitted or reworked parts of it. In Jn. 11.7–16, for instance, it is plausible to suppose that John reworked the incoherent elements of the source (reflected by canonical Mk. and the longer text) into a coherent preface to the resurrection of Lazarus. Reworking of the Johannine preface into the incoherent material now found in Mk. and the longer text is incredible. Again, neither Jn.'s omission of the nocturnal initiation nor the longer text's inclusion of it is proof that it was not—or was—in their common source.

But the facts that both Jn. and the longer text of Mk. do include the resurrection story, that both locate it at the same place in their outline, and that both introduce it and follow it by similar pieces of framework—these facts make it likely that the resurrection story was part of the common source on which both Mk. and Jn. were dependent. But if the story was in Mk.'s source it was probably in the earliest form of Mk. If so, we should suppose that the canonical text of Mk. was produced, at least in this instance, by abbreviation of the earlier, longer text. We shall have later to weigh this conclusion against the opposite one, reached above from consideration of the stylistic evidence.

Before leaving the relation of the Johannine Lazarus story to the resurrection story in the longer text, it should be noted that both have a number of parallels to the stories of Jesus' resurrection. This is easily explicable. The similarity of content would necessitate some, chance might account for others, the tendencies to assimilate the phrasing of similar stories and to regard Lazarus' resurrection as a prefiguring of Jesus' would produce yet more. Accordingly it is not surprising that a tomb located in a garden and closed by a stone which had to be rolled away should appear in the stories of both resurrections. (As we saw above on Jn. 11.37, John also included in his Lazarus story the same sort of polemic material which Mk. put in his crucifixion scene, and for the same purpose—dramatic irony before the resurrection.)[8]

8. But there is one further parallel between Jn. and canonical Mk. which deserves attention: Jn. insists that Lazarus was raised on his fourth day in the tomb (11.17,39, emphatic repetition). The passion prophecies of Mk. 8.31, 9.31, and 10.34 all date Jesus' resurrection $\mu\epsilon\tau\grave{a}$ $\tau\rho\epsilon\hat{\iota}\varsigma$ $\dot{\eta}\mu\acute{\epsilon}\rho\alpha\varsigma$, which might mean "on the fourth day." This is why the date was changed to $\tau\hat{\eta}$ $\tau\rho\acute{\iota}\tau\eta$ $\dot{\eta}\mu\acute{\epsilon}\rho\alpha$ by Matthew in all instances and by Luke in two. (In the third—9.44—Luke eliminated the date entirely. Note also the correction by the copyists of Mk., Williams, *Alterations* 45.) For the meaning of the expression in Mk. cf. Mk. 9.2, where $\mu\epsilon\tau\grave{a}$ $\dot{\eta}\mu\acute{\epsilon}\rho\alpha\varsigma$ $\ddot{\epsilon}\xi$ presumably means "on the seventh day"—as shown by the parallel in Ex. 24.16—no doubt for sabbatarian or numerological reasons (Lohmeyer, Grundmann). LXX uses $\mu\epsilon\tau\acute{a}$ with a number of days to indicate the day following the number given. [C.R. remarks that this is particularly clear from the parallelism in Hosea 6.2: $\dot{\upsilon}\gamma\iota\acute{a}\sigma\epsilon\iota$ $\dot{\eta}\mu\hat{a}\varsigma$ $\mu\epsilon\tau\grave{a}$ $\delta\acute{\upsilon}o$ $\dot{\eta}\mu\acute{\epsilon}\rho\alpha\varsigma$, $\dot{\epsilon}\nu$ $\tau\hat{\eta}$ $\dot{\eta}\mu\acute{\epsilon}\rho\alpha$ $\tau\hat{\eta}$ $\tau\rho\acute{\iota}\tau\eta$ $\dot{a}\nu\alpha\sigma\tau\eta\sigma\acute{o}\mu\epsilon\theta\alpha$.] (On this the third-day resurrection tradition may have been built.) See also Dan. 1.15 (LXX), with which cf. Theodotion; Gen 7.10; 8.3,6, etc. Luke seems to have understood Mk.'s $\mu\epsilon\tau\grave{a}$ $\dot{\eta}\mu\acute{\epsilon}\rho\alpha\varsigma$ $\ddot{\epsilon}\xi$ in 9.2 as meaning "on the seventh day," since his $\dot{\omega}\sigma\epsilon\grave{\iota}$ $\dot{\eta}\mu\acute{\epsilon}\rho\alpha\iota$ $\dot{o}\kappa\tau\acute{\omega}$ (9.28) are probably the 7 days of Mk. plus 1 for the day from which the count began (so, on Mk., Swete, followed by Lagrange and Klostermann; on Lk., Creed, followed by Luce; contra, Rengstorf). Later on, however, both Mk. (chs. 15–16) and Jn. (19–20) date the resurrection on the third day after the crucifixion. Therefore the expectation of a resurrection on the fourth day is so odd that its appearance in the Markan passion prophecies and the Johannine Lazarus story may be thought evidence for the hypothesis that John used a source like that of Mk.-plus-the-longer-text, in which the Lazarus story was closely connected to a resurrection prophecy of the Markan type. The only (?) other traces of the

D. *Relation of the new material to the structure of Mk.*

Now we turn to the evidence of Mk. itself as to whether or not the canonical text is an abbreviation of the longer one.

I. POSITION IN THE "HISTORICAL OUTLINE"

The longer text reports that the dead man's sister addressed Jesus publicly by the messianic title "son of David" and that the disciples rebuked her. This is an example of the Markan motif of the "messianic secret" which is always being let slip and then hushed up—the closest parallels are in 1.24f; 3.11f; 8.29f; 9.9,30f; 10.48; a recent discussion is Burkill's *Revelation* esp. 62ff. In canonical Mk. the title "son of David" first appears in 10.47 (the Bartimaeus story) and is difficult to explain there. People had not been saying that Jesus was the Messiah (Mk. 6.14f; 8.28). Only Peter had guessed it (8.29); and he and the others who heard him had been warned to keep it secret (8.30). How, then, did the title indicative of this secret get into the mouth of the beggar Bartimaeus, outside Jericho (10.47)? This question was asked by Ebeling (*Messiasgeheimnis* 92) with the confidence that it would be historically insoluble. The longer text does not supply a historical solution, but it does present a sequence of facts from which historical imagination can create an understandable sequence of events. For between Peter's confession and Bartimaeus' appeal it puts first the use of the title by one of the women of a family with which Jesus was intimate (Jn. 11.5) and then a visit by this woman to Jericho, where (or before which) she had some sort of difference with Jesus such that he did not "receive" or "welcome" her and her companions. By the time he left the city, even the beggar by the roadside knew he claimed to be the son of David.

This argument might have been well received fifty years ago. Today the reader will object: (1) Whatever may be thought of the primitive outline of Mk., the present order of events is not in detail historically reliable (Schmidt, *Rahmen*). (2) The introductory inventions in Jn. 11.1–5 are unreliable (see the comments above) and cannot be used to prove Jesus' intimacy with the family of the deceased; in the longer text of Mk. the sister appears without any introduction and her usage of the title "son of David" is no more explicable than Bartimaeus'. (3) A likely "historical" explanation which would account for a given sequence of events is not necessarily true. To demonstrate its truth one would have to demonstrate that no other explanation was equally likely and that what did happen was what was most likely to happen (often not the case). Such demonstration is impossible in the present instance, therefore this possibly historical construction is of little value as evidence for the question of whether the longer text was prior to the shorter one or vice versa.

---

expectation are Mt. 12.40; 27.63; and the western text of Acts 10.40—another example of the corruption of the western text by the influence of this section of Mk. (Stendahl, *School*, has argued that Mt. 12.40 is a later insertion. Trocmé, *Formation* 180 and n24, also remarked the difficulty and drew from it the conclusion that the original Mk. did not contain chs. 14–16. But if a later interpolator could overlook such contradictions, so could an original compiler. The material is better evidence for diversity of tradition than for details of literary history.)

2. PARALLELS TO THE TRANSFIGURATION AND PASSION STORIES

More important is the fact that insertion of the quotations from the longer text into canonical Mk., at the places Clement indicates, enables us to present three important sections of Mk. as parallel constructions showing the same basic pattern.

Mk. 8.29: Peter's confession of faith	Mk. 10.20: A man's profession of good works.	
(Mt. 16.17: Jesus' blessing of Peter.)	10.21: Jesus loved the man (a youth, Mt. 19.20).	(Lk. 22.31: Jesus' prayer for Peter.)[9]
Mk. 8.31: Jesus' prophecy of his passion.	10.21: Jesus' demand, *Forsake all and follow me.*	Mk. 14.27: Jesus' prophecy of his passion.
8.32: Peter rejects Jesus' teaching (an expression of his love for Jesus).	10.22: The man rejects Jesus' teaching.	14.29: Peter rejects Jesus' teaching (an expression of his love for Jesus).
8.33: Jesus calls Peter Satan.	10.23: Jesus declares that the man can hardly enter the kingdom.	14.30: Jesus' prophecy that Peter will deny him.
8.34: Jesus' demand, *Deny yourself and follow me, Lose your life for me.*	10.28: Peter's claim, *We have forsaken all and followed you.*	14.31: Peter's promise, *Though it cost me my life, I shall not deny you.*
8.34: Implies Jesus' passion.	10.32: Jesus' prophecy of his passion.	14.53ff: Jesus' passion.
9.1: Jesus' prophecy, *Some shall not taste death.*[10]	Longer Text: Resurrection of the man (a youth). His love for Jesus.	(Supposed but not reported: Jesus' resurrection.)
9.2: μετὰ ἡμέρας ἕξ.	LT: μεθ' ἡμέρας ἕξ.	16.1: διαγενομένου τοῦ σαββάτου.[11]
9.2ff: Transfiguration appearance (in white) to Peter, James, and John.	LT: Teaching of the mystery to the youth (in white).[12]	16.5: A youth in white appears, anouncing the resurrection.[13]

9. Note the similarity between Lk.'s prayer for Peter (that Satan shall not prevail over him, that he shall strengthen the brethren) and Mt.'s blessing of Peter (the Church shall be built on him and Hell shall not prevail over it). Furthermore, Lk.'s prayer follows Jesus' teaching that greatness is service and the promise that in Jesus' kindom the twelve shall sit on thrones. This is akin to the request of the sons of Zebedee to sit at Jesus' right and left hands in his kingdom and Jesus' reply that greatness is service. And this request and reply immediately follow the second passage shown here (Mk. 10.20–34 plus the longer text).

10. This verse is probably to be connected with the Lazarus story and the expectation that the beloved disciple would never die, an expectation also attributed to events in a resurrection appearance (Jn. 21.23). Eckhardt's denial of the relationship (*Tod* 16f) does not allow for the fluidity in form of traditional material nor the importance of the common tradition (demonstrated above) behind Mk. and Jn.

11. In its present Markan context this cannot mean μεθ' ἡμέρας ἕξ; yet σάββατον is used in the very next verse to mean "week," and both Matthew (28.1) and Luke (24.1) so changed the construction as to eliminate the ambiguity. Is it accidental that the rejected sense should accord so closely with the two parallels?

12. [K.S. suggests that Mk. 10.35–45 is related to 10.32–34 as is 8.32–33 to 8.31.] This I doubt. There is no rejection of Jesus and no curse on the apostles.

13. Note that Mk. 16.7 promises a resurrection appearance, presumably with some teaching (secret?). It may or may not be supposed that this was the appearance to Peter (Lk. 24.34; I Cor. 15.5) of which the disappearance is one of the most suggestive mysteries of early Christian tradition. (The attempted solution by Annand, *He Was Seen,* does not convince me.)

These texts seem to follow the same basic pattern: acceptance, blessing, demand for sacrifice, rejection, curse; renewed demand for sacrifice, Jesus' fulfilment of the demand, resurrection, and, one week later, revelation of the mystery.[14] Yet it would seem also that the expression of this basic pattern has been carried out with considerable differences even as to the most important points: Mk. 8.34 does not explicitly foretell or report Jesus' passion, but merely implies it, and Mk. 16.1ff merely implies the resurrection; but the implication is certain in both instances, so there is no denying the identity of the basic pattern. Similarly, in 8.29–9.10 and in 10.20–34 plus the longer text, the pattern is presented in concentrated form with relatively little extraneous material, whereas in 14.27–16.8 it is worked into the much larger passion story in which the earlier parts of it (14.27–31) appear as an excrescence unimportant to the course of the main action.

Thus the relation between these passages is somewhat similar to that between the variant forms of identical stories (discussed above) and the variant developments by Mark and John of a common narrative presumably given by tradition. But here there seems to be an important difference. It can hardly be supposed that the transfiguration, the Lazarus story, and the passion story are all variants of a single narrative. (Against the supposition that the transfiguration is an account of a resurrection appearance see above, p. 149). Nor do the stories of Peter's confession and the rich young ruler seem variants of a single original. Rather, the common pattern here is the result not of common origin, but of common purpose, which has three times put together pieces of different origins to express the same teaching. The teaching seems to be that of human depravity and the consequent vicarious atonement: Even those who accept Jesus (or the Law) and therefore receive his blessing cannot accept the demand for sacrifice, and therefore come under his curse; consequently he sacrifices himself, rises from the dead, and communicates to his unworthy followers the mystery of his resurrection. The parallels to this in Paul are well known (e.g., Rom. 5.8: God shows his love for us in that while we were yet sinners Christ died for us), and the *Hodayot* from Qumran have shown that even before Jesus' time some circles in Judaism were magnifying human depravity and God's salvation of his elect in spite of it (*Hodayot* I.20ff; III.24ff; IV.29ff; etc.).

However, in none of the three passages outlined above is the doctrine clearly expressed. Instead it is implied by the *sequence* of stories and sayings, of which no single one states it clearly. Only when the three pericopae are put side by side does the repetition of the pattern and thus its significance appear. The pattern can hardly be accidental—the parallels are too close; why, then, did the author not state its significance? Evidently he expected his book to be taught, and left the explanation of these patterns to the teacher. This is exactly what Clement's letter says Mark did (I.22–26). The same conclusion was reached by Bird (γάρ 174).

But the fact that Clement realized that there was latent teaching in Mk. does not prove that his account of the origin of the longer text is correct. And the above

14. K.S. comments: "Another complex is Thomas in Jn. 20 with a week's delay, coupled with Thomas' role in the *Gospel of Thomas*, where he receives the secret revelation in three words." This is perhaps important, especially because of the connection of Thomas with Salome, to be noted below.

demonstrated fact—that the longer text taken together with Mk. 10.20–32 embodies a pattern found in two pericopae of the canonical Gospel—suggests that the longer text was originally part of the Gospel, since the patterns are presumably the work of a redactor and the three instances of the same pattern look like three examples of the work of the same redactor. This is particularly so because the patterns are not explicit or even obvious; therefore one might say they would not have served as models for some later editor who added the material of the longer text to produce another example. But against this there is evidence that these patterns were recognized by later editors (who had the exegetic traditions of their churches to guide them). Matthew added to Mk. the blessing of Peter, Luke, the prayer for Peter, and both of these additions stand in exactly the right places to extend and emphasize the patterns; this can hardly be accident. (See, further, note 9 on the three texts outlined above.) Accordingly, it is not impossible that the material of the longer text should have been interpolated after 10.34 in order to produce another example of a pattern useful for exegetic purposes. However, the supposition that all three examples were produced by the same redactor seems more likely. The additions in Mt. and Lk. are comparatively minor and—although they embody independent tradition—their attachment to the pattern would have been suggested by its existence. In Mk. 10.20–32, on the contrary, the most important elements of the pattern are lacking; and the addition of the material of the longer text would not merely have filled out an existing example, but would have created a new one.

Postscript: On rereading this section in 1966, some three years and more since it was written, I must confess I am more dubious than ever, not only as to the significance of these parallels, but even as to their actual parallelism. Mk. 10.21 is not actually paralleled in Mk. 8 or 14, and even if the additions from Mt. and Lk. be supposed to have been derived from early tradition, love is neither a blessing nor a prayer. The rejection of Jesus in Mk. 10.22 is something quite different from Peter's expressions of loyalty in 8.32 and 14.29, and they, in turn, are different from each other. 10.28 is not a new demand for sacrifice, but a claim to have made the necessary sacrifice. In the longer text and in 9.1 we have the youth's resurrection, not Jesus'. Consequently—though the one resurrection was doubtless thought to prefigure the other—the proposed interpretation in terms of the vicarious atonement seems forced. A further fact which seems to me important is that these alleged parallels do not fit easily into the structure of Mk. revealed by the interpretation of Mk. 10, to be presented in the following section. But the interpretation of Mk. 10 is much better supported than the argument for the above parallels. Accordingly, I suspect the parallelism may be due not to "Mark's" intention but to my invention. But if I was deceived before, when I could see it, I may be deceived now, when I can't. Accordingly, I submit the problem to the reader.

3. RELATION TO THE BAPTISMAL CONCERN OF MK. 10.13–45

The judgment that the material of the longer text was probably coeval with 10.17–34 is further supported by the fact that they fit together as parts of a larger section,

10.13–45—a pericope designed to provide a textual basis for systematic teaching concerning baptism, teaching which followed the baptismal service point by point. Accordingly, the pericope may have been read at the baptismal service preceding the pascha. This was first pointed out to me by Richardson in a letter (of January 13, 1961) which furnished not only the thesis, but also some important items of the evidence I shall use to support it. Though the bulk of the following argument is mine, I have profited so greatly by discussions with Richardson that it would be impossible to indicate exactly the limits of his contributions. This general acknowledgment—with my thanks—must stand in place of many brackets and initials.[15]

The evidence for treating the whole passage, 10.13–45, as a baptismal pericope is as follows:

(a) Clement says the longer text was written εἰς τὴν τῶν τελειουμένων χρῆσιν (I.22) and was read πρὸς αὐτοὺς μόνους τοὺς μυουμένους τὰ μεγάλα μυστήρια (II.2). This proves its liturgical use in his church; and τὰ μεγάλα μυστήρια would most easily be referred to the pascha, the annual occasion for baptism. Clement sharply distinguishes ordinary baptism—τὸ λουτρόν—as the lowest stage of the Christian initiation, from τὰ μεγάλα μυστήρια—see the commentary on II.2; but Clement's church may have practiced a second baptism by which the believer achieved true gnosis. This question must be postponed to Chapter Five; here it is enough to remark that such higher initiatory rites were common in second-century Christianity (Acts 8.14–17; 19.1–7; Irenaeus (Harvey, I.14.1 = Stieren, I.21.1f). [C.R. thinks a second baptism unlikely; he would explain τὸ λουτρόν as baptism administered alone and τὰ μεγάλα μυστήρια as the entire paschal ceremony, including baptism.]

(b) The liturgical use of this pericope in a most important service in Clement's church would account for (1) the fact that almost half of Clement's quotations of Mk. come from chs. 9 and 10 (above, p. 79, and Appendix D); (2) the influence of this pericope on the western text (above, p. 122); (3) the frequency with which it is echoed by the other parts of Mk. (above, pp. 139ff); and (4) the fact that Luke ends his "great insertion" (9.51–18.14) and comes back to the text of Mk. precisely at the beginning of this pericope (Mk. 10.13 = Lk. 18.15).

(c) That the service—the μεγάλα μυστήρια—with which Clement associated this material was (or included) some sort of baptism may be indicated by the scriptural reminiscences with which he justifies himself for quoting the passage to Theodore (II.16ff): ἡμεῖς δὲ υἱοὶ φωτός ἐσμεν, πεφωτισμένοι τῇ ἐξ ὕψους ἀνατολῇ τοῦ πνεύματος τοῦ κυρίου· οὗ δὲ τὸ πνεῦμα τοῦ κυρίου, φησίν, ἐκεῖ ἐλευθερία, πάντα γὰρ καθαρὰ τοῖς καθαροῖς. The baptismal associations of these verses are familiar; the references in the commentary, above, could easily be multiplied.

(d) The structure of canonical Mk. can be seen as parallel to that of the paschal service: chs. 1–8.30 can be taken as exoteric teaching for those catechumens not yet ready for baptism. Then, with the creed (Peter's confession) and the consequent transfiguration would begin the esoteric teaching for those about to be baptized (so

15. A similar interpretation of the longer text alone as a baptismal lection was suggested by G.L., but this suggestion rested on interpretations of detail which I do not think plausible and therefore have not presented.

Riesenfeld, *Tradition* 162). Here the baptismal pericope would follow. After the baptism the story, like the service, proceeds to Jerusalem, the eucharist, passion, and resurrection, and closes with a hint of the *disciplina arcani* in 16.8. It must be admitted that this outline is obscured by numerous interpolations in Mk., but one could defend the proposition that it remains recognizable. Its recognition would confirm the hypothesis that 10.13–45 is a baptismal pericope: the section stands at the very place in Mk. where the general outline would require such a pericope.

(e) Finally, the details of Mk. 10.13–34 + the longer text + 35–45, and the order in which they occur, correspond to the content and order of the elements in the baptismal service. This I shall now demonstrate by a commentary (points i–xii):

(i) The pericope begins with Mk.10. 13–16, a pronouncement story of which the key verses are 14–15, ἄφετε τὰ παιδία ἔρχεσθαι πρός με, μὴ κωλύετε αὐτά, τῶν γάρ τοιούτων ἐστὶν ἡ βασιλεία τοῦ θεοῦ, (15) ἀμὴν λέγω ὑμῖν, ὃς ἂν μὴ δέξηται τὴν βασιλείαν τοῦ θεοῦ ὡς παιδίον οὐ μὴ εἰσέλθῃ εἰς αὐτήν. 15 is omitted by Mt. and may not have stood in his text; Bultmann (*Geschichte* 32), Lohmeyer, and Klostermann (both *ad loc.*) recognize it as a secondary addition. Mt. has a different version in 18.3 (the common supposition that this derives from Mk.—e.g., my *Comments* 45—is gratuitous). Another presumably underlies Jn. 3.3ff. Whatever the original sense of the saying, Jn. is conclusive evidence of its interpretation to refer to baptism, and the same interpretation probably explains its addition to the stories here and in Mt. 18 (cf. Mt. 11.25,29 ἄρατε τὸν ζυγόν = קבל עול מלכות שמים = δέχεσθαι τὴν βασιλείαν— the essential act of the convert. This explains the apparent contradiction: only those who accept the kingdom can enter it, Dodd, *Parables* 34.) Cullmann, *Baptism* 72ff, has established the likelihood that there was an early baptismal formula τί κωλύει; οὐδὲν κωλύει. Of this the μὴ κωλύετε in the text may be an echo. Baptism as rebirth, and the childlikeness of candidates and recipients, are commonplaces of early Christian literature; besides the passages cited above, see I Pet. 1.13f; 2.2; Hermas, *Mandates* II.1; *Similitudes* IX.29.1; *Acta Thomae* 132; *Gospel of Thomas* (Leipoldt) 22; *Clementine Homilies* VII.8; XI.26; *Sibylline Oracles* VIII.313ff; Grant, *Children* 71. Accordingly we need not enter the current controversy as to whether Mk. 10.13ff was written to justify *infant* baptism (so Jeremias, *Kindertaufe*; contra, Aland, *Säuglings-taufe*). Admittedly the passage was used in Tertullian's time to justify infant baptism (*De baptismo* XVIII), and when infant baptism was provided for, infants were baptized first (Hippolytus, *Apostolic Tradition* XXI.4), as Mk. 10.13ff stands first in the Markan pericope. But the position of the passage would be justified even in a pericope dealing solely with adult baptism, since it states a sine qua non. This is why its parallel also stands first in the discussion of baptism in Jn. 3. This was almost seen by Grund-mann, on Mk. 10.17–31: "One must reckon with the possibility that the pericopae concerning the blessing of the children and the rich young ruler, with the attached conversation with the disciples, had been put together in some pre-Markan tradition as answers to the question: How can one enter the kingdom of God?"

(ii) Having begun with the blessing of those who are like children (in what way need not concern us), the pericope in Mk. goes on to more specific requirements for baptism (verses 17–22): monotheism, observance of the Ten Commandments,

renunciation of property.[16] These are presented in answer to the question, "What shall I do to inherit eternal life?" Equivalent questions in Acts 16.30 and 2.37 lead directly to baptism; cf. also Acts 11.18, where baptism is τὴν μετάνοιαν εἰς ζωήν (with a preceding reference to the κωλύειν formula, as here). In Lk. 10.25 the same question is answered by the two great commandments, which also appear in the *Didache* as the first point of the instruction to be recited before baptism (I.2, cf. VII.1). Cf. Justin Martyr, *First Apology* 61.2, the preparation for baptism: ὅσοι ἂν πεισθῶσι καὶ πιστεύωσιν ἀληθῆ ταῦτα τὰ ὑφ᾽ ἡμῶν διδασκόμενα καὶ λεγόμενα εἶναι (that is, monotheism and the role of Jesus), καὶ βιοῦν οὕτως δύνασθαι ὑπισχνῶνται (according to the commandments of Jesus)—these proceed to baptism. Baptismal catechesis presumably lies behind the similar summary of Christian teaching in Aristides, *Apologia* 15.3–9 (monotheism, commandments, sharing property with the poor). Again, in the passages behind which Boismard, *Liturgie,* has recognized a baptismal catechism (I Pet. 1.3–12; Titus 2.12–14; I Jn. 3.1–11—especially this last) appears the same sequence as in Mk. 10. 13–22: children of God, the holiness of God, the consequent obligation to keep the commandments and to share with the poor (ποιεῖν δικαιοσύνην). On I Pet. 1.3–21 see also Windisch-Preisker, *Briefe* 157. Preisker likewise sees in this a prebaptismal διδαχή. Note also the sequence of themes in 17–21: the holiness and fatherhood of God, the fear (= obedience) of God, the worthlessness of silver and gold, the saving death and resurrection of Christ. This same sequence appears in Mk. 10.17–34. The evidence given by Preisker and Boismard seems to me to refute the contention of Robinson, *Survey,* that in NT times there was no prebaptismal instruction. Robinson's arguments are all based on silence; and the most impressive instances of silence, those in Acts, are not probative because most of them report baptisms resultant on miracles and therefore not to be taken as evidence of normal procedure.

(iii) In these passages used by Preisker and Boismard, however, the holiness of God is taken as an attribute to be realized also in the lives of his children. In Mk. 10.18 the goodness of God is sharply declared unique: τί με λέγεις ἀγαθόν; οὐδεὶς ἀγαθὸς εἰ μὴ εἷς ὁ θεός. This declaration is clearly an insertion irrelevant to the latter half of Jesus' reply (τὰς ἐντολὰς οἶδας, κ.τ.λ.) and to all the rest of the story. Only the latter half of Jesus' reply responds to the preceding question, and only this latter half is found in the independent version of the same story in Lk. 10.25f. Moreover, the *Didache* (I.2) parallel to Lk., introducing the commandments as ἡ ὁδὸς τῆς ζωῆς, suggests a pre-Christian, Jewish origin for the present question and answer in its Lucan form, and a variant of the same question and answer appears in many passages of rabbinic literature as an exegesis of Ps. 39.13ff (Margulies, *Wayyikra' Rabbah,* sec. 16.2). Accordingly, the insertion in the Markan form has to be explained. Why should an editor have inserted such a detail? To adapt the story to the requirements of baptismal catechesis. The catechesis required an initial proof text for monotheism, so a verbal detail ("good master") was seized on as an excuse to insert this irrelevant proof text. That

16. Walter, *Analyse,* has not persuaded me that the following account should be changed.

οὐδεὶς   ἀγαθός,
εἰ μὴ εἷς   ὁ θεός.

is a proof text is clear not only from its mnemonic form, but also from its background and its history in Christian exegesis. Its background is generally in acclamations of the εἷς θεός type (studied by Peterson, Εἷς), but more specifically in Philo, De mutatione nominum 7: Moses, πάντα διὰ πάντων ἐρευνήσας ἐζήτει τὸν τριπόθητον καὶ μόνον ἀγαθὸν τηλαυγῶς ἰδεῖν, and therefore prayed to see God (Ex. 33.13). Even more striking is De somniis I.148–149, ταῖς μὲν δὴ τῶν ἄκρως κεκαθαρμένων διανοίαις ἀψοφητὶ μόνος ἀοράτως ὁ τῶν ὅλων ἡγεμὼν ἐμπεριπατεῖ ... ταῖς δὲ τῶν ἔτι ἀπολουομένων, μήπω δὲ κατὰ τὸ παντελὲς ἐκνιψαμένων ... ἄγγελοι, λόγοι θεῖοι, φαιδρύνοντες αὐτὰς τοῖς καλοκἀγαθίας δόγμασιν. ὅσα δὲ ἐξοικίζεται κακῶν οἰκητόρων στίφη, ἵνα εἷς ὁ ἀγαθὸς εἰσοικίσηται, δῆλόν ἐστι. σπούδαζε οὖν, ὦ ψυχή, θεοῦ οἶκος γενέσθαι, ἱερὸν ἅγιον. The connections of this passage with the rhetoric of Christian baptism are so numerous that it may be thought additional evidence for the baptismal usage of the εἷς ὁ ἀγαθός/θεός phrase and consequently of the Markan pericope to which the phrase was added. As for the history of Mk. 10.18 in Christian exegesis, that shows the verse constantly used, as in this passage, to inculcate monotheism. It appears in Justin, First Apology 16.6f, as proof ὡς ... τὸς θεὸν μόνον δεῖ προσκυνεῖν, and Dialogue 101.1 as a proof text against the Marcionites—Jesus was saved by the God of the OT. Marcion, for his part, used it to prove that the true God, qua good, is superior to both Jesus and the demiurge (Hippolytus, Philosophumena VII.31). In Ptolemaeus it is proof of the nature of the τέλειος θεός ... ὁ πατήρ, ἐξ οὗ τὰ πάντα (Epiphanius, Panarion XXXIII.7.5f). Irenaeus (Harvey, I.13.2 = Stieren, I.20.2) reports that the Marcosians used it to the same purpose; so, too, the Naassenes in Hippolytus Philosophumena V.7 (fol. 30 verso). It was not only an important text in gnosticism (Grant, Gnosis 4), but also a favorite of Clement (Osborn, Philosophy 65)—again, as a proof of a single, supreme God τὸν ἀγαθὸν καὶ πρῶτον καὶ μόνον ζωῆς αἰωνίου ταμίαν, ἣν ὁ υἱὸς δίδωσιν ἡμῖν παρ᾽ ἐκείνου λαβών (III.164.11f—again a baptismal theme).

(iv) The use of the ten commandments in baptismal teaching, as in Mk. 10.19, appears already in the Didache (II.1–3) and probably in Pliny's epistle of the year 112 (X.96.7; Grant, Decalogue 11f); it was anticipated by their use in connection with the shemaʿ—the nearest thing in Israelite tradition to a confession of faith (Kuhn, Phylakterien; Grant, Decalogue 1). [Stendahl reminds me that in Christian baptismal practice not the whole decalogue was used, but only the latter half, as in Mk. 10.19. See his School 63.]

(v) ἐμβλέψας αὐτῷ ἠγάπησεν αὐτόν (Mk. 10.21) is not paralleled in either Mt. or Lk. Either the later evangelists deleted it as improper (so Wellhausen EM, ad loc.), or they did not find it in their texts of Mk. Its connection with the rest of the Markan story is difficult to explain. Does it imply that because Jesus loved the young man he told him that in order to be saved he must sell his belongings and follow him? If Jesus had not loved him would he have concealed this secret and let him go to hell? (So Lohmeyer!) Or does it imply that because Jesus loved him his fulfilment of the commandments, which would otherwise have sufficed for salvation, became insufficient

and this extra requirement (which he would not meet) was imposed on him by a special act of divine love? (So Lagrange!) Such "explanations" suggest (by their desperation) that the phrase here is intrusive. So does the fact that it is not in Mk.'s manner, when repeating himself, to transfer to one person what he says elsewhere of another. Such transferences are more common in the use of Markan material by the later evangelists (see above, p. 137). Accordingly, the phrase here is an interpolation and the longer text enables us to explain it. It was added here to identify this man with the youth of the following passage in the longer text, where the same phrase is used with a clear narrative function: the youth, looking at Jesus, loved him, *and therefore* begged to be with him, *and therefore* the two of them went to the youth's house. This makes sense. The same hand probably added ἦν γὰρ ἔχων κτήματα πολλά to the longer text (III.6) for the same purpose of identifying the two characters (and some copyist abbreviated it to ἦν γὰρ πλούσιος; see above, in the commentary, *ad loc.*). The editor who made these interpolations (both in canonical Mk. and in the longer text) seems to have worked after Matthew and Luke, but worked so early that his addition has probably left no trace in the MS tradition of Mk. 10.21. (The omission of ἠγάπησεν αὐτὸν καὶ by 11, 15, and 579 is more likely censorship.) However, it is notable that Mt. 19.20 makes the unidentified rich man of Mk. a "youth"—νεανίσκος —like the one in the following passage of the longer text, and thus effects the same identification as did the editor of Mk., but without the awkwardness of the intrusive phrase and the possibly objectionable attribution to Jesus of love for a man. Here we have perhaps another indication that Mt. knew the longer text (cf. the commentary on προσεκύνησεν, II.24, and on καὶ προσελθών, III.1, above). The motive for identifying the two characters was the baptismal use of the pericope, for ἠγάπησεν αὐτόν in 10.21 looks forward to the resurrection and the nocturnal initiation (baptism) in the longer text. Baptism is the gift of love. So Eph. 5.25ff ὁ χριστὸς ἠγάπησεν τὴν ἐκκλησίαν καὶ ἑαυτὸν παρέδωκεν ὑπὲρ αὐτῆς ἵνα αὐτὴν ἁγιάσῃ καθαρίσας τῷ λουτρῷ τοῦ ὕδατος ἐν ῥήματι. Apoc. 1.5, τῷ ἀγαπῶντι ἡμᾶς καὶ λύσαντι (λούσαντι, koine, *Pal.gig.vg.*) ἡμᾶς ἐκ τῶν ἁμαρτιῶν ἡμῶν ἐν τῷ αἵματι αὐτοῦ. Jn. 3.16 and 13.1ff. (Is footwashing a Johannine second baptism?)

(vi) The abandonment of property as a requirement for baptism was evidently a peculiarity of that church from which this material originally derived. The corollary and compensation of this primitive communism appear in verses 28–30: Whoever joins the group enjoys its common property and is a member of its common family. νῦν ἐν τῷ καιρῷ τούτῳ . . . μετὰ διωγμῶν is hardly explicable otherwise. So the ancient Church understood the passage (Cramer; Theophylact) and so, generally, do modern commentators (cited by Lagrange, *ad loc.*). Goguel's objection (*Persécutions* 275 n3) that community of goods was "never" realized is a *petitio principii*: it apparently was realized in the community from which this text came (cf. Lohmeyer, 214–219; Grundmann, *ad loc.*). The parallels discussed above, p. 165, if valid, would show that verse 28 (Peter's claim, "We have left all and followed") was already attached to the story in the earliest form of Mk. Verses 26–27 are clearly secondary (Bultmann, *Geschichte* 21). They reflect the abandonment of the original requirement and explain that, in spite of the famous saying about the camel, salvation is possible even for those

who keep their wealth. A similar modification appears in Mt. 19.21, where the un-
conditional requirement of Mk. is softened to a counsel of perfection: εἰ θέλεις τέλειος
εἶναι. Since the Markan requirement was thus soon abandoned, no survival of it is
to be expected in the baptismal teaching of the later Church. But it is in place in a
baptismal pericope, where later baptismal teaching substituted for it the requirement
of indiscriminate charity: Didache I.5, παντὶ τῷ αἰτοῦντί σε δίδου καὶ μὴ ἀπαίτει.
(Further passages cited above, ii, end.) The rewards in this world are the consequences
of church membership, effected by baptism (verses 28–30), "and, in the world to
come, eternal life," made available by baptism.

(vii) Hereupon follows the prophecy of the passion and resurrection because, in
the first place, it is the essential of the specifically Christian creed; and in the baptismal
service, as here, this creed follows the preliminary instructions in monotheism, commandments, and charity, which Christianity had in common with other forms of
Judaism (cf. the "Two Ways," in Didache I–VI). Mark also attached the passion and
resurrection prophecy to Peter's confession in ch. 8, of which it fills out the credal
content (verses 29–31): Son . . . suffered . . . dead . . . rose again. Like the creed, the
passion prophecy is here presented as a μυστήριον (Theophylact, ad loc.), "esoteric
teaching" (Bultmann, Geschichte 357). In the second place, Jesus' resurrection is the
assurance of the efficacy of baptism and the reliability of the promise—in the preceding verses—of reward in the world to come (I Cor. 15.12–22). Finally, Jesus'
passion, death, burial, and resurrection are, according to Paul, the essential content
of baptism; the effect of baptism is to make the initiate participate in these (Rom.
6.3f). And this same use of baptism as the symbol of passion, death, and burial appears in the immediately following section of Mk. (10.38, δύνασθε . . . τὸ βάπτισμα
ὃ ἐγὼ βαπτίζομαι βαπτισθῆναι;). It is therefore plausible to suppose that the passion
prophecy appears in this baptismal pericope not only as the assurance, but also as
the explanation of the rite's efficacy.

(viii) Chrysostom, De quatriduano Lazaro, treats the Lazarus story as the immediate
sequel and consequence of the prophecies of the passion, and so, too, it is here, in the
longer text of Mk. Chrysostom sees in it Jesus' demonstration of his power to raise
the dead, thus the antitype of his own resurrection. For the author of the longer text
it was probably also the antitype of the two resurrections of the believer, both the final
resurrection which will bring the life of the world to come, promised above—this
interpretation appears in Irenaeus (Harvey, V.13 = Stieren, V.13)—and also the
initial, baptismal resurrection of the sinner from the death of sin—this interpretation
appears in Origen, for example, in Homilia in Jeremiam IX.3 (ed. Klostermann,
GCS Origines, vol. 3, pp. 67f) and in Hippolytus Commentary on Jn. (ed. Bonwetsch and
Achelis, GCS Hippolytus, vol. 1.II, p. 216), where the interpretation of the story as a
preparation for baptism is explicit: on the statement that Lazarus was sick, Hippolytus comments, ὦ ἀσθένεια πυρετοὺς ψυχῶν ἀποσοβοῦσα καὶ ἰδρῶτας βαπτίσματος
δροσίζουσα, καὶ λαμπρὰς στολὰς ψυχῆς ἐξυφαίνουσα. Moreover, the interpretation of
baptism as resurrection from the dead seems to have been held already by the Carpocratians (below, p. 185) and is traceable through the hymn quoted in Eph. 5.14
back to the time and possibly to the affiliates of the Qumran sect; see Kuhn, Epheser-

brief 342–345. Accordingly, the story is perfectly in place where the longer text puts it in this baptismal pericope. The baptismal and the literal interpretations are conjoined in the second-century and perhaps Egyptian *Epistula Apostolorum*, 27(38), where Jesus says, "And therefore, *indeed*, I have gone down to

Abraham, Isaac, and Jacob,	⟨*the place of*⟩ *Lazarus, and have preached*
to your fathers the prophets,	⟨*to the righteous and*⟩ *the prophets*
and have brought them word	
that they might come out of	*that they might come out of*
the rest, which is beneath,	*the rest, which is beneath,*
into the heavens;	*and ascend to that which is* ⟨*above*⟩
and I have given	. . .
them the right hand	*right* ⟨*han*⟩*d on them* . . .

of the baptism of life and forgiveness and release, *freeing* from all evil, as *I have* also *done* for you, and from now on also for those who believe on me."[17] Here the saviour's entering the tomb (underworld) and reaching his hand to the dead agree with the longer text against Jn. Similar interpretation and agreements appear in the *Apocryphon of John* (edd. Krause and Labib, 195ff, 250ff) and in Methodius, *De resurrectione* I.23 end (ed. Bonwetsch, *GCS*, p. 248): In saving the wicked from sin πρέπει δὲ τῷ θεῷ ἀνοίγειν τὰ μνημεῖα ἑκάστου καὶ ἐξάγειν ἐκ τῶν μνημείων ἡμᾶς ἐζωοποιημένους, ὥσπερ ὁ σωτὴρ τὸν Λάζαρον εἵλκυσεν ἔξω. This agrees with the longer text against Jn. in making Jesus open the tomb himself and (probably) raise Lazarus by hand.

Thus the Lazarus story, in both its Johannine and Markan forms, was connected with baptismal resurrection. This perhaps explains why John prefaces his version of the story by a contrast of Jesus with the Baptist, continuing his polemic against the latter (1.26ff; 3.26ff; 4.1). In 10.40ff he has Jesus go to the Baptist's original territory and there emphasizes the differences between them: καὶ πολλοὶ ἦλθον πρὸς αὐτὸν καὶ ἔλεγον ὅτι Ἰωάννης μὲν σημεῖον ἐποίησεν οὐδέν, πάντα δὲ ὅσα εἶπεν Ἰωάννης περὶ τούτου ἀληθῆ ἦν. This leads directly to the raising of Lazarus, Jesus' greatest σημεῖον (that is, miracle, as in Jn. 11.47; 12.18; cf. Melito, *On the Passion* 12, line 38), but the intention may also be to contrast the miraculous resurrection effected by the Christian σημεῖον (sign = baptism: Clement III.138.15; cf. circumcision, Rom. 4.11) with Johannite baptism which—John implies—had no such supernatural effect; a similar contrast is made in Acts 19.1–7.

(ix) The baptismal concern which has thus far dominated the pericope makes it probable that the nocturnal initiation which follows the Lazarus story should be understood to be a baptism. This probability finds curious confirmation in a tradition reported from Ephraem Syrus by Dionysius bar Salibi, that Lazarus was raised in order to be baptized, and that after his baptism he was taken to Alexandria (where the longer text appears). Baumstark, *Lazarusakten*, from whose discussion I know the

17. My translation from Duensing's German. The italics are his and distinguish elements peculiar to the older, but imperfectly preserved, Coptic text, from the complete, but corrupt, Ethiopic. His revised translation (Hennecke-Schneemelcher I.141) presents no significant difference.

passage, thinks the source must have been a very early περίοδος, πράξεις, or μαρτύριον Λαζάρου (p. 211). Another trace of the same tradition perhaps appears in the *Iohannis Evangelium Apocryphum Arabice* (tr. I. Galbiati, Milan, 1957), LIII.8, etc., which refers to "the disciple whom Jesus loved and whom he instructed in his mysteries"; cf. Clement's description of the rich young ruler as ὑπὸ τοῦ κυρίου συντελειούμενος (II.221. 27). These passages may reflect knowledge of at least the content of the longer text, where the baptismal character of the initiation is indicated not only by the preceding context, surveyed above, but also by the details of the rite: it is *after six days*, it is *nocturnal*, the prescribed costume is *a sheet to be worn over the naked body*, and the content is *the mystery of the kingdom of God*. Let us examine these details one by one.

"THE SIX DAYS," Richardson wrote to me, "are the six days of the Alexandrine paschal feast (Dionysius of Alexandria, *Epistle to Basilides* 1 end). Cf. the transfiguration six days, Mk. 9.2, and the paschal six days of Jn. 12.1. The earlier custom of two days is in Mk. 14.1, *Didache* VII.4, and Hippolytus, *Apostolic Tradition* XX.7; XXIX.2, and is referred to by Dionysius, *loc. cit.*" However, Dionysius wrote of the length of the *fast* before the feast celebrating the resurrection, and his letter makes clear that even as to this there were variations of practice. Mk. 14.1, μετὰ δύο ἡμέρας, supposes a three-day preparation period (see above, p. 163 n8). Thus the story of the anointing, which it places on the first day, accords with the preparatory washing of the catechumens which Hippolytus, *Apostolic Tradition* XX.5, sets on Maundy Thursday, to be followed by the fast on Friday and Saturday. And Hippolytus XX.1–3 supposes that even before these three days there had been a preparatory period in which those set apart to be baptized had undergone examination, Gospel reading, and daily exorcism. A seven-day period of preparation for baptism is supposed in *Acta Thomae* 26 end. Jn. 12.1, which puts the anointing πρὸ ἓξ ἡμερῶν τοῦ πάσχα, probably presupposes such a period, and the importance in pre-Markan tradition of a six-day period prior to the initiatory revelation is strongly suggested by the similarities (set forth above, section 2) of Mk. 8.29–9.8; 10.20–32 plus the longer text; and 14.27–16.5. So it seems likely that the six days' preparation before baptism is even earlier than the two days' fast of the *Didache*. Both seven- and three-day periods of preparation are frequently required for magical operations; e.g., *PGM* III. 304; V. 228; VII. 334; XIII. 115, 118, 674.

NOCTURNAL: Hippolytus, *Apostolic Tradition* XXI.1, sets baptism at cockcrow, following an all night vigil. This is repeated by the later Church orders (e.g., *Apostolic Constitutions* V.19.3) and seems to have been common usage. Baptism is nocturnal in *Acta Petri et Andreae* 21 end; *Martyrium Matthaei* 8; *Acta Thomae* 27; and probably *Clementine Homilies* XIV.1. If the author of Acts 10.47 knew the geography of Palestine, he must have thought baptism nocturnal: Caesarea is 10 hours by horse from Joppa (Baedeker, *Palestine* 239) so Peter would have arrived in the evening. Baptism is again nocturnal in Acts 16.33. The footwashing in Jn. 13 (a variant of baptism) is nocturnal. Nicodemus, in Jn. 3, comes to Jesus by night and receives instruction concerning baptism as the means of entering the kingdom of God (3.3,5,13ff).

THE SHEET OVER THE NAKED BODY: Nudity in baptism is prescribed by Hippolytus *Apostolic Tradition* XXI.3,5,11, and was required by the Pharisees in proselyte baptism

as well as in immersions for purification (*Mikwa'ot* VIII end and IX; *B. Yebamot* 47b). Particularly close to the longer text, where the prescribed garment is a σινδών, is *Acta Thomae* 121, where the apostle has to baptize a young lady: ἐκέλευσεν τῇ τροφῷ αὐτῆς ἀποδύειν αὐτὴν καὶ σινδόνα αὐτὴν περιζῶσαι. Undressing for baptism appears also in *Acta Barnabae* 12 and *Martyrium Matthaei* 27. In the Johannine foot-washing (which Aphraates, *Demonstratio* XII.10, interpreted as a baptism) Jesus is naked except for a towel (λέντιον, 13.4), which the Syriac versions describe as a σινδών (ܟܬܢܐ). Is it by chance that the beggar in Mk. 10.50 (immediately after the second passage of the longer text) throws away his himation when he comes to Jesus to be cured? The gesture was understood as symbolic by the commentator in Cramer, *ad loc.* and may have been so understood by the author. That naked baptism was already customary in Paul's time is shown by his allegorizing the undressing for it and dressing after it: Col. 2.11f, ἐν τῇ ἀπεκδύσει τοῦ σώματος τῆς σαρκὸς, ἐν τῇ περιτομῇ τοῦ χριστοῦ . . . ἐν τῷ βαπτίσματι; Gal. 3.27, ὅσοι γὰρ εἰς χριστὸν ἐβαπτίσθητε χριστὸν ἐνεδύσασθε; further, I Cor. 15.33ff (as interpreted by *Odes of Solomon* 15.8, see Lietzmann, *Korinther, ad loc.*) and II Cor. 5.2. Similar allegorization (not apparently dependent on Paul) appears in the *Gospel of Thomas* (Leipoldt) 37; the *Gospel according to the Egyptians* (Clement, II.238.24ff); and *P. Oxy.* 655 end; and the same general theme recurs in the *Gospel according to Philip* (Schenke, 77, 101); *Clementine Homilies* VIII.22.4–23.1; Hippolytus, *Philosophumena* V.19 end (the Sethians); Irenaeus (Harvey, I.14.1–4 = Stieren, 1.21.1–5—the Valentinians); *Acta Thomae* 132 (text P only); Justin, *Dialogue* 116; Clement III.131.25ff (*Excerpta ex Theodoto*); 140.6ff; 143.24ff (*Eclogae*); *Apostolic Constitutions* VI.6; and many later Christian documents. This early dissemination of the theme argues an early origin.

The indicated baptismal practice (nudity and σινδών) lent itself particularly to Pauline exegesis because (as Lieberman pointed out to me) the initiatory σινδών (which LXX regularly uses to translate סדין) was also the regular burial garment; cf. *J. Kil'ayim* IX.4 (32b) = *J. Ketubot* XII.3 (35a) בסדין אחד נקבר רבי, "Rabbi ⟨Judah, the Patriarch⟩ was buried in a single σινδών" (and no other garment); *J. Terumot* VIII.10 (46b, inf.), יכרך המת בסדינו, "Let the dead man be wrapped in his σινδών" (that is, let the man be abandoned to his fate—a current saying). Accordingly, Jesus had been buried in a σινδών (Mk. 15.46 and parallels). Paul's interpretation of baptism as death and burial with Jesus suggests that the σινδών over the naked body was the customary costume as early as Paul's time.

The σινδών was not a "proper" garment, though it was worn occasionally. Crates, the cynic, when called down by the Athenian police for going about in a σινδών, offered to show them the great philosopher Theophrastus similarly attired. When they found this incredible, he took them to a barber shop and showed them Theophrastus in a σινδών having his hair cut (Diogenes Laertius, VI.90).

Accordingly, since the costume specified in the longer text is unusual and is associated with baptism, it can be used as an indication of baptism. This explains why the phrase of the longer text, περιβεβλημένος σινδόνα ἐπὶ γυμνοῦ, recurs verbatim in Mk. 14.51 (except that W *fam* 1 *c k Sy.*ˢ*·Cop.*ˢᵃ· have discreetly omitted ἐπὶ γυμνοῦ, while θ *fam* 13. 543.565.Sy.ᵖ·Aeth. have accidentally replaced it by the γυμνός of the

following verse). In 14.51, too, the subject is νεανίσκος τις—the young man who was with Jesus at the time of his arrest and who, on being seized, fled naked (an episode both Matthew and Luke chose to omit). As suggested in the commentary on III.8, above, the recurrence of the περιβεβλημένος phrase is to be explained as that of a fixed formula, probably a baptismal rubric. Mark's fondness for repetition as a means of cross-reference was noted above (p. 136); for example, his initial identification of the Baptist as Elijah merely by repeating ζώνην δερματίνην περὶ τὴν ὀσφὺν αὐτοῦ. And fixed formulas, especially those connected with baptism, frequently recur verbatim or are referred to by partial quotation in the NT and early Christian literature, for example, τὸ βάπτισμα Ἰωάννου, Mk. 11.30 and parallels; Lk. 7.29; Acts 1.22; 18.25; 19.3; (εἰς) ἄφεσιν ἁμαρτιῶν Mk. 1.4 and parallels; Mt. 26.28; Lk. 1.77; 24.47; Acts 2.38; 5.31; 10.43; 13.38; 26.18; Col. 1.14; εἰς τὸ ὄνομα τοῦ κυρίου Ἰησοῦ, Acts 8.16; 19.5; cf. 2.38 (ἐπὶ); 10.48 (ἐν); I Cor. 1.13f, etc.; τί κωλύει; οὐδὲν κωλύει, Cullmann, *Baptism* 72ff (to his evidence add *Clementine Homilies* XIII.11.1, where Peter's laughter is better explained if the previous speaker has unwittingly quoted a part of the formula of the rite). Further, Mk. 14.51 is echoed in Mk. 16.5, νεανίσκον . . . περιβεβλημένον στολὴν λευκήν, and again in the *Gospel of Peter* 55 (13), νεανίσκον . . . περιβεβλημένον στολὴν λαμπροτάτην; and the recurrent use of περιβεβλημένους στολὰς λευκάς and cognate phrases to describe the saints in the Apocalypse (3.5,18; 4.4; 7.9,13; 19.8) indicates that the expression and the white garment (σινδών = στολὴ λευκή) had some special significance in the early Church. From the longer text and the parallels above, we can conclude that the garment was the baptismal and burial garment. Thus the repetition in Mk. 14.51 (recognized by Bultmann as primitive tradition, by contrast with the "completely legendary" agony in 32–42; *Geschichte* 288ff) is an explanation, from an early Markan stratum, of what the young man was doing there (a problem for which no plausible solution has hitherto been suggested). The reader who had already read the longer text would realize that this youth, too, had come to be baptized. (On the stylistic difference between the story of the arrest and that of the agony, see Wohleb, *Beobachtungen* 190; the objections of Zerwick, *Untersuchungen* 4f are naive.)

However, a further question has to be answered: Why, then, is the same phrase used for the angels at the resurrection and the saints in the Apocalypse? Because the burial garment is also the resurrection garment. This is stated explicitly by the first two of the rabbinic passages cited above—*J. Kil'ayim* IX.4 (32b) = *J. Ketubot* XII.3 (35a): "A man is raised in the same clothes in which he is buried." (Such is, at least, the majority opinion). Accordingly, the baptismal shroud is also the robe of the saints and of the saviour, and hence of the *caelicoli* generally. This explains the stories in *Acta Thomae* 27, *Actus Petri cum Simone* 5 end, and *Acta Barnabae* 3, where baptism is followed by appearance of a young man in a white garment and a blaze of light: these are the angels whose appearance announces the initiate's resurrection by baptism. Finally, this conclusion is confirmed by and itself confirms the observations of Goodenough as to the symbolic importance of white robed figures in Jewish art (for example, Kraeling, *Dura* pl. LII, LIII, LXI, LXII, LXIII, etc.). Goodenough's point of departure had been the obvious importance of such figures in Philo and in

early Christian art (Goodenough, I.28ff and the indices, under *Robe*; further, IX.131–168, where the argument is pushed to absurdity but not thereby wholly invalidated).

THE MYSTERY OF THE KINGDOM OF GOD: This phrase, too, recurs in Mk., at 4.11. For the variants there and those of the Matthaean and Lucan parallels, see the commentary above, on III.10.

In Mt. and Lk. (as Lk. now stands) the plural "mysteries" which the disciples are given "to know" are the teachings of the Church—especially, in this instance, its interpretations of the parables. This misinterpretation was suggested by the context into which the logion was inserted in Mk. 4.11; it would also have been suggested by the use of ἐδίδασκεν in the longer text, if Matthew and Luke had read it.

That Mk. 4.11f is an old logion, not an invention by the compiler of Mk., was shown by Jeremias (*Gleichnisse* 7–12, partly anticipated by Lohmeyer, *ad loc.* and Manson, *Teaching* 77) and has since been widely accepted (Taylor; Cranfield; Grundmann; Gnilka, *Verstockung* 23; Boobyer's attempt in *Redaction* to defend the unity of the passage is not convincing). The compiler of Mk. knew or represented the logion as addressed to Jesus' circle (οἱ περὶ αὐτόν); a later glossator has added σὺν τοῖς δώδεκα (4.10; Bultmann, *Geschichte* 71). The compiler also took ἐν παραβολαῖς τὰ πάντα γίνεται to mean, "I teach only in parables," (cf. Mk. 4.33f), but Jeremias has argued that, once the logion is separated from its present context, this meaning is not necessary; he proposes to translate "ist alles rätselvoll"—"everything is puzzling," and this, too, has been widely accepted. If it be accepted, there is no need to refer τὰ πάντα exclusively to Jesus' verbal teaching (and such a reference would not be expected even in rabbinic Judaism, where students customarily learned from their masters' actions as well as from their words—e.g., B. ʿErubin 64b). τὰ πάντα may, therefore, mean "everything I do and say," or even "everything God does." Accordingly, one cannot define from τὰ πάντα the meaning of the μυστήριον to which it might or might not be sharply antithetical.

The μυστήριον, therefore, must be defined—if at all—from the general sense of the verse and the similar usages elsewhere in the NT and in related works. In the first place, it is clear that in Mk. 4.11 the μυστήριον cannot be the explanation that follows in 4.14–20, for it is something which already "has been given" in the past, something which Jesus' intimates have already received and which makes it possible for Jesus to give them now, as a further gift, the explanation of the parable. That they had already received the μυστήριον was what distinguished them from τοῖς ἔξω, which presumably meant for Mark what it means in I Cor. 5.12; Col. 4.5; I Thess. 4.12; that is, those outside the Church (cf. the parallels from philosophic schools cited by Bauer, *Wb.*, ἔξω, β). Now that "mystery" which "was given" to members of the Church, which distinguished them from nonmembers, and which enabled them to be given the secret teachings of the Church, was baptism.

The word μυστήριον in Eph. 5.32 probably refers to the spiritual union effected by baptism. The argument in verses 25–32 runs as follows: Christ *loved* the Church, washed it with water and the word, hallowed it, placed it beside him in glory, and *made it his own body*, therefore he *feeds* and *cherishes* it; men *make* their wives *their own bodies*, therefore they should *love, feed,* and *cherish* them. The first half of this argument

reflects the Pauline doctrine of baptism (including the enthronement with Christ; cf. Col. 2.12–3.4). Of this doctrine the words italicized at the beginning and the end were relevant to the author's purpose; the middle terms (washing, hallowing, and enthronement) were not. Why, then, did he include them? Presumably because they were fixed parts of the doctrine of baptism. Therefore when he concludes τὸ μυστήριον τοῦτο μέγα ἐστίν, ἐγὼ δὲ λέγω εἰς Χριστὸν καὶ εἰς τὴν ἐκκλησίαν, the "mystery" is presumably the spiritual union effected by baptism and thence the rite itself which makes the Church the body of Christ by making Christ's spirit live in the members. To this mystery the writer compares the spiritual union effected by physical intercourse in marriage, and he finds a reference to both these mysteries in Gen. 2.24.

The same use of "mystery" to refer to baptism is found in I Cor. 2.6f σοφίαν δὲ λαλοῦμεν ἐν τοῖς τελείοις ... λαλοῦμεν θεοῦ σοφίαν ἐν μυστηρίῳ, where it is utterly implausible to neglect the parallelism and to separate the initiated (τελείοις) from the initiation (μυστηρίῳ). Allo's objection (I Cor., ad loc.) that the Corinthian converts were not τέλειοι neglects the distinction between potential and actual salvation, which is basic to Paul's thought with its constant alternation between deity and depravity (Rom. 7–8, II Cor. 4, etc.) Baird's attempt to explain away the terminology (Mature) is built on the false antithesis: either "a special and esoteric doctrine reserved for ... the initiated" or "the Gospel, 'the word of the Cross.'" It never occurred to him that, to the ancients, baptism was an initiation—a τελετή, as Lucian said (Peregrinus 11). Anticipating arguments to be presented later, it may be said that a further reason for understanding the "mystery" in I Cor. 2.7 to be baptism lies in the fact that the "wisdom of God" revealed in it involves the secret of Christ's descent in disguise and his assumption of the body from the cosmic powers, for the purpose of subjugating them: σοφίαν ... ἣν οὐδεὶς τῶν ἀρχόντων τοῦ αἰῶνος τούτου ἔγνωκεν· εἰ γὰρ ἔγνωσαν, οὐκ ἂν τὸν κύριον τῆς δόξης ἐσταύρωσαν; cf. Ascension of Isaiah 10–11. This secret of descent in disguise underlies the Pauline interpretation of baptism in Col. 2.15, where the second half of the process, the stripping off in the ascent, is referred to. And the conclusion of the process in I Cor. 2.9, as in Col. 2.12–3.4, is the participation of the baptized in Christ's resurrection, ascension, and session in glory, ἃ ὀφθαλμὸς οὐκ εἶδεν καὶ οὖς οὐκ ἤκουσεν ... ὅσα ἡτοίμασεν ὁ θεὸς τοῖς ἀγαπῶσιν αὐτόν. (Note again, as in the longer text of Mk., the connection of baptism with ἀγάπη; cf. above, section v, end). Finally, the "wisdom of God" (I Cor. 2.7) given in the mystery is Christ (1.24,30) and Christ is given in baptism, therefore the mystery is baptism. This wisdom is given only by the spirit (2.11) and the gift of the spirit is the function of baptism (Acts 2.38 and often).

Since the "mystery" of I Cor. 2.7 is baptism, it is not unlikely that in I Cor. 4.1–6, where Paul speaks of himself, Kephas, and Apollos as οἰκονόμους μυστηρίων θεοῦ, he refers to their function not only in general, as agents of the grand secret strategy of God, but also in particular, as administrators of the mystery rites of baptism and the eucharist, and thus of the salvation effected by these rites. The same sense can be borne by the interpretation of this passage in Eph. 3.9 and of this in Ignatius, Trall. 2.3, where the contrast between the "mysteries" and "food and drink" is that of I Cor. 11 between the eucharist and ordinary eating and drinking; the reference is

particularly to 11.22. (Bauer's reference, *Ig.*, *ad loc.*, to Acts 6.2 is not justified by the text.)

All the above argument on μυστήριον has run counter to the common dogma that μυστήριον in the NT always has the sense of רז or סוד and that these always mean "secret," never "secret rite"; so Bornkamm, μυέω; Nock, *Mysterion*; Allo, *I Cor.*, on 5.7; Klostermann, Taylor, and Cranfield on Mk. 4.11; etc. But this dogma is false.

Paul sometimes did use μυστήριον to mean "secret," but there are a number of instances where he clearly did not: the "mystery of iniquity," that is, "the unlawful magic," in II Thess. 2.7 is not a secret, but a process—a secret process, no doubt, but the essential thing is not the secrecy but the process, which is already "working" to bring the coming of the evil one. So, too, μυστήριον in the magical papyri means not only "charm," but the whole magical ceremony and its consequences (*PGM* I.131; IV.476; etc.; contrast Rigaux, *Thess.*, on 2.7). Similarly in Col. 1.26f the mystery is not a secret but a process, χριστὸς ἐν ὑμῖν, the indwelling and working of Christ in the baptized; cf. *PGM* I.128ff, where τὸ μέγα τοῦτο μυστήριον means not only the whole magical ceremony by which one receives ὁ κύριος τοῦ ἀέρος (cf. Eph. 2.2) as an indwelling deity, but also all the consequences which follow from the reception: the continued possession and service of the deity, the status of an initiate, μα[κάρι]ε μύστα τῆς ἱερᾶς μαγείας. That Paul should have used μυστήριον to describe the process and consequences of Christ's indwelling in Christian initiates was probably a reflection of his use of the same term for the rite of initiation, baptism. As in *PGM*, the mystery produced the association of man and god, and the term was carried over loosely to its consequences. Nock's notion that Paul was not aware of the connection between μυέω, μύστης, and μυστήριον (*Mysterion* n1) seems to me incredible. That Paul was thinking of baptism in Col. 1.26f is indicated by the immediately preceding verses where he speaks of the body of Christ, the Church (25), ἧς ἐγενόμην ἐγὼ διάκονος κατὰ τὴν οἰκονομίαν τοῦ θεοῦ τὴν δοθεῖσάν μοι εἰς ὑμᾶς πληρῶσαι τὸν λόγον τοῦ θεοῦ, τὸ μυστήριον, etc. This is the vocabulary found in I Cor. 4.1 where Paul is speaking of his work as οἰκόνομος of the mysteries; and the concept of the Church as the body of Christ is that remarked above in connection with the references to baptism, since by baptism this embodiment was effected. Thus, the notion that Paul always uses μυστήριον to mean "secret" is false.

Further, the notion that when Paul does use μυστήριον to mean "secret" he cannot at the same time use it to mean "secret process" or "rite," is also false. This has been shown by the examples above. For some consequences of this false antithesis, see above, in the comment on μυστήρια in the body of the letter (II.2).

Finally, the notion that רז and סוד always refer to secrets and never to secret rites is also false. סוד in particular is not infrequently taken in rabbinic literature as a reference to the rite of circumcision; for example, *Tanhuma, Hayyé Sarah* 4, where Prov. 31.24, סדין עשתה, is glossed (by punning on סוד) with the words זו המילה שנאמר סוד יהוה ליראיו "this is circumcision, of which it is said, 'The mystery (סוד) of the Lord is given to those who fear him'"—Ps. 25.14. (A contributory element in the exegesis may have been the fact that סדין was the initiation garment, the σινδών; see

above). More important is the fact that both סוד and רז appear in *Hekalot Rabbati* (27.1; 28.3; 29.1,2,4; etc.) as descriptions of the magical technique by which one is enabled to ascend through the heavens and be seated in the throne of God. Though the present form of this text is late, Scholem, *Gnosticism*, has shown that speculations on the subject of the ascent go back to a syncretistic Judaism of the early first century A.D. at the latest; and his argument is now confirmed by the appearance of their peculiar angelology in the Qumran texts, 3Q 7.5 = *Discoveries* III.99. Further, I have shown (*Observations* end) that the account of the ascent in the *Hekalot* and that in the so-called "Mithras Liturgy" (*PGM* IV.475ff) go back to a common source of tradition, if not of writing. The "Mithras Liturgy" describes itself as μυστήρια (476), and means by this "initiation," for it prescribes that one may have a συνμύστης (line 732). The first reference to practice of a technique for ascent to the heavens may be that in Col. 2.18: "the angels whom he saw when going in." Into the heavens? (Cf. *Observations* 156). And ascent to the heavens and session with Christ on the right hand of God are described by Paul in the same context as the potential climax of the consequences of Christian baptism (Col. 3.1ff). So the supposition that רז and/or סוד could have been used by Paul to refer to the rite of baptism as a "mystery" is not unsupported.

Judaism was often considered a "mystery" religion (e.g., by Plutarch, *Quaestiones Convivales* IV.6: Jewish doctrines and ceremones are τὰ Ἑβραίων ἀπόρρητα and the unknown Jewish god is identified as Dionysus because of parallels between the Jewish and the Eleusinian mysteries). Paul's Jewish contemporary, Philo, frequently described the doctrines and ceremonies of Judaism as "mysteries" (Goodenough, *Symbols* VI.206–216; Wolfson, *Philo* I.43). And the rabbis took over the word μυστήριον with the full range of its Greco-Roman meanings.

On the one hand they used it to mean "spell" or "magic" and identified "the mystery of Israel," מיסטורין של ישראל, as the secret name of Yahweh. It was by pronouncing this that Moses killed the Egyptian: *Wayyikra' Rabbah* 32.4 end, and Margulies' note *ad loc.* As in Greek, the word can mean not only the essential charm, but the whole magical praxis in which it is used; thus the Shunnamite says to Elisha, עמדת במסטורין של אלהים מתחלה נתת לי בן אף עכשיו עמוד אתה במסטורין של אלהים והחיה אותו. "You practiced the mysteries of God when you gave me a son, to begin with, so now practice the mysteries of God and raise him from the dead." (*Shemot Rabbah* 19.1. This passage is of particular interest here because it shows these mysteries were conceived as means of resurrection, as was baptism.)

Besides this magical usage, the rabbis also took over, as Philo did, the usage of μυστήριον for "mystery initiation." They used it in this sense to refer to the initiatory rite of Judaism, circumcision. For this they found Biblical basis in Ps. 25.14, סוד יהוה ליראיו ובריתו להודיעם, which LXX had translated κραταίωμα κύριος τῶν φοβουμένων αὐτόν· καὶ ἡ διαθήκη αὐτοῦ δηλῶσαι αὐτοῖς, but Aquila translated ἀπόρρητον (Theodotion and *Quinta*, μυστήριον) κυρίου τοῖς φοβουμένοις αὐτόν· καὶ τὴν συνθήκην αὐτοῦ γνωρίσει (Theodotion, δηλώσει) αὐτοῖς, thus rendering סוד as "mystery" and equating the mystery and the covenant. Compare Is. 24.16, where רזי לי רזי לי was omitted by LXX but translated by Symmachus and Theodotion

τὸ μυστήριόν μου ἐμοί, τὸ μυστήριόν μου ἐμοί—a translation also reflected by an agraphon attributed to Jesus in Clement, the *Clementine Homilies*, and many later authors (see the commentary on I.12): τὰ μυστήρια ἐμοὶ καὶ τοῖς υἱοῖς τοῦ οἴκου μου. As observed in the commentary, this agraphon is introduced in the *Clementina* as if it came from Mk., but is interpreted, by analogy with the Matthaean and Lucan interpretations of Mk. 4.11, as referring to teachings. Ps. 25.14, however, is consistently taken in rabbinic literature as referring to circumcision. Thus *Tanhuma* on Gen. 17.2 (*Lek*, 19) comments: ואתנה בריתי ביני ובינך זש״ה סוד ה׳ ליראיו ובריתו להודיעם· איזה הוא סוד שגילה ליראיו· זו המילה שלא גילה הקב״ה מסטורין של מילה אלא לאברהם· —"'And I shall establish my covenant between us.' This is what is referred to by the verse, 'The mystery of Yahweh is for those who fear him and so is his covenant, to give them knowledge' (Ps. 25.14). What is this 'mystery' which he revealed 'to those who fear him'? This is the rite of circumcision. For the Holy One, blessed be He, did not reveal the mystery rite of circumcision to any save Abraham." This exegesis occurs as part of a homily beginning with the verse התהלך לפני והיה תמים (Gen. 17.1), which is taken to mean, "Do as I tell you and you shall be perfect." Here LXX and Philo rendered תמים by ἄμεμπτος, which Aquila corrected to τέλειος—a term cognate to the technical terms "to initiate" (τελέω), "initiation" (τελετή), etc. τέλειος is also the term used by Jesus in urging his followers to follow his law rather than the traditional commandments; he concludes (Mt. 5.48), ἔσεσθε οὖν ὑμεῖς τέλειοι ὡς ὁ Πατὴρ ὑμῶν ὁ οὐράνιος τέλειός ἐστιν; cf. Mt. 19.21, where, in the conversation with the rich young man of Mk. 10, Matthew's Jesus contrasts a man who merely keeps the Mosiac law with one who is τέλειος.

The difference between LXX and Philo on the one hand and Aquila, Symmachus, Theodotion, and Mt. on the other in the translations of Gen. 17.1 and Ps. 25.14 and Is. 24.16 (noted above) indicates that the interpretation of circumcision as a mystery is to be dated in the first or early second century. The sermon in *Tanhuma* goes on to declare this mystery the necessary means to happiness in the afterlife (as were, for example, the Eleusinian mysteries, and baptism). This exegesis was standard. It recurs in the parallel version of the *Tanhuma* (ed. Buber, *Lek* 20–27), which places even more emphasis on the notion that by circumcision the initiate becomes τέλειος (here שלם, 20 and 25), takes Abraham as prefiguring the Messiah (22), and explains that the mystery was given him in order that he might be made like God (23 end; cf. Mt. 5.48, above) and that its performance prevents the world's returning to chaos (24)—a notion derived from the mysteries of ancient Mesopotamia (and a reminder that this development need not be conceived as wholly the result of Greek influence). We have already seen this same exegetic complex referred to en passant in *Tanhuma* (*Sarah* 4) apropos of a mention of the σινδών which was probably the costume for the rite (זו המילה שנאמר סוד יי). A corrupt version was introduced into most MSS of *Bereshit Rabbah* 49.2; see Theodore's notes there. Finally, the theme is further developed in *Shemot Rabbah* 19.5–7. After emphasizing again that to have been circumcised is necessary and sufficient (save to heretics and the very wicked) for salvation, the text goes on to treat it as the precondition for participation in the sacred, secret, passover meal (6). Only one speaker is named—the Galliean, R. Simon

ben Halafta, of the beginning of the third century—but how much of the tradition can be attributed to him is not clear. The text commented upon is Ex. 12.43ff, זאת חקת הפסח כל בן נכר לא יאכל בו וכל ערל לא יאכל בו. . . . Particularly striking is the comment, "It is like a king who made a dinner for his friends ⟨לאוהביו = τοῖς ἀγαπῶσιν αὐτόν = τοῖς τελείοις . . . ἐν μυστηρίῳ, I Cor. 2.6–9; see above, page 179⟩. The king said, 'If there is anyone, of all those invited, on whom my seal does not appear, he is not to be admitted here.' ⟨Cf. Mt. 22.1–14. Circumcision is a "seal" in Rom. 4.11; baptism or chrism—probably—in Apoc. 7.2; 9.4. All these use σφραγίς, on which, and on its background in the mysteries, see Bauer, *Wb.*, *s.v.*, and the literature there.⟩ So God made a feast ⟨i.e., the passover⟩ . . . because he was delivering them from evil ⟨הצרה, cf. Mt. 6.13; Gal. 1.4⟩. He said to them, 'If the seal of Abraham is not in your flesh you shall not taste of it' ⟨Lk. 14.24, also *Didache* IX.5, none but the baptized may eat the eucharist⟩ . . . (7) 'No alien shall eat of it' . . . The Holy One, blessed be He, said to them, 'Let no other people participate in it, and let them not know the mystery ⟨מסטורין, accepting the emendation of Krauss, *Lehnwörter*, *s.v.*⟩, but let it be for you alone.'" The text goes on to describe the Passover in this world as an anticipation of the feast of the blessed in the world to come.

In sum, then, the rabbis often spoke of the initiatory ceremony of Judaism as a "mystery" which had been "given" to them. They thought this initiation prerequisite for participation in the sacred meal of the cult in this world, and for the life of the blessed—a glorified form of that sacred meal—in the world to come. Thus the clear evidence of the rabbinic material confirms the preceding interpretation of Paul. μυστήριον in Jewish usage regularly refers to the initiatory rite of circumcision, as in Paul's usage it refers to the initiatory rite of baptism which Paul equated with circumcision: Col. 2.11; τῇ περιτομῇ τοῦ χριστοῦ . . . τῷ βαπτίσματι.

Given the Pauline and the rabbinic usage, it is not surprising to find μυστήριον used as a technical expression for baptism in the community from which Mk. drew his material. Christian baptism is "the mystery of the kingdom of God" because it enables those to whom it is given to enter the kingdom—so Jn. 3, Nicodemus' nocturnal visit to Jesus (of which the similarity in content to the initiation in the longer text is no less striking than the total independence of the two passages). Therefore those to whom Christian baptism *has been* given (Mk. 4.11) are *in* the kingdom, as opposed to "those outside" (*ibid.*) like the Baptist (Lk. 7.28; Mt. 11.11; Acts 19.1–7), who have been born only of women, not of water *and* the spirit (Jn. 3.3–5).

The one difficulty in the way of a baptismal interpretation of "the mystery of the kingdom of God" in the longer text is the word ἐδίδασκε. In the light of the evidence reviewed above, I think this a corruption of an original ἔδωκεν. The corruption was probably made by a copyist influenced by the misinterpretation of Mk. 4.11 in Mt. 13.11 and Lk. 8.10, where "the mystery" becomes "the mysteries"—that is, the following interpretations of the parables, which "it is given" the disciples "to know." That misinterpretation, in turn, probably resulted from the rapid growth of Christianity, which made baptism an experience common to all members of a large group including many not completely saved; baptism therefore declined in prestige and there was a corresponding growth of secret teachings which professed to reveal

something more. This is the development reflected by the Matthaean and Lucan emendations of canonical Mk. and by the corruption of the longer text.

Apart from this, the details of the nocturnal initiation (the six days' preparation, the coming by night, the sheet and the nudity, and the mystery of the kingdom) all accord with the interpretation required by the clearly baptismal character of the preceding pericope. The rite was a form of baptism.

(f) This baptismal interpretation explains both the inclusion in the longer text of the story of the baptism and its omission from the canonical text if that was intended, as Clement says it was, for reading by the unbaptized.

The inclusion at the place where it stands is exactly in accord with the requirements of the pericope as a reading for the baptismal service. We have had the prerequisites—become as children, believe in the one good God, obey the commandments, forsake all, and join the Church—and the peculiarly Christian creed, the death and resurrection of Jesus, the Son of Man, which the initiates are now to share. We have had the evidence of resurrection and the antitype of baptism—the raising of Lazarus (the Gospel for the service, here *following* the creed—evidently because it belonged to the secret teaching of the church—see above on τοὺς μυουμένους in II.2). Now we come to the baptism itself, and here, as in the eucharist, *the essential is not a prayer, but a story* of what Jesus once did: ἐπέταξεν αὐτῷ . . . καὶ . . . ἔρχεται . . . καὶ ἔμεινε . . . ἔδωκεν γὰρ αὐτῷ . . . τὸ μυστήριον τῆς βασιλείας τοῦ θεοῦ (III.7–9). And with this the story ends as abruptly as the Markan account of the institution of the eucharist: ἐκεῖθεν δὲ ἀναστὰς ἐπέστρεψεν (III.10–11); cf. Mk. 14.26, ὑμνήσαντες ἐξῆλθον.

That this story should have been omitted in revision of the Gospel for exoteric use is in accord with John's omission of both Jesus' baptism and the eucharist (so Dodd, *Fourth Gospel* 309–310). It is remarked in Windisch-Preisker (*Briefe* 157) that in I Peter, between 1.21 and 1.22, "Der Taufakt selbst ist aus Arkandisziplin fortgelassen." Schille, *Tauflehre* 35, remarks a similar omission of advanced eschatological teaching in *Barnabas* 17.2: οὐ μὴ νοήσητε διὰ τὸ ἐν παραβολαῖς κεῖσθαι; cf. Mk. 4.11. Preisker, Boismard, and Schille represent I Peter and *Barnabas* as baptismal texts because of their outlines (above, page 170), and we have shown the extensive agreement of these outlines with that of Mk. 10. Therefore the omission in *Barnabas* 17 may help to explain the suppression in Mk. 10. Baptism, as the secret way of entering the kingdom (Jn. 3.5) was acutely eschatological. The most important secret about the kingdom was how to get in. Perhaps this was why, in canonical Mk., baptism was suppressed while the eucharist was not (cf. Moule, *Intention* 171f). This question, however, would lead to that of the structure and history of canonical Mk., which must indeed be restudied in the light of the longer text, but not here.

Returning to the role of the baptism story in the baptismal pericope, it should be noted that the liturgical interpretation of the whole pericope explains the seeming difficulty that the resurrection of the youth (the symbol of his baptism) precedes, by six days, his baptism. One might either compare Apuleius, *Golden Ass* XI.13–25 (where Lucius' restoration to human form precedes his initiation, of which it is the symbol), or quote the Pharisaic ruling on circumcision: "Separation from a foreskin is like separation from a tomb." הפורש מן הערלה כפורש מן הקבר (*Pesahim*

VIII.8; *'Eduyot* V.2), which puts a seven-day purification period (Num. 19.16) between circumcision and participation in the passover meal. But the Pharisaic ruling is not closely parallel, since the ceremonies it affects are not related as symbol and reality. And in Apuleius the duplication is due to the shift from allegory to auto-biography: having allegorized his uninitiated self as an ass, he had to restore himself to human form (that is, undergo allegoric initiation) before he could describe his actual initiation as a man. In the longer text of Mk., however, the resurrection story (allegoric initiation) anticipates the story of the actual baptism because the whole pericope is designed to correspond with a service in which the Gospel anticipates the actual ceremony, as the Gospel for the feast of Corpus Christi anticipates the canon of the mass. (Note that the roles of these elements in the baptismal pericope do not determine their relations in the smaller section—Mk. 10.20–34 plus the longer text, discussed above in pp. 165ff. Perhaps that pattern was worked into the pericope as a basis for yet more esoteric teaching.)

(g) At this point Clement tells Theodore, τὸ δὲ γυμνὸς γυμνῷ καὶ τἆλλα περὶ ὧν ἔγραψας οὐχ εὑρίσκεται; in other words, the longer text as used in Clement's church (or, as Clement chose to describe it) did not contain some material—including the phrase γυμνὸς γυμνῷ—which Theodore had reported as standing hereabouts in the Carpocratian text.

Since the Carpocratians had a reputation for sexual license (see Appendix B) and this section of the longer text reported that a youth came to Jesus περιβεβλημένος σινδόνα ἐπὶ γυμνοῦ and stayed with him all night, it is easy to suppose that the Carpocratians took the opportunity to insert in the text some material which would authorize the homosexual relationship Clement suggested by picking out γυμνὸς γυμνῷ. Similar developments might be thought to lie behind the celebration of baptism in *Acta Thomae* 27 as ἡ κοινωνία τοῦ ἄρρενος (cf. 132, text P, both lacking in the Syriac), and sayings like *Gospel of Thomas* (Leipoldt) 108, "Jesus said: 'He who will drink of my mouth will become like me, and I shall be he, and the hidden things shall be revealed to him.'" Cf. the longer text, ἐδίδασκεν γὰρ αὐτὸν τὸ μυστήριον τῆς βασιλείας τοῦ θεοῦ.

However, Clement does not explicitly say that the additional material was sexually offensive, and he would hardly have missed the chance to say so if it had been. Therefore the γυμνὸς γυμνῷ probably belonged to a fuller account of the ritual. Hippolytus, *Apostolic Tradition* XXI.11, after speaking of the catechumen and the presbyter who is to baptize him, goes on to specify, "And let them stand in the water naked." The Carpocratian text may have contained some similar provision, more explicitly phrased.

Another possibility is indicated by the fact that the Carpocratians interpreted baptism as a resurrection. This appears from Irenaeus (Harvey, II.48.2 = Stieren, II.31.2): After arguing that the Carpocratians perform their miracles by magic, and cannot perform major cures, he goes on to say, *tantum autem absunt ab eo ut mortuum excitent, quemadmodum Dominus excitavit et apostoli per orationem (et in fraternitate saepissime propter aliquid necessarium, ea quae est in quoque loco ecclesia universa postulante per jejunium et supplicationem multam, reversus est spiritus mortui, et donatus est homo orationibus*

sanctorum) ut ne quidem credant hoc in totum posse fieri; esse autem resurrectionem a mortuis agnitionem eius, quae ab eis dicitur, veritatis. On this Harvey aptly quotes Tertullian, *De resurrectione mortuorum* XIX.2ff. *resurrectionem . . . mortuorum manifeste adnuntiatam in imaginariam significationem distorquent, adserentes ipsam etiam mortem spiritaliter intellegendam. Non enim hanc esse in vero, quae sit in medio, discidium carnis atque animae, sed ignorantiam dei, per quam homo mortuus deo non minus in errore iacuerit quam in sepulchro. Itaque et resurrectionem eam vindicandam, qua quis adita veritate redanimatus et revivificatus deo ignorantiae morte discussa velut de sepulchro veteris hominis eruperit . . . exinde ergo resurrectionem fide consecutos cum domino esse, quem in baptismate induerint. Hoc denique ingenio etiam in conloquiis saepe nostros decipere consueverunt, quasi et ipsi resurrectionem carnis admittant: "Vae," inquiunt, "qui non in hac carne resurrexerit," ne statim illos percutiant, si resurrectionem statim abnuerint. Tacite autem secundum conscientiam suam hoc sentiunt: "Vae, qui non, dum in hac carne est, cognoverit arcana haeretica." Hoc est enim apud illos resurrectio. Sed et plerique ab excessu animae resurrectionem vindicantes, de sepulchro exire de saeculo evadere interpretantur, quia et saeculum mortuorum sit habitaculum, id est ignorantium deum, vel etiam de ipso corpore, quia et corpus vice sepulchri conclusam animam in saecularis vitae morte detineat.*

Given this interpretation of resurrection as initiation (and vice versa) it is easy to suppose that the Carpocratians added to the ritual of their baptismal initiation some sort of resurrection ritual like that suggested by the parallels adduced in the commentary on γυμνὸς γυμνῷ above (on III.13). Elisha's raising of the widow's son, II Kgs. 4.34, would have provided an OT precedent; its importance in Judaism of the Roman period is shown by its place on the front wall of the Dura synagogue (panel WC1, Kraeling, *Dura* pl. LXIII), and the comments by impressed visitors (Geiger, *Texts* nos. 49, 51, 55). At all events, the one thing certain about the Carpocratian text is also the one thing most important for our present purpose: it is fully compatible with the interpretation of the secret ceremony as a baptism.

(h) After the baptism comes the sermon, the postbaptismal instruction, which still stands in canonical Mk. 10.35–45. The "message" is as follows: The newly baptized should not feel themselves at a disadvantage vis à vis Christians of longer standing, for not even the original disciples were assured the highest places in the kingdom. All who enter must drink of Jesus' cup (communion—the commemoration of the passion—will follow) and be baptized (as the initiates just have been) with his baptism (his death and resurrection), but for the future he who would be greatest should follow the example of the Son of Man who made himself servant of all and gave his life for us. So practice humility, make yourselves useful in the church, and give what you can.

With this concern for church discipline and finance the baptismal pericope comes to its natural conclusion. In the dramatic situation, that is, as put into Jesus' mouth, the references to the baptism and the cup in verses 38–39 must be understood as prophecies of his own passion and death and therefore of those of the sons of Zebedee.[18]

18. The amusing exegeses contrived to avoid this conclusion (Bernard, *Study*; Delling, *Baptisma*; etc.) need not concern us; nor need the question whether or not the prophecy was fulfilled in the case of John. The writer of Mk. 10.39 may have yet expected its fulfillment or may have erroneously believed it to have been fulfilled.

But for that church which told the story, baptism and communion had become ritual means of participation in Jesus' death and resurrection (Rom. 6.3; I Cor. 11.24–28); so the question to the sons of Zebedee is now directed to all Christians, and their answer is the initiates' affirmation of faith in the magical identification with the saviour, effected by the rites of the mystery. To suppose the dramatic reference to the passion excludes the homiletic reference or the sacraments (Werner, *Einfluss* 137ff) is ridiculous. Equally ridiculous was the gnostic interpretation of the verses as referring to a second baptism (Irenaeus: Harvey, I.14.1 = Stieren, I.21.2), but it may have been accepted also by Clement's church in Alexandria (point a, above, p. 168).

This concludes the argument concerning the structure of Mk. 10.13–45 and its relation to the longer text. Since the argument has been complicated, it should be summarized here:

(a) Clement declares that the longer text was read in τὰ μεγάλα μυστήρια, probably the paschal service which included baptism.

(b) The liturgical use of the text would explain its importance to Clement, to the western text, to Lk., and to Mk.

(c) That τὰ μεγάλα μυστήρια were or included some sort of baptism is suggested by the baptismal reminiscences with which Clement introduces the text.

(d) The text stands at that place in canonical Mk. where baptismal material is to be expected.

(e) The details of Mk. 10.13–34 + the longer text + 10.35–45 show the whole pericope to be a baptismal lection, to which all its parts are essential:

(i) 10.13–16 states the general prerequisite of baptism: become as little children.

(ii–vi) 10.17–31 states specific requirements: monotheism, obedience to the commandments, renunciation of property; these correspond to the standard preliminary instruction for baptism.

(vii) 10.32–34, the credal prophecy of the passion and resurrection, provides both the assurance and the explanation of the rite's efficacy.

(viii) The "Gospel" for the service, the story of the raising of Lazarus, was from the second century on associated with baptism—both as a symbol of the initiates' resurrection from sin and as an example of the expected resurrection from death.

(ix) That the nocturnal initiation which follows the resurrection was understood to have been a baptism is argued by Ephraim's tradition concerning Lazarus and by the details reported: the six-day interval, the nocturnal character, the sheet and the nudity, and the communication of "the mystery of the kingdom of God," which seems to have been baptism.

(f) This baptismal interpretation explains both the inclusion of this material at this place in the longer text, and its omission from the shorter, exoteric text. It was included because the church for which the longer text was written performed baptism, as it performed the eucharist, by telling a story of what Jesus did. The story of the nocturnal initiation was the "canon" of the baptismal service, as the story of the nocturnal supper was—and is—the canon of the mass. Hence the omission from the exoteric text, comparable to the omission of the "words of institution" from John. Hence also the doubling of the account of baptism—first symbolic (resurrec-

tion) as the "Gospel" for the service, then actual (initiation) as the words accompanying the δρώμενα.

(g) The additions reported from the Carpocratian text also admit of baptismal interpretation, and this interpretation is made likely by reports of the Carpocratians' allegorizing of resurrection.

(h) Mk. 10.35–45 is best understood as postbaptismal instruction.

These arguments are cumulative. If even one of them be thought conclusive, it establishes the baptismal character of the section to which it applies, and thus strengthens the case for a baptismal interpretation of the adjacent sections. And even if none be thought conclusive, the fact that so many sections in sequence lend themselves so readily to the same interpretation will be difficult to explain away.

4. EVIDENCE FOR ABBREVIATION AT MK. 10.46

For the second quotation from the longer text I see no such structural argument. But it reports an incident located in Jericho, on Jesus' last trip to Jerusalem. Lk. 19.1–10 also reports an incident—the Zacchaeus story—and all the synoptics tell the story of blind Bartimaeus (doubled by Mt.) as something which happened near Jericho. So there were stories connected with the place, and Bultmann is inclined to consider these local connections as "old tradition" or even "höchst primitiv" (*Geschichte* 68f, 258, 364).

Moreover, the Zacchaeus story, like the preceding story in the longer text, is of a rich man who wished to see (cf. "be with") Jesus and therefore received him in his house and was saved. Other connections with the baptismal pericope in Mk. are his gift of (half of) his possessions to the poor (cf. Mk. 10.21) and the concluding sentence, ἦλθεν γὰρ ὁ υἱὸς τοῦ ἀνθρώπου ζητῆσαι καὶ σῶσαι τὸ ἀπολωλός; cf. the Markan conclusion (10.45, which Lk. omitted), καὶ γὰρ ὁ υἱὸς τοῦ ἀνθρώπου οὐκ ἦλθεν διακονηθῆναι ἀλλὰ διακονῆσαι καὶ δοῦναι τὴν ψυχὴν αὐτοῦ λύτρον ἀντὶ πολλῶν. One is tempted to suppose that in telling the Zacchaeus story Luke had in mind the preceding Markan pericope, *including* the passages from the longer text. This jibes with the evidence seen above that Matthew also knew the longer text (see the commentary on προσεκύνησε, II.24; καὶ προσελθὼν ἀπεκύλισε, III.11; and the argument above on page 172), and the first of these bits of Matthaean evidence implies knowledge of the second addition, that following Mk. 10.46a.

Therefore, it is interesting that there seems to be a gap in the text of Mk. 10.46, just at the place where Clement locates his quotation from the longer text. 10.46a reads καὶ ἔρχονται εἰς Ἱερειχω. 10.46b reads καὶ ἐκπορευομένου αὐτοῦ ἀπὸ Ἱερειχω (and the text goes on to tell the Bartimaeus story). Notice the change of number between ἔρχονται and ἐκπορευομένου αὐτοῦ, and the repetition εἰς Ἱερειχω ... ἀπὸ Ἱερειχω, which would be better understandable if something had intervened. Apparently the story of what happened *in* Jericho has been omitted. This appearance is strengthened by the way Matthew and Luke handled the Markan text: Matthew omitted 46a entirely, thus suppressing all reference to anything happening *in* Jericho; Luke changed 46a to ἐγένετο δὲ ἐν τῷ ἐγγίζειν αὐτὸν εἰς Ἱερειχω, omitted 46b, and told

the Bartimaeus story as something which happened before Jesus reached the city. He then went on, καὶ εἰσελθὼν διήρχετο τὴν Ιερειχω καὶ ἰδού, etc. (19.1f) and proceeded to tell his version of what happened *in* Jericho—the Zacchaeus story which, as we have just seen, has reminiscences of the baptismal pericope, including the longer text. So it seems that what happened *in* Jericho was something to which Matthew chose not to refer, and for which Luke had another, remotely cognate tradition which he preferred to Mk.

This appearance is strengthened by examination of the other passages where Mark begins a pericope with καὶ ἔρχεται/ἔρχονται εἰς. As noted above (commentary on II.23), this is one of Mark's favorite formulas and characteristic of his style as opposed to the other synoptists'. He used it in 3.20; 5.38; 6.1; 8.22; 10.1 (expanded); 10.46; 11.15; 11.27; 14.32; and he used the same construction with other verbs or tenses in 1.21; 3.1; 5.1; 9.33. In all of these the formula is introductory, and in all except 3.20 and 10.46 it is followed by an account of some event which occurred in the place entered. The text in 3.20 was omitted by Matthew and Luke and looks as if it were the introduction to another deleted section of the longer text. Perhaps 9.33 is another example of the same thing: καὶ ἦλθον εἰς Καφαρναουμ, καὶ ἐν τῇ οἰκίᾳ γενόμενος. What happened to "them" in Capernaum before "he" went to "the" (unexplained) house? According to Matthew, what happened was an encounter between Peter and a tax collector (the coin in the fish's mouth). Is this the only story in the Gospels to imply that Christians *need not* obey the civil law? If so, the fact that it was kept secret is understandable.

Mark is known for the loose ends—references to unexplained houses or boats or people—his text contains (e.g., 3.20; 4.1; 6.32; 15.21) and for passages which look like abbreviations or references to omitted material, e.g., 1.12–13; 3.6; 4.33f; 6.30,34; 7.31 (see Richardson's comment above, p. 161 n7); 10.1; 11.19; 16.7f). It is obvious that the text of canonical Mk. was abbreviated considerably by later revisers (Matthew and Luke), and other examples of abbreviation of Gospel material can readily be found (see above, page 94). Therefore it is not surprising that scholars of quite diverse views have supposed canonical Mk. produced by abbreviation: so Hilgenfeld, *Markus*; Parker, *Gospel*; Vaganay, *Problème*. But such theories are necessarily speculative. In the present instance we have a specific case where *expansion* is reported by early tradition, but where the present text looks as if it has been produced by abbreviation and, as remarked above, traces of the abbreviated material seem to appear in Mt. and Lk.

The case for abbreviation is further strengthened by the fact that the omitted material mentions Salome. Salome appears in the NT only in Mk. 15.40 and 16.1 —in both as a witness of an event of great importance to Christian claims (the crucifixion, the discovery of the empty tomb; see the commentary on III.16). For these events she seems to have been one of the chief original witnesses, all of whom were women (so Mk.; contrast the later Gospels).[19] Yet Luke (23.55; 24.1) omitted

19. The way these women witnesses are introduced in Mk. 15.41 suggests that they were not previously mentioned in the Gospel as the author of 15.41 left it. But the introduction also shows that the author of 15.41 knew other stories about them. Were they stories he had cut out of the Gospel?

both Markan lists of these women witnesses. [H.J.C. would prefer "rearranged," rather than "omitted"; cf. Lk. 8.3; 23.49,55; 24.10. But, though Luke did mention the other women elsewhere, he eliminated Salome's name.] Matthew deleted the name of Salome from the first list (27.56) and removed her figure entirely from the second (27.61; 28.1) and John also omitted her name (19.25). The Johannine text may come from a different tradition, but the omissions by Matthew and Luke were presumably deliberate. The presumption is that Salome was eliminated because persons of whom the canonical evangelists disapproved were appealing to her as an authority. For the late first century this is only a presumption. [H.J.C. compares Lk.'s variants in the lists of the twelve.] But for the second century there is no doubt that Salome was popular in heretical circles; we have Celsus' report that the Carpocratians appealed to her authority (Origen, *Contra Celsum* V.62). Salome appears as one of the interlocutors of Jesus in the *Gospel according to the Egyptians* (Hennecke-Schneemelcher, 109f), used by the encratites, Julius Cassianus, Theodotus the Valentinian, the Naassenes, and the Sabellians, as well as by *II Clement* and Clement of Alexandria. She also appears in the *Gospel of Thomas* (Leipoldt) 61b where she asks Jesus the curious question, "Who ⟨are you,⟩ man, as from the one? ⟨sic⟩ You get onto my bed." (The text has, understandably, been corrupted.) Again in the Chenoboskion gnostic documents she is found in the *First Apocalypse of James* (Böhlig-Labib, *KGA*, p. 50). *The Book of the Resurrection of Christ* (James, *ANT* 183) lists among the women who went to Jesus' tomb "Mary Magdalene, Mary the mother of James whom Jesus delivered out of the hand of Satan, Salome who tempted him, Mary who ministered to him and Martha her sister." Salome is one of the interlocutors in the gnostic *Pistis Sophia* (54, 58, 132, 145) and explains the mysteries. By contrast, the orthodox *Ethiopic Didascalia* (III.6) makes the apostles report that "there abode with us Mary Magdalene, and the sisters of Lazarus, Mary and Martha, and Salome, and others also with them; (and) since He ⟨Jesus⟩ commanded not them ⟨sic, Harden⟩ to teach along with us, neither is it right for other women to teach." (This occurs again in a Greek fragment of the *Didascalia Apostolorum* III.6, Connolly, p. xxvi, thinks Salome intrusive.) Of special interest is the double tradition found in the stories of the birth of Jesus. In the orthodox *Protevangelium Iacobi* XIX.3–XX.4 Salome was not the Virgin's midwife, but a woman who heard of the virgin birth only after it had taken place and would not believe it. She attempted to test Mary's virginity and was punished by the withering of her hand. In the less respectable *Liber de Infantia* there were two midwives, Zelomi and Salome (as Amann notes, *Protévangile* 325, these are two forms of the same name). Zelomi first made a manual test, proclaimed Mary's virginity, and gave glory to God; Salome refused to believe Zelomi's report, made a second manual test, and had her hand blasted. Finally, in a Coptic fragment quoted by Robinson (*Gospels* 196f) and in the Coptic *Discourse by Demetrius on the Birth of our Lord* (Budge, *Texts* 673ff), Salome was the only midwife; she immediately believed and became the first to proclaim the Gospel; and she followed the holy family and, later, Jesus everywhere, and—as Demetrius specifies—she saw everything. (A trace of this legend appears also in the *History of Joseph the Carpenter* VIII.3: Salome accompanied

the holy family to Egypt.) Obviously, Salome was a controversial figure. And it can be seen that the orthodox material has been edited to diminish her importance as a witness, for the oldest text of the *Protevangelium Iacobi* (which denies that she was the midwife) reports her cure with the words καὶ ἰάθη ἡ μαῖα ἐν τῇ ὥρᾳ ἐκείνῃ (Testuz, p. 108, lines 9–10, ca. A.D. 200). This shows reworking of an older form in which she was the midwife (a fact overlooked by Strycker, to say nothing of Testuz). The hostile orthodox tradition is further represented by Origen on Mt., *Commentariorum Series* 141 and 144, which admits that Salome watched the crucifixion from a distance, but denies that she was in at the resurrection—only Mary Magdalene and Mary the mother of James were admitted to that, "quasi maiores in caritate." Against this, the semignostic tradition favorable to Salome is represented by numerous Coptic texts on the assumption of the Virgin (Robinson, *Gospels* 51, 59, 60, 77) in which she appears as one of the Virgin's companions. (Some of these contain details reminiscent of the raising of Lazarus in the longer text.) Finally, in the *Psalms of Thomas* (note his connections) in the *Manichaean Psalm Book* II.222f, Salome appears as the equivalent of the OT "Wisdom" who builds her house, the Church.

[K.S. pointed out to me the similarity of Salome's disbelief and manual test of the virgin birth and Thomas' disbelief and manual test of the resurrection in Jn. 20.24–29. He also remarked (above, p. 166 n14) that Jn. 20.24–29 plus Thomas' reception of the secret revelation (in the *Gospel of Thomas*) make up a rejection-resurrection-revelation complex similar to those in Mk. 8.29ff; 10.20ff; 14.27ff discussed above, pp. 165ff.] Of this complex John chose to retain only the first element and to use that as polemic against the followers of Thomas. Thomas had indeed seen, but was less blessed that the evangelist who, presumably, had not seen. (The explicit counterclaim in I Jn. 1.1 is less convincing than the implicit admission in Jn. 20.29.) Here, as in the development of the Salome stories, the original figures of Jesus' circle are pushed aside by the authorities of the developing churches. The importance of this will appear in the following chapter.

The above survey covers almost all the early Christian reports concerning Salome. Omitted are only a set of notices in which Salome's name appears in lists of women who served the Lord or were related to the holy family or were involved in the resurrection stories. Such comparatively colorless material is directly derivable from the Markan references. Not so the tradition surveyed above. That tradition is almost entirely Egyptian (Strycker, 423, thinks Egypt the source of the *Protevangelium Iacobi*) and is sharply divided between (a) orthodox polemic and (b) glorification by "heretical" material and by Coptic material which, although sometimes nominally orthodox, perpetuates quite unorthodox elements of Egyptian background. Since the Carpocratians who appealed to Salome's authority (Origen, *Contra Celsum* V.62) also maintained that Jesus was a natural man, the son of Joseph (Irenaeus: Harvey, I.20 = Stieren, I.25), and since Salome in orthodox material was cursed for her denial of the virgin birth, it would seem that she had figured as an authority for esoteric traditions allied with a naturalistic account of Jesus' birth, and that the importance of the esoteric traditions for the Egyptian churches had been sufficient to save her from the polemic which the naturalism engendered and to transform

her into the first disinterested witness of the virgin birth. But whatever may be thought of the later history of the tradition, it is quite clear that the early material is so widespread and rich in content that it cannot be explained as derived from the two references in canonical Mk. There must have been other early traditions about Salome to explain the later developments. The later developments, in turn, suggest reasons for the suppression of the early material. That suppression is already visible in Mt. and Lk., and may therefore have operated in the editing of Mk.

E. *Conclusions*

Let us now review the points which have been made.

A. The resurrection story in the longer text is an example of the miracle-in-response-to-intercession story: its similarities in content to canonical examples of that type (e.g., the story of the Gerasene demoniac) are no more numerous than the similarities of the canonical examples to each other.

B. However, it is especially related to the story of Lazarus: the story in Jn. is a Johannine expansion of a later version of the story in the longer text. That the author of the longer text did not know the Johannine story is as nearly certain as anything based on source-analysis can be. That John did not know the longer text is probable.

C. When the longer text is added to Mk., the geographical outlines of Mk. 6.32–16.8 and Jn. 6.1–20.2a are so similar and the order of major events and the places of these events in relation to the geographical outlines are so similar as to indicate that Mark and John independently expanded and reworked what were probably independent translations of some ultimately common source. Clement locates his first quotation from the longer text exactly where it should be in Mk. had it been part of this source. Also, the piece of geographical framework with which it concludes is paralleled in Jn., but differs so far from the Johannine parallel that it cannot be explained as derived from Jn. Presumably both it and its Johannine parallel came from the source. That the source was Aramaic is not unlikely in view of the numerous Aramaic traits in the style of both Mk. and Jn., which have led a number of scholars to suppose them dependent, more or less directly, on Aramaic material (Burney, *Origin*; Black, *Aramaic*; Schlatter, *Sprache*; Torrey, *Four Gospels* and *Translated Gospels*, etc.).

D. The new material has particularly close structural ties with canonical Mk.:

1. It fits the "historical" outline traditionally found in Mk.

2. Mk. 10.20–34 plus the longer text shows an order of events paralleled in Mk. 8.29–9.8 and Mk. 14.27–16.5. These parallels do *not* seem to come from a common source, but from common editorial arrangement of diverse material. It may be that the same editor was responsible for all three instances of the pattern.

3. Mk. 10.13–34 + the longer text + 10.35–45 is a pericope of which the contents follow closely the order and contents of a baptismal service. Another

form of the first section, related to the longer text, stood in a *Gospel according to the Hebrews* (Klijn, *Question*). The Markan (+ longer text) pericope was designed as a basis for baptismal teaching and for reading in the service. In this design the resurrection and initiation stories of the longer text are essential elements and occur exactly where they should. Moreover, the interpretation of the initiation as a baptism is confirmed by and explains the details given, and these explain Mk. 14.51.

4. The second quotation from the longer text has been so bowdlerized by Clement or his predecessors that few conclusions can be drawn from it. However, Mt. seems to have known it where Clement located it in Mk. Luke also locates in Jericho a story which has important similarities to the longer text (it looks like a late version of the same tradition with moralizing substituted for miracles). The present text of Mk. seems to have suffered a deletion precisely where Clement locates the additional material. And the reference to Salome suggests a reason for the deletion.

Of the above points, B, C, and D concur to indicate that the longer text was the original text of Mk., and that canonical Mk. has been produced by abbreviation.

Against this conclusion must be set the conclusion reached from the stylistic study in the previous section (pp. 144–145, above).

The evident conflict of these bodies of evidence leads one to examine what can be said against either side.

Against the stylistic evidence it can be objected that the excess of parallelism might be accounted for by the convergence of many different elements—the similarity in content of resurrection stories as such; the self-repetition of Mark; the use of liturgical and narrative formulas; the influence exerted by an important text; deliberate interpolation and manuscript corruption; and mere chance. And most important of all is the fact that the sample is too short to afford conclusive stylistic evidence.

Against the evidence from content it can be said that interpolation is often concerned to produce texts useful for teaching, and interpolators often take advantage of small irregularities in texts interpolated. So the lacuna in Mk. 10.46 might have attracted an interpolator, and the concern to use earlier sections of the chapter for baptismal teaching, or for teaching of the vicarious atonement, might have led to their being filled out with appropriate material. Similarly, the fact that the resurrection story of the longer text shows a form older than the source of Jn.'s Lazarus story does not prove that the longer text was originally part of Mk.—early material could have been written down at a later date and interpolated in the canonical text. Thus the strongest piece of evidence for supposing the canonical text an abbreviation is the indication that the resurrection story stood in the common source of Mark and John. This argument could be eliminated by supposing John used the longer text of Mk.; but that supposition would have to be defended against the extremely strong case for John's independence of Mk., presented by Dodd in *Historical Tradition*.

If we suppose that John did not use Mk., but that both used different translations of a common source, it would still be possible to suppose that this common source was not used all at once. If the source was an esoteric document and if the first form of Mk. was written for beginners in Christianity—as Clement says—then the first form of Mk. might have been filled out at a later date by further selections from the esoteric source, and the editor who added these might have tried—particularly if he were translating from the Aramaic—to imitate as closely as possible the wording of the earlier Markan text. An Aramaic origin may be indicated by the attribution of another floating scrap of this material to a *Gospel according to the Hebrews* (Klijn, *Question*).

This theory seems to fit the evidence from style as well as that from content, but it still leaves unexplained the evidence that something was deleted from Mk. 10.46. However, there is no need to suppose that the editorial work on Mk. was limited to interpolation, or that all selections of the longer text—or all sections of canonical Mk.—had the same origin and history. The editor may have deleted as well as added; insertions may have been made by one editor and deletions by a second; other possibilities can easily be imagined.

Accordingly, if we were to shape our theory as closely as possible to the evidence, we should suppose that the latter part of Jn. and Mk. had as their remote source an Aramaic document which they knew in different translations and perhaps differently mutilated or interpolated or both. The earliest form of Mk., though using this source, did not include the resurrection and initiation stories now known from the longer text—although at least the former was in the source, and probably both were. However, a later editor cast these stories in a style constantly reminiscent of the Markan material he already knew, and added them to the Markan text. In doing this he was adding in written form material which had hitherto been kept secret and supplied orally in the teaching concerning baptism. The expanded text he produced was probably that used by Matthew. Whether it was later cut down again to form the present canonical text, or whether the canonical text was an older form which preserved its integrity alongside the interpolated text, there is no telling. But in 10.46, at least, the present canonical text seems to be an abridgment; and the longer text, as quoted by Clement, preserves the introductory phrases of the material cut out.

Postscript: Rereading this text in 1970, more than seven years after it was written and four years after its revision, I find the argument from style much weaker than that from content. Also I notice that I have not considered the likelihood that Clement, who had no reason to love the secret Gospel, might have been inclined to prefer an account representing it as a secondary expansion of the shorter text which in his day was well on its way to becoming "canonical." Perhaps, therefore, I have overestimated the reliability of his report. But the theory proposed above still seems to me the one which would best fit the evidence reviewed.

FOUR

The Background

A draft of this chapter was read by Professors Cyril Richardson and Gershom Scholem, to both of whom I am indebted for helpful discussion.

I. The question as to the historical value of the new Gospel text

Solution of the literary problem as to the relation between the new Gospel text and canonical Mk. does not solve the historical problem as to the reliability of the material contained in the new text. Since all first-century Christian authors drew on the traditions of their churches, as well as on their own imaginations, an early text may contain mere invention or a late one report old tradition. Therefore, although some of the material in the longer text probably came from a Gospel earlier than canonical Mk., and although some of it was probably cast in its present form a decade or so later than most of the stories in the canonical Gospel, neither of these probabilities is of much value as evidence of historical reliability. False statements may be primitive, and true statements may be secondary accretions to original errors.

Given this state of affairs, and given the evidence collected by Bultmann, *Geschichte*, *passim*, it would be naive to ask whether or not the events reported in the longer text "really happened." In dealing with the Gospels we have no prima facie criterion of truth save verisimilitude, and verisimilitude is not reliable. But we can ask how the new text is related to the historical problems which have been raised by the study of the canonical Gospels.

One of the most important of these problems is that of the source and significance of the secrecy motifs in the Gospels. With this we may conveniently begin, especially because Clement's letter, which quotes the new text, has revealed that Clement's church in Alexandria kept this Gospel secret and read it only to those being initiated into the "great mysteries." Moreover, the new text itself reports that Jesus administered to one of his followers a nocturnal initiation in which "Jesus taught him the mystery of the kingdom of God." How is this report related to the canonical Gospels' reports of Jesus' secret teaching?

II. Secrecy in ancient judaism

First, the background: Throughout the ancient world secrecy was practiced everywhere—in government and politics, in the trades and professions, in the philosophic schools, and, above all, in religion and magic. Secret rituals had been particularly common in ancient near eastern religions (Hooke, *Religion* 53), and the religion of Israel had been no exception in this respect: its official center was a temple of which the area around the altar might be entered only by members of the various grades of the priestly caste. None save the high priest himself was permitted to enter the adyton (Lev. 16; Num. 1.47–54; 4.1–15; 8.14–19; 17.1–5; 18.1–7; etc.).

Judaism not only perpetuated but developed these esoteric traits. The main court of the temple was now closed to gentiles (Bickerman, *Warning* 390–394, remarks on the similarity to pagan mysteries), and increased emphasis on purity law did much to cut off Jews from their gentile neighbors. The degree of separation has been greatly exaggerated in such works as Moore's *Judaism*, but the fact of it is undeniable. Consequent, the gentiles saw the religion of the Jews as a mystery religion and the Jews themselves represented it as such (see above, pp. 180ff).

Besides the assimilation of Judaism in general to the mystery religions, the several sects which grew up within Judaism kept their doctrines and rites secret from each other and from ordinary Jews. These sects probably originated in differences of legal theory and practice, particularly differences concerning the purity laws (see my *Sect*). Consequently, their meals, their houses, their schools, and their synagogues were apt to be closed to all "outsiders" (τοῖς ἔξω, Mk. 4.11), gentile and Jewish alike. (Accordingly, Strack-Billerbeck on Mk. 4.11 is mistaken. The commentary there contains only one really relevant passage—*Megillah* IV.8—and that one it misinterprets. The חיצונים are not "ketzerisch gerichtete Menschen"; on the contrary, they are sharply contrasted with the heretics, who are the adherents of מינות; the חיצונים are the ordinary Jews who are not members of the Pharisaic sect *or of any other*, while the heretics are members of competing sects—see the notes of Bertinoro and Yom Tov. But the precision here is determined by the contrast. When there is no such contrast, חיצונים means nothing more or less than "those outside"; what they are outside of must be determined from the context.)

Groups cut off from the outside world by such legal barriers usually developed further peculiarities of doctrine and observance, and among these was apt to be a deliberate affectation of secrecy concerning their teachings and practices. How far this was rooted in childish delight at having secrets, how far it was based on practical considerations of discipline and prudence, how far it was influenced by the examples of philosophic schools and mystery cults are questions which doubtless had different answers for each sect. Anyhow, it is clear from the disciplinary material in the Qumran finds that the pattern was well established in Palestine before the time of Jesus. See, for instance, *Manual of Discipline* IX.16f: It is a legal obligation to conceal the sense of the Law from wicked men. Again, VI.13–23: An initial examination and covenant is required before the outsider can even be instructed in the rules of the

sect, two years' probation before full admission. This material roughly agrees with the descriptions of the Essenes' practice of secrecy as found in Josephus, *BJ* II.119ff and Hippolytus, *Philosophumena* IX end (on which my *Description*), also Josephus, *AJ* XVIII.11ff. (That Jewish laws were to be kept secret, a fortiori, from the gentiles, is a notion probably older than the Essenes and more widely accepted than their practices; it appears already in the *Testaments of the Twelve Patriarchs, Judah* XVI.4.)

These agreements help secure credence for the account of the secret practices of a similar group in Egypt given by Philo in *On the Contemplative Life*. A society of would-be revolutionists whom Josephus describes as another "philosophical" sect (*BJ* II.118; *AJ* XVIII.23; etc.) must certainly have practiced a good deal of secrecy for prudential reasons; so must later revolutionary groups, of which the most famous were to be the "Zealots" (with whom Jesus' zealous disciple Simon (Lk. 6.15; Acts 1.13) had probably no connection). The tradition of doctrine and practice from which came the Merkabah literature (especially the *Hekalot* tracts) and the "Mithras Liturgy" (discussed above, p. 181) was certainly secret and must have existed in Palestine during Jesus' lifetime. The priests, particularly the upper priesthood, must have had a large body of secret traditions and practices; so must the Samaritans (among whom, in turn, were a number of secret sects). We hear of the Samaritans keeping secret, for instance, the principles by which they regulated their calendar (as did the Dead Sea Sect: Bowman, *Calendar* 27ff). But of all these groups we are badly informed. The one sect best known, the Pharisees, practiced secrecy in many fields. Jeremias (*Jerusalem* II.B.106ff) has shown they had secret doctrines about God, his name and his throne, the heavens, creation, the structure of the world, eschatology, the "reasons for the Law," sexual questions, magical formulas, discreditable traditions, and laws or legal provisions likely to be abused. He remarks that this "Arkandiziplin" played an even larger role in early Christianity, where it also involved Christology, the secrets of the divine nature, and the sacraments (*ibid.*, 109).

The material Jeremias collected could easily be increased (see, e.g., Jervell, *Imago* 20f, 72f, etc.). Moreover, these secrets are secrets which were kept even from ordinary members *within* the Pharisaic sect. Therefore, besides all this, it must be emphasized that vis-à-vis Judaism at large the Pharisaic sect itself was, in the first century A.D., an esoteric group. Melamed, *Leshe'elat* 118, shows that public teaching was prohibited (except as a demonstration in times of persecution) by the older interpretation of the Law (which Rabbi tried to maintain as late as the end of the second century). This secrecy produced in rabbinic material a form of "pronouncement story" which is also important in Mk.: An outsider asks a question of a rabbi, the rabbi gives him an inadequate or even false answer, later the rabbi's students ask him in private about the matter, and he gives them the true explanation; e.g., *Bereshit Rabbah* 8.9 and parallels. See, for example, the stories about Yohanan ben Zakkai, a younger contemporary of Paul and Jesus, in *Bemidbar Rabbah* 19.4; *Tanhuma'* (ed. Buber) *Hukat* 26; *J. Sanhedrin* I.2 (19b). (In the first group of these passages his secret teaching is that a dead body does not render the man who touches it impure, nor does the immersion legally prescribed for purification after contact with dead

bodies purify; but the laws are to be observed as arbitrary divine rulings. Cf. Jesus' saying, Mk. 7.15, οὐδέν ἐστιν ἔξωθεν τοῦ ἀνθρώπου εἰσπορευόμενον εἰς αὐτὸν ὃ δύναται κοινῶσαι αὐτόν. This in Mk. is followed by a private explanation to the disciples. On the story of Yohanan see Daube, *NTRJ* 141ff; Neusner, *Life* 61f.)

III. Reports about the secret teaching of Jesus

Stories of this same form—pronouncement, question in private, secret teaching to disciples—are told of Jesus in Mk. 4.10ff; 7.17ff; 9.28f; 10.10ff; 13.3ff. The private questions and answers in these passages have often been attributed to the redactor of Mk.: e.g., Bultmann, *Geschichte* 356; Seitz, *Criteria*. The latter (p. 220) affords an amusing example of "historical" criticism: it proves the secondary character of Mk. 7.18ff by the fact (!) that a special revelation from heaven was required to persuade Peter to go with a gentile. Admitting on literary grounds that the Markan secret explanations are redactional, one has to ask why the redactor chose to represent Jesus in this way. It is not enough to argue (as Seitz does) that the content of the secret explanations represents the wishes of the gentile church. Even if one were to accept the dubious distinction between the "primitive Palestinian" and "gentile" churches, one would have to explain why the secondary material was introduced as *secret* teaching. Why could the question not have been asked from the crowd and the answer given openly? To this the customary reply, since Reimarus, has been that doctrines falsely attributed to Jesus had to be presented as secret teaching because his public teaching was known and the intended dupes would remember that he had not publicly taught such things. But, first, it is unlikely that the public teaching of Jesus was so completely known to readers of the Gospels that they could confidently deny it had contained one or another element. And, second, if it be supposed that Jesus' teaching was clearly and fully remembered by the churches, they would have remembered also whether or not he taught in secret. So the fact that the editors of the Gospels chose to present some additions as secret teaching suggests their churches had a tradition that Jesus *did* teach in secret, and this tradition was older than the Gospels which relied on it to lend credit to their accounts of what he thus taught. This leads to the question, are there other traits in Mk. or in other early Christian documents which confirm these reports of secret teaching?

It is well known that there are such traits in Mk. Wrede has left a classic description of those which, as he says (*Messiasgeheimnis* 146ff), were noticed by many critics— Schleiermacher, Strauss, Keim, Hilgenfeld, and others—before his time: the taking aside of the sick, the manipulation and use of tangible means in the miracles, the magical overtones, the conception of miracles as mysteries, the conception of the disciples as initiates to whom the mystery has been given, the conception of Jesus as a god disguised in flesh, his mysterious, secret journeys, his traveling incognito, his going apart alone or with a few disciples—"scenes from the life of a magician." Moreover, Wrede declares, the earlier critics were right. All these *are* characteristics

of Mk. as opposed to the other Gospels. The earlier critics saw them because they looked at Mk. as it was; the later critics overlooked them because they came to Mk. with the preconceived notion that it was the earliest and most historical Gospel, the repository of Peter's memories, and therefore looked at it only to find material which would pass as historical and possibly Petrine. "Schleiermacher has already remarked that this Gospel approximates the characteristics of the apocryphal ones. How he meant this, is not here in question. But one thing seems to me certain: *If this Gospel came to light today, for the first time, in some grave, Schleiermacher's judgement would be approved by more than a few.*" (*Ibid.*, my italics.) Cf. Schille, *Formgeschichte* 18: "Why does Mark choose, in developing Jesus' speeches of revelation, a form which presumably was customary in the catechetic initiation of neophytes in the teaching of the Church, *as if Jesus like a hierophant led the twelve* and 'those around him' *step by step into the mysteries of the 'Church'*?" (His italics.) Even Wrede's enumeration does not exhaust the esoteric traits—there are, further, the teaching in parables, the disciples' failures to understand, the commands of secrecy, the actions performed before a few chosen witnesses, the contrast of the immediate circle with those outside, and so on. The early Christians recognized these traits and consistently pictured Jesus as teaching mysteries in secret, Cramer 311, 335, 353, etc.

Since Wrede's time this material in Mk. has commonly been discussed under the heading "the messianic secret." This is a pity because, as Wrede's list shows, the traits are too various to be explained by the sole secret that Jesus was the Messiah. What has that to do with—for instance—the use of magical techniques in the miracles? A further misfortune resultant from Wrede's brilliant study has been the tendency to treat these phenomena as peculiar to Mk. (See the review of theories in Boobyer, *Secrecy* 225f.) This was not Wrede's fault. He had examined the other Gospels, too, and had found in Mt. a different theory of a secret teaching, exemplified in such passages as 9.27ff; 11.25 and 12.18ff (*Messiasgeheimnis* 151–162) and in Lk.-Acts a theory closer to Mk.'s (165ff). Here he noted especially the report of Jesus' postresurrection teaching (Lk. 24.25f; Acts 1.3, τὰ περὶ τῆς βασιλείας τοῦ θεοῦ) but did not see that this was intended to authenticate some body of secret doctrine known to Luke. He also observed (188ff) traces of the Markan theory in Jn.

Jesus' claim in his trial, ἐν κρύπτῳ ἐλάλησα οὐδέν (Jn. 18.20), probably reflects a charge of secret teaching. Neglecting this claim, Jn. represents Nicodemus as coming to Jesus for secret instruction by night (ch. 3—the parallelism to the longer text of Mk. is clear), reports that Jesus had secret disciples (19.38f), and makes the last supper a long secret lecture. Also, the disciples in Jn., like those in Mk., repeatedly failed to understand: 2.22; 12.16; 13.7,28; 14.20; 16.12,25; 20.9. Only after Jesus' death came the spirit which was to recall to them all things Jesus had said (14.16f) and lead them into all truth (16.13); that is, into a revelation more revealing than John's Gospel, of which the last speech was still ἐν παροιμίαις (16.25).[1] This again

---

1. This closely resembles the relation which Clement said existed between the longer text of Mk. and the secret teachings: the longer text contained those stories and sayings the spiritual interpretation of which would lead the initiates to the hidden truth (Letter I.21–26, and commentary, also p. 166 above).

must be a claim to secret teaching or to private revelation which would immediately pass over into secret teaching (cf. Kragerud, *Lieblingsjünger* 84ff; Käsemann, *Ketzer* 302).

The identical claim is found in Paul, I Cor. 2.11, and there is no doubt that Paul has secret teachings which he will not reveal even to baptized Christians who are still "carnal" (*ibid.*, 3.1ff). Machen, *Origin*, has made a strong case for the supposition that the main elements of Paul's religion came from Jesus. We saw above (pp. 178ff) that Paul and Mk. were at one in their use of μυστήριον to refer to baptism. They are also at one in their belief that the teachings of Christianity include secrets to be revealed only to the few elect. A further point of agreement is their belief that Jesus was a supernatural power in disguise: Mark thought demons could recognize him but men could not (1.24,34; 3.11; etc.); Paul thought even demons were fooled (I Cor. 2.8, on which Macgregor, *Principalities*; cf. Phil. 2.7; Col. 2.15; Jn. 19.11); Paul's opinion was shared by the first-century (?) author of the *Ascension of Isaiah* 10–11. (A similar belief was probably held about Simon Magus by his followers: Acts 8.10; Cerfaux, *Gnose*, I.504f. See the remarks of Weiss, *Christianity* 758f.)

In sum, the Gospels all represent Jesus as teaching in secret; Paul certainly had secret doctrines and Lk. and Jn. presuppose them. When Christianity first appears in the writings of pagan authors it is described as a secret society (Pliny, *Epistulae ad Traianum* 96.7: *hetaeria*; Grant, *Pliny*; *PW sub voc.*) or an initiation (Lucian, *Peregrinus* 11: τελετή). These descriptions are completely in accord with its background in sectarian Judaism. Accordingly, we need not question the report in the new text that Jesus taught in secret, but we may reasonably inquire what he secretly taught.

IV.   QUESTIONS ABOUT THE CONTENT OF JESUS' SECRET TEACHING

But can we hope, at this remove, to discover what Jesus taught secretly? There is no scholarly agreement even as to what he taught in public. He has been represented as a rabbi, a philosopher, a pacifist, a revolutionary, a moral reformer, a prophet of the coming end of the world, an itinerant exorcist, and the son of God, come down to earth to reveal his own nature. This general disagreement as to his teachings suggests that some of them, at least, were secret. So does the cause of the general disagreement—the fact that the canonical Gospels contain considerable elements which give apparently contradictory pictures of their hero. These contradictions must be dealt with either by supposing one body of material "primary" and the rest "secondary" (the method which has produced the various "historical" pictures of Jesus listed above), or by supposing them all "secondary" (an act of faith, not to say credulity), or by supposing that they reflect different facets of a complicated character in which they were reconciled (more or less) by considerations not made public. Of these three methods the first and last are not mutually exclusive, but their possible combinations do not here concern us. Here the facts to be noted

are that any attempt to explore the area of secrecy in the Gospel tradition is necessarily speculative, but any attempt to deny it is necessarily wrong. Even texts like Mt. 10.27, "What I tell you in darkness, declare in the light, and what you hear in the ear, proclaim on the housetops," while intended to suggest that (all?) the content of the secret teaching has now been made public, admit implicitly that a secret teaching existed. Accordingly we must recognize both that we deal here with an extremely speculative area of study, and also that the preserved evidence necessitates speculation.

To the question "what did Jesus tell his disciples in darkness?" the answer has usually been "the messianic secret." This secret is divided by a recent study (Burkill, *Revelation*) into two parts: the secret fact—that Jesus was the Messiah—and the secret interpretation of the messiahship as a career of service, suffering, and death. As for the secret fact—it seems likely that Jesus did think he was the Messiah, and had obvious, prudential reasons to conceal his opinion. As for the secret interpretation, however—there is no clear reason why *that* should be kept secret, and Mk. insists that Jesus taught it publicly (8.31f). Moreover, it seems unlikely that he ever taught it at all: the prophecies of the passion look like prophecies *ex eventu*—the weakness of the opposite opinion has been demonstrated by Taylor's defense of it (*Origin*). And the report that Jesus set guards at Gethsemane (Mk. 14.32,34; cf. Lk. 22.40) indicates that he had no intention of giving his life as a ransom for any. The question of Shemtov ben Shaprut, reported by Krauss (*Leben* 269) is worth repeating: If Jesus gave himself freely to his sacrificial death, why did he say that Judas Iscariot betrayed him?

On the other hand, there is no reason to suppose Jesus had only one secret—the fact that he was the Messiah. The existence of other secrets may be indicated by obscurities in the tradition. One such obscurity is that covering the relation of the Messiah to the kingdom of God. And since Mk. 4.11 declares that "the mystery of the kingdom of God" has been given to the disciples (as opposed to "those outside"), and the new text represents Jesus as teaching this mystery to the youth who came to him for nocturnal initiation, we seem to have here another element of Jesus' secret teaching. We have already seen evidence indicating that the mystery was a baptism (above, pp. 178ff). We must now try to find out what this baptism was supposed to effect, why it was administered by Jesus, and why it was secret. But these questions presuppose another: If baptism was "the mystery of the kingdom of God," what was "the kingdom of God"?

V. The Kingdom of God

The discussion of the kingdom touched off by Dodd's *Parables* has practically ended with the recognition that "kingdom" meant primarily, "rule" (as מלכות —an abstract—would) but might, by extension, refer to the persons or organization or area ruled; cf. Lundström, *Kingdom* and Perrin, *Kingdom*. Of recent articles, Ladd,

Reign, is right as to the essential meaning but does not allow sufficiently for the extensions. Grant, *Idea* 442, gives a better account by comparing God's rule of all creation to the rule of the Great King: it had originally been complete, but since the time of Adam certain provinces (the demonic, human, and animal worlds) had been in revolt, and in Jesus' time apocalyptic writers had recently been foretelling that the revolt was soon to be suppressed and the rule restored. It was, later, the peculiarity of Jesus' followers to believe that the suppression had already begun; the Great King's rule had come back into the revolted provinces in the person of his representative, Jesus, it had been manifested in Jesus' acts of power, and it was continued in their own obedience, as they looked forward eagerly to his coming again "with power and great glory" to complete the restoration. This explains why the NT documents generally speak of the "kingdom" both as present and as future—it was both at once: It was present in Jesus, in the Church, and in God's eternal rule of the heavens; it was yet to come in the full resubjugation of the lower world (so Kümmel, *Eschatologie*).

That the Church is a manifestation of the "kingdom of God" confirms our previous interpretation of "the mystery of the kingdom" as baptism—the ritual of initiation into the Church. Stanley (*Kingdom*) has shown that in Mt. and Lk. the kingdom is sometimes the Church (so especially in Mt. 13.33,52), and the same sense appears in Paul (Col. 1.13; 4.11), the Apocalypse (1.6,9, etc.), and the Markan parable of the mustard seed (Mk. 4.30; cf. Dan. 2.35,44 and Jeremias, *Gleichnisse* 93).

A further point made clear by Grant's analogy is that God's rule of the heavens continued unchanged in spite of the rebellion of the lower provinces. God's throne either is in or is the heavens (Apoc. 4.2; Mt. 5.34; 23.22) and God himself is in the heavens (Mt. 6.1,9, etc.); the heavens are therefore his kingdom, κατ᾽ ἐξοχήν. This had been the opinion of the Psalmist (103.19, where ๅ is to be translated "even though"—cf. 115.16). In Wisdom, too, "the kingdom of God" is in the heavens, where it was shown to Jacob in his dream (10.10) and whence the divine word descended to destroy the wicked (18.15). So, too, in the pseudepigraphic apocalypses, God is customarily enthroned in the heavens and his kingdom is, by implication, there; the implication is made explicit in *III Baruch* (the Greek apocalypse) 11.1f, where the keys "of the kingdom of heaven" are identified as those to the gate of the fifth heaven. Compare Dan. 4.34, where God is "the King of the heavens." This explains the fact noted by Aalen, that in the NT "the kingdom of God" often has a local sense and evidently refers to "a confined area" (*Reign* 229). This "confined area" is in the heavens, the realm of God, as Riesenfeld noted (*ΠΑΡΑ*). There "in the kingdom of God" is Abraham (Mt. 8.11, Lk. 13.28), to whose bosom Lazarus was carried by angels immediately after death (Lk. 16.22; cf. Dodd, *Parables* 44). There (in the third heaven) is the Paradise to which Paul was taken up on his conversion (II Cor. 12.1–4; cf. Gal. 2.1), to which four second-century rabbis reportedly ascended (*J. Hagigah* II.1 [77b]), and to which Jesus promised to take, on the very day of their deaths, the thief who believed that he would yet come into his kingdom (Lk. 23.42f). It is in the heavens that the reward of the righteous is laid up—the kingdom prepared for them from the beginning of creation (Lk. 12.32–

34; Mt. 5.12; 6.20; 25.34). It is in the heavens that God's kingdom has come, that is, his will is done, already, as the Church prays it may come on earth (Mt. 6.10). So too the Synagogue prays, in a probably contemporary prayer: "May he who maintains peace in his heavens (במרומיו) maintain peace for us and for all Israel" (Baer, *Seder* 104). The keys of the kingdom of the heavens, which are to be given to Peter, will render his legal decisions binding in the heavens; compare the rabbinic claim that God's court in the heavens confirms the actions of rabbinic courts on earth (*B. Makkot* 23b and parallels, etc.). Before Abraham came, says *Sifré Devarim* 313 (on Dt. 32.10), God was, as it were, King only over the heavens; when Abraham came God began to rule also on earth. By taking away the key of knowledge the experts on the law locked the kingdom of the heavens in men's faces; they neither went in themselves nor permitted others to enter (Mt. 23.14; Lk. 11.52; *P. Oxy.* 655; Kraft, *Oxyrhynchus*; *Gospel of Thomas* (Liepoldt 39); *Clementine Homilies* XVIII.15–16). And finally the author of II Tim. 4.18 prays that the Lord will deliver him from every evil thing καὶ σώσει εἰς τὴν βασιλείαν αὐτοῦ τὴν ἐπουράνιον.

This demonstration that "the kingdom of God" may refer to a locality in the heavens has been protracted because the fact is usually ignored. Having established the fact—for which we shall later on bring further evidence—we can now return to the previous problem: what was Jesus' secret teaching about baptism, "the mystery of the kingdom"? Here we shall try to determine Jesus' position by comparison with the Baptist's on the one hand and Paul's on the other.

The interval between the work of the Baptist and the preserved letters of Paul is a mere 25 years (ca. A.D. 25–50). Therefore the work of Jesus can be defined functionally as that which, beginning from the Baptist, led to Paul. Accordingly, after some preliminary remarks on the difficulty of distinguishing Jesus' role from the Baptist's, we shall define as sharply as possible the work of the Baptist, then review the NT evidence that Jesus baptized, and then consider Paul's statements about baptism and try to discover in them the elements which derive from Jesus.

VI. The problem of Jesus' role in relation to the present kingdom

According to the Gospels, the important difference between Jesus and the Baptist was that Jesus was the Messiah, the Baptist, merely a forerunner of the Messiah. The Gospels are clear as to the role of Jesus in the future, when the kingdom will come "with power": then he, as Messiah, will be the chief executive (Mt. 25.31ff; Mk. 13.26ff; etc.). But in the present kingdom, the kingdom on earth in his day, he is generally represented as an advance agent: his function is to proclaim the coming of the kingdom and to exemplify its presence, to manifest its power in his miracles and its requirements in his preaching (so, for example, Dibelius-Kümmel, *Jesus*). But all this could have been done by any prophet and therefore, a fortiori,

by the Baptist, who was admittedly more than a prophet (Mt. 11.9ff; Lk. 7.26ff.—Jn. 10.41 is presumably partly polemic). Therefore we must ask whether Jesus thought his present role different from the Baptist's, and, if so, how.

It will do no good to say that with the Baptist the kingdom was yet to come but in Jesus' work it was present. For we have seen above that the kingdom is simply the rule of God, therefore it is present *whenever* God manifests his power or men obey him. So if the presence of the kingdom means only its presence in preaching and prediction and acts of power, it was present already in the work of the Baptist. And even if we were to suppose Jn. 10.41 correct in reporting that the Baptist did no miracles (an unlikely supposition), and if we should follow Mt. 11.2ff ‖ Lk. 7.18ff and Lk. 11.20 in supposing that Jesus saw in his own miracles the proof that the kingdom was coming in a new way, we should have still to ask what consequences he drew from this belief. Did he think his present role was merely to preach, prophesy, and perform miracles? And did he expect no response but belief, repentance, and expectation of the great change? (These were the responses expected by the Baptist, Mt. 3.1–12 and parallels.) Or did Jesus think of himself as having some further function; did he think there was something which he and his hearers could *do*, but which the Baptist and the Baptist's hearers could not?

Like the Baptist, Jesus was to be executed by the civil authorities and to rise from the dead (Mk. 6.16; 8.28), but he probably did not foresee these details of the divine plan until the last minute; therefore the Gospels contain little material explaining how the crucifixion was useful for or relevant to the kingdom, and what little they do contain probably dates from the period after Jesus' death. Another peculiarity of Jesus' work was the ceremony of the last supper, but this was reportedly performed only once, on the last evening of his life, and therefore does not represent the sort of thing we are looking for—something which the Messiah (as distinct from a prophet) could *do* for his followers, some *action* which his followers could take because *He* (and not merely another prophet) had come. It is not impossible that, as Schweitzer believed (*Leben-Jesu-Forschung* 421f), the stories of the feeding of the multitude reflect some sort of symbolic anticipation of the banquet of the righteous in the world to come; but the evidence for this interpretation is not convincing. So the problem as to Jesus' *messianic* function, in relation to the *present* kingdom, remains open.

VII.   THE ROLE OF THE BAPTIST

The problem of Jesus' function is the more acute because the Baptist certainly did have a notion of his own special function, by which he was to prepare his hearers for the coming of the kingdom, and of a special response (beyond belief, repentance, and reformation) by which his hearers could be prepared. His function was to administer a new rite, a "baptism of repentance for the remission of sins" (Mk. 1.4 and parallels).

From the NT it can at once be seen that the Baptist's work marked an epoch for early Christianity. Not only do Mk., Q, and Jn. represent it as "the beginning of the Gospel" (Mk. 1.1ff and parallels; Lk. 16.16b; cf. Jn. 1.6), but it seems to mark in fact the beginning of the Christian tradition, which contains no reliable report of anything earlier. Moreover, it is repeatedly referred to, in the traditional material, as the point from which the movement began: "The law and the prophets were until John." "From then on" is the Christian period (Lk. 16.16 || Mt. 11.12f). When a successor is chosen for Judas he must be one who was a member of the group throughout all Jesus' career "beginning from the baptism of John" (Acts 1.22). When Peter begins to explain the Gospel to Cornelius and company he assumes, "You know what has been happening throughout all the Jewish districts, beginning from Galilee, after the baptism which John proclaimed" (Acts 10.37).[2] When Paul presents the Gospel to the Jews of Pisidian Antioch he dates Jesus' work "after John had preached . . . the baptism of repentance to all the people of Israel" (Acts 13.24).

Moreover, from what the Gospels tell it can be seen that the Baptist's importance was not limited to the Christians. All Judea and Jerusalem (Mk. 1.5) and Transjordan (Q, Mt. 3.5 || Lk. 3.3) went out to him, in crowds (Mt. 11.7 || Lk. 7.24; Lk. 3.7,10; etc.). His teaching was accepted by masses of the common people (Lk. 7.29). Even the authorities of the Temple are said to have been afraid to speak against the Baptist, even after his death, because of his popular following (Mk. 11.32 and parallels). His disciples carried his sect as far as Alexandria and Ephesus (Acts 18.25; 19.3). In this matter the testimony of the NT is confirmed by Josephus, who had heard of John as a figure both influential (Herod Antipas had him executed for fear he might initiate a revolt) and popular (many Jews interpreted a subsequent defeat of Herod's army as a divine punishment for this execution, *AJ* XVIII.116ff).

The importance of the Baptist makes it not unlikely that he is the object of the polemic in the Qumran *Manual of Discipline* III.4ff against the notion that baptism can remit sins. The opponent is not named, but the passage seems to have one and to insist, against him, that men can be cleansed of their iniquities only by the holy spirit and by submission to the rules of the sect (III.7–8), and only *after* this spiritual cleansing can their flesh be cleansed of impurity by the regular OT method of sprinkling with water containing the ashes of a red heifer properly killed and burned (Num. 19.9,13, etc.).[3] That the object of the polemic was the Baptist is made very likely by the fact that Josephus, in the passage cited above, saw fit to defend him against such charges and to insist that he required repentance as a prerequisite for his physical cleansing. Evidently his teaching left some danger of *ex opere operato*—

2. For the translation of 'Ιουδαία see Burkitt, *Vestigia* 485f.

3. This passage has been repeatedly misunderstood by neglect of its polemic character, although that was recognized (but misinterpreted) by Gottstein, *Traits*. Against Flusser, *Sect*, and Betz, *Proselytentaufe*, it must be said that nothing in the Qumran documents implies the use by the sect of any type of immersion other than such as are prescribed in the OT for purification. In particular, the regulations for entrance to the sect, which are twice described in the *Manual of Discipline* (I and VI) and once in the *Damascus Document* (VI.14ff) say nothing of any special immersions, nor does Josephus mention any such rite of admission to the sect. See further Rowley, *Baptism*; Benoit, *Qumran* 280.

not to say libertine—interpretation (with the polemic in the *Manual of Discipline* III.4f, cf. Connolly, *Didascalia* VI.22, p. 254).

Admittedly, there is no being sure that the Qumran polemic was directed against the Baptist—rites of immersion were popular at the time, as Thomas, *Mouvement*, has shown. Nevertheless, his importance makes the hypothesis plausible; and so does the fact that his baptism was remembered as a distinct rite, "the baptism of John" (Mk. 11.30 and parallels; Lk. 7.29; Acts 1.22; 10.37; 13.24; 18.25; 19.3f), which was sharply differentiated from Christian baptism (Acts 18.25; 19.3f) and also from ordinary Jewish immersions for purification (Mk. 7.4, Heb. 9.10—the βαπτισμῶν διδαχή of Heb. 6.2 was presumably instruction as to the different sorts of baptisms then in competition; cf. Spicq, *ad loc.*).

The characteristics of the Baptist's rite have often been noticed: It was not something one could do for oneself; it had to be administered by the Baptist or one of his disciples, was perhaps public, was administered to Jews (whether or not to gentiles), *may* not have been repeatable, used water and probably required immersion, either required or effected repentance, was accompanied by confession of sins, effected remission of sins, demanded the performance of good works in the future, was performed as a preparation for the coming judgment or kingdom of God, and either was not connected with any teaching about the holy spirit, or supposed the spirit would be given (as a further "baptism") only at the last judgment (Acts 19.2 *vs.* Mk. 1.8 and parallels; see Best, *Spirit*). That it made the recipient a member of a new community is often said by the critics but never by the sources—there is no evidence that all those whom John baptized became his disciples; the reports of crowds coming to be baptized suggest that the rite entailed no membership in any society, and Josephus' βαπτίσμῳ συνιέναι is inadequate as an excuse for supposing the contrary (*vs.* Flemington, *Doctrine* 15). What was demanded of the few who did become disciples, we do not know.

It has already been remarked that no baptism of this kind appears in the Qumran documents. Attempts to derive it from Jewish proselyte baptism are equally mistaken. (See the distinctions made by Werblowsky, *Rite* 101f; Doeve, *Doop*; Michaelis, *Hintergrund*; Beasley-Murray, *Baptism* 40–42; and the chronological arguments of Taylor, *Beginning*.) It should be added that the rule "a proselyte is as a new born child" is a legal fiction meaning that the proselyte is freed from most legal liabilities —including the liability for transgressions—contracted in his earlier life, and also loses his prior legal claims—for example, he has no property. It does not mean— *pace* Werblowsky, *Rite* 102—that he is reborn as a child of Israel; Daube's examples, *Reflections* 51, show loss of prior legal ties, including family connections, but not acquisition of new ones. Rabbi ruled in *Bikkurim* I.4 that proselytes must continue to speak of the Patriarchs as "their fathers," not "our fathers." Though the contrary opinion of R. Judah (*J. Bikkurim* I.4 (64a), called to my attention by R. William G. Braude) subsequently prevailed, the fact that neither the *Mishnah* nor the *Tosephta* mentions it makes almost certain—so R. Saul Lieberman advises me—that the preference of it is a subsequent alteration of the law. In any event, R. Judah based his opinion on Gen. 17.5, "For I have made you the ancestor of a multitude of peoples,"

so he presumably considered the proselytes a different people than Israel and justified their reference to "our" fathers by the fact that they were descendants of Abraham, not of Jacob—this would have involved no change of ancestry. Moreover it seems likely that his opinion was a reply to Christian propaganda, see the use of the same verse by Paul, Romans 4.17ff, and the development of this by the fathers, for instance Aphraates, *Demonstratio* XI.10ff, who is evidently answering Jewish arguments.

Since, then, the Baptist's rite can be derived neither from Pharisaic baptism of proselytes nor from Qumran, we must look elsewhere for its origin. The true source is that indicated by Mk. 11.30: it was from "Heaven," that is, from God. This was what all the people believed (*ibid.*), and their belief presumably came from the Baptist's own claim—that he was a prophet (Mt. 11.9 and parallels) charged by God to institute a new rite, an immersion which would remit sins (cf. Kraft, *Anfänge* 401f).

To understand the importance of this one must realize that in Jewish law sin and impurity are different things. One may become highly impure by any number of accidents which involve no sin whatever—for example, by being present in a house when a death occurs there. Many sins, on the other hand—theft, for instance—do not render the sinner impure. Admittedly, by the Baptist's time the distinction had often been blurred. The prophets and psalmists had spoken of sins as impurities from which men could be cleansed (e.g., Ps. 51.4); the verb "to sin" had an intensive form which should have meant "to de-sin" but actually meant "to purify," and the water used for certain types of purification was known as "sin-water." But neither poetry nor etymology is valid in law. In law, impurity was removed by immersions (the "baptisms" of Mk. 7.4), and certain unintentional sins could be expiated by the sacrifices prescribed in the OT; but for the rest one could only trust to the general expiatory rites of the day of atonement, to the powers of repentance, restitution, reformation, and prayer, to the atonement effected by one's death, and to the mercy of God (*Yoma'* VIII.8f). Moreover, the possibilities for sacrifice to Yahweh in Palestine had been cut down sharply under the Maccabees; the destructions of the temples at Gerizim, Araq el Emir, and Lachish indicate what happened to lesser shrines. By John's time the only place in the country where Jews could legally offer sacrifices was Jerusalem, and its services were expensive. To introduce into this situation a new, inexpensive, generally available, divinely authorized *rite*, effective for the remission of all sins, was John's great innovation.[4] His warning of the coming judgment was nothing new; prophets had been predicting that for the past eight centuries. The new thing was the assurance that there was something the average man could easily *do* to prepare himself for the catastrophic coming of the kingdom. Therefore John was remembered not merely as a prophet, but as "more than a prophet"—as "the Baptist."

---

4. The Qumran sect had probably developed the doctrine that their life of obedience to the Law had the atoning power of the sacrifices (see Flusser, *Sect.* 229–236); but the devotion of an entire life to the observance of an ascetic law is a very different thing from the performance of one, quick, easy ceremony.

VIII.   Evidence from the Gospels that Jesus baptized

Since the Baptist's role in relation to the coming kingdom is so clearly definable, it is surprising that there should be such obscurity about the role of Jesus—who is said to have been thought, in his own lifetime, the Baptist redivivus (Mk. 6.14; 8.28 and parallels; cf., however, Kraeling, *Necromancy*).

Particularly surprising is the particular obscurity concerning Jesus' use of baptism. He himself was baptized; but the synoptics say nothing of his having baptized his followers, while the Fourth Gospel contradicts itself on this point (as on so many others): it says in 3.22 that he did baptize; it refers to reports of his baptizing in 3.26 and 4.1; but in 4.2 it adds καίτοι γε 'Ιησοῦς αὐτὸς οὐκ ἐβάπτισεν ἀλλ' οἱ μαθηταὶ αὐτοῦ. Here the accepted alternatives are either to eliminate 4.2 as a gloss (Bultmann, *Johannes* 128 n4; Dodd, *Fourth Gospel* 311 and *Historical Tradition* 237) or to accept it as a correction: Jesus did not himself baptize, but during an early ministry in Judea (unknown to the synoptics except for Lk. 4.44, on which cf. Acts 10.37—above, p. 206) he permitted his disciples to go on administering (the Baptist's?) baptism, a practice which he subsequently stopped (why?) but which the disciples nevertheless resumed as soon as he was out of the way, Acts 2.38. But here the function of the Baptist's rite—εἰς ἄφεσιν τῶν ἁμαρτιῶν—is combined with the Christian formula ἐπὶ τῷ ὀνόματι 'Ιησοῦ Χριστοῦ. How the disciples could baptize in Jesus' name if Jesus had stopped the practice is not easily explicable (see the wrigglings of Beasley-Murray, *Baptism* 70f; Flemington, *Doctrine* 30f, chose to ignore the problem).

These difficulties may perhaps justify a hypothesis of mistranslation. In Syriac 4.2 reads, ܝܡܘܙܝܕܐ ܐܠܐ .ܟܘܡ ܡܥܡܕ ܠܐ ܗܘ ܟܘܡ ܠܐ ܗܘ. It is only the medial period which prevents this from meaning, "Yet Jesus himself baptized none save his disciples." (A ܠ before ܬܠܡܝܕܘܗܝ would be desirable, but not necessary. Cf. the similarly possible mistranslation in Jn. 12.17, above, p. 157.) Variant forms of the tradition that Jesus baptized only his disciples are found in Clement (III.196.21ff) and later writers (Echle, *Baptism* 367f), and this is the meaning indicated by the context in Jn. 4.2. Jn. has been at its usual business of contrasting Jesus and the Baptist to the latter's disadvantage. It has just reported how the Pharisees heard ὅτι 'Ιησοῦς πλείονας μαθητὰς ποιεῖ καὶ βαπτίζει ἢ 'Ιωάννης. Here the Syriac reads ܕܫܡܥܘ ܦܪܝܫܐ ܥܠ ܕܣܓܝܐܐ ܬܠܡܝܕܐ ܥܒܕ ܘܡܥܡܕ ܝܬܝܪ ܡܢ ܝܘܚܢܢ. In any case the Greek should not be read as evidence that all whom the Baptist baptized became his disciples. The evangelist was talking about Jesus. He realized the ambiguity of his statement (which was to mislead Bultmann, *Johannes* 128 n7) and therefore went on to explain it by declaring, "Yet Jesus baptized *only* his disciples!"—while the Baptist (it is to be understood) baptized everybody who came to him—and even so Jesus' disciples were more numerous than the Baptist's here-today-and-gone-tomorrow penitents. This presumable exaggeration concludes the theme begun in 3.26 and formally stated in 3.30. (See also Dodd's arguments in *Historical Tradition* 285f, 292, and, further, from the themes of water and spirit in *Fourth Gospel* 308–311.) [Discussion with C.R. leaves me dubious about the above interpretation. It is possible that the author

(or glossator) meant, "*Yet* Jesus baptized only his disciples, and consequently the Pharisees were misinformed and their (suggested) plots unnecessary."]

Thus we have the statements of Jn. on one side, the silence of the synoptics on the other. To Jn.'s statements should be added the account of the footwashing in 13.1–15. The footwashing is to baptism as the feeding of the multitude is to the eucharist; for both sacraments Jn. has a chapter of theological exegesis (3 on baptism, 6 on the eucharist) and a story of a similar event which could be used by a teacher as a type of the rite. Aphraates, *Demonstratio* XII.10 understood the footwashing as a miraculous baptism, by anticipation, of the twelve, into Jesus' passion. As such he contrasted it with the Baptist's rite, which only produced remission of sins by repentance, and he thus explained why the Baptist's penitents were rebaptized, with the baptism of Jesus, by the apostles. But Jn., as usual, remains enigmatic. Synoptic evidence that Jesus baptized might be found in Mk. 1.8 and parallels (including Jn. 1.33), where the Baptist is made to declare that he can baptize only with water, but his greater successor will baptize with the holy spirit ("and with fire," Q); and also in Mk. 9.49 (correcting ἁλισθήσεται to βαπτισθήσεται, with Baarda). But Acts (1.5; 11.16) interprets the promise of baptism with spirit and fire as referring to Pentecost (Acts 2.3f,17), and Jn. 7.39 indicates that the spirit was not given until after Jesus' resurrection; so it could be that the whole of the Baptist's prophecy is an anachronistic invention of the Christian polemic against his followers. (The greater successor—whose shoelaces he was not worthy to untie—can hardly have been Yahweh, who has no body, parts, or shoelaces. Contrast Kraft, *Anfänge* 400.) Mk. 9.49, as a prophecy by Jesus, is, rather, evidence against his practice of any such rite. That MSS *c* and *e* at Lk. 23.5 add to the Jews' charges against Jesus, *et filios nostros et uxores avertit a nobis, non enim baptizantur sicut nos*, is dubious evidence at best, and the first phrase is attributed to Marcion by Epiphanius (*Panarion* XLII.11.6–8 scholion 70, ed. Holl, p. 116)—but the attributed phrase is in a slightly different form and place, so might be taken as collateral evidence for the tradition.

In sum, we come back again to the self-contradictory statements of Jn. and the silence of the synoptics. Jn.'s statements might be explained as polemic, to set Jesus above the Baptist, but self-contradiction is not a common polemic device, and one's general impression of Jn. is that it misrepresents more by exaggeration than by baseless invention. On the other hand, the strength of arguments from the silence of the synoptics has been weakened considerably by the evidence we have seen for thinking Mk. an exoteric work. Accordingly, since neither is conclusive, the contradictory evidence of Jn.'s statements and the synoptics' silence must be judged by relation to the larger problems of the history. These indicate that Jesus baptized.

Foremost among them is the obscurity, which we have been trying to penetrate, of Jesus' function in relation to the kingdom. We have seen his expected role in the final establishment, and his present role as advance agent. But we have also seen that these are inadequate, because they indicate nothing unusual for his hearers to *do* about his announcements—and this inadequacy is particularly glaring by contrast with the clear and practical function of the Baptist.

Moreover, against the supposition that Jesus gave up the practical rite of the Baptist and went back to the mere preaching of repentance traditional to the prophets stands the fact that the Gospels do not consistently represent him as a preacher of repentance. They contain no accounts of mass penitence produced by his preaching, and few of individuals' repentance (and those few are suspect—e.g., Lk. 19.1–10). The message which Mk. 1.15 and parallels put into Jesus' mouth is not his, but that of the later Christian preachers: μετανοεῖτε καὶ πιστεύετε ἐν τῷ εὐαγγελίῳ (that is, the gospel about Jesus; against Taylor see Lohmeyer, and Bultmann, *Geschichte*, 124). Accordingly, it is plausible to suppose the same origin for the reference to repentance in Mk. 6.12 (a late addition unknown to both Mt. and Lk.?). These two are the only references in Mk. to Christian preaching of repentance. Jn. never refers to μετάνοια or to μετανοεῖν. Q has the verb in its exegesis of the sign of Jonah (Lk. 11.32 ‖ Mt. 12.41—evidently posterior to the resurrection) and in the woes on the Galilean cities (Lk. 10.13 ‖ Mt. 11.21), which are thus the best evidence that Jesus occasionally did use the theme. It would be hard to believe that he did not, but it would be even harder to believe, in the face of this evidence, that he was *principally* a preacher of repentance.

The difficulty becomes even clearer when one remembers that against this exiguous evidence must be set not only the rarity of stories of repentance, and the rarity of any other examples of Jesus' preaching it (found only in Lk.), but also the presence of a great deal of material which represents Jesus and his followers as anything but penitents. The Baptist, who certainly did preach repentance, conducted himself as a penitent; Jesus, by contrast, "came eating and drinking" (Lk. 7.34 ‖ Mt. 11.19). The followers of the Baptist and those of the Pharisees fasted; Jesus' followers did not, and Jesus justified this by comparing them to the members of a bridal party (Mk. 2.18ff and parallels). He justified their laxity in observance of the Law by comparing them to the companions of David (Mk. 2.25 and parallels). He forgave sins freely, without demanding repentance (Mk. 2.5 and parallels). He blessed not the penitent and the fasting, but the poor and the hungry (Lk. 6.20ff ‖ Mt. 5.3ff). And so on—the theme is familiar and need not be developed at length: The Gospels simply do not represent Jesus as principally a preacher of repentance; in this respect he differed fundamentally from the Baptist, and the difference was noticed and criticized in his own time. It now has to be accounted for.

Ever since Dodd's *Parables* this difference has customarily been accounted for by saying that for the Baptist the kingdom is still in the future, for Jesus the kingdom is here. This position is now familiar and does not need exposition, but development. If the kingdom is simply the realm of obedience to God, then it should come whenever God is obeyed. Any prophet preaching repentance will restore it insofar as his preaching is successful, and repentance will be the primary step in its restoration. Therefore the emphasis placed by the Gospels on the fact that Jesus was not merely a prophet (Mk. 8.28f and parallels; Lk. 7.26ff ‖ Mt. 11.9ff; Jn. 4.19–26; 7.40ff; etc.), and the inconspicuous role of repentance in his teaching and his followers' practice, indicate some different notion of the way in which the kingdom is present and the consequence of its presence. This notion presumably concerns some special

function of Jesus in relation to the present kingdom, and also, in the light of the Baptist's career, some special, practical, probably ritual, response which could be made by Jesus' followers to his announcement of the kingdom's presence. Now a few elements in the synoptics represent the kingdom as already—in some respect—attainable, and the disciples as already in it:

Mk. 2.19	The members of the wedding party cannot be made to fast.
2.26	David gave those *who were with him* the holy bread.
	The disciples already need not observe the sabbath.
3.15	The twelve are empowered, already, to exorcise (again 6.7).
3.35	Those who do the will of God are already Jesus' kin.
4.11	The mystery of the kingdom *has been* given to the disciples.
4.30ff	The kingdom is already growing like a mustard seed.
7.2ff	The disciples already need not observe the purity laws.
9.2ff	The transfiguration.
9.18ff,28	The disciples practiced exorcism (9.38, so did others, in Jesus' name).
10.29f	The disciples will be rewarded now—but with persecutions.
14.22ff	The eucharist.

Q (The references are to Lk.; generally I follow Manson, *Sayings*.)

7.28	The least in the kingdom *is* greater than Jn.
9.60	The disciple should let the dead bury the dead (he is already alive).
10.9	The disciples are, already, to heal the sick and announce the kingdom; Mt. adds, raise the dead!
10.16	He that heareth you heareth me, etc.
10.21	The Father *has* revealed these things to babes (and hidden them from the wise).
10.22	The Father is now revealed by the Son.
11.10	Whoever asks receives now, etc.
11.52	Those who *were* entering (the kingdom, Mt. 23.14) were hindered by the lawyers.
12.3	The things told the disciples now in secret are someday to be proclaimed openly.
12.31	Seek first the kingdom, and the good things *of this world* will be added.
13.21	The kingdom is already spreading like leaven.
16.16	The law and the prophets were until John, thenceforth (i.e., now), everyone forces his way into the kingdom.
19.26	To him that *hath* shall be given.
Mt. 11.28	Come unto me and I will give you rest now.
11.29f	Take my yoke (*sc.* of the kingdom) now.
13.44	The field with the treasure can be purchased now.

13.46	The pearl can be purchased now.
13.52	A scribe can already be a disciple of the kingdom.
16.19	The keys of the kingdom shall be given to Peter now (so that what he binds *on earth* shall be also at once bound in heaven).
18.20	Where two or three are gathered in my name, I am among them now.
Lk. 10.17	The demons are already subject to the disciples, whose names are already written in heaven.
15.11ff	The repentant son is admitted at once to the feast.
17.21	The kingdom is in your power (Griffiths, *Within*).

Some of these elements are much clearer and more conclusive than others, but the clear ones indicate how the others should be interpreted. Many different sorts and strata of material are represented, but this shows that the notion is not a peculiarity of any one strand of the tradition. Its wide distribution argues an early, common source, and the argument is strengthened by the present union of the disciples with Jesus in Jn. (15.1ff, etc.), and the location of the believers *in* the kingdom by Paul (Col. 1.13) and by the Apocalypse (1.6, etc.). All in all, it would seem that Jesus somehow enabled at least some of his followers to enter the kingdom forthwith, and to enter it in some special fashion other than that of mere repentance and obedience to God—some fashion which would make them greater than the Baptist (who was presumably penitent and obedient), would exempt them from the Law, give them power over demons and diseases, and admit them at once to the feast. This admission was the special function of Jesus, the Messiah—the function which the Baptist, though more than a prophet, could not perform.

Now the recognized means of preparation for admission to the kingdom—recognized by Jesus himself, since he had used it—was baptism, and in the earliest Christian material we find baptism the means of admission to the Church, which is the kingdom present on earth. It is therefore reasonable to assume that Jesus effected the admission of his chosen followers to the kingdom by some sort of baptism. On the other hand, the Baptist's baptism evidently did not admit the recipient to the kingdom, so Jesus' baptism must have differed from it. First and foremost it differed in being not only private, but secret. Therefore, attempts to determine its other differences are necessarily speculative.

IX. Baptism according to Paul

As a check on speculation, it is helpful to compare the Baptist's baptism, which dates from about A.D. 25, with the Christian baptism as we find it in the earliest Christian documents—Paul's letters of about A.D. 50. There is admittedly some doubt as to when Paul is talking about baptism; here we shall follow the example of

Braumann, *Taufverkündigung*, and confine ourselves to passages where the reference is indubitable. Of these the most important are the following:

Rom. 6.3ff: Those of us who were baptized into Messiah Jesus were baptized into his death. That is to say, we were buried with him, through the baptism into death, in order that, just as Messiah was raised from the dead through the glory of the Father, thus we too should live a new life. For if we have been united with him in a death like his, let us be so, too, in a resurrection like his. For we know that the man we once were was crucified with him, in order that the body which belonged to sin might be made ineffective, so that we should no longer be slaves to sin. For when a man dies he is no longer answerable for his sins. And if we died with Messiah, we believe that we shall also continue to live with him, knowing that Messiah, having been raised from the dead, will never again die.

I Cor. 12.12f: For just as the body is one, but has many members . . . so also is the Messiah. And thus we all were baptized with one spirit to constitute one body—whether Jews or Greeks, whether slaves or freemen—and we were all given one spirit to drink.

Gal. 3.26ff: For all of you ⟨formerly gentiles⟩ are sons of God through faith in Messiah Jesus. For as many of you as were baptized into Messiah have been clothed with Messiah. In him there is neither Jew nor Greek, there is neither slave nor freeman, there is no male and female, for you all are one in Messiah Jesus. And if you are Messiah's, then you are the seed of Abraham and heirs of the promise ⟨made to Abraham by God⟩.

Col. 2.9ff: ⟨In the Messiah⟩ all the fullness of the divine dwells bodily. And you are fulfilled in him, since he is the head of every cosmic power and authority. In him you have also been circumcised, not with the physical image of circumcision, but with the stripping off of the body of flesh, with the circumcision of the Messiah, having been buried with him in baptism, in which you have also been resurrected together with him through faith in the working of God who raised him from the dead. Thus, when you were dead in your sins and in the foreskin of your flesh, God brought you to life together with him. Having forgiven us all our sins, he ⟨the Messiah⟩ has cancelled the bond with the legal demands which was against us and has set it aside, having nailed it to the cross. Having stripped off the cosmic powers and authorities he has made a public spectacle of them and led them, by means of the cross, as captives in his triumphal procession. Therefore let no man sit in judgment on you about food and drink, or in a matter of festival or new moon or sabbath, which are a shadow of the things to come, whereas the substance is of the Messiah. Do not let yourselves be condemned by anyone set on self-abasement and worship of angels, things he saw going in ⟨to the heavens⟩,[5] someone puffed up to no purpose by carnal imaginations, and not holding to the head from which all the body, nourished and knit together throughout all its joints and ligaments, grows the growth of God. If, dying with Messiah, you left behind the elemental spirits of the world, why do you live as if still in the world? . . . If you have been raised from the dead with the Messiah, seek the things above, where the Messiah is, sitting to the right of God. Fix your mind on the things above, not those on earth. For you have died, and your life has been hidden with the Messiah in God. When the Messiah, our life, shall be revealed, then you too will be revealed with him in glory.

Finally, we must add *I. Cor. 10.1–4*, although it does not speak directly of Christian baptism:

5. See my *Observations*, 156–157.

I would not have you ignorant, brethren, of the fact that our fathers were all under the cloud and all went through the sea and were all baptized into Moses in the cloud and in the sea, and all ate the same spiritual food and all drank the same spiritual drink, for they drank from the spiritual rock which followed them, and the rock was the Messiah.[6]

The above passages show at a glance the immense difference between the baptism of the Baptist and that of Paul. The former was analogous to earlier biblical immersions except that it was specially instituted by God through a new prophet and it removed sin, whereas they had removed impurity. The baptism of Paul, on the contrary, is essentially a means of uniting with the Messiah. Since the Messiah and the spirit are so closely related as to be practically identical—Paul once explicitly identifies them (II Cor. 3.17, "The Lord is the spirit," cf. I Cor. 15.45)—the union is conceived as possession by a spirit. The spirit dwells in the baptized ($οἰκεῖ ἐν$, Rom. 8.9, 11 bis; I Cor. 3.16; cf. I Cor. 6.19 and Philo, De somniis I.148f, cited above, p. 171), and acts through them (I Cor. 12 and passim; notice especially the spirit's "speaking" through the possessed—Rom. 8.26, $στεναγμοῖς ἀλαλήτοις$, cf. I Cor. 2.13 and all of ch. 12—a phenomenon often observed in schizophrenia; cf. Mk. 1.24; 5.7; 13.11; Philostratus, Vita Apollonii III.38). Thus the body of the possessed Christian is in effect a part of the body of the Messiah, the spirit which lives in each Christian and acts through him. All Christians together constitute the whole body of the Messiah, of which each individual body is a member (that is, an organ—a hand, or a foot, or whatever). As I Cor. 12.13 says, "we were baptized with one spirit to constitute ($εἰς$) one body." (Cf. Plutarch, De Iside 73 (380c): The soul of Typhon is divided among the various Typhonic animals.)

This central concept Paul develops in different ways to meet the needs of different situations. In Romans 6, where he is protesting against a libertine interpretation of his teachings, he argues that union with the Messiah involves participation in his death and resurrection; since the death was a death to sin, the new life is a life to God, from which sin is necessarily excluded. (Rom. 6.11f. The future in verse 5 is hortatory; that the resurrected life has already begun is clear from the context. The future is used in verse 8 because the present resurrected life will continue; cf. Moule, Idiom-Book 23; Sanday-Headlam, Romans 154–155 and n. on 6.8.) We shall see later that Paul's notion of baptism as death and resurrection may have resulted

---

6. Here it is a mistake to speak as Lietzmann (Korinther, ad loc.), does, of topology. The concluding explanation ("for . . . Messiah") must have been needed to explain why the food and drink were "the same." "The same" is repeated for emphasis. The same as what? The same as what we Christians now eat and drink, "for . . . the rock was the Messiah." This is the point of the whole passage: Baptism and communion will not make you wholly immune to the consequence of eating things offered to idols, for they did not produce such immunity in the generation of the exodus. This argument requires that baptism into Moses should be "the same" thing as baptism into Christ—not a mere type of it—and so it would be for any Christian who had formerly been a reader of Philo and knew that Moses had been, like Jesus, an incarnation of the Logos. Therefore Paul does not have to explain this as he does his notion about the rock, which depends more on Palestinian Jewish traditions (Allo, I Cor., ad loc.). This shows he expected most members of his Corinthian church to be familiar with exegesis of the Philonic type on the story of the exodus. This is evidence in favor of Goodenough's hypothesis (I.23–29) that such exegesis was once widespread in Greco-Roman Jewry.

from other causes as well as from the notion of union with Jesus. Here let it be noted only as a development both so important and so unlikely as to deserve attention. In *I Cor. 12*, where Paul is protesting against the arrogance of those who claimed special spiritual gifts, he argues that union with the Messiah implies that all Christians have the same spirit and are therefore parts of the same body and mutually dependent. In *Galatians 3*, where he is protesting against the pretensions of those who claimed to keep the Jewish law, he argues that union with the Messiah implies that all Christians are essentially identical, for all are the Messiah, the true seed of Abraham, the true heir of the promise. (Here his use of the metaphor "you have clothed yourselves in Messiah" is probably an allegorization of the clothing which followed baptism, and suggests that the baptism was naked. See above, pp. 175f; and, further, I Cor. 15.53, where the baptismal reference was already recognized by *Odes of Solomon* 15.8; also I Cor. 15.44–49, cf. Robinson, *Hymn* 62 and 72ff, esp. 77–78; also II Cor. 3.17f; 5.2.) Finally, in *Colossians 2–3*, where he is protesting against the introduction of some cult of the cosmic powers (which conceived of them as supernatural beings to be honored or placated by observance of rules of the Mosaic Law), he argues that union with the Messiah involves participation in his nature, his death, and his resurrection. By nature he was superior to all the cosmic powers, by death he stripped them off and subjected them, and by resurrection he ascended above them, and was hid in God, where the Christians are hidden with him until the end. Therefore they should not subject themselves to the laws of inferior beings. Notice the recurrence of the stripping-then-clothing motif in 2.11,15 and 3.9. Here it is connected with the legend of the descent of a supernatural being to the lower world, his assumption from it of a physical body or some other sort of disguise, and his return to the heavens, stripping off the disguise and resuming his true form (cf. Bousset, *Himmelsreisse* 139–141, 233 and n2). This legend was ancient and widespread in Orphic and Iranian mythology (Bidez, *Ecoles* 57f; Puech, *Où* 301ff; Cumont, *Religions* 282f n69), was popularized by Plato, and about Paul's time found expressions as different as *CH* I.12–26, the Naassene hymn in Hippolytus, *Philosophumena* V.10, and *The Hymn of the Soul* (cf. Preuschen, *Hymnen* 61f). Compare also the *Prayer of Joseph* (James, *Lost Apocrypha* 21ff; Nock, review of Schoeps 584—Nock's discussion of the descent legend, 584–590, is vitiated by a scholarly concern for details which prevented him from recognizing the common pattern variously adapted in the various stories). The legend was already used by Christians as an interpretation of Jesus' work in the pre-Pauline hymn quoted by Paul in Phil. 2.6ff. We have also remarked its use by Paul, Simon Magus, Mark (?), and the *Ascension of Isaiah* (see above, p. 201). It is also basic to the thought of Jn. (1.9–11; 16.28; 19.11) and Hebrews (1.2f), and is epidemic in gnosticism and neoplatonism (Bousset, *Hauptprobleme* 361ff).

X. Elements derived from Jesus in Pauline baptism

Some of these Pauline interpretations and applications of baptism are recognizably secondary. The notion that identification with Jesus involves participation in Jesus'

death and resurrection is obviously later than those events. (Contrast the Ebionite tradition that the essential for salvation is not the sacrifice of Jesus, but baptism: Schoeps, *Judenchristentum* 69, 84f. This at least *could* have been the teaching of Jesus.) Paul's deduction of mutual dependence from the analogy of the body looks like moralization produced to meet the needs of a developing community. Similarly, the argument that all members of the Messiah must be parts of the seed of Abraham can have been pressed only in a community where Jewish snobbery and gentile emulation were a problem. Finally, the identification of baptism into Jesus with baptism into Moses is a consequence of the Philonic type of logos theory, which does not seem to have been common in Jesus' circle. All these, therefore, are probably posterior developments.

The case is different for the essential Pauline notion that baptism results in the possession of the baptized by the spirit of Jesus. This reflects demonological beliefs which appear in the exorcisms in Mk. It may have its background in the same Palestinian milieu. Compare the way the Palestinian apocalyptic writers "explain inspiration ultimately in terms of possession," Russell, *Apocalyptic* 175. (Innumerable attempts have been made to find the origin of the Pauline notion in paganism, especially in the mysteries; these are reviewed and rejected by Wagner, *Problem*. The rejection was evidently predetermined, but nevertheless seems to me justified. Cf. Warnach, *Tauflehre*.)

Moreover, there are a number of reasons for thinking that Pauline baptism came not only generally from Palestine, but specifically from Jesus: A. It was essentially a means of uniting with Jesus. B. This union was effected by the spirit, which Jesus had. C. The closest analogies to the rite are found in magical material, and there is considerable evidence that Jesus practiced magic. D. Paul's rite was soon and widely connected with ascent to the heavens, with which Jesus was also credited. E. It freed the recipient from the obligations of the law, from which Jesus' disciples were freed. Let us examine these points in order.

A.   *The rite was a means of uniting with Jesus*

Because it was a means of uniting with Jesus, Pauline baptism was radically unlike any rite known from Palestinian Jewish tradition except the eucharist. If Goodenough be correct in supposing (I.6, etc.) that some rite was devised or interpreted to symbolize or effect union with the Logos, this provides an analogy. But the evidence is inconclusive and the analogy—if any—remote. The demonological character of Paul's concept indicates that his rite did not come from the philosophers of Alexandria, but from the magicians of Palestine. Its magical character was long ago remarked by Dieterich, *Mithrasliturgie* 178. On the prevalence of magic in Palestinian Jewry see Schürer, *Geschichte* III.407ff and Lieberman, *Greek* 91–114. The evidence is rich, from Jewish and pagan sources alike. Spells in which the magician identifies himself with a spirit are plentiful in the magical papyri. A good Jewish

example comes from *The Sacred Hidden Book of Moses called Eighth or Holy* (*PGM* XIII.343ff), lines 783ff:

"And Thou, lord of life, ruler of the heavens and the earth and all those dwelling in them, whose righteousness is not turned aside, whose glorious name the Muses hymn, whom the eight guards escort, Η, Ω, Χω, Χουχ, Νουν, Ναυνι, Ἀμουν, Ἀμαυνι, who hast the unerring truth: thy name and thy spirit rest upon the good; enter my mind and my thoughts for the whole time of my life and perform for me all the desires of my soul, for Thou art I and I am Thou. Whatever I say must happen, for I have thy name as sole amulet in my heart, and no disturbance of the flesh shall overpower me, no spirit shall oppose me, no demon nor visitation nor any of the evil beings of Hades, through thy name, which I have in my soul" (cf. Rom. 8.38f; Apoc. 3.12; 14.1; 22.4).

There is another ritual means of uniting with Jesus—the eucharist—which is even less compatible with the material commonly taken to represent "normative" Judaism (eat my body! drink my blood!), but which pretty certainly was introduced by Jesus and exemplifies the same sort of magical thought and practice. Cf. *DMP* XV.1–19:

One mingles various ingredients in a cup of wine and says over it an invocation: "I am he of Abydos.., as to which the blood of Osiris bore witness ... when it (the blood) was poured into this cup, this wine. Give it, blood of Osiris (that?) he (?) gave to Isis to make her feel love in her heart for him ... give it, the blood of N. born of N. ... to N. born of N. in this cup, this bowl of wine, today, to cause her to feel a love for him in her heart, the love that Isis felt for Osiris."

This type of magical procedure is standard; cf. *PGM* no. VII, lines 643ff, which comes even closer to "this is my body"; the wine is made into the flesh (σπλάγχνα) of Osiris and Iao (= Yahweh). On the relation of the eucharist to the mysteries see Nock, *EGC* and *Mysteries*. As in the case of baptism, the eucharist's obvious incompatibility with supposedly "normative" Judaism has led to repeated efforts to derive it from the mysteries. It is a fact that Dionysiac rites celebrating the god's gift of wine were practiced around Galilee in Jesus' time; see my article "On the Wine God in Palestine," in the forthcoming Festschrift for S. Baron. These rites probably derived from a native Syro-Palestinian cult of a wine god; the Greek myth associated with them referred to the wine as "blood"; the god was said to enter those who drank the wine; Jn. 2.1–11 was modelled on this myth; there are other traces of its influence in Jn. and the influence of the cult of the wine god can be traced in many elements of Palestinian Judaism from Genesis on. But the influence of the mysteries and the influence of magic are not mutually exclusive—indeed, magicians were commonly said to have established mysteries (Burkert, ΓΟΗΣ 39f; Lucian, *Alexander* 38; etc.), and certainly drew material from them (notably for the figures of Orpheus, Hecate, and Selene: Nilsson, *Zauberpapyri* 67, 71ff). Moreover, the Dionysiac myth is not enough to explain Jesus' institution of the eucharist: the myth tells of what a god once did, but provides no excuse for a man's doing it. That a man should undertake to identify *his own* blood with wine and give it to his followers to drink in order to unite them with himself—this goes far beyond the

mysteries; its only close parallels are in magic. And there is plenty of evidence that magic was common in Palestine; e.g., *B.Berakot* 53a (end); *Sifré Devarim* 26; *Sotah* IX.13; *J.Kiddushin* IV.11 (66c); Gressmann, *Aufgaben* 11–15.

Thus early Christianity has two rites for uniting the believer with Jesus. Both derive from the same type of magical practice, both show a similar break with traditional Judaism, and both must have been introduced within half a dozen years, if we are to accept Acts' stories of baptisms in the first days of the Jerusalem community and of the baptism of Paul. Of these two rites, one was certainly introduced by Jesus; the presumption that the other one also came from him is strong. If it be accepted, it enables us to understand in a new sense a number of sayings in which the unity of the disciples with Jesus is implied, e.g., Lk. 10.16f and parallel: He that heareth you heareth me.

B. *The union was effected by the spirit*

In Pauline baptism the union with Jesus was effected by the spirit. OT immersions have nothing to do with the spirit; neither does proselyte baptism. *The Manual of Discipline* III.4ff required cleansing by the spirit as a *prerequisite* for valid immersion for purity; so the immersion probably was not thought to give the spirit. The Baptist's baptism, too, is contrasted with Christian on the ground that it was only with water, not with the spirit. (So Mk. 1.8 and parallels; Acts 19.2ff. On 18.24–28 see Flemington, *Doctrine* 40.)

Whence, then, did the spirit come into connection with baptism? It first appears at the baptism of Jesus. The variety of the traditions which agree on this point suggests that some historical fact may lie behind it. Compare Mk. 1.11 and parallels (presumably Q); Jn. 1.33; *Ebionite Gospel; Gospel according to the Hebrews;* Col. 1.19 (?—see Münderlein, *Erwählung*). Jn. 1.33 is particularly interesting for our purpose. Though suppressing Jesus' baptism (because that subordinated him to the Baptist) it implies a connection between the descent of the spirit on Jesus and his power to give it to others. And both friends and enemies agreed that Jesus had a spirit—the only question was, which? The spirit possessed him and *drove* him into the wilderness to be tempted of the devil—another spirit (Mk. 1.10 and parallels). He made his reputation by casting out spirits (Mk. 1.23ff,27; 3.11; 5.2ff; 7.25; 9.17ff). He was accused of doing so by Beelzebub or some unclean spirit, but claimed that he did so by the holy spirit (Mk. 3.22ff); he gave his disciples power over spirits (Mk. 6.7) and assured them that the holy spirit would speak through them (as the spirits in the demoniacs spoke through them—Mk. 1.24; 5.7; 13.11). This Markan material is further developed in the other synoptics (e.g., Mt. 10.25; Lk. 10.17ff) and supported by apparently independent traditions in Jn. (e.g., 8.48; 10.20f—for the magical background of this see Dieterich, *Mithrasliturgie* 117) and the *Gospel according to the Hebrews.* (See, further, Samain, *Magie* 456ff.) Since spirits played such an important role in the life of Jesus, and since baptism had been the occasion when he—unlike most of those whom John baptized—was seized by a spirit, it is not

implausible to suppose that he was the one who transformed baptism into a regular means of his followers' getting a spirit. (The tradition in Jn. and Acts that the spirit was not given until after Jesus' death will be discussed below.)

C.   *The rite was magical*

The magical character of Pauline baptism also points back to Jesus. We have already seen (above, in A) that it jibes with the magical character of the eucharist, which Jesus instituted. However, the use of the term "magical" is sure to occasion misunderstanding and requires justification.

I.   THE TERM AND THE FACTS

In the Roman Empire the practice of magic was a criminal offense (Paulus, *Sententiae* V.23.14–18), and "magician" was therefore a term of abuse. It still is, but the connotation has changed: now it is primarily fraud; then it was social subversion (MacMullen, *Enemies* 124ff). The efficacy of magic was almost universally believed, and the magician was conceived as a man who, by acquiring supernatural powers, had become a potential danger to the established authorities and the order they sought to maintain. Consequently magic was widely practiced, but rarely admitted. For Judaism, a further limiting factor was the dogma that there was no god save Yahweh. But this did not lead to the denial of the efficacy of pagan magic; that was a matter of common knowledge, not to be denied. Nor did it prevent Jews from using the same magical practices as pagans; on the contrary, they were famous as magicians (Josephus, *AJ* VIII.46). The *Sepher ha-Razim*, newly discovered by Margalioth, shows how, as late as the fourth or fifth century, a Jew steeped in the OT and thoroughly at home in the poetry of the synagogue could still compose a magicians' handbook, listing pagan deities and Christ among the angels of the lower heavens, prescribing the prayers and sacrifices to be offered them in magical ceremonies (among the prayers, an invocation of Helios in transliterated Greek), and concluding, on reaching the seventh heaven, with a celebration of Yahweh as the sole (that is, supreme) god. The more scrupulous Jews distinguished their marvels —as performed by the power of the supreme god or of pure spirits—from those of the pagans, whose gods were demons and whose spirits, impure. Thus Rabbi Akiba, complaining of his own ill success in magic, said: "When a man fasts in order that an unclean spirit should rest upon him, the unclean spirit does so. A fortiori, therefore, when a man fasts in order that a pure spirit should rest upon him, it should do so. But what can I do, since our iniquities are the cause of our difficulties, as it is said, 'For your iniquities were dividing you from your God,'" *B. Sanhedrin* 65b end. (The context leaves no doubt of the magical reference; it goes on to report that Rabba created a homunculus—the implication being that the holy spirit rested upon him and communicated to him its creative power.) Of course neither Akiba nor Rabba is represented in the Talmuds as a magician. "Magician," as we said, was a term of abuse.

Given this state of affairs, it goes without saying that Jesus is not represented by the Gospels as a magician. For the Gospels he is the Son of God in disguise. But were his practices those of contemporary magic? That he should be represented as a supernatural being is the first suspicious item, for this was a common claim of magicians and result of magical operations. Thus in the "Mithras Liturgy" the magician begins with a prayer that the supreme being will "breathe into me the holy spirit," and then goes on to declare, "I am the Son." (*PGM* IV.487–535; cf. Mk. 1.11f.) Again, the letter of "Nephotes to Psammetichus" (*ibid.*, 154–221), begins with directions for uniting oneself with the sun, as follows:

At any dawn you wish, when it is the third day of the moon, going to the roof of a high building, spread on the earthen roof a clean sheet ⟨σινδόνιον—see above, pp. 176f⟩. Do this with a mystagogue. Then you yourself, wearing a wreath of black ivy, after eleven o'clock, when the sun is in the midst of the heaven, lie down naked ⟨γυμνός—*ibid.*⟩ on the sheet, looking upward, and order that your eyes be covered with a black band. Then, wrapping yourself up like a mummy, closing your eyes and keeping your face toward the sun, begin the following prayer: "Powerful Typhon, sovereign and ruler of the realm above, God of gods, King (αβεραμενθωου formula), thou who scatterest the darkness, bringer of thunder, stormy one, who dazzlest the night, who breathest warmth into the soul, shaker of rocks, earthquake-destroyer of walls, God of foaming waves and mover of the deep ʼΙωερβητανταυ-ιμηνι!, I am he who searched through the whole world with thee and found the great Osiris, whom I brought to thee a prisoner. I am he who fought as thine ally with the gods (other texts: against the gods). I am he who locked the double doors of heaven ⟨Mt. 16.19⟩ and put to sleep the invisible dragon, who stayed the sea, the tides, the streams of the rivers until thou mightest subdue this realm. I, thy soldier ⟨II Cor. 10.4⟩, have been defeated by the ⟨astral⟩ gods ⟨I Cor. 2.8⟩; I have been cast down because of vain wrath. Raise up, I beseech thee, thy friend, I entreat thee, and do not cast me on the earth, O King of gods αεμιναεβαρωθερρεθωραβεανιμεα! Fill me with power, I beseech thee, and grant me this grace, that, when I shall order one of those gods to come, he shall at my spells come and appear to me quickly ναινεβασαναπτατουεαπτουμηνωφαεσμηπαπτουμηνωφ· αεσιμη· τραναπτι· πευχρη· τραναρα· πτουμηφ· μουραι· ανχουχαφαπτα· μουρσα· αραμει· Ιαω ... Ιαω αηι αι Ιαω." When you say these things thrice the following sign of your union ⟨with the god⟩ will occur, but you, armed by your magic soul, should not be terrified. For a sea hawk, flying down, will strike you with his wings on your body ⟨Mk. 1.10 and parallels⟩, by this very sign indicating that you should arise. You, therefore, arise, clothe yourself in white garments, and burn uncut frankincense in drops on an earthenware incense altar, saying as follows: "I have been united with thy sacred form ⟨II Cor. 3.18; Phil. 2.6⟩. I have been empowered by thy sacred name ⟨Acts 3.16⟩. I have received the effluence of thy goodness, Lord, God of gods, King, Daimon, αθθουιν θουθουϊ ταναντι· λαω απτατω." When you have done this, descend, having attained that nature, equal to the God's ⟨ἰσόθεος φύσις—cf. Phil. 2.6; Jn. 5.18⟩, which is effected by this ritual union.[7]

It has seemed worthwhile to translate this section as a whole, not only because of the ritual parallels to the story in the longer text, but also to show that magic

7. The next five words in the Greek text are to be taken with σκέψις, which follows them.

does not necessarily compel the gods,[8] but is capable of prayer, of individual devotion to the deity, and of considerable religious feeling. Also, besides the parallels pointed out in the text, the main notion of the passage—that by union with the ruler of the gods the initiate can attain superiority to the astral deities—is precisely that of Paul in Col. 2.8–3.4, discussed above.

After these asides we return to the point—that Jesus was, for the authors of the Gospels, a supernatural being in human form does not prove their thought about him was not magical. On the contrary, it suggests that it was magical. Many magical operations were designed to produce such incarnate deities; if Jesus could be made the Son of God by having the spirit descend upon him after a ritual purification, so could other magicians. That Jesus did believe he owed his powers to the possession of such a spirit is strongly suggested by the story of his dying cry, "My god, my god, why hast thou forsaken me?" (Mk. 15.34 and parallels; cf. *Gospel of Peter* 19, which reads "my *dynamis*," equivalent to "my daimon.") From Mk. 14.50 and 15.40 it seems unlikely that any of Jesus' disciples was on hand to hear what—if anything —he actually said. The reported cry, therefore (Ps. 22.2) is their notion of what he should have said—an expression at once of messianic hope and magical Christology. It is plausible to suppose that the beliefs of disciples reflect those of their master.

2. THE QUESTION OF SPELLS

Since the Gospels represent Jesus as the Son of God, they credit him with the power to perform his miracles immediately. Thus he does not use charms, magical formulas, or special rituals, and this might be thought to distinguish him sharply from the magician, who is supposed to have used on every occasion the elaborate ceremonies of the magical papyri. This may have been the belief of the evangelists; Arnobius, *Adversus Nationes* I.43f, and Philostratus, *Vita Apollonii* VII.38 end, uses this argument to prove their heroes were not magicians. But many of the ceremonies in the magical papyri are initiations—means of getting a spirit. Once one has a spirit, no such rites are necessary. Thus *PGM* I.97–194, after describing at length the ceremonies by which one can get "the Lord of the air" (Eph. 2.2) as a familiar, concludes (lines 176ff): "When you die he will prepare your body for burial, as befits a god, but, taking up your spirit, he will lead it into the air, with himself ⟨I Thess. 4.17⟩, for an aerial spirit united with a mighty familiar will not go into Hades ⟨Acts 2.27ff⟩, for to such a one all things are subordinate ⟨I Cor. 15.27⟩. Now when you want him to do something, say into the air only his name and 'Come,' and you will see him, and standing near you. Then say to him, 'Do thus-and-so,'

---

8. The assertion that the magician attempts to compel the gods, the religious man to entreat them, is so common a commonplace that it seems worthwhile to quote the explicit denial of this by Iamblichus, *De mysteriis* III.18 end (ed. des Places, Paris, 1966): τὸ μὲν οὖν θεὸν ἢ δαίμονα ἢ ἄγγελον εἶναι τὸν ἀποτελοῦντα τὰ κρείττονα ἔργα συγχωρήσειεν ἄν τις· οὐ μὴν ἔτι γε δίδομεν ὃ σὺ προσέρριψας ὡς ὁμολογούμενον, ὅτι δι' ἡμῶν ἑλκόμενος ἀνάγκαις ταῖς τῆς κλήσεως ταῦτα ἐπιτελεῖ. κρείττων γὰρ ἀνάγκης ἐστὶν ὁ θεὸς καὶ πᾶς ὁ συναπτόμενος αὐτῷ τῶν κρειττόνων χορός, οὐ τῆς ἐξ ἀνθρώπων ἐπαγομένης μόνον, ἀλλὰ καὶ ὅση τὸν κόσμον κατείληφεν. κ.τ.λ. It must be added, however, that this philosophic protest proves the other opinion was widespread.

and he will do it at once and, when it is done, will say to you, 'What else do you want, for I haste to the heaven?' And if you do not have anything to command at once, say to him, 'Go, sir,' and he will go ⟨Mt. 8.9⟩. Accordingly, this god will be seen only by you, nor will any hear his voice save you only ⟨Acts 22.9⟩." Similar notions will be found in *PGM* IV.2081ff and elsewhere.

Of course there is no more historical probability that "the Lord of the air" ever came down to answer a magician than there is that "the holy spirit" ever descended upon Jesus; but that a magician who believed he had "the Lord of the air" could perform miracles expeditiously is no less likely than that Jesus could do so, as the result of his similar belief. Hence it is clear that the absence of elaborate magical formulas from the reports of Jesus' miracles is no evidence as to whether or not he was a magician.

3. MINOR MAGICAL TRAITS OF THE MIRACLE STORIES

To make up for the absence of elaborate spells and rituals, the miracle stories in the Gospels show a great many of the minor traits of magical procedures. These were studied by Bonner, *Technique* 171ff, who cited magical parallels for curing by touch, manipulation, looking upward, sighing or groaning (especially στεναγμός), the use of Aramaic phrases in a Greek context, the use of ἐμβριμάομαι (175ff) and of ταράσσω (177). Eitrem, *Demonology*, added evidence for the traits noted by Bonner and himself noted further traits: the anointing with a salve compounded with spittle (47), the emphasis on the use of the hand in touching, etc. (35; cf. the longer text III.3–4), and especially the touching of the tongue (48), the use of "the finger of God" (34), the use of ἐπιτάσσειν in exorcisms, and the prohibition of the demons' return (26f), the use of φιμοῦν (30f), the anger at the demons (41f), the commands that the patients or bystanders keep the matter secret (47), the requirement that the petitioner have faith (47), and the instruction to the disciples to pray and fast before exorcisms (38). These, as Eitrem remarked, "do not seem to fit well into the picture of a wonderworking Messianic Soter" (49). Nor do they exhaust the material. The requirement of three- or seven-day preparatory periods is frequent in *PGM*— e.g., IV.1100 (three days); IV.26,53,734–735; XIII.671 (all seven days); cf. Mk. 9.2; the longer text III.6–7; Mk. 16.1. The use of a σινδών, usually over the naked body, in magical initiations—and particularly as a costume for boys who are to serve as mediums—is a frequent and striking parallel to Mk. 14.51 and the longer text III.8 (cf. Eusebius, *Praeparatio Evangelica* V.9.6; *PGM* III.305,706ff; IV.88f, 170ff,3095; *DMP* III.12f; XXVIII.6; XXIX.23). Requiring the demon to tell his name is a familiar piece of magical technique (Mk. 5.9; *PGM* I.160; IV.3038; Lucian, *Philopseudes* 16)—and so on; the list could easily be lengthened.

Admittedly, there are traces of a tendency in the Gospels to increase the magical traits in the stories: Eitrem, *Demonology* 29, notes especially the way Mk. 1.29ff has been made an exorcism by Lk. 4.39; and he thinks the notion of binding, especially by Satan, in Lk. 13.16 (p. 37) and the introduction of anointing with oil into the charges to the apostles (38) are later developments. One might add that the Johannine

editor of the Lazarus story has built it up with magical traits: Jesus' prefatory declaration in 11.25 is like many prefaces in the magical papyri (e.g., *PGM* V.145ff, ἐγώ εἰμι ἡ ἀλήθεια, cf. Jn. 14.6), and his prayer before the raising (11.41f) has a parallel in *PGM* IV.1060f, εὐχαριστῶ σοι, κύριε . . . ἐπακούων μοι ἐπὶ τὸν τῆς ζωῆς μου χρόνον. So not even the magical traits in the Gospels can be taken as certainly primitive.

However, some of them must be: they are too many to be got rid of entirely. And besides, their presence is stronger evidence than the absence of more elaborate magical material. Quite apart from the prudential and theological motivation pointed out above, the Gospels were exoteric works and we should not expect them to describe Jesus' magical practices. Moreover, the tendency in the tradition to increase magical traits is more than matched by the tendency to diminish them—note the omission of both saliva miracles (Mk. 7.32ff; 8.22ff) by both Mt. and Lk. This latter tendency probably reflects an apologetic concern which later is well documented (Fridrichsen, *Problème* 59ff)—Jesus must not appear as a magician.

4. THE PREDOMINANTLY MAGICAL CHARACTER OF THE GOSPEL STORIES

Unfortunately for the would-be apologists, not only the minor traits of the Gospel stories, but also the essential content of most of them come from the world of magic. Jesus appears in Mk. as one possessed by a holy spirit and thereby made the son of a god; we have already seen the same sort of figure in the magical papyri (*PGM* IV.510, 535). Other stories say he was born of a god (Mt. 1.18ff); so was Apollonius of Tyana, whom the Christians, and ancient opinion generally, considered a magician —though his followers, like Jesus', denied the charge (Philostratus, *Vita Apollonii* I.4,6; IV.18; VII.38; cf. Dio Cassius LXXVII.18.4; Origen, *Contra Celsum* VI.41, with Chadwick's n3). At the beginning of his career Jesus, like Apollonius, was driven by the spirit (Mk. 1.12 and parallels; *V.Ap.* I.18) into the wilderness, where he was approached by an evil spirit but repulsed it (Mk. 1.13; Lk. 4.2ff; *V.Ap.* II.4). This accords with the general pattern of shamanic initiation. So does the mixture of traditions which represent Jesus now as possessing spirits, again as himself possessed (Eliade, *Shamanism* 33ff, esp. 236; Mk. 1.12f; 3.21-30; Mt. 9.34; 10.25; Jn. 7.20; 8.48f,52; 10.20). On returning to settled areas Jesus, like Apollonius, became a wandering preacher with an attendant circle of disciples (Mk. 1.21,36; 3.7-19; Lk. 6.20ff; *V.Ap.* IV.1ff,37; V.43 and *passim*), and the admirers of both later appealed to their religious teaching and its success as evidence that they were not magicians (*V.Ap.* IV.19, etc.; Origen, *Contra Celsum* I.38,68, where he overlooks Apollonius). Both, however, were distinguished from ordinary preachers by their miraculous powers; many of the same miracles appear in the stories about both of them; and most of the miracles reported of Jesus are those which are commonly reported of magicians and for which recipes are given in the magical papyri.

Thus we find (and the following references give merely a few examples of each):

The power to make anyone he wanted follow him: Mk. 1.16ff; 2.14 (cf. *V.Ap.* IV.20); *PGM* IV.1716ff; VII.300ff,620ff (from *The Diadem of Moses*); XIII.238 (from *The Eighth Book of Moses*); XXXIIa; etc.

Exorcism: Mk. 1.23,34; 3.11,22; 5.1ff, etc.; *V.Ap.* IV.10,20,25, etc.; Lucian, *Philopseudes* 16; Origen, *Contra Celsum* I.68; *PGM* I.115; IV.2170; V.96ff; VII.431ff, etc.; Tamborino, *Daemonismo* 18f.

Exorcism at a distance, remote control of spirits, and the power to order them about: Mk. 7.25ff; Lk. 7.1–10; *V.Ap.* III.38; Lucian, *Philopseudes* 13; *PGM* I.180ff; V.165ff.

Miraculous cures: Mk. 1.29ff (fever),34,40ff; 2.1ff; 3.1ff (withered hand); 3.10; 5.25ff (issue of blood), etc.; Lk. 7.18ff (lame, blind, etc.); *V.Ap.* VII.39 (lame, blind, a man with a withered hand); Lucian, *Philopseudes* 11(∥ Mk. 2.12, he took up his pallet and walked); Origen, *Contra Celsum* I.68; *PGM* XVIIIb; XXXIII (fever); XXII.1ff (issue of blood); VII.191–214,580 (πᾶσαν νόσον, cf. Mt. 4.23), 677, etc.; Heim, *Incantamenta*; *DMP verso, passim*.

Stilling storms: Mk. 4.35ff; *V.Ap.* IV.13; *PGM* I.120; V.137 (∥ Mk. 4.41); XXIX.

Raising the dead: Mk. 5.21–43, etc.; *V.Ap.* IV.45 (∥ Lk. 7.11ff); *PGM* XIII.278ff.

Giving his disciples power over demons: Mk. 6.7; *PGM* I.42ff,193ff; IV.475ff, 732–747,850, etc.

Miraculous provision of food: Mk. 6.35ff; 8.1ff; *V.Ap.* IV.25; Origen, *Contra Celsum* I.68; Lucian, *Philopseudes* 35; *PGM* I.103–115; XIII.998; *J. Sanhedrin* VI.9(23c) and parallels.

Walking on water: Mk. 6.48; Lucian, *Philopseudes* 13; *PGM* I.120ff; XXXIV.

Miraculous escapes (his body could not be seized): Lk. 4.30; Jn. 7.30,44; 8.20,59 (C, *koine*, etc.); 10.39; *V.Ap.* VII.38; VIII.30; *PGM* I.195–222; XXIIa.11f; XXXVI.320ff; Vienna National Library, Pap. gr. 323; Tamborino, *Daemonismo* 18.

Making himself invisible: Jn. 8.59; 12.36(?); Lk. 24.31; *V.Ap.* VIII.5; *PGM* I.102,222ff,247ff; VII.619ff; XIII.268f.

Possession of the keys of the kingdom: Mt. 16.19; *PGM* III.541; IV.189f.

Foreknowledge:

    Of his own fate: Mk. 8.31ff, etc.; *V.Ap.* XIII.38,41; *PGM* I.173f; XIII.700ff.

    Of disasters coming on cities: Lk. 10.13f; 13.34f; 23.28ff; Mk. 13.2; *V.Ap.* IV.4; V.13; *Sibylline Oracles, passim*.

    General: Mk. 5.39; Jn. 11.11ff; Mk. 14.13ff; *V.Ap.* IV.24; V.24; VI.32; *PGM* I.188ff (∥ Mk. 5.39); IV.231,250; V.288ff, etc.

Knowledge of others' thoughts: Mk. 2.8; 12.15; *V.Ap.* IV.25; VI.3; *PGM* I.176; III.330,459; V.228; etc.

Metamorphosis: Mk. 9.3; *PGM* I.117f,177; XIII.270ff. The tradition that Apollonius was the son of Proteus—*V.Ap.* I.4—suggests that he was credited with this accomplishment, for which Proteus was notorious—*Odyssey* IV.455ff. However, in these metamorphoses the new forms assumed are disguises, by which the magician attempts to prevent recognition of his true and familiar form; in the transfiguration the new form reveals Jesus' true, supernatural powers, of which his familiar form was a disguise; cf. *Odyssey* XIII.221ff,287ff. This motif of the deity in disguise was common in Greek mythology: for example, the Homeric *Hymn to Demeter* 91–280, whence it influenced both the legends

of hellenistic cults—cf. Plutarch, *De Iside* 14–16 (357)—and the claims and practices of magicians, Lucian, *Alexander* 40; *PGM* IV.1859. A form particularly important for NT thought was the descent-in-disguise legend, on which see above, p. 201. This is the more remote background of the transfiguration story, but its immediate background is in magical practice and apocalyptic theory. From these came the notion that the magician could ascend into the heaven (or the mountain) of the gods and assume their glory: Is. 14.13f; Ezekiel 28.13ff; *II Enoch* A 22.8ff; *Ascension of Isaiah* 7.25; 9.30; etc. In *PGM* IV.475–750 and in the *Hekalot* we have instructions for such an ascent, either alone or with a disciple (732ff). A disciple in whom suggestion produced the hallucination of such an ascent would have seen his master clothed in the garment of glory and talking with the inhabitants of the heavens.

Revealing supernatural beings to his disciples: Mk. 9.4; *PGM* IV.88ff,172,732ff, 897–922; V.1–40; VII.549; *DMP* II.1ff; VII.10; XIV.24f; etc.

Prescribing reforms of temple practices: Mk. 11.15ff; *V.Ap.* I.16; IV.1,23,24; etc.

Introducing a new rite, a meal by which his followers are united with him by partaking of food magically identified with his flesh and blood: Mk. 14.22ff; Jn. 6.56; I Cor. 10.16; 11.24f; cf. *V.Ap.* III.25,32,51; see above, section A. The role of magicians in introducing new religious rites is emphasized by Burkert, *ΓΟΗΣ* 39f, and exemplified by Lucian, *Alexander* 38. Cf. Diodorus V.64.4; Irenaeus—Harvey, I.7.1ff = Stieren, I.13.1ff.

Claiming to be united with his disciples, so that he is in them and they in him: Jn. 6.56; 14.20; 15.3ff,9 (union in love); etc.; *PGM* XXXIIa: "Adona(i), Abrasax, Pin(o)uti and Sabaoth, enflame the soul and heart of . . . Amonius . . . for Serapiacus . . . now, now, quickly, quickly . . . Forthwith mingle together the souls of both and make . . . Amonius . . . one with Serapiacus . . . every hour and every day and every night. Therefore Adonai, highest of gods, . . . set to it, Adonai!"

Claiming to be a god or a son of a god, or united with some god or supernatural entity (notably in statements beginning "I am"): Mk. 14.62; cf. 13.6; (Mt. 26.63, ὁ υἱὸς τοῦ θεοῦ τοῦ ζῶντος C*WΔΦ 090 al. ff²; *DMP* XX.33, "I am the son of the god who liveth"); *V.Ap.* III.18; Jn. 10.36, υἱὸς τοῦ θεοῦ εἰμί. *PGM* IV.535, ἐγώ εἰμι ὁ υἱός. Jn. 14.6, ἐγώ εἰμι ἡ . . . ἀλήθεια. *PGM* V. 148, ἐγώ εἰμι ἡ ἀλήθεια (cf. *DMP* IX.14). Jn. 8.12, ἐγώ εἰμι τὸ φῶς τοῦ κόσμου. *PGM* XII.232, ἐγώ εἰμι ὁ Ἥλιος ὁ δεδειχὼς φῶς. Jn. 17.21 (to the Father), σύ . . . ἐν ἐμοὶ κἀγὼ ἐν σοί. *PGM* VIII.50 (to Hermes), ἐγώ . . . σὺ καὶ σὺ ἐγώ.

This list by no means exhausts the material. There are many other traits in the Gospels' picture of Jesus—particularly, but by no means exclusively, in the Johannine picture—which are common in magical material: the magician is the only one who knows his god (Lk. 10.22; Jn. 7.29; 17.25; *PGM* I.186ff ‖ Jn. 5.37; XIII.580ff, 841–888) and is known by his god (Lk. 10.22; Jn. 10.15; *PGM* VIII.49); those who see him see the invisible god, of whom he is the visible image (Jn. 1.18; *PGM*

XII.229,235); and so on. But these similarities in sayings (and, a fortiori, mere similarities of terminology, like the uses of κύριος and σώζειν remarked by Robinson, *Text* 252f) are less important for our purpose than the fact that the *stories* of the Gospels are mostly stories about things a magician would do. They are not mostly stories about things the Messiah would do. (Who ever heard of the Messiah's being an exorcist—let alone being eaten?) The closest parallels in the OT material are to be found in the stories of the prophets, but here, too, the exorcistic and the sacramental elements are completely lacking. The sacramental side, too, is wholly lacking from the reports about the rabbis. Jesus doubtless was, as was Apollonius, involved in arguments about the proper observance of religious laws, he did behave like a prophet and was thought to be one, and he probably came to think himself the Messiah (certainly other people thought him so and their opinion cost him his life); but neither his messianic nor his legal opinions, nor even his imitations of the prophets, account for the most important of the stories about him, which are stories of a man who did the things magicians claimed to do. This fact was recognized in antiquity even by the Christian apologists: Justin, *First Apology* 30; Tertullian, *Apology* XXI.17; Origen, *Contra Celsum* II.49ff.

Moreover, after Jesus' death his followers continued to credit him with typically magical activities. He appeared to his followers after his death (Jn. 20, etc.; *V.Ap.* VIII.31 ‖ Acts 9.3ff). He could, at will, make himself unrecognized or invisible (Lk. 24.16,31; see above). He came through locked doors (Jn. 20.19,26; *PGM* XII. 279; XIII.1064ff; XXXVI.312ff). He gave his followers power to handle serpents and drink poison without being harmed (Mk. 16.18; *PGM* I.115; IV.2175; XIII.253). He gave them the holy spirit by breathing it into them (Jn. 20.22; Tamborino, *Daemonismo* 81, 102; Origen, *Contra Celsum* I.68; *PGM* IV.3007–3085). And finally, he ascended into the heavens (Lk. 24.51; Acts 1.9f; *V.Ap.* III.51; VI.11 end; VIII.30 end; *PGM* I.178; IV.475ff) and was worshiped as a god (*V.Ap.* VII.21; VIII.5,7.vii, 31 end; *PGM* I.191f) and as a magician: Many sects in the gnostic wing of Christianity not only practiced magic, but remembered and revered Jesus as the great magician (Anz, *Frage* 5–9; Irenaeus, Harvey, I.19.2—I.20 = Stieren, I.24–25; etc.). The apocryphal gospels and acts, it is well known, add many magical traits to the picture of Jesus: e.g., *Gospel of Peter* 19; *Gospel of Thomas* (Leipoldt), heading, 13, 19, etc.; *Acta Ioannis* 87–105; *Pistis Sophia, passim*; etc. Whether these traits came from tradition (as is possible) or from invention (as is commonly taken for granted) or from both (as is likely) they at all events show that many, perhaps most, Christians thought of Jesus as doing the things a magician would do in the ways a magician would do them. Even in the comparatively "orthodox" catacombs and mosaics he is customarily represented with the magician's rod (Goodenough IX.160f, with recognition of the Mosaic parallel but not of the reason for it).

5. THE RELATION OF "MAGICIAN" TO θεῖος ἀνήρ AND "SON OF GOD"

It is not to be thought that the destined occupants of the catacombs, or even most of the gnostics, would have *described* Jesus as a "magician." For his believers, he

was "the Son of God"; sceptical but reverent pagans would probably have called him "a divine man," θεῖος ἀνήρ. Both terms were applied to a good many wonder-working religious teachers, some of them men who lived in the Roman empire, others ancient worthies like Pythagoras and Moses, whose stories were retold with the embellishments then fashionable. (For "Son of God," Wetter, *Sohn*, is still most valuable; the apologetic quibbles of Bieneck, *Sohn*, need not be read; Kramer, *Christos, non vidi*. For the θεῖος ἀνήρ see Bieler, with the remarks of Nilsson, II.527ff; Lévy (*Légende*) demonstrated the influence of the type on Jewish thought, but pushed his arguments too far; a recent recognition of its influence on the Gospels' picture of Jesus will be found in Robinson's *Problem . . . Reconsidered* 136f.) In spite of the original diversity of these heroes and the diversity of theological explanations and consequent titles imposed on them, their stories, as now retold, follow a relatively uniform pattern (compare the "biographies" summarized in *Heroes and Gods*), but are not directly or even—in many cases—indirectly derived from each other. There-fore the uniformity may in part be explained by the fact that the authors were describing a single social type, and Wetter's chapter "The Son of God as Antitype of the Magician" (*Sohn* 73ff) leaves no doubt as to what that type was. The magician claims the powers which the "divine man" or "Son of God" is thought to possess.

The difference between these figures is one of social status and success. A wandering quack to whom servant girls go for potions or poisons has little chance to pass himself off (even to himself) as a deity in disguise. But let him begin to succeed and Lucian, *Alexander*, will tell you how he can become the founder of a new cult and the spiritual director of Roman senators. He can then represent himself not only as the prophet, but also as the son, of a god (*Alexander* 11, 39). He can also come to believe his own representations (especially if his success has not been achieved by such conscious, mechanical devices as Alexander used, but has resulted from abnormal elements in his own personality which he himself would understand as evidence of supernatural powers). His enemies, however, will continue to call him a magician (γόης, Lucian, *Alexander* 1, cf. Burkert, ΓΟΗΣ; μάγος, *Alexander* 6, cf. Nock, *Magus*; the different connotations of the words do not here concern us. For alternation of the terms προφήτης (by friends) and γόης (by enemies) see Nock, *Alexander* 162.)

"Magician" thus covers a larger range than θεῖος ἀνήρ or "son of a god"; it includes the market quack (Origen, *Contra Celsum* I.68) and even the individual who practices in private (Lucian, *Lucius* 4), whereas the θεῖος ἀνήρ or "son of a god" must be a man of considerable public reputation and theosophic pretensions. With the difference of pretensions goes a supposed difference of technique which we have already noticed: the hole-in-the-corner magicians peddle spells and ceremonies and materia magica, therefore they have a different set for each different purpose (and customer). The θεῖος ἀνήρ has his own spirit who has only to be ordered and will at once obey. The son of a god is himself a spirit who can command others. To guess what these differences meant in terms of actual experience is a risky, albeit tempting, game. One may begin with the notion that "miracles" (including magical cures and the like), when they do happen, are usually the results of suggestion (often hypnotic) and therefore depend both on the practitioner's "power of suggestion"

and the patient's "suggestibility" (for which the ancient terms—of equally obscure meaning—were "spirit" and "faith"). Both of these can be augmented by various factors among which are rituals, practice, previous success, and consequent reputation. As the two latter increase, the dependence on rituals diminishes and the practitioner also rises in social position, self-esteem, and consequent claims. The change is a gradual one and the magical papyri therefore contain a medley of material, from simple charms for particular purposes through the more complex rites necessary to gain control over one or another spirit, to the elaborate initiations which will enable the magician himself to enter the heavens, become a god or the son of a god, and command all the spirits inferior to himself. The difference reflects that between the do-it-yourself world of the peasants and the slave service available to the rich. Theologically (or, demonologically?), however, as the magical texts show, this difference is one of form, not of essential content. And this fact is reflected by the terminology. Once the requirements of social status and decorum are met, the same man will customarily be called a θεῖος ἀνήρ, or son of a god, by his admirers, a magician by his enemies. Within this area all three terms refer to a single social type, and that type is the one characterized by the actions listed above, which make up by far the greatest part of the Gospels' reports about Jesus.

6. JEWISH AND PAGAN OPINIONS OF JESUS

From what has been said it follows that Jesus would be described, by those who did not accept his claims, as a magician. This description in fact appears repeatedly in both the pagan and the Jewish traditions about him, which have generally been disregarded by Christian scholarship on the grounds that they were pagan or Jewish. Yet surely the historical study of any man should take account of, not only the reports of his adherents, but also those of his opponents, and especially those of comparatively indifferent observers.

The judgment of Jesus' opponents is reported already by the Gospels: Mk. 3.22 and parallels. The scribes who came down from Jerusalem said, "He has ⟨control over⟩ Beelzebub," and "he drives out demons by the ruler of the demons." A different version of the same tradition appears in Mt. 9.32. From Mt. 10.25 it seems that Jesus was actually nicknamed "Beelzebub." Other traces of the same tradition appear in the arguments to refute it, which Mt. 12.27 and Lk. 11.19 derived from Q. Other, independent, traditions to the same effect, but ignorant of Beelzebub, are stated or reflected in Mk. 3.28f; Lk. 12.10 and parallel (probably Q); possibly Mk. 6.14 (see Kraeling, *Necromancy*); and certainly Jn. 7.20; 8.48,52; 10.20 (on the typical alternation between possession and being possessed see above, section 4, and also Samain, *Magie* 475). It is significant that neither Jesus nor his followers denied the charge that he "had" a spirit; on the contrary, they admitted it, but claimed that the spirit was a holy one (Jn. 1.32ff; Mk. 1.10 and parallels; 3.28f and parallels; etc.; and *The Gospel according to the Hebrews*). This charge would explain Jesus' "recurrent warnings against being 'scandalized' at him, or being ashamed of him, or denying him before men" which appear in both Jn. and the synoptics

and were thought perhaps historical by Dodd (*Historical Tradition* 221), though he was unable to suggest an adequate reason for them. After Jesus' death the charge that he had been a magician continued common in both Jewish and pagan circles (e.g., Justin, *First Apology* 30; *Dialogue* 69.7; Origen, *Contra Celsum* I.6; Tertullian, *Apology* XXI.17; Arnobius, *Adversus Nationes* I.43; *B. Sanhedrin* 43a as quoted by Strack, *Jesus* 1; the Talmudic references to Jesus as Balaam (Bileam), e.g., Strack, *Jesus* 5; *J. Shabbat* XII.4(13d)—ben Stada is probably Jesus—cf. Origen, *Contra Celsum* 1.28; Krauss, *Leben* 40ff; the Clementine *Recognitiones* I.58). *B. Sanhedrin* 107b and *B. Sotah* 47a represent Jesus as a pupil of Rabbi Joshua ben Perahyah who appears in Babylonian magic as a great magician who had ascended into heaven and mastered all the demons, Montgomery, *Incantation Texts* 225ff and texts 8, 9, 17, 32, 33. Birds of a feather . . .

These accusations were of course denied but were not fundamentally countered by Jesus' followers, of whom some (as remarked above, section 4 end) not only admitted, but celebrated his achievements as a magician, while all perpetuated and many added to the magical traits of the stories and pictures in which he was represented. Once again, the question was not his control of spirits, but only the means by which he had achieved it.

This evidence is further strengthened by that of comparatively indifferent observers —both Jews and pagans—who did not become followers of Jesus, but admitted his magical powers and attempted to make use of them in their own operations. Even in his own lifetime, if we are to believe Mk. 9.38f, men who were *not* his followers were using his name to cast out demons. Similar usage continued in Palestine as late as the second century, when *T. Hullin* II.22 and parallels show us one Jacob, of the village of Sama in Galilee, offering to cure snakebite "with the name of Jesus." This does *not* prove Jacob a Christian! Jesus' reported magical powers led pagan magicians also to use his name in their charms: *PGM* XII.192 and 391f. (For discussion and additional examples see Eitrem, *Demonology* 4–9.) Bickerman called to my attention Augustine, *De consensu evangelistarum* I.11ff, esp. 14f: there are pagans who think Jesus a man who attained the highest wisdom; they attribute to him letters to Peter and to Paul (!) pretending to teach the magic (*exsecrabiles*) arts by which he did his miracles. Particularly important is the story in Acts 19.13ff, that Jewish exorcists in Ephesus were using the name of Jesus in their exorcisms by A.D. 55 and that some of them used the formula "I conjure you by the Jesus whom Paul proclaims." To this the demon is represented as replying, "Jesus I know and Paul I am acquainted with, but who are you?" This is intended as testimony that Jesus and Paul are supernatural powers prominent in the demonic world: Jesus because he has the holy spirit, and Paul because he has Jesus. That the demoniac thereupon jumped on the would-be exorcists and drove them away in disgrace is said to have produced great reverence for the name of Jesus among "all the Jews and Greeks dwelling in Ephesus . . . And many of the believers ⟨the Christians⟩ began to confess and declare their magical practices. And a large number of those who had been practicing the occult arts brought together their books and burned them publicly, and when their prices were reckoned up they came to 50,000 pieces

of silver." Here the writer's intention is not only edification but also admonition. What had happened in Ephesus was to be an example to the churches which the writer had in mind—presumably those of Asia Minor. He suspected or knew that they were thick with magicians, and—as Paul in Colossians—he reminded them that Jesus is more efficacious in magic than are the demonic powers. There is also a strong element of party propaganda: the only safe use of Jesus' name is that by proper representatives of the Pauline party.

7. MAGIC IN THE PRACTICE OF JESUS' FOLLOWERS

It must again be insisted that the practices and teachings of a man's followers are at least some indication of what he practiced and taught. If so, the accounts of Jesus' followers indicate strongly that he practiced and taught magic. His followers are said to have begun exorcising demons and performing cures already during his lifetime, and of course by the use of his name (Mk. 6.7,13,14 and parallels; Lk. 10.17). After his death they reportedly continued and developed these practices (Acts 3.6; 5.5,9,15f; etc.). Paul is credited with them, too, and also—as were Jesus and Peter—with miraculously effective curses, another hallmark of the magician (Acts 3.6; 5.5,9,15f; 13.9ff; 14.8ff; 16.16ff; Mk.11.13ff,20ff and parallels; Lk. 9.54; PGM XIII.248,261ff; etc.) Paul wrote to the Corinthians that he had been present in Corinth in the spirit and so had judged and "handed over to Satan, for destruction of the flesh"—that is, for affliction with some illness, a common magical procedure (see Audollent, passim)—a libertine member of the Corinthian church (I Cor. 5.3ff). Consequently, Alexander and Hymenaeus were "given over to Satan" by pseudo-Paul in I Tim. 1.20. Here, probably, is to be found the explanation of Paul's claim to have some strange power over his congregations (I Cor. 4.19f; 5.3ff; II Cor. 6.7; 10.3ff; 12.19–13.7), as well as his fear that the initiates in Jerusalem might invalidate his work (Gal. 2.2 and my comments in Problems 116f). The keys given to Peter could lock as well as open (Mt. 16.19). Also, like Jesus, both Peter and Paul were believed to have such supernatural powers resident in their bodies that even the shadow of Peter (Acts 5.15) or clothes which had touched the body of Paul (Acts 19.12) might work wonders. The great importance of exorcism in Jewish Christianity is noted by Schoeps, AFZ 65f. The widespread practice of magic in the gnostic wing of Christianity is notorious from the accusations made by other Christians (Irenaeus, I passim; Hippolytus, Philosophumena, passim) and Bauer, Rechtgläubigkeit, has given strong reasons for his opinion that in the late first and early second centuries the gnostic wing was larger than that which subsequently became "orthodox."

Far more important, however, than such occasional phenomena as exorcisms, blessings, curses, and cures, more important, also, than the extraordinary gnostic ceremonies of which the self-styled "catholics" complained, was the essentially magical nature of the fundamental rites of initiation (baptism) and communion (eucharist) by which practically all Christian communities were constituted and held together. To the Christians, of course, these rites were the sacred mysteries instituted by the Son of their God, but this is no argument against their magical

character. The parallel rites are also represented by the magical papyri as sacred mysteries, divinely revealed. The magical character of baptism is made particularly clear by Paul's reference in I Cor. 15.29 to "those who are baptized on behalf of the dead"—a piece of substitutionary magic Paul evidently approved, since he used its unquestioned efficacy as an argument to prove that the dead must be raised. This sort of thought about Christian ceremonies continued down to the time of Clement, who objects to women wearing wigs because, when the presbyter lays his hands on a wig and gives his blessing, the blessing will not go to the wearer of the wig but to the head which provided the hair (I.271.20—this was pointed out to me by H.C.).

The fundamental position of baptism and the eucharist testifies that this sort of thought was not secondary in Christianity, but primitive. Such, too, is the testimony given by the essential character of the stories in the Gospels, reviewed above. The same conclusion follows from Paul's account of Christianity as, essentially, salvation by possession; this, too, has been pointed out above, but we may add here the evidence afforded by the practice of "speaking with tongues" in the Pauline churches. As I Cor. 12 makes clear, this was the utterance of incomprehensible sounds, thought by the believers to be the speech of the spirit which possessed the speakers. As already remarked in section IX this is a common symptom of schizophrenia. In the church at Corinth it had become so common that it was disrupting the worship, and those especially gifted with it were giving themselves insufferable airs. Therefore Paul has to insist that it is not the greatest of the gifts of the spirit. The spirit gives also wisdom, knowledge, faith, and the ability to perform cures, do miracles, prophesy, distinguish good from evil spirits, and interpret things spoken in "tongues." And practically all of these Paul treats—on this occasion—as superior to the gift of "tongues." This obviously does not reduce the importance of magic in Paul's view of the world. On the contrary, it extends it to the whole of normal, as well as abnormal psychology. Everything good is the work of "the spirit." Another thing to be noticed is that even in this letter Paul thanks God that he speaks with tongues "more than all of you" (14.18), and elsewhere, when this problem of church discipline is not uppermost in his thought, he treats "speaking with tongues" as the supreme prayer of the Church—Rom. 8.26f. τὸ γὰρ τί προσευξώμεθα καθὸ δεῖ οὐκ οἴδαμεν, ἀλλὰ αὐτὸ τὸ πνεῦμα ὑπερεντυγχάνει στεναγμοῖς ἀλαλήτοις· ὁ δὲ ἐρευνῶν τὰς καρδίας οἶδεν τί τὸ φρόνημα τοῦ πνεύματος, ὅτι κατὰ θεὸν ἐντυγχάνει ὑπὲρ ἁγίων. ἀλάλητος is not "unutterable"—they were uttered—but "inarticulate"; vs. LSJ see Bauer, Wb. ad loc. This fact, and the phenomenon of glossolalia, were tactfully overlooked by Dietzel, Beten, whose denial of the relation between Christian and magical prayer overlooks the main problem—to explain, not why the spirit spoke to the churches, but why it spoke to them in jabberwocky. στεναγμός was noted above (section 3) as a characteristic form of magical utterance. Such στεναγμοὶ ἀλάλητοι are preserved in great quantities in the magical papyri, of which they are perhaps the most noticeable peculiarity. These are the "magical words," of which a few are fixed formulas with secret significance, but most are apparently meaningless combinations of letters by which the magician calls the spirit in the spirit's own language, or, by speaking

in the spirit's language, shows that the spirit is already in him and acting through him. These combinations perhaps were not intended merely for repetition, but were indications of the "tune"—the sort of phonetic combinations and interspersed names—appropriate to the spirit invoked.[9] A number of examples of this have been given in the passage already quoted from *PGM* in section 1; more are to be found on almost every page of that collection. The same sort of thing appears in *Pistis Sophia* in the concluding prayers of Jesus, presumably representative of the secret prayers of the church that preserved this material: "Then ⟨after the resurrection⟩ Jesus stood with his disciples . . . and called on ⟨the Father with⟩ this prayer . . . 'Hear me, my Father, Thou Father of all paternity, Thou endless light, αεηιουω· ϊαω· αωϊ· ωϊα·[10] ψινωθερ· θερνωψ· νωψιτερ·[11] ζαγουρη· παγουρη·[12] νεθμομαωθ· νεψιομαωθ· μαραχαχθα· θωβαρραβαυ· θαρναχαχαν· ζοροκοθορα· ϊεου·[13] σαβαωθ.'"[14] (ch. 136, my translation from Schmidt-Till; more in ch. 142.) Harnack, *Pistis-Sophia* 89, recognized these passages as representations of speaking with tongues; Anz, *Frage* 8, as incantations, combinations of "magical words" typical of the spells in the magical papyri. Both were right. The spirit which spoke through the Christians and the spirits which spoke through the pagan magicians spoke the same characteristic language.

Not only is this fact recognizable now; it was already recognized in antiquity and its recognition resulted in many of the persecutions which Christianity every-

---

9. Similar variation of formulas appears in the *defixiones* and on the magical gems. In the case of the latter, this has been noticed by A. Delatte and P. Derchain, *Les Intailles magiques gréco-égyptiennes*, Paris (Bibliothèque Nationale), 1964, p. 234: "There is little chance, naturally, that one should ever find an object ⟨magical gem⟩ exactly in agreement with the ancient description ⟨in the magical papyri⟩, for magic was still living at the time of the redaction of the papyri and at the time when the gems were engraved. Consequently, on comparing them with each other, one finds that the formulas show innumerable variations about which the magicians hardly bothered at all."

10. Such variations on the seven vowels are common in *PGM*, in which all these individual combinations occur—e.g., no. II. lines 14–16; III.230,436; IV.487,917, etc.; XII.72,102,119; XIII.209, 895,936; and often elsewhere. 'Ιαω (the commonest Greek name of יהוה) is particularly frequent. In the indices to *PGM*, which the late Prof. Preisendanz kindly put at my disposal, there are three columns full of references to 'Ιαω—far more than to any other deity. (The runners up are 'Αδωναϊ and 'Ερμῆς with about two columns each.)

11. *PGM* III.186a–b νωψιθ[ερ] θερνωψι; IV.828f ψινωθερ νωψιθερ θερνωψι; VII.316 ψινωθ βερ.

12. *PGM* V.479; XXXVI.308; 348–353; Kropp, *AKZ* no. XIII line 7, cf. vol. III.127 n5. All these give the combination ζαγουρη παγουρη or vice versa (with various misspellings). Both words also occur alone; e.g., *PGM* XXXVI.10,64 ζαγουρη; VII.597,606 παγουρη.

13.
PGM XIII.959–963 νεθμομαω μαρχαχθα . . . θαρνμαχαχ ζαροκοθαρα . . . ηεου θωβαρραβαυ
Audollent no. 267.9ff [ν]εθμομαω μαρχαχον . . . ζαρακ[α]θαρα θωβαρραβαυ θαρναχαχα.
νεθμομαωθ (and variants) alone: *PGM* II.119 (μαϊραχαχθα follows in 120); III.153 (οροκοτοθρο in 154); Audollent no. 242.31.
νεψι- combinations do not appear elsewhere; this is probably a corruption.
θωβαρραβαυ (and variants) alone: *PGM* VII.977; XIXa.42; Audollent no. 242.18; etc.
ιεου alone: *PGM* II.137; VII.476; XII.189; XIII.810; etc.

14. *PGM* VII.605; IX.7; XII.207 and *passim* (almost a full column of references in Preisendanz' index).

where called forth. These persecutions require explanation both because of their frequency and because of the general tolerance throughout the Roman empire for cults of oriental gods and deified men. Occasional exceptions to this tolerance might be explained by peculiar local circumstances; but the consistent opposition to Christianity evidently resulted from something characteristic of the new religion. What was it? The common answer is, the Christians' refusal to worship other gods. But other worshipers of Yahweh—the Jews and the Samaritans—also refused to worship other gods, and they were not generally persecuted. Consequently, the Christians had to explain the persecutions as inspired either by the demons or by the Jews who, they said, denounced them to the authorities (Acts 13.50; 14.2; 17.6,13; 18.12; etc.; I Thess. 2.15; Apoc. 2.9; *Martyrdom of Polycarp* XII.2; XVII.2; Justin, *Dialogue* 17). But for what could the Jews denounce them? Certainly not for refusing to worship other gods—that was the hallmark of Jewish faith generally. Perhaps for political conspiracy? But there is no evidence that the Christians were, generally, subversive in politics—not, at least, after the year 70 (cf. Brandon, *Fall*)—and they were not generally accused of plotting political revolution. What they were accused of was the practice of magic and other crimes associated with magic: human sacrifice, cannibalism, and incest (*Vita Apollonii* VIII.5; Bidez-Cumont, *Mages* 78ff). The accusation of magic probably appears already in Suetonius, *Nero* 16.3: *Afflicti suppliciis Christiani, genus hominum superstitionis novae ac maleficae*, since a *maleficus* is par excellence a magician. Suetonius indicates how Tacitus, *Annals* XV.44, should be interpreted: *quos per flagitia invisos vulgus Christianos appellabat . . . exitiabilis superstitio . . . atrocia aut pudenda . . . primum correpti qui fatebantur*. What did they—under torture—confess? Probably firing the city, probably being Christians, but probably also magic. Magic figures conspicuously in charges against Christians from the second century on (Origen, *Contra Celsum* I.6; VI.40f; *Passio Perpetuae* 16; *Acta Acacii* V.2f; Tertullian, *Ad uxorem* II.5.2; Eus., *HE* III.26.4; IV.7.10f). Moreover, as the passages from Eusebius show—and they could be paralleled by many more from Irenaeus, Hippolytus, and Epiphanius—the Christians made considerable use of this charge against each other. Presumably they knew what they were talking about. Magic has been commonly neglected in discussions of the persecutions (recently Speyer, *Vorwürfen*; Grégoire, *Persécutions*; Sherwin-White, *Letters*, 691ff, 772ff; but cf. Freudenberger, *Verhalten*, 165ff) because these have commonly been based on the apologists and the acts of the martyrs and have neglected the heresiologists. But the apologists chose to defend Christianity from charges of which most Christians were not guilty; magic would have been an embarrassing topic, therefore they do not mention it and in refuting the charge of cannibalism they are careful to avoid the question of what actually happens in the eucharist. And the acts of the martyrs are propaganda pieces, mostly intended to represent the Christians as innocent victims martyred solely because of monotheism; therefore they usually say nothing of any of the *flagitia cohaerentia nomini* (Pliny, *Epistulae* X.96.2). Commonly the only questions are, are you a Christian, and, will you sacrifice to the gods or the emperor. References to magic are rare, but references to incest and cannibalism are even rarer. History should not use such material uncritically.

8. RECAPITULATION AND CONCLUSIONS

It has now been argued: (1) The fact that Jesus is not represented as a magician by the Gospels is insignificant; "magician" was a dirty word. The significant fact is that he is represented as the possessor of the holy spirit and as "the Son of God," a supernatural being recognized by demons as able to command them; he is represented as a successful magician would have represented himself. (2) That Jesus is not represented by the Gospels as using long spells or magic rites is insignificant. Once a magician "had" his spirit, he need only command and it would instantly obey. Here too, the Gospels represent Jesus as a successful magician would have represented himself. (3) The miracle stories are shot through with minor traits of magical practice. (4) The Gospels' stories generally are stories of things magicians claimed to do, and they add up to an account of a magicians' life: Jesus' career began when he was possessed by a spirit which drove him into the wilderness (Mk. 1.9–12; Eliade, *Shamanism* 33f, 64, etc.). After surviving the ordeals to which the spirits there subjected him (Mk. 1.13f; Lk. 4.1–13 and parallel) he returned to Galilee, where he made his reputation as an exorcist (Mk. 1.21–27) and miracle worker (Jn. 2.11) and developed it by cures of which the magical traits have been mentioned. He then empowered his disciples to exorcise and perform similar cures (Mk. 6.7–13). His fame thus became so great that magicians outside the circle of his followers began to use his name in their exorcisms (Mk. 9.38f). He introduced a τελετή—a secret meal in which his followers were united with him by being given bread and wine which were declared to be his flesh and blood (Mk. 14.17–25). In all these respects his work can be paralleled from the claims and careers of other magicians. (The career most fully reported is that of Apollonius of Tyana, but if the facts were known a closer parallel would perhaps be found in that of Jesus' contemporary Simon, the Samaritan magician, who also did miracles, claimed to be a power come down from heaven, and was credited with the introduction of mystery rites; Acts 8.9ff; Irenaeus, Harvey, I.16.1ff = Stieren, I.23.1ff; see my *Account*). Finally, Jesus claimed to be the Messiah and, somehow, to be able to admit his followers to the kingdom of God, and this claim resulted in his execution by the Romans. In these respects, too, his career has magical parallels. Josephus reports that in Palestine at this period there was a plague of messianic magicians who similarly raised men's hopes for the coming of the kingdom, and who came to similarly bad ends at the hands of the Romans: *BJ* II.258ff; *AJ* XX.97, 188; Eisler, *Messiah* 328,360. (5) and (6) As in the case of Simon and Apollonius and other magicians, Jesus' followers believed him a supernatural being—either a "divine man" or the son of a god—but by his enemies he was repeatedly accused of magic, and these accusations were continued in later reports. Magicians also believed him a magician. (7) Similar accusations were often made against his followers and were an important contributory element in a long series of legal actions against them. Considerable groups of his followers admittedly did practice magic and claimed that he was the source of their practice.

In addition to all this evidence, the hypothesis that Jesus practiced magic helps

to explain some of the major problems raised by the Gospels' account of his career. From that account it appears, as we have said, that Jesus claimed to be the Messiah and bringer of the kingdom of God. But there is no clear indication of his functional relation to the kingdom as already present. This is the more surprising because even in the sketchy stories given by Josephus (in the passages just cited) about the other messianic magicians, their functions in relation to the kingdom are clear— they will use their magical powers to protect their followers and overthrow the Romans. So, too, the functional relation of the Baptist to the kingdom he foretold was clear (above, pp. 205ff). So, the silence of the Gospels on Jesus' functional relation to the kingdom is amazing. It requires an explanation.

A considerable number of Jesus' sayings imply that not only he, but also some of his disciples are already in the kingdom (above, pages 211ff). A few of these sayings indicate that there is a definite, practical way to get in. That the mystery of the kingdom *has been given* to the disciples (Mk. 4.11) suggests there was some initiatory rite. Some evidence indicates that this rite was a baptism (above, pp. 178ff), which Jesus administered secretly to a chosen few of his followers (above, pages 209ff). Notice how the Q statement, Lk. 7.28 and parallel, fits together with Jn. 3.3ff. Q says, none born of women is greater than the Baptist, but the least in the kingdom is greater than he. We naturally ask: What, then, was the least in the kingdom born of? John answers, of water and the spirit, for only those born of water and the spirit (as opposed to those born of the flesh) can enter the kingdom. "Of water and the spirit" is evidently a reference to Jesus' baptism, which gave the spirit, as opposed to the Baptist's baptism, which did not (above, pp. 207, 219). But the gift of the spirit is not prima facie identical with admission to the kingdom, so we ask: How did Jesus' baptism admit his followers to the kingdom? If they "entered" the kingdom, the kingdom was presumably an area in space. This agrees with what we have seen, that the kingdom was par excellence in the heavens (above, pp. 202ff). And we have also seen some reason to believe that there was in Palestine in Jesus' time a magical technique for ascending and causing others to ascend into the heavens (p. 181). If we suppose Jesus practiced such a technique, then we can explain the famous Q statement that, "the Law and the prophets were ⟨in force⟩ until John ⟨the Baptist⟩; since then the good news about the kingdom of God has been proclaimed and anyone can force his way into it" (Lk. 16.16; Mt. 11.12; notice the connection in Mt. with the statement that the least in the kingdom is greater than John). Here Dodd's despairing comment on Mt. 11.12 ("the kingdom of heaven suffers violence"), "whatever that may mean," (*Parables* 40) and such fantastic explanations as Danker's (*Lk. 16.16*) are alike unnecessary. In the magical techniques of ascent to the heavens the magician must overcome the resistance of the demonic or angelic guards who bar the way (e.g., *Hekalot, passim*). These powers Jesus has overcome (Col. 2.9ff). Therefore the kingdom of God, the kingdom in the heavens, suffers violence, because its guards are now overcome by those who have been magically united with the spirit of Jesus in the baptism of Jesus—"the mystery of the kingdom of God," the mystery which enables them to force their way into the kingdom of God in the heavens.

It was while performing such a baptism that Jesus was arrested. The rite was secret. He chose a lonely garden, through which a stream still flows, and went there late at night, after the ceremony of the eucharist had assured the magical union of his circle of initiates. Since he did not wish to be interrupted (this is essential in magic) he set guards (Mk. 14.32–34). He had no intention of being arrested if he could help it. The agony, therefore, has no likelihood, and it was witnessed by no one. (On its homiletic motivation see my *Comments* 22f.) When the guards fell asleep and the police arrived unexpectedly they surprised both Jesus and the initiate, νεανίσκος τις ... περιβεβλημένος σινδόνα ἐπὶ γυμνοῦ (Mk. 14.51)—the proper magical costume in the proper magical setting. If this was not an initiation, what was the young man doing with Jesus at such an hour, in such a place, and in such a costume? The author of *Acta Ioannis* 94ff understood what was going on and supplied an account of the initiation, unfortunately imaginative.

D.   *The rite was a means of ascent to the heavens*[15]

By this time the reader will have forgotten that the long argument about magic was only the third point of a yet longer argument to show that important elements in the Pauline concept of baptism were derived from Jesus. That argument went as follows: Paul interpreted baptism as a means of uniting with Jesus—the one baptized was possessed by Jesus' spirit. This notion looks as if it came from Palestinian demonology. And there are five traits which point to Jesus as its source. Of these five we have now considered three: (A) as a means of uniting with Jesus baptism is essentially like communion, which he introduced; (B) it is effected by the spirit, and the spirit is distinctive of Jesus' ministry, as opposed to that of the Baptist; (C) it is a magical ceremony, and Jesus practiced magic. These points established, we can now go on to the fourth: (D): Pauline baptism was conceived as a means of ascent to the heavens (above, pp. 214ff) and in Christianity this notion of ascent seems also to go back to Jesus.

Here I shall try to show: (1) the notion of ascent to the heavens was an important element in Jesus' Palestinian background and had led to the development of a technique for ascent which Jesus might have practiced. (2) There is a good deal of indirect evidence indicating that Jesus did practice such a technique. (3) A number of passages in the Gospels are best understood as records of his practice and consequent teaching.

15. The following section was written before Scholem brought to my attention Daniélou's *Traditions*, which has demonstrated the existence in Christianity, from Paul's time on, of a secret tradition concerning ascent through the celestial spheres. Daniélou supposes the tradition came into Christianity through Paul, from his Jewish background (p. 213). But it is too widely distributed to have come through Paul alone. Most important is the extensive agreement of the conclusions of two studies made independently and from standpoints so diverse as Daniélou's and my own. For this reason I have not here repeated Daniélou's arguments and evidence, but leave it to the reader to look at his article and see for himself at once the independence of the methods and the agreement of the results.

I. BACKGROUND

The notion of ascent to the heavens is ancient (Kees, *Himmelsreise*; *ANET* 101f; 118; 446f; Oppenheim, *Interpretation* 259, 267, 282, 287) and widespread (Eliade, *Shamanism* 115–144, 181–288, 392ff, 477ff, 487ff, etc.). Since 1897, when its fundamental importance in gnosticism was pointed out by Anz, *Frage*, it has been repeatedly discussed; see the remarks of Lewy, *Oracles* 413ff. The studies cited above (section IX, end), and those referred to below are only the ones I have found most useful for the present argument. I have been careful not to refer to some others, particularly the pan-Iranian anachronisms of Reitzenstein and the inaccurate work of Widengren. Many of the previous discussions have dealt with origins and transmission. Here we need concern ourselves only with those forms in which the notion of ascent to the heavens may have been current in the Greco-Roman, Hebrew, and Aramaic material circulating in Palestine during the first centuries B.C. and A.D.

In the eastern Mediterranean world the notion had early appeared in two forms not always separate, but roughly distinguishable. One was that of the soul's ascent into the heavens after death, the other that of ascent by living individuals either carried aloft bodily or in dream or ecstasy leaving their bodies below and returning to them later (cf. Bousset, *Himmelsreise* 136). It would be a mistake to try to differentiate the stories too sharply. Paul, who claimed to have had such an experience, said he did not know whether, at the time, he was in the body or not (II Cor. 12.2).

The notion of the soul's ascent at some time after death was given classical expression by Plato and was popularized by Posidonius and by the influence of astrology (Cumont, *Lux* ch. 3). During the first centuries B.C. and A.D. it was widely held all over the Greco-Roman world, including Palestine where the expectation that the righteous dead will shine as the stars appears in Dan. 12.3 and their ascent to heaven is anticipated in many other apocalypses (e.g., *Enoch* 39.4f; 104.2; *Assumption of Moses* 10.8ff; *II Enoch* 8–9; *II Baruch* 51.10ff; *III Baruch* 10.5; *IV Ezra* 7.90–100). Josephus attributes the same anticipation to the Essenes (*BJ* II.154ff). It thus provided a widespread background for the other notion—more important for our present purpose—of ascent to the heavens by living men.

Claims of ascent by living men seem to be attacked already in Is. 14.13f and Ezek. 28, esp. verses 1,6,9,13–17. With "the mountain of God" cf. Mt. Sinai in the story of Moses' enthronement as κοσμοκράτωρ (Ezekiel *tragicus* in Eusebius, *Praeparatio Evangelica* IX.29.4f) and the mountains of the temptation and the transfiguration (Mt. 4.8; Mk. 9.2–13; and parallels) and notice how many early Christian revelations were located on mountains—*Apocryphon of John*, *Pistis Sophia*, *Gospel of Eve*, *Great Questions of Mary* (Epiphanius, *Panarion* XXVI.3.1; 8.1ff) etc. The OT attacks show that those who ascended were thought to become like the gods in form (cf. Phil. 2.6) and to be enthroned in the heavens (cf. Col. 3.1; Heb. 1.3; this is the goal of the *Hekalot* mystics). A similar claim is made on behalf of (probably) Simon Maccabeus in Ps. 110.1: "The Lord said unto my Lord, 'Sit thou at my right hand.'" (This is perhaps related to the stories of the enthronement of Moses, cited above, and the ascension of Levi, *Testaments of the Twelve Patriarchs, Levi* II.6–V.3.) Such notions were so important to the religious and political thought of the

times that they were made the basis for the imperial cult. Indeed, from the beginning of the second century A.D. the Roman government regularly used magical techniques to effect the bodily apotheosis of the dead emperor (Bickerman, *Kaiserapotheose* esp. 5ff). Stories like those of the bodily assumptions in supernatural chariots of the wonder-worker Elijah (II Kgs. 2.11) and the magician Medea (Roscher, *Lexikon* s.v., II.2.2484ff) had been allegorized already by Parmenides as types of the ascent in philosophic contemplation (Diels, 28 B1). This allegory was powerfully developed by Plato in the *Phaedrus* 244–257, and the type became a commonplace (Pippidi, *Recherches* 170 n2). For the great importance of the Elijah story as an archetype of the Christian experience, see Schrade, *Ikonographie* 81–89, where the connections with magic are made clear. Besides these myths specifying the means of transportation, there were simpler stories deriving directly from ecstatic or cataleptic experience; and these, too, Plato made part of the literary tradition known to all educated men by his use of the story of Er in the *Republic* (614ff) as the vehicle for his great myth of the travels of the soul (cf. Dieterich, *Mithrasliturgie* 199). Similar pictures of the heavens and the afterlife, as seen by living travelers, abound both in subsequent Greek and Latin literature (for example, from the first century B.C., Cicero's *Somnium Scipionis*), and appear in Judaism both in the work of Philo (e.g., *De opificio* 23 end) and in the originally Hebrew or Aramaic Palestinian apocalypses from the late third or early second century B.C. and thereafter (*Vita Adae* 25; *Enoch* 14.8; 39.3; 71.1,5; *II Enoch* 3.1; 67.1; *Testament of Abraham* 10; *Apocalypse of Abraham* 15; *Testaments of the Twelve Patriarchs, Levi* II.6ff; *III Baruch* 2ff; etc.). For the connection of these with Christian and rabbinic traditions see Scholem, *Gnosticism* ch. III.

These Palestinian stories of heavenly travels probably reflect not only the influence of Greek literature and near eastern legend, but also, as has long been recognized, some sort of experience deliberately cultivated in pietistic circles (Eppel, *Piétisme* 66f; Scholem, *Gnosticism* ch. III). Just when this deliberate cultivation first took the form of a definite technique there is no telling. In the Qumran *Hodayot* and *Manual of Discipline* the entrance of the members of the sect into the company of the angels is often celebrated as something already accomplished. The members are "together with the angels of the presence, and there is no need of an interpreter between them" (*Hodayot* VI.13; cf. III.20ff; XI.10ff; XIII.27ff; frag. 2.10ff; frag. 5; *Manual of Discipline* XI.5–10).[16] It is not unlikely that this state of affairs was thought to be brought about by some special ceremony, probably that (ἀπ)αθανατισμός referred to by Josephus, *AJ* XVIII.18: ἀθανατίζουσι τὰς ψυχάς, περιμάχητον ἡγούμενοι τοῦ δικαίου τὴν πρόσοδον. Bousset, *Himmelsreise* 143, remarks that this probably refers to demonic opposition, encountered by those who would enter the heavens, and explains the Essenes' desire to know the names of the angels, which commonly serve as passwords for the journey (*Hekalot, passim*; Josephus, *BJ* II.142; contrast the forced translations and implausible conjectures discussed by Feldman, *Josephus*, at *AJ* XVIII.18). περιμάχητον here has the same background as Eph. 6.11ff, "Put

16. *I Q 28b*, cols. III and IV, shows the same notions projected into the future. Not only do the members of the sect have access to the assemblies of heaven, but the angels come down to those of earth: *War Scroll* X.9ff; XII.7ff.

on the whole armour of God ... for our battle is ... against the cosmic rulers of this darkness, the spiritual powers of evil in the heavens." ἀθανατίζουσιν, accordingly, means "make immortal" by some rite which provided the soul with the necessary purification and information (angelic names and spells)—the armour required for the περιμάχητον πρόσοδον in which, if unarmed, it would be destroyed. For a magical ἀπαθανατισμός introducing the initiate into the company of the gods, see the "Mithras Liturgy," *PGM* IV.647f,741,747,771; also XXIIb.24, προσευχὴ Ἰακώβ; etc.

That such a magical technique for ascent into the heavens had developed in some Jewish circles during the first century B.C. is also shown by the fact that this date is the latest possible one for the common ancestor of the *Hekalot* literature and the "Mithras Liturgy" cited above. Scholem in *Gnosticism* 41f argued that the common ancestor of these traditions must be dated not later than the early second century A.D. and Nock (review of Scholem's *Gnosticism*) accepted this argument. In my *Observations* 155ff, I brought evidence for the practice of the technique in the mid-first century A.D. (Col. 2.18) and for its relation to the Essenes; but I did not see clearly its role in early Christianity.[17] Now Strugnell (*Angelic Liturgy*) has published a text full of the terminology and constructions of the *Hekalot* hymns. The second of his fragments in particular is rich in such parallels and, to judge from them, describes the wonders of the heavens which the initiate, in his ascent, was expected to see. This text proves the tradition represented by the *Hekalot* and the "Mithras Liturgy" was in development at Qumran during the first century B.C., from which Strugnell would date two of the four MSS he used. Consequently there is nothing unlikely in the supposition that Jesus may have practiced such a technique for ascent to the heavens. Moreover, a number of considerations indicate that he did so.

2. INDIRECT EVIDENCE OF JESUS' PRACTICE

First of all, such an ascent was the goal anticipated by much early Christian teaching. We saw above (pp. 203f) that for the Gospels the kingdom of God, the

17. I had not noticed the evidence for Jesus' ascent, and was led by ἁρπαγέντα (II Cor. 12.2) to think Paul's ascent an involuntary ecstatic experience, peculiar to him. (I neglected the indication that his opponents claimed similar experiences.) Also, I drew a sharp distinction between ascent and instances when the initiate remained on earth but saw heavenly beings or saw the heavens opened (as did ben Zakkai and his disciples, *B. Hagigah* 14b and parallels, on which Neusner, *Life* 97ff; cf. Mk. 1.10). But the connection between vision and ascent was very close (e.g., Apoc. 4.1ff), and I doubt that such hallucinations can be sharply distinguished. As for ἁρπαγέντα, I wonder if it may not be an indication of what Paul experienced in his involuntary conversion. (The account in Acts is exoteric and may be fictitious.) Baptism as administered by Jesus was presumably a vivid, hypnotic experience of ascent. The stages by which it passed from this to a sacramental fiction are unknown and probably differed in each different chain of tradition, as different disciples had more or less of Jesus' hypnotic power. To Paul's churches the gift of the spirit (in baptism?) seems still to have been a matter of vivid experience; but from the way Paul had to remind the members of their death, resurrection, and ascension with Jesus, it would seem that these had already become things which baptism "was supposed to do," rather than experiences actually produced. Within half a century after Paul even the gift of the spirit had probably dwindled to a legal fiction for most of the "orthodox." The gnostics still strove for actual experience, and some may have succeeded in maintaining it well into the second century—hence came some of the charges that they practiced magic.

sphere of divine rule, is κατ' ἐξοχήν in the heavens. Accordingly, it is to the heavens that Jesus is represented as ascending, at or after his resurrection (Col. 3.1; Jn. 20.17; Acts 1.9; Lk. 24.51 ABC; etc.; Paul probably equated the resurrection with the ascension—Weiss, *Christianity* 84—Jn. and Lk. distinguished them). And it is to the heavens that many Christians hope to ascend, either at the End (I Thess. 4.17; Lk. 12.8f and parallel; Jn. 14.2f, cf. 6.38; 16.28) or immediately after death (Lk. 6.23; 12.33 and parallels; 16.22; 23.43—cf. II Cor. 12.4—Mk. 10.21 and parallels; II Cor. 5.1–10; Phil. 3.20; Col. 1.5; II Tim. 4.18; I Pet. 1.4; Apoc. 3.21, 7.9–17; etc.)—or even, somehow, in this life (Heb. 12.22f). Jesus, ascending thither, went as the leader of his followers and showed them the way (Heb. 2.10; Jn. 14.1–5). This orientation of the sect might derive from its founder.

In the second place, it appears that claims *to have ascended* into the heavens were frequently made by Jesus' followers and played an important role in their competition for prestige and authority. One example of such a claim has come down to us—that of Paul in II Cor. 12.1–5. But from the context there it appears that Paul's claim was not unique (Schmithals, *Gnosis* 174ff). It was made as vindication of his apostolic status in answer to the claims of his competitors, who presumably were alleging their ascents as proofs of their superiority to Paul (cf. 11.21ff; 12.11ff; I Cor. 9.1ff). These opponents were "Hebrews, Israelites, seed of Abraham," and ὑπερλίαν ἀπόστολοι; therefore it is not implausible that their claims went back to Palestinian Christian circles. Such claims, put in the mouth of Simon Magus, are repeatedly attacked by the *Clementina* (*Hom.* XVII.14,19, etc.). Paul's opponent in Colossians also claimed to have ascended into the heavens, and linked his claims with observance of the OT holy days (Col. 2.18, on which my *Observations* 156). There may be a touch of polemic against similar teachings in Rom. 10.6. The author of the Apocalypse (4.1ff) claimed to have been taken up into heaven, and to report what he had heard and seen there. II Peter 1.11 recommends that its recipients practice various virtues because οὕτως . . . πλουσίως ἐπιχορηγηθήσεται ὑμῖν ἡ εἴσοδος εἰς τὴν αἰώνιον βασιλείαν. Here πλουσίως has its normal meaning, "abundantly, plentifully," with reference to repeated entries (contrast Windisch-Preisker, *Briefe, ad loc.*; they were forced to make of it "ein glänzender Einzug," although the proof passage they cite from Philo, *De vita contemplativa* 35, shows the normal reference to plurality). Aphraates, *Demonstratio* IV.5, says that Jacob saw in his vision (Gen. 28.11ff) the gate of heaven, which gate is Christ, and the ladder to heaven, which is "the mystery of ⟨instituted by?⟩ our saviour, by which righteous men ascend from the lower ⟨world⟩ to the ⟨world⟩ above." Another interpretation, preferred by Aphraates (*ibid.* 6), took the ladder as the cross. The notion that "the mystery of our saviour" means a rite or technique instituted by him is made more likely by the fact that in the contemporary *Hekalot* material the technique for ascent to the heavens is also described as a ladder.

In the third place, the supposition that these claims by Jesus' followers reflect some similar claim by Jesus himself is thoroughly in accord with the magical character of Jesus' career, as set forth in the preceding section. The Christian story of Simon Magus charges Simon with magical ascent to the heavens; the Jewish story of Jesus makes the same charge against Jesus (*Actus Petri cum Simone* 32; Krauss, *Leben* 43;

etc.). Eliade, *Shamanism*, has shown (*passim*) that the claim to have ascended to the heavens and thereby attained supernatural powers is characteristic of a type of magician found all over Asia and the Americas. This type of magician we now begin to find along the Palestine-Syria coast, and soon elsewhere in the Roman empire. The *Vita Apollonii* represents ascent to the heavens as the greatest achievement of the Indian magicians and the ultimate triumph of Apollonius (VI.11 end; VIII.30 end). In Lucian, *Philopseudes* 13, it is the conclusive proof by which the (pseudo) sceptic claims that a Hyperborean magician (from the territory of the shamans) overcame his doubts. The magical papyri represent it as the means to achieve magical powers, the reward of their achievement, and the ultimate goal of the magician's career (*PGM* IV.537ff; I.118ff; XXXIV.7f; I.178ff).

In the fourth place, the supposition that Jesus practiced some such technique for ascent enables us to explain both the secret character of his baptism and the way he got his disciples into the kingdom of God. Both the *Hekalot* and the "Mithras Liturgy" give directions for performing the ascent with a companion or assistant, and provision for a boy as assistant is very frequent in the magical papyri (e.g., *PGM* IV, *passim*; *DMP, passim*). Most often the boy is the medium; the magician *causes him to see* the gods. This technique lent itself for development into an initiation, a "mystery of the kingdom of God," by which chosen disciples could be made to believe they had literally "entered the kingdom." Hence the claim to have experienced such an ascent appears as accreditation of the apostolate and as authority for teaching, *both* in Paul and in his Judaizing and Jewish opponents. And how else is this fact to be explained? What authority other than Jesus was both early enough and important enough to give both Paul and his opponents not only the odd notion that they could ascend to the heavens, but the amazing one that such an ascent was necessary to make them apostles of Jesus?

In the fifth place, Paul's interpretation of baptism as a means of ascent to the heavens (Col. 2.9ff; above, pp. 214ff) has to be explained. Acts 9.18 reports that Paul found baptism an established practice in the church in Damascus about fourteen years before his correspondence with the Corinthians (II Cor. 12.2)—that is, within half a dozen years of Jesus' death. Presumably his teaching concerning baptism reflected at least the essentials of the teaching given him when he was baptized. The burden of proof may be left to those who would deny this. They will have to show whence, if not from Jesus, came the Pauline interpretation of baptism as a means of union with Jesus and of ascent to the heavens.

Finally, we have here another contact with shamanism. Eliade (*Shamanism* 33, 64, 288, etc.) has shown that the traditional scheme of a shamanic initiation involves hallucinations of passion, death, and resurrection prior to the ascent to the heavens. One of the most striking developments of Paul's, as opposed to the Baptist's, baptism was the notion that it was an initiation ceremony in which the candidate died, was buried, and rose again (above, pp. 214ff). Can it be accidental that the followers of a magician credited with shamanic ascent to the heavens came to see in their initiation ceremony the essentials of a shamanic initiation? It can. This particular magician had been caught and put to death, his followers had seen visions of him

after his death, and these historical accidents may have led to a reinterpretation of the baptism he administered: originally a rite of union with him and participation in his ascent to the heavens, it later came to include also participation in his death, burial, and resurrection. This, at least, has been my assumption thus far; so I have treated all NT references to Jesus' death and resurrection as later reflections of those alleged events. But the theme of deliverance from death, couched in terms suggesting a resurrection, was familiar in the Psalms (e.g., 30.4; 49.16; 86.13) and in the Qumran *Hodayot* (II.32; III.10,19; V.6; IX.4ff; X.33f; XVII.13?) as an expression of deliverance from illness or danger, and, in the *Hodayot*, from the corruption natural to man. It is possible, therefore, that such elements may have figured in Jesus' magical teaching and practice. If so, they would have prepared for the disciples' resurrection experiences. In any event, Paul's interpretation of baptism as death, resurrection, and ascension, and his claim (and the claims of his Christian competitors) to have ascended into the heavens, fit together as pieces of a recognizable pattern. Therefore it seems likely that their common source—the teaching and practice of Jesus—contained at least the most important element of the pattern, the ascent to the heavens. (The possibility of a connection with Shamanism has not been disproved by Goldammer's defense of it in *Shamanismus*.)

3. RECORDS OF JESUS' PRACTICE

The above indirect evidence is supported by some direct evidence from NT passages, chief of which is the story of the transfiguration. This direct evidence is not conclusive, but conclusive evidence about a secret magical practice is hardly to be expected. What we have are several puzzling passages which can all be explained by this one hypothesis more satisfactorily than they have hitherto been by diverse hypotheses.

a.   The transfiguration

The transfiguration is one of the most puzzling stories in the synoptics. Scholars have often noticed its resemblance to four other stories: the baptism (Feuillet, *Perspectives*), the scene in Gethsemane (Kenny, *Transfiguration*; Burkill, *Revelation* 241), the resurrection, and the ascension (see above, pp. 149, 165). To these can now be added the initiation story from the longer text of Mk. This complex set of relations has often led to attempts at source analysis (recently Müller, *Verklärung*), none of them convincing. In this group of related stories, the Gethsemane scene differs sharply from the rest because of its central section, the agony, and its historical conclusion, the arrest. The first of these differences confirms the supposition that the agony is a homiletic insert filling the gap produced by the *disciplina arcani*, which prohibited a report of the initiation Jesus was performing that night (see above, pp. 177 and 237). The historical conclusion, on the other hand, indicates that this type of story had some basis in some type of event recurrent in Jesus' life: it is not pure myth. The nature of the event is indicated by the agreements of the stories: a preparatory period or ceremony (John's baptism of Jesus, the last supper, the burial), a small group of participants (in the first baptism, only the Baptist and Jesus?),

a revelation (except in the Gethsemane story, where the police arrive instead). In the two fullest accounts—the transfiguration and the ascension—the revelation involves an ascent, a vision of the glorified Messiah, an entering into a cloud. The first of the stories is the account of Jesus' baptism, and the story in the longer text of Mk. states that the thing revealed was "the mystery of the kingdom of God," that is (as we have seen), a baptism, leading to entrance of the heavens. Paul supposed entering into a cloud to be a form of baptism (I Cor. 10.2); neither Allo, *I Cor.*, nor Lietzmann, *Korinther*, could gues why.

One could make sense of this data by supposing that Jesus, when baptized by John, had some sort of ecstatic experience in which he saw the heavens opened and the spirit took possession of him (Mk. 1.10), and that using the magical discipline of his day he developed his spiritual gift into a technique by which he was able to ascend to the heavens and also to give others the same experience and similar spiritual powers. Evidence for this might be found in the *Gospel according to the Hebrews*: "My mother, the holy spirit, seized me by a hair of my head and carried me off to the great mountain, Tabor." Lk. 10.17ff: "The demons are subject to us . . . I saw Satan falling from the heaven like lightning. Behold. I have given you authority . . . over every power of the enemy . . . But do not rejoice in this, that the spirits are subject to you; rather rejoice that your names are written in the heavens." Jn. 1.51: "You shall see the heaven opened and the angels of God ascending and descending on the Son of Man." It was seen by Burney, *Origin* 115ff that the Son of Man is here the ladder of Gen. 28.12, by which ascent to the heavens is made possible. So in *Bereshit Rabbah* 68.12 the angels ascend and descend on Jacob, the mediator (cf. Aphraates, *Demonstratio* IV.5, quoted in the preceding section). As the first step in this technique Jesus continued to use the water baptism of the Baptist, since it removed sin and presumably also impurity (which was automatically removed by immersion in sufficient running water) and thus made the initiate fit to enter the heavens. What Jesus added we can guess from Paul, the *Hekalot*, and the "Mithras Liturgy." What the initiates experienced can be guessed also from the partial, remote, and deliberately secretive reflections in our group of stories. These experiences which Jesus' disciples had during his lifetime probably produced and shaped their visions of him after his death. Thus the resurrection and ascension stories are reflections of the transfiguration experiences which were produced in "the mystery of the kingdom of God." (The ancient world saw the development of many such magical rites and mysteries which purported to make the initiate ascend into the heavens; see the material collected by Lewy, *Oracles* 177ff. Schrade, *Ikonographie* 87, saw that recollection of initiatory experience might lie behind the story of the transfiguration.)

b. Phil. 2.5–11; I Tim. 3.16; Jn. 3

These three NT passages imply that Jesus had ascended into the heavens before his death. All three of them may be plausibly connected with baptism. Let us consider first the hymn quoted by Paul in Phil. 2.6–11 (and therefore earlier than Paul's letter): ⟨Messiah Jesus⟩ ἐν μορφῇ θεοῦ ὑπάρχων οὐχ ἁρπαγμὸν ἡγήσατο τὸ εἶναι ἴσα θεῷ, ἀλλὰ ἑαυτὸν ἐκένωσεν μορφὴν δούλου λαβών, ἐν ὁμοιώματι ἀνθρώπων γενόμενος, καὶ σχήματι

εὑρεθεὶς ὡς ἄνθρωπος, ἐταπείνωσεν ἑαυτὸν γενόμενος ὑπήκοος μέχρι θανάτου, θανάτου δὲ σταυροῦ· διὸ καὶ ὁ θεὸς αὐτὸν ὑπερύψωσεν καὶ ἐχαρίσατο αὐτῷ τὸ ὄνομα τὸ ὑπὲρ πᾶν ὄνομα, ἵνα ἐν τῷ ὀνόματι Ἰησοῦ πᾶν γόνυ κάμψῃ ἐπουρανίων καὶ ἐπιγείων καὶ καταχθονίων, καὶ πᾶσα γλῶσσα ἐξομολογήσηται ὅτι κύριος Ἰησοῦς Χριστὸς εἰς δόξαν θεοῦ πατρός. The credal character of this is obvious and its connection with baptism not unlikely. It has commonly been understood (e.g., by Käsemann, *Analyse*; Jervell, *Imago* 212f, 227ff) by reference to Col. 1, Jn. 1, Heb. 1, etc., as beginning with an account of the incarnation. But this neglects the fact that it is an account of what was done by *Jesus*, not by "the Son" (Col. and Heb.) or "the Logos" (Jn.). Nor can it be said that "Jesus" here is a mere slip of the pen by Paul, who carelessly attributed to Jesus a hymn celebrating some pre-existent entity. On the contrary, as is obvious from the conclusion (and as Käsemann has shown at great length) the hymn is a celebration of *Jesus*. Moreover, Paul expresses similar ideas about *Jesus* in II Cor. 8.9: δι' ὑμᾶς ἐπτώχευσεν πλούσιος ὤν. Of course Paul believed in a pre-existent Messiah, but that is not in question here. In both these passages Paul is proposing an example which his disciples can and should follow—the example of their fellow man, Jesus. Therefore, we must ask: when was *Jesus* in the form (μορφή) of God and either "as God" (ἴσα θεῷ) or able "to grasp at equality with God," and when could *he* have voluntarily relinquished this glory and taken the form of a minister (δοῦλος = עבד) of God—specifically, of a man?[18] The answer is: after his ascent to the heavens. After the Helios initiation, quoted above in section C, the initiate is described as ἰσοθέου φύσεως κυριεύσας, and he gives thanks with the words συνεστάθην σου τῇ ἱερᾷ μορφῇ, ἐδυναμώθην τῷ ἱερῷ σου ὀνόματι (*PGM* IV.216–221; for parallels from rabbinic literature and the relation to Phil. 2.6ff see my discussion in *Image* 478ff). Having seen Christian baptism as a magical union of the initiate with Jesus and therefore a magical participation in Jesus' ascent, we can now see the force of Phil. 2.5 as an argument for humility and good behavior (which it is in its context, cf. 2.2ff; 2.12ff). Paul here, as so often, is arguing against a libertine interpretation of the Gospel. When he says τοῦτο φρονεῖτε ἐν ὑμῖν ὃ καὶ ἐν Χριστῷ Ἰησοῦ he concedes that the Philippians have, as a result of baptism, been, like Jesus, ἐν μορφῇ θεοῦ. But they should not attempt, as would the libertines, τὸ εἶναι ἴσα θεῷ. On the contrary they should now—like Jesus—come down to earth and make themselves serviceable and obedient to their fellow Christians (among others, to Paul).

Moreover, in this instance we can specify the apocalyptic tradition by which the magical practice was interpreted: it is that of Enoch. Enoch began his apocalyptic career as a holy man who was taken up to heaven to see the rewards and punishments reserved for the righteous and wicked, then sent back to earth for a one-year ministry

---

18. The specification was necessary because the angels are also δοῦλοι τοῦ θεοῦ, Apoc. 19.10. On the other hand, no significance whatever can be attached to the distinctions of meaning to be found between μορφή, ὁμοίωμα, and σχῆμα. This is devotional poetry, not philosophic prose. (And even for philosophic prose, see the observations of Wolfson on the laxity of Philo's usage, *Philo* I.102.) In the hymn paraphrased by Paul in Philippians the choice of words was probably determined more by metrical considerations than by those of content. σχῆμα and ὁμοίωμα probably represent Aramaic terms which were once equated, since the verse in which they stand still shows its original *parallelismus membrorum*.

to warn men of the judgment (= rule, kingdom) to come: *I Enoch* 81.5). In 71.11 it is mentioned that he was transfigured when taken on high. This theme is developed in *II Enoch*, where his transfiguration makes him look exactly like an angel (22.10— this could be ἴσα θεῷ or ἐν μορφῇ θεοῦ, since angels are often called "gods" in Jewish tradition; e.g., *Image* 477; Käsemann's statement that ἴσα θεῷ could not come from Judaism is mistaken). This time, when Enoch was sent down on his saving mission to men (ch. 36), he had to be changed back to a form men could bear to see (ch. 37). *II Enoch* probably dates from sometime in the late first century (Scholem, *Gnosticism* 17) and is therefore approximately contemporary with the *Ascension of Isaiah* where, as in Phil. 2, we have the Enoch story adapted to Christianity. In the *Ascension of Isaiah*, the prophet is transfigured on the way up and becomes like an angel (7.25; 9.30). Then the descent of the Lord is foretold: it involves a whole series of transformations, first to the likeness of the angels of the lower heaven and eventually into human form (ch. 10). Finally Isaiah is ordered to return into his garment of flesh (= σχῆμα ἀνθρώπου) and go back to earth (11.35). He is to be a martyr for God and for the salvation of men (ὑπήκοος μέχρι θανάτου). Last of all comes *III Enoch* (closely connected with the *Hekalot* literature and its doctrine of magical ascent). Here Enoch is transformed into the angel Metatron and is given the name "Yahweh" (ch. 12, cf. 15), as is Jesus in Phil. 2.9–11 ("Yahweh" = κύριος); and all the powers of heaven fall prostrate before him (ch. 14), as they do before Jesus in Philippians. These parallels suffice to show from what tradition the hymn in Philippians has come. The parallels from the *Hermetica* to which Jervell, *Imago* 228ff, appeals are less similar in content and more remote from Palestinian tradition. Here again the closest and earliest parallels to Paul's ideas about Jesus are to be found in Palestinian material. Such parallels establish a strong presumption that Paul got these ideas from Jesus' Palestinian followers, who got them from Jesus himself.

These parallels also make it probable that the similar hymn in I Tim. 3.16, ὃς ἐφανερώθη ἐν σαρκί, ἐδικαιώθη ἐν πνεύματι, ὤφθη ἀγγέλοις, ἐκηρύχθη ἐν ἔθνεσιν, ἐπιστεύθη ἐν κόσμῳ, ἀνελήμφθη ἐν δόξῃ, reflects the same tradition: the gift of the spirit is immediately followed by the first ascension, then comes the ministry on earth, and finally the second ascension in glory. This hymn shows the "adoptionist Christology" (deriving from the historical tradition that Jesus' messianic delusion began with his baptism) combined with the "pre-existent Christology" which eventually won out. The two theories can be reconciled in any number of ways; their combination may go back to Jesus himself: he would not have been the only man in antiquity to think himself the son or incarnation of a supernatural power (Wetter, *Sohn* ch. 1).

This interpretation of Phil. 2.6–11 and I Tim. 3.16 is strengthened by the fact that the same outline of Jesus' career appears more explicitly in Jn. 3 where the connection with baptism is indubitable. After having declared that to enter the kingdom of God one must be reborn of water and of the spirit (verses 3ff—for the rebirth imagery see *CH* XIII and Festugière's notes *ad loc.*), Jesus goes on to describe the magical powers of one who possesses the spirit: Like the spirit itself he can go about invisible; his motions cannot be traced. (So *PGM* I.222ff; 247ff; etc.; the

superstition goes back to Plato's ring of Gyges, *Republic* 359f. John probably meant this both symbolically and literally; his Jesus could walk on water, 6.19, and through crowds of men who wished to seize him, 7.44, 8.59, 10.39; and through locked doors, 20.19.) Nicodemus' request for an explanation suggests disbelief (verse 9). Jesus replies (10ff) that all this is well known in Jewish tradition (where magical practices were long established) and that he is speaking from personal experience (ὃ ἑωράκαμεν μαρτυροῦμεν). He then goes on, εἰ τὰ ἐπίγεια εἶπον ὑμῖν καὶ οὐ πιστεύετε, πῶς ἐὰν εἴπω ὑμῖν τὰ ἐπουράνια πιστεύσετε; καὶ οὐδεὶς ἀναβέβηκεν εἰς τὸν οὐρανὸν εἰ μὴ ὁ ἐκ τοῦ οὐρανοῦ καταβάς, ὁ υἱὸς τοῦ ἀνθρώπου. Then comes a reference to the Son's future crucifixion and an account of his role as a means of salvation. This lecture on baptism is followed by the report that Jesus went forth and baptized (verse 22), which leads to the Baptist's "testimony" to Jesus (27ff): Jesus is the bridegroom who has the bride (*sc.* the spirit, Wetter, *Sohn* 54); he comes from "above," that is, from God (= "the heaven"), and is therefore above all and ὃ ἑώρακεν καὶ ἤκουσεν, τοῦτο μαρτυρεῖ (verse 32).

Here Barrett (on verse 13) takes καὶ οὐδεὶς ἀναβέβηκεν, κ.τ.λ., as a comment made by the Church, while Bultmann (*Johannes* 108) sees it in a prophecy of the resurrection and ascension—one of the "heavenly things" Nicodemus could not believe. But the plain sense of the passage is: "You do not believe what I tell you of earthly things ⟨like the miraculous powers of the baptized⟩, how will you believe if I tell you of heavenly things ⟨the ascent into the kingdom⟩? Yet ⟨I am the only one qualified to declare such things, for⟩ no one *has ascended* into the heaven except he who ⟨first⟩ came down from heaven, the Son of Man ⟨that is, I⟩." So, again, verse 32. Here we have, as in I Tim. 3.16, the combination of "adoptionist" and "pre-existent" Christologies. For John, Jesus is the incarnation of the pre-existent logos. But this does not prevent John from preserving and reworking material which has come to him from an earlier and more historical tradition, and to such material we owe this recollection that Jesus in his lifetime claimed to have gone up to heaven and to speak of it from firsthand knowledge. (Contrast Sidebottom's contorted attempt to explain away the reference of the ascent.) Parallels to Jn. 3.3 in the *Clementine Homilies* XI.26.2 and Macarius (*Neue Homilien* XVI.3, p. 83) show such agreements against Jn. that Quispel (*Syrian Thomas* 230f) argues that this material was handed down independently by a Jewish-Christian Gospel tradition akin to that of the *Gospel of Thomas*. One of the most important characteristics of this tradition, in Quispel's opinion, was the belief "that eschatology has been realized here and now and that this has implications for marriage and possessions" (p. 235). The possible relevance of this will become apparent later, when we speak of the libertine side of early Christianity.

Other references to the tradition of Jesus' ascent are probably to be found in Jn. 6.38,42,58,62, since it is this tradition—that Jesus had been taken up into heaven, transformed into a supernatural being, and sent back into the world as the messenger of the Father—which explains why the Jews both do and do not know whence he comes: they know his earthly origin but not his heavenly mission. The same tradition, again, lies behind 10.36, where Jesus speaks of himself as one "whom the Father

hallowed and sent into the world." This description fits a figure like Enoch, who was first a man, then was taken up into heaven, hallowed, and sent back to earth. It does not fit the Logos, which from the beginning "was God" (1.1) and therefore could never have been hallowed. The commentators, from St. Cyril of Alexandria down to Bultmann and Barrett, who try to avoid the difficulty by equating sanctification with commission, probably understand the verse as the author intended it to be understood. But the Johannine context imposes on the words a meaning which they ordinarily would not carry.

Finally, in Hebrews the secret doctrine to which the believers should go on (leaving behind the elementary, exoteric teaching—6.1ff) is that of Jesus' ascent to the heavens (9.11ff), which enables the baptized to follow him thither (10.19ff). Here, as in Paul, the doctrine has been reinterpreted in the light of the passion—Jesus has been made the high priest bearing the sacrifice of his own blood into the heavenly adyton; but this reinterpretation may disguise a teaching rooted in Jesus' magical practice.

E. The rite liberated its recipients from the Mosaic law

We turn now to the fifth of the traits of Pauline baptism which were listed as probably derived from Jesus. This is the fact that it results in liberty from the Mosaic Law. Paul expresses this as a consequence of the death of Jesus: By his death Jesus satisfied the demands of the Law, so that it had no further claim on him; the baptized, being united with him, are also beyond its claims (e.g., Rom. 7.4). There has been much speculation as to how Paul—reportedly a Pharisee—came to hold such a theory, so alien to his training and his moralizing temperament and therefore probably not his own invention. Perhaps the most brilliant presentation of the problem remains that by Machen, *Origin*, who argues that Paul got the main ideas by tradition from Jesus. Here we shall begin by distinguishing between Paul's explanation of *why* baptism results in liberty from the Law, and the mere teaching *that* it does so. Paul's explanation presupposes Jesus' death and therefore can hardly go back to Jesus himself. But the mere teaching makes no presupposition. Therefore it might be supposed to have come from Jesus if there were good evidence of his belief that he and his disciples had been freed from the requirements of the Law. We should then suppose that his freedom began with his identification with "the Son" as a result of his possession by the spirit at his baptism, and that the freedom of his disciples resulted from their identification with him through their possession by his spirit, in the baptism which he administered (cf. II Kgs. 2.9ff, where Elisha gets a double portion of Elijah's spirit as a result of seeing him taken up to heaven in a chariot of fire and/or a whirlwind). It would be plausible also to connect both Jesus' and his disciples' possession by the spirit and consequent freedom from the Law with their entrance of the kingdom, conceived as a passage from this world or age (subject to the Law) to the coming world or age (of liberty). A century later Rabbi Elisha ben Abuyah was believed to have learned how to enter the paradise

in the heavens, and this was thought the cause of his throwing over the Law and becoming a libertine (*B. Hagigah* 14bff and parallels. Like Jesus, even after he had become a libertine he continued to be consulted as an authority on legal questions, *ibid.*, 15a–b).

The evidence on Jesus' attitude toward law is complex. Here all that can be done is to indicate the major elements. (See further *Jesus' Attitude*.)

First, the law of the state: Jesus was condemned and executed for criminal sedition; he was arrested at a nocturnal meeting (to which at least one of his followers had come armed, Mk. 14.47 and parallels, cf. Lk. 22.38). Sometime before his arrest he had created a disturbance in the Temple markets (Mk. 11.15f and parallels), and he was accused of plotting to destroy the Temple (Mk. 14.58 and parallel; Jn. 2.19). As to his teaching about taxes, we have contrary reports: Mk. 12.17 and parallels (render unto Caesar); Mt. 17.26f (his followers are free but may pay if they wish, from policy). The charge that he forbade payment of taxes appears in one report of his trial, Lk. 23.2.

Second, the Mosaic Law: The evidence is again contradictory. First there are a series of sayings implying that the Mosaic Law is still in force. These are notoriously conspicuous in Mt. (5.17,20; 23.2; etc.) but they occur also in Q and Mk.—Mt. 5.18 ‖ Lk. 16.17—it is easier for heaven and earth to pass away than for one iota to fall from the Law. Mt. 23.23 ‖ Lk. 11.42: one should do justice and love mercy *and also* tithe. Mk. 10.19: obedience to the ten commandments is the way of life; cf. Mk. 12.34.

The same implication—that the Mosaic Law is still in force—is to be seen in a series of stories and sayings in which Jesus interprets one or another commandment either more or less strictly than do his contemporaries; for example, the stories of preparing food and healing on the Sabbath, Mk. 2.23ff; 3.1ff; Lk. 13.10ff; 14.1ff; Jn. 5.1ff; 9.1ff. In most of these Jesus defends his action by arguments from the OT or from precedents in Jewish tradition. These arguments presuppose the validity of the Mosaic Law which they interpret; thus Mk. 2.25ff; Mt. 12.5,11; Lk. 13.10ff; Jn. 7.22. The same validity is presupposed by most of the material in Mt. 5 and 23 and parallels. This large and clear body of evidence determines the interpretation of what otherwise might be dubious cases, where Jesus' exegesis is so drastic as to practically annul a provision of the Mosaic Law; e.g., Mk. 10.1ff; Mt. 5.38; "Jn." 8.1ff. These are to be understood as corrections of detail (*tikkunim*) which do not call into question the validity of the general system. (All this is familiar and is documented in Strack-Billerbeck and Bonsirven, *Textes*.)

On the other hand, there is an important series of sayings in which the coming of the kingdom in Jesus and his disciples is represented as the beginning of a new age, sharply distinguished from the old age of the Law. "The Law and the prophets were until John, from then on the kingdom of God is proclaimed" and is available to those who will use violence (Mt. 11.12f ‖ Lk. 16.16). Consequently, the least in the kingdom is greater than Jn. (Mt. 11.11 ‖ Lk. 7.28). The new kingdom is the new garment which is not to be cut to patch up the antiquated fabric of Judaism (Lk. 5.36); it is the new wine not to be put in the old bottles (Mk. 2.22). Therefore

the Son of Man is lord of the Sabbath (Mk. 2.28) and has authority on earth to forgive sins (Mk. 2.1ff and parallels; Lk. 7.47ff); and his companions, as he celebrates his marriage with the spirit, may not fast (Mk. 2.19). As opposed to the Baptist, who represented the Law and therefore came "in the way of righteousness"—that is, asceticism (Mt. 11.18; 21.32), he comes eating and drinking and is called a gluttonous man and a winebibber, a friend of publicans and sinners (Mt. 11.19 ‖ Lk. 7.34), in whose homes he is a frequent guest (Mk. 2.15 and parallels; Lk. 15.1f; 19.1ff). His yoke, by contrast to that of the law, is light (Mt. 11.28ff; Acts 15.10). As John said, the Law came by Moses, grace by Jesus (1.17). With the coming of grace came a new commandment, to love one another (Jn. 13.34; 15.12; Mt. 5.44ff). Accordingly, worship at Gerizim and Jerusalem was to be replaced by worship in spirit and in truth (Jn. 4.21ff). For the Son had now revealed to his chosen the hitherto unknown Father (Mt. 11.27 ‖ Lk. 10.22 ‖ Jn. 1.18), and it was at last possible to assure the initiate, "You shall know the truth, and the truth will make you free" (Jn. 8.32). "Free" from what? The saying is directed "to the Jews" (8.31), so the implication is, "free from the Law."

Between these opposing bodies of material there is a large no-man's-land of sayings which can be interpreted one way or the other—either as expressions of a liberal legal position, or as manifestations of the freedom of the new age. The neglect of washing before meals is a recurrent example (Mk. 7.5 and parallel; Lk. 11.38). But in spite of this (and of other complicating factors) the difference of the two main bodies of tradition is clear. It is also clear that both are so widely represented in the preserved documents that neither can safely be dismissed as secondary. No doubt it was true (as I argued in *Elements*) that the rapprochement between the Jerusalem church and Pharisaism in the forties and thereafter contributed not a little to the reformation of Jesus. And the legal arguments to justify the sabbath healings are separable and perhaps secondary. But the bulk of the legalistic material, and the consistency with which it appears in *all* the sources, rule out any attempt to eliminate it from the primary evidence. On the other hand, the sayings on the presence of the kingdom are now generally recognized as reflections of the most peculiar and original element in Jesus' teaching.

What is needed, therefore, is some explanation of the coexistence of these two bodies of material. And from what we have seen above, the explanation can be supplied. The legalistic material represents Jesus' exoteric teaching. For "those without" (Mk. 4.11) the law was still binding, and for them Jesus interpreted it as did the lawyers of his time, holding with more lenient opinions in some instances, with stricter ones in others. (Such variation appears in the opinions of every ancient rabbi.)[19] His secret teaching was only for those to whom the mystery of the kingdom

19. How it came about that Jesus was consulted as a legal authority (e.g., Mk. 10.2; Lk. 12.13) we do not know. It is not impossible that he had some legal training. As the *Hekalot* tracts, the stories of Yohanan ben Zakkai (on which Neusner, *Life* 97, etc.), and the magical material newly discovered by Margalioth demonstrate, the halakic tradition, even in rabbinic Judaism, has close connections with the study of magic, including the practice of ascents to the heavens. That these could be combined with libertinism, too, and that the successful magician and notorious libertine could remain a great legal authority, is shown in the case of Rabbi Elisha ben Abuyah. On the other hand, anyone in first-century

had been given (*ibid.*). He had no intention of giving that which was holy to the dogs, or of casting his pearls before swine (Mt. 7.6). The contradictions of the present Gospels may result from seepage of secret material into originally exoteric texts. Of this we should now have a further example in the additions of the longer text to Mk. More evidence might be seen in the fact that material suggesting the presence of the kingdom, as a radically new regime exempt from the laws of the former age, is more prominent in Q and L than in Mk.—it was added to Mk. by Matthew and Luke. Later additions may be found in Jn. 8.1ff and in the western text (D) at the end of Lk. 6.4: "On the same day, seeing a man working on the sabbath, he said to him, 'Man, if you know what you are doing, you are blessed, but if you do not know, you are accursed and a transgressor of the Law.'"

More of the esoteric teaching is found in the epistles of Paul, the oldest Christian documents and those most surely written for reading within the closed circles of the churches. Within those circles there were still distinctions in degree of initiation (I Cor. 3.1ff)—esoterism is rarely content with a simple inside-outside contrast, but loves to elaborate secrets within secrets to the thirty-third degree. Nevertheless, Paul enables us to glimpse the true beliefs of the congregations to which he writes, and he is to be preferred, as a source for early Christian thought, to the later, comparatively exoteric Gospels.

XI. Consequences of Jesus' baptismal practice

Through the preceding studies of the relations of Jesus' work to that of the Baptist and of Paul, we have arrived at a definition of "the mystery of the kingdom of God": It was a baptism administered by Jesus to chosen disciples, singly, and by night. In this baptism the disciple was united with Jesus. The union may have been physical (see above, commentary on III.13 and pp. 185f—there is no telling how far symbolism went in Jesus' rite), but the essential thing was that the disciple was possessed by Jesus' spirit. One with Jesus, he participated in Jesus' ascent into the heavens; he entered the kingdom of God and was thereby set free from the laws ordained for and in the lower world.

This understanding of the mystery of the kingdom enables us to understand in the history of the early Church a number of problems which hitherto have gone either without solution or without recognition. The failure to recognize and the inability to solve them have in part been due to the influence of Acts, a partizan document often shown to be incomplete (it neither reports the foundations of the churches of Rome and Alexandria nor the survival of Christianity in Galilee,

---

Palestine who had messianic pretensions would have had to give decisions on legal questions. In *Jesus' Attitude* I discuss the whole problem further and propose (p. 244) a threefold division of Jesus' hearers: ordinary Jews, for whom the Mosaic Law is still binding, those who would be perfect, who are still subject to the Law but with additional requirements and also with special exemptions, and those who have been admitted to the kingdom, who are free from the Law.

cf. Lohmeyer, *Galiläa*; etc.), confused (5.19 is a doublet of 12.7ff; Peter's miracles are doublets of Jesus'; the chronology of Paul's career is hardly to be reconciled with Gal. 1 and 2), and misrepresentative (it minimizes doctrinal differences in order to present a single, original, united Christian Church, of which Paul was the fully approved representative—cf. Weiss, *Christianity* 260; Brandon, *Fall* 208ff; on the Hellenists, Cullmann, *Significance*; Simon, *Stephen*, *vs.* Haenchen, *Apostelgeschichte*, on 6.1). But the blame cannot be laid entirely on Acts. Bauer, *Rechtgläubigkeit*, has shown that the NT as a whole is a partizan collection, made to present and support the views of that party which became predominant within the Church in the late second century and finally triumphed in the third. Accordingly, *the picture of early Christianity given by the NT has constantly to be supplemented by pictures of the parties it opposes, and has frequently to be explained by reference to factors it attempts to conceal.* One of these concealed factors is Jesus' practice of baptism as "the mystery of the kingdom." Therefore a number of consequences of this practice appear in the history of early Christianity as unexplained phenomena or are "explained" by stories of miracles. These can now be explained historically by recognition of their source in Jesus' practice.

A.   *The coming of the spirit*

Most critical scholarship has uncritically taken for granted that "the spirit"—that is, the schizophrenic behavior—just "came," and has not tried to explain its coming. Acts "explained" it as a miracle (Pentecost). But the coming of the spirit presupposes a group with peculiar preparation. The holy spirit did not descend on the disciples of Rabbi Akiba after he was executed for treason; at most they heard a heavenly voice (*B. Berakot* 61b). But Jesus' disciples had been prepared for the phenomena of group possession by their experience of individual possession in his baptism. It must be remembered that he had a peculiar attraction for and power over schizophrenics. Hence his exorcisms and his following of "women who had been cured of evil spirits," Lk. 8.2. The stories of his disciples' sudden, total abandonment of their ordinary lives, to follow him—Mk. 1.16ff; 2.14; Jn. 1.43; cf. Lk. 9.59ff—probably reflect the same power and explain not only the disciples' suitability for possession in baptism, but also their visions of the resurrected Lord. These same psychological characteristics were perpetuated in the Pauline churches (above, p. 215).

This explains also why the spirit is identified with Jesus, as it is in Paul (I Cor. 6.18; 15.45; II Cor. 3.17f). Jesus had originally been the source of it. When the type of personality disturbance originally connected with him recurred as a group phenomenon in the circle of those who had depended on him for it, he was of course supposed to be the cause. This, however, was a historical inference, and as time went on and personal memories of Jesus faded, the spirit became an independent personality and pushed Jesus aside. This can be seen happening already in Paul. For, unlike Jesus, the spirit was alive and present: it spoke to the churches (Apoc. 2.7,11,17, etc.), did miracles, and was the source of knowledge and wisdom (I Cor. 12.8ff)

and the guide of private life (Gal. 5.18,22, etc.). Therefore, as the churches grew, the importance of the present, active spirit grew with them, while its connection with Jesus receded into the background—a memory for the few he had initiated, a dogma for the many new converts.

Accordingly, for Acts the spirit is something Jesus gives *after* his death, resurrection, and ascension. The prophecy of Jesus' baptizing by the spirit, which Mk. 1.8 put into the mouth of the Baptist, is made by Acts to refer to the beginning of the group experience after Jesus' death: 1.5; 11.16. (Another factor in the account given by Acts is secrecy. Luke's silence about the baptismal teaching of Jesus, like his silence about Paul's theology, can hardly be explained save as deliberate reticence. For further evidence on this point, see *Reason.*)

Development has gone even further in the latest stratum of Jn., which insists that the spirit was *not* given until after Jesus' death and ascension (7.39; cf. 14.17, 26; 15.26; 16.7,13; 20.22). The insistence looks like polemic and is perhaps to be explained along the line suggested by Kragerud (*Lieblingsjünger*) and Käsemann (*Ketzer*): John is appealing to the newly given spirit for authorization, against opponents who had better claims than he to human traditions about Jesus. New problems required a new authority, so the development of the doctrine of the Third Person of the Trinity was under way, though its progress was soon to be slowed. As the original enthusiasm of the Christian communities wore off, the temporary attacks of schizophrenia which had been the most conspicuous gift of the spirit became rarer. Also, their practical importance presumably declined as the frequent foolishness of the promptings they produced became evident, as the churches developed fixed routines for worship and daily life, and as control of the churches fell more and more into the hands of professional administrators who are not, as a class, much given to ecstasy and have often viewed ecstatics with hostility as possible competitors for authority. From the mid-second century on, therefore, the active guidance of the spirit is characteristic of groups soon thereafter to be declared "heretical."

B.   *The adoption and development of baptism by the early churches*

A second problem explained by Jesus' practice of baptism is that posed by the fact that Jesus' followers practiced a baptism of the Baptist's type, yet claimed that it would not only remit sins, but also give the spirit. If Jesus never baptized (and, even more, if he deliberately stopped baptizing) it would be very difficult to explain why his followers took up the practice (above, pages 209f). And even if we neglect this difficulty and suppose they did take over the practice from the Baptist's followers, where did they get the notion that baptism gave the spirit, which the Baptist's baptism did not (Acts 19.1–6)? The most probable explanation is that the first element of Jesus' baptismal rite had been an immersion like the Baptist's for remission of sins and also for the purity necessary to approach the heavenly kingdom. (Until baptism the candidate was still of this world and therefore bound to obey the Law.) What Jesus had done beyond the Baptist's immersion was something dependent

on his peculiar powers of suggestion. But even if some of the early disciples succeeded in repeating Jesus' rite of possession and ascension, their initiations of a few individuals, one by one, were soon overshadowed by the phenomena of group possession in the meetings of the churches. The spirit now united the believer to the life of the Church, not to the person of Jesus, and the entrance to the kingdom in the heavens was replaced by the entrance of the Church, the kingdom present in this world (above, pp. 202f). Consequently, the developments which Jesus had added to the Baptist's baptism fell into disuse or were preserved as "great mysteries" for more advanced candidates. But the Baptist's baptism was preserved as the necessary ceremony for entrance to the Church. Since the Church was the kingdom of God on earth, entrance required that the initiate be pure and sinless. Since the Church was also the body inhabited by Jesus' spirit (I Cor. 12.12f), ceremonial entrance of the Church came to be credited with effecting possession of the spirit. This interpretation we find already in Paul, but Acts reflects the tradition that although Christian baptism is normally followed by the gift of the spirit (2.38; 19.5f), nevertheless it need not be so. The coming of the spirit may be delayed for some time after baptism (8.12ff) or may even precede it (10.47; cf. 11.15ff; Flemington, *Baptism* 39ff).

C. *The libertine tradition in early Christianity*

A third consequence of Jesus' baptismal practice was libertinism. The Christian libertine tradition, because of its early date and wide extent, is best explicable as the consequence of Jesus' teaching that those who have entered the kingdom are free of the law. Something has already been said of this as the source of Pauline theology, and the importance of Paul's doctrine needs no exposition. What has not generally been realized is that Paul as an exponent of Christian liberty was neither unique nor extreme. On the contrary, he was a comparatively conservative and mediating figure, consistently attacking and attacked by representatives of the libertine side. The libertine party or parties, whose tradition derived from Jesus himself, must have been widespread and influential, since evidence of their importance is to be found in almost every book of the NT and in most of the extracanonical Christian literature of the first two centuries. However, since all of their own writings have been destroyed, the very existence of the movement has too often been overlooked. Consequently, it seems worthwhile here to sketch at some length the major elements of the evidence.

I. THE PERSECUTION OF THE EARLY CHURCHES

This problem has been pointed out above (p. 234), but deserves further consideration.

As reported by Acts, the history of the early church of Jerusalem was a series of persecutions. But why should Jesus' followers have been persecuted? To believe that the Messiah had come, or to expect that he would soon come again, were not offenses punishable by Jewish law. And a man like Paul would not have taken an active

part in a persecution (as he himself testifies that he did—Gal. 1.23; I Cor. 15.9) without serious cause.

The concern of the temple authorities to stop the apostles' preaching in Jesus' name because "you wish to bring upon us the blood of this man" (Acts 5.28) is understandable if it means "you are inciting the mob to riot and punish us for handing him over to the Romans." But this can hardly be taken as the Christian message; neither will it explain the persecution by Paul, a Pharisee, who presumably had little concern for the welfare of the Sadducean high priests. Again we are told that the Sadducees were "grieved at their proclaiming in Jesus the resurrection from the dead" (Acts 4.2). If this meant simply "teaching that there would be a resurrection of the dead, and using Jesus as an example," it would not have been grounds for legal action, since the Pharisees also taught the resurrection of the dead and the appeal to an example does not alter the teaching. Perhaps the author wished to represent the Sadducees as acting illegally and thus expressed his hostility to the Sadducees, by contrast to the Pharisees whom he represented as not always unfriendly (so Blass, *Acta, ad loc.*, comparing 5.17,34; 23.6ff). Another possibility, however, is suggested by Paul's warning the Thessalonians against those who taught that the day of the Lord is already here (II Thess. 2.2). If the teaching in Jerusalem was that "the resurrection" had already come "in Jesus," it might have led—as it did in Thessalonica (3.6ff)—to irregularities of behavior which could have occasioned legal action.

In Acts 6.14 Stephen is charged with having said that Jesus would destroy the temple and abolish (or, change?) the Mosaic Law. Stephen proceeds to deliver a speech which tends to justify these charges, and is lynched. Here again, while his prediction of such events in the future *might* have moved a Jewish audience to lynch him, the action would have been more understandable had he been teaching that the end was already come and the law already abolished for those in Jesus. It was this latter teaching which almost got Paul lynched in the same place about twenty years later (Acts 21.21,28), and something similar is attributed to Jesus half a dozen years earlier (Mk. 2.10,19,28) in a body of material intended to lead up to and explain the Pharisees' plot against his life (Mk. 2.1–3.6).

Finally, no explanation at all is offered for the beginning of the persecution under Herod Agrippa I (A.D. 41–44), but it began with the beheading of James, the brother of John (12.2), and even in first-century Palestine capital punishment usually required serious grounds. Acts says the persecution was continued "because it was pleasing to the Jews." But some fifteen years later, when Paul comes to Jerusalem in Acts 21, we find the church on excellent terms with its neighbors and making "tens of thousands of converts . . . all of whom are zealots for the law" (21.20). Perhaps the change was begun by Herod's persecutions, which drove Peter underground and so allowed the leadership of the Jerusalem community to pass to James, Jesus' brother (Acts 12.17—Acts' first mention of James). The question of cause of the persecutions is thus related to the question of the parties in the Jerusalem church, where, it would seem, the libertine wing was originally important but was expelled by outside pressure and by developments within the Christian group. The leaders of the legalist

party within the church may have asked their friends in other Jewish parties—particularly the Pharisees, who had much influence with Herod Agrippa I—for a little timely persecution to help get rid of their libertine rivals. See further *Reason*.

2. THE PARTIES IN THE EARLY CHURCHES

The same picture emerges from the preserved evidence about the parties in the Jerusalem Church. This evidence is presumably incomplete, and what is preserved is none too good. Even among the accepted Gospels the lists of the twelve closest followers of Jesus differ slightly; the libertine parties may have appealed to other figures like Salome (above, pp. 189ff) or Glaucias and Theodas (Clement III.75.15ff), whose names have been eliminated from the accepted tradition. Trocmé, *Formation* 42ff, 90–108, etc., sees in Mk. a tradition which emphasized the role of Jesus as a miracle worker, not to say magician, and was hostile to the "respectable" tradition which appealed to Peter and John and represented them as the authoritative apostles. But we need not speculate as to what has been lost (though we must always remember that much certainly has been); there is plenty of evidence in the preserved material for the relation of different figures of the Jerusalem church to different parties.

John is particularly hostile to Jesus' brothers; he goes out of his way to state that they did not believe in Jesus during his lifetime (7.5). But none of the Gospels represents them as part of his following. We may suppose that they came into the movement after his death; as members of the family of an alleged pretender to the throne, they were involved in his disaster whether they liked it or not. The probability therefore is that James (like the other converts made since Jesus' death) had never received Jesus' initiation. His succession to leadership of the Jerusalem church will have marked the triumph of the converts over Jesus' original circle. Significantly, his authority had to be supported by the story that he had seen the risen Lord (I Cor. 15.7)—Paul was not the only one who appealed to posthumous revelations. After James' triumph, the antinomian aspect of Jesus' original teaching was obscured. Jerusalem became the center of a legalistic interpretation of the Gospel. Repercussions of this in the mission field are seen in Galatians and in Acts 21.15ff, from which it is customary to distinguish four positions.

First is the position of the legalists, whom James is trying to pacify and for whose sake he urges Paul to show that he still observes the law (Acts 21.20ff; Gal. 2.3f). Since this party maintained that the law was still binding, they must have denied either that the kingdom could as yet be entered, or that entrance to it put one beyond the law.

Second, the position of James: the *appearance* of obeying the law is to be maintained. This concern for appearance (מראית העין) is of great importance in Jewish law (e.g., *Kil'ayim* III.5; IX.2; *Shebi'it* III.4; *Shabbat* XIX.6; *Bekorot* VII.3,5). If Acts 21.24ff can be trusted, James and Paul were agreed that full observance of the law by gentile converts was not required, and James presumably had few illusions about Paul's practice outside Jerusalem (21.21, cf. Gal. 2.12). What he urged and Paul accepted was an act of "occasional conformity." Cf. Gal. 6.13 and Paul's argument to deter the Galatians, 5.3, which is proof that they were being asked to

obey only a few conspicuous commandments. Another concern perhaps relevant here is that for living at peace with one's neighbors (דרכי שלום *Shebi'it* IV.3; V.9; *Gittin* V.9; *Shekalim* I.3). But evidence as to rabbinic law in this period is so unreliable that there is no point in trying to define closely the legal positions of the several parties.

Third, the position of Paul: there is no need to appear to obey the law unless apparent disobedience of it would lead you into danger or your fellow Christians into sin (I Cor. 8.9ff; 10.14–31). However, one is free to obey when obedience seems politic (I Cor. 9.19ff), provided that one does so with clear understanding that obedience and disobedience are of no importance for salvation (I Cor. 8.7f).

Fourth is a mediating position (?) represented by Peter and Barnabas, who felt no obligation to preserve appearances among the lax but wanted to keep on good terms with James (Gal. 2.11–13).

On this customary analysis, two observations must be made. The first is that James' position practically presupposes that the doctrine about the liberty of those in the kingdom will be kept secret. The legalist party in James' church was probably the source of pronouncements like Mt. 23.2: "The scribes and the Pharisees sit on Moses' seat; all things whatsoever that they say unto you, these do and observe." Such a party could hardly have lived at peace with another which held that obedience to the law was optional, unless the latter opinion was masked by obedience and kept secret. Similarly, the position of Paul is congenial to secrecy, though it does not require it (cf. *Reason*). The existence in his churches of members who do not know that the eating of things sacrificed to idols is harmless (I Cor. 8.7ff) implies that his doctrine of Christian liberty had been kept to an inner group. I Cor. 3.1 indicates that he had teaching reserved for more advanced believers and kept secret from "babes." These "babes" were ignorant of the mysteries revealed by the spirit (I Cor. 2.6–16), of the things to be revealed at the end (13.8–13), and of their own freedom from the law (*ibid.*; 8.7). (How such ignorants got into a Pauline church is a question to be noted in passing for its indication of the difference between what Paul preached when he first came to a community and what he taught later.)

This leads to the second observation on the customary catalogue of parties, given above. The catalogue follows Acts and therefore neglects one important factor in the situation, the libertine party or parties to the left of Paul—groups like that against which Paul defends himself in I Cor. 8ff. Acts says nothing of this side of Christianity (save for an occasional veiled reference, like 20.29ff), and its silence is not accidental. One of the author's purposes was to persuade his Roman readers that Christianity was morally admirable and politically innocent (18.14f; 23.29; 25.25; 26.31). Therefore the libertinism, usually scandalous and occasionally criminal, was concealed. Consequently scholars have neglected it, and have treated the references to it in the NT as references to particular abuses in practice or corruptions in doctrine peculiar to the single church in connection with which they are mentioned. Admittedly, as Köster has remarked (*Häretiker*, sec. 3 end), it is not safe to suppose that every warning against moral turpitude implies the existence of a libertine sect. Sin occurs also in the most legalistic communities, as Meleager of Gadara happily

observed: ἔστι καὶ ἐν ψυχροῖς σάββασι θερμὸς "Ερως (*Anthologia Palatina* V.160.4). Nevertheless, the arguments of Jude or I Cor. cannot be explained by individual offenses unconnected with theological theory. And the existence of clear cases of theoretical libertinism requires that other cases be examined for their relevance. Accordingly, we now turn to these.

3. DIRECT EVIDENCE OF LIBERTINISM

Here is a list of the passages in which polemic against libertinism is fairly clear:

Mt. 5.19. Those who *teach* others to break the commandments, and are therefore the least *in* the kingdom, are evidently libertine teachers. This indicates the interpretation of 5.11,13,17ff, etc., and also of Matthew's additions of δικαιοσύνη to Q sayings like Mt. 5.6 and 6.33—to say nothing of the emphasis on the need for good works which runs throughout the sermon on the mount.

Mt. 7.15–27. These teachers pretend to observe the law, but their secret teaching is contrary to it. They are false prophets and are conspicuous for their magical powers, displayed in prophecies, exorcisms, and miracles done "in Jesus' name" (cf. Col. 3.17), but they are also ἐργαζόμενοι τὴν ἀνομίαν.

Mk. 9.42. Whoever scandalizes one of the "little ones" among the believers would be better off dead. Cf. I Cor. 8.9–12. This may indicate for whom the editor intended the warnings of Mk. 9.43ff.

Lk. 7.36–50. This has been edited. From the premise "he who is forgiven more will love more," the conclusion to be drawn is that the greatest sinners (who have most to be forgiven) are capable of the greatest love. This Luke has replaced by less dangerous doctrine. He has similarly edited the saying "I came not to call the righteous, but sinners" by adding "to repentance" (5.32 ‖ Mk. 2.17b; Mt. 9.13). However, he preserves a lot of peculiar material which suggests that the kingdom is primarily for sinners (15.8ff, the lost coin; 15.12ff, the prodigal son; 16.1ff, the unjust steward). This looks like a source. It had some material in common with Q (15.4ff, the lost sheep ‖ Mt. 18.12f; 15.10, joy in heaven over one repentant sinner ‖ Mt. 18.13—here again Luke has edited: Mt. has *more* joy over one repentant sinner *than over ninety-nine righteous*.) This material is not necessarily libertine (cf. *Barnabas* 5.9), but is patient of libertine interpretation; and Luke's care to specify that the sinners were to be called "to repentance" is evidence that such interpretation troubled him.

Acts 20.29f. Paul's *ex eventu* prophecy to the Ephesians of the wolves among the sheep attacks teachers of "twisted things" and is interesting because it is related both to Mt. 7.15ff (*supra*) and to II Thess., where, as here, Paul is attacking men who live on the congregations and refuse to work (II Thess. 3.6ff). These men should probably be connected with the belief that "the day of the Lord is already here" (II Thess. 2.1f). This belief was being foisted on Paul by epistles forged in his name (*ibid.*).

Further references to the same theme appear in II Tim. 2.16ff and perhaps II Peter 3.3f; see below. This may also have been the belief of those in Corinth who denied the resurrection and, it seems, claimed to have received salvation "in this life" (I Cor. 15.19); they, too, were a libertine group (15.32–34). See also below, on Apoc. 2.

Rom. 3.8. "Let us do evil that good may come" looks from the context as if it were said by libertines who claimed that Paul's teaching agreed with theirs; cf. also Rom. 6.1,15–23. Another quotation may be 8.1. In 8.12 the notion that we are not debtors to the flesh appears suddenly and without relevance to what has preceded. Who said we were debtors to the flesh, that Paul should deny it? Mt. 5.25f ‖ Lk. 12.58f ("agree with your creditor quickly") was understood by unnamed teachers, whom Clement opposed, to refer to the body (II.290.10ff); the Carpocratians understood it to refer to the demonic ruler of this world, the creator of the body (Irenaeus: Harvey, I.20.2 = Stieren, I.25.4; cf. Tertullian, *De anima* XXXV). Thus, through the first part of Romans the argument often seems to have been framed with reference to libertine arguments; this makes it plausible that the same reference may explain some of the moral counsels in the second half. (They can hardly refer to particular circumstances in the Roman church, which Paul did not know.)

I Cor. 5.2. This is unmistakable; the Corinthians were proud that incest was being practiced in their church. (This anticipates the accusations against Christians reported by the apologists of the next century.) 6.9f, "do not be deceived," indicates the existence of an opposed teaching; and 6.12, "all things are permissible," is probably one of its premises—one Paul is not prepared to deny but attempts to "explain." Another premise, that knowledge (of what?) has freed the initiates from the Law, appears through 8.1ff. Cf. Jn. 8.32: You shall know the truth and the truth shall make you free. Paul finds it necessary, in 9.1, to remind the Corinthians of his own freedom, presumably to equal the claims of his opponents. 10.1ff proves that they based their claims on the supposed effect of baptism and communion— no doubt because these rites gave them the spirit, and the spirit had the knowledge (I Cor. 2.6ff)—but also probably because baptism included resurrection. Hence their denial of a future resurrection (15.12), claim of salvation already in this life (15.19), and consequent libertinism (15.32–34); cf. above, on Acts 20.29f, and below, on Apoc. 2.

Gal. 5.13ff. Here it appears that Paul was aware of the libertine interpretation as a danger to which his doctrine laid itself open. This awareness was probably the result of experience, which probably continued and got worse, see above, on Rom. 3.8. That libertinism was an immediate danger to the Galatians is not suggested.

Phil. 3.18f. "The enemies of the cross of the Messiah, whose end is destruction, whose god is the belly and whose glory is in their shame" are probably libertines. Since verse 17 seems to take up a new subject, they are not to be identified with the κατατομή of verses 2–16, that is, those who teach that the observance of the Law is still necessary. "Enemies of the cross" probably refers to docetism (cf. Jn.

259

19.17); "whose god is their belly" may refer to magical practices (cf. ἐγγαστρίμυθος) and "whose glory is in their shame" to their pride in shameful actions as signs of liberty (cf. I Cor. 5.2, above). Paul's explanation in the preceding section (3.12), οὐχ ὅτι ἤδη ἔλαβον ἢ ἤδη τετελείωμαι, may be an anticipation, in arguing against the legalists, of the dangers of the libertine interpretation (cf. Gal. 5.13).

II Thess. 3.6ff. See above, on Acts 20.29f.

Eph. 5.1–20. This attacks specific opponents. It is shameful even to say what they do in secret (verse 12); they try to deceive the Ephesians and to persuade them that sexual license is not incompatible with the kingdom of God (verses 5f); they practice "fruitless works of darkness" (verse 11, nocturnal ceremonies?) in which the Ephesians should not participate, since they have been raised from the dead (in baptism) to participate in light (11–14). The specific reference is also proved by comparison with the generalizing morality of Col. 3.5–17, which the author of Eph. was reworking.

I Tim. 1.19f. Hymenaeus and Alexander, by rejecting conscience, made shipwreck of their faith; consequently (pseudo) Paul gave them over to Satan that they might be taught not to blaspheme. This is presumably directed against their followers, whom it taunts with some of their teachers' misfortunes believed to have been caused by Paul's magic. "Rejecting conscience" is a vague charge, and the rest of the letter seems to be directed against legalists (1.7ff; 4.1ff); so this passage would hardly belong in the present list were there not a likelihood that the Hymenaeus here is to be identified with the Hymenaeus in II Tim. 2.16, below. (6.3ff and 6.20f are of uncertain reference; all Christians claimed knowledge and most wanted to get rich.)

II Tim. 2.16–4.4. Hymenaeus and Philetus said the resurrection had already taken place (probably magically, in baptism) and therefore did not abstain from unrighteousness (verse 18). Their teachings probably provided opportunities for the indulgence of youthful desires (22) and for idle controversies (23). They have been caught in the snare of the devil and are doing his will (26). They are apparently examples of a much larger class whose members have all the vices (3.2ff) and are particularly successful in their libertine mission with women, to whom they promise secret knowledge (3.6f). They are magicians, like Iannes and Iambres (3.8,13), and teach myths (4.4). The teaching that the resurrection has already taken place links these men to the group(s?) attacked in II Thess. 3.6ff. Acts 20.29, etc.; see above.

James 2.14ff. The argument here is against someone who claims to have faith but does not have good works (14) and evidently thinks good works unnecessary for salvation. Cf. 3.13–18 ‖ Mt. 7.21 (above). The opponent may be Paul, but there is so much evidence for libertine teaching that the identification is dubious.

I Peter 2.11–16. This is mere moral exhortation, not directed against anybody. But the final warning, that Christian liberty should not be made a cloak for wrongdoing, shows that the author was aware of libertinism, though he did not consider it a real and present danger to the group for which he was writing.

II Peter 1.5–11. The insistence that one must have virtue as well as faith, and conti-
nence as well as gnosis, is probably aimed at some libertine teacher (attacked in
verse 9) and is backed up by the promise that virtue will be rewarded by frequent
ecstatic experiences (entries to the kingdom, 11).

II Peter 2–3 and Jude. This tract was evidently popular with the victorious party,
since two versions were canonized. The popularity indicates that there was considerable need for it—hence that the libertine wing of Christianity was strong and
widespread. The "false prophets" of II Pet. 2.1 recall Mt. 7.15ff. The denial of
Jesus may be docetism (cf. Phil. 3.18; I Jn. 2.22f). The ἀσέλγεια (2) is the hallmark
common to most passages. That the libertines give Christianity a bad reputation anticipates the excuses of the second-century apologists. Their contempt for the cosmic
powers (10ff ‖ Jude 8ff) is a new and surprising charge; it suggests that the tract may
originally have come from a semilegalist teacher like the one attacked in Col. 2.16.
So does the *haggadah* (fallen angels, Noah, Sodom, Lot, Michael and the body of
Moses, Cain, Balaam, Enoch. The Balaam theme has recently been linked with
an early Syrian center of Christianity with which Stephen's speech declaring the
abolition of the law, Mt., Simon Magus, and the Nicolaïtans of Acts may also have
been connected: Daniélou, *Etoile* 133–136). What the libertines understood physically,
to their consequent corruption, may have been sayings about the freedom in the
kingdom. Agreement between II Peter and Jude ends with the statement that their
opponents are mockers intent on their own desires (II Pet. 3.3; Jude 18). To this
Jude adds that they are ψυχικοί, πνεῦμα μὴ ἔχοντες; II Peter, that they deny the
second coming; the latter may be a different form of the claim that "the day of
the Lord is already here"; cf. above, on Acts 20.29.

I Jn. 1.6,8. 1.6 might be ordinary morality; but 1.8, the claim to be sinless, must
come from a liar, a fool, or a theologian. The author opted for the first and second
of these possibilities, but the third is not thereby excluded. We may suppose that
perfectionist, libertine theology was one of the writer's targets. Confirmation for
the supposition can be found in 1.10; 2.4,18f (they are antichrists), 22f (also docetists,
see above; Phil. 3.18; II Pet. 2.1; Jude 4); 3.7–10 (they commit sinful actions);
4.1ff (they are false prophets, cf. II Pet. 2.1, Mt. 7.15ff); 4.5 (they have considerable
success in their missionary work). More of the same appears in II Jn. 7.

Apoc. 2.6,14f,20ff. Nicolaïtans are established in Pergamum, hated in Ephesus;
they have irregular sexual practices and eat things sacrificed to idols, thus following
the teaching of Balaam (see above on II Pet. and Jude). In Thyatira there is a woman
whom the author calls Jezebel, who calls herself a prophetess and teaches the same
practices. She has been at it for some time and has not taken the opportunity to
repent. Her followers claim to know "the deep things of Satan" (or perhaps simply
"the deep things," if "of Satan" be the author's comment). The complaint about
eating things offered to idols suggests that these letters, like the tract behind II Pet.
and Jude, come from a comparatively legalistic circle.

The above list has been limited to passages of which the purport is reasonably
clear. Both discussion of disputed details and bibliographical data have been excluded,

since the most important thing in this evidence is the cumulative force. (For a recent bibliography see Köster, *ΓΝΩΜΑΙ* 283 n8, and for the variety and importance of different trends in the early churches see the whole article.) The passages listed above show that libertine Christianity was widespread and ancient. It is attested in Ephesus, Corinth, Thessalonica, Pergamum, and Thyatira, and must have been important in Syria, too (Mt., the tract used by II Pet. and Jude). The connection of the Nico-laïtans of the Apocalypse with the Nicholas of Acts 6.5 is suggested by what is said in Clement (II.207.18ff) and asserted by Irenaeus (Harvey, I.23 = Stieren, I.26.3); it involves no improbability. Hippolytus, *De resurrectione* (*Werke, GCS* vol. 1.II, p. 251), says the basis of Nicolas' libertinism was the belief that resurrection occurs in baptism (a belief Hippolytus does not contest). This looks like correct information; cf. above, on Acts 20.29f; I Cor. 15; II Pet. 2–3. The Nicholas of Acts 6.5 was one of the deacons appointed to appease the Hellenists; and some scholars have supposed that the Hellenists, if a libertine or laxist group, stood closer to Jesus' teachings than did the Hebrews (Conzelmann, *Apostelgeschichte* 43; cf. the remarks on Jesus by Gärtner, *Temple* 120ff). The connection of libertinism with docetism cannot be used to prove the former late; the connection may be secondary. Moreover, the hymn quoted by Paul in Phil. 2.6ff is probably docetic in supposing that Jesus' resumption of humanity after his ascension was in appearance only—*pace* Käsemann, *Analyse* 340—and the Enoch tradition is certainly so in the *Ascension of Isaiah*, which is probably first century. Finally, whatever may be thought of such arguments, the fact remains that the libertine tradition is attacked by Mt., Mk., Lk., Acts, Paul (in five letters), Ephesians, I and II Tim., James, I and II Pet., I and II Jn., Jude, and Apoc.

4. SOURCE AND DISPERSION OF THE LIBERTINE TRADITION

The fact that the libertine tradition was so early so widespread is evidence that it derives from Jesus' baptismal practice. To try to explain all of it as resultant from misunderstanding of Paul is implausible. Paul protests that his name and his sayings are being misused by the libertines (above on Acts 20.29, Rom. 3.8). He complains not of misunderstanding, but of deliberate misrepresentation, and he does not write as if the persons concerned were his former disciples. But if the misinterpretation was deliberate it was probably in the interest of some already existing position. (Paul was also misrepresented, by the opposite side, as preaching circumcision, Gal. 5.11.) Moreover, there is another figure to whom all the early and widespread branches of the libertine tradition can plausibly be traced, since attacks on his liber-tine teaching and practice are prominent in the reports of his work. He broke the sabbath, he neglected the purity rules, he refused to fast, made friends with publicans and sinners, and was known as a gluttonous man and a winebibber. He not only taught his disciples that the law had come to an end with the Baptist and that the least of those in the kingdom was greater than the Baptist, but he also administered a baptism—"the mystery of the kingdom of God"—by which he enabled some of his disciples, by union with himself, to enter the kingdom and to enjoy his own freedom from the law.

Therefore, in our picture of pre-Pauline Christianity, alongside the legalistic interpretation of the religion we must set the libertine. The legalistic interpretation went back to the (principally Pharisaic?) converts of the Jerusalem church, and appealed to the tradition of Jesus' exoteric teaching. The libertine interpretation went back to Jesus himself and preserved elements of his esoteric teaching. It was dominant in the Jerusalem church in the earliest days, but lost its hold as the small group of Jesus' original, initiated disciples was outnumbered by the new converts under the leadership of Jesus' brother James. We see the leader of the old disciples —Peter—challenged by the legalists in Acts 11; he disappears from the city in Acts 12; in Acts 15 is he back again—but is Acts 15 historical? Anyhow, James presides at the meeting. In Acts 21 only James remains. When Paul visits the city he is persuaded to make a public pretense of keeping the law. Paul, by virtue of his donations, was doubtless a highly valued member of the Church, moreover he could recall and might report the traditions of the original apostles, so James was willing to make adjustments—for Paul. As for his general policy, however, the mere appearance of his representatives in Antioch was enough to frighten Peter out of eating with gentiles (Gal. 2.12). At least in Jerusalem the libertine tradition would be a secret doctrine.

D. The "loss" of all writings of Jesus' immediate followers

This leads to a fourth consequence of Jesus' baptismal practice, this time an indirect consequence: the "loss" of all writings from Jesus and his immediate disciples. That they were all illiterate is improbable. They founded a sect and the survival of the sect makes the disappearance of all works of its founders a noteworthy problem (Brandon, *Fall* 9f). Having seen how Jesus' immediate disciples disappeared from the Jerusalem church, we may suppose that their writings went with them. The libertine consequences of Jesus' baptismal practice probably helped James and his party to get rid of both the apostles and their writings.

James's works, if any, have also disappeared and we have nothing from the legalist Jerusalem church of A.D. 40–66, but these facts are largely explained by the great revolts of 66–73 and 132–135 in Palestine and of 115–117 in Egypt, Cyrene, Cyprus, Syria, and Mesopotamia, which must have ruined most of legalistic Christianity (so Brandon, *Fall*). Asia Minor was the only area in the Near East where a large Jewish population survived relatively undisturbed, and Asia Minor had been the scene of Paul's most successful work. This probably was a major cause of the predominance of Pauline material both in the NT canon and in the entire corpus of early Christian material.

However, besides this external cause it is plausible to attribute the success of Pauline Christianity to its practical nature. In the conflict between the libertine and the legalist interpretations, Paul represents the safe and sane and socially acceptable compromise. He accepts the realized eschatology of the libertines (Rom. 14.17; Col. 1.13) but rejects those who make it an excuse for refusing to work (II Thess.

2.1ff, 3.6ff). He also accepts the expectant eschatology congenial to the legal inter-pretation (I Thess. 5.1ff; II Thess. 1; etc.) but he tacitly drops the nationalistic and political side of it which were to involve the legalists in the military disasters of the rest of Judaism (Brandon, *Fall* 167ff, esp. 180). He also rejects the revolutionary implications of Christianity in the political and social fields. Jesus' record on taxes is equivocal, at best (above, p. 249); Paul is explicit: they are to be paid (Rom. 13.6). Subjection to the existing political authorities is not only a wise policy, but a moral obligation (Rom. 13.5). Wives, obey your husbands; slaves, your masters (Col. 3.18,22). In matters of personal morality he reverences the Mosaic Law (which had immense prestige)—it is holy, just, and spiritual (Rom. 7.12,14)—but he rejects the observance of it and especially of circumcision and the food laws, which did so much to hinder the growth of Judaism and to isolate the Jews as a peculiar people—a dangerous social position. Rejection of the rules of the law leaves him free, and the claim of freedom was highly valued in a world much influenced by the Stoics and the Cynics. But Paul's liberty is guided by the spirit, and by common sense (I Cor. 11.14, "nature itself"); and the spirit (very much like common sense), teaches industry, thrift, obedience, good citizenship, moral propriety, and all those other requirements which must be observed if the individual is to succeed in society, or if a small society—in this case, a local church—is to succeed in the larger world. What early Christianity was like in the areas from which no material has been preserved can be inferred from the things Paul opposed in his letters, and this explains why no material was preserved.

E.   *Second-century silence about Paul's doctrine of baptism*

Finally, we may consider as a more remote consequence of Jesus' baptismal practice the disappearance of the baptismal teaching of Paul himself from the works of the second-century Christian writers of the party ultimately triumphant ("ortho-dox"). As Benoit, *Baptême*, shows, the *orthodox* references to baptism throughout this period consistently stress the remission of actual sin*s* (not original sin), and the gift of the spirit as an earnest of future life (not a present spiritual power and source of moral behavior, but a vague deposit to be protected by moral behavior). Notions of new birth, illumination, and exorcism occur but are comparatively unimportant. The essential Pauline theme of death and resurrection with Christ is totally absent. Benoit insists (p. 228) that this is not due to misunderstanding of Paul; there are no reminiscences of his works. Hence Benoit concludes that orthodox second-century Christianity came largely from non-Pauline sources, and he inclines to agree with Bauer (*Rechtgläubigkeit* 221, 227, 230) that Paul was most venerated in heretical circles (p. 229).

But this will not do, because most of the evidence for the early history of Chris-tianity is connected with Asia Minor: *Lk.-Acts*, Jn., and the Johannine epistles, *the Pauline epistles, the pseudo-Pauline epistles* (including *Hebrews*), *I Peter*, James, the Apocalypse, *the Ignatian epistles, Polycarp*, Papias, the epistle of Pliny, the *Martyrdom*

of Polycarp, Marcion, Justin's Dialogue (laid in Ephesus), Melito, Polycrates, *Avircius Marcellus and his anti-Montanist correspondent* (Eus., *HE* V.16f), *the presbyters of Irenaeus, Irenaeus* himself—all are examples which immediately come to mind, and the list could be extended. All of the writers and works italicized in this list show clear Pauline influence. More than that, the predominance of this material in the corpus of early Christian evidence and the predominance of Pauline material in the NT are mutually confirmatory evidence. As remarked above, the NT is a product of selection—it shows which, of the many first-century Christian documents, the party that became predominant in the late second century chose to keep. So, to a lesser degree, is and does the remainder of the preserved corpus of early Christian material (Goguel, review of Bauer 164). The material chosen by the triumphant party was predominantly Pauline.

Consequently the disappearance of Paul's theology of baptism from second-century Christianity cannot be explained as Benoit proposes—by ignorance. It must have been deliberate. But if Paul represented safe, sane, and successful Christianity, and if it is for this reason that the Pauline tradition dominates the canon of the NT and the corpus of early Christian literature, why did second-century Christianity drop his doctrine of baptism?

The answer, I think, must be sought along the lines indicated above. Paul's doctrine had been a safe compromise by comparison with the competing extremes of his day, but for baptism he had substantially preserved the teaching of Jesus; and as the potentialities of this teaching became apparent, it also became apparent that Paul had not been safe enough. (A similar explanation has now—1965—been given by Barrett, *Things Sacrificed*.) The Jewish revolts had ruined forever the legalistic interpretation of Christianity, but the libertine interpretation was flourishing and it found in Paul's doctrine of baptism everything needed to justify its inclinations: identification with Jesus, possession by his spirit, ascent to the heavens in his ascension, and consequent liberation from the law. Accordingly, the gnostic teachers, who now emerged from the libertine tradition, made great use of Paul (Harnack, *Quellenkritik* 27, 29, etc.); and Grant, *Gnosticism* 149, finds it difficult to decide whether his teaching "is more adequately reinterpreted by these gnostic teachers, or by such second-century 'orthodox' teachers as the apologists and Irenaeus." Buri, *Clemens*, has shown in detail how drastically Paul's concept of freedom was remodeled by the orthodox in the interests of social acceptability. The process can be seen in its simplest form in Acts, where Paul's career is reported, his theology omitted. That the letters had been esoteric documents to begin with made matters easier.

XII.   CONCLUSION: THE HISTORICAL VALUE OF THE NEW TEXT

It has now been argued that the interpretation of "the mystery of the kingdom of God" as a baptism with Jesus' spirit, effecting entrance of the kingdom, will

explain (A) the coming of the spirit in the early churches; (B) their adoption and development of baptism; (C) the primitive and widespread libertine tradition within Christianity and the consequent persecution of the early churches, as well as their internal political struggles; (D) the "loss" of all writings of Jesus' immediate followers; and (E) the abandonment of Paul's doctrine of baptism by the predominantly Pauline "orthodox" churches of the second century. In the course of the argument it has become evident that this interpretation would also explain the extent and importance of secret doctrine in the early churches, and would indicate the content of the most important secrets. Will the reader please offer another explanation for all these problems?

While awaiting another explanation, we shall consider the history of Christianity, in the first and second centuries, as a vector of the conflict between the libertine tradition and its opponents—in the first period the legalists in Jerusalem and Paul in the Aegean area; later the developing institutionalism of the established churches and the ascetic movement probably to be explained by influence from Greek philosophy. The situation in the later period has been given classic description by Bauer, *Rechtgläubigkeit*. The state of affairs he discovers in the early second century is inexplicable unless we suppose a massive libertine development in the first century; and such a development at so early a date must be taken as indicative of something in the origins of the movement.

It is against this background that the problem of the origin of the Gospels must be seen; and against this background the new text would seem to be of the highest historical value.

XIII. CARPOCRATES

Of the several parties in this background, the libertine has been the least studied. The Carpocratian sect was one of its most extreme representatives, and is directly involved in the history of the longer text of Mk. Therefore it seems worthwhile to review here the evidence concerning the Carpocratians. The texts are collected in Appendix B.

A. *Names*

Καρποκράτης with K is an extremely rare name, but a woman, Καρποκρ[άτη(?)], appears in *P.Oxy.* 1473 line 24 (A.D. 201), and Κα[ρποκρά]της as the name of the deity appears in the hymn to Isis, on Ios (3 c. B.C., *SIG* 1267). Ἁρποκράτης or Ἁρποχράτης with the rough breathing is somewhat commoner (*P. Teb.* I, no. 83; Viereck, *Ostraka* no. 365; etc.). Epiphanes as a personal name is not uncommon (*P. Erlangen*, no. 60 line 9; *SEG* XIV.685.3; *P. Teb.* III.1.811 line 23; etc.).

B. *Date*

As to the date of Carpocrates we have three types of evidence. First, explicit statements: Eus. (*HE* IV.7.9) says Irenaeus said Carpocrates was a contemporary of Saturninus and Basilides. Irenaeus does not say so in his preserved works, and the probability is that Eusebius was arguing from the fact that in Irenaeus' account of heretics Carpocrates immediately follows Saturninus and Basilides (so Usener, *Weihnachtsfest* 116). But Irenaeus did not treat the heretics in chronological order: for example, he puts Cerinthus after Carpocrates and Carpocrates after Basilides, although he himself tells of Polycarp's report of a near-encounter between Cerinthus and John the apostle (Harvey, III.3.4 = Stieren, III.3.4) whereas Basilides, commonly placed in the third generation of Simon Magus' line, probably flourished in the time of Hadrian (117–138—Clement III.75.13ff). Theodoret (*Compendium* I.5 end) says flatly that Carpocrates and Epiphanes flourished in the reign of Hadrian; he may have derived this information by inference from Eusebius, or he may have had some other source. Michael Syrus dates Carpocrates in the time of Bar Kosibah and "the prince Antinoüs," Hadrian's favorite, but Michael was certainly using Eusebius.

In the second place there are statements about the history of the sect. The often repeated statements that Cerinthus was Carpocrates' successor or that Carpocrates followed Basilides merely reflect the order of names in Iranaeus (or his source), which, as we have seen, is not chronological. Epiphanius declares that Epiphanes, Carpocrates' son, who died at the age of 17 or 18, joined the sect of Secundus, the disciple of Valentinus. But Epiphanius is an extremely unreliable writer, and in this instance his statement is probably based on a misunderstanding of Irenaeus' reference to an ἐπιφανὴς διδάσκαλος of the Valentinians. (So Holl in *GCS* on Epiphanius, *Panarion* XXXII.3, referring to Irenaeus—Harvey, I.5.2 = Stieren, I.11.3.) Far more important is Irenaeus' statement that Marcellina, a member of Carpocrates' sect, came to Rome under Anicetus (ca. 150–165) and had great success there (Harvey, I.20.4 = Stieren, I.25.6). The branch of the sect which followed Marcellina differed so greatly from the original that Celsus, about 175, thought them different sects (Origen, *Contra Celsum* V.62). Accordingly, a date for Carpocrates no later than the generation preceding Marcellina (i.e., ca. 125) is indicated. (Praedestinatus' statement that the apostle Barnabas condemned the Carpocratians in Cyprus is probably worthless as evidence of an early date.)

Finally, there is the evidence from the lists of heretics. A conspectus of the older lists is given at the beginning of Appendix B, where the different symbols, marking the different groups of heretics which commonly are listed together and in the same order, show clearly the sources (whether documents or oral traditions is immaterial) from the which present lists have been put together. The core was a list of Simon Magus and his successors: Menander, Basilides, Satornilus. This is understandable: at the beginning, as Justin makes clear, Simon had been the great competitor (*First Apology* 56). Next comes a group composed of Carpocrates (with or without Marcellina), Cerinthus, and Ebion. (To this Epiphanius adds some Jewish-Christian

heresies.) Around these two central groups (Simonians and Carpocratians) different groups have been added in different places by different writers. The group of Samaritan and Jewish heresies, when added, is of course put first; but it is certainly an accretion, absent from Justin, Celsus, Irenaeus, and Hippolytus. The Valentinian group is also secondary, as shown by the variation of its position. It was added in front of the Simonians by Irenaeus and Hippolytus, for whom Valentinus was the major, present competitor, but was moved behind the Carpocratian group by pseudo-Tertullian, Epiphanius, and Filastrius, who wrote when the Valentinian peril was past. The Ophites and their ilk are added sometimes at the end (Irenaeus), sometimes at the beginning (Hippolytus, Filastrius), sometimes at one or another place in the middle (pseudo-Tertullian, Epiphanius). Finally, the schools associated with Marcion and Tatian are always placed at or near the end, in accord with the general opinion as to their relative date.

The surprising thing about these lists, for our purposes, is not only the early date they indicate for Carpocrates, but also their persistent classification of him with the Jewish-Christian sects of Cerinthus (on whom Dionysius of Alexandria, in Eus., *HE* VII.25) and the Ebionites. This is odd, since the Platonic traits in Carpocratianism have often been remarked—recently, e.g., by Festugière, *Révélation* III.25—and were noticed as early as Irenaeus (Harvey, II.50f = Stieren II.33f) and Clement (II.200.16ff). A further peculiarity is the fact that this tradition puts Carpocrates at the head of the Jewish-Christian group, although Cerinthus and the Ebionites were presumably earlier. We must look for explanations of these facts, and shall do so by examining in sequence the testimonia collected in Appendix B—with first a word about Jude and II Pet.

C. *Testimonia*

Clement (II.200.24ff) says that Jude in his epistle "spoke prophetically" of the Carpocratians and similar heretics; and in the letter, I.3–6, he identifies the erring stars of Jude 13 as Carpocratians and says they claim to know the deep things of Satan—a claim which in Apoc. 2.24 is attributed to the followers of Jezebel of Thyatira. Its transference to the Carpocratians is rhetorical. What justification there was for the rhetoric is unknown. The notion that Jude refers to the sect may be correct. Does II Pet. also refer to them and was the reference intended by the common source of Jude and II Pet.? These questions are insoluble, therefore the details in Jude and II Pet. cannot safely be used as evidence of Carpocratian teaching although they may be so. But in order to explain Clement's interpretation, we must suppose the general picture given by Jude bore some similarity to Carpocratianism; this is important since the source of Jude and II Pet. may have had connections with early Syrian Christianity.

Now for the texts printed in Appendix B:

Heracleon (ca. A.D. 160) quoted by Clement in *Eclogae propheticae* 25.1 (III.143.22ff) spoke of certain Christians who branded their ears and who justified the practice

by allegorization of Lk. 3.17 ‖ Mt. 3.12. That he referred to the Carpocratians is not certain, but it is made likely by the context of the following reference in Celsus.

Celsus' report (ca. 175) must be disentangled from the comments of Origen, who pretends (*Contra Celsum* V.64) that only by misunderstanding I Tim. 4.1–3, ἐν ὑστέροις καιροῖς ἀποστήσονταί τινες τῆς πίστεως, προσέχοντες πνεύμασι πλάνοις καὶ διδασκαλίαις δαιμονίων, ἐν ὑποκρίσει ψευδολόγων, κεκαυστηριασμένων τὴν οἰκείαν συνείδησιν, κωλυόντων γαμεῖν, ἀπέχεσθαι βρωμάτων, and also misunderstanding those who used these apostolic words against heretics, could Celsus have been led to believe that some Christians would call others such horrid things as Κίρκας . . . κύκηθρα αἱμύλα . . . ἀκοῆς καυστήρια . . . αἰνίγματα . . . Σειρῆνας ἐξορχουμένας . . . σοφιστρίας, κατασφραγιζομένας τὰ ὦτα, καὶ ἀποσυοκεφαλούσας τοὺς πειθομένους.

Here Origen is misrepresenting Christian party polemics. There is no reason to doubt that Celsus got these phrases from a Christian tract which must have antedated his work. Heretics are compared to sirens by Hippolytus, *Philosophumena* VII.13. The reference to branding the ears, together with libertinism (Circes . . . making pigs of their followers), suggests that the polemic was directed against the Carpocratians. Branding is reported of *some* branches of the sect by Irenaeus (Harvey I.20.4 = Stieren I.25.6); and became notorious. Besides the numerous references in the later testimonia, see Minucius Felix 9: *Eruenda prorsus haec et exsecranda consensio. Occultis se notis et insignibus noscunt et amant mutuo, paene antequam noverint; passim inter eos velut quaedam libidinum religio miscetur, ac se promisce appellant fratres et sorores, ut etiam non insolens stuprum intercessione sacri nominis fiat incestum.* On the other hand, it is unlikely that I Tim. 4.1ff refers to the Carpocratians, since, as the context shows, the opponents observe food taboos. The "branding of their consciences" is probably a sneer at some initiatory branding; if so the practice was not limited to the Carpocratians. Dölger, *Sphragis* 77f, found evidence suggesting similar practice, in later sects, interpreted as a baptism of fire (to fulfill Mt. 3.11, Lk. 3.16, contrast Heracleon). Dölger thought this a second baptism (*ibid.,* 75ff). Jerome, *Luciferianos* 23 end, would then be mistaken—not an unlikely supposition: in the same sentence he mistook Ebion for a personal name: see Vallarsi's pathetic note, *ad loc.*

On the other hand, Dölger was probably mistaken in supposing the rite came from the Greek world; he overlooked the OT provision for piercing the ear of a slave as a sign of perpetual servitude (Dt. 15.16f)—in this instance of Christ—because he loves his master and finds life good *in his master's house.* This practice was still in force in rabbinic times (*T. Baba' Kama'* VII.5; *Sifré Devarim* 121; etc.). Moreover, Bousset, *Antichrist* 25 and 200ff, has shown that the expectation of sealing is probably part of the pre-Christian apocalyptic tradition, cf. the rabbinic tradition that Jesus (? = בן סטדא) came back from Egypt with magical names or signs tattooed on his skin (*J. Shabbat* XII.4(13d), *B. Shabbat* 104b). Such marking of the body as part of initiation into societies of magicians is probably prehistoric.

Origen's quotation from Celsus gives a list of the sects to which Celsus referred ca. 175 to prove the varieties and self-contradictions of Christianity—no doubt the sects best known in his environment. Origen says he called "the Church" (*sc.*

Origen's party) οἱ ἀπὸ τοῦ πλήθους; these are they who say their god is the same as the god of the Jews (V.61). Besides these there are some unnamed dualists, then the Valentinians, Gnostics, Ebionites, Sibyllists, Simonians from Helen, Marcellians from Marcellina, Harpocratians from Salome, others from Mariamme (Ophites: Hippolytus, *Philosophumena* V.7.1; X.9.3), others from Martha, and finally the Marcionites. Notice the number of libertine sects (Gnostics, Simonians, Marcellians, Harpocratians, Ophites, and possibly others), the number "from" women, and the importance of the Carpocratians, who account for two of the eleven. The importance of women in the practice of magic appears already in *Enoch* 7.1ff: it was to women that the fallen angels first taught the black arts. In rabbinic literature it is a commonplace: even the purest of women practices magic (*J. Kiddushin* IV.11 [66c end]); a woman being punished in public is automatically supposed to have practiced magic or committed adultery (*Sifré Devarim* 26 ‖ *Wayyikra' Rabbah* 31.4); see further *B. Berakot* 53a end; *B. 'Erubin* 64b end; *Sotah* IX.13; etc. Hence the importance of women in libertine Christianity and in the circle of Jesus' disciples (Lk. 8.1ff, etc.; above, commentary on II.23) is probably significant. Salome, in particular, indicates some connection between the Carpocratians and the Gospels of Mark, *Thomas*, and *the Egyptians* (see above, pp. 189ff).

Origen's statement that he has never met any of "these" is of uncertain reference —and veracity. However, the libertine wing of Christianity does seem to have diminished sharply in the early third century, perhaps because of police action. In Celsus' comparison with the worshipers of Antinoüs, where does the similarity stop and the polemic begin? The main point of similarity is immoral behavior; this fits later Christian reports of the Carpocratians; so do the repeated references to ear-marking in Celsus' source. τοὺς παραχαράττοντας τὰ Χριστιανισμοῦ, if it came from Celsus' source, may be echoed in the letter of Clement I.14, but is too common to prove relationship.

Hegesippus, ca. 180, in Eus. *HE* IV.22.4ff, derives *all* Christian heresies from Samaritan and Jewish-Christian sects, and therefore is not a strong witness for this derivation. The order agrees with Justin's (*Dialogue* 35.6) save for the presence of the Carpocratians; unfortunately, it is probably not chronological.

Irenaeus, ca. 185, provides the only account of Carpocratian theology which can pretend to reliability. Clement's reports are mostly limited to questions of ethics, and the later writers have little, if any, independent knowledge of the sect. The theology described by Irenaeus has many apparently Platonic traits: the creation of the world by inferior beings, salvation for the pure soul able to remember what it saw when moving in the celestial sphere, transmigration as a penalty for souls which have not attained perfection. It also uses the Stoic notion that physical actions are indifferent by nature, good or bad only by opinion.

But in the first place, some of the apparently Platonic traits may not have come from Platonism. For instance, the creation of the world by inferior beings may be one consequence of that awareness of the importance of intermediaries which appears

in every field of thought during the imperial period and is probably a reflection of the imperial administration: it appears where Platonism does not—for instance, in Paul's notion that God gave the law through intermediaries (Gal. 3.19).

In the second place, the Platonic traits are superficial and explanatory; beneath them is the structure found in Col. 2.8–3.4, and in the Typhon initiation quoted above, on page 221: the soul's escape from the rulers of this world by union with a spirit which gives it magical powers (and, in Col. and Carpocrates, enables it to ascend into the heavens). Platonism helped make this sort of thought respectable, but the practice was magical and, in Carpocrates' case, Christian. That libertine Christianity was Platonized in Alexandria is understandable; the Platonic and Stoic traits in the system of Carpocrates are no more proof of Platonic or Stoic origin than are those in the systems of Clement and Philo.

Turning to details: the report that Jesus was begotten by Joseph shows the Carpocratians holding to an early tradition the majority abandoned.[20] Hilgenfeld, *Evangeliorum* 18 and 36, conjectures that they used Mt. with the Sinaitic Syriac reading at 1.16 (cf. Epiphanius, *Panarion* XXX.14). The report of Jesus' training and escape is given by Irenaeus from two, mutually explanatory, sources printed below in parallel columns. The words added in Greek are from Hippolytus (*Philosophumena* VII.32) who evidently read them in his text of Irenaeus though they are not in the present Latin translation. Epiphanius, *Panarion* XXVII.2.2, paraphrased the same passage of Irenaeus; his paraphrase shows that he also found these words in the text.

A	B
Jesum autem . . .	*Jesu autem animam*
distasse a reliquis ⟨hominibus⟩	
γεγονότα δικαιότερον τῶν λοιπῶν	*in Judaeorum consuetudine nutritam*
secundum id quod anima ejus firma et munda cum esset	
commemorata fuerit quae visa essent sibi . . . ingenito Deo	*contempsisse eos* (cf. the following sentence: *contemnere mundi . . . archontas*)
et propter hoc	*et propter hoc*
ab eo missam esse ei virtutem	*virtutes accepisse*
uti mundi fabricatores effugere posset	
et per omnes transgressa et in omnibus liberata	*per quas evacuavit quae fuerunt in poenas passiones*
ascenderet ad eum	

20. Another primitive element may be their denial of the physical resurrection. Richardson suggests that the diversity and disagreements of the resurrection stories in the Gospels (striking by contrast with the close agreements of the preceding passion stories) indicate that the stories of a bodily resurrection are accretions to the original preaching, which declared only, "he is alive again"—*sc.* as a life-giving spirit (Acts 25.19; I Cor. 15.45).

That Jesus was brought up and excelled in the observance of Jewish law would explain why he appears in the Gospels as a legal authority—a problem which has no other clear answer. It would fit also with Mk.'s location of the dispute stories, and Jn.'s of the cleansing of the temple, early in Jesus' career. The Platonizing explanations in text A (*anima . . . munda . . . commemorata*, etc.) tell how Jesus was enabled to see through the cosmic powers (equated in text B, as in Col. 2.16–23, with Jewish observances). The reward of this philosophic penetration is the descent of the holy spirit—the *virtus* of text A (= δύναμις, which leaves Jesus only at crucifixion, *Gospel of Peter* 19 ‖ θεός, Mk. 15.34; Χριστός, Cerinthus in Irenaeus [Harvey, I.21 end = Stieren I.26.1]; Simon Magus also was or had a δύναμις, Acts 8.10; further, Vaganay, *Evangile* 108). The spirit makes it possible for Jesus to overcome the cosmic powers (which text B now identifies with the passions) and so to ascend to God. *Per omnes transgressa et in omnibus liberata*, the means of victory, reflects the ascension theory discussed above, pages 238ff. Each cosmic sphere had its proper demonic ruler, physical element, and psychological passion. Consequently, ascent involved not only movement through space and victory over the demons, but also change in physical nature and victory over the passions. But in order to overcome a passion, one must experience it. The consequences of this belief appear in Carpocrates' theology and in that of the contemporary(?) Epistle to the Hebrews, 2.9ff and 4.14ff. (χωρὶς ἁμαρτίας, tagged to the end of verse 15 as a safeguard, suggests the author knew libertine developments of the theory and was trying to avoid them.) Another common belief was that the spirits of ἄωροι—persons who died before their time, especially before marriage—became earthbound demons subject to magicians and to the chthonic gods. Hence Carpocrates' teaching that complete experience of this life is necessary for liberation from it. The Carpocratians' support for this theory —their interpretation of Mt. 5.25 ‖ Lk. 12.58 ("agree with your creditor quickly . . .") —seems to have been current in Paul's time (above, p. 259). On the antiquity of other demonological exegeses handed down in secret tradition, see Daniélou, *Traditions* 200.

Apart from this basic structure of Carpocrates' theology, the most important things for our purpose in Irenaeus are his reference to Carpocratian texts containing secret teachings of Jesus—this accords with the report in Clement's letter—and the indirect evidence he provides for the influence of the Carpocratian sect in his environment. He says (Harvey, I.26.2 = Stieren I.28.2) that Basilides and Carpocrates provided the starting points of all the libertine sects. Again (Harvey II.48–53 = Stieren II.31–33), after explaining that his refutation of the Valentinians refutes by implication all other heretics, he deals first with elements common to the Carpocratians and other sects (creation by inferior angels, possession of supernatural powers, and ability to do miracles) and next with claims primarily Carpocratian: that one must experience everything, that they have souls from the same sphere as Jesus' soul, that Jesus did his miracles by magical delusions (φαντασιωδῶς), that souls are punished by transmigration. This extended attack on the Carpocratians shows that Irenaeus thought them the most important of the libertine sects against which he had to argue.

Clement (ca. 190) was of the same opinion. When he came, in *Stromateis* III, to deal with the libertine heresies, he took the Carpocratians first and treated them at far greater length than any of the others. Yet—and this is typical of Clement—he gives no systematic account of the Carpocratian position. He represents Epiphanes, Carpocrates' son, as the source of both "the monadic gnosis" and "the Carpocratian sect" (II.197.26ff). The letter shows that the second part of this is polemic: the sect came also from Carpocrates and had behind it the longer text of Mk. (above, p. 84). And the first part of Clement's statement is no more reliable. Chadwick has pointed out (*Alexandrian Christianity* 27) that the monadic gnosis probably had behind it "an apocryphal work ... the mother of their licentiousness" (II.209.17ff).

From Epiphanes' *On Justice* Clement quotes a considerable passage representing the physical world as the work of a just—that is, egalitarian—god, interpreting Mt. 5.45 as evidence of this, and consequently describing Ex. 20.17 ("thou shalt not covet") as "ridiculous" and the law in general as an occasion of sin because it runs counter to divinely established communism. (Here Clement saw a misunderstanding of Rom 7.7.) This might be thought to contradict Irenaeus' statement that Carpocrates said the world was made by inferior angels; but Epiphanes, being a Platonist, probably held that daimones had created the world according to a divinely given form; he could therefore speak without self-contradiction of divinely ordained patterns in the demonic creation.

Next Clement reports the orgiastic *agapai* of the Carpocratians. Jude 12 (cf. II Pet. 2.13) declares the heretics it attacks particularly active in *agapai*. Clement's report is suspiciously similar to those that contemporary pagans were spreading about all Christians (cf. Tertullian, *Apology* VII.1), but he adds that in such *agapai* they seek communion (II.200.12) and later, when discussing the libertine sects generally, he protests the use of κοινωνία μυστική for sexual connection and he lets slip ταύτην οἴονται εἰς τὴν βασιλείαν αὐτοὺς ἀνάγειν τοῦ θεοῦ (II.208.10ff; 24f), showing that the primitive functional connection of the sacraments with the kingdom persisted in the sect. (Here, by the way, we have another reference to the Carpocratians as οἱ παραχαράσσοντες τὴν ἀλήθειαν, as in the letter, I.14.)

Besides their ritual copulation in the *agapai*, Clement says, they also ask of any women they wish performance of the "divine law" (II.200.13ff), which he suggests they derived from a "misunderstanding" of Plato. But eight pages later, in a passage where the Carpocratians are not named (the same passage which contains the information about κοινωνία quoted above), the "divine law" turns out to be Jesus' saying "give to him who asketh of thee," which the wicked quote from Scripture (γέγραπται). Clement's attribution to Plato was a smoke screen.

After remarks on several particular sects, Clement proceeds to more general discussion and for the purpose divides all heresies into two groups, the ascetic and the libertine. Much of what he says about the libertines probably refers to the Carpocratians, whom he had taken as the first major example of the type. It is probably they who appeal to the sayings "the Son of Man is Lord of the Sabbath" (II.214.17), "all things are permissible" (*ibid.*, 19), and "you were called to liberty"

(*ibid.*, 28f). (The Pauline contexts of the two latter sayings are notably favorable to Clement's purpose and unfavorable to libertinism; perhaps the sayings were agrapha which Paul was explaining away and which the libertines quoted as agrapha, not as Pauline.) The attack on those who maintain ἐπιθυμίᾳ χαριστέον καὶ τὸν ἐπονείδιστον βίον ἀδιάφορον ἡγητέον suggests the whole passage is aimed at the Carpocratians. This fits Irenaeus (Harvey I.20.3 end = Stieren I.25.5): the Carpocratian report of Jesus' secret teaching was *per fidem enim et caritatem salvari; reliqua vero, indifferentia.*

In II.221.6ff Clement mentions the Carpocratians and attacks their interpretation of "give to him who asketh." This develops into a defense of wealth as the prerequisite of charity, and the defense makes it seem that Clement's Carpocratians practiced economic, as well as sexual, community of goods. They evidently appealed to Mt. 19.21f: "If you wish to be perfect, sell what you have and give to the poor"—we met the Markan parallel in the baptismal pericope. (Above, pp. 172f. This may explain why ἢ γυναῖκα has disappeared from Mk. 10.29; cf. Theophylact on 10.30, ἆρα οὖν καὶ γυναῖκας ἑκατονταπλασίονας λήψεται; ναί, κἂν ὁ κατάρατος Ἰουλιανὸς ἐκωμῴδει τοῦτο. Julian's joke may have referred to stories derived from Carpocratian practice. Cf. also Origen, *Exhortatio ad martyrium* 16.)

In II.224.10ff we again have an attack on those who advocate ἀδιαφορίαν. This time they appeal to Rom. 6.14 and do not believe in the last judgment. In the concluding section of book III (II.244.21ff), the community of wives and economic communism recur, together with some new traits: the Carpocratians' notion of τὴν διαθήκην τὴν καινήν, their use of baptism, and their importance as a cause of the bad reputation of Christians in general. This section has a number of traits also found in the letter's attack on Carpocratians (πάντα καθαρὰ τοῖς καθαροῖς, εἰς τὸ ἐξώτερον σκότος, etc.). On all the material in *Stromateis* III see now Bolgiani, *Polemica*. Further passages in Clement's works may also refer to the Carpocratians; for instance, III.143.12ff: Ὅτε χοϊκοὶ ἦμεν; Καίσαρος ἦμεν. Καῖσαρ δέ ἐστιν ὁ πρόσκαιρος ἄρχων, οὗ καὶ εἰκὼν ἡ χοϊκὴ ὁ παλαιὸς ἄνθρωπος, εἰς ὃν ἐπαλινδρόμησεν. τούτῳ οὖν τὰ χοϊκὰ ἀποδοτέον, ἃ "πεφορέκαμεν ἐν τῇ εἰκόνι τοῦ χοϊκοῦ," καὶ "τὰ τοῦ θεοῦ τῷ θεῷ·" ἕκαστον γὰρ τῶν παθῶν ὥσπερ γράμμα καὶ χάραγμα ἡμῖν καὶ σημεῖον. ἄλλο χάραγμα νῦν ὁ κύριος ἡμῖν καὶ ἄλλα ὀνόματα καὶ γράμματα ἐνσημαίνεται, πίστιν ἀντὶ ἀπιστίας, καὶ τὰ ἑξῆς. οὕτως ἀπὸ τῶν ὑλικῶν ἐπὶ τὰ πνευματικὰ μεταγόμεθα "φορέσαντες τὴν εἰκόνα τοῦ ἐπουρανίου." This might be interpreted to fit Carpocratian doctrine; and it immediately precedes, in the *Eclogae propheticae*, Clement's quotation from Heracleon referring to the sectarians who branded their ears. Moreover, 14ff explains the equivalence of demons and passions in Irenaeus' accounts of Carpocratian teaching, quoted above. As John of Damascus would have said, the demons are one in form with the passions they have given us. Like the orthodox, the Carpocratians were groping for philosophical explanations of the gospel sayings—and of the magical practices—which had come down to them from their Palestinian origin.

After Clement the material in Appendix B affords almost no reliable information about the Carpocratians.

Tertullian exploits Irenaeus, *Hippolytus* abbreviates him, *Epiphanius* inflates him. Occasionally Hippolytus and Epiphanius make it possible to improve the text used by the Latin translation of Irenaeus (the most important example was given above.)

Epiphanius furnishes additional material, but because furnished by him it is so unreliable that it does not add to our knowledge. Thus, when he makes the Carpocratian god ἀρχὴ, ἄγνωστος, ἀκατονόμαστος and declares that the angels revolted from him before creating the world, he may be importing traits from other gnostic systems; when he specifies the Carpocratians' wicked actions, he is probably indulging his libidinous imagination; and when he credits them with two kinds of images of Jesus—a secret set modeled on Pilate's and another used with the images of philosophers—he is probably confused. That, when Carpocratians are known, gentiles will have nothing to do with Christians, is probably his own improvement of the scandal story. That Carpocratians come near Christian groups only to snare souls may be his excuse for the fact that none are to be seen (Origen, over a century earlier, seemed to say he had never been able to meet one, and he may have been telling the truth). Epiphanius' connection of Epiphanes with Secundus is merely a muddle, and his statement that the Origenians resemble the sect of Epiphanes means only that they had filthy practices. Perhaps his report that the Carpocratians used Mt., with the genealogy, to prove the human birth of Jesus, is reliable, but even about this there is no being sure.

From the minor authors in Appendix B there is even less to glean.

Pseudo-Tertullian's notion that Jesus' ascent to the heavens, according to the Carpocratians, took place after his death is a new specification and, from the evidence we have seen, presumably a misunderstanding: Jesus' role in Carpocratian theology as revelator requires that he have already ascended and seen what he reveals—the more so since the Carpocratians held to the historical fact of his human nature; contrast John 1.1ff.

Eusebius we have already spoken of. He adapts Irenaeus' information to his own apologetic interests, using the Carpocratians to explain the scandalous charges— including incest—which have been brought against the Christians.

Athanasius reflects Irenaeus.

Marcellus of Ancyra gives a list of sects in unusual sequence, but his originality results from confusion, not knowledge.

Gregory's remark shows that the sect had disappeared quite a while before the rise of the Arian controversy, but was remembered as one of the six or seven main

gnostic sects. This may be due to the prominence given it in the accounts of Irenaeus and Clement, not to knowledge of its actual size.

The later fathers furnish repetitions and confusions.

Filastrius' Florian Carpocratians are the most conspicuous confusion.

Praedestinatus is exceptional. His report must have come from some *Acts of Barnabas* (not the preserved text) written at a time and in a place where the Carpocratians were important enough to call down the pseudo-apostle's rebuke, and old enough to make it seem possible. Third-century Cyprus would be a likely guess.

"Cyril's" Discourse on Mary is another exception. It shows that Ebionite and Carpocratian literature lived on in fourth-century Palestine and was developed in accordance with the developing superstitions of the time. "My mother the holy spirit" of the *Gospel according to the Hebrews* has now been identified with Mary *and* Michael! But the Carpocratians and the Ebionites are still connected, and the retort, "Harpocrates used to cast out devils" is probably the last item which should be added to our picture of this all-too-primitive Christian.

D. *Studies*

This review of the evidence has shown the connection of Carpocratian doctrine with the original libertine tradition of Christianity. Both connection and tradition were ignored by the principal studies of Carpocrates in the past century. The tone was set by the *DCB* article (1877) which saw in Carpocrates a Platonic philosopher, discussed the Platonic elements of his work in some detail and paid little attention to the rest. Hilgenfeld, *Ketzergeschichte* (1884), followed the same line, adding discussion of the sources and defending the historicity of Clement's account against the unlikely hypotheses of Volkmar. Classic statement of the conservative position was given by Krüger's article in *RTK* (1901), supported by a full collection of references to the sources. Bareille in *DTC* added nothing; nor did Bousset's extensive study of near eastern mythological elements in gnosticism (*Hauptprobleme*, 1907) contribute much to the background of Carpocratianism. His material on marking initiates (286ff) and, more generally, on baptism (278ff), on the saviour (238ff), and on obscene mysteries (314f) either deals with peripheral details or does not reveal close connections, and this fact is significant: Carpocratianism had its background not in mythology but in magic, an adjacent but not identical field. Neither its basis in Palestinian practice nor the veneer of Platonism it acquired in Alexandria was dependent on mythology, and its most obviously mythological elements—the *cosmocratores*, for instance—probably began as mere demons over whom the magician gained control and were made cosmic powers by secondary development. That secondary development had already taken place in Col. 2, and did not substantially change the character of the essential practice.

Leclerq's article in *DACL* recognized the connection of Carpocratianism with magic, but spoiled the recognition by attempting to attribute to Carpocratianism the *Eighth Book of Moses* (*PGM* XIII.1ff), which has nothing in common with Carpocratianism save its alternative title, *Monas,* and the usual characteristics of magical literature. By contrast, de Faye, *Gnostiques* (1913[1], 1925[2]), tried to deny the relation between the Carpocratian school and the work of Epiphanes which Clement quoted. This is not impossible, but not likely. It is more difficult to suppose that Clement confused two Carpocrates than to suppose that the doctrines of Epiphanes' *On Justice* and of Carpocrates as reported by Irenaeus were somehow reconciled. Irenaeus reports on the Marcellinist branch of the sect after a generation of development in Rome, and Clement, apart from his quotations of Epiphanes, shows us the Alexandrian branch after two generations of development there; differences are expectable.

Fendt (*Gnostiche Mysterien,* 1922) did not deal directly with Carpocratianism, but his study of other obscene interpretations of communion is helpful for an understanding of the libertine tradition and its consequently secret doctrines. Buonaiuti's *Fragments* (1924) followed the usual line, adding the unlikely suggestion that the statue of the teaching "Christ" in the Museo delle Terme might be of Carpocratian origin (p. 57). Leisegang, *Gnosis* (1924), did little more than translate the principal testimonia and add a brief account of the Greek tradition concerning transmigration of souls. Dölger's valuable study, *Sphragis* (1929), has been discussed above.

Liboron (*Die Karpokratianische Gnosis,* 1938) wrote the first monograph on the Carpocratians, giving a sensible if somewhat superficial account of the sect. An important advance from earlier studies was the recognition that the Carpocratians would have found many elements in the Gospels congenial to their doctrines (pp. 45ff: Liboron selects Mt. 5.21ff; 4.8; 16.25; Jn. 8.23f and 44; 15.19; 17.25; Mk. 9.23; Mt. 22.40; Jn. 13.34; Mk. 4.11; Mt. 13.11). All that was lacking was the realization that these are not chance similarities, but that the Carpocratians derived from and continued the primitive libertine Christian tradition; this is why they have neither the elaborate cosmology of the philosophic gnostics like Basilides and Valentinus, nor the fantastic mythology of sects like the Naassenes and the Ophites. Failure to realize this led Liboron (p. 52) to treat the sect as a simplification of gnosticism, whereas it was in fact a slightly philosophizing continuation of a sort of Christianity which often developed into or took up gnosticism. (Consequently works on the nature of gnosticism—recently Jonas, *Religion,* and Wilson, *Problem*—have relatively little to do with Carpocratianism. It was closer to magic, and while magic was an important element in many gnostic systems, it was not itself a system, but a practice, older than gnosticism and more widespread.)

Bardy in his articles on Carpocrates and Carpocratianism in *DHGE* (1949) recognized the connection of Carpocratianism with magic, but not that with Christianity (though the latter is proved by theological structure and constant use of the dicta of Jesus and Paul). Peterson, in *Enciclopedia Cattolica* (also 1949) added references from Michael Syrus and the *Apostolic Constitutions* and explained the Carpocratians' exegesis of Mt. 5.25f and of their use of images (which he connected

with pagan use of amulets). Schoeps, *AFZ* (262ff—1950), emphasized rightly the number and variety of libertine sects in early Christianity and also the connection between libertinism and the notion of deliverance from the world, but he failed to realize what these facts indicate as to the early, eschatological origin of the libertine movement. By contrast, Kraft, *Gab* (1952), began with historical error ("the tiny and insignificant sect of the Carpocratians," p. 434) and progressed by hypotheses for which there is no reliable evidence (the sect's identification of Christ with Harpocrates) and by neglect of part of the little evidence there is (the material in Clement and Irenaeus outside the primary passages) to the absurd conclusion that Carpocrates never existed. This thesis need not be discussed; it has been refuted by Chadwick, *Alexandrian Christianity* (1955, p. 27), who also gives a good survey of the discussion of Volkmar's lunar theory (26, cf. Bolgiani, *Polemica* 95 n13) and a clear account of the major sources. Kretschmar, *RGG*[3] (1959) adds nothing.

Perhaps the best evaluation of Carpocrates, however, was that by Daniélou, *Théologie* (1958, pp. 97f). He recognized that Carpocrates might have got from Judaism the notions that the world was created by inferior angels and that the soul could ascend above them. He also saw that Carpocrates, by his belief that Jesus was a normal human being begotten by Joseph, was connected with the Ebionites rather than the later gnostics, and that his treatment of Jesus as a model for other men was a further Jewish-Christian trait. He therefore suggested that even the sexual indifferentism and the notion of reincarnation might have come from Jewish sources. (For evidence of Jews who believed in reincarnation he refers to Origen, *Commentarii in Evangelium Ioannis* VI.7.) His conclusions (p. 98) deserve quotation: "Consequently the case of Carpocrates is quite remarkable. He seems to depend essentially on a heterodox Jewish gnosis, which admitted that the angels had created the world and that metempsychosis took place. But on the other hand he has no relation to Samaritan gnosticism. We have to do with a strictly Jewish gnosticism. Moreover, Carpocrates is a heterodox Jew become a follower of Christ, but after the fashion of the Ebionites, that is to say, he sees in him only a prophet and a model. Finally, he seems to have been affected by Zealot messianism. His son, Epiphanes, will Hellenize this Jewish gnosticism, as Valentinus will, at the same time, the Samaritan gnosticism, and Justin the orthodox gnosis." This lacks only the realization that Jesus also was a heterodox Jew. Both Daniélou's observations and Chadwick's study were neglected by Camelot, whose article in *LTK* (1960) follows Kraft instead of the evidence. This is what comes of relying on "the latest study of the subject." Mention should be made in conclusion of the penetrating remark by Grant, *Gnosticism* 96 (1959), that in Carpocratianism "counsels of eschatological perfection have been transmuted into a kind of Cynicizing gnosis."

FIVE

The History of the Text

I. EGYPT AND MARK

The preceding discussion of the magical and libertine elements in early Christianity, and of the practices of secrecy they entailed, was necessary because these elements and practices have commonly been ignored (so Clasen, *Arkandiziplin* 56ff, 100ff). They have been ignored because the adherents of the Pauline and Matthaean forms of the religion, the forms which ultimately triumphed, destroyed the documents and denied the authenticity of the competing traditions. The extent of the destruction can be judged by the poverty of Christian literature from the century between 35 and 135 and by the evidence collected in Bauer's *Rechtgläubigkeit*.

Because of the loss of the documents it is impossible to write a history of Christianity before the latter half of the second century. Therefore in the preceding chapter I made no attempt to present a history of the libertine side of the religion or to define precisely the affiliations of the longer text of Mk. to the various parties within Christianity. Restraint was dictated by what Weiss, quoting Harnack, has called "our nearly complete ignorance of Christianity in Alexandria and Egypt before the year 180" (Christianity 658). This Egyptian darkness has not been much illuminated by such works as I have seen (Bauer, *Rechtgläubigkeit*, 1934; Till, *Gnosis*, 1949; Bell, *Cults*, 1953; Roberts, *Christianity*, 1954; Plumley, *Christianity*, 1957; Hornschuh, *Anfänge*, 1958, and *Studien*, 1965; Barnard, *Stephen*, 1960, and *Mark*, 1964; Pericoli-Ridolfini, *Origini*, 1962).

Moreover, besides our general ignorance of the history of Christian groups in Egypt, we ignore the particular circumstances which produced both canonical Mk. and the longer text. The study in Chapter Three led to the conclusion that the preserved sections of the longer text were written by someone who knew most of the canonical text and was anxious to cast older material, perhaps from an Aramaic

source, in the same style. Hornschu's arguments for a Jewish Christianity, perhaps of Essene background, in early second-century Egypt (*Studien* 79f, 93ff, 111ff, 116f) would make it not unlikely that an Aramaic text should have been reworked there. But we were also led to conclude that canonical Mk. showed traces of revision which could best be explained by supposing it had been produced by abbreviation from the longer text (so, the addition of ἐμβλέψας αὐτῷ ἠγάπησεν αὐτόν in Mk. 10.21— above, pp. 171f; the omission of something from Mk. 10.46—above, pp. 188ff; the cross-reference to the longer text in Mk. 14.51—above, pp. 176f). It would seem that canonical Mk. is the end product of a number of editorial reworkings, in the course of which it was sometimes expanded, sometimes cut down. That the preserved evidence would suffice for determination of the details of these reworkings is improbable, and the attempt to determine them would involve a complete restudy of canonical Mk., which cannot be undertaken here. For the present, the origin of the longer text must remain part of the larger unsolved problem of the origin of canonical Mk.

At most, the appearance of the longer text in Egypt is some reason for thinking the canonical text may have originated there and for questioning its traditional connection with Rome, a connection which might have resulted from an apologetic concern to authenticate the Gospel by attaching it to Peter. The traditional arguments for the Roman origin of Mk. must be re-examined and against them must be set the evidence connecting Mark with Alexandria. Supporting evidence may be found in the fact that the Christians seem to have introduced the codex form of manuscript into Egypt (Roberts, *Codex*),[1] but the strongest element remains the early tradition, of which the chief witnesses were collected by Parker in his aforementioned report on the longer text; additional material has been pointed out by Pericoli-Ridolfini (*Origini* 318ff). Thus the following passages have been adduced:

Eus., *HE* II.16f: "They say that this Mark was the first to be sent to preach in Egypt the Gospel which he had also put into writing, and was the first to establish churches in Alexandria itself. The number of men and women who were there converted at the first attempt was so great, and their asceticism both so extreme and so philosophic, that Philo thought it right to describe their conduct and assemblies and meals and all the rest of their manner of life. Philo is also said to have talked at Rome, in the time of Claudius, with Peter, who was then preaching to the people there." (The Philonic work referred to is the account of the Therapeutae.)

Eus., *HE* II.24: "In the eighth year of the reign of Nero, Annianus was the first after Mark the Evangelist to receive the charge of the community in Alexandria."

These passages are matched by two notices in Eusebius' *Chronicon* (ed. Helm, pp. 179, 183) and similar notices, with minor variations, in other editions and versions of the work. Jerome's *Commentarii in Matthaeum*, *Prooemium* 6 and *De viris inlustribus* 8 evidently derive from Eusebius and Papias; the conjunction is interesting if Eusebius' account also came from Papias, as was suggested above (commentary on I.15). A variant is provided by Ado of Vienne (died 875) *Breviarium Chronicorum*

---

1. Followed by Barnard, *Mark*, with other (feeble) arguments in support of the tradition.

6, which has Mark preaching first at Aquileia before going to Alexandria—an example of the adaptability of ecclesiastical tradition to local interest.

The Alexandrian *Liturgy of St. Mark* (*The Ante-Nicene Fathers*, VII.556), the Alexandrian *Synaxarion*, and the history of the patriarchs of Alexandria (bibliographical data in Pericoli-Ridolfini, *Origini* 317f) agree in representing Mark as the founder of the church in Alexandria; the Roman martyrology for April 25 makes him the first bishop of the city. This tradition is probably older than Eusebius; it might even be older than Papias, but this is a matter for which there is no direct evidence. Other reports which perhaps, in spite of their considerable differences, derive from the Alexandrian or Eusebian traditions, are Epiphanius, *Panarion* LI.6; *Apostolic Constitutions* VII.46; *Acta Barnabae* end; and prefaces to several MSS of the Vulgate (Wordsworth and White, p. 173). Particularly interesting in the light of the new evidence is Chrysostom's statement that Mark composed his Gospel in Egypt (*Proöemium in Matthaeum*); whatever source Chrysostom may have had for the statement is unknown.

It must be added that these passages adduced by Parker and Pericoli-Ridolfini do not exhaust the early evidence for the tradition of Mark's work in Alexandria. Others can easily be found—Eus., *Theophany* IV.6; Ephraem, *Commentary on the Diatessaron* (Armenian version) end; the *Acta and Martyrium Marci* (*Acta Sanctorum Aprilis III*, Apr. 25); the *Doctrine of the Apostles* (ed. Cureton, *ASD*, pp. 32f of the Syriac text). But none of this material is reliable and nothing can be built on it.

II.   EVIDENCE FOR THE EXISTENCE OF THE LONGER TEXT OF MK.

Wherever produced, the longer text was known at a very early date. The indications that it was used by Mt. (above, commentary on II.24 and III.1–2, and pp. 171f) and Lk. (above, p. 188) are inconclusive, but suffice to establish at least the likelihood of its use by Mt. On the other hand, Clement's statement that it was used by Carpocrates is probably correct and implies a date before 125 (above, p. 90); I believe this is the earliest at which any knowledge of Mk. in Egypt can be demonstrated. Soon thereafter must be dated the influence exercised by the longer text on the western text of the canonical Gospels. For this the evidence seems to me almost conclusive (above, pp. 122f) and accords with the supposition that the western text arose in Egypt before 150.

The similarities between the longer text and Hippolytus, Methodius, *De resurrectione*, and the *Epistula apostolorum* (above, p. 174), the *Gospel according to the Egyptians* (the role of Salome), and Coptic texts on the *transitus Mariae* (p. 191) do not suffice to prove knowledge of the longer text: it seems a priori almost certain that in early Christianity similar traditions circulated independently, and all these works may have derived from similar traditions. On the other hand, this possibility does not suffice to disprove knowledge of the longer text. The question must be left open and perhaps—for the older Egyptian material—the hypothesis of knowledge may be thought the more likely. By contrast, the *Acts of Lazarus* hypothecated by

Baumstark and the *Iohannis Evangelium Apocryphum Arabice* (above, pp. 174f) probably derived from similar traditions, as did *Actus Petri* 29 (cf. pseudo-Hegesippus, *De bello iudaïco* III.2): A boy whom Peter raised from the dead would not leave him; since Peter, though invited, would not go to his house, he went to spend the night at the house where Peter was. This transfers to Peter the story told by the longer text of Mk. about Jesus, as Acts 9.36–42 transfers to Peter the story told about Jesus by canonical Mk. 5.35–43.

Celsus charges that Christians persuade boys to go apart with them privately ἵνα τὸ τέλειον λάβωσι (Origen, *Contra Celsum* III.55). This may reflect hearsay knowledge of the longer text, as may his statement that the "Harpocratians" derive from Salome (V.62) and Irenaeus' reference to Carpocratian documents reporting the secret teachings of Jesus (Harvey I.20.3 = Stieren I.25.5), a reference to which Clement affords a parallel (III.199.19ff).

On the other hand, direct knowledge of the longer text is probably reflected by Theodotus, quoted in Clement, III. 128.24ff: ὁ σωτὴρ τοὺς ἀποστόλους ἐδίδασκεν, τὰ μὲν πρῶτα τυπικῶς καὶ μυστικῶς, τὰ δὲ ὕστερα παραβολικῶς καὶ ᾐνιγμένως, τὰ δὲ τρίτα σαφῶς καὶ γυμνῶς κατὰ μόνας. By comparison with the Carpocratian γυμνὸς γυμνῷ (above, pp. 185f) this looks like secondary allegorizing. κατὰ μόνας is certainly physical, referring to the conditions of the teaching, not the exposition; therefore γυμνῶς at first was probably also physical. Theodotus or some earlier Valentinian has provided the preceding exegesis to transform γυμνῶς into a metaphorical description of the content of the teaching and thus explain away an element of the tradition which might otherwise be an occasion of sin. Clement, always puritanical, welcomed this interpretation and therefore quoted it from Theodotus, although he or some predecessor had deleted γυμνὸς γυμνῷ from the longer text of Mk. used in his church. The Carpocratians kept the original text (in this respect) and remembered the original magical significance. This is, at least, a likely reconstruction of the course of events.

This brings us to the time of Clement and his statements concerning the text. It also completes the list of passages which seem to reflect knowledge of the longer text or of similar traditions. From the list it appears that the longer text was influential at a very early date: Mt., Lk.(?), Carpocrates, the western text. Knowledge of it persisted in Egypt, in esoteric circles: *Epistula apostolorum*(?), *G. Egyptians*(?), Celsus (hearsay), Theodotus, Clement. Elsewhere, only Irenaeus has heard of the Carpocratians having such a text. After Clement there is no certain trace of it—to my knowledge. Now that the text is known, references to it may be discovered in later writers. For the sake of the argument, however, let us suppose the last reference to it is the account in the letter of Clement.

III. THE ACCEPTANCE AND DISAPPEARANCE OF THE LONGER TEXT

This poses two problems: First, how did Clement's church come to use this text; second, how did the text disappear from later Christian literature, especially that of Egypt?

As to the use of the text by Clement's church: For lack of evidence there can be no history of the parties in Egyptian Christianity before Clement's time. Even Clement's church is a vague entity. Its use of the longer text in its "great mysteries" was probably an established practice before Clement joined it (commentary on I.23). The letter apparently distinguishes between "those being instructed" (or "the catechumens," I.18) and "those being initiated" (or "perfected," I.22); the latter are probably "those being initiated in the great mysteries" (II.2). This suggests two initiations—the second perhaps a second baptism for the true gnostics, distinct from the rank and file.

Such a practice might have resulted from the coming together—perhaps under the pressure of persecution—of congregations originally distinct. A more hellenized congregation, holding to a philosophical interpretation of the religion and familiar with the practices of the mysteries, might have tried to maintain its individuality as an *ecclesiola in ecclesia* and have admitted candidates from the larger church only after a special course of training, and administration of its peculiarly significant sacraments. Another possibility is that we have here a late example of the way many Christian churches first quarantined and then eliminated the libertine tradition. The dangerous secrets of realizable eschatology—of the immediate accessibility of the kingdom and the liberty of those who entered it—were limited to a few, shut away from the rest by special requirements, and at last quietly forgotten. It is recognized that the disappearance of realized eschatology (and of much that went with it) is one of the fundamental differences between the Christian explosion of the first century and the Christian organization of the third. Perhaps in Clement's letter we have one glimpse of a church in transition.

Such speculations are indemonstrable. The facts are that Clement's church in Alexandria had the longer text of Mk. and that thereafter nothing was heard of it. How is the disappearance to be explained?

Again we have no certain information; any answer must be speculative. A basis for speculation is Eusebius' report (*HE* VI.1) that a persecution under Septimius Severus hit hard in Alexandria, and that Origen at 18 became head of the catechetical school because all older teachers had been driven out of the city (VI.3.1–3). In this persecution both Clement's church and its "official" copy of the longer text of Mk. (letter, I.28–II.2) may have been destroyed. Whether or not other copies existed in orthodox circles is uncertain. They would not have been numerous and all may have been wiped out at the same time. Book-burning was a regular feature of ancient religious conflicts (*I Macc.* I.56f, etc.) and was conspicuous in Roman persecutions of the Christians (Eus., *HE* VIII.2, etc.) as well as intra-Christian disputes (Acts 19.19, with Wetstein's commentary) see below, p. 345.

Besides, as Bickerman has pointed out to me, ancient books were so perishable that any work not copied would normally disappear within a generation or two. What usually requires explanation is not the disappearance of an ancient work, but its preservation. Why was it copied? Clement's letter shows that the "secret Gospel" was an occasion of some embarrassment to him, particularly because the Carpocratians also had it and evidently found in it material to support the libertine

interpretation of Christianity. Moreover, as Mondésert remarked, appeal to secret traditions ran counter to the philosophic conception of Christianity as the teaching of universal reason, and to the more important institutional definition of Christian tradition as that determined by the bishop (*Clément* 57f). Also, most of the competing Christian sects had their own Gospels, of which many were represented as transcripts of secret traditions. Thus, appeal to such authorities was discredited, not to say discreditable. In these circumstances what had preserved the longer text of Mk. in Clement's church was probably its ritual use in "the great mysteries." But the raison d'être of these mysteries was the existence of an inner circle with special teachings—libertine or magical or philosophic or all three. If this circle was broken up by the Severan persecution, there would have been no further ritual use in Clement's church for the longer text of Mk., and its disappearance would probably have followed from mere neglect, if not from precaution. (Consider what Clement says of the danger of secret writings falling into the wrong hands—II.11.4f). How many other churches had copies? We do not know.

As for the disappearance of the longer text outside Egypt, the only strong evidence we have for knowledge of it outside Egypt is Irenaeus' report that the Carpocratians had such a document and the indications that it was used by Mt. and perhaps Lk. (above, section II). For the disappearance of the Carpocratian text no special explanation is required. What has become of the rest of Carpocratian literature, or of the many gnostic documents used by Hippolytus in his *Philosophumena*—most of them apparently unknown to all other Christian writers (Stähelin, *Quellen* 7ff)? For the disappearance of the text used by Mt. and Lk. we have the analogous problem of the fate of Q, discussed by Kilpatrick, *Disappearance*. The connection of the longer text with the libertine and magical side of primitive Christianity, which the developing organization was more and more anxious to disown, is sufficient to explain the disappearance. (I refer again to the importance of charges of libertinism in persecutions of Christians: Justin, *First Apology* 10, 23, 26, 27; *Second Apology* 12; *Dialogue* 17. And in spite of the claims of the apologists, the libertine tradition remained a danger even within the "orthodox" Christian organization; compare the claims of Tertullian before he became a Montanist—*Apology* XXXIX—with his charges afterward—*De jejunio* XVII.)

Returning to the disappearance of the longer text from Egypt: The strongest evidence for dating this at the Severan persecution is Origen's ignorance of the text. Admittedly, he did not write down everything he knew, and much of what he wrote is lost and more is edited. Nevertheless, had he known the text we should have expected a reference. But if the text disappeared early in the Severan persecution when Origen was about eighteen (on Eusebius, *HE* VI.1–3; cf. Barnes, *Origen*; Koch, *Origenes* 1037), and if Clement was driven out of the city at the same time, Origen may never have known the text. That he was a pupil of Clement is dubious, in spite of Eusebius' claims (Munck, *Untersuchungen* 173ff; cf. Völker, 36). They differ in their canons of scripture (for example, Clement accepted as Petrine the *Kerygma Petri* and *Apocalypse of Peter*, which Origen rejected—Kutter, 89ff), their textual traditions (Clement used a western text at least for Lk.—Swanson, *Text*), their

exegesis of many particular passages (e.g., Prov. 5.16—cf. II.116.27ff with Origen, *Homilia in Genesin* XIII.4; *Homilia in Numeros* XII.1), and major aspects of their theology (Clement did not believe in metempsychosis). Such differences might be due to the independent development of Origen. More important is the fact that Origen, when speaking of his predecessors in the philosophic interpretation of Christianity, specifies Pantaenus but says nothing of Clement (Eus., *HE* VI.19.13). Apparently he never mentioned Clement, since Eusebius, attempting to prove that Clement was Origen's teacher, is forced to argue by inference from their temporal proximity (*HE* VI.6) and to quote a letter of Alexander of Jerusalem to Origen in which Alexander refers to Clement (then deceased) as formerly known to Origen and as one through whom he himself had made Origen's acquaintance (*HE* VI.14.8f). But this only makes Origen's silence about Clement more significant. It would seem that the two were not close, and that if Clement ever was Origen's teacher, it was only for a short period when Origen was fifteen or sixteen. Consequently Origen's ignorance of the longer text is understandable.

IV. The history of the letter of Clement

As a result of the early disappearance of the longer text, our knowledge of it depends almost entirely on Clement's letter. The date and destination of the letter are alike uncertain. Its many parallels to *Stromateis* III suggest that it dates from about the same time, that is, roughly the last decade before the Severan persecution; but the parallels are largely due to the subject matter, and Clement may have long continued to say the same things about the Carpocratians. That the letter was found in Palestine suggests that its recipient, Theodore, lived there. This suggestion is supported by the facts: (1) that the name Theodore (translating names like Nathaniel) was popular with Christians of Jewish ancestry; (2) that Clement had studied in Palestine under a Christian teacher of Jewish ancestry (II.8.23 = Eus., *HE* V.11.4f); (3) that one of Clement's warmest admirers, Alexander, afterward became bishop of Jerusalem, and Clement dedicated to him a work against Judaizing heretics (*HE* VI.13.3; Photius 111); (4) that a collection of Clement's letters existed at Mar Saba when John of Damascus, who worked there from 716 to 749, quoted three passages from the collection in his *Sacra Parallela* (Stählin, III.223–224; cf. Stählin's notes, III.LXff); (5) that no certain trace of Clement's letters is found anywhere else. Accordingly, we may suppose that the letter to Theodore was sent to some address in Palestine.

Sometime after its arrival in Palestine the letter was incorporated into a collection of Clement's letters. This is almost certain from the heading of the present text, ἐκ τῶν ἐπιστολῶν τοῦ ἁγιωτάτου Κλήμεντος. The collection known to John of Damascus had at least twenty-one letters (Stählin, III.223f). The making of the collection may plausibly be assigned to Clement's friend, the bishop Alexander. He had ample precedent; collections of the letters of eminent Christians had been

common ever since the appearance of the Pauline and Ignatian corpora. Clement used a collection of Valentinus' letters (II.223.12), and Eusebius knew collections of the letters of a number of Clement's contemporaries (*HE* VI.12.1; 14.8; etc.). Moreover, Eusebius reports that Alexander founded the library in Jerusalem and that it was rich in collections of letters, which he himself used for his history (*HE* VI.20.1ff, on which Ehrhard, *Bibliothek* 217f). But if Alexander made the collection or had it made, and if it was in the Jerusalem library which Eusebius used, how are we to account for the fact that Eusebius did not know it? He would certainly have mentioned it had he known it. Dubious material in one letter would not have prevented his using the others or his including the collection in his list of Clement's works (*HE* VI.13.1ff). Perhaps the book had been misplaced or mistitled or somehow separated from the library and thus escaped his attention. Alternatively, one might suppose that the collection was made elsewhere (Ehrhard, *Bibliothek* 219) or at a later date.

A later date might be suggested by the use of ἁγιώτατος for an ecclesiastical writer, found in the heading of the present text. This seems to appear first in the time of Athanasius. The use of ὁ στρωματεύς for Clement (except for the instance dubiously attributed to Sextus Julius Africanus) is even later (commentary on I.1). But the heading is conventional and might be the work of any excerpter down to the time of the present MS; it cannot be used to date the collection from which the text was taken. And it is hard to find a later time at which Clement was sufficiently popular to occasion the collection. So, at least, one would judge from the rarity with which works of Clement were cited, copied, and forged. A cluster of citations comes from the late fifth, sixth, and seventh centuries (Socrates, Stephen Gobarus, John Moschus, Maximus, Antiochus of Mar Saba, Anastasius of Sinai, etc.), but if the collection had not been made before then it is unlikely that any letters would have been left to collect. Early MSS of Clement are rare; the present text of the *Stromateis* depends for the most part on a single eleventh-century manuscript and its derivatives. Of the spuria given by Stählin most are the result of misattribution, not forgery; forgery accounts only for the ἀπόδειξις περὶ τοῦ πάσχα (III.LII), the source of fragments 70–74, and possibly the homily on the prodigal son printed in Potter's edition. The ὅροι probably began by drawing on Clement for material and ended with misattribution (for ὁ φιλόσοφος see III.LXVI, on fragment 52). The three forgeries are evidently late and isolated; they do not testify to any general interest in Clement at any time when forgery of the present text would have been credible. Note the comparative rarity of references to Clement in Grant's account of the use of early fathers as authorities (*Appeal* 15ff). Accordingly, it seems more likely that the collection was made early and thereafter neglected, than that it was made late.

That such a collection should have existed for centuries without being cited, and that John of Damascus, who did cite it, should have passed over in silence the reference to the longer text of Mk., are phenomena paralleled in the history of Byzantine literature. Procopius' *Secret History*, for instance, was written in the sixth century but not referred to until the tenth. Far from collecting dubious traditions about Jesus, ecclesiastical writers were unwilling to preserve them. Epiphanius, for

instance, when copying Irenaeus' account of the Carpocratians, deliberately omitted their report of Jesus' secret teaching (both Irenaeus' and Epiphanius' texts are given in Appendix B). In this matter Jerome was an exception; he translated the *Gospel according to the Hebrews* into Greek. But Jerome never mentions the Jerusalem library (Ehrhard, *Bibliothek* 247); perhaps even before his quarrel with the bishop of Jerusalem he had little access to it. And it is significant for the attitude of succeeding generations that his translation of the *Gospel according to the Hebrews* has not been preserved. *The Gospel according to the Egyptians* has also disappeared. So had the *Gospel of Thomas* and the *Gospel of Peter* until they turned up in chance finds of ancient MSS. We have already mentioned the disappearance of Q and of the gnostic works used by Hippolytus (a disappearance which led Stähelin, *Quellen*, into the error of thinking them fakes). The same principle explains the long list in Hennecke-Schnee-melcher of Gospels which church fathers referred to by name, but of which they did not choose to preserve—or chose to destroy—the content. Theodoret boasted of having destroyed more than two hundred copies of the *Diatessaron* (*Haereticarum fabularum compendium* I.20 end).

To prevent foreseeable stupidities, it must be said at once that the lack of reference to the letter is no argument against attribution of the letter to Clement. In the first place, even those who think it is not by Clement recognize it to be ancient. Völker thinks it must date from the time of the gnostic controversy (the third century); Nock thought it on stylistic grounds not later than the fourth century; Munck thought it propaganda for the church of Alexandria and would presumably not have placed it later than the Christological controversies of the fifth century. Even if we accept the latest of these dates we must admit that the letter went unmentioned for fifteen hundred years. So the attribution to Clement does not much augment—proportionately—the period of neglect. And the neglect is easier to explain if the letter be genuine than if not. If genuine it was, to begin with, a private and confidential letter of which no mention was to be expected in the years immediately after it was written—that is, if we have dated it correctly, the years before or after the Severan persecution (c. 201? or 210?). But if we can trust Origen (*Contra Celsum* V.62) the Carpocratians must have become rare and insignificant shortly after that persecution—perhaps as a result of it. Once they had become unimportant the letter would interest no one save a historian. But historians were few in the medieval Church, and historians willing to report aberrant traditions from the early fathers were fewer. Thus the lack of any reference to the letter would be explicable. On the other hand, if the attribution to Clement be false and the letter a forgery, it must have been written and attributed to Clement for some purpose of propaganda; that is, it was intended to be circulated and to attract attention. In this event the failure of anyone to comment on it—or at least the fact that no comment has been preserved—is more difficult to explain. So the total neglect of the letter through seventeen centuries argues for its authenticity. Nor is the neglect incompatible with the literary activities of the monks of Mar Saba. They excelled in hymnody and in the production of ascetic works and martyrologies; see the accounts by Vailhé (*Ecrivains*) and Phokylides (*Laura*).

At what time the collection containing the letter got into the library of Mar Saba is uncertain. The foundation of the library was probably almost contemporaneous with that of the monastery in the late fifth century, so any date from that time on is possible. Even the citation by John of Damascus does not provide an absolutely certain terminus ante quem, since it is conceivable that John might have cited from a MS not directly related to that from which our excerpt derives. The likelihood, however, is that John's MS was the ancestor of that from which the surviving (eighteenth-century) excerpt was made and that the collection was at Mar Saba throughout all the intervening period.

The continuous—or practically continuous—existence of the monastic community has been strongly defended by Phokylides. In particular, he has conclusively refuted Ehrhard's statement (*Kloster* 37) that the site was abandoned from 1450 to 1540 (Phokylides, *Laura* 506–521; see also Papadopoulos-Kerameus, II.703). Ehrhard's opinion (uncritically repeated by Strzygowski, *Kloster* 3, and Vailhé, *Ecrivains* 2) was based on the report of Sophronius (Khitrowo, *Itinéraires* I.274). To the remarks of Phokylides it should be added that Sophronius' report, when read in full, is apparently based on stories told him at the monastery; these stories seem to have been invented by the Vlachs, who were then in control, as a bid for Russian support against the Greeks, who did not regain control until 1612 (Phokylides, *Laura* 541).

Another point made by Phokylides (*Laura* 477), but requiring further emphasis, is the failure of occasional pillaging or even "destruction" of the monastery to destroy the books there. The buildings of the community were almost entirely of stone; many were caves with stone facings. Codices dispersed in the cells were not likely to be burned nor to be taken as loot by bedouin; consequently they have been found in the ruins of abandoned cells (Papadopoulos-Kerameus III.316). Also it is reported that when attacks seemed imminent the most important MSS were hidden in nearby caves (*ibid.*; Phokylides, *Laura* 477f). These reports are confirmed by the analogy of the finds from the Qumran community (near the end of the Wadi en-Nur on which Mar Saba is located) and from the nearby monastery of Khirbet Mird (Milik, *Inscription* 527), as well as by finds of Greek biblical and apocryphal documents (fifth- to eighth-century) in caves of the Wadi en-Nur itself (de Vaux, *Fouille* 85). Compare the story told by Curzon of his visit to a Coptic monastery of which only "the crumbling walls" remained and which had not been inhabited by monks for at least a generation, but of which the most valued MSS were still in existence—concealed from the Moslems in a subterranean tomb and guarded by a local peasant, who showed them to Curzon (*Visits* 130). *Se no è vero, è bene trovato.*

Given such evidence, there is nothing improbable in the hypothesis that MSS existed at Mar Saba at all periods of its history, and that the archetype(s) of the present text may have been there ever since the time of John of Damascus. But this hypothesis cannot be made an essential part of the history of the present text, since there is nothing improbable, either, in the supposition that during the centuries between John of Damascus and the last copyist the text migrated half a dozen times from one monastery to another in southern Palestine. Many texts did so. Perhaps

the strongest reason for thinking this one remained at Mar Saba is (after the fact that it was found there) the absence of any known reference to its content. This suggests that it did not circulate, but lay neglected in some corner of a single library.

As to the ultimate fate of the collection of Clement's letters, the likelihood is that it perished in the great fire which Phokylides, *Laura* 477, dates in the early years of the eighteenth century. The fire burned out the contents of a cave in which many of the antiquities and the oldest MSS of the monastery had been stored. Since the fire was in a cave the air supply must have been limited. Present monastic tradition says the fire smouldered for two weeks before the monks could get through the smoke to put it out. Even under the most favorable circumstances books are difficult to burn; they usually char around the edges and then go out. Therefore it is presumable that after the fire a large number of loose leaves, almost undamaged, were salvaged from the unburned centers of old MSS. Papadopoulos-Kerameus remarks on the "great number of isolated leaves" and, again, "innumerable quaternions of codices which had gone to pieces" (II.695) in the Mar Saba material. Numbers of such isolated leaves are still found, either loose (Papadopoulos-Kerameus, II, nos. 701–704; my Ἑλληνικὰ χειρόγραφα end), or inserted in other MSS (Papadopoulos-Kerameus, II, nos. 2, 9, 13, 16, 18, 19, etc.) or used for bookbinding (Monasteries, 174, 177).

The fragmentary state of the present letter is best explained by supposing it a copy of such an isolated leaf. Ehrhard (*Kloster* 67) remarks on the large amount of copying of older MSS which went on at Mar Saba in the seventeenth and eighteenth centuries. No doubt someone's attention was attracted by the surprising content of this isolated folio. He studied the text, corrected it to the best of his ability, and then copied it into the back of the monastery's edition of the letters of Ignatius, since it resembled them in being a letter from an early father, attacking gnostic heretics. For analogies reference may be made to the loss in a fire at Strassburg of the only MS of the *Epistle to Diognetus*, to the preservation of the *Muratorian Canon* (also a fragment) on the last pages of a volume of Ambrose, and to the insertion of the Syriac translations of the apocryphal psalms into an empty space in the middle of a MS of the *Ketaba de durrasha* (Noth, *Fünf* 3). The oldest MS containing these psalms dated from 1340—until the discovery of the Dead Sea documents. For an example of the correction of the text by the copyist, there is the acid remark of the hegoumenos Joasaph that one Seraphim, who worked at Mar Saba in the late seventeenth century, was an ignoramus who spoiled old MSS by trying to correct them (Phokylides, *Laura* 562f). Note also the correction of itacisms in fifteenth- and eighteenth-century MSS of Marcarius (*Neue Homilien* p. XVIII). [B.E. remarks: "The correctness may be due to the person who copied the text you saw, or it may be due to some predecessor. Thus in the case of the MSS of Plutarch, Planudes introduced a correctness of spelling and accentuation that persists in the MSS derived from his edition."] As remarked in Chapter One, the occasional errors of transcription in the present text are probably due to the haste of the copyist.

In conclusion, it must be reiterated that the most to be claimed for the above account is plausibility, and plausibility is not proof. Things might well have happened thus, but they could have happened otherwise. It is a pity that there is no adequate

catalogue of the contents of the Mar Saba library prior to its transfer to Jerusalem in 1865. Of the earlier catalogues known to Papadopoulos-Kerameus, the most nearly complete listed only 536 MSS; he found over 700 in the Jerusalem material brought from Mar Saba (Papadopoulos-Kerameus, II.695). Similarly, a list of books dated 1910 which I found in the Mar Saba library (no. 76 of my Ἑλληνικὰ χειρόγραφα) lists only 191 titles; the library at present must have at least double that number. In *Monasteries*, 172, 175, I discuss reasons for the inadequacy of the earlier catalogues; Papadopoulos-Kerameus makes similar observations (II.695). Since the catalogues are incomplete, their silence cannot be used as an argument against the existence of material in the monastery at the time when they were made (particularly material extant on isolated leaves).

Thus we have, in the last analysis, no *proof* that the present text was or was not copied in Mar Saba, or that the MS from which it was copied was or was not in the Mar Saba library. The above history of the text, like most histories, cannot pretend to be more than an account of probabilities.

APPENDICES

INDICES

ABBREVIATIONS AND WORKS CITED

THE FRAGMENT: PLATES, TRANSCRIPTION, AND TRANSLATION

APPENDIX A

PALAEOGRAPHIC PECULIARITIES

Abbreviations: Medial: $\overset{\text{᾽}}{\alpha}\text{ν}\overset{\prime\sim}{\omega}\text{ν}$ = ἀνθρώπων

ﷲ = κυρίου

Terminal: ⌐ = αν

– = ος

≈ = ᾽ ους

⌐ = ται

⌐ = ῶν

≈ = ᾽ ων

Ligatures: $\mathcal{S}$ = ἀ, $\alpha\mathcal{S}$ = ἀν, $\alpha\mathcal{S}$ = αὐ, $\alpha\mathcal{S}$ = ας

$\mathcal{V}^{\alpha}$ = γα, $\mathcal{V}^{\iota}$ = γι, $\mathcal{V}^{o}$ = γο

$\mathcal{J}\epsilon$ = δε, $\mathcal{J}_{\xi}$ = δη, $\mathcal{J}_{\xi}$ = δι

$\sqrt{}$ = ει, $\mathcal{J}$ = ει, $\mathcal{W}$ = ἐν, $\mathcal{O}$ = ευ, $\mathcal{OW}$ = ευσ

$\mathcal{Z}\rho$ = ζο

$\mathcal{U}_{\eta}$ = και, $\mathcal{Z}$ = και (at the end of a line)

γ = ου, $\mathcal{J}$ = οὐ or οῦ

$\mathcal{U}$ = πι, $\mathcal{U}\sigma$ = πο

$\mathcal{C}\alpha$ = ρα, $\mathcal{C}\Lambda$ = ρι, $\mathcal{C}\mathcal{J}$ = ρο, $\mathcal{S}\upsilon$ = ρυ

$\mathcal{C}_{\varsigma}$ = σας, $\mathcal{C}_{\upsilon}$ = σιν, $\mathcal{O}$ = σι, $\mathcal{Z}$ = στ

$\mathcal{U}\alpha$ = τα, $\mathcal{U}_{\xi}$ = ται, $\mathcal{Z}$ = τε, $\mathcal{J}$ = τη, $\mathcal{Z}$ = το, $\mathcal{Y}$ = τοῦ

$\mathcal{J}$ = .ῦ, $\mathcal{U}$ = υς

$\mathcal{C}\alpha$ = φα, $\mathcal{G}_{\eta}$ = φη

Note that initial $\mathcal{J}$ is a small ι. $\mathcal{f}$ is ψ.
At the ends of ligatures o may be σ, and τ, $\mathcal{Z}$.
Between letters ε sometimes becomes w. $\mathcal{Z}\mathcal{J}$ = εται.

APPENDIX B

THE EVIDENCE CONCERNING CARPOCRATES

The following pages contain all the reasonably certain references to Carpocrates that I have found in patristic literature. A discussion of this evidence will be found in Chapter Four.

The older lists of heretics (see pp. 267ff)

Justin	Hegesippus in Eus. HE IV.22.5	Const. Apos. VI.6ff	Irenaeus	Hippolytus	Pseudo-Tertullian Adv. om. haer.	Epiphanius	Filastrius
				× Νασσηνοί = Γνωστικοί			× Ofitae
				× Περάται			× Caiani
				× Σηθιανοί			× Sethiani
				× Ἰουστῖνος			
					◆ Dositheus	◆ Samaritans (including ◆ Dositheus)	◆ Dositheus
	◆ Jewish sects (among them ◆ Μασβωθαῖοι ★ Ἐβιωναῖοι)	◆ Jewish sects			◆ Jewish sects	◆ Jewish sects	◆ Jewish sects
	◆ Θεβουθίς						
■ Σίμων (I Ap. 26)	■ Σίμων	■ Σίμων		■ Σίμων	■ Simon	■ Σίμων	■ Simon
	■ Κλεόβιος	■ Κλεόβιος	◐ Valentinus	◐ Οὐαλεντῖνος			
	◆ Δοσίθεος	◆ Δοσίθεος	◐ Secundus	◐ Σεκοῦνδος			
	◆ Γορθαῖος	★ Κήρινθος	◐ Ptolemaeus	◐ Πτολεμαῖος			
	◆ Μασβώθεοι			◐ Ἡρακλέων			
	● Μάρκος	● Μάρκος	● Marcus	◐ Μάρκος			
			■ Simon	◐ Κολάρβασος			
■ Μένανδρος	■ Μένανδρος	■ Μένανδρος	■ Menander	■ Μένανδρος	■ Menander	■ Μένανδρος	■ Menandrus
	■ Μεναδριανισταί						
● Μαρκιανοί (Dialogue 35)	● Μαρκιανοί						
	★ Καρποκρατιανοί						
◐ Οὐαλεντινιανοί	◐ Οὐαλεντινιανοί						
			■ Saturninus	■ Σατορνεῖλος	■ Saturninus	■ Σατορνιλιανοί	■ Saturnilus
■ Βασιλειδιανοί	■ Βασιλειδιανοί	■ Βασιλείδης	■ Basilides	■ Βασιλείδης	■ Basilides	■ Βασιλειδιανοί	■ Basilides
■ Σατορνιλιανοί	■ Σατορνιλιανοί	■ Σατορνῖλος		■ Μένανδρος			
		■ Νικολαῖται			■ Nicolaus	■ Νικολαΐται	■ Nicolaus
				● Μαρκίων	× Ophitae	× Γνωστικοί	
				● Πρέπων	× Cainei	(7 names)	
					× Sethoitae		
Celsus V.61f unnamed dualists							Judas

	◑ οἱ ἀπό	* Carpocrates	* Καρποκράτης	* Carpocrates	* Καρποκρατιανοί	* Carpocras
	Οὐαλεντίνου	* Marcellina			* Μαρκελλίνα	
		* Cerinthus	* Κήρινθος	* Cerinthus	* Κηρινθιανοί	* Cerinthus
	× Γνωστικοί				* Ναζωραῖοι	
	* Ἐβιωναῖοι	* Ebionaei	* Ἐβιωναῖοι	* Ebion	* Ἐβιωναῖοι	* Hebion
	◆ Σιβυλλισταί		* Θεόδοτος			
	■ Σιμωνιανοί		× Θεόδοτος II			
	* Μαρκελλιανοί		× (Γνωστικοί)	◑ Valentinus	◑ Οὐαλεντῖνοι	◑ Valentinus
	* Ἁρποκρατιανοί	■ Nicolaitae	■ (Νικόλαος)	◑ Ptolomaeus	◑ Σεκουνδιανοί	◑ Ptolemeus
	× οἱ ἀπὸ			◑ Secundus	◑ Πτολεμαῖοι	◑ Secundus
	Μαριάμμης			◑ Heracleon	◑ Μαρκώσιοι	◑ Heracleon
	× οἱ ἀπὸ Μάρθας			◑ Marcus	◑ Κολορβάσιοι	◑ Marcus
				◑ Colarbasus	◑ Ἡρακλεωνῖται	◑ Colorbasus
					× Ὀφῖται	
					× Καϊανοί	
					× Σηθιανοί	
					× Ἀρχοντικοί	
I Ap. 26		• Cerdon	• Κέρδων	• Cerdon	• Κερδωνιανοί	• Cerdon
• Μαρκίων	• Μαρκιωνισταί	• Marcion	• Μαρκίων	• Marcion	• Μαρκιωνισταί	• Marcion
			• Λουκιανός	• Lucanus	• Λουκιανισταί	• Lucanus
			• Ἀπελλῆς	• Appelles	• Ἀπελλῆϊανοί	• Apelles
			Δοκῆται		• Σευηριανοί	
			Μονόϊμος			
		◒ Tatianus	◒ Τατιανός	◒ Tatianus	◒ Τατιανοί	◒ Tatianus
		× Gnostici				
		× Ophitae				
		× Cajani				

Clement, *Eclogae propheticae* 25.1 (ed. Stählin III.143)

p. 143 20   Ὁ Ἰωάννης φησίν, ὅτι »ἐγὼ μὲν ὑμᾶς ὕδατι βαπτίζω, ἔρχεται δέ **25, 1**
μου [ὁ] ὀπίσω ὁ βαπτίζων ὑμᾶς ἐν πνεύματι καὶ πυρί.« πυρὶ δὲ
οὐδένα ἐβάπτισεν· »ἔνιοι δέ«, ὥς φησιν Ἡρακλέων, »πυρὶ τὰ ὦτα
τῶν σφραγιζομένων κατεσημήναντο«, οὕτως ἀκούσαντες τὸ ἀποστο-
λικόν. »τὸ γὰρ πτύον ἐν τῇ χειρὶ αὐτοῦ τοῦ διακαθᾶραι τὴν ἅλω,
25 καὶ συνάξει τὸν σῖτον εἰς τὴν ἀποθήκην, τὸ δὲ ἄχυρον κατακαύσει
πυρὶ ἀσβέστῳ.« πρόσκειται οὖν τῷ »διὰ πυρὸς« τὸ »διὰ πνεύματος«, **2**
ἐπειδὴ ⟨ὡς⟩ ὁ σῖτος ἀπὸ τοῦ ἀχύρου διακρίνεται (τουτέστιν ἀπὸ τοῦ
ὑλικοῦ ἐνδύματος) διὰ πνεύματος | καὶ τὸ ἄχυρον χωρίζεται διὰ τοῦ **347 S**
πνεύματος λικμώμενον, οὕτως τὸ πνεῦμα διαχωριστικὴν ἔχει δύναμιν
30 ἐνεργειῶν ὑλικῶν.

20f vgl. Matth. 3, 11; Luk. 3, 16.   22f Herakleon Fr. 49 Brooke; vgl.
Iren. I 25, 6 (= Hippol. Philos. VII 32 p. 404, 35f).   **24–26** Matth. 3, 12;
Luk. 3, 17.

21 [ὁ] Sy.   **23** κατεσημήναντο Sy κατεσημήνατο L.   **26** τῷ L¹ τὸ L*.
27 ⟨ὡς⟩ ὁ σῖτος St τὸν σῖτον L.   διακρίνεται St διακρῖναι L.   **30** ἀγεννήτου
Arcerius ἀγενήτου L.

Origen, *Contra Celsum* V.62–64 (ed. Koetschau II.65–67)

p. 65   LXII. Εἶτα σωρὸν καταχέων ἡμῶν ὀνομάτων φησὶν εἰδέναι
15 τινὰς καὶ Σιμωνιανούς, οἳ τὴν Ἑλένην ἤτοι διδάσκαλον
Ἕλενον σέβοντες Ἑλενιανοὶ λέγονται. . . .
26   οἶδε καὶ Μαρκελλιανοὺς ἀπὸ Μαρκελλίνας καὶ
p. 66 Ἀρποκρατιανοὺς ἀπὸ Σαλώμης καὶ ἄλλους ἀπὸ Μαριάμμης
καὶ ἄλλους ἀπὸ Μάρθας· ἡμεῖς δὲ οἱ διὰ τὴν κατὰ τὸ δυνατὸν
ἡμῖν φιλομάθειαν οὐ μόνα τὰ ἐν τῷ λόγῳ καὶ τὰς διαφορὰς τῶν
ἐν αὐτῷ ἐξετάσαντες, ἀλλ' ὅση δύναμις καὶ τὰ τῶν φιλοσοφησάντων
5 φιλαλήθως ἐρευνήσαντες οὐδέ ποτε τούτοις ὡμιλήσαμεν. ἐμνήσθη
δ' ὁ Κέλσος καὶ Μαρκιωνιστῶν, προϊσταμένων Μαρκίωνα.
    LXIII. Εἶθ' ἵνα δοκῇ καὶ ἄλλους εἰδέναι παρ' οὓς ὠνόμασε,
φησὶν ἑαυτῷ συνήθως ὅτι ἄλλοι ἄλλον διδάσκαλόν τε καὶ δαίμονα, κακῶς πλαζόμενοι καὶ καλινδούμενοι κατὰ σκότον

p. 65   26 Vgl. Irenaeus, Adv. haer. I 20, 4. Epiphan., Panar. I 27, 6.

p. 66   1 Vgl. A. Hilgenfeld, Die Ketzergesch. des Urchrist. S. 397–408. 548 u.
Novum test. extra can. rec. fasc. IV p. 45, 26 sqq.—Vgl. Hippolyt, Philos,
V 7. X 9.   6 Vgl. A. Hilgenfeld, Die Ketzergesch. des Urchrist. S. 316–341.

p. 66   1 Ἀρποκρατιανούς] Καρποκρατιανούς vermutet Sp. (Annotat. p. 71); dagegen
verteidigt R. A. Lipsius (Die Quellen der ältest. Ketzergesch. 1875 S. 86 Anm.)
mit Recht die überlieferte Lesart | μαριάμμης A μαριάμνης M^corr· Ausgg.   **5**
ἐρευνήσαντες] υ übergeschr. A¹.

10 πολὺν τῶν Ἀντίνου τοῦ κατ' Αἴγυπτον | θιασωτῶν ἀνομώ- 627
τερόν τε καὶ μιαρώτερον. καὶ δοκεῖ μοι ἐπαφώμενος τῶν πραγμάτων ἀληθές τι εἰρηκέναι, ὅτι τινὲς ἄλλοι ἄλλον δαίμονα κακῶς
πλαζόμενοι καὶ καλινδούμενοι εὕραντο προστάτην κατὰ
πολὺν τὸν τῆς ἀγνοίας σκότον. περὶ δὲ τῶν κατὰ τὸν Ἀντί-
15 νουν, παραβαλλόμενον ἡμῶν τῷ Ἰησοῦ, ἐν τοῖς πρὸ τούτων εἰπόν-
τες οὐ παλιλλογήσομεν.

καὶ βλασφημοῦσι δέ, φησίν, εἰς ἀλλήλους οὗτοι πάν- Ph. 88, 31
δεινα ῥητὰ καὶ ἄρρητα· καὶ οὐκ ἂν εἴξαιεν οὐδὲ καθ' ὁτιοῦν εἰς ὁμόνοιαν, πάντῃ ἀλλήλους ἀποστυγοῦντες. καὶ
20 πρὸς ταῦτα δ' ἡμῖν εἴρηται ὅτι καὶ ἐν φιλοσοφίᾳ ἔστιν εὑρεῖν αἱρέσεις αἱρέσεσι πολεμούσας καὶ ἐν ἰατρικῇ...

p. 67
ἔτι δὲ ⟨οἱ⟩ τὸ ,,μακά-
ριοι οἱ εἰρηνοποιοὶ" νοήσαντες καὶ τὸ ,,μακάριοι οἱ πραεῖς" οὐκ ἂν
ἀποστυγήσαιεν τοὺς παραχαράττοντας τὰ χριστιανισμοῦ οὐδὲ
Κίρκας καὶ κύκηθρα αἱμύλα λέγοιεν τοὺς πεπλανημένους.

LXIV. Παρακηκοέναι δέ μοι φαίνεται τῆς τε ἀποστολικῆς λέξεως
10 φασκούσης· ,,ἐν ὑστέροις καιροῖς ἀποστήσονταί τινες τῆς πίστεως,
προσέχοντες πνεύμασι πλάνοις καὶ διδασκαλίαις δαιμονίων, ἐν ὑποκρίσει ψευδολόγων, κεκαυστηριασμένων τὴν οἰκείαν συνείδησιν, κωλυόντων γαμεῖν, ἀπέχεσθαι βρωμάτων, ἃ ὁ θεὸς ἔκτισεν εἰς μετά-
ληψιν μετ' εὐχαριστίας τοῖς πιστοῖς," παρακηκοέναι δὲ καὶ τῶν ταύ-
15 ταις τοῦ ἀποστόλου ταῖς λέξεσι χρησαμένων κατὰ τῶν παραχα-
ραξάντων τὰ χριστιανισμοῦ· διόπερ εἶπεν ὁ Κέλσος ἀκοῆς καυσ-
τήριά τινας ὀνομάζεσθαι παρὰ Χριστιανοῖς. αὐτὸς δέ φησι
τινὰς καλεῖσθαι αἰνίγματα, ὅπερ ἡμεῖς οὐχ | ἱστορήσαμεν. ἀλη- 628
θῶς δὲ τὸ τοῦ σκανδάλου ὄνομα πολὺ ἐν τοῖς γράμμασι τούτοις
20 ἐστίν, ὅπερ εἰώθαμεν λέγειν περὶ τῶν διαστρεφόντων ἀπὸ τῆς
ὑγιοῦς διδασκαλίας τοὺς ἁπλουστέρους καὶ εὐεξαπατήτους. Σειρῆ-

---

p. 66   **15** Vgl. oben III 36–38.   **20** Vgl. oben III 12f V 61.
p. 67   **6** Matth. 5, 4.   **7** Vgl. oben V 52, S. 56 Z. 20.   **9 u. 14** Vgl. unten
V 65, S. 68 Z. 25.   **10** I Tim. 4, 1–3.   **15** Vgl. oben V 52 u. 63 a. E.
16 Vgl. Irenaeus, Adv. haer. I 20, 4. Epiphan., Panar. I 27, 5 und A. Hilgenfeld, Die Ketzergesch. des Urchrist. S. 399 Anm.   **19** Vgl. Matth. 18, 6–9.
Mark. 9, 42–47. Luk. 17, 1. 2.   **21** Vgl. Homer, Od. XII 39–54. 158–200.

p. 66   **13** εὕραντο A εὕροντο M^corr· Ausgg.   **14** πολὺν Ausgg. πολύ, dahinter kleine
Rasur, A.   **16** παλιλλογήσομεν A.   **17** καὶ βλασφημοῦσι bis S. 67 Z. 7
χριστιανισμοῦ = Philokalia, Cap. XVI 4 (p. 88, 31–89, 18 ed. Rob.).   **18**
εἴξαιεν] ἤξαιεν CD.   **19** ἀποστοιγοῦντες Pat.   **20** δ' AAusgg. Rob. δὲ Φ
| ἔστιν] ἐστὶν Del. Rob.
p. 67   **6** vor νοήσαντες + οἱ νοήσαντες Del.   **7** mit χριστιανισμοῦ endigt die
Philokalia, Cap. XVI 4 (p. 89, 18 ed. Rob.).   **8** Κίρκας] ρκ in Correctur
A | κύκηθρα] über η ist ῖ geschrieben A¹.   **12** κεκαυτηριασμένων Hö. am
Rand, Sp. Del. im Text.   **19** vor ὄνομα ein Buchst. ausradiert A.

p. 67   νας δέ τινας ἐξορχουμένας καὶ σοφιστρίας, κατασφραγιζομένας τὰ ὦτα καὶ ἀποσυοκεφαλούσας τοὺς πειθομένους,
ἡμεῖς οὐκ ἴσμεν ὀνομαζομένους, οἶμαι δ' ὅτι οὐδ' ἄλλος τις τῶν
25 ἐν τῷ λόγῳ οὐδ' ἐν ταῖς αἱρέσεσιν.

p. 67   22 Vgl. Homer, Od. X 239.   p. 67   22 καταφραγιζομένας Α.

Eusebius, *HE* IV.22.4ff, quoting Hegesippus (= ὁ δ' αὐτός)
(ed. Schwartz II.1.370 and 372)

p. 370   ὁ δ' αὐτὸς καὶ τῶν κατ' αὐτὸν αἱρέσεων τὰς ἀρχὰς ὑποτίθεται 4
διὰ τούτων

»καὶ μετὰ τὸ μαρτυρῆσαι Ἰάκωβον τὸν δίκαιον, ὡς καὶ ὁ κύριος,
10 »ἐπὶ τῷ αὐτῷ λόγῳ, πάλιν ὁ ἐκ θείου αὐτοῦ Συμεὼν ὁ τοῦ Κλωπᾶ
»καθίσταται ἐπίσκοπος, ὃν προέθεντο πάντες, ὄντα ἀνεψιὸν τοῦ
»κυρίου δεύτερον. διὰ τοῦτο ἐκάλουν τὴν ἐκκλησίαν παρθένον, οὔπω
»γὰρ ἔφθαρτο ἀκοαῖς ματαίαις· ἄρχεται δὲ ὁ Θεβουθις διὰ τὸ μὴ 5
»γενέσθαι αὐτὸν ἐπίσκοπον ὑποφθείρειν ἀπὸ τῶν ἑπτὰ αἱρέσεων,
15 »ὧν καὶ αὐτὸς ἦν, ἐν τῷ λαῷ, ἀφ' ὧν Σίμων, ὅθεν Σιμωνιανοί,
»καὶ Κλεόβιος, ὅθεν Κλεοβιηνοί, καὶ Δοσίθεος, ὅθεν Δοσιθιανοί,
»καὶ Γορθαῖος, ὅθεν Γοραθηνοί, καὶ Μασβωθεοι. ἀπὸ τούτων
p. 372   »Μενανδριανισταὶ καὶ Μαρκιανισταὶ καὶ Καρποκρατιανοὶ καὶ Οὐαλεν-
»τινιανοὶ καὶ Βασιλειδιανοὶ καὶ Σατορνιλιανοὶ ἕκαστος ἰδίως καὶ
»ἑτεροίως ἰδίαν δόξαν παρεισηγάγοσαν, ἀπὸ τούτων ψευδόχριστοι, 6
»ψευδοπροφῆται, ψευδαπόστολοι, οἵτινες ἐμέρισαν τὴν ἕνωσιν τῆς
5 »ἐκκλησίας φθοριμαίοις λόγοις κατὰ τοῦ θεοῦ καὶ κατὰ τοῦ Χριστοῦ
»αὐτοῦ«.

p. 370   ΑΤΕΡΒDΜΣΛ
9–10 ὡς—λόγωι] wie wir auch gesagt haben [אמרן für מרן] Σ.   10 αὐτοῦ
DM | τοῦ θείου M | συμεὼν ΠΛ vgl. zu 268, 8. 270, 2 | cleophae Λ קליופא Σ.
12 δεύτερον Π, auf ἐπίσκοπος bezogen Σ > Λ; unrichtig.   13 δὲ Τ^cΤ^rERD
δ' B aber Σ sed Λ γὰρ ΑΤ¹ > M | θεβουθὶς B θεβουθὴσ D θέβουθισ A θαιβουθὶσ
TER θεοβουθὴσ M theobutes und thobutes Λ HSS תאבותיס Σ.   15 ὧν
Τ^cERBDM ὦν ΑΤ^rΣ > T¹ qui erat ex septem haeresibus in populo constitutus Λ |
ὅθεν BD ὅθεν οἱ ATERM.   16 κλεοβιηνοί ΑΣΛ οἱ καιηνοί Τ¹Ε οἱ καιανοί
Τ^rR καιηνοί B κλεὶηνοί DM | καὶ—Δοσιθιανοί > D, + nach Γοραθηνοί | ὅθεν
καὶ M.   17 γορθέοσ D γόρθιοσ M גוראתינוס Σ^b גוראתגוס Σ^a |
κοραθηνοὶ Τ¹ γορθηνοὶ Τ^c | μασβωθεοι TE μασβωθεοί R μασβωθαῖοι B μασβωθέοι
D μασβωθηνάιοι M μασβώθεοι [ε in ras. Α¹] ὅθεν Α מסבותיס mit Pluralpunkten
Σ et Masbutheus, unde Masbutheni Λ καὶ Μασβώθεοι scheint eine alte Interpolation zu sein·

p. 372   1 μενανδριανισταὶ TERBDM ἀδριανισταὶ A [vgl. Theodoret. haer. fab. 1, 1]
Μαρκιανισταὶ καὶ > D | μαρκιανισταὶ ΑΤ¹M μαρκιωνισταὶ Τ^cERBΛ מרקיונו
Σ.   1–2 οὐαλεντιανοί Τ¹ corr. Τ^cΤ^r οὐαλεντίνοι M > Σ.   2 βασιλιδιανοί
ΑΤΕRB¹ | ἕκαστος ἰδίως > B.   3 ἑτεροίωσ TERDM ἕτεροι ὡσ BΣ ἑτέρωσ
A | παρεισηγάγοσαν A παρεισήγαγον B¹M παρήγαγον D παρεισήγαγεν TERB^c.
4 καὶ ψευδοπροφῆται καὶ ψευδαπόστολοι DM.

p. 372 ἔτι δ᾽ ὁ αὐτὸς καὶ τὰς πάλαι γεγενημένας παρὰ ᾽Ιουδαίοις αἱρέ- 7
σεις ἱστορεῖ λέγων

»ἦσαν δὲ γνῶμαι διάφοροι ἐν τῇ περιτομῇ ἐν υἱοῖς ᾽Ισραηλιτῶν
10 »κατὰ τῆς φυλῆς ᾽Ιούδα καὶ τοῦ Χριστοῦ αὗται· ᾽Εσσαῖοι Γαλιλαῖοι
»᾽Ημεροβαπτισταὶ Μασβωθεοι Σαμαρεῖται Σαδδουκαῖοι Φαρισαῖοι«.

καὶ ἕτερα δὲ πλεῖστα γράφει, ὧν ἐκ μέρους ἤδη πρότερον ἐμνη- 8
μονεύσαμεν, οἰκείως τοῖς καιροῖς τὰς ἱστορίας παραθέμενοι, ἔκ τε τοῦ
καθ᾽ ῾Εβραίους εὐαγγελίου καὶ τοῦ Συριακοῦ καὶ ἰδίως ἐκ τῆς
15 ῾Εβραΐδος διαλέκτου τινὰ τίθησιν, ἐμφαίνων ἐξ ῾Εβραίων ἑαυτὸν πεπι-
στευκέναι, καὶ ἄλλα δὲ ὡς ἐξ ᾽Ιουδαϊκῆς ἀγράφου παραδόσεως μνημο-
νεύει.

p. 372 **9** nach περιτομῆι 4 Buchstaben getilgtB | ᾽Ισραηλιτῶν Valois ἰσραὴλ ἡ τῶν
AT¹M ἰσραὴλ τῶν T durch Rasur corr., ERBDΣΛ.   **10** αὗται ΠΣ > Λ
nach Conjectur, Heg. schrieb αὐτῆς.   **11** μασβωθεοι TE μασβωθέοι R
μασβωθαῖοι BDM μασβώθεοι A מזבותיא Σ.   **13** παρατιθέμενοι DM.   **16**
ὣσ BDM ὣσ ἂν ATER.

Irenaeus: Harvey, I.20–22 = Stieren, I.25–26.2
(ed. Harvey I.204–213)

CAP. XX.

Quæ est Carpocratis doctrina, et quæ operationes
ipsorum, qui ab eo sunt, omnia [omnium].

p. 204   1. CARPOCRATES autem et qui ab eo, mundum quidem, et   M. 103.
ea quæ in eo sunt, ab Angelis multo inferioribus ingenito Patre
factum esse dicunt. Jesum autem e Joseph natum, et qui
similis reliquis hominibus fuerit, distasse a reliquis secundum id,
quod anima ejus firma et munda cum esset, commemorata
fuerit quæ visa essent sibi in ea circumlatione, quæ fuisset
ingenito Deo: et propter hoc ab eo missam esse ei virtutem,
uti mundi fabricatores effugere posset, et per omnes transgressa,
et in omnibus liberata, ascenderet ad eum, et eas, quæ similia ei
p. 205   amplecterentur, similiter. Jesu autem dicunt animam in Judæ-
G. 100.   orum consuetudine nutritam contempsisse eos, et propter hoc
virtutes accepisse, per quas evacuavit quæ fuerunt in pœnis
[*l.* pœnas] passiones, quæ inerant hominibus. Ea [*l.* eam]
igitur, quæ similiter atque illa Jesu anima, potest contemnere
mundi fabricatores archontas, similiter accipere virtutes ad
operandum similia. Quapropter et ad tantum elationis pro-
vecti sunt, ut quidam quidem similes se esse dicant Jesu:
quidam autem adhuc et secundum aliquid illo fortiores, qui
sunt [*l.* quidam et] distantes amplius quam illius discipuli,
ut puta quam Petrus et Paulus, et reliqui Apostoli: hos autem
p. 206   in nullo deminorari a Jesu. Animas enim ipsorum ex eadem
circumlatione devenientes, et ideo similiter contemnentes mundi

fabricatores, eadem dignas habitas esse virtute, et rursus in idem abire. Si quis autem plus quam ille contempserit ea quæ sunt hic, posse meliorem quam illum esse.

2. Artes enim magicas operantur et ipsi, et incantationes, philtra quoque et charitesia, et paredros, et oniropompos, et reliquas malignationes, dicentes se potestatem habere ad dominandum jam principibus et fabricatoribus hujus mundi: non solum autem, sed et his omnibus, quæ in eo sunt facta. Qui et ipsi ad detrectationem divini Ecclesiæ nominis, quemadmodum et gentes, a Satana præmissi sunt, uti secundum alium et alium modum, quæ sunt illorum audientes homines, et putantes omnes *p. 207* nos tales esse, avertant aures suas a præconio veritatis: aut et videntes quæ sunt illorum, omnes nos blasphement, in nullo eis communicantes, neque in doctrina, neque in moribus, neque in quotidiana conversatione. Sed vitam quidem luxuriosam, sententiam autem impiam ad velamen malitiæ ipsorum nomine abutuntur, *quorum judicium justum est*, recipientium dignam Rom. iii. 8. suis operibus a Deo retributionem. Et in tantum insania effrænati sunt, uti et omnia quæcunque sunt irreligiosa et impia, in potestate habere et operari se dicant. Sola enim M. 104. humana opinione negotia mala et bona dicunt. Et utique secundum transmigrationes in corpora oportere in omni vita, et in omni actu fieri animas: (si non præoccupans quis in uno adventu omnia agat semel ac pariter, quæ non tantum dicere et audire non est fas nobis, sed ne quidem in mentis conceptionem venire, nec credere, si apud homines conversantes in his quæ sunt secundum nos civitates, tale aliquid agitatur,) uti, secundum quod scripta eorum dicunt, in omni usu vitæ factae animæ *p. 208* ipsorum, exeuntes, in nihilo adhuc minus habeant; adoperandum autem in eo, ne forte propterea quod deest libertati aliqua res, cogantur iterum mitti in corpus. Propter hoc dicunt Luc. xii. 58. Jesum hanc dixisse parabolam: *Cum es cum adversario tuo in via,* G. 101. & Matt. v. 25, *da operam, ut libereris ab eo, ne forte te det judici et judex minis-* 26. *tro, et mittat te in carcerem. Amen dico tibi, non exies inde, donec reddas novissimum quadrantem.* Et adversarium dicunt unum Cf. p. 198. ex Angelis qui sunt in mundo, quem diabolum vocant, dicentes factum eum ad id, ut ducat eas quæ perierunt animas a mundo ad principem. Et hunc dicunt esse primum ex mundi fabricatoribus, et illum altero angelo, qui ministrat ei, tradere tales animas, uti in alia corpora includat: corpus enim dicunt esse *p. 209* carcerem. Et id quod ait: *Non exies inde, quoadusque novissi-* Hipp. *mum quadrantem reddas,* interpretantur, quasi non exeat quis a Philos. vii. 32. potestate Angelorum eorum, qui mundum fabricaverunt; sed sic transcorporatum semper, quoadusque in omni omnino opera-

302

tione, quæ in mundo est, fiat: et quum nihil defuerit ei, tum liberatam ejus animam eliberari ad illum Deum, qui est supra angelos mundi fabricatores; sic quoque salvari, et omnes animas sive ipsæ præoccupantes in uno adventu in omnibus misceantur operationibus, sive de corpore in corpus transmigrantes, vel immissæ in unaquaque specie vitæ adimplentes, et reddentes debita, liberari, uti jam non fiant in corpore.

3. Et si quidem fiant hæc apud eos, quæ sunt irreligiosa, et injusta, et vetita, ego nequaquam credam. In conscriptionibus autem illorum sic conscriptum est, et ipsi ita exponunt; Jesum dicentes in mysterio discipulis suis et apostolis seorsum locutum, *p. 210* et illos expostulasse, ut dignis et assentientibus seorsum hæc traderent. Per fidem enim et caritatem salvari; reliqua vero, indifferentia cum sint, secundum opinionem hominum quædam quidem bona, quædam autem mala vocari, cum nihil natura malum sit.

4. Alii vero ex ipsis signant, cauteriantes suos discipulos in posterioribus partibus exstantiæ dextræ auris. Unde et Marcellina, quæ Romam sub Aniceto venit, cum esset hujus doctrinæ, multos exterminavit. Gnosticos se autem vocant: M. 105. etiam imagines, quasdam quidem depictas, quasdam autem et de G. 102. reliqua materia fabricatas habent, dicentes formam Christi factam a Pilato, illo in tempore quo fuit Jesus cum hominibus. Et has coronant, et proponunt eas cum imaginibus mundi philosophorum, videlicet cum imagine Pythagoræ, et Platonis, et Aristotelis, et reliquorum; et reliquam observationem circa eas similiter ut gentes faciunt.

p. 211

CAP. XXI.

Qualis est doctrina Cerinthi.

Et Cerinthus autem quidam in Asia [*l.* Ægypto], non a primo Deo factum esse mundum docuit, sed a virtute quadam valde separata, et distante ab ea principalitate quæ est super universa, et ignorante eum qui est super omnia Deum. Jesum autem subjecit, non ex virgine natum, [impossibile enim hoc ei visum est], fuisse autem eum Joseph et Mariæ filium, similiter ut reliqui omnes homines, et plus potuisse justitia, et prudentia, et sapientia ab omnibus. Et post baptismum descendisse in eum, ab ea principalitate quæ est super omnia, Christum figura columbæ; et tunc annunciasse incognitum Patrem, et virtutes perfecisse; in fine autem revolasse iterum Christum de Jesu, et *p. 212* Jesum passum esse, et resurrexisse: Christum autem impassibilem perseverasse, exsistentem spiritalem.

CAP. XXII.

Quæ est Ebionitarum doctrina.

QUI autem dicuntur Ebionæi, consentiunt quidem mundum a Deo factum: ea autem quæ sunt erga Dominum, non simi-
p. 213 liter ut Cerinthus et Carpocrates opinantur. Solo autem eo quod est secundum Matthæum Evangelio utuntur, et aposto-lum Paulum recusant, apostatam eum legis dicentes. Quæ
G. 103. autem sunt prophetica, curiosius exponere nituntur; et circum-ciduntur ac perseverant in his consuetudinibus, quæ sunt secun-dum legem, et Judaico charactere vitæ, uti et Hierosolymam adorent, quasi domus sit Dei.

Irenaeus: Harvey, I.26.2 = Stieren, I.28.2 (ed. Harvey I.221)

The *alii* are heretical sects and are contrasted, qua libertine, with the ascetic sects just previously mentioned, which sprang up from the teachings of Saturninus and Marcion.

p. 221   2. Alii autem rursus a Basilide et Carpocrate occasiones accipientes, indifferentes coitus, et multas nuptias induxerunt, et negligentiam ipsorum quæ sunt idolothyta ad manducan-dum, non valde hæc curare dicentes Deum. Et quid enim? non est numerum dicere eorum, qui secundum alterum et alte-rum modum exciderunt a veritate.

Irenaeus: Harvey, II.48–53 = Stieren, II.31–33.4 (ed. Harvey I.369–379)

p. 369   CAP. XLVIII.

Quomodo ea quæ adversus Valentinum dicuntur, omnem evertunt hæresin.

1. DESTRUCTIS itaque his qui a Valentino sunt, omnis hæreticorum eversa est multitudo. Quæ enim et quantum adversus Pleroma ipsorum et ad ea quæ extra sunt diximus, ostendentes quoniam concludetur et circumscribetur Pater universorum ab eo quod extra eum est, (si tamen extra eum aliquid sit); et quoniam necesse est multos quidem Patres, multa autem Pleromata, et multas mundorum fabricationes, ab aliis quidem cœptas ad alteras autem deficientes, esse secundum omnem partem; et universos perseverantes in suis propriis, non curiose agere de aliis, in quibus neque participatio, neque communio aliqua est eis; et nullum alium omnium esse Deum, sed solam esse omnipotentis appellationem:

M. 164. et adversus eos qui sunt a Marcione, et Simone, et Menandro, vel quicunque alii sunt, qui similiter dividunt eam quæ secundum nos est conditionem a Patre, similiter erit ad eos aptatum. Quanta autem rursus diximus adversus eos, qui dicunt omnia quidem comprehendere Patrem universorum; eam autem quæ sit secundum nos conditionem non ab eo esse factam, sed a Virtute quadam altera; vel ab Angelis ignorantibus Propatorem, in immensa magnitudine universitatis circumscriptum centri vice, velut maculam in pallio; ostendentes quoniam non est verisimile alium quemdam eam quæ secundum nos est conditionem fecisse quam Patrem universorum; et adversus eos qui sunt a Saturnino, et a Basilide, et Carpocrate, et reliquos Gnosticorum, qui eadem similiter dicunt, idem dicetur. Quæ autem de prolationibus dicta sunt, et Æonibus, et deminoratione, et quemadmodum instabilis Mater ipsorum, similiter evertit Basilidem, et omnes qui falso cognominantur agnitores, aliis nominibus eadem similiter dicentes; magis autem quam hi qui ea quæ sunt extra veritatem transferentes ad

G. 186. characterem suæ doctrinæ. Et quæcunque sunt quæ de numeris diximus, adversus omnes, qui in hujusmodi speciem deducunt quæ

p. 370 sunt veritatis, et dicentur. Et quæcunque dicta sunt de Demiurgo, ostendentia quod his solus est Deus et Pater universorum; et quæcunque adhuc dicentur in sequentibus libris, adversus omnes dico hæreticos; eos quidem qui sunt mitiores eorum et humaniores avertes et confundes, ut non blasphement suum conditorem, et factorem, et nutritorem, et Dominum, neque de labe et ignorantia genesin ejus affingere: feroces autem, et horribiles, et irrationabiles effugabis a te longe, ne amplius sustineas verbositates eorum.

2. Super hæc arguentur qui sunt a Simone, et Carpocrate, et si qui alii virtutes operari dicuntur: non in virtute Dei, neque in veritate, neque in beneficiis hominibus facientes ea quæ faciunt; sed in perniciem et errorem, per magicas elusiones et universa fraude, plus lædentes quam utilitatem præstantes his, qui credunt eis, in eo quod seducant. Nec enim cæcis possunt donare visum, neque surdis auditum, neque omnes dæmones effugare, præter eos qui ab ipsis immittuntur, si tamen et hoc faciunt; neque debiles, aut claudos, aut paralyticos curare, vel alia quadam parte corporis vexatos, quemadmodum sæpe evenit fieri secundum corporalem infirmitatem; vel earum quæ a foris accidunt infirmitatum bonas valetudines restaurare; tantum autem absunt ab eo ut mortuum excitent, quemadmodum Dominus excitavit, et Apostoli per orationem, et in fraternitate sæpissime propter aliquid necessarium, ea quæ est in quoquo loco Ecclesia universa postulante per jejunium et supplicationem multam, reversus est spiritus mortui, et donatus est homo orationibus sanctorum, ut ne quidem credant

hoc in totum posse fieri: esse autem resurrectionem a mortuis, agnitionem ejus quæ ab eis dicitur, veritatis.

p. 371 3. Quando igitur apud eos quidem error, et seductio, et magica phantasia in speculatu hominum impie fiat; in Ecclesia autem miseratio, et misericordia, et firmitas, et veritas ad opitulationem hominum, non solum sine mercede et gratis perficiatur, sed et nobis ipsis quæ sunt nostra erogantibus pro salute hominum, et ea, quibus hi qui curantur indigent, sæpissime non habentes, a nobis accipiunt: vere et per hanc speciem arguuntur a divina substantia, et benignitate Dei, et virtute spiritali in totum extranei; fraude autem universa, et adinspiratione apostatica, et operatione dæmoniaca, et phantasmate idololatriæ per omnia repleti, præcursores vero sunt draconis ejus, qui per hujusmodi phantasiam abscedere faciet in cauda tertiam partem stellarum, et dejiciet Rev. xii. 4. eas in terram: quos similiter atque illum devitare oportet, et quanto majore phantasmate operari dicuntur, tanto magis observare eos, quasi majorem nequitiæ spiritum perceperint. Quam prophetiam si observaverit quis, [*adj.* et] eorum diurnam conversationis operationem, inveniet unam et eandem esse eis cum dæmoniis conversationem.

G. 187. 4. Et hæc autem quæ est erga operationes impia ipsorum
M. 165. sententia, quæ dicit oportere eos in omnibus operibus etiam quibuslibet malis fieri, ex Domini doctrina dissolvetur: apud quem Matt. v.
p. 372 non solum qui mœchatur, expellitur, sed et qui mœchari vult: et 21. et seq. non solum qui occidit, reus erit occisionis ad damnationem, sed et qui irascitur sine causa fratri suo: qui et non solum non odire homines, sed et inimicos diligere jussit: et non solum non pejerare, sed nec jurare præcepit; et non solum [non] male loqui de proximis, sed ne quidem *racha* et fatuum dicere aliquem; si quo minus, reos esse hujusmodi in ignem gehennæ: et non tantum non percutere, sed et ipsos percussos etiam alteram præstare maxillam: et non solum non abnegare quæ sunt aliena, sed etiam si sua auferantur, illis non expostulare: et non solum non lædere proximos, neque facere quid eis malum, sed et eos qui male tractantur magnanimes esse, et benignitatem exercere erga eos, et orare pro eis, uti pœnitentiam agentes salvari possint; in nullo imitantes nos reliquorum contumeliam, et libidinem, et superbiam. Quando igitur ille, quem isti magistrum gloriantur, et eum multo meliorem et fortiorem reliquis animam habuisse dicunt, cum magna diligentia quædam quidem jussit fieri quasi bona et egregia, quibusdam autem abstinere non solum operibus, sed etiam his cogitationibus quæ ad opera ducunt, quasi malis et nocivis et nequam: quemadmodum magistrum dicentes talem fortiorem et meliorem reliquis, deinde quæ sunt contraria ejus doctrinæ manifeste præcipientes, non confundantur? Et si quidem nihil esset mali aut

rursus boni, opinione autem sola humana, quædam quidem injusta
Matt. xiii. 43. quædam autem justa putarentur, non utique dixisset dogmatizans,
[id est docens:] *Justi autem fulgebunt sicut sol in regno Patris eorum:*
Matt. xxv. 41. Marc. ix. 44, 46, 48. injustos autem et qui non faciunt opera justitiæ, mittet *in ignem*
æternum, ubi vermis ipsorum non morietur, et ignis non exstinguetur.

CAP. XLIX.

Eversio Hæreticorum omnium in iis, quibus non com-
municant cum Valentino.

1. ADHUC etiam dicentes, oportere eos in omni opere et in
omni conversatione fieri, ut, si fieri possit, in una vitæ adven-
tatione omnia perficientes ad perfectum transgrediantur; eorum
quidem quæ sunt ad virtutem pertinentia, et laboriosa et gloriosa
et artificialia, quæ etiam ab omnibus bona approbantur, nequaquam inveniuntur conati facere. Si enim oportet per omne opus,
et per universam ire operationem; primo quidem oportebat
p. 373 omnes se ediscere artes, quæcunque illæ sive in sermonum rationibus, sive in operibus consumantur, sive per continentiam edocentur,
et per laborem, et meditationem, et perseverantiam percipiuntur;
ut puta omnem speciem Musicæ, et Computationis, et Geo-
metriæ, et Astronomiæ, et universa quæ in sermonum rationibus
occupantur: adhuc etiam Medicinam universam, et herbarum
scientiam, et eas quæ ad salutem humanam sunt elaboratæ; et
picturam, et statuarum fabricationem, et ærariam artem, et mar-
morariam, et similes his: ab his autem omnem speciem rustica-
tionis, et veterinariæ, et pastoralis, et opificum artes, quæ dicuntur
pertransire universas artes, et eas quæ erga mare vacant, et
corpori student, et venatorias, et militares, et regales, et quot-
G. 188. quot sunt, quarum nec decimam, nec millesimam partem in tota
vita sua elaborantes ediscere possunt. Et horum quidem nihil
conantur addiscere, qui in omni dicunt semetipsos oportere fieri
opere, ad voluptates autem et libidinem, et turpia facta dever-
gentes, a semetipsis judicati cum sint secundum doctrinam suam;
quoniam enim desunt eis quæ prædicta sunt omnia, ad correp-
tionem ignis adibunt. Qui quidem Epicuri philosophiam, et
Cynicorum indifferentiam æmulantes, Jesum magistrum gloriantur, qui non solum a malis operibus avertit suos discipulos, sed
etiam a sermonibus et cogitationibus, quemadmodum ostendimus.

2. Dicentes autem, se ex eadem circumlatione cum Jesu
habere animas, et similes ei esse, aliquando autem et meliores, ad
opera producti quæ ille ad utilitatem hominum et firmitatem
p. 374 fecit, et nihil tale nec simile, neque secundum aliquid in compara-
tionem quod venire possit, perficere inveniuntur. Sed et si aliquid
faciunt, per magicam, quemadmodum diximus, operati, fraudu-

lenter seducere nituntur insensatos: fructum quidem et utilitatem nullam præstantes, in quos virtutes perficere se dicunt; adducentes autem pueros investes, et oculos deludentes, et phantasmata ostendentes statim cessantia, et ne quidem stillicidio temporis perseverantia, non Jesu Domino nostro, sed Simoni M. 166. mago similes ostenduntur. Et ex hoc autem quod Dominus surrexit a mortuis in tertia die, firmum esse, et discipulis se manifestavit, et videntibus eis receptus est in cœlum, quod ipsi morientes, et non resurgentes, neque manifestati quibusdam, arguuntur in nullo similes habentes Jesu animas.

3. Si autem et Dominum per phantasmata hujusmodi fecisse dicunt, ad prophetica reducentes eos, ex ipsis demonstrabimus, omnia sic de eo et prædicta esse, et facta firmissime, et ipsum solum esse Filium Dei. Quapropter et in illius nomine, qui vere illius sunt discipuli ab ipso accipientes gratiam, perficiunt ad *p. 375* beneficia reliquorum hominum, quemadmodum unusquisque accepit donum ab eo. Alii enim dæmones excludunt firmissime et vere, ut etiam sæpissime credant ipsi qui emundati sunt a nequissimis spiritibus, et sint in Ecclesia: alii autem et præscientiam habent futurorum, et visiones, et dictiones propheticas. Alii autem laborantes aliqua infirmitate, per manus impositionem curant, et sanos restituunt. Jam etiam, quemadmodum diximus, et mortui resurrexerunt, et perseveraverunt nobiscum annis multis. Et quid autem? Non est numerum dicere gratiarum, quas per universum mundum Ecclesia a Deo accipiens, in nomine Christi Jesu, crucifixi sub Pontio Pilato, per singulos dies in opitulationem gentium perficit, neque seducens aliquem, nec pecuniam ei auferens. Quemadmodum enim gratis accepit a Deo, gratis et ministrat. Nec invocationibus angelicis facit aliquid, nec *p. 376* incantationibus, nec reliqua prava curiositate; sed munde et pure et manifeste orationes dirigentes [dirigens] ad Dominum, qui omnia fecit, et nomen Domini nostri Jesu Christi invocans, virtutes secundum utilitates hominum, sed non ad seductionem perfecit. Si itaque et nunc nomen Domini nostri Jesu Christi beneficia præstat, et curat firmissime et vere omnes ubique credentes in eum, sed non Simonis, neque Menandri, neque Carpocratis, nec alterius cujuscunque, manifestum est, quoniam homo factus, conversatus est cum suo plasmate, vere omnia fecit ex virtute Dei, secundum placitum Patris universorum, quomodo prophetæ prædixerunt. Quæ autem erant hæc, in his quæ sunt ex propheticis ostensionibus narrabuntur.

CAP. L.

Ostensio quod non transeant animæ in alia corpora.

DE corpore autem in corpus transmigrationem ipsorum sub- M. 167.
vertamus ex eo, quod nihil omnino eorum quæ ante fuerint,
meminerint animæ. Si enim ob hoc emittebantur, uti in omni
fierent operatione, oportebat eas meminisse eorum quæ ante
facta sunt, uti ea quæ deerant adimplerent, et non circa eadem
semper volutantes continuatim, miserabiliter laborarent. Non
enim poterat corporis admixtio in totum universam ipsorum, quæ
ante habita erant, extinguere memoriam et contemplationem; et
maxime ad hoc venientes. Quomodo enim nunc soporati et
requiescente corpore, quæcunque anima ipsa apud se videt, et in
p. 377   phantasmate agit, et horum plura reminiscens communicat cum
corpore; et est quando et post plurimum temporis, quæcunque
per somnium quis vidit, vigilans annuntiat: sic utique reminisceretur et illorum, quæ, antequam in hoc corpus veniret, egit.
Si enim hoc, quod in brevissimo tempore visum est, vel in
phantasmate conceptum est, et ab ea sola per somnium,
postquam commixta sit corpori, et in universum membrum
dispersa, commemoratur, multo magis illorum reminisceretur,
in quibus, temporibus tantis et universo præteritæ vitæ
sæculo immorata est.

CAP. LI.

Ostensio quod non bibant, secundum Platonem, oblivionis
poculum.

G. 190.   AD hæc Plato vetus ille Atheniensis, qui et primus sententiam
hanc introduxit, cum excusare non posset, oblivionis induxit
p. 378   poculum, putans se per hoc aporiam hujusmodi effugere: ostensio-
nem quidem nullam faciens, dogmatice autem respondens, quoniam
introeuntes animæ in hanc vitam, ab eo qui est super introitum
dæmone, priusquam in corpora intrent, potantur oblivione. Et
latuit semetipsum in alteram majorem incidens aporiam. Si enim
oblivionis poculum potest, posteaquam ebibitum est, omnium
factorum obliterare memoriam, hoc ipsum unde scis o Plato, cum
sit nunc in corpore anima tua, quoniam, priusquam in corpus
introeat, a dæmone potata est oblivionis medicamentum? Si enim
dæmonem, et poculum, et introitum reminisceris, et reliqua
oportet cognoscas: si autem illa ignoras, neque dæmon verus,
neque artificiose compositum oblivionis poculum.

CAP. LII.

Ostensio quoniam corpus non est oblivio.

ADVERSUS autem eos, qui dicunt ipsum corpus esse oblivionis medicamentum, occurret hoc: Quomodo igitur quodcunque per semetipsam anima videt, et in somniis et secundum cogitationem, mentis intentionem, corpore quiescente, ipsa reminiscitur, et renuntiat proximis? Sed ne quidem ea quæ olim agnita sunt, aut per oculos, aut per auditum, meminisset anima in corpore exsistens, si esset corpus oblivio; sed simul atque ab inspectis abesset *p. 379* oculus, auferretur utique et ea quæ esset de his memoria. In ipsa enim oblivione exsistens anima nihil aliud cognoscere poterat, nisi solum illud quod in præsenti videbat. Quomodo autem et divina disceret, et meminisset ipsorum exsistens in corpore, quando sit, ut aiunt, ipsum corpus oblivio? Sed et prophetæ ipsi cum essent in terra, quæcunque spiritaliter secundum visiones cœlestium vident vel audiunt, ipsi quoque meminerunt in hominem conversi, et reliquis annuntiant: et non corpus oblivionem efficit animæ eorum quæ spiritaliter visa sunt; sed anima docet corpus, et participat de spiritali ei facta visione.

CAP. LIII.

Quoniam in corporis communione non amittit suas
virtutes anima.

G. 191.   NON enim est fortius corpus quam anima, quod quidem ab illa spiratur, et vivificatur, et augetur, et articulatur; sed anima possidet et principatur corpori. Tantum autem impeditur a sua velocitate, quantum corpus participat de ejus motione; sed non M. 168. amittit suam scientiam. Corpus enim organo simile est; anima autem artificis rationem obtinet. Quemadmodum itaque artifex velociter quidem operationem secundum se adinvenit, in organo autem tardius illam perficit, propter rei subjectæ immobilitatem, et illius mentis velocitas admixta tarditati organi temperatam perficit operationem: sic et anima participans suo corpori, modicum quidem impeditur, admixta velocitate ejus in corporis tarditate; non amittit autem in totum suas virtutes; sed quasi vitam participans corpori, ipsa vivere non cessat. Sic et de reliquis ei communicans, neque scientiam ipsorum perdit, neque memoriam inspectorum.

Clement, *Stromateis* III.2 (ed. Stählin II.197–200)

p. 197

II. Οἱ δὲ ἀπὸ Καρποκράτους καὶ Ἐπιφάνους ἀναγόμενοι κοινὰς 5, 1
εἶναι τὰς γυναῖκας ἀξιοῦσιν, ἐξ ὧν ἡ μεγίστη κατὰ τοῦ ὀνόματος
ἐρρύη βλασφημία. Ἐπιφάνης οὗτος, οὗ καὶ τὰ συγγράμματα κομί- 2
ζεται, υἱὸς ἦν Καρποκράτους καὶ μητρὸς Ἀλεξανδρείας τοὔνομα τὰ
20 μὲν πρὸς πατρὸς Ἀλεξανδρεύς, ἀπὸ δὲ μητρὸς Κεφαλληνεύς, ἔζησε
δὲ τὰ πάντα ἔτη ἑπτακαίδεκα, καὶ θεὸς ἐν | Σάμῃ τῆς Κεφαλληνίας 184 S
τετίμηται, ἔνθα αὐτῷ ἱερὸν ῥυτῶν λίθων, βωμοί, τεμένη, μουσεῖον
ᾠκοδόμηταί τε καὶ καθιέρωται, καὶ συνιόντες εἰς τὸ ἱερὸν οἱ Κεφαλλῆνες κατὰ νουμηνίαν γενέθλιον ἀποθέωσιν θύουσιν Ἐπιφάνει, σπέν-
25 δουσί τε καὶ εὐωχοῦνται καὶ ὕμνοι ᾄδονται. ἐπαιδεύθη μὲν οὖν 3
παρὰ τῷ πατρὶ τήν τε ἐγκύκλιον παιδείαν καὶ τὰ Πλάτωνος, καθη- 512 P
γήσατο δὲ τῆς μοναδικῆς γνώσεως, ἀφ' οὗ καὶ ἡ τῶν Καρποκρατιανῶν αἵρεσις. λέγει τοίνυν οὗτος ἐν τῷ Περὶ δικαιοσύνης »τὴν 6, 1

p. 198

δικαιοσύνην τοῦ θεοῦ κοινωνίαν τινὰ εἶναι μετ' ἰσότητος. ἴσος γέ
τοι πανταχόθεν ἐκταθεὶς οὐρανὸς κύκλῳ τὴν γῆν περιέχει πᾶσαν,
καὶ πάντας ἡ νὺξ ἐπ' ἴσης ἐπιδείκνυται τοὺς ἀστέρας, τόν τε τῆς
ἡμέρας αἴτιον καὶ πατέρα τοῦ φωτὸς ἥλιον ὁ θεὸς ἐξέχεεν ἄνωθεν ἴσον
5 ἐπὶ γῆς ἅπασι τοῖς βλέπειν δυναμένοις, οἳ δὲ κοινῇ πάντες βλέπουσιν,
ἐπεὶ μὴ διακρίνει πλούσιον ἢ πένητα, δῆμον ἢ ἄρχοντα, ἄφρονάς τε 2
καὶ τοὺς φρονοῦντας, θηλείας ἄρσενας, ἐλευθέρους δούλους. ἀλλ'
οὐδὲ τῶν ἀλόγων παρὰ τοῦτο ποιεῖταί τι, πᾶσι δὲ ἐπ' ἴσης τοῖς
ζῴοις κοινὸν αὐτὸν ἐκχέας ἄνωθεν ἀγαθοῖς τε καὶ φαύλοις τὴν
10 δικαιοσύνην ἐμπεδοῖ μηδενὸς δυναμένου πλεῖον ἔχειν μηδὲ ἀφαιρεῖσθαι
τὸν πλησίον, ἵν' αὐτὸς κἀκείνου τὸ φῶς διπλασιάσας ἔχῃ. ἥλιος 3
κοινὰς τροφὰς ζῴοις ἅπασιν ἀνατέλλει, δικαιοσύνης [τε] τῆς κοινῆς
ἅπασιν ἐπ' ἴσης δοθείσης, καὶ εἰς τὰ τοιαῦτα βοῶν γένος ὁμοίως
γίνεται ὡς αἱ βόες καὶ συῶν ὡς οἱ σύες καὶ προβάτων ὡς τὰ πρό-
15 βατα καὶ τὰ λοιπὰ πάντα· δικαιοσύνη γὰρ ἐν αὐτοῖς ἀναφαίνεται ἡ 4

p. 197 16–S. 199, 13. 199, 29–200, 4 vgl. Hilgenfeld, Ketzergeschichte S. 402ff. 18–
28 vgl. Epiph. Haer. 32, 3 I S. 442, 4–18; Lipsius, Zur Quellenkritik des Epiph.
S. 161f.; Usener, Weihnachtsfest S. 111 Anm. 10. 23f zur monatl. Geburts-
tagsfeier vgl. Rohde, Psyche² I p. 234f; Schürer, ZntW 2 (1901) S. 48ff;
Wissowa, Hermes 37 (1902) S. 157ff; Collitz, Dialektinschr. 1801, 5f (von einer
Freigelassenen): στεφανωέτω τὰν Φίλωνος εἰκόνα καθ' ἕκαστον μῆνα δὶς δαφνίνω
στεφάνω πλεκτῶ νουμηνίαι καὶ ἑβδόμαι.

p. 198 12 vgl. I Clem. ad Cor. 20, 4 (Fr).

p. 197 19 ἀλεξανδρίας L. 20 ἀπὸ Κεφαλληνίας μὲν τὸ πρὸς πατρὸς γένος ὤν Epiph.
Κεφαλλὴν Cobet S. 511 (vgl. Z. 23f). 23 nach τε καὶ ist σον von L¹ getilgt.
25 καὶ ὕμνοι ᾄδονται Wi καὶ ὕμνοι λέγονται L ὕμνους τε αὐτῷ ᾄδουσι Epiph.

p. 198 6 δῆμον ἢ St ἢ δήμου L ἢ δημότην ⟨καὶ⟩ Hiller. 7 [τοὺς] Wi. 8 ποιεῖται:
Medium ist richtig, denn es bedeutet hier „einschätzen" (Fr). 9 αὐτὸν L.
11 τὸ κἀκείνου L κἀκείνου τὸ ~ Wi. 12 ἀνατέλλει Sy ἀνατέλλειν L [τε] Hiller.
14 οἱ σύες] αἱ σύες Hilg.

κοινότης. ἔπειτα κατὰ κοινότητα πάντα ὁμοίως κατὰ γένος σπείρεται,
τροφή τε κοινὴ χαμαὶ νεμομένοις ἀνεῖται πᾶσι τοῖς κτήνεσι καὶ πᾶσιν
ἐπ᾽ ἴσης, οὐδενὶ νόμῳ κρατουμένη, τῇ δὲ παρὰ τοῦ διδόντος ⟨καὶ⟩
κελεύσαντος χορηγίᾳ συμφώνως ἅπασι δικαιοσύνῃ παροῦσα. ἀλλ᾽ οὐδὲ **7, 1**
20 τὰ τῆς γενέσεως νόμον ἔχει γεγραμμένον (μετεγράφη γὰρ ἄν), σπεί-
ρουσι δὲ καὶ γεννῶσιν ἐπ᾽ ἴσης, κοινωνίαν ὑπὸ δικαιοσύνης ἔμφυτον
ἔχοντες. κοινῇ πᾶσιν ἐπ᾽ ἴσης ὀφθαλμὸν εἰς τὸ βλέπειν ὁ ποιητής
τε καὶ πατὴρ πάντων δικαιοσύνῃ νομοθετήσας τῇ παρ᾽ αὐτοῦ παρ-
έσχεν, οὐ διακρίνας θήλειαν ἄρρενος, οὐ λογικὸν ἀλόγου, καὶ
25 καθάπαξ οὐδενὸς οὐδέν, ἰσότητι δὲ καὶ κοινότητι μερίσας τὸ βλέπειν
ὁμοίως ἑνὶ κελεύσματι πᾶσι κεχάρισται. οἱ νόμοι δὲ«, φησίν, »ἀν- **2**
θρώπων ἀμαθίαν κολάζειν μὴ δυνάμενοι παρα|νομεῖν ἐδίδαξαν· ἡ 513 P
γὰρ ἰδιότης τῶν νόμων τὴν κοινωνίαν τοῦ θείου νόμου κατέτεμεν
καὶ παρατρώγει,« μὴ συνιεὶς τὸ τοῦ ἀποστόλου ῥητόν, λέγοντος
30 »διὰ νόμου τὴν ἁμαρτίαν ἔγνων«· τό τε ἐμὸν καὶ τὸ σόν φησι διὰ **3**
τῶν νόμων παρεισελθεῖν, μηκέτι εἰς κοινότητα [κοινά τε γὰρ] καρπουμένων μήτε γῆν μήτε κτήματα, ἀλλὰ μηδὲ γάμον. »κοινῇ γὰρ **4**
p. 199   ἅπασιν ἐποίησε τὰς ἀμπέλους, αἳ μή⟨τε⟩ στρουθὸν μήτε κλέπτην ἀπαρ-
νοῦνται, καὶ τὸν σῖτον οὕτως καὶ τοὺς ἄλλους καρπούς. ἡ δὲ κοινωνία παρανομηθεῖσα καὶ τὰ τῆς ἰσότητος ἐγέννησε θρεμμάτων καὶ
καρπῶν κλέπτην. κοινῇ τοίνυν ὁ θεὸς ἅπαντα ἀνθρώπῳ ποιήσας **8, 1**
5 καὶ τὸ θῆλυ τῷ ἄρρενι κοινῇ συναγαγὼν καὶ πάνθ᾽ ὁμοίως τὰ ζῷα
κολλήσας τὴν δικαιοσύνην ἀνέφηνεν κοινωνίαν μετ᾽ ἰσότητος. οἱ δὲ **2**
γεγονότες οὕτω τὴν συνάγουσαν κοινωνίαν τὴν γένεσιν αὐτῶν
ἀπηρνήθησαν καὶ φασιν· ὁ μίαν ἀγόμενος ἐχέτω, δυναμένων κοινω-
νεῖν ἁπάντων, ὥσπερ ἀπέφηνε τὰ λοιπὰ τῶν ζῴων.« ταῦτα εἰπὼν **3**
10 κατὰ λέξιν πάλιν ὁμοίως αὐταῖς ταῖς λέξεσιν ἐπιφέρει· »τὴν γὰρ
ἐπιθυμίαν εὔτονον καὶ σφοδροτέραν ἐνεποίησε τοῖς ἄρρεσιν εἰς τὴν
τῶν γενῶν παραμονήν, ἣν οὔτε νόμος οὔτε ἔθος οὔτε ἄλλο ⟨τι⟩ τῶν
ὄντων ἀφανίσαι δύναται. θεοῦ γάρ ἐστι δόγμα.« καὶ πῶς ἔτι οὗτος **4**
ἐν τῷ καθ᾽ ἡμᾶς ἐξετασθείη λόγῳ ἄντικρυς καὶ τὸν νόμον καὶ τὸ
15 εὐαγγέλιον διὰ τούτων καθαιρῶν; ὁ μὲν γάρ φησιν· »οὐ μοιχεύσεις,« **5**
τὸ δὲ »πᾶς ὁ προσβλέπων κατ᾽ ἐπιθυμίαν ἤδη ἐμοίχευσεν« λέγει. τὸ **5**
γὰρ »οὐκ ἐπιθυμήσεις« πρὸς τοῦ νόμου λεγόμενον τὸν ἕνα δείκνυσι
θεὸν διὰ νόμου καὶ προφητῶν καὶ εὐαγγελίου κηρυσσόμενον· λέγει

p. 198   **30** Rom 7, 7.
p. 199   **15** Exod 20, 13.   **16** Mt 5, 28.   **17–19** Exod 20, 17.

p. 198   **16** ἔπειτα] ἐπεὶ oder ἐπειδὴ St.   **17** κοινῇ Hilg.   **18** [διδόντος] Heyse, Hilg.
⟨καὶ⟩ Hiller.   **19** χορηγίᾳ L χορηγεῖν Schw ἅπασι ~ nach δικ. Heyse δικαιοσύνῃ
Ρο -η L [δικαιοσύνῃ] Sy.   **31** [κοινά τε γὰρ] Ma κοινὸν τί γὰρ Hilg. (κοινά τε
γάρ) Ρο.   **31f** καρπουμένων ⟨ἡμῶν⟩ St.
p. 199   **1** μή⟨τε⟩ St μὴ L.   **3** καὶ τὰ (vgl. S. 198, 20; 200, 2)] κατὰ Hilg.   **7** συνέχουσαν (vgl. S. 200, 2) St.   **8** φασιν Hilg. φησὶν L ἔφασαν St ὁ Sy εἰ L.   **12**
⟨τι⟩ He.   **13** δόγμα] δόμα Bernays πῶς ⟨ἂν⟩ Ma.   **15** καθαιρῶν Sy καθαίρων
L.

γάρ· »οὐκ ἐπιθυμήσεις τῆς τοῦ πλησίον.« ὁ πλησίον δὲ οὐχ ὁ Ἰου- 6
20 δαῖος τῷ Ἰουδαίῳ, ἀδελφὸς γὰρ καὶ ταυτότης τοῦ πνεύματος, λείπε-
ται δὴ πλησίον τὸν ἀλλοεθνῆ λέγειν. πῶς γὰρ οὐ πλησίον ὁ οἷός
τε κοινωνῆσαι τοῦ πνεύματος; οὐ γὰρ μόνων Ἑβραίων, ἀλλὰ καὶ
ἐθνῶν πατὴρ Ἀβραάμ. εἰ δὲ ἡ μοιχευθεῖσα καὶ ὁ εἰς αὐτὴν πορνεύσας 9, 1
θανάτῳ κολάζεται, δῆλον δήπου τὴν ἐντολὴν τὴν λέγουσαν »οὐκ
25 ἐπιθυμήσεις τὴν γυναῖκα τοῦ πλησίον« περὶ τῶν ἐθνῶν διαγορεύειν,
ἵνα τις κατὰ νόμον καὶ τῆς τοῦ πλησίον καὶ τῆς ἀδελφῆς ἀποσχό-
μενος ἄντικρυς ἀκούσῃ παρὰ τοῦ κυρίου· »ἐγὼ δὲ λέγω, οὐκ ἐπιθυ-
μήσεις·« ἡ δὲ | τοῦ »ἐγώ« μορίου προσθήκη προσεχεστέραν δείκνυσι 514 P
τῆς ἐντολῆς τὴν ἐνέργειαν, καὶ ὅτι θεομαχεῖ ὅ τε Καρποκράτης ὅ τ' 2
30 Ἐπιφάνης, ⟨ὃς⟩ ἐν αὐτῷ τῷ πολυθρυλήτῳ βιβλίῳ, τῷ Περὶ δικαιοσύνης
λέγω, ὧδέ πως ἐπιφέρει κατὰ λέξιν· »ἔνθεν ὡς γελοῖον εἰρηκότος τοῦ 3
νομοθέτου ῥῆμα τοῦτο ἀκουστέον »οὐκ ἐπιθυμήσεις« πρὸς τὸ γελοιό-
p. 200 τερον εἰπεῖν »τῶν τοῦ πλησίον·« αὐτὸς γὰρ ὁ τὴν ἐπιθυμίαν δοὺς
ὡς συνέχουσαν τὰ τῆς γενέσεως ταύτην ἀφαιρεῖσθαι κελεύει μηδενὸς
αὐτὴν ἀφελὼν ζῴου· τὸ δὲ »τῆς τοῦ πλησίον γυναικὸς« ἰδιότητα τὴν
κοινωνίαν ἀναγκάζων ἔτι γελοιότερον εἶπεν« |

5 Καὶ ταῦτα μὲν οἱ γενναῖοι Καρποκρατιανοὶ δογματίζουσι. τού- 10, 1
τους φασὶ καί τινας ἄλλους ζηλωτὰς τῶν ὁμοίων κακῶν εἰς τὰ   185 S
δεῖπνα ἀθροιζομένους (οὐ γὰρ ἀγάπην εἴποιμ᾽ ἂν ἔγωγε τὴν συνέ-
λευσιν αὐτῶν), ἄνδρας ὁμοῦ καὶ γυναῖκας, μετὰ δὴ τὸ κορεσθῆναι
(»ἐν πλησμονῇ τοι Κύπρις«, ᾗ φασι) τὸ καταισχῦνον αὐτῶν τὴν
10 πορνικὴν ταύτην δικαιοσύνην ἐκποδὼν ποιησαμένους φῶς τῇ τοῦ
λύχνου περιτροπῇ, μίγνυσθαι, ὅπως ἐθέλοιεν, αἷς βούλοιντο, μελετήσαντας δὲ ἐν τοιαύτῃ ἀγάπῃ τὴν κοινωνίαν, μεθ᾽ ἡμέραν ἤδη παρ᾽
ὧν ἂν ἐθελήσωσι γυναικῶν ἀπαιτεῖν τὴν τοῦ Καρποκρατείου, οὐ
γὰρ θέμις εἰπεῖν θείου, νόμου ὑπακοήν. τοιαῦτα δὲ οἶμαι ταῖς κυνῶν
15 καὶ συῶν καὶ τράγων λαγνείαις νομοθετεῖν τὸν Καρποκράτην ἔδει.
δοκεῖ δέ μοι καὶ τοῦ Πλάτωνος παρακηκοέναι ἐν τῇ Πολιτείᾳ φαμέ- 2
νου κοινὰς εἶναι τὰς γυναῖκας πάντων, κοινὰς μὲν | τὰς πρὸ τοῦ 515 P
γάμου τῶν αἰτεῖσθαι μελλόντων, καθάπερ καὶ τὸ θέατρον κοινὸν
τῶν θεωμένων φάσκοντος, τοῦ προκαταλαβόντος δὲ ἑκάστην ἑκάστου
20 εἶναι καὶ οὐκέτι κοινὴν τὴν γεγαμημένην. Ξάνθος δὲ ἐν τοῖς ἐπι- 11, 1

p. 199   **21f** vgl. Strom. II 42, 1.   **22f** vgl. Rom 4, 16f; Gen 17, 5.   **23f** vgl. Lev
20, 10; Deut 22, 22.   **24f** Exod 20, 17.   **27f** Mt 5, 28.

p. 200   **9** Euripides Fr. inc. 895.   **16–20** vgl. Epiktet fr. 15 Schenkl.   **16f** vgl.
Plato Rep. V p. 457 D.   **20–24** Xanthos Fr. 28 FHG I p. 43; vgl. Tatian 28
p. 29, 21 Schw.; Minuc. Fel. Oct. 31, 3.

p. 199   **20** καὶ ⟨ᾧ ἡ⟩ Schw.   **30** ⟨ὃς⟩ Wi.   **31** λέγω Sy λέγων L.   **32f** τούτου
ἀκουστέον· ⟨τοῦ δ᾽⟩ »οὐκ ἐπιθ.« προσέτι γελ. εἶπεν Sch πρὸς τῷ Μü.

p. 200   **3** ⟨εἰς⟩ ἰδιότητα Ρο ἰδιότητα ⟨γενέσθαι⟩ Schw.   **4** ἀναγκάζον Schw.   **6**
κακιῶν Sy.   **9** τοι Κύπρις, ᾗ Di aus Athen. VI p. 270 C τῇ κυπρίσῃ L φασι ⟨οἱ
παροιμιαζόμενοι⟩ Cobet S. 439.   **18** καρποκρατίου L.

γραφομένοις Μαγικοῖς »†μίγνυνται δὲ« φησὶν »οἱ Μάγοι μητράσι καὶ
θυγατράσι καὶ ἀδελφαῖς μίγνυσθαι θεμιτὸν εἶναι κοινάς τε εἶναι τὰς
γυναῖκας οὐ βίᾳ καὶ λάθρᾳ, ἀλλὰ συναινούντων ἀμφοτέρων, ὅταν
θέλῃ γῆμαι ὁ ἕτερος τὴν τοῦ ἑτέρου.« ἐπὶ τούτων οἶμαι καὶ τῶν 2
25 ὁμοίων αἱρέσεων προφητικῶς Ἰούδαν ἐν τῇ ἐπιστολῇ εἰρηκέναι·
»ὁμοίως μέντοι καὶ οὗτοι ἐνυπνιαζόμενοι« (οὐ γὰρ ὕπαρ τῇ ἀληθείᾳ
ἐπιβάλλουσιν) ἕως »καὶ τὸ στόμα αὐτῶν λαλεῖ ὑπέρογκα.«

21f vgl. Cyrill v. Al. C. Jul. IV (PG 76,680D); Fr. in ZntW 36(1937)89.   26f
Iud 8, 16

21 μίγνυνται] ἀποφαίνονται Schw ἡγοῦνται St.

Hereupon follows *Stromateis* III.3, in which Clement turns to Marcion. Some of
his criticisms, especially his insistence that Plato was the source of the heresy, may
have been intended to tell against Carpocrates also. In III.4 (25.1ff) he pairs the
two in his resume:

p. 207 6   IV. Τῶν δὲ ἀφ' αἱρέσεως ἀγομένων Μαρκίωνος μὲν τοῦ Πον- 25, 1
τικοῦ ἐπεμνήσθημεν δι' ἀντίταξιν τὴν πρὸς τὸν δημιουργὸν τὴν
χρῆσιν τῶν κοσμικῶν ·παραιτουμένου. . . . ἐπεμνήσθημεν δὲ καὶ τῆς 5
18 κατὰ Καρποκράτην ἀθέσμου γυναικῶν κοινωνίας, περὶ δὲ τῆς Νικολάου ῥήσεως διαλεχθέντες ἐκεῖνο παρελίπομεν. . .

p. 208 10   Εἰσὶν δ' οἳ τὴν πάνδημον Ἀφροδίτην κοινωνίαν μυστικὴν ἀνα- 27, 1
γορεύουσιν ἐνυβρίζοντες καὶ τῷ ὀνόματι· λέγεται γὰρ καὶ τὸ ποιεῖν 2
τι κακὸν ἐργάζεσθαι, ὥσπερ οὖν καὶ τὸ ἀγαθόν τι ποιεῖν ὁμωνύμως
ἐργάζεσθαι, ὁμοίως δὲ καὶ ἡ κοινωνία ἀγαθὸν μὲν ἐν μεταδόσει ἀργυρίου καὶ τροφῆς καὶ στολῆς, οἳ δὲ καὶ τὴν ὁποίαν δήποτ' οὖν
15 ἀφροδισίων συμπλοκὴν κοινωνίαν ἀσεβῶς κεκλήκασιν. φασὶ γοῦν 3
τινα αὐτῶν ἡμετέρᾳ παρθένῳ ὡραίᾳ τὴν ὄψιν προσελθόντα φάναι·
»γέγραπται › παντὶ τῷ αἰτοῦντί σε δίδου‹«, τὴν δὲ σεμνῶς πάνυ
ἀποκρίνασθαι μὴ συνιεῖσαν τὴν τἀνθρώπου ἀσέλγειαν· »ἀλλὰ περὶ |
γάμου τῇ μητρὶ διαλέγου.« ὢ τῆς ἀθεότητος· καὶ τῶν τοῦ κυρίου 524 P 4
20 φωνῶν διαψεύδονται οἱ τῆς ἀσελγείας κοινωνοί, οἱ τῆς λαγνείας
ἀδελφοί, ὄνειδος οὐ φιλοσοφίας μόνον, ἀλλὰ καὶ παντὸς τοῦ βίου,
οἱ παραχαράσσοντες τὴν ἀλήθειαν, μᾶλλον δὲ κατασκάπτοντες ὡς
οἷόν τε αὐτοῖς· οἱ γὰρ τρισάθλιοι τὴν [τε] σαρκικὴν καὶ [τὴν] συνου- 5

p. 208   10f Theodoret Haer. fab. I 6; vgl. Platon Symp. p. 180 D ff [s. auch Theodor.
a. a. O V 27 (PG 83, 545 B) μυστικὴν κοινωνίαν ὠνόμασαν τὴν ἀσέλγειαν (Fr)].
17 Lc 6, 30; Mt 5, 42.   17-19 vgl. Cobet S. 511.   23-S. 209, 1 Theodoret
a. a. O.

p. 208   12 οὖν Schw ἂν L.   13 μὲν Hiller δὲ καὶ L.   13f ἀργυρίου Hervet ἀργύριον L.
18 [μὴ] St.   23 οἱ γὰρ Theod. οἵ γε τρισάθλιοι ⟨ὄντες⟩ Hiller τε < Theod.
[τὴν] Ma σαρκικὴν καὶ Theod. σαρκίνην κατὰ L.

σιαστικὴν κοινωνίαν ἱεροφαντοῦσι καὶ ταύτην οἴονται εἰς τὴν βασι-
25 λείαν αὐτοὺς ἀνάγειν τοῦ θεοῦ. εἰς τὰ χαμαιτυπεῖα μὲν οὖν ἡ τοιάδε 28, 1
εἰσάγει κοινωνία καὶ δὴ συμμέτοχοι εἶεν αὐτοῖς οἱ σύες καὶ οἱ
τράγοι, εἶεν δ' ἂν ἐν ταῖς μείζοσι παρ' αὐτοῖς ἐλπίσιν αἱ προεστῶσαι
p. 209 τοῦ τέγους πόρναι ἀνέδην εἰσδεχόμεναι τοὺς βουλομένους ἅπαντας.
»ὑμεῖς δὲ οὐχ οὕτως ἐμάθετε τὸν Χριστόν, εἴ γε αὐτὸν ἠκούσατε καὶ 2
ἐν αὐτῷ ἐδιδάχθητε, καθώς ἐστιν ἀλήθεια ἐν Χριστῷ Ἰησοῦ, ἀπο-
θέσθαι ὑμᾶς τὰ κατὰ τὴν προτέραν | ἀναστροφὴν τὸν παλαιὸν ἄν- 188 S
5 θρωπον τὸν φθειρόμενον κατὰ τὰς ἐπιθυμίας τῆς ἀπάτης· ἀνανε- 3
οῦσθε δὲ τῷ πνεύματι τοῦ νοὸς ὑμῶν καὶ ἐνδύσασθε τὸν καινὸν
ἄνθρωπον τὸν κατὰ θεὸν κτισθέντα ἐν δικαιοσύνῃ καὶ ὁσιότητι τῆς
ἀληθείας,« κατὰ τὴν ἐξομοίωσιν τοῦ θείου. »γίνεσθε οὖν μιμηταὶ 4
τοῦ θεοῦ, ὡς τέκνα ἀγαπητά, καὶ περιπατεῖτε ἐν ἀγάπῃ, καθὼς καὶ
10 ὁ Χριστὸς ἠγάπησεν ὑμᾶς καὶ παρέδωκεν ἑαυτὸν ὑπὲρ ἡμῶν προσ-
φορὰν καὶ θυσίαν τῷ θεῷ εἰς ὀσμὴν εὐωδίας. πορνεία δὲ καὶ πᾶσα 5
ἀκαθαρσία ἢ πλεονεξία μηδὲ ὀνομαζέσθω ἐν ὑμῖν, καθὼς πρέπει
ἁγίοις, καὶ αἰσχρότης καὶ μωρολογία.« καὶ γὰρ ἀπὸ τῆς φωνῆς 6
ἁγνεύειν μελετᾶν διδάσκων ὁ ἀπόστολος γράφει· »τοῦτο γὰρ ἴστε
15 γινώσκοντες, ὅτι πᾶς πόρνος« καὶ τὰ ἑξῆς ἕως »μᾶλλον δὲ καὶ
ἐλέγχετε.«

Ἐρρύη δὲ αὐτοῖς τὸ δόγμα ἔκ τινος ἀποκρύφου, καὶ δὴ παρα- 29, 1
θήσομαι τὴν λέξιν τὴν τῆς τούτων ἀσελγείας μητέρα· καὶ εἴτε αὐτοὶ
τῆς βίβλου συγγραφεῖς (ὅρα τὴν ἀπόνοιαν, εἰ καὶ θεοῦ διαψεύδονται
20 δι' ἀκρασίαν), εἴτε ἄλλοις περιτυχόντες τὸ καλὸν τοῦτο ἐνόησαν
δόγμα διεστραμμένως ἀκηκοότες· ἔχει δὲ οὕτως τὰ τῆς λέξεως· »ἐν 2
ἦν τὰ πάντα· ἐπεὶ δὲ ἔδοξεν αὐτοῦ τῇ ἑνότητι μὴ εἶναι μόνη, ἐξῆλθεν ἀπ' αὐτοῦ ἐπίπνοια, καὶ ἐκοινώνησεν αὐτῇ καὶ ἐποίησεν τὸν
ἀγαπητόν· ἐκ δὲ τούτου ἐξῆλθεν ἀπ' αὐτοῦ ἐπίπνοια, ᾗ κοινωνήσας
25 ἐποίησεν δυνάμεις μήτε ὁραθῆναι μήτε ἀκουσθῆναι δυναμένας« ἕως
»ἐπ' ὀνόματος ἰδίου ἑκάστην.« εἰ γὰρ καὶ οὗτοι καθάπερ οἱ ἀπὸ 3
Οὐαλεντίνου πνευματικὰς ἐτί|θεντο κοινωνίας, ἴσως τις αὐτῶν τὴν 525 P
ὑπόληψιν ἐπεδέξατ' ⟨ἄν⟩· σαρκικῆς δὲ ὕβρεως κοινωνίαν εἰς προφη-
τείαν ἁγίαν ἀνάγειν ἀπεγνωκότος ἐστὶ τὴν σωτηρίαν.

p. 209   2–8 Eph 4, 20–24.   8–13 Eph 5, 1–4.   14–16 Eph 5, 5. 11.   21–26 vgl.
C. Schmidt TU NF. V 4 S. 54.

p.208   25 θεοῦ] Χριστοῦ Theod.   χαμαιτυπία L.   26 εἶεν ⟨ἄν⟩ Di Theod.
p. 209   1 ἀναίδην L ἐκδεχόμεναι Theodor.   5f ἀνανεοῦσθε L¹ ἀνανεοῦσθαι L*.   10
ὑμᾶς] ἡμᾶς Paed. III 94, 4.   19 συγγραφεῖς Sy συγγραφῆς L εἰ] ἦ Mü.   20
ἄλλως Sy ἐνόησαν L¹ (wie Po) ἐνόησαν L* Ausgg.   21 δὲ ⟨οὖν⟩ Schw δὴ Po.
28 ἐπεδέξατ' ⟨ἄν⟩ Ma ἐπεδέξατο L.

Note also the next sentence: τοιαῦτα καὶ οἱ ἀπὸ Προδίκου ψευδωνύμως γνωστικοὺς
σφᾶς αὐτοὺς ἀναγορεύοντες δογματίζουσιν.

Clement, *Stromateis* III.5 (ed. Stählin II.214–216)

p. 214

V. Ἵν᾽ οὖν μὴ ἐπὶ πλεῖον ὀνυχίζοντες τὸν τόπον πλειόνων **40, 1**
ἀτόπων αἱρέσεων ἐπιμεμνώμεθα μηδ᾽ αὖ καθ᾽ ἑκάστην αὐτῶν λέγειν
πρὸς ἑκάστην ἀναγκαζόμενοι αἰσχυνώμεθά τε ἐπ᾽ αὐτοῖς καὶ ἐπὶ
10 μήκιστον τὰ ὑπομνήματα προάγωμεν, φέρε εἰς δύο διελόντες τάγματα ἁπάσας τὰς αἱρέσεις ἀποκρινώμεθα αὐτοῖς. ἢ γάρ τοι ἀδια- **2**
φόρως ζῆν διδάσκουσιν, ἢ τὸ ὑπέρτονον ᾄδουσαι ἐγκράτειαν διὰ
δυσσεβείας καὶ φιλαπεχθημοσύνης καταγγέλλουσι. πρότερον δὲ περὶ **3**
τοῦ προτέρου διαληπτέον τμήματος. εἰ πάντα ἔξεστιν ἑλέσθαι βίον,
15 δῆλον ὅτι καὶ τὸν μετ᾽ ἐγκρατείας, καὶ εἰ πᾶς βίος ἀκίνδυνος ἐκλεκτῷ,
δῆλον ὅτι ⟨ὁ⟩ μετὰ ἀρετῆς καὶ σωφροσύνης πολὺ μᾶλλον ἀκίνδυνος·
δοθείσης γὰρ ἐξουσίας τῷ κυρίῳ τοῦ σαββάτου, εἴπερ ἀκολάστως **4**
βιῶσαι, ἀνεύθυνον εἶναι, πολλῷ μᾶλλον ὁ κοσμίως πολιτευσάμενος
οὐχ ὑπεύθυνος ἔσται· »πάντα μὲν γὰρ ἔξεστιν, ἀλλ᾽ οὐ πάντα συμ- **5**
20 φέρει«, φησὶν ὁ ἀπόστολος. εἰ δὲ καὶ πάντα ἔξεστι, δῆλον ὅτι καὶ
τὸ σωφρονεῖν. ὥσπερ οὖν ὁ τῇ ἐξουσίᾳ εἰς τὸ κατ᾽ ἀρετὴν βιῶσαι **41, 1**
συγχρησάμενος ἐπαινετός, οὕτω πολὺ μᾶλλον ὁ τὴν ἐξουσίαν ἡμῖν
δεδωκὼς ἐλευθέραν καὶ κυρίαν καὶ συγχωρήσας ἡμῖν βιοῦν ὡς βου-
λόμεθα σεμνὸς καὶ προσκυνητός, μὴ ἐάσας δουλεύειν ἡμῶν κατὰ
25 ἀνάγκην τὰς αἱρέσεις καὶ τὰς φυγάς. εἰ δὲ τὸ ἀδεὲς ἑκάτερος ἔχει, **2**
ὅ τε ἀκρασίαν ὅ τε ἐγκράτειαν ἑλόμενος, ἀλλὰ τὸ σεμνὸν οὐχ ὅμοιον.
ὁ μὲν γὰρ εἰς ἡδονὰς ἐξοκείλας σώματι χαρίζεται, ὁ δὲ σώφρων τὴν
κυρίαν τοῦ σώματος ψυχὴν ἐλευθεροῖ τῶν παθῶν. κἂν »ἐπ᾽ ἐλευ- **3**
θερίᾳ κεκλῆσθαι« λέγωσιν ἡμᾶς, μόνον μὴ »τὴν ἐλευθερίαν εἰς ἀφορ-
30 μὴν τῇ σαρκὶ« παρέχωμεν κατὰ τὸν ἀπόστολον· εἰ δὲ ἐπιθυμίᾳ **4**
χαριστέον καὶ τὸν ἐπονείδιστον βίον ἀδιάφορον ἡγητέον, ὡς αὐτοὶ
λέγουσιν, ἤτοι πάντα ταῖς ἐπιθυμίαις πειστέον, καί, εἰ τοῦτο, τὰ
ἀσελ|γέστατα καὶ ἀνοσιώτατα πρακτέον ἅπαντα ἑπομένους τοῖς ἀνα- 530 P

p. 215

πείθουσιν ἡμᾶς· ἢ τῶν ἐπιθυμιῶν τινὰς ἐκκλινοῦμεν καὶ οὐκέτι **5**
ἀδιαφόρως βιωτέον οὐδὲ ἀνέδην δουλευτέον τοῖς ἀτιμοτάτοις μέρεσιν
ἡμῶν, γαστρὶ καὶ αἰδοίοις, δι᾽ ἐπιθυμίαν κολακευόντων τὸν ἡμέτερον
νεκρόν. τρέφεται γὰρ καὶ ζωοποιεῖται διακονουμένη εἰς ἀπόλαυσιν **6**
5 ἐπιθυμία, καθάπερ ἔμπαλιν κολουομένη μαραίνεται. πῶς δέ ἐστι **42, 1**
δυνατὸν ἡττηθέντα τῶν τοῦ σώματος ἡδονῶν ἐξομοιοῦσθαι τῷ κυρίῳ
ἢ γνῶσιν ἔχειν θεοῦ;

p. 214 **17** vgl. Mt 12, 8; Mc 2, 28; Lc 6, 5.   **19f** I Cor 6, 12; 10, 23.   **28–30**
vgl. Gal. 5, 13.

p. 214 **7** πλέον Di.   **8** ἐπιμεμνώμεθα Sy ἐπιμεμνήμεθα L.   **9** ἀναγκαζόμενοι (νοι
in Ras.) L¹.   **10** προάγωμεν Sy προάγοιμεν L.   **10f** τάγματα St πράγματα
L.   **11** ἢ γὰρ τὸ Mü.   **12** ᾄδουσαι (vgl. Strom. II 123, 2) Schw ἄγουσαι L.
16 ⟨ὁ⟩ Hiller.   **17** vgl. Strom. III 30, 1.   **23** βιοῦν L³ βιοῦς L* aber ν
am Rand L¹.   **24** σεμνὸς L¹ σεμνῶς L*.   **29** κεκλῆσθαι (αι in Ras.) L¹.
32 πειστέον Di πιστέον L. *p. 21* * *p. 215*   **2** ἀναίδην L.

Clement, *Stromateis* III.6 end (ed. Stählin II.221–222)

p. 221   Ἡ δὲ Καρποκράτους δικαιοσύνη καὶ τῶν ἐπ' ἴσης αὐτῷ τὴν   **54, 1**
ἀκόλαστον μετιόντων κοινωνίαν ὧδέ πως καταλύεται. ἅμα γὰρ τῷ
φάναι »τῷ αἰτοῦντί σε δός« ἐπιφέρει· »καὶ τὸν θέλοντα δανείσασθαι
μὴ ἀποστραφῇς«, ταύτην διδάσκων τὴν κοινωνίαν, οὐχὶ δὲ τὴν
10 λάγνον. πῶς δὲ ὁ αἰτῶν καὶ λαμβάνων καὶ δανειζόμενος ἀπὸ μη-   **2**
δενὸς ὑπάρχοντος τοῦ ἔχοντος καὶ διδόντος καὶ δανείζοντος; τί δ'   **3**
ὅταν | ὁ κύριος φῇ· »ἐπείνασα καὶ ἐχορτάσατέ με, ἐδίψησα καὶ ἐπο-   193 S
τίσατέ με, ξένος ἤμην καὶ συνηγάγετέ με, γυμνὸς καὶ περιεβάλετέ
με.« εἶτα ἐπιφέρει· »ἐφ' ὅσον ἐποιήσατε ἑνὶ τούτων τῶν ἐλαχίστων,
15 ἐμοὶ ἐποιήσατε.« οὐχὶ δὲ τὰ αὐτὰ καὶ ἐν τῇ παλαιᾷ διαθήκῃ νομο-   **4**
θετεῖ; ὁ διδοὺς πτωχῷ δανείζει θεῷ« καὶ »μὴ ἀπόσχῃ εὖ ποιεῖν
ἐνδεῆ« φησίν. καὶ πάλιν »ἐλεημοσύναι καὶ πίστεις μὴ ἐκλιπέτωσάν   **55, 1**
σε« εἶπεν. »πενία δὲ ἄνδρα ταπεινοῖ· χεῖρες δὲ ἀνδρείων πλουτί-
ζουσιν.« ἐπιφέρει δέ· »ἰδοὺ ἀνήρ, ὃς οὐκ ἔδωκεν ἐπὶ τόκῳ τὸ ἀρ-
20 γύριον αὐτοῦ, ἀποδεκτὸς γίνεται.« καὶ »λύτρον ψυχῆς | ἀνδρὸς ὁ   537 P
ἴδιος πλοῦτος κρίνεται« οὐχὶ διασαφεῖ ἄντικρυς; ὡς οὖν ἐξ ἐναντίων
ὁ κόσμος σύγκειται ὥσπερ ἐκ θερμοῦ καὶ ⟨ψυχροῦ⟩ ξηροῦ τε καὶ
ὑγροῦ, οὕτω κἀκ τῶν διδόντων κἀκ τῶν λαμβανόντων. πάλιν τε   **2**
αὖ ὅταν εἴπῃ· »εἰ θέλεις τέλειος γενέσθαι, πωλήσας τὰ ὑπάρχοντα
25 δὸς πτωχοῖς,« ἐλέγχει τὸν καυχώμενον ἐπὶ τῷ »πάσας τὰς ἐντολὰς
ἐκ νεότητος τετηρηκέναι·« οὐ γὰρ πεπληρώκει τὸ »ἀγαπήσεις τὸν
πλησίον σου ὡς ἑαυτόν«. τότε δὲ ὑπὸ τοῦ κυρίου συντελειούμενος
ἐδιδάσκετο δι' ἀγάπην μεταδιδόναι. καλῶς οὖν πλουτεῖν οὐ κεκώ-   **56, 1**
λυκεν, ἀλλὰ γὰρ τὸ ἀδίκως καὶ ἀπλήστως πλουτεῖν· »κτῆσις« γὰρ
30 »ἐπισπευδομένη μετὰ ἀνομίας ἐλάττων γίνεται.« »εἰσὶ« γὰρ »οἳ σπεί-
p. 222   ροντες πλείονα ποιοῦσι, καὶ οἳ συνάγοντες ἐλαττοῦνται« περὶ ὧν
γέγραπται· »ἐσκόρπισεν, ἔδωκεν τοῖς πένησιν, ἡ δικαιοσύνη αὐτοῦ
μένει εἰς τὸν αἰῶνα.« ὁ μὲν γὰρ »σπείρων καὶ πλείονα συνάγων«   **2**
οὗτός ἐστιν ὁ διὰ τῆς ἐπιγείου καὶ προσκαίρου μεταδόσεως τὰ οὐράνια
5 κτώμενος καὶ τὰ αἰώνια, ἕτερος δὲ ὁ μηδενὶ μεταδιδούς, κενῶς δὲ

---

p. 221   **7** vgl. Strom. III 27, 3.   **8f** Mt 5, 42.   **10f** vgl. Qu. div. salv. 13, 1.
12–15 ebda 30, 2; Mt. 25, 35f. 40.   **16** Prov 19, 14 (17).   **16f** Prov
3, 27.   **17f** Prov 3, 3.   **18f** Prov 10, 4.   **19f** vgl. Ps 14, 5; Ez 18, 8.
20f Prov 13, 8.   **24–27** Mt 19, 21. 20. 19; Mc 10, 21. 20; 12, 31; Lc 18, 22.
21. 20.   **25–28** ἐλέγχει—μεταδιδόναι Ath fol. 97ʳ.   **29f** Prov 13, 11.
30f Prov 11, 24.

p. 222   **2** vgl. auch Paed. III 35, 5.   **2f** Ps 111, 9.   **4** vgl. Mt 19, 21.

p. 221   **10** λάγνον (o in Ras. für ω) L¹ ἀπο⟨λείπεται⟩ Schw.   **17** ἐνδεῆ Prov. ἐνδεεῖ
L.   **18** ἀνδρείων Prov. und Paed. II 129, 1 ἀνδρῶν L.   **19** ἰδοὺ ἀνήρ Sy
ἤδ' (corr. aus ἤδ') ἂν L τόκωι (ωι in Ras. für ον) L¹.   **22** ⟨ψυχροῦ⟩ Sy.
28 ⟨τὸ⟩ καλῶς Mü (unnötig, weil variatio vorliegt Fr)   **29** τὸ L¹ τῶν L*.

p. 222   **1** οἱ L.   **3** μὲν über d. Z. L¹.   **5** κενὸς καὶ oder κενῶς [καὶ] Heyse δὲ
Ma καὶ L.

»θησαυρίζων ἐπὶ τῆς γῆς ὅπου σὴς καὶ βρῶσις ἀφανίζει« (περὶ οὗ
γέγραπται· »συνάγων τοὺς μισθοὺς συνήγαγεν εἰς δεσμὸν τετρυπη-
μένον«), τούτου τὴν χώραν εὐφορῆσαι λέγει ἐν τῷ εὐαγγελίῳ ὁ κύ-   **3**
ριος, ἔπειτα τοὺς καρποὺς ἀποθέσθαι βουληθέντα, οἰκοδομησόμενον
10 ἀποθήκας μείζονας κατὰ τὴν προσωποποιίαν εἰπεῖν πρὸς ἑαυτόν·
»ἔχεις ἀγαθὰ πολλὰ ἀποκείμενά σοι εἰς ἔτη πολλά, φάγε, πίε,
εὐφραίνου· ἄφρον οὖν, ἔφη, ταύτῃ γὰρ τῇ νυκτὶ τὴν ψυχήν σου ἀπαι-
τοῦσιν ἀπὸ σοῦ. ἃ οὖν ἡτοίμασας, τίνι γένηται;«

p. 222   **6** Mt 6, 19.   **7f** Agg 1, 6.   **8–13** vgl. Lc 12, 16–20.

Clement, *Stromateis* III.8 (ed. Stählin II.224)

p. 224 10   VIII. Ἐπεὶ δὲ οἱ τὴν ἀδιαφορίαν εἰσάγοντες βιαζόμενοί τινας **61, 1**
ὀλίγας γραφὰς συνηγορεῖν αὐτῶν τῇ ἡδυπαθείᾳ οἴονται, ἀτὰρ δὴ
κἀκείνην »ἁμαρτία γὰρ ὑμῶν οὐ κυριεύσει· οὐ γάρ ἐστε ὑπὸ νόμον,
ἀλλ᾽ ὑπὸ χάριν« (καί τινας ἄλλας τοιαύτας, ὧν ἐπὶ τοιούτοις μεμνῆ-
σθαι οὐκ εὔλογον· οὐ γὰρ ἐπισκευάζω ναῦν πειρατικήν), φέρε δὴ διὰ
15 βραχέων διακόψωμεν αὐτῶν τὴν ἐγχείρησιν. αὐτὸς γὰρ ὁ γενναῖος **2**
ἀπόστολος τῇ προειρημένῃ λέξει ἐπιφέρων ἀπολύσεται τὸ ἔγκλημα·
»τί οὖν; ἁμαρτήσωμεν, ὅτι οὐκ ἐσμὲν ὑπὸ νόμον, ἀλλ᾽ ὑπὸ χάριν;
μὴ γένοιτο.« οὕτως ἐνθέως καὶ προφητικῶς καταλύει παραχρῆμα
τὴν σοφιστικὴν τῆς ἡδονῆς τέχνην. οὐ συνιᾶσιν οὖν, ὡς ἔοικεν, ὅτι **62, 1**
20 »τοὺς πάντας ἡμᾶς φανερωθῆναι δεῖ ἔμπροσθεν τοῦ βήματος τοῦ
Χριστοῦ, ἵνα κομίσηται ἕκαστος διὰ τοῦ σώματος πρὸς ἃ ἔπραξεν,
εἴτε ἀγαθὸν εἴτε κακόν,« ἵνα ἃ διὰ τοῦ σώματος ἔπραξέν τις ἀπο-
λάβῃ. »ὥστε εἴ τις ἐν Χριστῷ, καινὴ κτίσις,« οὐκέτι ἁμαρτητική· **2**
»τὰ ἀρχαῖα παρῆλθεν«, ἀπελουσάμεθα τὸν βίον τὸν παλαιόν· »ἰδοὺ
25 γέγονε καινά«, ἁγνεία ἐκ πορνείας, [καὶ] ἐγκράτεια ἐξ ἀκρασίας, δικαιοσύνη ἐξ ἀδικίας. »τίς γὰρ μετοχὴ δικαιοσύνῃ καὶ ἀνομίᾳ; ἢ τίς κοινωνία
φωτὶ πρὸς σκότος; τίς δὲ συμφώνησις Χριστοῦ πρὸς Βελίαρ; τίς **3**
μερὶς πιστῷ μετὰ ἀπίστου; τίς δὲ συγκατάθεσις ναῷ θεοῦ μετὰ εἰδώ-
λων; ταύτας οὖν ἔχοντες τὰς ἐπαγγελίας καθαρίσωμεν ἑαυτοὺς ἀπὸ
30 παντὸς μολυσμοῦ σαρκὸς καὶ πνεύματος, ἐπιτελοῦντες ἁγιωσύνην ἐν
φόβῳ θεοῦ.«

p. 224   **12f** Rom 6, 14.   **17f** Rom 6, 15.   **20–22** II Cor 5, 10.   **22** ἃ̶–ἔπραξεν
lesen II Cor 5, 10 D*FG u. a. statt τὰ διὰ τοῦ σ. πρὸς ἃ ἔπραξεν.   **23–25** II
Cor 5, 17.   **26–31** II Cor 6, 14–16; 7, 1.

p. 224   **11** αὐτῶν L.   **19** συνιᾶσιν Di συνιεῖσιν L.   **21f** [ἵνα κομίσηται—κακόν] Ma
als Glosse, welche den wörtl. Text der Cor-Stelle zu den Worten des Clem.
schrieb; aber das zweite ist Paraphrase zum ersten.   **25** [καὶ] Ma.

Clement, *Stromateis* III.18 (ed. Stählin II.244–247)

p. 244   XVIII. Τὴν δικαιοσύνην τοίνυν καὶ τὴν ἁρμονίαν τοῦ σωτηρίου **105, 1**
σεμνὴν οὖσαν καὶ βεβαίαν οἱ μὲν ἐπέτειναν, ὡς ἐπεδείξαμεν, βλασφή-
μως ἐκδεχόμενοι μετὰ πάσης ἀθεότητος τὴν ἐγκράτειαν, ἐξὸν ἑλέσθαι
τὴν εὐνουχίαν κατὰ τὸν ὑγιῆ κανόνα μετ' εὐσεβείας, εὐχαριστοῦντα
25 μὲν ἐπὶ τῇ δοθείσῃ χάριτι, οὐ μισοῦντα δὲ τὴν κτίσιν οὐδὲ ἐξου-
θενοῦντα τοὺς γεγαμηκότας· κτιστὸς γὰρ ὁ κόσμος, κτιστὴ καὶ ἡ
εὐνουχία, ἄμφω δὲ εὐχαριστούντων ἐν οἷς ἐτάχθησαν, εἰ γινώσκουσι
καὶ ἐφ' οἷς ἐτάχθησαν. οἱ δὲ ἀφηνιάσαντες ἐξύβρισαν, »ἵπποι θηλυ- **2**
μανεῖς« τῷ ὄντι »γενόμενοι καὶ ἐπὶ τὰς τῶν πλησίον χρεμετίζοντες«,
30 αὐτοί τε ἀκατασχέτως ἐκχεόμενοι καὶ τοὺς πλησίον ἀναπείθοντες
φιληδονεῖν, ἀθλίως ἐπαΐοντες ἐκείνων τῶν γραφῶν, »τὸν σὸν κλῆρον
p. 245   βάλε ἐν ἡμῖν, κοινὸν δὲ βαλλάντιον κτησώμεθα πάντες καὶ μαρσίπ-
πιον ἓν γενηθήτω ἡμῖν.« διὰ τούτους ὁ αὐτὸς προφήτης συμβου- **106, 1**
λεύων ἡμῖν λέγει· »μὴ πορευθῇς ἐν ὁδῷ μετ' αὐτῶν, ἔκκλινον τὸν
πόδα σου ἐκ τῶν τρίβων αὐτῶν· οὐ γὰρ ἀδίκως ἐκτείνεται δίκτυα
5 πτερωτοῖς· αὐτοὶ γὰρ αἱμάτων μετέχοντες θησαυρίζουσιν ἑαυτοῖς
κακά,« τουτέστι τῆς ἀκαθαρσίας ἀντιποιούμενοι καὶ τοὺς πλησίον τὰ
ὅμοια ἐκδιδάσκοντες, »πολεμισταί, πλῆκται ταῖς οὐραῖς αὐτῶν,« κατὰ
τὸν προφήτην, ἃς κέρκους Ἕλληνες καλοῦσιν. εἶεν δ' ἂν οὓς αἰνίσ- **2**
σεται ἡ προφητεία, καταφερεῖς, ἀκρατεῖς, οἱ ταῖς οὐραῖς αὐτῶν πολε-
10 μισταί, σκότους καὶ »ὀργῆς τέκνα«, μιαιφόνοι αὐτῶν τε αὐθένται καὶ
τῶν πλησίον ἀνδροφόνοι. »ἐκκαθάρατε τὴν παλαιὰν ζύμην, ἵνα ἦτε **3**
νέον φύραμα,« ὁ ἀπόστολος ἡμῖν ἐμβοᾷ. καὶ πάλιν ἀσχάλλων ἐπὶ
τοιούτοις τισὶ διατάττεται »μὴ συναναμίγνυσθαι, ἐάν τις ἀδελφὸς
ὀνομαζόμενος ᾖ πόρνος ἢ πλεονέκτης ἢ εἰδωλολάτρης ἢ λοίδορος ἢ
15 μέθυσος ἢ ἅρπαξ, τῷ τοιούτῳ μηδὲ συνεσθίειν.« »ἐγὼ γὰρ διὰ νόμου **4**
νόμῳ ἀπέθανον,« λέγει, »ἵνα θεῷ ζήσω. Χριστῷ συνεσταύρωμαι·
ζῶ δὲ οὐκέτι ἐγώ,« ὡς ἔζων κατὰ τὰς ἐπιθυμίας, »ζῇ δὲ ἐν ἐμοὶ

---

p. 244   **22f** vgl. S. 214, 12ff.   **25** zu χάριτι vgl. I Cor 7, 7.   **28f** Ier 5, 8.
31–S. **245, 2** Prov 1, 14.

p. 245   **3–6** Prov 1, 15–18.   **7** woher? vgl. Apc 9, 10. 19.   **10** Eph 2, 3.
11f I Cor 5, 7.   **13–15** I Cor 5, 11.   **15–20** Gal 2, 19f.   **17–20** ζῶ
δὲ–θεοῦ Cat. zu Gal 2, 20 in Vatic. 692 fol. 82ʳ Inc. Κλήμεντος· ζῶ δὲ,
φησίν, οὐκέτι expl. θεοῦ.

p. 244   **29** χραιμετίζοντες L.   **30** ἐκχεόμενοι (vgl. Iud 11) St Münzel ἐχόμενοι
L ἔχοντες Ma ἑπόμενοι Bywater ⟨ἡδονῆς⟩ ἐχόμενοι Schw ἑλόμενοι Wi [die
Konjektur ἐκχεόμενοι wird durch die ihren Urhebern unbekannte Stelle
Polyb. 32, 11, 4 (p. 1269, 9 Hultsch) οἱ μὲν γὰρ εἰς ἐρωμένους τῶν νέων, οἱ δ'
εἰς ἑταίρας ἐξεκέχυντο gestützt, ἐχόμενοι ist jedoch nicht ganz unmöglich,
vgl. den Ausspruch des Aristipp., Strom. II 118, 2 (S. 177, 1) (Fr)].

p. 245   **1** βαλάντιον L.   **6** τοὺς Sy τοῖς L.   **9** καταφερεῖς (vgl. S. 196, 6; Strom.
VII 33, 4) Bywater.   **11** nach πλησίον ist κληρονόμοι getilgt L¹.   **14** ᾖ
I Cor ᾗ L.

Χριστὸς « διὰ τῆς τῶν | ἐντολῶν ὑπακοῆς ἁγνῶς καὶ μακαρίως· ὥστε 561 P
τότε μὲν ἔζων ἐν σαρκὶ σαρκικῶς, » ὃ δὲ νῦν ζῶ ἐν σαρκί, ἐν πίστει
20 ζῶ τῇ τοῦ υἱοῦ τοῦ θεοῦ.« »εἰς ὁδὸν ἐθνῶν μὴ ἀπέλθητε καὶ εἰς 107, 1
πόλιν Σαμαρειτῶν μὴ εἰσέλθητε,« τῆς ἐναντίας πολιτείας ἀποτρέ-
πων ἡμᾶς ὁ κύριος λέγει, ἐπεὶ »ἡ καταστροφὴ ἀνδρῶν παρανόμων
κακή. καὶ αὖταί εἰσιν αἱ ὁδοὶ πάντων τῶν συντελούντων τὰ ἄνομα.«
»οὐαὶ τῷ ἀνθρώπῳ ἐκείνῳ,« φησὶν ὁ κύριος· »καλὸν ἦν αὐτῷ εἰ μὴ 2
25 ἐγεννήθη, ἢ ἕνα τῶν ἐκλεκτῶν μου σκανδαλίσαι· κρεῖττον ἦν αὐτῷ
περιτεθῆναι μύλον καὶ καταποντισθῆναι εἰς θάλασσαν, ἢ ἕνα τῶν
ἐκλεκτῶν μου διαστρέψαι·« »τὸ γὰρ ὄνομα τοῦ θεοῦ δι᾽ αὐτοὺς
βλασφημεῖται.« ὅθεν γενναίως ὁ ἀπόστολος »ἔγραψα ὑμῖν« φησὶν 3
_p. 246_ »ἐν τῇ ἐπιστολῇ μὴ συναναμίγνυσθαι πόρνοις« ἕως »τὸ δὲ σῶμα οὐ
τῇ πορνείᾳ, ἀλλὰ τῷ κυρίῳ, καὶ ὁ κύριος τῷ σώματι.« καὶ ὅτι οὐ | 4
τὸν γάμον πορνείαν λέγει, ἐπιφέρει· »ἢ οὐκ οἴδατε ὅτι ὁ κολλώμενος 203 S
τῇ πόρνῃ ἓν σῶμά ἐστιν;« ἢ πόρνην τις ἐρεῖ τὴν παρθένον πρὶν ἢ
5 γῆμαι; »καὶ μὴ ἀποστερεῖτε«, φησίν, »ἀλλήλους, εἰ μὴ ἐκ συμφώνου 5
πρὸς καιρόν,« διὰ τῆς »ἀποστερεῖτε« λέξεως τὸ ὀφείλημα τοῦ γάμου,
τὴν παιδοποιίαν, ἐμφαίνων, ὅπερ ἐν τοῖς ἔμπροσθεν ἐδήλωσεν εἰπών,
»τῇ γυναικὶ ὁ ἀνὴρ τὴν ὀφειλὴν ἀποδιδότω, ὁμοίως δὲ καὶ ἡ γυνὴ
τῷ ἀνδρί,« μεθ᾽ ἣν ἔκτισιν κατὰ τὴν οἰκουρίαν καὶ τὴν ἐν Χριστῷ 108, 1
10 πίστιν βοηθός, καὶ ἔτι σαφέστερον εἰπών· »τοῖς γεγαμηκόσι παραγ-
γέλλω, οὐκ ἐγώ, ἀλλ᾽ ὁ κύριος, γυναῖκα ἀπὸ ἀνδρὸς μὴ χωρισθῆναι
(ἐὰν δὲ καὶ χωρισθῇ, μενέτω ἄγαμος ἢ τῷ ἀνδρὶ καταλλαγήτω) καὶ
ἄνδρα γυναῖκα μὴ ἀφιέναι. τοῖς δὲ λοιποῖς λέγω ἐγώ, οὐχ ὁ κύριος·
εἴ τις ἀδελφὸς« ἕως »νῦν δὲ ἅγιά ἐστι.« τί δὲ λέγουσι πρὸς ταῦτα 2
15 οἱ τοῦ νόμου κατατρέχοντες καὶ τοῦ γάμου ὡς κατὰ νόμον συγκεχωρημένου μόνον, οὐχὶ δὲ καὶ κατὰ τὴν διαθήκην τὴν καινήν; τί πρὸς
ταύτας εἰπεῖν ἔχουσι τὰς νομοθεσίας οἱ τὴν σπορὰν καὶ τὴν γένεσιν
μυσαττόμενοι; ἐπεὶ καὶ »τὸν ἐπίσκοπον τοῦ οἴκου καλῶς προϊστά-
μενον« νομοθετεῖ τῆς ἐκκλησίας ἀφηγεῖσθαι, | οἶκον δὲ κυριακὸν 562 P
20 »μιᾶς γυναικὸς« συνίστησι συζυγία. »πάντα οὖν καθαρὰ τοῖς καθα- 109, 1

_p. 245_ **20f** Mt 10, 5. **22f** Prov 1, 18f. **24–27** I Clem. ad Cor. 46, 8; vgl.
Mt 26, 24; 18, 6f; Mc 9, 42; Lc 17, 2; dazu E. Nestle, Einführ. in d. Griech.
Neue Test.[2] S. 121. **27f** Rom 2, 24. **28f** I Cor 5, 9.

_p. 246_ **1f** I Cor 6, 13. **2f** vgl. S. 218, 21 (Tatian). **3f** I Cor 6, 16. **5f**
I Cor 7, 5. **8f** I Cor 7, 3. **10** vgl. Gen 2, 18 (βοηθός). **10–14** I Cor
7, 10–12. 14. **18–20** I Tim 3, 2. 4; vgl. Strom. III 79, 6; 90, 1. **20**
Tit 1, 6. **20–22** Tit 1, 15.

_p. 245_ **19** ἐκ σαρκί[1]] + ἵνα εἴπῃ Cat. **26** εἐς] + τὴν Clem. Rom. **27** ἐκλεκτῶν
—διαστρέψαι (wohl veranlaßt durch I Clem. ad Cor. 46, 9 τὸ σχίσμα ὑμῶν
πολλοὺς διέστρεψεν)] μικρῶν—σκανδαλίσαι Clem. Rom. **27f** βλασφημεῖται
δι᾽ αὐτοὺς Zeichen der Umstellung L[1].

_p. 246_ **8** ὀφειλὴν (zwischen λ u. η 4 Buchst. ausrad.) L. **10** ἔτι Sy εἴ τι L. **13**
vor ἐγώ 3 Buchst. ausrad. **14** ἅγιά ἐστι I Cor ἁγία ἐστί L. **15f**
συγκεχωρημένου, μονονουχὶ L.

ροῖς,« λέγει, »τοῖς δὲ μεμιαμένοις καὶ ἀπίστοις οὐδὲν καθαρόν, ἀλλὰ
μεμίαται αὐτῶν καὶ ὁ νοῦς καὶ ἡ συνείδησις.« ἐπὶ δὲ τῆς παρὰ τὸν 2
κανόνα ἡδονῆς »μὴ πλανᾶσθε« φησίν· »οὔτε πόρνοι οὔτε εἰδωλολάτραι οὔτε μοιχοὶ οὔτε μαλακοὶ οὔτε ἀρσενοκοῖται οὔτε πλεονέκται
25 οὔτε κλέπται, οὐ μέθυσοι, οὐ λοίδοροι, οὐχ ἅρπαγες βασιλείαν θεοῦ
οὐ κληρονομήσουσιν. καὶ ἡμεῖς μὲν ἀπελουσάμεθα,« οἱ ἐν τούτοις
γενόμενοι, οἱ δέ, εἰς ταύτην ἀπολούοντες τὴν ἀσέλγειαν, ἐκ σωφροσύνης εἰς πορνείαν βαπτίζουσι, ταῖς ἡδοναῖς καὶ τοῖς πάθεσι χαρί-
ζεσθαι δογματίζοντες, ἀκρατεῖς ἐκ σωφρόνων εἶναι διδάσκοντες καὶ
30 τὴν ἐλπίδα τὴν σφῶν ταῖς τῶν μορίων ἀναισχυντίαις προσανέχοντες,
ἀποκηρύκτους εἶναι τῆς βασιλείας τοῦ θεοῦ, ἀλλ' οὐκ ἐγγράφους τοὺς
φοιτητὰς παρασκευάζοντες, »ψευδωνύμου γνώσεως« προσηγορίᾳ τὴν
p. 247   εἰς τὸ ἐξώτερον σκότος ὁδοιπορίαν ἐπανηρημένοι. »τὸ λοιπόν, 3
ἀδελφοί, ὅσα ἀληθῆ, ὅσα σεμνά, ὅσα δίκαια, ὅσα ἁγνά, ὅσα προσφιλῆ,
ὅσα εὔφημα, εἴ τις ἀρετὴ καὶ εἴ τις ἔπαινος, ταῦτα λογίζεσθε· ὅσα
καὶ ἐμάθετε [ἃ] καὶ παρελάβετε καὶ ἠκούσατε καὶ ἴδετε ἐν ἐμοί, ταῦτα
5 πράσσετε· καὶ ὁ θεὸς τῆς εἰρήνης ἔσται μεθ' ὑμῶν.« καὶ ὁ Πέτρος 110, 1
ἐν τῇ ἐπιστολῇ τὰ ὅμοια λέγει· »ὥστε τὴν πίστιν ὑμῶν καὶ ἐλπίδα
εἶναι εἰς θεόν, τὰς ψυχὰς ὑμῶν ἡγνικότες ἐν τῇ ὑπακοῇ τῆς ἀληθείας, ὡς τέκνα ὑπακοῆς, μὴ συσχηματιζόμενοι ταῖς πρότερον ἐν τῇ 2
ἀγνοίᾳ ὑμῶν ἐπιθυμίαις, ἀλλὰ κατὰ τὸν καλέσαντα ὑμᾶς ἅγιον καὶ
10 αὐτοὶ ἅγιοι ἐν πάσῃ ἀναστροφῇ γενήθητε, διότι γέγραπται· ⟩ ἅγιοι
ἔσεσθε, διότι ἐγὼ ἅγιος.⟨«

Ἀλλὰ γὰρ πέρα τοῦ δέοντες ἡ πρὸς τοὺς ψευδωνύμους τῆς γνώ- 3
σεως ὑποκριτὰς ἀναγκαία γενομένη ἀπήγαγεν ἡμᾶς καὶ εἰς μακρὸν
ἐξέτεινε τὸν λόγον ἀντιλογία. ὅθεν καὶ ὁ τρίτος ἡμῖν τῶν κατὰ
15 τὴν ἀληθῆ φιλοσοφίαν γνωστικῶν ὑπομνημάτων Στρωματεὺς τοῦτο
ἔχει τὸ πέρας. |

p. 246   23-26 I Cor 6, 9-11.   30 vgl. Phil 3, 19.   31 vgl. Apc 20, 12. 15; 21, 27.
32 vgl. I Tim 6, 20.
p. 247   1 vgl. Mt 8, 12; 22, 13; 25, 30.   1-5 Phil 4, 8f.   6-11 I Petr 1, 21f.
14-16 (16 = Lev 11, 44; 19, 2; 20, 7).

p. 246   22 μεμίανται Cobet S. 512 wie Tit.

p. 247   4 [ἃ] St (als Variante zu ὅσα).   9 ἀγνοίᾳ I Petr ἁγνείᾳ L.   13f ἀπήγαγεν
ἡμᾶς καὶ εἰς μακρὸν ἐξέτεινε τὸν λόγον ἀντιλογία (α β γ üb. d. Z. von L³).

Subscriptio: στρωμά γ̄:—

Clement, *Eclogae propheticae* 25

See above, p. 298. Discussed under *Heracleon*, p. 268.

Tertullian, *De anima* XXIII.2 (ed. Waszink *CC* II.815)

p. 815   XXIII. **1.** Quidam de caelis deuenisse se credunt tanta persuasione quanta et illuc indubitate regressuros repromittunt, ut Saturninus Menandri Simoniani discipulus. . . . **2.** Sed et Carpocrates tantundem sibi de superioribus uindicat, ut discipuli eius animas suas iam et Christo, nedum apostolis, et peraequent et cum uolunt praeferant, quas perinde de sublimi uirtute conceperint despectrices mundipotentium principa-
15 tuum.

XXIII. **1** VNDE ANIMA *AB* VNDE ANIMA, ADVERSVS HAERETI-
COS QVI EAM DE COELIS DEFERVNT *Gel.*   **2** et *om. B Gel.*   **3**
Saturnus *B* Saturnius *Rig₁₋₂.*   **13** proinde *B Gel* de *om. A.*   **14** despec-
trices *scripsi*] despectrice *AB Gel* mundi potentium *AB.*   **14–15** principatum
A.

Tertullian, *De anima* XXXV.1–5 (ed. Waszink, *CC* II.836–837)

p. 836   XXXV. **1.** Sed non tibi soli metempsychosis hanc fabulam instruxit: inde etiam Carpocrates utitur, pariter magus, pariter fornicarius, etsi Helena minus. Quidni? cum propter omnimodam diuinae et humanae disciplinae euersionem con-
5 stituendam recorporari animas asseuerauerit; nulli enim uitam istam rato fieri, ‖ nisi uniuersis quae arguunt eam f. 147ᵛ expunctis, quia non natura quid malum habeatur, sed opinione. Itaque metempsychosin necessarie imminere, si non in primo quoque uitae huius commeatu omnibus inlicitis
10 satisfiat (scilicet facinora tributa sunt uitae!), ceterum totiens animam reuocari habere quotiens minus quid intulerit, reliquatricem delictorum, d o n e c e x s o l u a t n o u i s s i m u m q u a d r a n t e m detrusa identidem in carcerem corporis. **2.** Huc enim temperat totam illam allegorian domini certis
15 interpretationibus relucentem et primo quidem simpliciter intellegendam. Nam et ethnicus homo aduersarius
p. 837   noster est, incedens in eadem uia uitae communis. Ceterum oportebat nos de mundo exire, si cum illis conuersari non

XXXV. **12** Mtth. 5, 26.   **18** I Cor. 5.10.

XXXV. **1** AD (ADVERSVS *Gel*) CARPOCRATIS OPINIONEM *AB*
Gel.   **3** etsi . . . Quidni?] "praestat includi notis parentheseos" *Iun.*
5 adseuerauerit *B Gel.*   **7** quia] qua *Seml.*   **8** necessariae *A.*   **14**
allegoriam *B Gel.*   **16** intellegendum *A* et *om. A.*
17 incaedens *A*   in *del. Rig* eandem *Rig*   uiam *A Rig.*

liceret. Huic ergo boni animi praestes iubet (diligite
20 enim inimicos uestros, inquit, et orate pro
maledicentibus uos), ne aliquo commercio negotio-
rum iniuria prouocatus abstrahat te ad suum iudicem, et ad
custodiam delegatus ad exsolutionem totius debiti arteris.
3. Tum si in diabolum transfertur aduersarii mentio ex ob-
25 seruatione comitante, cum illo quoque moneris eam inire
concordiam quae deputetur ex fidei conuentione; pactus es
enim renuntiasse ipsi et pompae et angelis eius. Conuenit
inter uos de isto. Haec erit amicitia obseruatione sponsionis,
ne quid eius postea re|sumas ex his quae eierasti, quae illi V 361
30 reddidisti, ne te ut fraudatorem, ut pacti transgressorem
iudici deo obiciat, sicut eum legimus alibi sanctorum crimina-
torem et de ipso etiam nomine diaboli delatorem, et iudex te
tradat angelo exsecutionis, et ille te in carcerem mandet in-
fernum, unde non dimittaris nisi modico quoque delicto mora
35 resurrectionis expenso. Quid his sensibus aptius? Quid his
interpretationibus uerius? 4. Ceterum ad Carpocraten: si
omnium ‖ facinorum debitrix anima est, quis erit inimicus et f. 148
aduersarius eius intellegendus? Credo, mens melior, quae
illam in aliquid innocentiae inpegerit adigendam rursus ac
40 rursus in corpus, donec in nullo rea deprehendatur bonae
uitae. Hoc est ex malis fructibus bonam arborem intellegi, id
est, ex pessimis praeceptis doctrinam ueritatis agnosci.

19 Mtth. 5, 44 (Luc. 6, 27).   **21** Mtth. 5, 25/6 (Luc. 12, 58/9).
30 Mtth. 5, 25/6 (Luc. 12, 58/9).   **31** Apoc. 12. 10.   **45** Mtth. 17,
12.   **46** Mtth. 11, 14.

19 boni *A*; *approbant Gomperz 73*; *Th. St. T. 3, 33/4*] bonum *B Gel* praestes]
praesto esto *Gomperz 73* praesto es(se) *Stowasser ap. Gomperz 73*; *lectionem
traditam uindicat Th. St. T. 3, 33/4* iubet *om. A.*   **20** enim *om. A* et *om. Gel.*
21 commertio *A.*   **22–23** in custodiam *B Gel.*   **23** exsoluitionem *A.*
25 comitantem *Gomperz 74.*   **27** renunciasse *A* renuntiare *B Gel.*   **28**
de obseruatione *Rfd susp.* obseruatio *Bmg.*   **29** ei eierasti *B Gel.*   **29–30** eie reddidisti (eie *inductum*) *A.*   **31** sicuti *Pam.*   **32** diaboli *om.*
A.   **33** executionis *B Gel.*   **36** ad *A*; *approbat Lfst. Z. Spr. T. 87*; *sed
cf. comm.*] apud *B Gel* Carpocratem *Gel.*   **38** mens] meus *B.*   **39**
aliquid innocentiae] aliud quid nocentiae *Rfd susp.*

Hippolytus, *Philosophumena* VII.6 (ed. Wendland 190)

Items in a table of contents.

p. 190   6. Πῶς Καρποκράτης ματαιάζει, καὶ αὐτὸς ὑπὸ ἀγγέλων τὰ ὄντα
φάσκων γεγενῆσθαι.

Hippolytus, *Philosophumena* VII.31 end–33
(ed. Wendland 217–221)

This follows Hippolytus' account of Marcion (= τούτου).

p. 217 ἀλλ' ἐπεὶ καὶ τὰ τούτου ἱκανῶς ἡμῖν δοκεῖ ἐκτεθεῖσθαι, ἴδωμεν τί
λέγει Καρποκράτης.

p. 218 32. Καρποκράτης τὸν μὲν κόσμον καὶ τὰ ἐν αὐτῷ ὑπὸ ἀγγέλων 1
πολὺ ὑποβεβηκότων τοῦ ἀγενήτου πατρὸς γεγενῆσθαι λέγει, τὸν δὲ
Ἰησοῦν ἐξ Ἰωσὴφ γεγεννῆσθαι καὶ ὅμοιον τοῖς ἀνθρώποις γεγονότα
δικαιότερον τῶν λοιπῶν γενέσθαι, τὴν δὲ ψυχὴν αὐτοῦ εὔτονον καὶ
5 καθαρὰν γεγονυῖαν διαμνημονεῦσαι τὰ ὁρατὰ μὲν αὐτῇ ἐν τῇ μετὰ
τοῦ ἀγενήτου θεοῦ περιφορᾷ, καὶ διὰ τοῦτο ὑπ' ἐκείνου αὐτ(ῇ) κατα-
πεμφθῆναι δύναμιν, ὅπως τοὺς κοσμοποιοὺς ἐκφυγεῖν δι' αὐτῆς δυ-
νηθῇ· ἣν καὶ διὰ πάντων χωρήσασαν | ἐν πᾶσί τε ἐλευθερωθεῖσαν f. 99ᵛ 2
⟨ἀν⟩εληλυθέναι πρὸς αὐτόν, ⟨καὶ ὁμοίως τὴν⟩ τὰ ὅμοια αὐτῇ ἀσπα-
10 ζομένην. τὴν δὲ τοῦ Ἰησοῦ λέγουσι ψυχὴν ἐννόμως ἠσκημένην ἐν
Ἰουδαϊκοῖς ἔθεσι καταφρονῆσαι αὐτῶν καὶ διὰ τοῦτο δυνάμεις †εἰλη-
φέναι,† δι' ὧν κατήργησε τὰ ἐπὶ κολάσει πάθη προσόντα τοῖς ἀνθρώποις. τὴν οὖν ὁμοίως ἐκείνῃ τῇ τοῦ Χριστοῦ ψυχῇ δυναμένην κατα- 3
φρονῆσαι τῶν κοσμοποιῶν ἀρχόντων ὁμοίως λαμβάνειν δύναμιν πρὸς
15 τὸ πρᾶξαι τὰ ὅμοια. διὸ καὶ εἰς τοῦτο τὸ τῦφος κατεληλύθασιν,
p. 219 ὥστε [αὐ]τοὺς μὲν ὁμοίους αὐτῷ εἶναι λέγουσι τῷ Ἰησοῦ, τοὺς δὲ καὶ
ἔτι ⟨κατά τι⟩ δυνατωτέρους, τινὰς δὲ καὶ διαφορωτέρους τῶν ἐκείνου
μαθητῶν, οἷον Πέτρου καὶ Παύλου καὶ τῶν λοιπῶν ἀποστόλων·
τούτους δὲ κατὰ μηδὲν ἀπολείπεσθαι τοῦ Ἰησοῦ. τὰς δὲ ψυχὰς αὐτῶν 4
5 ἐκ τῆς ὑπερκειμένης ἐξουσίας παρούσας καὶ διὰ τοῦτο ὡσαύτως καταφρονούσας τῶν κοσμοποιῶν [διὰ] τῆς αὐτῆς ἠξιῶσθαι δυνάμεως καὶ
αὖθις εἰς τὸ αὐτὸ χωρῆσαι· εἰ δέ τις ἐκείνου πλέον καταφρονήσειεν
τῶν ἐνταῦθα, δύνασθαι διαφορώτερον αὐτοῦ ὑπάρχειν. τέχνας οὖν 5
μαγικὰς ἐξεργάζονται καὶ ἐπαοιδάς, φίλτρα τε καὶ χαριτήσια, παρέ-
10 δρους τε καὶ ὀνειροπόμπους καὶ τὰ λοιπὰ κακουργήματα, φάσκοντες
ἐξουσίαν ἔχειν πρὸς τὸ κυριεύειν ἤδη τῶν ἀρχόντων καὶ ποιητῶν
τοῦδε τοῦ κόσμου, οὐ μὴν ἀλλὰ καὶ τῶν ἐν αὐτῷ ποιημάτων ἁπάν-
των· οἵτινες καὶ αὐτοὶ εἰς διαβολὴν τοῦ θείου τῆς ἐκκλησίας ὀνόμα- 6

p. 218 1 Titel καρποκράτης rot P. 3 γεγενῆσθαι P. 5 ἑωραμένα αὐτῇ We.
(s. Iren.). 6 αὐτῇ] η ausradiert in P. 9 ἀνεληλυθέναι Gö., vgl. Iren.:
ἐληλυθέναι P ⟨ ⟩ Gö. (Iren.) αὐτῇ Iren. Gö.: αὐτῆς P. 11f εἰληφέναι Iren.
Gö.: †ἐπιτετελεκέναι P, doch s. Z. 14. 12 κολάσεσι Iren. Gö. 15 τοῦ
τύφου? We.

p. 219 1 τοὺς Gö.: αὐτοὺς P ὁμοίως P λέγειν We. 2 + κατά τι Iren. Gö. τινὰς
δὲ P: τινάς, ὄντας δὲ Gö. 4 μηδένα P. 5 ἐκ τῆς αὐτῆς περιφορᾶς Iren.
Cruice, doch s. S. 220, 14 καὶ > Cruice. 5f καταφρονούσας Iren. Gö.:
καταφρονεῖν P. 6 διὰ > Gö., διὰ τὸ Miller. 9 ἐξεργάζονται Gö.
(Iren., + καὶ αὐτοί): ἐξεργαζόμενον P χαρητήσια P.

τος πρὸς τὰ ἔθνη ὑπὸ τοῦ σατανᾶ προεβλήθησαν, ἵνα κατ' ἄλλον
15 καὶ ἄλλον τρόπον τὰ ἐκείνων ἀκούοντες ἄνθρωποι καὶ δοκοῦντες
ἡμᾶς πάντας τοιούτους ὑπάρχειν ἀποστρέφωσι τὰς ἀκοὰς αὐτῶν ἀπὸ
p. 220 τοῦ τῆς ἀληθείας κηρύγματος, ⟨ἢ καὶ⟩ βλέποντες τὰ ἐκείνων ἅπαντας
ἡμᾶς βλασφημῶσιν. εἰς τοσοῦτον | δὲ μετενσωματοῦσθαι φάσκουσι f. 100ʳ 7
τὰς ψυχάς, ὅσον πάντα τὰ ἁμαρτήματα πληρώσωσιν· ὅταν δὲ μηδὲν
λείπῃ, τότε ἐλευθερωθεῖσαν ἀπαλλαγῆναι πρὸς ἐκεῖνον τὸν ὑπεράνω
5 τῶν κοσμοποιῶν ἀγγέλων θεόν, καὶ οὕτως σωθήσεσθαι πάσας τὰς
ψυχάς. [εἴ] τινὲς δὲ φθάσασαι ἐν μιᾷ παρουσίᾳ ἀναμιγῆναι πάσαις 8
ἁμαρτίαις οὐκέτι μετενσωματοῦνται, ἀλλὰ πάντα ὁμοῦ ἀποδοῦσαι τὰ
ὀφλήματα ἐλευθερωθήσονται τοῦ μηκέτι γενέσθαι ἐν σώματι. τούτων τινὲς καὶ καυτηριάζουσι τοὺς ἰδίους μαθητὰς ἐν τοῖς ὀπίσω
10 μέρεσι τοῦ λοβοῦ τοῦ δεξιοῦ ὠτός. καὶ εἰκόνας δὲ κατασκευάζουσι
τοῦ Χριστοῦ λέγοντες ὑπὸ Πιλάτου τῷ καιρῷ ἐκείνῳ γενέσθαι.

33. Κήρινθος δέ τις, αὐτὸς Αἰγυπτίων παιδείᾳ ἀσκηθείς, ἔλεγεν 1
οὐχ ὑπὸ τοῦ πρώτου ⟨θεοῦ⟩ γεγονέναι τὸν κόσμον, ἀλλ' ὑπὸ δυνά-
μεώς τινος κεχωρισμένης τῆς ὑπὲρ τὰ ὅλα ἐξουσίας καὶ ἀγνοούσης
15 τὸν ὑπὲρ πάντα θεόν. τὸν δὲ Ἰησοῦν ὑπέθετο μὴ ἐκ παρθένου
γεγενῆσθαι, γεγονέναι δὲ αὐτὸν ἐξ Ἰωσὴφ καὶ Μαρίας υἱὸν ὁμοίως
p. 221 τοῖς λοιποῖς ἅπασιν ἀνθρώποις, καὶ δικαιότερον γεγονέναι καὶ σοφώ-
τερον. καὶ μετὰ τὸ βάπτισμα κατελθεῖν εἰς αὐτὸν ἀπὸ τῆς ὑπὲρ τὰ 2
ὅλα αὐθεντίας τὸν Χριστὸν ἐν εἴδει περιστερᾶς, καὶ τότε κηρῦξαι
τὸν ἄγνωστον πατέρα καὶ δυνάμεις ἐπιτελέσαι, πρὸς δὲ τῷ τέλει
5 ἀποπτῆναι τὸν Χριστὸν ἀπὸ τοῦ Ἰησοῦ, καὶ τὸν Ἰησοῦν πεπονθέναι
καὶ ἐγηγέρθαι, τὸν δὲ Χριστὸν ἀπαθῆ διαμεμενηκέναι πνευματικὸν
ὑπάρχοντα.

34. Ἐβιωναῖοι δὲ ὁμολογοῦσι ⟨μὲν⟩ τὸν κόσμον ὑπὸ τοῦ ὄντως 1
θεοῦ γεγονέναι, τὰ δὲ περὶ τὸν Χριστὸν ὁμοίως τῷ Κηρίνθῳ καὶ
10 Καρποκράτει μυθεύουσιν.

---

p. 220   **1** + ἢ καὶ Iren. Bunsen I 371 (I 60) ἅπαντας Sauppe: ἅπαντα P.   **2** βλα-
σφημοῦσιν P.   **3** ὅσον] ἕως ἄν Sauppe.   **4** ἐλευθερωθείσας Miller, doch
s. Iren.   **6** εἴ > Iren. Gö. εἰ—ἀνεμίγησαν Bunsen I 372 (I 60).   **12**
Titel κήρινθος rot P ⟨καὶ⟩ αὐτὸς Miller, doch s. H.   **13** + θεοῦ H Bunsen I
373 (I 62).   **16** υἱὸν H Iren. Bunsen: οἷον P.

p. 221   **1** δικαιώ́τερον P.   **2** ἀπὸ Cruice: τὸν P, τὸν ἐκ Scott, ἐκ H Bunsen.   **4**
ἄγνωστον H: γνωστὸν P.   **5** ἀποπτῆναι H Bunsen (Iren): ἀποστῆναι (nicht
ἀποστῆσαι) P (Theodoret I 3 ἀποστῆναι μὲν τὸν Χριστόν) Ἰησοῦ Iren. Bunsen:
χριστοῦ P.   **6** πνευματικὸν Iren. Bunsen: πατρικὸν P, πνεῦμα κυρίου H.
8 Titel ἐβιωναῖοι schwarz B μὲν Iren. Gö. vgl. H: > P.

Origen, *Contra Celsum* V.62–64

See above, pp. 298–300. Discussed under *Celsus*, pp. 269f.

Pseudo-Tertullian, *Adversus omnes haereses* III.1–3
(ed. Kroymann, *CC* II.1405)

p. 1405   III. 1. Carpocrates praeterea hanc tulit sectam: unam esse
dicit uirtutem in superioribus principalem. Ex hac prolatos V 219
angelos atque uirtutes, quos distantes longe a superioribus
[uirtutum] mundum istum in inferioribus partibus condidisse;
Christum non ex uirgine Maria natum, sed ex semine Ioseph
5 hominem tantummodo genitum, sane prae ceteris iustitiae
cultu, uitae integritate meliorem. Hunc apud Iudaeos passum,
solam animam ipsius in caelo receptam, eo quod et infirmior
et robustior ceteris fuerit; ex quo colligi retenta anima-
rum sola salute nullas corporis resurrectiones. 2. Post hunc
10 Cerinthus haereticus erupit, similia docens. Nam et ipse mundum
institutum esse ab angelis dicit; Christum ex semine Ioseph
natum proponit, hominem illum tantummodo sine diuinitate
contendens, ipsam quoque legem ab angelis datam perhibens,
Iudaeorum deum non dominum, sed angelum promens. 3. Huius
15 successor Ebion fuit, Cerintho non in omni parte consentiens,

---

1 esse dicit *NR*, esse discit *P*, dicit esse *F*.   3 uirtutum *seclusi*, uirtutibus *GR*³ V219
condidisse *PN*, contumeliis *F*.   5 homine *F*.   6 cultu, uitae *GR*³, cultu
iustiae *N*, cultu *P* (*in mg.* uitae *add. R*), uitae *F*   integritatem *F*.   7 receptam
PN, rectam *F* infirmior *PNF*, firmior *R uulgo*.   8 ceteris *Gel*: ex ceteris *PNF*
ex quo *R*³, et quo *PNFR*¹ colligi *Eng*: colligeret *PN*, colligere *F*, colligere
est Iun retenta *scripsi*: tentata *P*, temptata *N*, temptatam *F*, retentata
Oehlerus.   9 solam salutem *F*.   nullas *R*³, multas *PNFR*¹   resurrectionem *F*.
10 Cerinthus *R*³, corinthus *PNFR*¹ prorupit *N*.   11 angelis *Eng*: illis *PNF*.
15 Cerintho *R*³, corintho *PNFR*¹ non *om. F*.   16 a deo *PN*, ab eo *F*.

Eusebius, *HE* IV.7.9–11 (ed. Schwartz II.1.310 and 312)

This follows Eusebius' report of Saturninus and Basilides.

p. 310 25   Γράφει δὲ καὶ Εἰρηναῖος συγχρονίσαι τούτοις 9
Καρποκράτην, ἑτέρας αἱρέσεως τῆς τῶν Γνωστικῶν ἐπικληθείσης
πατέρα· οἳ καὶ τοῦ Σίμωνος οὐχ ὡς ἐκεῖνος κρύβδην, ἀλλ' ἤδη καὶ
εἰς φανερὸν τὰς μαγείας παραδιδόναι ἠξίουν, ὡς ἐπὶ μεγάλοις δή,

25-S. 312, 8 Iren. 1, 25.

ΑΤΕΡΒΔΜΣΛ

25 *IA* ER | ὁ εἰρηναῖοσ M.   28 δή] τισὶ T*.

p. 312   μόνον οὐχὶ καὶ σεμνυνόμενοι τοῖς κατὰ περιεργίαν πρὸς αὐτῶν ἐπι-
τελουμένοις φίλτροις ὀνειροπομποῖς τε καὶ παρέδροις τισὶ δαίμοσιν
καὶ ἄλλαις ὁμοιοτρόποις τισὶν ἀγωγαῖς· τούτοις τε ἀκολούθως πάντα
δρᾶν χρῆναι διδάσκειν τὰ αἰσχρουργότατα τοὺς μέλλοντας εἰς τὸ τέ-
5 λειον τῆς κατ᾽ αὐτοὺς μυσταγωγίας ἢ καὶ μᾶλλον μυσαροποιίας
ἐλεύσεσθαι, ὡς μὴ ἂν ἄλλως ἐκφευξομένους τοὺς κοσμικούς, ὡς ἂν
ἐκεῖνοι φαῖεν, ἄρχοντας, μὴ οὐχὶ πᾶσιν τὰ δι᾽ ἀρρητοποιίας ἀπονεί-
μαντας χρέα. τούτοις δῆτα συνέβαινεν διακόνοις χρώμενον τὸν   **10**
ἐπιχαιρεσίκακον δαίμονα τοὺς μὲν πρὸς αὐτῶν ἀπατωμένους οἰκτρῶς
10 οὕτως εἰς ἀπώλειαν ἀνδραποδίζεσθαι, τοῖς δ᾽ ἀπίστοις ἔθνεσιν πολλὴν
παρέχειν κατὰ τοῦ θείου λόγου δυσφημίας περιουσίαν, τῆς ἐξ αὐτῶν φήμης εἰς τὴν τοῦ παντὸς Χριστιανῶν ἔθνους διαβολὴν κατα-
χεομένης. ταύτῃ δ᾽ οὖν ἐπὶ πλεῖστον συνέβαινεν τὴν περὶ ἡμῶν   **11**
παρὰ τοῖς τότε ἀπίστοις ὑπόνοιαν δυσσεβῆ καὶ ἀτοπωτάτην διαδί-
15 δοσθαι, ὡς δὴ ἀθεμίτοις πρὸς μητέρας καὶ ἀδελφὰς μίξεσιν ἀνοσίαις
τε τροφαῖς χρωμένων.

ΑΤΕΡΒΔΜΣΛ

1 καὶ TᶜTʳERBDM > AT¹. | **3** ἄλλοισ BD | ὁμοτρόποισ TE | τισὶν > BD.
5 αὐτοὺσ ABDMΣ αὐτὸν TER.   **12** χριστιανῶν ἔθνοσ BDM ἔθνους
χριστιανῶν ATER

Athanasius, *Oratio I contra Arianos* 56 (Migne, *PG* 26.129)

col. 129   Οὐκοῦν εἰ μὲν τῶν γενητῶν (20) ἄλλος ἐστί, τῆς δὲ
τοῦ Πατρὸς οὐσίας μόνον ἴδιον γέννημα ὁ Υἱός, με-
ματαίωται τοῖς Ἀρειανοῖς ἡ περὶ τοῦ "γενόμενος"
πρόφασις. Κἂν γὰρ ἐν τούτοις αἰσχυνθέντες βιάζων-
ται πάλιν λέγειν συγκριτικῶς εἰρῆσθαι τὰ ῥητά, καὶ
διὰ τοῦτο εἶναι τὰ συγκρινόμενα ὁμογενῆ, ὥστε τὸν
Υἱὸν τῆς τῶν ἀγγέλων εἶναι φύσεως· αἰσχυνθήσονται
μὲν προηγουμένως ὡς τὰ Οὐαλεντίνου καὶ Καρποκράτους (21) καὶ τῶν ἄλλων αἱρετικῶν ζηλοῦντες καὶ
φθεγγόμενοι, ὧν ὁ μὲν τοὺς ἀγγέλους ὁμογενεῖς εἴ-
ρηκε τῷ Χριστῷ· ὁ δὲ Καρποκράτης ἀγγέλους τοῦ
κόσμου δημιουργοὺς εἶναί φησι. Παρ᾽ αὐτῶν γὰρ
ἴσως (22) μαθόντες καὶ οὗτοι, συγκοίνουσι τὸν τοῦ
θεοῦ Λόγον τοῖς ἀγγέλοις.

327

Marcellus of Ancyra, *De sancta ecclesia* 4–7
(published as the work of Anthemius of
Nicomedia in *Studi e Testi* V [1901])

4. Οὐκοῦν ἀναγκαῖον εἰπεῖν πόθεν καὶ παρὰ τίνων τὰς ἀφορμὰς
λαβόντες οἱ αἱρετικοὶ παρὰ αἱρετικῶν κατηνέχθησαν εἰς τὸ τῆς ἀπω-
λείας βάραθρον· ἔθος γὰρ τοῖς αἱρετικοῖς τὰ ἀλλήλων ὑφαιρεῖσθαι καὶ
προσεξευρίσκειν καινότερα—αὐχοῦντες εἶναι διδάσκαλοι ἀλλήλων.
30 5. καὶ πρῶτον μὲν συγχωρήσει θεοῦ Σαδδουκαῖοι ἐκ τῶν Ἰουδαίων
ὄντες ἐκήρυξαν μὴ εἶναι ἀνάστασιν μήτε πνεῦμα ἅγιον ὁμολογοῦντες
μήτε ἀγγέλους μήτε προφήτας· ἀφ' ὧν Κήρινθος μικρὰ παραμείψας
παραδίδωσι τοῖς Ἐβιωναίοις. 6. πάλιν οἱ ἀπὸ Σίμωνος γνωστικοὶ λεγόμενοι Μένανδρος καὶ Σατορνῖνος καὶ Βασιλείδης, Μάρκος τε καὶ Κολόρ-
35 βασος καὶ οἱ λοιποὶ καινότερα ἀλλήλων παρεπενόησάν τε καὶ παρέδωκαν τοῖς ὑπ' αὐτῶν ἠπατημένοις, ὅθεν καὶ γνωστικοὺς ἑαυτοὺς
προσηγόρευσαν· ἐξ ὧν ἔλαβον οἵ τε Ὀφίται καὶ Καϊανῖται, Σηθῖται
τε καὶ οἱ Ἑρμοῦ καὶ Σελεύκου καὶ ὁ λοιπὸς ὄχλος τῶν αἱρετικῶν
τῶν τὰ τοιαῦτα ληρούντων, ὡς ἀπὸ Νικολάου Καρποκρᾶς καὶ Πρόδικος   A 32ᵛ
40 καὶ Ἐπιφανής, οἳ καινότερα καὶ αὐτοὶ ἐπενόησαν. 7. πάντες δὲ οὗτοι
παρὰ Ἑρμοῦ καὶ Πλάτωνος καὶ Ἀριστοτέλους τῶν φιλοσόφων τὰς
ἀφορμὰς τῆς ἀσεβείας εἰλήφασι.

26–30 Ουκουν—μεν A: πόθεν δὲ τὰς ἀφορμὰς ἕκαστος ἔλαβεν; πρῶτοι S.   29
αυχουντας ... διδασκάλους? S.   30 Σαδδ. συγχ. θεου S.   32 μικρα παραμ.
A: τινα παραλείψας S.   33 Σιμ.: γνωστοί ἤ add. S; num γνώσται? λεγομενοι
om. S.   34 Βασιλ.—Κολορβ. A: Βασιλίδης καὶ Μάρκος, Κολόβαρσός τε S.
35 καινοτέραν S. παρεπ. τε και om. S.   37 εξ A: ἀφ' S. λαβόντες A. σιθιται A.
38 οἱ λοιποί S.   38–39 οχλος—ληρουντων om. S.   39–40 Καρπ.—
καινοτερα A: Καρποκράτους καὶ Προδίκου καὶ Ἐπιφανίου καὶ νοταρίου S.   40
επενοησαν: ἢ ὡς ἀπὸ Κέρδωνος Μαρκίων καὶ Λουκιανός, ἀφ' ὧν Μανιχαῖοι
ἀφορμὰς λαβόντες καὶ νοταρίοις (corr. καινότερα) παρέδωκαν add. S.   41 των
φιλοσοφων om. S.   42 της ασεβειας om. S.

Epiphanius, *Panarion* XXVII–XXVIII.1 (ed. Holl I.300–313)

p. 300   Κατὰ Καρποκρασίων ζ, τῆς δὲ ἀκολουθίας κζ.
20   1. Καρποκρᾶς τις ἕτερος γίνεται, συστήσας ἑαυτῷ ἀθέμιτον δι-   1, 1
δασκαλεῖον τῆς ψευδωνύμου αὐτοῦ γνώμης, χείρονας πάντων οὗτος
τοὺς τρόπους κεκτημένος. ἐκ πάντων γὰρ τούτων, Σίμωνός τε καὶ   2
Μενάνδρου, Σατορνίλου τε καὶ Βασιλείδου καὶ Νικολάου καὶ αὐτοῦ

V M

19 κατὰ Καρποκρασίων ἑβδόμη, ἢ καὶ κζ V κατὰ Καρποκρασίων ζ, τῆς δὲ ἀκολουθίας
κζ M.   20f διδασκαλί///αν aus διδασκαλεῖον Vᶜᵒʳʳ διδασκάλιον M.   21
χείρους M.   22 ἐχέκτητο M.   23 τε < M | βασιλείδους M.   23f αὐτοῦ
τοῦ] αὐτοῦ auf Rasur Vᶜᵒʳʳ τοῦ τοῦ M.

p. 301   τοῦ Καρποκρᾶ, ἔτι δὲ ἐκ προφάσεως Οὐαλεντίνου ἡ τῆς ψευδωνύ-
μου | γνώσεως ἐφύη αἵρεσις, ἥτις Γνωστικοὺς τοὺς αὐτῆς ὠνόμασεν,   Ö 204
ἀφ' ἧς οἱ Γνωστικοὶ ἤδη μοι δεδήλωνται, κατάγνωστοι ὄντες τὸν
τρόπον.

5   2. Οὗτος δὲ πάλιν ἄνω μὲν μίαν ἀρχὴν λέγει καὶ πατέρα τῶν **2, 1**
ὅλων [καὶ] ἄγνωστον καὶ ἀκατονόμαστον ἴσα τοῖς ἄλλοις εἰσάγειν
βούλεται, τὸν δὲ κόσμον καὶ τὰ ἐν τῷ κόσμῳ ὑπὸ ἀγγέλων γεγενῆσθαι, τῶν πολύ τι [ὑπὸ] τοῦ πατρὸς τοῦ ἀγνώστου ὑποβεβηκότων·
τούτους γὰρ λέγει ἀποστάντας ἀπὸ τῆς ἄνω δυνάμεως οὕτω τὸν | D 63
10 κόσμον πεποιηκέναι. Ἰησοῦν δὲ τὸν κύριον ἡμῶν ἀπὸ Ἰωσὴφ λέγει **2**
γεγεννῆσθαι, καθάπερ καὶ πάντες ἄνθρωποι ἐκ σπέρματος ἀνδρὸς καὶ
γυναικὸς ἐγεννήθησαν. εἶναι δὲ αὐτὸν ὅμοιον τοῖς πᾶσι, βίῳ δὲ
διενηνοχέναι, σωφροσύνῃ τε καὶ ἀρετῇ καὶ βίῳ δικαιοσύνης. ἐπειδὴ **3**
δέ, φησίν, εὔτονον ἔσχε ψυχὴν παρὰ τοὺς ἄλλους ἀνθρώ|πους καὶ P 103
15 ἐμνημόνευεν τὰ ὁραθέντα ὑπ' αὐτῆς ἄνω, ὅτε ἦν ἐν τῇ περιφορᾷ
τοῦ ἀγνώστου πατρός, ἀπεστάλθαι ὑπὸ τοῦ αὐτοῦ πατρός, φησίν,
εἰς τὴν αὐτοῦ ψυχὴν δυνάμεις, ὅπως τὰ ὁραθέντα αὐτῇ ἀναμνημο- **4**
p. 302 νεύσασα καὶ ἐνδυναμωθεῖσα φύγῃ τοὺς κοσμοποιοὺς ἀγγέλους ἐν τῷ
διὰ πάντων χωρῆσαι τῶν ἐν τῷ κόσμῳ πραγμάτων καὶ πράξεων
τῶν ὑπὸ τῶν ἀνθρώπων γινομένων καὶ ἐν παραβύστῳ ἀτόπων ἔργων
καὶ ἀθεμίτων, καὶ ὅπως διὰ πασῶν τῶν πράξεων ἐλευθερωθεῖσα ἡ **5**
5 αὐτὴ ψυχή, φησί, τοῦ Ἰησοῦ ἀνέλθῃ πρὸς τὸν αὐτὸν πατέρα τὸν
ἄγνωστον, τὸν δυνάμεις αὐτῇ ἀποστείλαντα ἄνωθεν, ἵνα διὰ πασῶν
τῶν πράξεων χωρήσασα καὶ ἐλευθερωθεῖσα διέλθοι πρὸς αὐτὸν ἄνω.

   οὐ μὴν δὲ ἀλλὰ καὶ τὰς ὁμοίας αὐτῇ ψυχάς, ⟨τὰς⟩ τὰ ἴσα αὐτῇ ἀσπα- **6**
σαμένας, τὸν αὐτὸν τρόπον ἐλευθερωθείσας ἄνω πτῆναι πρὸς τὸν
10 ἄγνωστον πατέρα, ἐν τῷ τὰς πάσας πράξεις πράξασας ὁμοίως ⟨τε⟩
τῶν πάντων ἀπαλλαγείσας λοιπὸν ἐλευθερωθῆναι. τὴν δὲ ψυχὴν **7**
τοῦ Ἰησοῦ ἐν τοῖς τῶν Ἰουδαίων ἔθεσιν ἀνατραφεῖσαν καταφρονῆσαι
αὐτῶν καὶ διὰ τοῦτο δυνάμεις εἰληφέναι, δι' ὧν τὰ ἐπὶ κολάσεσι
πάθη προσόντα τοῖς ἀνθρώποις δυνηθεῖσα † πρᾶξαι ὑπερβῆναι τοὺς
15 κοσμοποιοὺς ἴσχυσεν. οὐ μόνον δὲ αὐτὴν τὴν ψυχὴν τοῦ Ἰησοῦ τοῦτο **8**
δεδυνῆσθαι, ἀλλὰ καὶ τὴν δυναμένην διὰ ⟨πασῶν⟩ τῶν πράξεων
χωρῆσαι ὑπερβῆναι τοὺς κοσμοποιοὺς αὐτοὺς ἀγγέλους· καὶ αὐτὴ ἐὰν
λάβῃ δυνάμεις καὶ τὰ ὅμοια πράξῃ, * καθάπερ ἡ τοῦ Ἰησοῦ, ὡς
προεῖπον. ὅθεν εἰς τῦφον μέγαν οὗτοι ἐλη|λακότες οἱ ὑπὸ τοῦ **9** D64
V M

p. 301   **3** καταγνωστικοὶ V.   **5** ἄνω μὲν] ἄνωθεν M.   **6** [καὶ]* | ἀκατονόμαστον M |
εἰσάγειν < M.   **7** βουλόμενος aus βούλεται V^corr.   **7f** γεγεννῆσθαι M.
8 [ὑπὸ]* | τοῦ² < M | ὑπερβεβηκότων M.   **14** φησίν < M.

p. 302   **3** ἀνθρώπων] ἀγγέλων M.   **4–7** ἐλευθερωθεῖσα—πράξεων < M.   **8** ⟨τὰς⟩*.
10 πραξάσας < M | ⟨τε⟩*.   **14** δυνηθεῖσα *] δυνηθεὶς VM | † πρᾶξαι] lies
wohl καταργῆσαι*, vgl. Hippolyt.   **16** δυναμένην + ⟨ὁμοίως αὐτῇ⟩? Jül. |
⟨πασῶν⟩*.   **17** χωρῆσαι*] χωρήσασαν VM.   **18** * ⟨ἄνω πτήσεται⟩ * | ἡ <
V.   **19** μέγα V.

p. 303   ἀπατεῶνος τούτου ἀπατηθέντες ἑαυτοὺς προκριτέους ἡγοῦνται καὶ
αὐτοῦ τοῦ Ἰησοῦ. ἄλλοι δὲ ἐξ αὐτῶν οὐκ Ἰησοῦ φασιν, ἀλλὰ Πέτρου 10
καὶ Ἀνδρέου καὶ Παύλου καὶ τῶν λοιπῶν ἀποστόλων ἑαυτοὺς ὑπερ-
φερεστέρους εἶναι διὰ τὴν ὑπερβολὴν τῆς γνώσεως καὶ τὸ περισσό-
5 τερον τῆς διαπράξεως διαφόρων διεξόδων· ἄλλοι δὲ ἐξ αὐτῶν φά-
σκουσι μηδὲν διενηνοχέναι τοῦ κυρίου ἡμῶν Ἰησοῦ Χριστοῦ. αἱ γὰρ 11
ψυχαὶ | ἐκ τῆς αὐτῆς περιφορᾶς εἰσι καὶ ὁμοίως κατὰ τὴν τοῦ Ἰησοῦ Ö 206
πάντων ̣ αταφρόνησιν ποιησάμεναι *. καὶ ⟨γὰρ⟩ αἱ πᾶσαι, φησί, ψυχαὶ
τῆς αὐ ̣ ̣ δυνάμεως ἠξιώθησαν ἧς καὶ ἡ τοῦ Ἰησοῦ ἠξίωται· διὸ
10 καὶ ταῦτα⟨ς⟩ φασὶ χωρεῖν διὰ πάσης πράξεως, καθάπερ ἀμέλει καὶ ἡ
τοῦ Ἰησοῦ διελήλυθεν. εἰ δὲ καί | τις πάλιν δυνηθείη ὑπὲρ τὸν Ἰη- P 104
σοῦν καταφρονῆσαι, διαφορώτερος ἔσται αὐτοῦ.

    3. Ἐπιχειροῦσι δὲ οἱ τῆς ἀθεμίτου ταύτης σχολῆς παντοίας ἐπι- 3, 1
χειρήσεις δεινῶν ἔργων καὶ ὀλετηρίων. μαγεῖαι γὰρ’ παρ’ αὐτοῖς
15 ἐπινενόηνται, ἐπῳδάς τε διαφόρους πρὸς πᾶσαν μηχανὴν ἐφηύραντο,
[πρὸς] φίλτρα ⟨τε⟩ καὶ ἀγώγιμα. οὐ μὴν δὲ ἀλλὰ καὶ παρέδρους δαί-
μονας ἑαυτοῖς ἐπισπῶνται, εἰς τὸ διὰ πολλῆς μαγγανείας ἐν ἐξουσίᾳ
μεγάλῃ πάντων ⟨γενέσθαι⟩, ⟨ὥστε⟩, φησί, κυριεύε ̣ ̣ ̣ ̣ τε ἂν ἐθέλοι ἕκαστος καὶ ᾗ πράξει ἐπιχειρεῖν τολμήσειε· δῆθεν ἑαυτοὺς ἐξαπατῶντες 2
20 πρὸς πληροφορίαν τῆς τετυφλωμένης αὐτῶν διανοίας, ὅτι αἱ τοιαῦτα
ἐγχειρήσασαι ⟨ψυχαί⟩, κατισχύσασαι διὰ τῶν τοιούτων πράξεων καὶ
καταφρονήσασαι τῶν κοσμοποιῶν ἀγγέλων καὶ τῶν ἐν τῷ κόσμῳ,
ὑπερβαίνουσι τὴν τῶν αὐτῶν μυθοποιῶν (οὐ γὰρ ἂν εἴποιμι κοσμοποιῶν) ἐξουσίαν, ὅπως ἂν τὴν ἄνω ἐλευθερίαν ἀσπάσωνται καὶ τὴν
25 ἄνω πτῆσιν κτήσαιντο. εἰσὶ δὲ ἐκ τοῦ Σατανᾶ παρεσκευασμένοι 3
p. 304 καὶ προβεβλημένοι εἰς ὄνειδος καὶ σκάνδαλον τῆς τοῦ θεοῦ ἐκκλησίας. ἐπέθεντο γὰρ ἑαυτοῖς ἐπίκλην Χριστιανοί, τοῦτο τοῦ Σατανᾶ
παρασκευάσαντος πρὸς τὸ σκαν|δαλίζεσθαι τὰ ἔθνη δι’ αὐτῶν καὶ D 65
ἀποστρέφεσθαι τὴν τῆς ἁγίας τοῦ θεοῦ ἐκκλησίας ὠφέλειαν καὶ τὸ
5 ἀληθινὸν κήρυγμα διὰ τὰς ἐκείνων ἀθεμιτουργίας καὶ ἀνηκέστου⟨ς⟩
κακοπραγίας, εἰς τὸ τὰ ἔθνη κατανοοῦντα αὐτῶν τὰ ἐπάλληλα ἔργα 4
τῶν ἀθεμιτουργιῶν, νομίσαντα καὶ τοὺς τῆς ἁγίας τοῦ θεοῦ ἐκκλησίας τοιούτους εἶναι, ἀποστρέφειν ὡς καὶ προεῖπον τὴν ἀκοὴν ἀπὸ

V M
p. 303 3 Παύλου καὶ Ἀνδρέου M.   5 διὰ πράξεως M.   6 διενηνοχέναι M.   8
* etwa ⟨καὶ εἰς τὸ αὐτὸ χωρήσουσιν⟩ *, nach Iren. Hipp. | ⟨γὰρ⟩ *.   9 ἡ < V.
10 ταῦτα⟨ς⟩ *.   14f μαγεία . . . ἐπινενόηνται V.   15 ἐφεύροντο, ο aus α V.
16 [πρὸς] * | ⟨τε⟩ *.   18 ⟨γενέσθαι⟩, ⟨ὥστε⟩ *.   20f τοιαῦτα ἐγχειρήσασαι
⟨ψυχαί⟩ *] τοιαῦτα ἐγχειρήσεις V M.   21 τοσούτων V.   22 καταφρονῆσαι
M.

p. 304 V M 2-5 Niceph. Antirrhet. bei Pitra Spicileg. Solesm. IV 297, 8ff

2 ὅτι ἐπίκλην ἑαυτοῖς ἔθεντο Χριστιανούς Niceph. (dadurch ist der vorliegende
Gebrauch von ἐπίκλην für Epiph. gesichert).   2f τοῦτο τοῦ Σατανᾶ παρα-
σκευάσαντος Niceph.] < V M.   3 δι’ αὐτῶν < Niceph.   5 διὰ τὰς *] διὰ
τῆς V M | ἀνηκέστου⟨ς⟩ *] ἀνικάστου aus ἀνηκέστου V^corr ἀνηκέστου M.

τῆς τοῦ θεοῦ κατὰ ἀλήθειαν διδασκαλίας ἢ καὶ ὁρῶντά τινας *
10 πάντας ⟨ἡμᾶς⟩ ὁμοίως βλασφημεῖν. καὶ τούτου ἕνεκα οἱ πλείους τῶν 5
ἐθνῶν ὅπου δἂν ἴδωσι τοιούτους οὔτε ἐπὶ κοινωνίᾳ ἡμῖν προσφέρον-
ται ληψοδοσίας ἢ γνώμης ἢ ἀκοῆς λόγου θείου οὔτε τὴν ἀκοὴν ἐντι-
θέασιν, ἐπτυρμένοι ἀπὸ τῆς τῶν ἀθεμίτων ἀνοσιουργίας.

4. Εἰσὶ δὲ ἐν ἀσωτίᾳ διατελοῦντες οὗτοι καὶ πᾶν ὁτιοῦν ἐργαζό- 4, 1
15 μενοι πρὸς εὐπάθειαν σωμάτων, ἡμῖν δὲ ὅλως οὐ προσεγγίζοντες, εἰ
μή τι ἂν πρὸς τὸ δελεάσαι ψυχὰς ἀστηρίκτους τῇ αὐτῶν κακοδιδα-
σκαλίᾳ. εἰς οὐδὲν γὰρ ἡμῖν ὁμοιοῦνται ἢ μόνον ὀνόματι καλεῖσθαι
σεμνύνονται, ὅπως διὰ τοῦ ὀνόματος τὸ ἐπίπλαστον τῆς ἑαυτῶν
κακίας θηράσωνται. »τὸ δὲ κρίμα τούτων« | κατὰ τὸ γεγραμμένον 2 P 105
20 »ἔνδι|κόν ἐστιν«, ὡς ὁ ἅγιος ἀπόστολος Παῦλος ἔφη· διὰ γὰρ τὰς Ö 208
p. 305 κακὰς αὐτῶν πράξεις τὸ ἀνταπόδομα ἀποδοθήσεται αὐτοῖς. ἀδεῶς 3
γὰρ τὸν νοῦν αὐτῶν εἰς οἶστρον ἐκδεδωκότες πάθεσιν ἡδονῶν μυρίων
ἑαυτοὺς παραδεδώκασι. φασὶ γὰρ ὅτι ὅσα νομίζεται παρὰ ἀνθρώποις
κακὰ εἶναι οὐ κακὰ ὑπάρχει, ἀλλὰ φύσει καλά (οὐδὲν γάρ ἐστι φύσει
5 κακόν), τοῖς δὲ ἀνθρώποις νομίζεται εἶναι φαῦλα. καὶ ταῦτα πάντα 4
ἐάν τις πράξῃ ἐν τῇ μιᾷ ταύτῃ παρουσίᾳ, οὐκέτι μετενσωματοῦται
αὐτοῦ ἡ ψυχὴ εἰς τὸ πάλιν ἀντικαταβληθῆναι, ἀλλὰ ὑπὸ ἐν ποιήσασα
πᾶσαν πρᾶξιν ἀπαλλαγήσεται, ἐλευθερωθεῖσα καὶ μηκέτι χρεωστοῦσά
τι τῶν πρὸς πρᾶξιν ἐν τῷ κόσμῳ. ποίαν δὲ πρᾶξιν δέδια πάλιν | 5 D 66
10 εἰπεῖν, μὴ βορβόρου δίκην κεκαλυμμένου ὀχετὸν ἀποκαλύψω καί τισι
δόξω λοιμώδους δυσοδμίας ἐργάζεσθαι τὴν ἐμφόρησιν. ἀλλ' ὅμως
ἐπειδήπερ ἐξ ἀληθείας συνεχόμεθα τὰ παρὰ τοῖς ἠπατημένοις ἀπο-
καλύψαι, σεμνότερον εἰπεῖν τε καὶ τῆς ἀληθείας μὴ ἔξω βαίνειν
ἐμαυτὸν καταναγκάσω. τί δὲ ἀλλ' ὅτι πᾶσαν ἀρρητουργίαν καὶ 6
15 ἀθέμιτον πρᾶξιν, ἣν οὐ θεμιτὸν ἐπὶ στόματος φέρειν, οὗτοι πράτ-
τουσιν καὶ πᾶν εἶδος ἀνδροβασιῶν καὶ λαγνιστέρων ὁμιλιῶν πρὸς
γυναῖκας ἐν ἑκάστῳ μέλει σώματος· μαγείας τε καὶ φαρμακείας καὶ 7
εἰδωλολατρείας ἐκτελοῦντες τοῦτο εἶναί φασιν ἐργασίαν ἀποδόσεως
p. 306 τῶν ἐν τῷ σώματι ὀφλημάτων εἰς τὸ μηκέτι ἐγκαλεῖσθαι ἢ μέλλειν
τι πράξεως ἔργον ἀπαιτεῖσθαι, καὶ τούτου ἕνεκα μὴ ἀποστρέφεσθαι

V M

7-9 ἐκκλησίας—τοῦ θεοῦ < M.   9 ὁρῶντα *] ὁρῶντας V M | * etwa ⟨οὕτως
ἀνοσιουργοῦντας⟩ *.   10 πάντως V | ⟨ἡμᾶς⟩ Jül., vgl. Hipp.   13 ἐ|||πτυρ-
μένοι, 1-2 Buchstaben hinter ἐ ausradiert V.   15 οὐχ ἐγγίζοντες V.   16
ἄρα aus ἂν Vcorr | vor τῇ + ἐν V.   18 τοῦ ἐπιπλάστου aus τὸ ἐπίπλαστον Vcorr |
vor τῆς + τὰ V.   19 ἐργάσωνται aus θηράσωνται Vcorr θηράσονται M.   20
ὁ ἅγιος Παῦλος ὁ ἀπόστολος V.

p. 305   1 ἀνταποδοθήσεται M.   3 παρεδώκασι, αδ Vcorr.   6 πράξῃ ἐν] πράξειεν V.
7 ἀλλ' M.   9f εἰπεῖν δέδια πάλιν V.   11 δείξω M | δυσοσμίας M.
12 ἐξ] ἐπ'? *, aber vgl. S. 319, 8.   14 ἀλλ' ὅτι aus ἄλλο τι Vcorr ἄλλο τι
M; ἀλλ' + ⟨ἢ⟩? *.   18 καὶ vor τοῦτο hineingeflickt Vcorr < M | ἀποδόσεων M.
p. 306   1 ὀφειλημάτων aus ὠφλημάτων Vcorr.

331

τὴν ψυχὴν μετὰ τὴν ἐντεῦθεν ἀπαλλαγὴν καὶ πάλιν εἰς μετενσωμά-
τωσιν καὶ μεταγγισμὸν χωρεῖν.

5   5. Οὕτως γὰρ ἔχει τὰ αὐτῶν συντάγματα ὡς ἀναγνόντα τὸν   5, 1
συνετὸν θαυμάζειν καὶ ἐκπλήττεσθαι καὶ ἀπιστεῖν εἰ ταῦτα οὕτως
ὑπὸ ἀνθρώπων γενήσεται, οὐ μόνον τῶν καθ' ἡμᾶς πόλιν κατοι-
κούντων, ἀλλὰ καὶ τῶν μετὰ θηρῶν καὶ ὁμοίων θηρσὶ καὶ κτήνεσι
* καὶ σχεδὸν εἰπεῖν τὰ κυνῶν καὶ ὑῶν πράττειν τολμώντων. φασὶ   2
10 γὰρ δεῖν πάντως πᾶσαν χρῆσιν τούτων ποιεῖσθαι, ἵνα μὴ ἐξελθοῦσαι
καὶ ὑστερήσασαί τινος ἔργου τούτου ἕνεκα καταστραφῶσιν εἰς σώματα
πά|λιν αἱ ψυχαὶ εἰς τὸ πρᾶξαι αὖθις ἃ μὴ ἔπραξαν. καὶ τοῦτό ἐστι,   3 P 106
φασίν, ὅπερ ὁ Ἰησοῦς ἐν τῷ εὐαγγελίῳ εἶπεν διὰ τῆς παραβολῆς ὅτι
»ἴσθι εὐνοῶν τῷ ἀντιδίκῳ σου ἐν ᾧ εἶ ἐν τῇ ὁδῷ μετ' αὐτοῦ καὶ
15 δὸς ἐργασίαν ἀπηλλάχθαι ἀπ' αὐτοῦ, μή πως ὁ ἀντίδικος πα-
ραδῷ σε τῷ κριτῇ καὶ ὁ κριτὴς τῷ ὑπηρέτῃ, καὶ ὁ ὑπηρέτης
βάλῃ σε εἰς φυλακήν· ἀμὴν λέγω σοί, οὐ μὴ ἐξέλθῃς ἐκεῖθεν,
ἕως ἂν ἀποδῷς τὸν ἔσχατον κοδράντην«. μῦθον δέ τινα | 4 D 67
p. 307   πλάττουσιν οἱ αὐτοὶ πρὸς ἐπίλυσιν τῆς | παραβολῆς ταύτης καὶ φασιν Ö 210
εἶναι τὸν ἀντίδικον ἐκεῖνον τῶν τὸν κόσμον πεποιηκότων ἀγγέλων
ἕνα καὶ εἰς αὐτὸ τοῦτο κατεσκευάσθαι, εἰς τὸ ἀπάγειν τὰς ψυχὰς πρὸς
τὸν κριτὴν τὰς ἐντεῦθεν ἐξερχομένας ἐκ τῶν σωμάτων ἐκεῖσε
5 δὲ ἐλεγχομένας· μὴ ποιησάσας δὲ πᾶσαν ἐργασίαν παραδίδοσθαι
ἀπὸ τοῦ ἄρχοντος τῷ ὑπηρέτῃ. ἄγγελον δὲ εἶναι τὸν ὑπηρέτην,   5
ἐξυπηρετούμενον τῷ κριτῇ τῷ κοσμοποιῷ εἰς τὸ φέρειν τὰς ψυχὰς
πάλιν καὶ εἰς σώματα καταγγίζειν διάφορα. εἶναι δὲ τὸν ἀντίδικον
τοῦτον, ὃν ἔφημεν τὸν κύριον εἰρηκέναι ἐν τῷ εὐαγγελίῳ, [ὃν] οὗτοι
10 ἄγγελον ἕνα τῶν κοσμοποιῶν φασιν, ὄνομα ἔχοντα Διάβολον. φασὶ   6
γὰρ εἶναι τὴν φυλακὴν τὸ σῶμα. τὸν δὲ ἔσχατον κοδράντην θέλουσιν
εἶναι τὴν μετενσωμάτωσιν· * καθ' ἑκάστην παρουσίαν σωμάτων ἐπιτελεῖν ἐσχάτην πρᾶξιν καὶ μηκέτι ὑπολείπεσθαι πρὸς τὸ ἀθέμιτόν τι
πρᾶξαι. δεῖ γάρ, φασίν ὡς προείπαμεν, πάντα ⟨δι⟩ελθοῦσαν καὶ πρά-
15 ξασαν καθ' ἕκαστον καὶ ἐλευθερωθεῖσαν ἀνελθεῖν πρὸς τὸν ἄνω
ἄγνωστον, ὑπερβᾶσαν τοὺς κοσμοποιοὺς καὶ τὸν κοσμοποιόν. φασὶ   7
δὲ πάλιν ὅτι δεῖ κἄν τε ἐν μιᾷ παρουσίᾳ τῆς μετενσωματώσεως πρα-
ξάσας λοιπὸν ἄνω ἐλευθερωθείσας ἀπιέναι· εἰ δὲ μὴ ἐν μιᾷ παρουσίᾳ
πράξωσι, καθ' ἑκάστην παρουσίαν μετενσωματώσεως κατὰ βραχὺ
20 ποιησάσας ἑκάστου ἔργου ἀθεμίτου τὴν ἐργασίαν λοιπὸν ἐλευθερω-
p. 308   θῆναι. λέγουσι δὲ πάλιν ὅτι τοῖς ἀξίοις ταῦτα καταξιοῦμεν διη-   8
γεῖσθαι, ἵνα πράξωσι τὰ δοκοῦντα εἶναι κακά, οὐκ ὄντα δὲ φύσει

V M

5 ἔχειν M.   7 τῶν] τὴν M.   9 * etwa ⟨διαιτωμένων⟩ *.   10 δεῖ V.
13 διὰ τῆς παραβολῆς angeflickt V^corr.   14 εἶ] εἰς V.   17 vor φυλακὴν +
τὴν M | ἀμὴν zweimal V.
p. 307   4 τῶν < V.   5 δὲ hinter ποιησάσας *, hinter παραδίδοσθαι V M.   7 τῷ²
< M.   8f τούτον τὸν ἀντίδικον M.   9 [ὃν] * | αὐτοὶ aus οὗτοι V.   10
ἄβολον V.   12 * ⟨χρῆναι δὲ⟩ *.   14 ⟨δι⟩ελθοῦσαν *.   19 πράξουσι M.

κακά, ἵνα μαθόντες ἐλευθερωθῶσι. σφραγῖδα δὲ ἐν καυτῆρι ἢ δι' **9**
ἐπιτηδεύσεως ξυρίου ἢ ῥαφίδος ἐπιτιθέασιν οὗτοι οἱ ἀπὸ Καρποκρᾶ
5 ἐπὶ τὸν δεξιὸν λοβὸν τοῦ ὠτὸς τοῖς ὑπ' αὐτῶν ἀπατωμένοις. | P 107
   6. ῏Ηλθεν δὲ εἰς ἡμᾶς ἤδη πως Μαρκελλίνα τις | ὑπ' αὐτῶν ἀπα- **6, 1**
τηθεῖσα, ἣ πολλοὺς ἐλυμήνατο ἐν χρόνοις Ἀνικήτου ἐπισκόπου Ῥώμης,   D 68
τοῦ μετὰ τὴν διαδοχὴν Πίου καὶ τῶν ἀνωτέρω. . .

p. 310   'Εν **8**
χρόνοις τοίνυν, ὡς ἔφημεν, Ἀνικήτου ἡ προδεδηλωμένη Μαρκελλίνα | P 108
ἐν Ῥώμῃ γενομένη τὴν λύμην τῆς Καρποκρᾶ διδασκαλίας ἐξεμέσασα
πολλοὺς τῶν ἐκεῖσε λυμηναμένη ἠφάνισε. καὶ ἔνθεν γέγονεν ἀρχὴ
Γνωστικῶν τῶν καλουμένων. ἔχουσι δὲ εἰκόνας ἐνζωγράφους διὰ **9**
15 χρωμάτων, ἀλλὰ καὶ οἱ μὲν ἐκ χρυσοῦ καὶ ἀργύρου καὶ λοιπῆς ὕλης,
p. 311 ἅτινα ἐκτυπώματά φασιν εἶναι τοῦ Ἰησοῦ καὶ ταῦτα ὑπὸ Ποντίου
Πιλάτου γεγενῆσθαι, τουτέστιν τὰ ἐκτυπώματα τοῦ αὐτοῦ Ἰησοῦ ὅτε
ἐνεδήμει τῷ τῶν ἀνθρώπων γένει. κρύβδην δὲ τὰς τοιαύτας ἔχουσιν, **10**
ἀλλὰ καὶ φιλοσόφων τινῶν, Πυθαγόρου καὶ Πλάτωνος καὶ Ἀριστο-
5 τέλους καὶ λοιπῶν, μεθ' ὧν φιλοσόφων καὶ ἕτερα ἐκτυπώματα τοῦ
Ἰησοῦ τιθέασιν, ἱδρύσαντές τε προσκυνοῦσι καὶ τὰ τῶν ἐθνῶν ἐπιτελοῦσι μυστήρια. στήσαντες γὰρ ταύτας τὰς εἰκόνας τὰ τῶν ἐθνῶν
ἔθη λοιπὸν ποιοῦσι. τίνα δέ ἐστιν ⟨τὰ⟩ ἐθνῶν ἔθη ἀλλ' ἢ θυσίαι
καὶ τὰ ἄλλα; ψυχῆς δὲ εἶναι μόνης σωτηρίαν φασὶ καὶ οὐχὶ σω- **11**
10 μάτων.
   7. Δεῖ τοίνυν τούτους ἀνατρέπειν παντὶ σθένει· μηδεὶς γὰρ κατα- **7, 1**
φρονείτω λόγου καὶ μάλιστα κατὰ ἀπατεώνων.

Epiphanius' refutation adds nothing substantial to his report concerning the sect;
it is therefore omitted.

p. 313   Κατὰ Κηρινθιανῶν ἤτοι Μηρινθιανῶν η̄, τῆς δὲ ἀκολουθίας κ̄η.
   1. Κήρινθος δὲ αὖθις, ἀφ' οὗπερ οἱ Κηρινθιανοὶ λεγόμενοι, ἀπὸ **1, 1**
ταύτης τῆς θηριώδους σπορᾶς τὸν ἰὸν τῷ κόσμῳ φέρων ἥκει· σχεδὸν
δὲ οὐδὲν ἕτερον παρὰ τὸν προειρημένον Καρποκρᾶν, ἀλλὰ τὰ αὐτὰ
10 τῷ κόσμῳ κακοποιὰ φάρμακα ἐκβλυστάνει. τὰ ἴσα γὰρ τῷ προει- **2**
ρημένῳ εἰς τὸν Χριστὸν συκοφαντήσας ἐξηγεῖται καὶ οὗτος, ἐκ Μαρίας
καὶ ἐκ σπέρματος Ἰωσὴφ τὸν Χριστὸν γεγεννῆσθαι καὶ τὸν κόσμον

p. 310 V M **14**–S. **311, 7** frei wiedergegeben von Nicephorus Antirrhet. bei Pitra
Spicil. Solesm. IV 297 εἰκόνας Χριστοῦ ἔχουσιν ἐκ διαφόρων ὑλῶν ἅς φασιν εἶναι
τοῦ Ἰησοῦ καὶ ὑπὸ Ποντίου Πιλάτου γεγενημένας ὅτε ἐπεδήμει τῷ τῶν ἀνθρώπων
γένει, εἶτα καὶ φιλοσόφων Πυθαγόρου καὶ Πλάτωνος καὶ Ἀριστοτέλους καὶ ἑτέρων·
ἃς δὴ καὶ ἱδρυσάμενοι προσκυνοῦσι καὶ τὰ ἐθνῶν ἐπιτελοῦσι μυστήρια.

p. 308 **4** ξυρίου Pet.] ξηρίου V M | ὑπὸ V.   **5** λωβὸν, ω aus ο V^corr | ὑπ' αὐτὸν M.
6 δὲ] μὲν V | ἀπ' M.   **7** ἢ hineingeflickt V^corr.

p. 310 **2** καὶ < M.   **5** αὖθις] ἄν τις M.   **9** οὕτως] τούτων M.   **11** ἢ < M.
13 τῶν < M | ἔνθεν aus etwas anderem hergestellt V^corr.   **15** ἀλλὰ καὶ οἱ μὲν
durchgestrichen, dafür am Rande τινὲς δὲ V^corr.

p. 313 **6** κατὰ Κηρινθιανῶν ἤτοι Μηρινθιανῶν ὀγδόη ἡ καὶ κ̄η V.   **8** φέρειν M.   **10**
ἐκβλυσθάνει V ἐμβλυστάνει M.

ὁμοίως ὑπὸ ἀγγέλων γεγενῆσθαι. οὐδὲν γὰρ οὗτος παρὰ τὸν πρῶ- 3
τον διήλλαξε τῇ εἰσαγωγῇ τῆς αὐτοῦ διδασκαλίας ἀλλ' ἢ ἐν τούτῳ
15 μόνον, ἐν τῷ προσέχειν τῷ Ἰουδαϊσμῷ ἀπὸ μέρους. φάσκει δὲ οὗτος
τὸν νόμον καὶ τοὺς προφήτας ὑπὸ ἀγγέλων δεδόσθαι, τὸν δὲ δεδω-
κότα τὸν νόμον ἕνα εἶναι τῶν ἀγγέλων τῶν τὸν κόσμον πεποιηκότων.

13 γεγεννῆσθαι M.   14 ἀλλά M.   16 δὲ hineingeflickt V^corr < M.

Epiphanius, *Panarion* XXX.14 (ed. Holl I.351)

In a discussion of the Ebionites.

p. 351   14. Ὅρα δὲ τὴν παρ' αὐτοῖς παραπεποιημένην πανταχόθεν δι- 14, 1
δασκαλίαν, πῶς πάντα χωλά, λοξὰ καὶ οὐδεμίαν ὀρθότητα ἔχοντα.
ὁ μὲν γὰρ Κήρινθος καὶ Καρποκρᾶς, τῷ αὐτῷ χρώμενοι δῆθεν παρ' 2
10 αὐτοῖς εὐαγγελίῳ *, ἀπὸ τῆς ἀρχῆς τοῦ κατὰ Ματθαῖον εὐαγγελίου διὰ
τῆς γενεαλογίας βούλονται παριστᾶν ἐκ σπέρματος Ἰωσὴφ καὶ Μαρίας
εἶναι τὸν Χριστόν. οὗτοι δὲ ἄλλα τινὰ διανοοῦνται. παρακόψαντες 3
γὰρ τὰς παρὰ τῷ Ματθαίῳ γενεαλογίας ἄρχονται τὴν ἀρχὴν ποιεῖσθαι ὡς προείπομεν, λέγοντες ὅτι »ἐγένετο« φησίν »ἐν ταῖς ἡμέραις
15 Ἡρῴδου βασιλέως τῆς Ἰουδαίας ἐπὶ ἀρχιερέως Καϊάφα, ἦλθέν τις Ἰωάννης ὀνόματι βαπτίζων βάπτισμα μετανοίας ἐν τῷ Ἰορδάνῃ ποταμῷ« καὶ
τὰ ἑξῆς· ἐπειδὴ γὰρ βούλονται τὸν μὲν Ἰησοῦν ὄντως ἄνθρωπον 4
εἶναι, ὡς προεῖπον, | Χριστὸν δὲ ἐν αὐτῷ γεγενῆσθαι τὸν ἐν εἴδει P 139
περιστερᾶς καταβεβηκότα (καθάπερ ἤδη καὶ παρ' ἄλλαις αἱρέσεσιν
20 εὑρήκαμεν) συναφθέντα ⟨τε⟩ αὐτῷ, καὶ εἶναι | αὐτὸν τὸν Χριστὸν * ἐκ D 107
σπέρματος ἀνδρὸς καὶ γυναικὸς γεγεννημένον.

V M

1 ὁ Tischendorf] ὃν V M.   2 κύριε < M.   7f die Reihenfolge πανταχόθεν
διδασκαλίαν durch Zahlen hergestellt V^corr διδασκαλίαν πανταχόθεν M.   9
χρόμενοι M.   10 * ⟨κατὰ Ματθαῖον λεγομένῳ⟩ *, vgl. S. 349, 2.   15 ἐπὶ
ἀρχιερέως Καϊάφα < S. 350, 9.   15 u. 16 τις u. ὀνόματι < S. 350, 9 u. 10.
17f εἶναι ἄνθρωπον M.   18 γεγεννῆσθαι V.   20 εὑρήκαμεν *] εὑρίσκομεν
V M | ⟨τε⟩ * | * ergänze etwa nach haer. 28, 1, 5 ⟨ἐκ τοῦ ἄνω θεοῦ, τὸν δὲ
Ἰησοῦν⟩ *

Epiphanius, *Panarion* XXXII.3–7 (ed. Holl I.441–446)

In ch. 32 Epiphanius discusses one Secundus, a follower of Valentinus, whose
peculiarity was to describe the ogdoad as composed of a right hand tetrad, which
he called "light," and a left hand tetrad, which he called "darkness." Epiphanius
advances philosophical arguments against this theory and then continues as follows:

p. 441 15   3. Ἵνα δὲ μὴ παραλείψωμέν τι τῶν παρά τισιν γινομένων τε   **3, 1**
καὶ λεγομένων, κἄν τε ἐν ἑκάστῃ πολλοὶ | εἶεν οἱ ἔξαρχοι καὶ αὐ-   D 192
χοῦντες ἕτερα ἀνθ᾽ ἑτέρων ὑπὲρ τοὺς αὐτῶν διδασκάλους μυθοποι-
εῖσθαι, ἔτι ἐπιμενῶ ὑφηγούμενος τοὺς ἐν αὐτῇ τῇ αἱρέσει ὄντας,
ἕτερα δὲ παρὰ τούτους λέγοντας, φημὶ δὲ περὶ Ἐπιφάνους τοῦ Ἰσι-   **2**
20   δώρου, ἐκ προφάσεως παραινετικῶν ῥημάτων ἑαυτὸν ἔτι εἰς περισ-
σότερον βυθὸν ταλαιπωρίας καταγαγόντος, τἀληθῆ μὲν εἰπεῖν ἀπὸ
Καρποκράτους τοῦ ἰδίου πατρὸς κατὰ σάρκα εἰληφότος τὰς προφάσεις,
p. 442   συνημμένου δὲ τῇ αἱρέσει τοῦ προειρημένου Σεκούνδου καὶ αὐτοῦ
τῶν Σεκουνδιανῶν ὑπάρχοντος. πολλὴ γὰρ ἑκάστου τῶν πεπλανη-   **3**
μένων πρὸς τὸν ἕτερον διαφορὰ καὶ συρφετώδης ὡς εἰπεῖν πολυ-
μιξία κενοφωνίας. οὗτος γὰρ ὁ Ἐπιφάνης, ὡς ἔφην, υἱὸς ὢν Καρ-   **4**
5   ποκράτους, μητρὸς δὲ Ἀλεξανδρείας οὕτω καλουμένης, τούτοις ὡς
προεῖπον συνάπτεται· ἀπὸ Κεφαλληνίας μὲν τὸ πρὸς πατρὸς γένος
ὤν, ἑπτακαιδεκαετῆ ⟨δὲ⟩ βιώσας χρόνον θᾶττον τὸν βίον κατέ-
στρεψεν, τοῦ κυρίου ὥσπερ ἀκάνθας τοὺς φαύλους ἀπαλλάσσοντος,
κρεῖττόν τι περὶ τῆς οἰκουμένης προνοοῦντος. μετὰ δὲ τὴν αὐτοῦ   **5**
10   τελευτὴν οἱ πρὸς αὐτοῦ πεπλανημένοι τῆς ἀπ᾽ αὐτοῦ πληγῆς οὐκ
ἀπέσχοντο. ἐν Σάμῳ γὰρ ὡς θεὸς ἔτι καὶ εἰς δεῦρο τιμᾶται· τέμε-   **6**
νος γὰρ αὐτῷ | ἱδρύσαντες οἱ ἐπιχώριοι θυσίας καὶ τελετὰς ἐπιτελοῦσι   P 211
κατὰ νεομηνίαν, βωμοὺς δὲ αὐτῷ ἔστησαν καὶ μουσεῖον εἰς ὄνομα
αὐτοῦ περίπυστον ἀνεστήσαντο, τὸ δὴ Ἐπιφάνους μουσεῖον καλού-
15   μενον. θύουσι γὰρ αὐτῷ οἱ Κεφαλλῆνες εἰς τοσαύτην πλάνην ἐλη-   **7**
λακότες καὶ σπένδουσι καὶ ἐν τῷ ἱδρυμένῳ αὐτοῦ τεμένει εὐωχοῦνται ὕμνους τε αὐτῷ ᾄδουσι. δι᾽ ὑπερβολὴν δὲ τῆς ἐκείνου παιδείας,   **8**
ἐγκυκλίου τε καὶ Πλατωνικῆς, ἡ πᾶσα τοῖς προειρημένοις κατά τε
τὴν αἵρεσιν καὶ κατὰ τὴν ἑτέραν πλάνην, λέγω ⟨δὲ⟩ τὴν εἰς εἰδωλο-
20   μανίαν τοὺς ἐπιχωρίους τρέψασαν, γέγονεν ἀπ᾽ αὐτοῦ ἀπάτη. συνήπ-   **9**
τετο | γοῦν οὗτος ὁ Ἐπιφάνης Σεκούνδῳ καὶ τοῖς ἀμφ᾽ αὐτόν. τὴν γὰρ   D 193
αὐτοῦ ἰοβολίαν ἀπεμάξατο, λέγω ⟨δὲ⟩ τὴν τῆς ἀδικούσης ἑρπετώδους
p. 443   φθορᾶς περιττολογίαν. 4. Ἰσίδωρον δὲ φάσκουσιν ἐν παραινέσεσι   **4, 1**
τῆς αὐτοῦ μοχθηρίας αἴτιον γεγενῆσθαι. εἰ δὲ καὶ αὐτὸς τὰ ἴσα
φρονῶν καὶ ἐξ αὐτῶν ὁρμώμενος ἐτύγχανεν ἢ ἐκ φιλοσόφων μαθὼν
παραινετικός τις καὶ αὐτὸς ὑπῆρχεν, οὐ πάνυ σαφῶς περὶ τοῦ Ἰσιδώ-
V M

p. 441   **18** ἐπιμενῶ Pet.] ἐπιμένων V M.   **19** τούτους Dind.] τούτων V M.   **19f** τοῦ
Ἰσιδώρου] καὶ Ἰσιδώρου Dind. Öh., falsch; Ἐπιφάνης ὁ Ἰσιδώρου soll im Mund des
Epiph. ähnliches bedeuten, wie etwa Εὐσέβιος ὁ Παμφίλου.   **21** εἰπεῖν *] οὖν
V M.

p. 442   **1** συνημμένου aus συνημμένον V^corr.   **3** συρφετώδη/// , s wegradiert V^corr.   **6**
Κεφαλ^ληνίας, λ oben drüber V^corr.   **7** ⟨δὲ⟩ *.   **11** καὶ hineingeflickt V^corr.
15 Κεφαλῆνες V.   **17** τε Dind.] δὲ V M.   **19** ⟨δὲ⟩ *.   **20** συνέπετο aus
συνήπετο V^corr. συνείπετο M.   **22** ⟨δὲ⟩ * | ἀδικούσης durchgestrichen V^corr < M |
ἑρπετώδου, s drüber V^corr.

p. 443   **4** καὶ αὐτὸς angeflickt V^corr.

335

5 ρου γνῶναι ἠδυνήθημεν. πλὴν | οὗτοι πάντες καττύουσι τὴν ἴσην Ὅ 392
πραγματείαν.

Πρῶτον μὲν οὖν ἐνομοθέτει αὐτὸς ὁ Ἐπιφάνης σὺν τῷ αὐτοῦ 2
πατρί τε καὶ προστάτῃ τῆς αἱρέσεως Καρποκράτει καὶ τοῖς ἀμφ'
αὐτὸν κοινὰς εἶναι τὰς τῶν ἀνθρώπων γυναῖκας, ἔκ τε τῶν Πλά-
10 τωνος Πολιτειῶν τὴν πρόφασιν λαβὼν καὶ τὴν ἰδίαν ἐπιθυμίαν ἐκ-
τελῶν. ἐντεῦθεν δὲ τὴν ἀρχὴν ποιεῖται λέγων, ὡς ἐν τῷ εὐαγγελίῳ 3
ἐμφέρεται τοῦ σωτῆρος φάσκοντος τρεῖς μὲν εὐνούχους εἶναι, τόν τε
ἐξ ἀνθρώπων εὐνουχιζόμενον καὶ τὸν ἐκ γεννητῆς καὶ τὸν διὰ τὴν
βασιλείαν τῶν οὐρανῶν ἑαυτὸν ἑκουσίως εὐνουχίσαντα, καί φησιν·
15 »οἱ τοίνυν κατὰ ἀνάγκην, οὐ κατὰ λόγον εὐνοῦχοι γίνονται. οἱ δὲ ἕνεκα τῆς 4
βασιλείας τῶν οὐρανῶν ἑαυτοὺς εὐνουχίσαντες, διὰ τὰ ἐκ τοῦ γάμου συμβαίνοντα, φασί, τὸν ἐπιλογισμὸν ⟨τοῦτον λαμβάνουσιν, τὴν περὶ τὸν πορι-
σμὸν⟩ τῶν ἐπιτηδείων ἀσχολίαν δεδιότες. ⟨καὶ τῷ⟩ »βέλτιον γαμῆσαι ἢ 5
πυροῦσθαι, μὴ εἰς πῦρ ἐμβάλῃς τὴν ψυχήν σου«, φησὶ λέγειν τὸν ἀπό-
20 στολον· ἡμέρας καὶ νυκτὸς ἀντέχων καὶ φοβούμενος, μὴ τῆς ἐγκρατείας ἀποπέσῃς. πρὸς γὰρ τὸ ἀντέχειν γινομένη ψυχὴ μερίζεται τῆς
ἐλπίδος«. »ἀντέχου τοίνυν« ὡς ἤδη προεῖπον, τῆς παραινέ|σεως εἰς 6 Ρ 212
p. 444 μέσον φέρων τὸν λόγον φησὶ κατὰ λέξιν ὁ Ἰσίδωρος ἐν τοῖς Ἠθικοῖς
»μαχίμης γυναικός, ἵνα μὴ ἀποσπασθῇς τῆς χάριτος τοῦ θεοῦ, τό τε πῦρ
ἀποσπερματίσας εὐσυνειδήτως προσεύχου. ὅταν δέ, φησίν, | ἡ εὐχαριστία Δ 194
σου εἰς αἴτησιν ὑποπέσῃ καὶ στῇς ⟨εἰς⟩ τὸ λοιπόν, οὐ κατορθώσας, [μὴ]
5 σφαλῆναι, γάμησον«. εἶτα πάλιν φησίν »ἀλλὰ νέος τις ἢ πένης ἐστὶν 7
ἢ κατωφερὴς (τουτέστιν ἀσθενὴς) καὶ οὐ θέλει γῆμαι κατὰ τὸν λόγον,
οὗτος τοῦ ἀδελφοῦ μὴ χωριζέσθω«. αἰσχρὰς δέ τινας ὑπονοίας ἑαυτῷ
προσποριζόμενος δραματουργεῖ ὁ τάλας »λεγέτω« ⟨γάρ⟩ φησιν »ὅτι εἰσε- 8
λήλυθα ἐγὼ εἰς τὰ ἅγια, οὐδὲν δύναμαι παθεῖν«. »ἐὰν δὲ ὑπόνοιαν ἔχῃ,
10 εἰπάτω· ἀδελφέ, ἐπίθες μοι χεῖρα, ἵνα μὴ ἁμαρτήσω, καὶ λήψεται βοή-

V M   15–S. 445, 5 Clemens Al.

7 οὖν *] ὅτι V M.   8 τε καὶ πρωτοστάτῃ, τε καὶ πρω auf Rasur V^corr.   9
τῶν² Dind.] τοῦ V M.   13 εὐνουχιζόμενον V | γενετῆς aus γεννητῆς V^corr γεννητῆς
M.   15f τῆς βασιλείας τῶν οὐρανῶν] τῆς αἰωνίου βασιλείας Clemens Al.   16
εὐνουχίσαντες ἑαυτοὺς Clemens Al.   16f συμβαίνοντα, νοντα auf Rasur V^corr.
17 φασί hinter γάμου (Z. 16) Clemens Al.   17f ⟨τοῦτον—πορισμὸν⟩ Clemens Al.
18 ⟨καὶ τῷ⟩ *] καὶ τὸ Clemens Al. | βέλτιον ἄμεινον Clemens Al.   19 φησὶ <
Clemens Al.   20 νυκτὸς καὶ ἡμέρας Clemens Al.   21 τὸ] viell. vorclement-
inischer Fehler ür τῷ * | γενομένη Clemens Al.   22 ἀντέχου Clemens Al.]
ἀνέχου V M.   22f ὡς ἤδη—τὸν λόγον < Clemens Al.

p. 444   3 προσεύχῃ Clemens Al. | φησίν hinter εὐχαριστία σου Clemens Al.   4 ὑποπέσοι
V M | στῇς ⟨εἰς⟩ *; στῇς ⟨εἰς⟩ τό . . . σφαλῆναι gehört zusammen = du im Begriff
bist zu fallen] τῆς M αἰτῆς Hilgenfeld Stählin.   4f οὐ κατορθῶσαι, ἀλλὰ μὴ
σφαλῆναι Clemens Al.   4 [μὴ] *; viell. noch besser οὐ zu streichen u. μὴ
κατορθώσας zu schreiben Jül.   5 εἶτα πάλιν φησίν < Clemens Al. | ἐστιν hinter
νέος τις Clemens Al.   6 κατωφερὴς Clemens Al.] καταφερὴς V M | τουτέστιν
ἀσθενὴς < Clemens Al.   7f αἰσχρὰς δὲ—ὁ τάλας < Clemens Al.   8 ⟨γάρ⟩ * |
φησίν < Clemens Al.   10 vor χεῖρα + τὴν Clemens Al.

θειαν καὶ νοητὴν καὶ αἰσθητήν. θελησάτω μόνον ἀπαρτίσαι τὸ καλὸν καὶ
ἐπιτεύξεται«. εἶτα πάλιν φησιν »ἐνίοτε τῷ μὲν στόματι λέγομεν· οὐ 9
θέλομεν ἁμαρτῆσαι, ἡ δὲ διάνοια ἔγκειται εἰς τὸ ἁμαρτάνειν. ὁ τοιοῦτος
διὰ φόβον οὐ ποιεῖ ὃ θέλει, ἵνα μὴ ἡ κόλασις αὐτῷ ἐλλογισθῇ. ἡ δὲ ἀν-
15 θρωπότης ἔχει ἀναγκαῖά τινα καὶ φυσικά, ⟨τινὰ δὲ φυσικὰ⟩ μόνα· ἔχει
τὸ περιβάλλεσθαι [τὸ] ἀναγκαῖον καὶ φυσικόν, φυσικὸν δὲ καὶ τὸ τῶν ἀφροδισίων, ⟨οὐκ⟩ ἀναγκαῖον δέ«·

5. »Ταύτας παρεθέμην τὰς φωνάς«, ⟨φησὶν⟩ ὅ κατὰ τούτων γράψας, 5, 1
»εἰς ἔλεγχον τῶν | μὴ βιούντων ὀρθῶς«, καὶ Βασιλειδιανῶν καὶ Καρποκρα- Ö 394
20 τιανῶν καὶ τῶν ἀπὸ Οὐαλεντίνου καὶ τῶν Ἐπιφάνους καλουμένων,
ᾧ δὴ συνήφθη Σεκοῦνδος ὁ προτεταγμένος. ἐξ ἀλλήλων γὰρ ἕκαστος, 2
ἤτοι οὗτος ἐκείνῳ μεταδοὺς ἢ ἐκεῖνος τούτῳ, τὰ δεινὰ ἀπεμπολή-
p. 445 σαντες καὶ εἴς τι πρὸς ἀλλήλους διαφερόμενοι, ὅμως ἐν μιᾷ αἱρέσει
ἑαυτοὺς κατέθεντο, »ὥστε καὶ ἔχειν ἐξουσίαν ἐδογμάτισαν καὶ τοῦ ἁμαρ- 3
τάνειν διὰ τὴν τελειότητα, ἢ πάντως γε σωθησομένων φύσει, κἄν τε νυνὶ
ἁμάρτωσι, διὰ τὴν ἔμφυτον ἐκλογήν, ἐπεὶ μηδὲ τὰ αὐτὰ αὐτοῖς πράττειν
5 συγχωροῦσιν οἱ προπάτορες τῶν δογμάτων τούτων«.

»Φασὶ δὲ καὶ οὗτοι ὡς ἐπὶ τὸ ὑψηλότερον καὶ γνωστικώτερον ἐπεκ- 4
τεινόμενοι τὴν πρώτην τετράδα οὕτως· ἔστι τις πρὸ πάντων προαρχὴ
προανεννόητος, ἄρρητός | τε καὶ ἀνονόμαστος, ἣν ἐγὼ Μονότητα καλῶ. D 195
ταύτῃ τῇ Μονότητι συνυπάρχει δύναμις, ἣν καὶ αὐτὴν ὀνομάζω | Ἑνό- P 213
10 τητα. αὕτη ἡ Ἑνότης ἥ τε Μονότης, τὸ Ἕν οὖσαι, προήκαντο, μὴ προέ- 5
μεναι, ἀρχὴν ἐπὶ πάντων νοητήν, ἀγέννητόν τε καὶ ἀόρατον, ἣν ἀρχὴν ὁ
λόγος Μονάδα καλεῖ. ταύτῃ τῇ Μονάδι συνυπάρχει δύναμις ὁμοούσιος 6
αὐτῇ, ἣν καὶ αὐτὴν ὀνομάζω τὸ Ἕν. αὗται αἱ δυνάμεις, ἥ τε Μονότης
καὶ Ἑνότης, Μονάς τε καὶ τὸ Ἕν, προήκαντο τὰς λοιπὰς προβολὰς τῶν
15 αἰώνων«.

V M   Clemens Al.

12 εἶτα πάλιν φησίν < Clemens Al.   **13** εἰς] ἐπὶ Clemens Al.   **14** ἡ hineingeflickt
V^corr.   **15** τινὰ ἀναγκαῖα Clemens Al. | ⟨τινὰ δὲ φυσικὰ⟩ *] ⟨καὶ φυσικὰ⟩ Schwartz
⟨ἄλλα δὲ φυσικὰ⟩ Stählin.   **16** [τὸ] < Clemens Al. | καὶ² < Clemens Al.
17 οὐκ ἀναγκαῖον δὲ Clemens Al.] ἀναγκαίως δέ, als Anfang zum Folgenden gezogen
V M.   **18** ⟨φησὶν⟩ * | ⟨φησὶν⟩ ὅ κατὰ τούτων γράψας < Clemens Al.   **19** εἰς
ἔλεγχον τῶν Clemens Al.] ἐλέγχων V M | καὶ¹ < Clemens Al.   **19–S. 445, 2** καὶ
Καρποκρατιανῶν—κατέθεντο < Clemens Al.   **20** καλουμένων Dind.] καλουμένου
V M.

p. 445   **1** εἴς τι] ἔστι M.   **2** ἐκτέθεντο M | ὥστε καὶ—ἐδογμάτισαν] ὡς ἤτοι ἐχόντων
ἐξουσίαν Clemens Al. | καὶ τοῦ Clemens Al.] καὶ τὸ V M.   **2f** ἁμαρτεῖν Clemens
Al.   **3** πάντως Clemens Al.] πάντων V M | φύσει Clemens Al.] φυσικῶν V M | κἄν
τε νυνὶ] κἄν νῦν Clemens Al.   **4** τὰ αὐτὰ] ταῦτα Clemens Al.   **5** τούτων <
Clemens Al.   **6** φασὶ δὲ καὶ οὗτοι] alius vero quidam, qui et clarus est magister ipsorum
lat.   **7** ἔστι—προαρχὴ] ἣν ἡ πρώτη ἀρχὴ Hipp. | τις] quidem lat.   **8** προανεννόη-
τος] proanennoetos lat. ἀνεννόητος Hipp. inexcogitabilis Tert., vgl. S. 446, 4 | ἀνο///νόμα-
στος, ο aus ω V^corr | καλῶ *, vgl. S. 446, 5] ἀριθμῶ V M voco lat. καλεῖ (vorher ἐγὼ <)
Hipp. nomino Tert.   **10** ἑνό///τητος, ο aus ω V^corr | τὸ Ἕν οὖσαι < Hipp. | μὴ]
nihil lat.   **11** ἀγέν///ητον ν ausradiert V^corr.   **11f** ἀρχὴν ὁ λόγος < Hipp.
13 αὗται + autem at. | αὗται αἱ + τέσσαρες, dafür ἥ τε—τὸ Ἕν (Z. 14) < Hipp.
14f τῶν αἰώνων προβολὰς Hipp.

337

6. Εἶτα οἱ καλῶς συγγραψάμενοι τὴν ἀλήθειαν ⟨περὶ⟩ τούτων ἐν 6, 1
τοῖς σφῶν αὐτῶν συγγράμμασιν ἤλεγξαν ⟨αὐτούς⟩, Κλήμης τε, (ὅν
φασί τινες Ἀλεξανδρέα, ἕτεροι δὲ Ἀθηναῖον), ἀλλὰ καὶ ὁ ἱερὸς Εἰρη- 2
ναῖος καταγελῶν αὐτῶν τὸ τραγικὸν ἐκεῖνο [ὃ] ἐπὶ τοῖς προειρη-
20 μένοις εἰς μέσον φέρων ἧκεν ⟨τό⟩· »ἰοὺ ἰού« καὶ »φεῦ φεῦ.« τό 3

p. 446 τραγικὸν ὡς ἀληθῶς ἐπειπεῖν ἔστιν ἐπὶ τῇ τοιαύτῃ συμφορᾷ τῶν τὰ γελοιώδη ταῦτα γεγραφότων τῆς τοιαύτης ὀνοματοποιίας καὶ τῇ τοσαύτῃ τόλμῃ,
ὡς ἀπερυθριάσας τῷ ψεύσματι αὐτοῦ ὀνόματα τέθεικεν. ἐν γὰρ τῷ λέ- 4
γειν »ἔστιν τις προαρχὴ πρὸ πάντων προανεννόητος, ἣν ἐγὼ Μονότητα
5 καλῶ«, καὶ πάλιν »ταύτῃ τῇ Μονότητι συνυπάρχει δύναμις, ἣν καὶ αὐτὴν
ὀνομάζω Ἑνότητα«, σαφέ|στατα ὅτι τε πλάσμα αὐτοῦ ἐστι τὰ εἰρημένα Ö 396
ὡμολόγηκε καὶ ὅτι αὐτὸς ὀνόματα τέθεικε τῷ πλάσματι, ὑπὸ μηδενὸς
πρότερον ἄλλου τεθειμένα. καὶ σαφές ἐστιν ὅτι αὐτὸς ταῦτα τετόλμηκεν 5
ὀνοματοποιῆσαι, καὶ εἰ μὴ παρῆν τῷ βίῳ αὐτός, οὐκ ἂν ἡ ἀλήθεια εἶχεν
10 ὄνομα. οὐδὲν οὖν κωλύει καὶ ἄλλον τινὰ ἐπὶ τῆς αὐτῆς ὑποθέσεως 6
οὕτως ὁρίσασθαι ὀνόματα· εἶτα λοιπὸν εἰς ταῦτα ὁ αὐτὸς μακάριος 7
Εἰρηναῖος, ὥς γε προείπαμεν, γελοιώδη ῥήματα καὶ αὐτὸς † προεῖπεν,
ἑτερωνυμίαν ἀφ᾿ ἑαυτοῦ ὡς ἀντάξια τῆς αὐτῶν ληρῳδίας χαριεντιζό-
μενος, πεπόνων γένη καὶ σικύων καὶ κολοκυνθῶν ὡς ἐπὶ | ὑποκει- D 196
15 μένων τινῶν ἐπιπλασάμενος, † ὡς τοῖς φιλολόγοις σαφὲς ἂν εἴη ἀφ᾿
ὧν προανέγνωσαν.

V M lat. von Z. 17 an auch Hipp.

16 ⟨περὶ⟩ *.   **17** ἤλλεγξαν, erstes λ getilgt V^corr | ⟨αὐτούς⟩ *.   **19** [ὃ] Dind.
Öh.   **20** ⟨τό⟩ *.

p. 446   **1** τραγικὸν + γὰρ V.   **1f** ἐπὶ τῇ—ὀνοματοποιίας] super hanc nominum factionem lat. |
γελλοιώδη, erstes λ getilgt V^corr.   **3** ὀνόματα Ausgg., vgl. Z. 7] ὄνομα V M nomina
lat.   **4** τις < lat. | μονότητα Ausgg.] μονάδα V M monoteta lat.   **5** μονότητι
Ausgg.] μονάδι V M monotete lat.   **6** ἑνότητα ὀνομάζω V M voco Henotetem lat.,
vgl. S. 445, 9 | πλάσμα] figmenta lat. | αὐτοῦ zu εἰρημένα gezogen lat.   **8** πρότερον
< lat.   **8f** καὶ σαφές—ὀνοματοποιῆσαι < lat.   **9** καὶ εἰ μὴ—αὐτός] qui nisi
haec auderet lat. | οὐκ ἂν + hodie lat. | ἀλήθεια + secundum eum lat.   **10** ὄνομα]
nomina lat.   **12** † προεῖπεν] lies wohl προφέρει *.   **14** γένη] γένημα M.   **15**
† ὡς] lies etwa ὧν ⟨τὸ εὔλογον⟩ *.

Epiphanius, *Panarion* LXIII.1 (ed. Holl II.398–399)

p. 398   1. Ὡριγένιοί τινες καλοῦνται, οὐ πανταχοῦ δὲ τοῦτο τὸ γένος 1, 1
15 ὑπάρχει· καθεξῆς δὲ οἶμαι τούτων τῶν αἱρέσεων καὶ αὕτη ἡ δηλου-
μένη ⟨ἀνεφύη⟩. καλοῦνται δὲ Ὡριγένιοι, οὐ πάνυ δὲ σαφῶς ἴσμεν 2
τίνος ἕνεκα· εἰ ἀπὸ Ὡριγένους τοῦ Ἀδαμαντίου καλουμένου τοῦ συν-
τάκτου ἢ | ἄλλου τινὸς ⟨ἔλαχον τὸ⟩ εἶναι, ἀγνοῶ. ὅμως τοῦτο τὸ D 582

M U

14 καλοῦνται τινὲς U | πανταχοῦ] παντὶ U.   **16** ⟨ἀνεφύη⟩ *.   **17** εἰ *] ἢ
M U.   **18** ⟨ἔλαχον τὸ⟩ *.

ὄνομα κατειλήφαμεν.

20 Ἡ αἵρεσις | δέ, ⟨ἣ⟩ παρ' αὐτοῖς νομι[σ]τεύεται, ὥσπερ ἀπεικαζο-   3 Ö 222
μένη τῇ τοῦ Ἐπιφάνους ⟨τοῦ⟩ ἄνω μοι προδεδηλωμένου ἐν ταῖς κατὰ
τοὺς Γνωστικοὺς αἱρέσεσι. γραφὰς δὲ οὗτοι ἀναγινώσκουσι διαφόρους
καινῆς καὶ παλαιᾶς διαθήκης. ἀθετοῦσι δὲ γάμον καὶ οὐ παύεται
ἀπ' αὐτῶν ἡ λαγνεία. τινὲς δὲ ἔφασαν αὐτὴν περὶ Ῥώμην καὶ Ἀφρι-

p. 399   κὴν γεγενῆσθαι. μολύνουσι δὲ ἑαυτῶν τὸ σῶμα καὶ τὸν νοῦν καὶ   4
τὴν ψυχὴν ἐν ἀσελγείᾳ. οἱ μὲν γάρ εἰσι προσχήματι μοναζόντων, αἱ
δὲ σὺν αὐτοῖς οὖσαι | προσχήματι μοναζουσῶν. ἐφθαρμένοι δέ εἰσι   P 521
τοῖς σώμασι, τὴν μὲν ἐπιθυμίαν αὐτῶν ἐκτελοῦντες, τῷ δὲ ἔργῳ

5 κεχρημένοι (ἵνα σεμνότερον εἴπω) τοῦ υἱοῦ τοῦ Ἰούδα τοῦ Αὐνὰν
καλουμένου. ὡς γὰρ ἐκεῖνος τῷ σώματι μὲν τῇ Θάμαρ συνήπτετο   5
καὶ τὴν ἐπιθυμίαν ἐξετέλει, εἰς καταβολὴν δὲ σπέρματος κατὰ τὴν
ὑπὸ θεοῦ δοθεῖσαν παιδοποιίαν οὐκ ἐτελεσιούργει, ἀλλὰ ἑαυτὸν ἠδίκει,
ᾧ τρόπῳ ⟨αὐτὸς⟩ τὸ πονηρὸν εἰργάζετο, οὕτω καὶ οὗτοι κέχρηνται

10 μὲν ταῖς νομιζομέναις *, τελοῦντες ταύτην τὴν ἀθέμιτον ἐργασίαν.
πεφιλοτίμηται γὰρ παρ' αὐτοῖς οὐχ ἡ ἁγνεία, ἀλλ' ὑποκριτικὴ μὲν   6
ἁγνεία τῷ ὀνόματι καλουμένη, φιλοτίμησις δὲ ἕως τοῦ μὴ ἐγκυμονῆ-
σαι τὴν ὑπὸ τοῦ δοκοῦντος * ἐφθαρμένην γυναῖκα, ἢ κατὰ τὸ μὴ
παραστῆσαι τεκνογονίαν ἐν τῷ κόσμῳ ἢ ἵνα μὴ φωραθῶσιν ὑπὸ

15 ἀνθρώπων, βουλόμενοι ἐν τιμῇ εἶναι διὰ τὴν νομιζομένην παρ' αὐτοῖς τῆς ἁγνείας ἄσκησιν· ὅμως τοῦτο αὐτῶν ἐστι τὸ ἔργον, ἕτεροι   7
δὲ αὐτὸ τοῦτο φιλοτιμοῦνται τὸ μυσαρὸν ἐπιτελεῖν οὐχὶ διὰ γυναικῶν, ἀλλὰ καὶ ἑτέροις τρόποις, ἰδίαις χερσὶ μολυνόμενοι. καὶ ὡσαύ-   8
τως μιμοῦνται τὸν προειρημένον υἱὸν τοῦ Ἰούδα, τὴν γῆν ταῖς ἀθε-

20 μίτοις αὐτῶν ἐργασίαις καὶ μυσαραῖς σταγόσιν ἐπιμολύνοντες καὶ
ποσὶν ἑαυτῶν | τὰς ῥύσεις ἑαυτῶν ἀνατρίβοντες ἐν τῇ γῇ, ἵνα μὴ   D 583
δῆθεν ἁρπαγῶσι τὰ αὐτῶν σπέρματα ὑπὸ ἀκαθάρτων πνευμάτων εἰς
ὑποδοχὴν ἐγκυμονήσεως δαιμόνων.

M U

20 ⟨ἣ⟩ * | νομι[σ]τεύεται *.   **21** ⟨τοῦ⟩ * | ἄνω μοι] ἀνόμου M.   **24f** τινὲς
—γεγενῆσθαι < U; wohl vom Rand her an die falsche Stelle geratener Satz;
hinter κατειλήφαμεν Z. 19 einzuschieben?

p. 399   **1** αὐτῶν M.   **3** πεφθαρμένοι U.   **5** σεμνώτερον U | Αὐνάνου M.   **6**
συνῆπτο M.   **7** σπέρματος *] παιδοποιίας M U.   **9** ⟨αὐτὸς⟩ *.   **10**
* etwa ⟨μοναζούσαις⟩ *.   **11** vor ὑποκριτικὴ + ἡ M.   **13** ὑπὲρ M |
* etwa ⟨ἀσκητοῦ⟩ * | ἐφθαρμένην *] ἐφθάρθαι M πεφθάρθαι U | κατὰ] εἰς? *.
14 ἢ < M.   **16** αὐτῶν] αὐτὸ M.   **17** μυσερὸν M | οὐ M.   **18** ἑτέροις]
ἄλλοις U.   **19** μιμοῦνται < M.   **20** μυσεραῖς M.   **22** δῆθεν < U |
ἑαυτῶν U.   **23** δαιμόνων < U.

Gregory Theologus, *Oratio* 25.8 (ed. Maurists I.458–459)

p. 459   η. Ἦν ὅτε γαλήνην εἴχομεν ἀπὸ τῶν αἱρέσεων, ἡνίκα Σίμωνες
μὲν, καὶ Μαρκίωνες, Οὐαλεντῖνοί τέ τινες, καὶ Βασιλεῖδαι, καὶ Κέρδωνες,
Κήρινθοί τε καὶ Καρποκράτεις, καὶ πᾶσα ἡ περὶ ἐκείνους φλυαρία
τε καὶ τερατεία, ἐπὶ πλεῖστον τὸν τῶν ὅλων Θεὸν τεμόντες, καὶ
ὑπὲρ τοῦ ἀγαθοῦ τῷ δημιουργῷ πολεμήσαντες, ἔπειτα κατεπόθησαν
τῷ ἑαυτῶν βυθῷ, καὶ τῇ σιγῇ παραδοθέντες, ὥσπερ ἦν ἄξιον.

Constitutiones Apostolorum (*Apostolic Constitutions*) VI.10.3
(ed. Funk I.323 and 325)

The author is listing the teachings of the various heresies. He saves the Carpocratians for the end, perhaps as a climax of wickedness. The underlined words are not paralleled in the *Didascalia Apostolorum*.

p. 323   Ἄλλοι δὲ ἀναίδην ἐκπορνεύειν καὶ παραχρᾶσθαι τῇ σαρκὶ ἐδίδασκον
p. 325   καὶ διὰ πάσης ἀνοσιουργίας ἰέναι, ὡς οὕτως καὶ μόνως ἐκφεύξεσθαι
τὴν ψυχὴν τοὺς κοσμικοὺς ἄρχοντας. οὗτοι δὲ πάντες τοῦ διαβόλου
ὄργανα τυγχάνουσιν καὶ „υἱοὶ ὀργῆς".

Jerome, *Adversus Luciferianos* 23 end (ed. Vallarsi[2], II.1.197–198)

col. 197   Ad eos venio hæreticos, qui Evangelia laniaverunt. Saturninum
quemdam, & Ophitas, & Cainæos, & Setthoitas, & Carpocratem,
& Cerinthum, & hujus fuccefforem Ebionem, & cæteras peftes,
quorum plurimi vivente adhuc Joanne Apoftolo eruperunt, &
tamen nullum eorum legimus rebaptizatum.

Filastrius, *Diversarum hereseon liber* VII–VIII (ed. Marx 19)

Filastrius locates Carpocrates after Judas (= istum).

VII

p. 19   Post istum Carpocras nomine surrexit, et ipse dicens unum XXXV
10 principium, de quo principio, id est de deo, prolationes
factae sunt, inquit, angelorum atque uirtutum: ‖ quae autem

uirtutes deorsum sunt, fecerunt creaturam istam uisibilem
ubi nos, inquit, consistimus. Christum autem dicit non de 2
Maria uirgine et diuino spiritu natum, sed de semine Ioseph
15 hominem natum arbitratur, deque eo natum carnaliter, sicut
omnes homines, suspicatur. Qui post passionem, inquit, 3
melior inter Iudaeos uita integra et conuersatione inuentus
est; cuius animam in caelum susceptam praedicant, carnem| 4
uero in terram dimissam aestimant, animique salutem soli*us*,
20 carnis autem non fieri salutem opinantur.

VIII

Cerinthus successit huius errori et similitudini uanitatis, XXXVI
docens de generatione itidem saluatoris deque creatura
angelorum, in nullo discordans ab eo, nisi quia ex parte
25 solum legi consentit, quod a deo data sit, et ipsum deum
Iudaeorum esse aestimat qui legem dedit filiis Israhel.

11 uirtutem *A*.　　**12** deorsum *Fabricius*] deorum.　　　**14** uirgine maria *B*
sed *om A*.　　**15** arbitrantur *A*[1].　　**18** suscepta predicans *A*.　　　**19**
animeq: *B*[1] solis *A* solum *B*.　　**20** canis *A*[1].　　**22** Cerynthus *B* Cherentus
A.　　**23** de generatione itidem *B* degenerationem *A*.　　　**26** iudeorum *A*
iudaeos *B* esse *om A* isrł *B*.

Filastrius, *Diversarum hereseon liber* XXIX (ed. Marx 30)

XXIX

p. 30　　10　　Alii sunt qui Floriani siue Carpocratiani dicuntur, qui et LVII
Milites uocantur, quia de militaribus fuerunt, negantes iudi-
cium atque resurrectionem, Christum natum de uirgine non
credentes, omnemque resurrectionem in filiorum procreatione
nefandi coitus aestimantes consistere, ut in ecclesia sua post
15 occasum lucernis extinctis misceri cum mulierculis non dubi-
tauerint, ‖ legis praeceptum implere putantes: Nascimini et 2
multiplicamini, Iudaismo potius et paganitati parere
nefandae quam Christianae ueritati adquiescere properantes,
pecudumque uitam potius et amentiam detinentes, quos et
20 scriptura uitae pecudum comparauit.

16 Genes. I 28.　　**19** II Petr. II 12 Iud. 10.

11 quia *B* qui *A*.　　**14** coetus *B* ut *om A*.　　**15** occasum *A* occasum
solis *B*.　　**16** nascemini *B* et *om A*.　　**17** parare *A*.　　**18** xpiana
ueritate *A*.　　**19** pecodumque uita *A*.　　**20** pecodum *A*.

Didymus of Alexandria, *De Trinitate* III.42
(Migne, *PG* 39.992a–b)

Didymus is explaining that the Manichaean heresy derives from that of Simon, who was succeeded by Menander and Satornilus, then by Basilides, then by Carpocrates, then by Valentinus. He summarizes what was added to the doctrine by each.

col. 992   καὶ ὑπὸ Καρποκράτους, τοῦ καὶ ὕστερον χρόνοις κρατύναντος
ταῦτα, καὶ ἐν προσθήκης μέρει μιαρίας ἀπαγγείλαντος, ὡς εἰ
μή τις διὰ παντὸς ἐπιτηδεύματος ἁμαρτίας ἐλθών, τῶν δαιμόνων
ὅλων τὸ θέλημα ἐκτελέσῃ, οὐ δύναται παρελθεῖν τὰς ἀρχὰς
καὶ ἐξουσίας, καὶ εἰς τὸν ἀνώτατον φθάσαι οὐρανόν· ἔτι μὴν
καὶ Οὐαλεντίνου. . . .

Cyril of Jerusalem (?), *Discourse on Mary Theotokos*
(ed. Budge, *Texts* 58ff [Coptic], 628 and 636ff [English])

The attribution to Cyril is accepted by Burch, *Gospel*, and Waitz, *Evangelien* 17, doubted by Vielhauer, *Evangelien* 88, and denied by James, review of Hennecke[2] 185, and Altaner, *Patrologie*[6] 279. Supposing it to be false, the text would nevertheless come from southern Palestine, and probably from the century after Cyril's death (386).

p. 628   This is the day | wherein the Queen, the mother of the King of Life, tasted death like every other human being, because she was flesh and blood. And, moreover, she was begotten by a human father, and brought forth by a human mother, like every other man. Let Ebiôn now be ashamed, and Harpocratius, these godless heretics who say in their madness that 'she was a force (or, abstract power) of God which took the form of a woman, and came upon the earth, and was called "Mary", and this force gave birth to Emmanuel for us'. Doth it not follow from thy imaginative words, which are wholly incongruous, that Christ did not take flesh upon Himself? Without flesh and without body 'forces' would be beings without bodies, and they could not die like mortal men. Notwithstanding [this], come hither ye deaf and blind and foolish, O Biôn (*sic*) and Harpocration, and I will question you. If ye say that Mary is a 'force', Fol. 3 b   a 'force' will die. Who is it then | whose falling asleep the

5 whole of the inhabited world commemorateth by keeping a festival this day? Is it not Saint Mary, the mother of our Lord Jesus the Christ?

p. 636 And now I wish to relate to you an incident that happened to me. There was a certain monk who lived in the neighbourhood of Maiôma of Gaza, who had received instruction in the heresy of Biôn and of Harpocratius his master, of whose books he obtained possession, and he expounded them publicly, and he became filled with blasphemies and with falsehoods, and he masqueraded with great pride and arrogance, and he deceived all the poeple who were in that neighbourhood by his pretensions, through those who used to come to the holy places
Fol. 11 *a* there to pray. And the things which he proclaimed | in his
K̄λ corrupt heterodoxy were repeated to me, and I sent two ministers to the Bishop of Gaza, and I said unto him, 'I beseech thee to seek out on my behalf a certain monk who is in the neighbourhood of Maiôma, and do thou send him to me, together with his books.'

And when the bishop had received the letter and read it, he caused search to be made for that monk everywhere. And when they had brought him to the bishop he said unto him, 'My son, rise up and go to Jerusalem to the archbishop. If thou dost not go he will send for thee and thy books. He knoweth about thy doctrine, and about thy preaching, and whose it is.' And the monk replied, 'I will take my books and I will go to him in Jerusalem.' And the two ministers took him to Jerusalem to the archbishop, who said unto him, 'We have heard, O brother, that thou art teaching a strange doctrine, and that thou art changing the voices of the Holy Gospels.' The monk, [who was called]
Fol. 11 *b* Annarikhus, said unto him, 'My teaching (or, doctrine) is
[K̄B] not a strange doctrine, | but is that of our Fathers the
p. 637 Apostles, and our own Fathers taught it everywhere as sound doctrine.' And Apa Cyril said unto him, 'Who were thy Fathers?' And the monk said, 'Satôr, and Ebiôn, who succeeded him.' And the archbishop said unto him, 'Thou hast become a disciple and hast made thyself a mule-like beast under the stupid yoke of the chariot of the Devil.' And the monk said unto him, 'Harpocratius used to cast out devils.' And the archbishop said unto him, 'Shew me by what means thou dost cast out devils, and in what way thou dost preach the Gospel, and what thou dost say concerning Christ and His Birth according to the flesh, and concerning His mother who brought Him forth, and concerning His

343

death, which was full of salvation, and His resurrection from the dead after the third day.'

Fol. 12 *a*
$\overline{\text{КГ}}$
And that monk replied, 'It is written in | the [Gospel] to the Hebrews that when Christ wished to come upon the earth to men the Good Father called a mighty "power" in the heavens which was called "Michael", and committed Christ to the care thereof. And the "power" came down into the world, and it was called Mary, and [Christ] was in her womb for seven months. Afterwards she gave birth to Him, and He increased in stature, and He chose the Apostles, who preached Him in every place. He fulfilled the appointed time that was decreed for Him. And the Jews became envious of Him, they hated Him, they changed the custom of their Law, and they rose up against Him and laid a trap and caught Him, and they delivered Him to the governor, and he gave Him to them to crucify Him. And after they had raised Him up on the Cross the Father took Him up into heaven unto Himself.' And the Patriarch Cyril said unto the monk, 'Who sent thee about to teach these things?' And that monk said unto him, 'The Christ said, Go ye

Fol. 12 *b*
$\overline{\text{КΔ}}$
p. 638
forth | into all the world, and teach ye all the nations in My Name, in every place.'[1] And Apa Cyril said unto him, 'Dost thou take the Gospels literally?' And the monk said, 'Yea, absolutely, my lord Father.' And the archbishop answered and said, 'Where in the Four Gospels is it said that the holy Virgin Mary, the mother of God, is a "force"?' And the monk answered and said, 'In the [Gospel] to the Hebrews.' And Apa Cyril answered and said, 'Then, according to thy words, there are Five Gospels?' And that monk replied, 'Yea, there are.' And Apa Cyril answered and said, 'What is the name of the fifth Gospel? for I should like to know whence this doctrine concerning Christ is derived, and to understand it. The Four Gospels have written above them: "[The Gospel] according to Matthew"; "[The Gospel] according to Mark"; "[The Gospel] according to Luke"; "[The Gospel] according

Fol. 13 *a*
$\overline{\text{КЄ}}$
to John." | Whose is the fifth Gospel?' And that monk said unto him, 'It is [the Gospel] that was written to the Hebrews.' And Saint Cyril answered and said, 'If thou speakest the truth, O brother, must we not then reject the teaching of the Christ, and follow the misleading doctrine of the Hebrews? God forbid! The Hebrews wish for doctrine of this kind greatly, so that they may cast a blemish upon our purity and

---

1 Matt. xxviii. 19, 20.

honour, even as it was said by the Christ in times of old, "Thou castest out devils by Berzeboul."[1] And is it not written, "He who doth not confess that Jesus the Christ hath come in the flesh is a deceiver and an Antichrist, like thyself"?[2] And again, "Whosoever shall come unto thee, and bring a doctrine that is different from thine, receive him not into thy house, neither say unto him, Hail!"[3] And again, "If they were of us they would have been like unto us; they came forth from us, but they are not of us."[4] Which meaneth

Fol. 13 *b*

K͞S͞

p. 639

that they utter the Name of Christ with their mouths only, and that they make a pretence in their hearts. They heap up wrath for themselves in the day of the Judgement of Truth and the wrath that is from Jesus the Christ. The doctrine of the Jews cannot be joined unto the doctrine of Christ. What connection can there be between the agreement of the [Gospel to the] Hebrews and the agreement of the Holy Gospels? But those heresies must spring up which Epiphanius describes in his work Ἀγκυρωτός, saying, "The error in each one of them is different, but evil is implanted in them all."' And Annarikhus the monk said unto Apa Cyril, 'The night cannot contend against the day, neither can darkness stand before the light. I am vanquished by thy great wisdom, and I know that I have made a mistake. Let thy fatherhood grant repentance unto me! And all these things which I have overthrown I will build up again. But take my books, and burn them in the fire, and my possessions do thou give to the poor. My heart followeth thy words and [those of] the Holy Gospel.'

And when I (i.e. Cyril) had burned his books, I said unto

Fol. 14 *a*

K͞Θ͞

him, | 'Who . . .

[One leaf wanting]

'He to Whom no form can be assigned was born [in the form of] a son. He was the Beginning, and He Who had no beginning was brought forth. Now there was a beginning to that humanity, but the Godhead had no beginning, and was without form. And no addition took place to the Trinity in such wise that the Trinity, which consisteth of Three [Persons], became Four [Persons]. One σύνοδος entered one who was of two natures, and one son was brought forth, a unity of the flesh without any diminution. For He was neither changed in His nature, nor reduced in His strength,

---

1 Matt. xii. 24; Mark iii. 22; Luke xi. 15.   **2** 2 John 7.   **3** 2 John 10.
4 1 John ii. 19.

nor was He separated from His Ancient Begetter, that is to say, the Beginning. But the oneness of the flesh of God received one Nature. As for the coming to us of the blessed Offspring God the Word, it is the miracle that was hidden in God from eternity, I mean the miracle of God Who made Himself man. An impenetrable mystery is the Nature that abolished the curse and destroyed the sentence of death, *p. 640* and taught us concerning the foundation, which had no beginning, of the Only-begotten One, Jesus the Christ, our Lord, the production, according to the flesh, of the womb of Saint Mary, the perpetual Virgin, in whose holy house we Fol. 14 *b* are | gathered together this day to commemorate the day of ⲗ̄ her death. If thou wilt confess these things with a true and sincere belief then we will prepare to receive thee into the fold of all the sheep of the loving Shepherd Christ. Have no doubt about the matter; thou must either follow the words which I have taught thee or thou must get outside this place.' And Annarikhus opened his mouth and anathematized the heresy of Ebiôn and Harpocratius, saying, 'Anathema be every heresy; the things which thou [Ebiôn] hast said unto me are not to be believed. And now, O my father, receive thou me into good fellowship with thyself.' And when I knew that his mind had received the light I baptized him in the name of the Lady of us all, Saint Mary, whose day is this day. Finally he went to a monastery in the Mount of Olives, and he builded upon the foundation of the Apostles until the day of his death.

Augustine, *De haeresibus* 7 (ed. Maurists, second Paris ed., VIII.1.40)

col. 40   VII. CARPOCRATIANI sunt a Carpocrate, qui docebat omnem turpem operationem, omnemque adinventionem peccati: nec aliter evadi atque transiri principatus et potestates, quibus hæc placent, ut possit ad cœlum superius perveniri. Hic etiam Jesum hominem tantummodo, et de utroque sexu natum putasse perhibetur, sed accepisse talem animam, qua sciret ea quæ superna essent, atque nuntiaret. Resurrectionem corporis simul cum Lege abjiciebat. Negabat a Deo factum, sed a nescio quibus virtutibus mundum. Sectæ ipsius fuisse traditur quædam Marcellina, quæ colebat imagines Jesu et Pauli et Homeri et Pythagoræ, adorando incensumque ponendo.

Augustine, *Contra adversarium legis et prophetarum* 40 end
(ed. Maurists, second Paris ed., VIII.1.926–927)

Augustine interprets I Jn. 2.18, "Nunc antichristi multi facti sunt," as referring to heretics.

col. 926   Eos autem dicebat haereticos, qui temporibus Apostolorum esse jam cœperant. Hi autem cœperunt esse post ascensionem duntaxat in cœlum Domini Jesu Christi, ab illo Simone mago, quem legimus in Actibus Apostolorum baptizatum. Post hunc

col. 927   autem fuerunt nonnulli discipuli ejus, in eadem impietate posteriores prioribus succedentes: quorum in successione quartus exstitit Basilides, qui primus apertius ausus est dicere, Deum quem gens Judæa coluit, non fuisse verum deum. Post istos fuit quidam etiam Carpocrates, qui negavit istum visibilem mundum a summo Deo creatum, sed a quisbudam virtutibus dæmoniorum: negans etiam Legem quæ per Moysen data est, Deum dedisse. Cerdon postea surrexit, qui primus invenitur dixisse duos deos, unum bonum, et alterum malum, longe antequam hæresis Manichæorum emersisset, quorum in hoc furioso deliramento error est notior. Hujus Cerdonis Marcion discipulus fuit. Appelles quoque talia docuit. Fuerunt etiam a quodam Patricio nonnulli Patriciani, vel sunt, similiter adversantes divinis veteribus Libris. Hi omnes apertissime contra Deum sentiunt Legis et Prophetarum, hoc est, Deum verum, a quo factus est mundus. De aliqua istorum hæresi est iste: nam non eum puto esse Manichæum.

[Cyril of Alexandria, *Fragmenta in epistolam ad Hebraeos*, in *Cyrilli . . . in d. Joannis evangelium* (ed. P. Pusey, Oxford, 1872, III.371)

This is taken from Athanasius, *Oratio I contra Arianos* 56, *q.v. supra*, p. 327 of this appendix]

Theodoret, *Haereticarum fabularum compendium* I.5
(ed. Schulze IV.293–295)

p. 293   Ὁ δὲ Καρποκράτης, Ἀλεξανδρεὺς ὢν τὸ γένος, ὑπὸ μὲν ἀγγέλων καὶ αὐτὸς τὴν κτίσιν ἔφησε γεγενῆσθαι· τὸν δὲ Κύριον Ἰησοῦν ἐκ τοῦ Ἰωσὴφ καὶ τῆς Μαρίας γεννηθῆναι τοῖς ἄλλοις ἀνθρώποις παραπλησίως, ἀρετῇ δὲ αὐτὸν διαπρέψαι, καὶ καθαρὰν ἐσχηκότα

ψυχὴν, καὶ μεμνημένην τῆς μετὰ τοῦ ἀγεννήτου διαγωγῆς. φησὶ
δὲ καὶ τοὺς ἐκείνῳ παραπλησίως, τῶν κοσμοποιῶν ἀγγέλων
καταφρονήσαντας, ὁμοίως λαμβάνειν δύναμιν πρὸς τὸ πρᾶξαι τὰ
ὅμοια. εἰ δὲ καὶ καθαρωτέραν τις σχοίη ψυχὴν, ὑπερβήσεται, φησί,
p. 294 καὶ τοῦ Υἱοῦ τὴν ἀξίαν. Εἰς τοσαύτην τύφου μανίαν ἐξώκειλαν
ἄνδρες, γοητείᾳ μὲν χρώμενοι, καὶ τὰς τῶν δαιμόνων ἐπικλήσεις
ποιούμενοι, τὴν δὲ ἀσέλγειαν συγκαλύπτειν οὐκ ἀνεχόμενοι, ἀλλὰ
νόμον τὴν ἀκολασίαν ποιούμενοι. δόξῃ γάρ φησιν, οὐκ ἀληθείᾳ,
τὰ μὲν τῶν πραγμάτων κακὰ εἶναι δοκεῖ, τὰ δὲ ἀγαθά. ἀλλὰ
γὰρ ἐνταῦθα γενόμενος, οὐκ οἶδ' ὅπως ὑπερπηδήσω τὴν τῆς ἀσελγείας
νομοθεσίαν. τὰς γὰρ πυθαγορικὰς μετενσωματώσεις εἰσδεξάμενοι,
τὸν συνεζευγμένον οὐ προσεδέξαντο λόγον. ὁ μὲν γὰρ Πυθαγόρας
τὰς ἡμαρτηκυίας ψυχὰς ἔφησεν εἰς σώματα πέμπεσθαι, ὥστε καὶ
δίκας δοῦναι, καὶ καθαρθῆναι σπουδῇ. οὗτοι δὲ τῆς μετενσωματώσεως
αἰτίαν εἶναι φασι τῆς πυθαγορικῆς ἐναντίαν ἐκ διαμέτρου. λέγουσι
γὰρ εἰς τὰ σώματα πέμπεσθαι τὰς ψυχὰς, ὥστε πᾶν εἶδος ἀσελγειῶν
ἐπιτελέσαι. τὰς οὖν ἐν τῇ μιᾷ καθόδῳ πεπληρωκυίας, ἑτέρας μὴ
χρῄζειν ἀποσολῆς· τὰς δὲ ὀλίγα ἡμαρτηκυίας, καὶ δὶς ἐκπέμπεσθαι,
καὶ τρὶς, καὶ πολλάκις, ἕως ἂν ἐκπληρώσωσιν ἅπαντα τῆς κακίας
τὰ εἴδη. ἵνα δὲ μήτις ὑποπτεύσῃ με ταῦτα πλάττεσθαι κατ' αὐτῶν,
Εἰρηναίου, τοῦ τὴν ἑσπέραν φωτίσαντος ἀνδρὸς ἀποσολικοῦ, παρα-
θήσομαι μαρτυρίαν. λέγει δὲ οὗτος ἐν τῷ πρώτῳ βιβλίῳ τῶν εἰς
τὰς αἱρέσεις συγγραφέντων αὐτῷ· καὶ εἰ μὲν πράσσεται παρ' αὐτοῖς
τὰ ἄθεα, καὶ ἔκθεσμα, καὶ ἀπειρημένα, ἐγὼ οὐκ ἂν πιστεύσαιμι. ἐν
δὲ τοῖς συγγράμμασιν αὐτῶν οὕτως ἀναγέγραπται, καὶ αὐτοὶ οὕτως
p. 295 ἐξηγοῦνται, τὸν Ἰησοῦν λέγοντες ἐν μυστηρίῳ τοῖς μαθηταῖς αὐτοῦ
καὶ ἀποστόλοις κατ' ἰδίαν λελαληκέναι, καὶ αὐτοὺς ἀξιῶσαι τοῖς ἀξίοις
καὶ τοῖς πειθομένοις ταῦτα παραδιδόναι. διὰ πίστεως γὰρ καὶ ἀγάπης
σώζεσθαι, τὰ δὲ λοιπὰ ἀδιάφορα ὄντα, κατὰ τὴν δόξαν τῶν ἀνθρώπων, πῇ μὲν ἀγαθὰ, πῇ δὲ κακὰ νομίζεσθαι, οὐδενὸς φύσει κακοῦ
ὑπάρχοντος. ταῦτα μὲν οὖν ὁ θαυμάσιος Εἰρηναῖος περὶ αὐτῶν
ἔφη. τὰ δὲ ἑξῆς οὐ προστέθεικα. ὑπερβολὴν γὰρ ἔχει μανίας. Καὶ
Ἐπιφάνης δὲ τούτου παῖς, διὰ πλατωνικῆς ἠγμένος παιδείας, τὴν
τούτου μυθολογίαν ἐπλάτυνεν. Ἀδριανοῦ δὲ καὶ οὗτοι βασιλεύοντος
τὰς πονηρὰς αἱρέσεις ἐκράτυναν.

See also the beginning of I.6: Πρόδικος δὲ τοῦτον διαδεξάμενος . . . προφανῶς λαγνεύειν
τοῖς Καρποκράτους προστέθεικε δόγμασι.

Praedestinatus, *De haeresibus* 7 (ed. Oehler, *Haeresiologici* 234–235)

p. 234 Carpocratianorum septima est haeresis, a Carpocrate inventa,
qui docebat potestates tenebrarum transire non posse, nisi solos

348

eos qui omni se turpitudini miscuissent. Hi dominum nostrum Iesum de utroque sexu genitum adserebant, sed talem animam accepisse quae superna caelorum sciret. Resurrectionem corporis denegantes prophetas testamenti veteris condemnabant. Habebant autem Marcellinam quandam, quae imagines Iesu et Pauli et Pythagorae philosophi ponebat in medio populi quem decipiebat, et *p. 235* faciebat eos his imaginibus honorem deitatis exhibere, et incensum ponere. Hos damnavit apud Cyprum beatus Barnabas Christi discipulus, docens eos ministros esse Satanae, et non debere constituit Christianum penitus cum his habere sermonem.

Pseudo-Jerome, *Indiculus de haeresibus* 10 (ed. Oehler, *Haeresoilogici* 290–291)

p. 290 Carpocras, [1]Cerinthus et Evion, hi tres sibi successerunt, dicentes omnia secundum legem, [2]circumcidi, observare sabbatum et dies festos Iudaicos; Christus enim [3]haec *cum* omnia observavit, sufficere dicentes ita [4]esse *ut* doctorem, ut magistrum. Christum autem negant per spiritum sanctum a Maria virgine natum, sed a *p. 291* Ioseph conceptum ut hominem nuptiali coitu; habuisse autem illum spiritum prophetalem, et venturum ac iudicaturum vivos et mortuos.

p. 290

Cap. X.—**1** Cherinthus *Men.* **2** circumcidii *Men.* **3** haec cum omnia *ego.* haec omnia *Men.* **4** esse ut doctorem *ego.* esse doctorem *Men.*

Isidore of Seville, *Originum* VIII.6.7 (ed. Oehler, *Haeresiologici* 304 = VIII.5.7 in W. Lindsay, *Isidori hispalensis episcopi etymologiarum . . . libri XX* [Oxford, n.d.])

p. 304 **7.** Carpocratiani a Carpocrate quodam vocantur, qui dixit Christum hominem fuisse tantum, et de utroque sexu progenitum.

[Honorius of Augustodunum, *De haeresibus libellus* 22 (ed. Oehler, *Haeresiologici* 328) = Isidore of Seville (with minor differences of wording)]

Sophronii Patriarchae Hierosolymorum (Sophronius of Jerusalem), *Epistola Synodica ad Sergium Patriarchum Constantinopolitanum* (ed. Migne, *PG* 87.3, col. 3189)

Ἀνάθεμα τοίνυν εἰσαεὶ καὶ κατάθεμα ἀπὸ τῆς ἁγίας καὶ ὁμοουσίου καὶ προσκυνητῆς Τριάδος, Πατρὸς καὶ Υἱοῦ καὶ ἁγίου Πνεύματος, ἔστωσαν, πρῶτον μὲν Σίμων ὁ Μάγος, ὁ πασῶν πρῶτος κακίστων κακίστως ἄρξας αἱρέσεων· μεθ' ὃν καὶ Κλεόβιος, Μένανδρος, Φίλητος, Ἑρμογένης, Ἀλέξανδρος ὁ Χαλκεὺς, Δοσίθεος, Γόρθεος, Σατορνῖνος, Μασβόθεος, Ἀδριανὸς, Βασιλείδης, Ἰσίδωρος ὁ τούτου υἱὸς καὶ τὴν μανίαν ὑπέρτερος, Ἐβίων, Καρποκράτης, Ἐπιφανὴς, Πρόδικος, Κήρινθός τε καὶ Μήρινθος, Οὐαλεντῖνος, Φλωρῖνος, Βλαστὸς, Ἀρτέμων, Σεκοῦνδος . . . (the list goes on for three columns).

John of Damascus, *De haeresibus compendium* 27 (ed. Lequien I.82)

p. 82 κζ. *ΚΑΡΠΟΚΡΑΤΙΑΝΟΙ·* οἱ ἀπὸ Καρποκράτους τινὸς τῶν ἐν τῇ Ασία. οὗτος ἐδίδασκε πᾶσαν αἰσχρουργίαν ἐκτελεῖν, καὶ πᾶν ἐπιτήδευμα ἁμαρτίας. εἰ μήτις, φησί, διὰ πάντων παρέλθῃ, καὶ τὸ θέλημα πάντων τῶν δαιμόνων καὶ ἀγγέλων ἐκτελέσῃ, οὐ δύναται ὑπερβῆναι τὸν ἀνώτατον οὐρανὸν, οὐδὲ τὰς ἀρχὰς, καὶ τὰς ἐξουσίας παρελθεῖν. ἔλεγεν δὲ τὸν Ιησοῦν ψυχὴν νοερὰν εἰληφέναι· εἰδότα δὲ τὰ ἄνω ἐνταῦθα καταγγέλλειν· καὶ εἴ τις πράξειεν ὅμοια τῷ Ιησοῦ, κατ' αὐτὸν εἶναι. τόντε νόμον σὺν τῇ τῶν νεκρῶν ἀναστάσει, ἀπηγόρευσεν, ὡς οἱ ἀπὸ Σίμωνος, καὶ αἱ δεῦρο αἱρέσεις. τούτου γέγονεν ἡ ἐν Ρώμῃ Μαρκελλίνα· εἰκόνας δὲ ποιήσας ἐν κρυφῇ Ιησοῦ, καὶ Παύλου, καὶ Ομήρου, καὶ Πυθαγόρα, ταύταις ἐθυμία καὶ προσεκύνει.[1]

1 See also *p. 81, λβ. ΣΕΚΟΥΝΔΙΑΝΟΙ·* οἷς συνάπτεται Ἐπιφανὴς καὶ Ἰσίδωρος ταῖς αὐταῖς κεχρημένοι συζυγίαις, τὰ ὅμοια Οὐαλεντίνῳ πεφρονηκότες· ἕτερα δὲ παρ' αὐτῶν ποσῶς διηγούμενοι. ἀπαγορεύουσι δὲ καὶ αὐτοὶ τὴν σάρκα.

Michael Syrus, *Chronique* VI.4 (ed. Chabot I.2.177)

p. 177 A cette époque parut Carpocrate, le chef de l'hérésie des Gnostiques, qui pratiquaient la magie de Simon, et se vantaient des guérisons faites par les démons parmi eux. Ils se réjouissaient d'abominables obscénités. A cette époque, les chrétiens furent accusés, par de faux apôtres, d'abuser de leurs mères et de leurs sœurs. Cette odieuse opinion s'éteignit promptement, et la vérité fut établie.

APPENDIX C

CLAUSULAE

I. Possible arrangements of long and short syllables in groups of five, and their occurrences in the sentence endings of *Stromateis* III and of the letter:

Arrangement	Occurrences in Stromateis III	In the letter
− − − − −	卌 IIII	−
v − − − −	卌 II	−
− v − − −	卌 IIII	III
− − v − −	卌 卌 IIII	I
− − − v −	卌 卌 卌 卌 卌 III	III
− − − − v	卌 IIII	−
v v − − −	卌 卌 I	−
v − v − −	卌	−
v − − v −	卌 卌 卌 卌 卌 I	I
v − − − v	卌 卌	II
− − − v v	卌 卌 卌 III	II
− − v − v	卌 II	−
− v − − v	卌 卌 卌 IIII	II
− v v − −	卌 I	−
− v − v −	卌 卌 II	I
− − v v −	卌 III	−
v v v − −	IIII	II
v v − v −	卌 卌	I
v v − − v	卌 卌 I	I
v − v v −	卌 III	−
v − v − v	卌 卌 I	−
v − − v v	卌 IIII	I
− v v v −	卌 卌 卌 II	I
− v v − v	II	−
− v − v v	卌 III	−
− − v v v	II	−
v v v v −	卌 I	I
v v v − v	IIII II	−
v v − v v	卌 卌 I	II
v − v v v	II	−
− v v v v	IIII	−
v v v v v	IIII	−

Totals 32   314   24

Note that this list does not include the endings of quotations, sentences introducing quotations, rhetorical questions of less than five syllables, and passages textually corrupt.

Number of possible arrangements: 32
Number of occurrences in *Stromateis* III: 314
Number of occurrences in the letter: 24

II. Clement's preferred and avoided patterns, followed by the numbers of their occurrences in *Stromateis* III and in the letter:

Preferred		*Avoided*	
– – – v –	28/3	– v v – v	2/0
v – – v –	26/1	– – v v v	2/0
– v – – v	19/2	v – v v v	2/0
– – – v v	18/2	– v v v v	4/0
– v v v –	17/1	v v v v v	4/0
– – v – –	14/1	v v v – –	4/2
		v – v – –	5/0
		– v v – –	6/0
		v v v v –	6/1
Totals:	122/10		35/3

Proportional relations: $\dfrac{122}{314} : \dfrac{10}{24} :: \dfrac{4}{12} : \dfrac{5}{12}$

$\dfrac{35}{314} : \dfrac{3}{24} :: \dfrac{1}{9} : \dfrac{1}{8}$

APPENDIX D

CLEMENT'S QUOTATIONS FROM MK.

This list contains all the passages listed by Stählin as quotations of Mk.; the passages he lists as mere reminiscences are not included.

The items enclosed in parentheses Stählin should not have listed as quotations of Mk.; either their wording or their context shows clearly that they are quotations of passages from other works (most often Matthew). At most they show some similarity to Markan wording and belong in Stählin's other category, that of reminiscences.

The passages not enclosed in parentheses, but not starred, might be quotations of Mk.; but in most instances they probably are not, since they are cases where the text of Mk. is so similar to that of at least one other Gospel, or the text of Clement so remote from both, that there is no telling which is being quoted (and, in such cases, it is almost always more probable that the more popular Gospel—that is, not Mk.—was in the writer's mind).

Finally, the passages starred are undoubtedly quotations of Mk. "Undoubtedly" —except for III.141.5, on which see the note. The great majority of these (12 out of 16) occur in *QDS* in the discussion of Mk. 10.17–31. Several of these are Matthaean phrases which now stand in Clement's text of Mk. Whether he found them there or put them there is dubious. There is one instance, however, where the intrusion of a Matthaean phrase was surely his work: III.166.24, πώλησον τὰ ὑπάρχοντά σου. In his quotation of the Markan text as a whole Clement had written πώλησον ὅσα ἔχεις (III.162.26), but as he went on in his exegesis he slipped into the Matthaean wording. I suppose the phrase must be included in this list of quotations from Mk., since Clement presents it as such, and one cannot deny him the privilege of misquoting his own Gospel text.

I.9.18, Mk. 1.3 = Mt. & Lk. No reference to source.
I.165.16, Mk. 1.6 = Mt. No ref. to source.
II.363.16f, Mk. 1.7 = Lk. No ref. to source.
I.105.6, Mk. 1.11 = Lk. & Mt. (western text). No ref.
III.199.7–16, Mk. 1.44 = Mt. & Lk. No ref.
(II.153.22f, Mk. 1.40 = Mt. & Lk. No ref.; probably not a reference to any canonical Gospel.)
(I.93.19–21, Mk. 2.11f = Mt. & Lk. No ref. Dubious parallel to canonical Gospels.)
(III.142.13f, Mk. 3.35. No. Mt. & Lk. closer. No ref.)

353

(II.379.18, Mk. 4.11. No. Mt. 13.11. No ref. Clearly Mt., but has τὸ μυστήριον in singular as Mk.)

(II.9.16ff, Mk. 4.21. No. Half Lk. 8.16 & 11.33, half Mt. 5.15. Dubious if from canonical Gospels.)

(II.10.21, Mk. 4.25. No. Mt. 25.29, Lk. 19.26. No ref. Dubious if from canonical Gospels. Cf. following.)

(II.100.1f, Mk. 4.25. No. Closer to the above but clearly from noncanonical source. No ref.)

(II.263.25f, Mk. 4.25. No. The noncanonical source above combined with Mt. 6.33. No ref.)

(III.41.7, Mk. 4.25. No = II.10.21 above. No ref.)

II.319.22, Mk. 5.34 = Lk. 8.48. No ref.[1]

II.486.14, Mk. 5.34 = Mt. & Lk. No ref.

II.134.28ff, Mk. 7.6f = Mt. 15.8f = Is. 29.13. No ref.

II.146.11f, Mk. 7.6f = Mt. 15.8f = Is. 29.13. No ref.

II.262.17f, Mk. 7.6f = Mt. 15.8f = Is. 29.13. No ref.

(I.187.10f, Mk. 7.15. No. No parallel. No ref.)

(I.187.10f, Mk. 7.20. No. Mt. 15.18. No ref.)

III.127.10f, Mk. 8.31 = Lk. 9.22(?). Dubious if from canonical Gospels. No ref.

II.172.13f, Mk. 8.35 = Mt. & Lk. No ref.

II.488.9f, Mk. 8.36 = Mt. & Lk. No ref.

*II.280.1–4, Mk. 8.38. No ref. (*Strom.* IV.)

(III.106.23f, Mk. 9.1. No. Mt. 16.28. No ref.)

*I.148.1f, Mk. 9.7. No ref. (*Paed.* I.)

(III.107.5 & 10, Mk. 9.9. No. Mt. 17.9. No ref.)

?*III.141.5, Mk. 9.29. No parallel save in Mk. but not close to Mk. Dubious if from noncanonical Gospel, but a version of the Markan story. No ref. (*Eclog. proph. 12.*)

II.245.24ff, Mk. 9.42 = Lk. 17.1f. Closer to Lk., but has one Markan trait. No ref.

I.274.24, Mk. 9.47 = Mt. 18.9. No ref.

II.217.21, Mk. 10.9 = Mt. 19.6. No ref.

II.217.31–218.4, Mk. 10.3–12 = Mt. 19.4–9. Closer to Mt., but has some Markan traits. No ref.

II.218.31, Mk. 10.9 = Mt. 19.6. No ref.

(II.193.6f, Mk. 10.11. No. Mt. 19.9. No ref.)

(II.193.11–13, Mk. 10.11–12. No. Quite different. Noncanonical source? No ref.)

I.97.1–5, Mk. 10.13f = Mt. 19.13ff. Closer to Mt. No ref.

(I.284.26ff, Mk. 10.17,19. No. Lk. 10.25–38 with Markan contamination. No ref.)

---

1. Swanson, *Text* 97, accepts this as a certain quotation of Mk. But Mk. has ὕπαγε (εἰς εἰρήνην), Lk. has πορεύου, and Clement has ἄπελθε with no indication from which (if either) of the canonical Gospels he took this cliché.

*III.162.19–163.12, Mk. 10.17–31. ταῦτα μὲν ἐν τῷ κατὰ Μᾶρκον εὐαγγελίῳ γέγραπται·
καὶ ἐν τοῖς ἄλλοις δὲ πᾶσιν ⟨τοῖς⟩ ἀνωμολογημένοις ὀλίγον μὲν ἴσως ἑκασταχοῦ τῶν
ῥημάτων ἐναλλάσσει, πάντα δὲ τὴν αὐτὴν τῆς γνώμης συμφωνίαν ἐπιδείκνυται. (QDS.)

I.132.13, Mk. 10.18 = Lk. 18.19 (western text.)

I.133.5f, Mk. 10.18 = Lk. 18.19 (western text.)

(I.284.27, Mk. 10.19. No. Contamination of Lk. 4.5.)[2]

(I.178.22f, Mk. 10.21. No. Mt. 19.21. No ref.)

(II.221.24f, Mk. 10.21. No. Mt. 19.21. No ref.)

*III.165.25, Mk. 10.21. No. Mt. 19.21. No ref. However, this is part of the exegesis
of Mk. 10.17–31. Clement has the Matthaean phrase in his Markan text.

*III.166.4, Mk. 10.21. No. Lk. 13.22. As above, but Lk. for Mt.

*III.166.24, Mk. 10.21. Actually Mt. No ref. Still in the exegesis.

*III.169.33f, Mk. 10.21 = Mt. & Lk. No ref. Still in the exegesis.

*III.173.2, Mk. 10.26 = Mt. & Lk. Still in the exegesis.

*III.173.7f, Mk. 10.26. Still in the exegesis.

*III.174.1, Mk. 10.28 = Mt. 19.27. Still in the exegesis.

II.255.18–20, Mk. 10.29f = Mt. 19.29. No ref.

*III.174.11–13, Mk. 10.29f. Still in the exegesis. More Matthaean traits.

*III.175.28–30, Mk. 10.30. Still in the exegesis.

*III.176.26, Mk. 10.30. Still in the exegesis (= Lk. 18.30).

*III.176.27, Mk. 10.31 = Mt. 19.30. Still in the exegesis.

I.139.30ff,32f, Mk. 10.45 = Mt. 20.28. No ref.

II.498.33, Mk. 10.48 = Lk. 18.39 (etc.). No ref.[3]

(I.286.15f, Mk. 12.17. No. Mt. 22.21. No ref.)

II.218.3f, Mk. 12.25 = Mt. & Lk. No ref.

II.503.5, Mk. 12.25 = Mt. & Lk. (Closer to a variant of Lk.) No ref.

I.183.17f, Mk. 12.30f = Mt. & Lk. No ref.

(I.284.22f, Mk. 12.30f = Mt. & Lk. No ref. Shown by the sequel to be Mt.)

(II.150.23–25, Mk. 12.30f = Mt. & Lk. No ref. Shown by the sequel to be Mt.)

(I.77.18f, Mk. 12.30f. No. Synthesis of Mt. 18.18 & Lk. 10.27. No ref.)

(I.125.4, Mk. 12.30f. No Quotation of Dt. 6.5; see context. No ref.)

III.178.6f, Mk. 12.30f = Mt. & Lk. Slightly closer to Mk., but close to none.
No ref.

I.77.20f, Mk. 12.31 = Mt. 22.39. No ref.

I.229.16, Mk. 12.31 = Mt. 22.39. No ref.

(II.221.26f, Mk. 12.31 = Mt. 22.39. No ref. Context refers to the OT command.)

II.281.20, Mk. 13.13 = Mt. 24.13. No ref.

III.181.21, Mk. 13.13 = Mt. 24.13. No ref.

II.219.3f, Mk. 13.17 = Mt. & Lk. No ref.

I.195.3f, Mk. 14.20 = Mt. 26.23. Closer to Mt., but some Markan traits. No ref.

---

2. Swanson, Text 97ff, takes μὴ μοιχεύσῃς, μὴ φονεύσῃς in III.44.10f as a certain quotation of
Mk.10.19, but it looks more like Lk. 18.20.

3. Swanson, Text 97ff, accepts this as a certain quotation of Mk., but the words quoted are identical
with those in Lk.

I.176.7f, Mk. 14.25 = Mt. 26.29. Closer to Mt., but some Markan traits. No ref.

(I.66.1, Mk. 14.36 = Rom. 8.15. Shown to be Romans by the context. No ref.)

II.119.6f, Mk. 14.38 = Mt. 26.41. No ref.

II.268.21, Mk. 14.38 = Mt. 26.41. No ref.

*III.209.9–11, Mk. 14.61f. Introduced by the words: "In evangelio verum secundum Marcum interrogatus dominus," etc. The context goes on to contrast the Markan report with that in the other Gospels. (*Adumbrationes in epistulas canonicas.*)

APPENDIX E
GOSPEL PHRASES AND THEIR PARALLELS

° = Parallel to a Markan use.

καὶ ἔρχονται

Mk.2.18; (3.19 ΑℵᶜCLΔΘΠΣΦϞ Minusc.pler.it.pauc.vg.Sy.ᵖᵉˢʰ. ἔρχεται ℵ*BWΓ Cop.ˢᵃ·ᵇᵒ·Sy.ˢ·); 3.31 (ἔρχεται ℵDGWΘ fam.1. 330,565,569.892.it.pler.); 5.15, 38; 8.22; 10.46 (ἔρχεται D 61. 258.481, it.pler.Sy.ˢ·Or.ᵇⁱˢ);11.15 (ἔρχεται ΝΣ 517.700.892.l.18.l. 19.al. b f ff i r aur.; εἰσελθών D Sy.ˢ·); 11.27 (ἔρχεται DX 225. 252ᵐˢ· 565. it. plur. Cop. ᵇᵒ·⁽¹ᴹˢ⁾); 12.18; 14.32 (ἐξέρχονται W, ἔρχεται Θ pc.); (16.4 DΘ 565.it. pc.Sy.ˢ·ʰⁱᵉʳ·)

Mt. 21.17°; 26.6°

Lk. 19.29°; 24.50

καὶ ἔρχονται εἰς

Mk. (3.19); 5.38; 8.22; 10.46; 11.15; 11.27; 14.32 (variants as above)

καὶ ἔρχονται εἰς Βηθανίαν

(Mk. 8.22 D 262*.it.pl. Βηθσαϊδάν rell.)

Βηθανία

Mk. (8.22, see above); 11.1 (ἐξῆλθεν εἰς Β.), 11,12; 14.3

Mt. 2.15

καὶ ἦν ἐκεῖ

Mk. 3.1

εἰς / μία / ἕν for τὶς (these include εἰς alone and εἰς with following genitive or prepositional phrase, as well as the adjectival use given separately below)

Mk. 5.22 (τὶς DW 50.348.472.474. it.vg.); 6.15; 8.28; 9.17; 10.17; 12.28; 12.42; 13.1; 14.10 (see Taylor ad loc.); 14.18,20,43.47 (εἰς τὶς BCΔΘ et al. fam.13.22. 28.118.157.543.565.892.1071.al.

Mt. 5.19(?); 6.29(?); 8.19; 9.18° (τὶς FGLUT al., om. ℵ*C*DEMNWXΔΘΣΦ al.); 16.14°, 18.24,28; 19.16°; 20.13; 21.19; 22.35; 26.14,21°, 47°, 51°,69°; 27.48; (18.2 D Sy.ᶜ·ˢ·)

Lk. 5.3,12,17; 8.22; 12.27; 13.10; 15.15,19,(21 BℵD al.),26; 17.22; 20.1; 22.47°; 24.18; (9.19 D)

	Mk.	Mt.	Lk.
εἷς / μία / ἕν for τὶς (continued)	pl.it.vg.Sy.hl. So Taylor, cf. Legg); 14.66; (15.36 ACDNPYΓΘΠΣ⸃ fam.1.22.28.33.al.pler.it.vg.Sy.s. pesh.hl.Cop.Aeth.Aug.)		
εἷς / μία / ἕν for τὶς, used adjectivally, as in the secret Gospel	Mk. 12.42 μία χήρα	Mt. 8.19 εἷς γραμματεύς; 9.18 ἄρχων εἷς (see above); 21.19 συκῆν μίαν; 26.69 μία παιδίσκη; (18.2 v.s.)	
redundant αὐτός: οὗ ... αὐτοῦ / ἧς ... αὐτῆς	Mk. 1.7 Mk. 7.25 (om. אDWΔΘ𝔭45 fam.1, fam.13 [exc. 124] 28.225.237-253. 475**.565.569.700.al.pauc.it.vg. Cop.sa.bo.Geo.)	Mt. 3.12	Lk. 3.16°,17
ὧν ... αὐτῶν			
καὶ ἐλθών + finite verb	Mk. 1.29 καὶ εὐθὺς ... ἐξελθόντες ἦλθαν Mk. 9.14 καὶ ἐλθόντες ... εἶδαν Mk. 11.13 καὶ ἐλθὼν ἐπ' αὐτὴν οὐδὲν εὗρεν (om. ἐπ' αὐτὴν D it. Sy.s.pesh.) Mk. 12.14 καὶ ἐλθόντες λέγουσιν αὐτῷ Mk. 12.42 καὶ ἐλθοῦσα μία χήρα πτωχὴ ἔβαλεν	Mt. 2.11 interrupted; 2.23 καὶ ἐλθὼν κατῴκησεν; 8.14° interrupted; 12.44 καὶ ἐλθὸν εὑρίσκει; 13.4 interrupted; so 13.54; 14.12 καὶ ἐλθόντες ἀπήγγειλαν; 16.5 interrupted; 18.31 καὶ ἐλθόντες διεσάφησαν; 20.10 interrupted; so 26.43 and 27.33f	Lk. 13.1 Lk. 11.25 καὶ ἐλθὸν εὑρίσκει; 14.9 interrupted; so 15.6 and 16.21 and 19.23; (so also 5.27 and 19.45, both D)
προσκυνεῖν (* = with ἔρχομαι or one of its compounds; *! = following a participle of ἔρχομαι or one of its compounds; ac. = with the accusative)	Mk. 5.6 ac. (dative אDWΘΠΣΦ⸃ fam.1,fam.13,28.33.157.565. 579.1071.al.pler.), 15.19 (ac.472. 579.it.vg. Aug.; om. D)	Mt. 2.2*; 2.8*!; 2.11; 4.9; 4.10 ac.; 8.2*!; 9.18*!; 14.33;*!C*D LPWXΓΔΠΦ⸃ 33.157.al.pler. also Θ fam.13.543.517.al.Geo. *it.pler.vg.Sy.Arm.); 15.25*!; 18.26; 20.20*; 28.9*!; 28.17 (ac. Γ 4.28.al.pler.Sy.pesh.hl.hier.Cop. sa.bo.Aeth.Arm.Geo.)	Lk. 4.7; 4.8 ac.; (24.52 ac. אABWΘ fam.1, fam.13,pl.vg.pt.)

	Mk.	Mt.	Lk.
καὶ λέγει αὐτῷ	Mk. 1.41; 1.44; 2.14; 5.9; 7.28; 7.34; 14.30; 14.61	Mt. 4.6; 8.4°; (8.7 *om.* καὶ B 700. *l.*47.*it.pauc.*vg.*pauc.*Sy.ᶜ·ˢ·ᵖᵉˢʰ. Cop.ˢᵃ·ᵇᵒ·ᵖᵃᵘᶜ·Arm.); 8.20; 9.9°; 14.31; 22.12	
υἱὲ Δαβὶδ ἐλέησόν με	Mk. 10.47 υἱὲ Δαυεὶδ Ἰησοῦ ἐλέησόν με. ὁ υἱός AWXYΓΠΦ ⸆ *fam.*1.22.157 *al.pler.* υἱός DK *fam.*13.543.245.349.409.565. Or. Δαυεὶδ BDΨ 579.δαβὶδ *vel* δᾱδ *Uncs.pler.Minusc.pler.* Ἰησοῦ *om.* L 47.108.127.*al.l.*18.*l.*19.*al.*Sy.ˢ·ᵖᵉˢʰ.Geo.	Mt. 9.27 ἐλέησον ἡμᾶς υἱὲ Δ. + κύριε N *Minusc.pauc.* υἱός BG-UWYΠ ο 47.237-238.*al.* Mt. 15.22 ἐλέησόν με, κύριε, υἱός Δαυεὶδ. υἱός BDWΘ 0119.700. 945. υἱέ *Uncs.rell.Minusc.pler.*	Lk. 18.38° Ἰησοῦ υἱὲ Δαυεὶδ ἐλέησόν με. 18.39° υἱὲ Δαυεὶδ ἐλέησόν με. Ἰησοῦ *before* υἱέ ℵ *fam.*1.*fam.*13.*pauc.*
	Mk. 10.48 υἱὲ Δαυεὶδ ἐλέησόν με. υἱός DF. ὁ υἱός *fam.*1. Ἰησοῦ υἱέ *fam.*13(*exc.*124).543.1342	Mt. 20.30° κύριε ἐλέησον ἡμᾶς υἱὲ Δ. *om.* κύριε ℵDΘ 118.209.*fam.* 13.*al.it.pler.*Sy.ᶜ·ʰⁱᵉʳAeth.Arm. Geo.υἱός BGHKMSUVWXYZ ΓΔΠ² *Minusc.pler.*Or.*bis.* Ἰησοῦ υἱέ ℵLNΘΣ 69.124.543.*al.it.* *pauc.*Sy.ʰⁱᵉʳ.Cop.ᵇᵒ.Aeth.Arm. Geo. Mt. 20.31° = 20.30 κύριε *post* ἡμᾶς CNOWXΓΔΠΣΦ 𝔭⁴⁵ᵛⁱᵈ·⸆ *Minusc.pler.it.pauc.*Sy.ʰˡ. Geo.² Sy.° *om.* κύριε *Minusc.pauc.* υἱός BWXZΓΔΠ⸆ *Minusc.pler.*	
οἱ δὲ μαθηταί (initial + verb)	Mk. (2.23 565.*it.pauc.* καὶ οἱ *rell.*); 10.13; 10.24; (14.4 DΘ 565.*it.* *pler.*Arm. ἦσαν δέ τινες *rell.*) (*In the last three instances* DΘ *it.pler. add* αὐτοῦ)	Mt. 12.1; (14.26 *verb does not follow immediately, text dubious*); 19.13°; 28.16 (+ ἕνδεκα)	

359

	Mk.	Mt.	Lk.
ἐπιτιμάω (always with dative, unless used absolutely) † = ἐπετίμησεν/αν	Mk. 1.25†; 3.12; 4.39†; 8.30†; 8.32; 8.33†; 9.25†; 10.13 (ἐπετίμησαν† אBCLΔΨ579.892. Sy.ˢ·Cop.ˢᵃ·ᵇᵒ· ἐπετίμων ADNW XYΓΘΠΣΦϨ Minusc. rell. it. vg. Sy.ᵖᵉˢʰ·ʰˡ· Geo. Aeth. Arm. Bas.); 10.48	Mt. 8.26°†; 12.16°†; 16.20°† (so B*D d.e.Sy.ᶜ·Arm., διεστείλατο rell.); 16.22°; 17.18°†; 19.13°†; 20.31°†	Lk. 4.35°†; 4.39†; 4.41°; 8.24°†; 9.21°; 9.42°†; 9.55†; 17.3; 18.15°; 18.39°; 19.39; 23.40
οἱ δὲ μαθηταὶ ἐπετίμησαν	Mk. 10.13 (אB, etc., see above)	Mt. 19.13°	
καί + participle in nom. + finite vb., as basic sentence structure, in Mk. 1–3 and 10; Mt. 4,8,9 and 19–20; Lk. 4–6,11 and 18	Mk. 1.10,16,18,19,20,21,26,29,31, 41,43; 2.4,5,8,12,14,17; 3.5,15, 21,23,33,34; 10.1,2,16,23,32,41, 42.47.49.51	Mt. 4.2,3,13,21°; 8.3°,14°,19,25, 34; 9.1°,2°,4°,7°,9°,11,19,23; 19.15; 20.3,10,24°,32°	Lk. 4.5,8,12,13,17,20,29,39,41; 5.5,11°,13°,19°,20°,25°,28°,31°; 6.3,8,10°; 18, *none*
καί + nom. participle + ὁ Ἰησοῦς + vb., without interruption, in the same sections as above	Mk. 2.17; 10.23; 10.49; (2.14 FGHΓΩ 346.2.12.29.237.al. pler.)	Mt. 9.19; 20.32°	Lk. 4.8; 5.31°
ὀργισθείς	(Mk. 1.41 D it.pauc.cf.Tat.Ephr.; rell. σπλαγχνισθείς)		
ἀπῆλθεν μετά (with genitive)	Mk. 5.24	Mt. 18.34	Lk. 14.21
ἀπῆλθεν	Mk. 1.35; 1.42; 5.20; 5.24; 6.46; 7.24; 8.13; 10.22; 14.10; (6.1 and 15.46 D)	Mt. 4.24; 9.7; 13.25; 16.4°; 19.22°; 21.29; 27.60; (14.25 D)	Lk. 1.23; 1.38; 5.13°; 5.25; 8.39°; 24.12
κῆτος			Lk. 13.19
ὅπου ἦν	Mk. 2.4; 5.46		(Lk. 4.16; 5.19° D)
καὶ εὐθύς (initial) (The MSS cited are those which read or omit εὐθύς; all others read εὐθέως)	Mk. 1.10 אBLΔ 33.579 *om.* D it. Cop.ᵇᵒ· Mk. 1.12 אBLWΓΔΣΦϨ (exc. E*K) *fam.*13.*al.* Mk. 1.18 אLΘ 33.565-579.892 Mk. 1.20 אBL 33.565-579.892 *om.* WDΘ it.	Mt. 21.2° אLZ *om.*482.*al.*it.Cop.ᵇᵒ· Mt. 26.74° BLΘ (Mt. 13.5° D *om.* L)	(Lk. 5.6 D *d* [*e* Sy.ˢ·])

καὶ εὐθύς (initial) (continued)

Mk. 1.21 אL *fam.*1.28.33.565.700. *al.*Or.*semel*

1.23 א**BL** *fam.*1(exc.118).33.579. Cop.^{sa.bo.}Or. *om.* ACDWΓΔΘΠ ΣΦҁ 118.22.*fam.*13.543.*al.pler.* it.vg.Sy.Geo.

1.29 א**BLΔΣ** *fam.*1(exc.118).*fam.* 13(exc.124)28.33.543.565.*al.* *om.* DW Sy.Geo.Aeth.

1.30 א**BDL** *fam.*13.28.33.543.*al.* *om.* W it.Sy.Geo.Aeth.

1.42 א**BL**Θ 33.164

2.8 א**BL**Θ 33.700 *om.* DW 28.64.*al.* it.Sy.^{pesh.}Aeth.

2.12 א**BC*****L** 33 *om.* ΘW it.

4.5 א**BCDL**Δ 892 *om.* Sy.^{s.}

5.29 א**BCL**ΔΘ 33.349.517.579.*al.*

5.30 א**BCL**ΔΘ 33.349.517.*al.* *om.* it.

5.42 א**BL**ΔΘ 33.349.517.892 *om.* Cop.

6.27 א**BCL**ΔΘ 892.*l.*1596 *om.* it. vg.Sy.^{s.}

6.45 א**BL**WΔΘ 28.579.892. *om.* 238.*c*

8.10 א**BCL**WΔ *fam.*1,*fam.*13(exc. 124),28.253. *al.*

9.15 א**BCL**WΔΘΨ *fam.*1,*fam.*13 (exc.124),28.543.565.700.*al.*

10.52 א**BL**ΔΨ 892.1342.*om.*61

11.2 א**BL**ΔΨ 579.892.1342.Or.

11.3 א**BCDL**ΔΨ 579.892.1342.Or.^{semel}

καὶ εὐθύς (initial) (continued)

14.43 ℵBCLΔΨ 0112.579.892.
1342. om. DWΣ fam.1.fam.13
(exc.124),543.565.700.it.vg.Sy.
Cop.Geo.
14.72 ℵBL om. ACNXYΓΔΠΣΨ⸀
(exc.G),fam.1.22.28.33.al.pler.
Sy.Cop.
15.1 ℵBCLΔΨ 892.1342. om.it.
pauc.Sy.ˢ.Cop.ˢᵃ.Aeth.

καὶ εὐθύς + finite verb

Mk. 1.20,23,30,42; 4.5; 5.29,42;
6.45; 10.52

Mt. 21.2°

ἠκούσθη

Mk. 2.1

Mt. 2.18(= LXX Jer. 38.15 =
Heb. 31.15)

φωνὴ μεγάλη

Mk. 1.26; 5.7; 15.34; 15.37

Mt. 24.31 BDXΓΠΣΦ⸀ Minusc.
pler.Sy.ʰˡ.ⁿⁱᵉʳ.it.vg. Cop.ˢᵃ.Aeth.
om.rell.; 27.46°; 27.50°

Lk. 4.33°; 8.28°; 17.15; 19.37
(om.Dit.pauc.vg.(1)Cop.ᵇᵒ.⁽¹⁾);
23.23; 23.46°; (1.42 D)

καὶ προσελθών (initial)

Mk. 1.31; (14.35 ACDEGHLSU
VXYΓΔΠ²ΣΨ 0116 fam.1,fam.
13.543.71.157.299.300.al.plur.
Sy. προελθών rell.)

Mt.4.3;8.19;(20.28DΦit.vg.Sy.ᶜ);
25.20; (26.39° ℵACDLWΓΔΘ
Π²Σ* 067.074,⸀(exc.Ω),pap.
Mich.6652 fam.1.1582.69.124.
543.28.al.plur.Sy.προελθώνrell.);
28.2,18

Lk. 7.14; 10.34

καὶ προσελθὼν ὁ Ἰησοῦς (initial)
καὶ προσελθὼν ἀπεκύλισε τὸν λίθον

Mt. 28.18

ἀποκυλίειν ... τὸν λίθον

Mk. 16.3 (c. ἐκ ℵABLXΓΔΠΣ⸀
Minusc.pler. ἀπό CDWΘΨ fam.
13(exc.124),543.al.pauc.it.vg.);
16.4(exc. ℵBL it. ἀνακυλίω)

Mt. 28.2 (om. καὶ ADΓΔΘΠΦ⸀
Minusc.pler.Sy.ʰˡ.Arm.Geo.)

Lk. 24.2° (c. ἀπό); (24.1° D 0124
Cop.ˢᵃ.)

Mt. 28.2

ἀποκυλίειν ... τὸν λίθον ἀπὸ τῆς θύρας τοῦ μνημείου

Mk. 16.3 (the MSS cited above for
ἀπό; those cited for ἐκ have the same
reading except for the preposition)

Mt. 28.2 (see following entries)

	Mt.	Mk.	Lk.
ἀπεκύλισε τὸν λίθον ἀπὸ τῆς θύρας	Mt. 28.2 (om. ἀπὸ τῆς θ. ℵBD 544.700.892.1555.it.pler.vg.Sy.ˢCop.ˢᵃAeth. ἐκ 28.213		
ἀπεκύλισε τὸν λίθον ἀπὸ τῆς θύρας τοῦ μνημείου	Mt. 28.2 (om. τοῦ μν. the above and ACE*GHKM*SVWYΔΠΦΩ 69.124.28.al.pler.it.pauc.Sy.ᵖᵉˢʰ. Arm.Geo¹. read τοῦ μ. E²FLM² UΓΘΣ 047.fam.1.1582.22.346. 543.al.pler.Sy.ʰⁱ·ⁿⁱᵉʳ·Cop.ᵇᵒ·Geo.² Eus.)		
καὶ εἰσελθών (initial)	Mt. 26.58	Mk. 2.1 (ℵBDLΘ 28.33.59.471. al.Cop.ˢᵃ·Arm.it.pauc.); 5.39; 6.25 (εἰσελθοῦσα); 7.24; 11.15; 16.5 (εἰσελθοῦσαι); (11.15 iter. D Sy.ˢ.)	Lk. 1.28; 7.36; 19.1; 19.45°; (8.51 D)
καὶ εἰσελθὼν εὐθύς (initial)		Mk. 6.25 (εἰσελθοῦσα)	
νεανίσκος		Mk. 14.51; 16.5	
ἐκτεῖναι τὴν χεῖρα	Mt. 19.20; 19.22	Mk. 1.41; 3.5 bis; (1.31 DW it. pauc.)	Lk. 7.14
ἐξέτεινεν τὴν χεῖρα	Mt. 8.3°; 12.13 bis°; 12.49; 14.31; 26.51		Lk. 5.13°; 6.10°; 22.53 (6.10 iterum D; 22.51 D)
	Mt. 12.13 it.pler.Sy.		
ἤγειρεν		Mk. 1.31; 9.27 (+ αὐτόν)	Lk. 1.69
κρατήσας τῆς χειρός		Mk. 1.31 (om. DW it.pauc.Sy.ˢ.); 5.41; 9.27	Lk. 8.54°
χείρ (instrument of supernatural power)	Mt. 8.3°; 8.15°; 9.18°; 9.25°; 14.31; 19.13; 19.15°	Mk. 1.31 (om. D etc.v.sup.); 1.41; 5.23; 5.41; 6.2; 6.5; 7.32; 8.23; 8.25; 9.27; 10.16; (16.18. om. ℵB Sy.ˢ·Geo.ˡᵉᵗᴬ Aeth.Arm.)	Lk. 1.66; 4.40; 5.13°; 8.54°; 13.13; (22.51 D it.)
ἐμβλέψας (with following verb)	Mt. 19.26°	Mk.10.21;10.27;14.67 (ἐμβλέψασα αὐτῷ λέγει. ἐμβλέψας ΚΜΔ 33.59.282.al.om.αὐτῷ Dit.pauc.)	Lk. 20.17
ἀγαπάω	Mt. 5.43; 5.44; 5.46 bis; 6.24; 19.19; 22.37°; 22.39°	Mk. (7.6 DW it.pauc.Tert.τιμᾷ rell.); 10.21; 12.30; 12.31; 12.33 bis	Lk. 6.27; 6.32 quater; 6.35; 7.5; 7.42; 7.47 bis(om. D it.pauc.); 10.27; 11.43; 16.13

	Mk.	Mt.	Lk.
ἤρξατο / ἤρξαντο (with infinitive)	Mk. 1.45; 2.23; 4.1; 5.17 (om. DΘ 225-255.al.a); 5.20; 6.2; 6.7(om. D 565 it.Sy.ˢ·Aeth.); 6.34; 6.55; 8.11; 8.31; 8.32; 10.28; 10.32; 10.41(om. A91 q. vg.Aeth.); 10.47; 11.15; 12.1; 13.5 (om. DΘ 68.108.218.219. 237.al.l.18,l.19it.pauc.Sy.ˢGeo.² Arm.);14.19;14.33;14.65;14.69; 14.71; 15.8; 15.18; (5.18 D it. plur.vg.; 8.25 Dit.plur.vg.; 14.72 DΘ 565 it.vg.Sy.ˢ·pesh.ni.Cop. sa.bo.Geo.Arm.Aug.)	Mt. 4.17; 11.7; 11.20; 12.1°; 16.21°; 16.22°; 26.22°; 26.37°; 26.74°	Lk. 4.21; 5.21; 7.15; 7.24; 7.38; 7.49; 9.12; 11.29; 11.53; 12.1; 14.18; 14.30; 15.14; 15.24; 19.37; 19.45°; 20.9°; 22.23?; 23.2; (5.14°D; 6.1°D; 11.38 D pauc.it.vg.Sy.°·Marcion; 15.28 D)
παρακαλεῖν (meaning "entreat"); ◇ = with following ἵνα clause and subjunctive	Mk. 1.40 (ἐρωτῶν D);5.10◇;5.12; 5.17; 5.18◇; 5.23◇?; 6.56◇; 7.32◇;8.22◇	Mt. 8.5°; 8.31°; 8.34°; 14.36◇◇; 18.29;18.32;(20.28DΦit.vg.Sy. °·);26.53	Lk.7.4(πρώτων ℵDfam.13.700.al.); 8.31◇; 8.32◇; 8.41°; 15.28; (5.8 D it.Sy.pesh.)
καὶ ἐξελθόντες(-ών,etc.)initial with following finite verb († here = with ἔρχομαι and ◇ = with ἐκ)	Mk. 1.29†◇ (δὲ DW it.pler.); 3.6 (δὲ DWit.plur.vg.Cop.ˢª.);6.12; 6.24 (δὲ ACDNWYΓΠΣΦ⅄ Minusc.pler.it.vg.Sy.ˢ.); 6.34; 7.31†◇; 9.30◇; 16.8 (ἀκούσασαι ΘW Sy.ˢ·Cop.ˢª·Geo.)	Mt. (12.14° D 517.659.al.it. δὲ rell.); 14.14° (om. G it.plur Sy.°· pesh.Cop.ˢª.); 15.21◇; 20.3; 22.10; 24.1 (◇B 4.1093.al.); 26.75◇; 27.53†◇ (ἀπὸ Σ 047. 213) (c. τῶν μνημείον); (28.8° ἀπελθοῦσαι ℵBCLΘfam.13.543. 33.443.al.pauc.) (c.τοῦ μνημείου)	Lk. 22.39;22.62° (om.017;it.pler.)
οἰκία (historical) († here = after ἔρχομαι εἰς)	Mk. 1.29† (Σίμωνος κ. Ἀνδρέου); 2.15 (Λευεί);7.24†(τυνός);9.33 (τυνός;); 10.10 (τυνός;); 14.3 (Σίμωνος τοῦ λεπροῦ); (5.38†D 565.700 οἶκον rell.; 7.17† D 474. 565 οἶκον rell.)	Mt. 2.11 (τυνός;); 8.6 (τοῦ ἑκατο-ντάρχου);8.14†°(Πέτρου);9.10° (Μαθθαίον[?]); 9.23† (τοῦ ἄρχοντος); 9.28† (τυνός;); 13.1 (τυνός;) (om. D it.pler.Sy.ˢ·); 13.36† (+ αὐτοῦ 1.118.209.al. Or.); 17.25† (+ αὐτοῦ Sy.ˢ·); 26.6° (Σίμωνος τοῦ λεπροῦ)	Lk. 4.38†° (Σίμωνος); 5.29° (Λε-νεί); 7.6 (τοῦ ἑκατοντάρχου); 7.37 (Σίμωνος τοῦ φαρισαίου); 7.44† (eiusdem); 8.51† (τοῦ Ἰαεί-ρου); 10.38 (τῆς Μαρθᾶς) (οἶκον ADWΘ fam.1,fam.13,plΙ.it.vg. om.𝔭⁴⁵B); 22.10 (τυνός;); 22.11 (eiusdem);22.54 (τοῦ ἀρχιερέως); (8.41 D, οἶκον rell.)

	Mk.	Mt.	Lk.
ἦν/ἦσαν γάρ (introducing an appended explanation)	Mk. 1.16; 1.22; 2.15; 5.42 (ἦν δὲ D 565.569.it.vg.Sy.pesh.(1MS)); 6.31; 6.48; (6.52 ADNWXΓΠΣ Φϩ (ex.M²S).it.vg.Sy.s.hl.pesh. Aeth.Arm.Geo.); 10.22; 14.40; 16.4 (= 16.3 DΘ 565.it.plur.vg.Sy.s.hier.)	Mt. 4.18°; 7.29°; 14.24'; 19.22'; 26.43°	Lk. 8.40; 9.14; 14.24'; 19.22'; 18.23° (+ πλούσιος 23.8; (8.30 D)
πλούσιος	Mk. 10.25; 12.41; (10.17 AKMW ΘΠ fam.13.543.28.59.229.330. 470.482.565.700.1071.al.multi.c Geo.²Sy.hl.mg.Cop.sa.Arm.)	Mt. 19.23; 19.24°; 27.57	Lk. 6.24; 12.16; 14.12; 16.1; 16.19; 16.21; 16.22; 18.23; 18.25°; 19.2; 21.1°
μετά (with precise numbers of days)	Mk. 8.31 (ἐν c) (dative W fam.1,fam. 13.28.33.565.al.it.pauc.Sy.s.pesh. Geo.Aeth.Arm.);9.2(אBC^vid.DL Δ 892* μεθ' rell.); 9.31 (dative AC³NWXYΓΘΠΣΦϩ Minusc. pler.it.pauc.vg.Sy.Geo.Aeth. Arm.); 10.34 (dative ANWXY ΓΘΠΣΦϩ fam.1,fam.13.22.28. 157.565.al.pler.it.pauc.vg.Sy.Geo. Aeth.Arm.Or.); 14.1	Mt. 17.1°; 26.2°; 27.63; (16.21° D d.Cop.bo. dative rell.; 17.23° D it.Sy.s.Cop.bo.)	Lk. 2.46; 9.28 (c. ὡσεί)°?; (9.22° Dit.Marcion)
ἐπιτάσσειν († here = ἐπέταξεν)	Mk. 1.27; 6.27†; 6.39†; 9.25		Lk. 4.36°; 8.25; 8.31; 14.22; (8.55† D)
καὶ ἐπέταξεν ὁ Ἰησοῦς αὐτοῖς	Mk. 6.39 D a b d f g² vg.(5MSS). om. ὁ Ἰησοῦς rell.		
ὀψίας γενομένης (gen. absolute at beginning of sentence)	Mk. 1.32; 6.47 (καὶ ὀ.γ.); 14.17 (καὶ ὀ.γ.); 15.42 (καὶ ἤδη ὀ.γ.)	Mt. 8.16°; 14.15; 14.23°; 16.2 (om. אBVXYΓΩ* 13.124*.157. 230.267.al.Sy.°.s.Cop.Arm.); 20.8; 26.20°; 27.57°	
ἔρχεται (historical present)	Mk. 1.40; 3.19 (א*BWΓ it.(pauc.) Cop.sa.bo.Sy.s.); 5.22; 6.1 (ἦλθεν ADNΠΣΦϩ fam.1,fam.13.28.33.	Mt. 25.19; 26.36; 26.40°; 26.45°	Lk. 8.49

	Mk.	Mt.	Lk.
ἔρχεται (historical present) (continued)	157.al.pler.it.Sy.pesh.hl.hier Cop. Geo.); 6.48; (8.22 א*ANXΓΠΣ Φכ fam.1.22.157.565,al.pler.Sy.); 10.1(ἦλθεν Ν Sy.Cop.Geo.Aeth); (10.46 D 61.258.481.it.Sy.s.Or); (11.27 DX 225.565.it.plur.); 14.17; 14.37; 14.41; 14.66		Lk. 1.43; 6.47; 7.7; 8.35°; 14.26; 15.20; 18.3†; 18.16°; 22.45
πρός after ἔρχομαι († here = πρὸς αὐτόν) (Moulton-Geden citations only)	Mk. 1.40†; 1.45†; 2.3†; 2.13†; 3.8†; 5.15; 6.48; 9.14; 10.14; 10.50'; 11.27†; 12.18†; (14.66† DΘ a c f ff k q Eus.)	Mt. 3.14; 7.15; 14.25°; 14.28; 14.29; 17.14; 19.14°; 21.32; 25.36; 25.39; 26.40; 26.45; (21.1 ?)	
περιβάλλω (of clothing)	Mk. 14.51; 16.5	Mt. 6.29,31; 25.36,38,43 (om. א* 124.21.127*.1194.1424.1604)	Lk. 12.27; 23.11
σινδών	Mk. 14.51; 14.52; 15.46 bis	Mt. 27.59	Lk. 23.53
γυμνός	Mk. 14.51 (om. W fam.1 c k Sy.s. Cop.sa.); 14.52	Mt. 25.36,38,43 (om. as above, in περιβάλλω), 44	
μένω († here = ἔμενε[ν])	Mk. 6.10; 14.34	Mt. 10.11°; 11.23†; 26.38°	Lk. 1.56†; 8.27†; 9.4°; 10.7; 19.5; 24.29 (bis)
ἐδίδασκεν (of Jesus) († here = followed by αὐτούς)	Mk. 1.21 (+ αὐτούς DΘ 700.it. pler.vg.); 2.13†; 4.2†; 9.31; 10.1†; 11.17	Mt. 5.2†; 13.54†	Lk. 4.15; 5.3?; (5.27 D)
ἐκεῖθεν (with participle at beginning of sentence) († here = followed by ἀναστάς)	Mk. 7.24† (καί prefixed ANXΓΘΠ ΣΦכ fam.1.22.fam.13.543.28.33. 157.565.579.700.al.pler. l r² vg. Sy.hl.Cop.bo.Geo.²Arm.; ἀναστὰς ἐκεῖθεν D f ff g¹ q r¹ Geo.¹ Aeth., om. ἐκεῖθεν W a bᶜ i n Sy.s.); 10.1†; (6.53 D 45 b c ff q; with ἐκεῖθεν [inde] preceding the ppl. a); (10.46 DΘ a b f ff i q r¹, ἐκεῖθεν after μαθητῶν αὐτοῦ 565.700)	Mt.4.21; 9.9 (interrupted by ὁ Ἰησοῦς; om. ἐκεῖθεν א*L 71.692.1574. lectionaria aliqua Cop.bo.(1MS)); 9.27; 12.9 (ἐκεῖθεν precedes in a b c ff¹.² l vg.); 15.21°; 15.29	

ἀναστάς (the participle used pleon-astically with a following finite verb) (variants not checked; Moulton-Geden and Yoder refs. only)

Mk. 1.35; 2.14; 7.24; 10.1; 14.57(?); 14.60(?)

Mt. 9.9°; 26.62°

Lk. 1.39; 4.29; 4.38; 5.28°; 6.8; 15.18; 15.20; 17.19; 22.46(?); 23.1; 24.12; 24.33

πέραν († τὸ π; * with following genitive; ★ followed by τοῦ Ἰορδάνου)

Mk. 3.8★; 4.35†; 5.1†* (om. following gen. D 13.69.543. b f ff d i q r¹); 5.21† (om.р.⁴⁵vid.); 6.45† (om. W fam.1 q Sy.ˢ·); 8.13†; 10.1★ (+ τοῦ ΑΝΧΥΓ ΠΣ*vid.Φﭪ (exc.G).157.569.575. al.pler.Sy.ⁿⁱ·Aeth.)

Mt. 4.15★; 4.25★°; 8.18†°; 8.28†°; 14.22†°; 16.5†°; 19.1★°

Lk. 8.22†*°

367

APPENDIX F

CLEMENT'S QUOTATION OF MK. 10.17–31
(showing contaminations from Mt. and Lk.)

Clement, III.162.19–163.12 (*QDS*, 4.4–10)

ἐκπορευομένου αὐτοῦ εἰς ὁδὸν
προσελθών τις ἐγονυπέτει λέγων·

διδάσκαλε ἀγαθέ, τί ποιήσω,
ἵνα ζωὴν αἰώνιον κληρονομήσω;
ὁ δὲ ᾿Ιησοῦς λέγει·
τί με ἀγαθὸν λέγεις;
οὐδεὶς ἀγαθὸς εἰ μὴ εἷς ὁ Θεός.
τὰς ἐντολὰς οἶδας·
μὴ μοιχεύσῃς, μὴ φονεύσῃς,
μὴ κλέψῃς, μὴ ψευδομαρτυρήσῃς,
τίμα τὸν πατέρα σου καὶ τὴν μητέρα.
ὁ δὲ ἀποκριθεὶς λέγει αὐτῷ·
πάντα ταῦτα ἐφύλαξα.
ὁ δὲ ᾿Ιησοῦς ἐμβλέψας ἠγάπησεν αὐτὸν
καὶ εἶπεν· ἕν σοι ὑστερεῖ
εἰ θέλεις τέλειος εἶναι,
πώλησον ὅσα ἔχεις καὶ διάδος πτωχοῖς,
καὶ ἕξεις θησαυρὸν ἐν οὐρανῷ,
καὶ δεῦρο ἀκολούθει μοι.
ὁ δὲ στυγνάσας ἐπὶ τῷ λόγῳ
ἀπῆλθε λυπούμενος·
ἦν γὰρ ἔχων χρήματα πολλὰ καὶ ἀγρούς.
περιβλεψάμενος δὲ ὁ ᾿Ιησοῦς
λέγει τοῖς μαθηταῖς αὐτοῦ·
πῶς δυσκόλως οἱ τὰ χρήμα⟨τα⟩ ἔχοντες
εἰσελεύσονται εἰς τὴν βασιλείαν τοῦ Θεοῦ.
οἱ δὲ μαθηταὶ ἐθαμβοῦντο ἐπὶ τοῖς λόγοις αὐτοῦ.
πάλιν δὲ ὁ ᾿Ιησοῦς ἀποκριθεὶς λέγει αὐτοῖς·
τέκνα, πῶς δύσκολόν ἐστι
τοὺς πεποιθότας ἐπὶ χρήμασιν

Mk. 10.17–31 (Nestle-Kilpatrick)

καὶ ἐκπορευομένου αὐτοῦ εἰς ὁδὸν
προσδραμὼν εἷς καὶ γονυπετήσας αὐτὸν ἐπηρώτα
αὐτόν,
διδάσκαλε ἀγαθέ, τί ποιήσω
ἵνα ζωὴν αἰώνιον κληρονομήσω;
ὁ δὲ ᾿Ιησοῦς εἶπεν αὐτῷ.
τί με λέγεις ἀγαθόν;
οὐδεὶς ἀγαθὸς εἰ μὴ εἷς ὁ Θεός.
τὰς ἐντολὰς οἶδας.
μὴ φονεύσῃς, μὴ μοιχεύσῃς;
μὴ κλέψῃς, μὴ ψευδομαρτυρήσῃς, μὴ ἀποστερήσῃς,
τίμα τὸν πατέρα σου καὶ τὴν μητέρα.
ὁ δὲ ἔφη αὐτῷ, διδάσκαλε,
ταῦτα πάντα ἐφυλαξάμην ἐκ νεότητός μου.
ὁ δὲ ᾿Ιησοῦς ἐμβλέψας αὐτῷ ἠγάπησεν αὐτὸν
καὶ εἶπεν αὐτῷ, ἕν σε ὑστερεῖ·
ὕπαγε,
ὅσα ἔχεις πώλησον καὶ δὸς τοῖς πτωχοῖς,
καὶ ἕξεις θησαυρὸν ἐν οὐρανῷ,
καὶ δεῦρο ἀκολούθει μοι.
ὁ δὲ στυγνάσας ἐπὶ τῷ λόγῳ
ἀπῆλθεν λυπούμενος,
ἦν γὰρ ἔχων κτήματα πολλά.
καὶ περιβλεψάμενος ὁ ᾿Ιησοῦς
λέγει τοῖς μαθηταῖς αὐτοῦ.
πῶς δυσκόλως οἱ τὰ χρήματα ἔχοντες
εἰς τὴν βασιλείαν τοῦ Θεοῦ εἰσελεύσονται.
οἱ δὲ μαθηταὶ ἐθαμβοῦντο ἐπὶ τοῖς λόγοις αὐτοῦ.
ὁ δὲ ᾿Ιησοῦς πάλιν ἀποκριθεὶς λέγει αὐτοῖς.
τέκνα, πῶς δύσκολόν ἐστιν

εἰς τὴν βασιλείαν τοῦ Θεοῦ εἰσελθεῖν·
εὐκόλως διὰ τῆς τρυμαλιᾶς τῆς βελόνης
κάμηλος εἰσελεύσεται
ἢ πλούσιος εἰς τὴν βασιλείαν τοῦ Θεοῦ.
οἳ δὲ περισσῶς ἐξεπλήσσοντο καὶ ἔλεγον·

τίς οὖν δύναται σωθῆναι;
ὁ δὲ ἐμβλέψας αὐτοῖς εἶπεν·
ὅτι παρὰ ἀνθρώποις ἀδύνατον, παρὰ Θεῷ δύνατον.

ἤρξατο ὁ Πέτρος λέγειν αὐτῷ·
ἴδε ἡμεῖς ἀφήκαμεν πάντα καὶ ἠκολουθήσαμέν σοι.

ἀποκριθεὶς δὲ ὁ Ἰησοῦς λέγει:
ἀμὴν ὑμῖν λέγω, ὃς ἂν ἀφῇ τὰ ἴδια
καὶ γονεῖς καὶ ἀδελφοὺς καὶ χρήματα

ἕνεκεν ἐμοῦ καὶ ἕνεκεν τοῦ εὐαγγελίου,
ἀπολήψεται ἑκατονταπλασίονα.
νῦν ἐν τῷ καιρῷ τούτῳ
ἀγροὺς καὶ χρήματα καὶ οἰκίας καὶ ἀδελφοὺς

ἔχειν μετὰ διωγμῶν εἰς ποῦ;
ἐν δὲ τῷ ἐρχομένῳ ζωή[ν] ἐστιν αἰώνιος.
[ἐν δὲ] ἔσονται οἱ πρῶτοι ἔσχατοι
καὶ οἱ ἔσχατοι πρῶτοι.

εἰς τὴν βασιλείαν τοῦ Θεοῦ εἰσελθεῖν·
εὐκοπώτερόν ἐστιν κάμηλον
διὰ τῆς τρυμαλιᾶς τῆς ῥαφίδος διελθεῖν
ἢ πλούσιον εἰς τὴν βασιλείαν τοῦ Θεοῦ εἰσελθεῖν.
οἱ δὲ περισσῶς ἐξεπλήσσοντο λέγοντες πρὸς ἑαυτούς,

καὶ τίς δύναται σωθῆναι;
ἐμβλέψας αὐτοῖς ὁ Ἰησοῦς λέγει, παρὰ ἀνθρώποις
ἀδύνατον, ἀλλ᾽ οὐ παρὰ Θεῷ·
πάντα γὰρ δυνατὰ παρὰ τῷ Θεῷ
ἤρξατο λέγειν ὁ Πέτρος αὐτῷ,
ἰδοὺ ἡμεῖς ἀφήκαμεν πάντα καὶ ἠκολουθήκαμέν σοι.

ἔφη ὁ Ἰησοῦς
ἀμὴν λέγω ὑμῖν, οὐδείς ἐστιν ὃς ἀφῆκεν
οἰκίαν ἢ ἀδελφοὺς ἢ ἀδελφὰς ἢ μητέρα ἢ πατέρα
ἢ τέκνα ἢ ἀγροὺς
ἕνεκεν ἐμοῦ καὶ ἕνεκεν τοῦ εὐαγγελίου,
ἐὰν μὴ λάβῃ ἑκατονταπλασίονα
νῦν ἐν τῷ καιρῷ τούτῳ
οἰκίας καὶ ἀδελφοὺς καὶ ἀδελφὰς καὶ μητέρας
καὶ τέκνα καὶ ἀγροὺς
μετὰ διωγμῶν,
καὶ ἐν τῷ αἰῶνι τῷ ἐρχομένῳ ζωὴν αἰώνιον.
πολλοὶ δὲ ἔσονται πρῶτοι ἔσχατοι
καὶ οἱ ἔσχατοι πρῶτοι.

Clement agrees with either Mt. or Lk. or both in the readings underlined in his text and in omission of the words underlined in the text of Mk.

APPENDIX G

TYPE, FREQUENCY, AND DISTRIBUTION OF PARALLELS

The purpose of this appendix is to indicate graphically the parallels to individual phrases (*not* single words) by underlining the phrases paralleled. To prevent the indications from becoming uselessly complex, it has been necessary to neglect many possible distinctions between different kinds of parallels. Two kinds are of chief importance for our purpose: verbatim parallels, which suggest literary dependence and should therefore be noted even when isolated; multiple parallels to a single phrase, which show (even when they are not verbatim) that the phrase is commonplace in the usage of the author whose work furnishes the parallels. But if a phrase is commonplace, there is little need to indicate which of the parallels are verbatim, which are not. Accordingly, the following charts show (1) single, verbatim parallels, and (2) multiple parallels, whether verbatim or only approximate.

(1) Single parallels are not noted unless read by Nestle-Kilpatrick. When they are noted, the chapter and verse are specified after the underlining. The requirement that they be verbatim has usually been taken to mean not only the same words, but also the same number, gender, case, etcetera; the differences most often tolerated have been those of word order, and these have usually been marked by v.v. (= *vice versa*). Sometimes the requirement of exactitude has been slightly misrepresentative; thus in section III (parallels to Mk. 1.29–32) ἤγειρεν αὐτήν appears as unparalleled because its single parallels in Mk. 9.27 and Jn. 12.17 read ἤγειρεν αὐτόν; again in section V (Mt. 9.27–34) ἐν ὅλῃ τῇ γῇ ἐκείνῃ appears as only partially paralleled because Mt. 9.31 has εἰς ὅλην, and so on. To make up for such cases, not infrequently a series of exact parallels interrupted by different details has been indicated by a series of solid lines under the elements paralleled, connected by dotted lines under the differing elements; thus γυνὴ ἧς ὁ ἀδελφὸς αὐτῆς ἀπέθανεν· καὶ ἐλθοῦσα (Mk. 7.25) indicates that Mk. has verbatim the words solidly underlined, but has different (though functionally equivalent) words in places indicated by the dotted lines. Single parallels produced by direct synoptic copying have been excluded as irrelevant. This, too, sometimes has curious consequences: Thus εἰς τοὺς χοίρους in Mk. 5.12 appears with three single parallels, Mt. 8.32, Mk. 5.13 and Lk. 8.33; when the same phrase recurs in Mk. 5.13 it has only one parallel because this time the ones from Mt. and Lk. are the synoptic counterparts.

(2) When a phrase has multiple parallels in any one Gospel, only the number of parallels in that Gospel is given. Here approximate as well as verbatim ones have been counted, and all instances listed by Moulton-Geden have been included,

regardless alike of their textual support and of whether or not they stand in passages synoptically parallel. The statements made at the beginning of Chapter Three, section II, as to the difficulty of searching a concordance for parallels, and the consequent expectable inaccuracy of the data, should be recalled. In this appendix the numbers of the multiple parallels reported for the longer text will be slightly higher than the numbers of those reported for the canonical passages, because the phrases of the longer text were hunted more carefully and also because the hunt for them took into account the major variant readings recorded by Legg, whose editions were not consulted for the canonical passages.

I. THE LONGER TEXT OF MK., FIRST QUOTATION:

καὶ ἔρχονται εἰς Βηθανίαν   καὶ ἦν ἐκεῖ   μία γυνὴ ἧς ὁ ἀδελφὸς αὐτῆς
_____ Mk. 6/7[1]   _____ Mk. 3.1   _____
_____ Mk. 4   _____ Mt. 2.15

ἀπέθανεν· καὶ ἐλθοῦσα προσεκύνησε τὸν Ἰησοῦν, καὶ λέγει αὐτῷ·   υἱὲ Δαβὶδ
_____ _____ Mk. 7.25   _____ Mk. 8   _____
     _____ Mk. 5   _____ Mt. 6/7 _____
     _____ Mt. 12   _____
     _____ Lk. 5
         _____ Mt. 6

ἐλέησόν με.   οἱ δὲ μαθηταὶ ἐπετίμησαν αὐτῇ.   καὶ ὀργισθεὶς ὁ Ἰησοῦς
_____ Mk. 2 _____ Mk. 10.13 _____ Mt. 18.34
_____ Mt. 4 _____ Mt. 19.13
_____ Lk. 2 _____ Mk. 2/3
         _____ Mt. 4

ἀπῆλθεν μετ' αὐτῆς   εἰς τὸν κῆπον ὅπου ἦν τὸ μνημεῖον· καὶ εὐθὺς ἠκούσθη
_____ Mk. 5.24   _____ Mk. 2   _____ Mk. 25
     _____ Jn. 6   _____ Mt. 2

ἐκ τοῦ μνημείου   φωνὴ μεγάλη·   καὶ προσελθὼν ὁ Ἰησοῦς
_____ Jn. 3 _____ Mk. 4   _____ Mt. 28.18
     _____ Mt. 2/3 _____ Mk. 1/2
     _____ Lk. 6 _____ Mt. 4/6
     _____ Jn. 11.43 _____ Lk. 2

ἀπεκύλισε τὸν λίθον ἀπὸ   τῆς θύρας τοῦ μνημείου,   καὶ εἰσελθὼν εὐθὺς
_____ Mt. 28.2   _____ Mk. 6/8
_____ Mk. 16.3 _____ Mt. 26.58
         _____ Lk. 4

1. Means "6 or 7"; so hereafter, throughout Appendix G.

ὅπου ἦν ὁ νεανίσκος ἐξέτεινεν τὴν χεῖρα καὶ   ἤγειρεν αὐτόν,
_____ Mk. 2   _____ Mk. 3/4 _____ Mk. 2
_____ Jn. 6   _____ Mt. 6
                       _____ Lk. 3/5

κρατήσας τῆς χειρός. ὁ δὲ νεανίσκος ἐμβλέψας αὐτῷ ἠγάπησεν αὐτόν,
_____ Mk. 2/3   _____ Mk. 10.21
_____ Lk. 8.54   _____ Mk. 2

καὶ ἤρξατο   παρακαλεῖν αὐτὸν   ἵνα μετ' αὐτοῦ ᾖ·
_____ Mk. 10 _____ Mk. 5.17 _____ Mk. 2
_____ Lk. 4

καὶ ἐξελθόντες ἐκ τοῦ μνημείου, ἦλθον εἰς τὴν οἰκίαν τοῦ νεανίσκου·
_____ Mk. 3   _____ Mk. 1.29
_____ Mt. 3/4   _____ Mt. 6
                 _____ Jn. 3

ἦν γὰρ πλούσιος.   καὶ μεθ' ἡμέρας ἓξ   ἐπέταξεν αὐτῷ ὁ Ἰησοῦς
_____ Lk. 18.23 _____ Mk. 9.2
____ Mk. 5
____ Mt. 3
____ Lk. 2
____ Jn. 4

καὶ ὀψίας γενομένης ἔρχεται ὁ νεανίσκος πρὸς αὐτὸν περιβεβλημένος σινδόνα
_____ Mk. 14.17   _____
_____ Mk. 3
_____ Mt. 6
_____ Mt. 2
          _____------------_____ Mk. 6/8

ἐπὶ γυμνοῦ   καὶ ἔμεινε σὺν αὐτῷ τὴν νύκτα ἐκείνην, ἐδίδασκεν γὰρ
_____ Mk. 14.51   _____ Mk. 9.31

αὐτὸν ὁ Ἰησοῦς τὸ μυστήριον τῆς βασιλείας τοῦ Θεοῦ.
          _____ Mk. 4.11
          _____ Mt. 4
          _____ Mk. 14
          _____ Lk. 31

ἐκεῖθεν δὲ ἀναστὰς   ἐπέστρεψεν εἰς τὸ πέραν τοῦ Ἰορδάνου.
_____ Mk. 7.24 _____ Lk. 2.39
                             _____ Mk. 5
                             _____ Mt. 4
                             _____ Lk. 3
                                         _____ Mk. 2
                                         _____ Mt. 3
                                         _____ Jn. 3

II.   The longer text of Mk., second quotation:

καὶ ἦσαν ἐκεῖ ἡ ἀδελφὴ τοῦ νεανίσκου ὃν ἠγάπα αὐτὸν ὁ Ἰησοῦς
                             _____------_____ Jn. 4

καὶ ἡ μήτηρ αὐτοῦ   καὶ Σαλώμη   καὶ οὐκ ἀπεδέξατο αὐτὰς ὁ Ἰησοῦς.
_____ Mk. 3.31 _____ Mk. 2
_____ Mt. 13.55
_____ Lk. 3/4
_____ Jn. 3

III.   Mk. 1.29–32, "Peter's wife's mother":

καὶ εὐθὺς ἐκ τῆς συναγωγῆς ἐξελθόντες ἦλθον   εἰς τὴν οἰκίαν
_____ Mk. 25   _____ Mt. 8.32 _____ Mt. 5
_____ Mt. 2   _____ Mk. 2
                                         _____ Lk. 6

Σίμωνος καὶ Ἀνδρέου μετὰ Ἰακώβου καὶ Ἰωάννου. ἡ δὲ πενθερὰ
                           _____ Mk. 4
                           _____ Lk. 3

Σίμωνος κατέκειτο πυρέσσουσα. καὶ εὐθὺς   λέγουσιν αὐτῷ
              _____ Mk. 25 _____ Mt. 12
              _____ Mt. 2 _____ Mk. 9
                            _____ Lk. 17.37

περὶ αὐτῆς.   καὶ προσελθὼν   ἤγειρεν αὐτὴν κρατήσας τῆς χειρός.
_____ Jn. 8.5 _____ Mk. 6   _____ Mk. 2
                   _____ Lk. 2   _____ Lk. 8.54

καὶ ἀφῆκεν αὐτὴν ὁ πυρετός καὶ διηκόνει αὐτοῖς.

IV. Mκ. 5.1–16, the Gerasene demoniac:

καὶ ἦλθον εἰς τὸ   πέραν τῆς θαλάσσης   εἰς τὴν χώραν τῶν Γερασηνῶν.
———— Mt. 21.1 ————————— Jn. 3 ———— Mt. 2
———— Mk. 5.14 ————————————— Jn. 11.54
———————— Mk. 2
          ———————— Mt. 4
          ———————— Mk. 4
          ———————— Lk. 3

καὶ ἐξελθόντος αὐτοῦ   ἐκ τοῦ πλοίου, εὐθὺς   ὑπήντησεν αὐτῷ
-- Mk. 6.54 ————————— Jn. 3
     ———— Lk. 11.53———————— Lk. 5.3

ἐκ τῶν μνημείων   ἄνθρωπος ἐν πνεύματι ἀκαθάρτῳ, ὃς τὴν κατοίκησιν εἶχεν
————————— Mt. 2——————————————— Mk. 1.23
            ———————— Mt. 3
            ———————— Lk. 4
                ———————— Mk. 9
                ———————— Mt. 10.1
                ———————— Lk. 2

ἐν τοῖς μνήμασιν   καὶ οὐδὲ ἁλύσει οὐκέτι οὐδεὶς ἐδύνατο αὐτὸν δῆσαι,
———————— Mk. 5.5 ———— Mk. 3 ———— Mk. 3
                    ———————— Mt. 22.46
                    ——————— Jn. 5

διὰ τὸ αὐτὸν πολλάκις πέδαις καὶ ἁλύσεσιν δεδέσθαι, καὶ διεσπάσθαι ὑπ' αὐτοῦ τὰς ἁλύσεις
——— (c. inf.) Mt. 3   ———————— Mt. 2
——— (c. inf.) Mk. 2   ———————— Mk. 1.5
——— (c. inf.) Lk. 8   ———————— Lk. 6

καὶ τὰς πέδας συντετρίφθαι, καὶ οὐδεὶς ἴσχυσεν αὐτὸν δαμάσαι. καὶ διὰ παντὸς νυκτὸς καὶ
         ———————— Mt. 4   ———————Mt. 18.10
         ———————— Mk. 2   ———————— Lk. 24.53
         ———————— Lk. 6

ἡμέρας ἐν τοῖς μνήμασιν καὶ ἐν τοῖς ὄρεσιν ἦν κράζων καὶ κατακόπτων ἑαυτὸν λίθοις.
         ———————— Mk. 5.3
         ———————— Lk. 8.27

καὶ ἰδὼν τὸν Ἰησοῦν ἀπὸ μακρόθεν ἔδραμεν καὶ προσεκύνησεν αὐτόν.

———— Mt. 8   ———— Mt. 2   ———— Jn. 9.38

———— Mk. 7   ———— Mk. 4

———— Lk. 6   ———— Lk. 2

καὶ κράξας φωνῇ μεγάλῃ λέγει·   τί ἐμοὶ καὶ σοί, Ἰησοῦ υἱὲ τοῦ Θεοῦ τοῦ ὑψίστου;

———— Mk. 9.26   ———— Jn. 2.4

———— Mt. 27.50 ————————— Mk. 1.24

———— Mt. 2   ————————— Lk. 2

———— Mk. 2

———— Lk. 5

ὁρκίζω σε τὸν Θεόν, μή με βασανίσῃς. ἔλεγεν γὰρ αὐτῷ,

———————— Mt. 14.5

———— Mt. 9.21

———— Mk. 4

———————— Mk. 7

——————— Lk. 3

ἔξελθε τὸ πνεῦμα τὸ ἀκάθαρτον ἐκ τοῦ ἀνθρώπου. καὶ ἐπηρώτα αὐτόν, τί ὄνομά σοι;

—————————————————— Mk. 2 (exorcisms) ———————— Mk. 14

———————— Mk. 6   ———————— Lk. 4

———————— Lk. 2

———————— Mk. 2

καὶ λέγει αὐτῷ, Λεγιὼν ὄνομά μοι, ὅτι πολλοί ἐσμεν. καὶ παρεκάλει αὐτὸν πολλὰ ἵνα μὴ

———————— Mt. 7   ———————————— Mk. 5.23

———————— Mk. 7   ———————— Mt. 2

———————— Lk. 3

———————————— Mk. 2

αὐτὰ ἀποστείλῃ ἔξω τῆς χώρας. ἦν δὲ ἐκεῖ πρὸς τῷ ὄρει ἀγέλη χοίρων μεγάλη βοσκομένη·

———— Mt. 27.61

———— Jn. 2

καὶ παρεκάλεσαν αὐτὸν λέγοντες, πέμψον ἡμᾶς εἰς τοὺς χοίρους

———————————— Mt. 6   ———————— Mt. 8.32

———————————— Mk. 12.18   ———————— Mk. 5.13

———————————— Lk. 2   ———————— Lk. 8.33

ἵνα εἰς αὐτοὺς εἰσέλθωμεν. καὶ ἐπέτρεψεν αὐτοῖς.

καὶ ἐξελθόντα   τὰ πνεύματα τὰ ἀκάθαρτα εἰσῆλθον εἰς τοὺς χοίρους, καὶ ὥρμησεν ἡ

—————— Mt. 9 —————————— Mk. 6 —————— Mk. 5.12

—————— Mk. 7 —————————— Lk. 2

—————— Lk. 2

ἀγέλη κατὰ τοῦ κρημνοῦ εἰς τὴν θάλασσαν, ὡς δισχίλιοι, καὶ ἐπνίγοντο

ἐν τῇ θαλάσσῃ. καὶ οἱ βόσκοντες αὐτοὺς ἔφυγον καὶ ἀπήγγειλαν

—————— Mt. 8.24   —————— Mk. 6.30

—————— Mk. 2   —————— Lk. 2

—————— Lk. 17.6

εἰς τὴν πόλιν   καὶ εἰς τοὺς ἀγρούς·   καὶ ἦλθον ἰδεῖν   τί ἐστιν

—————— Mt. 6 —————— Lk. 15.15 —————— Mt. 21.1 —————— Mt. 3

—————— Mk. 2 ——--- —————— Mk. 2   —————— Mk. 3 —————— Mk. 2

—————— Lk. 2   —————— Lk. 2

τὸ γεγονός.   καὶ ἔρχονται πρὸς τὸν Ἰησοῦν, καὶ θεωροῦσιν τὸν δαιμονιζόμενον καθή-

—————— Lk. 4 —————————— Mk. 2

—————— Mk. 9

μενον ἱματισμένον καὶ σωφρονοῦντα, τὸν ἐσχκότα τὸν Λεγιῶνα, καὶ ἐφοβήθησαν.

                                                 —————— Mk. 4.41

                                                 —————— Lk. 2.9

                                                 —————— Jn. 6.19

V. Mt. 9.27–34, THE TWO BLIND MEN AND THE DUMB DEMONIAC:

καὶ παράγοντι ἐκεῖθεν τῷ Ἰησοῦ ἠκολούθησαν δύο τυφλοὶ

—————-------- —————-------- Mt. 9.9   —————— Mt. 20.30

—————— Mk. 2 —————————— Jn. 1.37 (v.v.)

κράζοντες καὶ λέγοντες,   ἐλέησον ἡμᾶς, υἱὸς Δανειδ.

—————— Mt. 7 —————————— Mt. 4

—————— Mk. 4 —————————— Mk. 2

—————— Jn. 2 —————————— Lk. 2

ἐλθόντι δὲ εἰς τὴν οἰκίαν   προσῆλθον αὐτῷ οἱ τυφλοί,

—————————— Mt. 4 —————————--- —————— Mt. 21.14

—————— Mt. 6 —————— Mt. 14

—————— Mk. 3 —————— Mk. 2

—————— Lk. 6

καὶ λέγει αὐτοῖς ὁ Ἰησοῦς   πιστεύετε ὅτι δύναμαι τοῦτο ποιῆσαι;
_____ Mt. 13 _____ Mk. 11.24
_____ Mk. 3   _____ Mt. 26.53
_____ Jn. 26

λέγουσιν αὐτῷ, ναί, κύριε. τότε ἥψατο τῶν ὀφθαλμῶν αὐτῶν λέγων,
_____ Mt. 2   _____ Mt. 20.34
_____ Jn. 3
_____ _____ Mk. 7.28

κατὰ τὴν πίστιν ὑμῶν γενηθήτω ὑμῖν.   καὶ ἠνεῴχθησαν αὐτῶν οἱ ὀφθαλμοί.
_____ _____ Mt. 2 _____ Jn. 6
                                        _____ Lk. 24.31

καὶ ἐνεβριμήθη αὐτοῖς   ὁ Ἰησοῦς λέγων,   ὁρᾶτε μηδεὶς γινωσκέτω.
_____ Mk. 2 _____ Mt. 3   _____ Mt. 4
                _____ Mk. 1.25 _____ Mk. 8.15
                _____ Lk. 2   _____ Lk. 12.15
                                        _____ Mk. 5.43

οἱ δὲ ἐξελθόντες διεφήμισαν αὐτὸν ἐν ὅλῃ τῇ γῇ ἐκείνῃ. αὐτῶν δὲ ἐξερχομένων
_____ Mt. 8.32   _____ Mt. 4.23
                _____ Lk. 2

ἰδοὺ προσήνεγκαν αὐτῷ   κωφὸν δαιμονιζόμενον καὶ ἐκβληθέντος
_____ Mt. 9.2 _____ Mt. 12.22 (v.v.)
_____ Mt. 7

τοῦ δαιμονίου ἐλάλησεν ὁ κωφός. καὶ ἐθαύμασαν οἱ ὄχλοι λέγοντες,
_____ Lk. 11.41
                _____ _____ Mt. 21.20

οὐδέποτε ἐφάνη οὕτως   ἐν τῷ Ἰσραηλ.   οἱ δὲ φαρισαῖοι ἔλεγον,
_____ _____ Mk. 2.12 _____ Mt. 8.10 _____ Mt. 9.11
        (v.v.)   _____ Lk. 4   ____ _____ Mk. 2.24
                                _____ Mt. 12.2
                                _____ Lk. 7.30

ἐν τῷ ἄρχοντι τῶν δαιμονίων ἐκβάλλει τὰ δαιμόνια.
_____ Mk. 3.22
_____ Lk. 11.15
_____ Mt. 12.24 (v.v.)

VI. Formulas in the *Iliad*, A.1–25, from Parry, *Studies* 118–119:

ΙΛΙΑΔΟΣ Α

Μῆνιν¹ ἄειδε θεὰ Πηληϊάδεω Ἀχιλῆος²

οὐλομένην ἥ³ μυρί'⁴ Ἀχαιοῖς ἄλγε' ἔθηκε,⁵

πολλὰς δ' ἰφθίμους ψυχὰς Ἄιδι προίαψεν⁶

ἡρώων, αὐτοὺς δὲ⁷ ἑλώρια τεῦχε κύνεσσιν

οἰωνοῖσί τε πᾶσι, Διὸς δ' ἐτελείετο βουλή⁸   5

ἐξ οὗ δή⁹ τὰ πρῶτα διαστήτην ἐρίσαντε

Ἀτρείδης τε¹⁰ ἄναξ ἀνδρῶν¹¹ καὶ δῖος Ἀχιλλεύς.¹²

   Τίς τ' ἄρ σφωε θεῶν ἔριδι¹³ ξυνέηκε μάχεσθαι;¹⁴

Λητοῦς καὶ Διὸς υἱός· ὁ γὰρ βασιλῆι χολωθείς¹⁵

νοῦσον ἀνὰ στρατὸν ὦρσε¹⁶ κακήν, ὀλέκοντο δὲ λαοί¹⁷   10

οὕνεκα τὸν Χρύσην ἠτίμασεν ἀρητῆρα

Ἀτρείδης· ὁ γὰρ ἦλθε θοὰς ἐπὶ νῆας Ἀχαιῶν¹⁸

λυσόμενός τε θύγατρα φέρων τ' ἀπερείσι' ἄποινα¹⁹

στέμμα τ' ἔχων ἐν χερσὶν²⁰ ἑκηβόλου Ἀπόλλωνος²¹

χρυσέωι ἀνὰ σκήπτρωι²² καὶ λίσσετο πάντας Ἀχαιούς,²³   = A 372–5   15

Ἀτρείδα δὲ μάλιστα²⁴ δύω κοσμήτορε λαῶν·²⁵

Ἀτρείδαι τε καὶ ἄλλοι²⁶ ἐυκνήμιδες Ἀχαιοί,²⁷   = Ψ 272, 658.

ὑμῖν μὲν θεοὶ δοῖεν Ὀλύμπια δώματ' ἔχοντες²⁸

---

¹ Cf. μῆνιν ἀλευάμενος ἑκατηβόλου Ἀπόλλωνος Π 711.   ² Πηληϊάδεω Ἀχιλῆος A 322, I 166, Π 269, 653, Ω 406, λ 467, ω 15.   ³ οὐλομένην ἧι E 876, ρ 287, 474.   ⁴ Cf. μυρί' Ὀδυσσεὺς ἐσθλὰ ἔοργε B 272. ⁵ ἄλγε' ἔθηκε Χ 422.   ⁶ πολλὰς ἰφθίμους κεφαλὰς (v l. ψυχὰς) Ἄιδι προίαψειν Λ 55; Ἄιδι προϊάψει Ζ 487. ⁷ Cf. ἡρώων τοῖσίν τε E 747, Θ 391, a 101.   ⁸ Διὸς δ' ἐτελείετο βουλή λ 297.   ⁹ ἐξ οὗ δή ξ 379. ¹⁰ Ἀτρείδης δέ Γ 271, 361, I 89, N 610, T 252, δ 304.   ¹¹ ἄναξ ἀνδρῶν A 172, 442, B 402, 441, 612, Γ 81, 267, 455, Δ 148, 255, 336, E 38, Z 33, 37, 162, 314, Θ 278, I 114, 672, K 64, 86, 103, 119, 233, Λ 99, 254, Ξ 64, 103, 134, Σ 111, T 51, 76, 172, 184, Ψ 161, 895, θ 77.   ¹² καὶ δῖος Ἀχιλλεύς A 7, Υ 160; δῖος Ἀχιλλεύς A 121, 292, B 688, E 788, Z 414, 423, I 199, 209, 667, Λ 599, Ο 68, Π 5, P 402, Σ 181, 228, 305, 343, T 40, 364, 384, Υ 177, 386, 388, 413, 445, Φ 39, 49, 67, 149, 161, 265, 359, Χ 102, 172, 205, 326, 330, 364, 376, 455, Ψ 136, 140, 193, 333, 534, 555, 828, 889, Ω 151, 180, 513, 596, 668.   ¹³ θεῶν ἔριδι Υ 66.   ¹⁴ ξυνέηκε μάχεσθαι Η 210.   ¹⁵ καὶ Διὸς υἷι Χ 302.   ¹⁶ Cf. ἀνὰ στρατόν εἰσι Κ 66.   ¹⁷ Cf. ἀρετῶσι δὲ λαοί τ 114; δαινῦτό τε λαὸς Ω 665; etc.   ¹⁸ ἦλθε θοὰς ἐπὶ νῆας Ἀχαιῶν A 371; θοὰς ἐπὶ νῆας Ἀχαιῶν B 8, 17, 168, Ζ 52, Κ 450, 514, Λ 3, Ω 564; θοὴν ἐπὶ νῆα γ 347, κ 244.   ¹⁹ λυσόμενος . . . φέρω δ' ἀπερείσι' ἄποινα Ω 502; ἀπερείσι' ἄποινα A 372, Ζ 49, 427, I 120, Κ 380, Λ 134, T 138, Ω 276, 502, 579. ²⁰ ἔχων ἐν χειρί Θ 221, Ξ 385.   ²¹ ἑκηβόλωι Ἀπόλλωνι A 438, Π 513, Ψ 872.   ²² Cf. χρυσέωι ἐν δαπέδωι Δ 2; χρυσέωι ἐν δέπαι Ω 285.   ²³ πάντας Ἀχαιούς A 374, Γ 68, 88, Η 49, Θ 498, I 75, Ξ 124, Ψ 815, γ 137, 141, δ 288, ω 49, 438.   ²⁴ Cf. Αἴαντι δὲ μάλιστα Ξ 459.   ²⁵ κοσμήτορε λαῶν Γ 236. ²⁶ Cf. Ἀτρείδη τε καὶ ἄλλοι ἀριστῆες Παναχαιῶν Η 327.   ²⁷ καὶ ἄλλοι ἐυκνήμιδες Ἀχαιοί Ξ 49; ἐυκνήμιδες Ἀχαιοί B 331, Δ 414, Ζ 529, Η 57, 172, Μ 141, N 51, Σ 151, T 74, Ψ 721, Ω 800, β 72, γ 149, σ 259. ²⁸ Ὀλύμπια δώματ' ἔχοντες B 13, 30, 67, E 383, Ο 115, υ 79, ψ 167.

ἐκπέρσαι Πριάμοιο πόλιν,²⁹ εὖ δ' οἴκαδ' ἱκέσθαι·³⁰

παῖδα δ' ἐμοὶ λύσαιτε φίλην, τὰ δ' ἄποινα δέχεσθαι   20

ἁζόμενοι³¹ Διὸς υἱὸν ἑκηβόλον Ἀπόλλωνα.³²

"Ενθ' ἄλλοι μὲν πάντες³³ ἐπευφήμησαν Ἀχαιοί³⁴

αἰδεῖσθαί θ' ἱερῆα καὶ ἀγλαά δέχθαι ἄποινα·   } = A 376–9

ἀλλ' οὐκ³⁵ Ἀτρείδηι Ἀγαμέμνονι³⁶ ἥνδανε θυμῶι,³⁷

ἀλλὰ κακῶς ἀφίει, κρατερὸν δ' ἐπὶ μῦθον ἔτελλε.³⁸   25

---

²⁹ Πριάμοιο πόλιν Σ 288, Χ 165, γ 130, λ 533, ν 316.   ³⁰ οἴκαδ' ἱκέσθαι Ι 393, 414, Ω 287, ι 530, ο 66, 210, φ 211, χ 35.   ³¹ Cf. εὐχόμενος δ' ἄρα εἶπεν ἑκηβόλωι Ἀπόλλωνι Π 513.   ³² Διὸς υἷι ἑκηβόλωι Χ 302; ἑκήβολον Ἀπόλλωνα Α 438, Π 513, Ψ 872.   ³³ ἔνθ' ἄλλοι μὲν πάντες Ω 25, α 11, β 82, δ 285, ε 110, 133, θ 93, 532, ρ 503.   ³⁴ Cf. ἀφορμηθεῖεν Ἀχαιοί Β 794; ἐφοπλίζωμεν Ἀχαιοί Δ 344; etc.   ³⁵ Cf. οὐδ' ἄρ' ἔτ' Αἴαντι μεγαλήτορι ἥνδανε θυμῶι Ο 674.   ³⁶ Ἀτρείδεω Ἀγαμέμνονος Β 185, Λ 231, ι 263.   ³⁷ ἥνδανε θυμῶι Ο 674, κ 373.   ³⁸ κρατερὸν δ' ἐπὶ μῦθον ἔτελλε Α 326, Π 199.

THE VOCABULARY OF THE TEXT

Words are cited by the plate and line on which they begin. Three classes are distinguished: words from the heading, words from the letter of Clement, and words from the quotations of the secret Gospel. The lemmata "Heading," "Letter," and "SG" indicate these three classes. Note that the words listed as "Letter" thus include those of all the quotations in the text except the ones from the secret Gospel. Words from quotations are followed in parentheses by the source of the quotation, thus: ἀστήρ Letter: I.3 (Jude 13). This is done even when the letter quotes the source in a form not now preserved, so that some of the words in the quotation are not to be found in the presently accepted text of the source given, thus: καί Letter: I.14 (Lk. 14.34), though Lk. has δέ instead of καί. When the letters C and A precede a listing, they indicate that the word appears in Stählin's index to Clement and in Müller's *Lexicon Athanasianum*, respectively. When numbers follow these letters, they indicate the numbers of usages reported; these are not given unless one or the other index reported 5 or under.

C6	A3	ἄβυσσος	Letter: I.4
C	A	ἀγαπάω	SG: III.4; III.15
C	A	ἅγιος	Letter: II.8
C1	A42	ἁγιώτατος	**Heading: I.1**
C	A	ἀδελφή	SG: III.15
C	A	ἀδελφός	SG: II.23
C9	A2	ἄδυτον	Letter: I.26
C	A	αἴρω	Letter: II.16 (Mt. 25.29)
C	A	ἀκούω	SG: III.1
C	A	ἀκροατής	Letter: I.25
C2	A2	ἅλας[1]	Letter: I.14 (Lk. 14.34)
C	A	Ἀλεξάνδρεια	Letter: I.19; II.1; II.5
C	A	ἀλήθεια	Letter: I.9 (bis); I.10; I.11; I.26; II.15
C	A	ἀληθής	Letter: I.8; I.9; I.10; I.12; I.13; II.13; II.13 (Philo, *Questions ... on Genesis* IV.67); III.18 (bis)

1. ἅλας is not cited by Stählin, but is used by Clement, I.281.25; III.183.23.

C	A	ἀληθῶς	Letter: I.13
C	A	ἀλλά	Letter: I.17; I.24; II.12
C	A	ἄλλος	Letter: I.24; III.13; III.17
C	A	ἁμαρτία	Letter: I.4
C	A	ἀμέλει	Letter: II.20
C	A	ἄν	Letter: I.9
C	A	ἀναβαίνω	Letter: II.21 (Mk. 10.32)
C	A	ἀναγινώσκω	Letter: II.1
C	A	ἀναγράφω	Letter: I.16
–	–	ἀναιδέστατος²	Letter: II.8
C4	–	ἀναμίγνυμι	Letter: II.8
C	A	ἀνατολή	Letter: II.17
C1	–	ἀνδραποδώδης	Letter: I.7
C	A	ἀνθίστημι	Letter: I.7
C	A	ἀνθρώπινος	Letter: I.10
C	A	ἄνθρωπος	Letter: II.3
C	A	ἀνίστημι	Letter: II.22 (Mk. 10.34)
			SG: III.10
C	A	ἅπας	Letter: II.12 (Philo, *Q.G.* IV.67)
C10	–	ἀπατηλός	Letter: II.4
–	–	ἀπέρατος³	Letter: I.4
C2	A60	ἀπέρχομαι	*SG: II.26*
C	A	ἀπό	Letter: I.3
			SG: III.2
–	–	ἀπόγραφον	Letter: II.6
C	A	ἀποδέχομαι	*SG: III.16*
C	A	ἀποθνῄσκω	Letter: I.28
			SG: II.23
C	A	ἀποκρίνω	Letter: II.14 (Prov. 26.5); II.19
–	–	ἀποκυλίω	*SG: III.1*
C15	A1	ἀπόρρητος	Letter: I.22
C15	A4	ἀπορρίπτω	Letter: I.6
–	–	ἀπροφυλάκτως	Letter: I.27
C	A	ἀρνέομαι	Letter: II.12
C	A	ἄρρητος	Letter: I.2
C	A	ἄρχω	*SG: III.5*
C	A	ἀστήρ	Letter: I.3 (Jude 13)
C1	A5	ἀσφαλῶς	Letter: II.1
C	A	αὔξησις	Letter: I.17
C100 +⁴	A2	αὐτίκα	Letter: II.15

2. A has the absolute only, 4 times; C has absolute and comparative, 7 times.

3. A has ἀπέραντος, i.e. *infinitum*, 3 times; C has it once and ἀπεράτωτος once.

4. Entries are marked + when Stählin gives only the number of instances indicated but marks his entry as incomplete.

C	A	αὐτός	Letter: I.9; I.19; I.20; I.22; I.28; II.2; II.4; II.6; II.7; II.11; II.14; (Prov. 26.5); II.20; III.12 (Mk. 10.35)
			SG: II.23; II.24; II.25; II.26; III.3; III.4 (bis); III.5 (bis); III.7; III.8; III.9 (bis); III.15; III.16 (bis)
C	A	ἄχραντος	Letter: II.8
C	A	βάθος	Letter: I.5 (Apoc. 2.24)
C	A	βασιλεία	*SG: III.10*
–	Aı	βηθανία	*SG: II.23*
C	A	βιβλίον	Letter: I.20
C	A	βλάσφημος	Letter: II.7
C	A	γάρ	Letter: I.3; I.5; I.8; I.9; I.13; II.12 (Philo, *Q.G.* IV.67); II.18
			SG: III.6; III.9
C	A	γένος	Letter: II.3
C	A	γίγνομαι	Letter: I.7
			SG: III.7
C	A	γνῶσις	Letter: I.5; I.21
C	A	γοῦν	Letter: I.15
C	A	γράφω	Letter: III.13; III.17
C	A	γυμνός	*SG: III.8*
			SG (Carpocratian version): III.13 (bis)
C	A	γυνή	*SG: II.23*
C	A	Δαβίδ	*SG: II.24*
C	A	δαίμων	Letter: II.3
C	A	δέ	Letter: I.12; I.18; II.2; II.8; II.9; II.16 (Mt. 25.29); II.17; II.18 (II Cor. 3.17); II.21 (Mk. 10.32); III.13; III.14; III.17
			SG: II.25; III.4; III.10
C	A	δεῖ	Letter: II.15
C	A	δή	Letter: I.14
C	A	διά	Letter: II.13 (bis); II.20
C7	A3	διατριβή	Letter: I.15
C	A	διδασκαλία	Letter: I.2; I.23
C	A	διδάσκω	Letter: II.4; II.15
			SG: III.9
C	A	δόγμα	Letter: II.10
C	A	δόξα	Letter: I.10; II.7
C	A	δοῦλος	Letter: I.7
C	A	ἑαυτός	Letter: I.6
C	A	ἐγείρω	*SG: III.3*
C	A	ἐγώ	Letter: I.27
			SG: II.25

C	A	εἰ	Letter: I.8; I.12
C5	A4	εἴκω	Letter II.10
C	A	εἰμί (sum)	Letter: I.7; II.11; II.17; II.21 (Mk. 10.32); III.17
			SG: II.23; II.26; III.3; III.5; III.6; III.14
C	A	εἰς	Letter: I.4; I.5 (bis); I.19; I.20; I.22; I.26; II.21 (Mk. 10.32); III.14 (Mk. 10.46)
			SG: II.23; II.26; III.6; III.11
C	A	εἷς	SG: II.23
C	A	εἰσέρχομαι	SG: III.2
C6	A1	εἰσέτι	Letter: II.1
C	A	ἐκ	**Heading: I.1**
			Letter: I.20; II.14 (Prov. 26.5); II.17
			SG: III.1; III.5
C	A	ἐκεῖ	Letter: II.18 (II Cor. 3.17)
			SG: II.23; III.15
C	A	ἐκεῖθεν	SG: III.10
C	A	ἐκεῖνος[5]	SG: III.9
C	A	ἐκκλησία	Letter: I.28; II.5
C37	A4	ἐκλέγω	Letter: I.17
C	A	ἐκτείνω	SG: III.3
C	A	ἐλέγχω	Letter: II.20
C	A	ἐλεέω	SG: II.25
C	A	ἐλευθερία	Letter: II.18 (II Cor. 3.17)
C	A	ἐλεύθερος	Letter: I.7
–	A1	ἐμβλέπω	SG: III.4
C	A	ἐν	Letter: I.15; I.28; II.5; II.16 (Eccles. 2.14); II.21 (Mk. 10.32)
C1	A2	ἐνσώματος	Letter: I.4
C	A	ἐντολή	Letter: I.3
C	A	ἔξ	SG: III.7
C1	A2	ἐξαγγέλλω	Letter: I.16
C1	–	ἐξαντλέω	Letter: II.9
C	A	ἐξέρχομαι	SG: III.5
C	A	ἐξηγέομαι	Letter: II.7
C12	–	ἐξήγησις	Letter: I.25; III.18
C	A	ἐξῆς	Letter: II.22
C3	A2	ἐξορχέομαι	Letter: I.23
C	A	ἐπάγω	Letter: III.14
C	A	ἐπί	Letter: III.11
			SG: III.8

5. No listing in Müller, *Lexicon*.

C	A	ἐπιθυμία	Letter: I.7
C	A	ἐπικρύπτω	Letter: II.15
C	A	ἐπίσταμαι	Letter: I.25
C	A	ἐπιστολή	**Heading: I.1**
C3	A1	ἐπιστομίζω	Letter: I.2
C	A	ἐπιστρέφω	*SG: III.11*
C1 +	A2	ἐπιτάσσω	*SG: III.7*
C	A	ἐπιτίθημι	Letter: I.24
C4	A10	ἐπιτιμάω	*SG: II.25*
C	A	ἐπιφέρω	Letter: II.22
C	A	ἕπομαι	Letter: III.11
C1	–	ἑπτάκις	Letter: I.26
C12	–	ἐραστής	Letter: I.9
C	A	ἔρχομαι	Letter: III.14 (Mk. 10.46)
			SG: II.23; II.24; III.6; III.7
C	A	ἐρωτάω	Letter: II.19
C	A	ἔτι	Letter: I.24; II.7
C	A	εὖ	Letter: II.1
C	A	εὐαγγέλιον	Letter: I.12; I.21; II.6; II.12; II.20
C	A	εὐθύς	*SG: III.1; III.2*
C	A	εὑρίσκω	Letter: III.13
C	A	ἔχω	Letter: II.16 (Mt. 25.29)
C	A	ἕως	Letter: II.22
C2	–	ζόφος	Letter: I.6 (Jude 13)
C	A	ἡμεῖς	Letter: II.16
C	A	ἡμέρα	Letter: II.22 (Mk. 10.34)
			SG: III.7
C1	A44	Θεόδωρος	**Heading: I.1**
C4	A13	θεόπνευστος	Letter: I.11
C	A	θεός	Letter: II.13
			SG: III.10
C	A	θρυλέω	Letter: I.11
C	A	θύρα	*SG: III.2*
C	A	Ἰάκωβος	Letter: III.12 (Mk. 10.35)
C1	A1	Ἰεριχώ	Letter: III.14 (Mk. 10.46)
C6	A4	Ἰεροσόλυμα[6]	Letter: II.21 (Mk. 10.32)
C1	–	ἱεροφαντικός	Letter: I.23
C	A	Ἰησοῦς	*SG: II.24; II.26; III.1; III.7; III.10;*
			III.15; III.16
C	A	ἵνα	*SG: III.5*
C	A	Ἰορδάνης	*SG: III.11*
C	A	Ἰωάννης	Letter: III.12 (Mk. 10.35)

6. A and C usually use Ἰερουσαλήμ.

C	A	καθαρός	Letter: II.18 (Titus 1.15); II.19 (*ib.*)
C	A	καθώς	Letter: II.10
C	A	καί	Letter: I.4; I.6; I.8 (bis); I.12; I.14 (Lk. 14.34); I.19 (bis); I.24; I.27; II.4; II.6; II.7; II.8 (bis); II.10; II.12; II.16; II.21; III.11 (Mk. 10.35); III.12 (Mk. 10.35); III.12; III.13; III.14 (Mk. 10.46); III.17 (bis); III.18 *SG: II.23 (bis); II.24 (bis); II.25; II.26; III.1; III.2; III.3; III.4; III.5; III.6; III.7; III.8; III.14; III.15; III.16 (bis)*
C	A	καλύπτω	Letter: I.26
C	A	καλῶς	Letter: I.2
C6	A2	Καρποκράτης	Letter: II.3
C2	–	Καρποκρατιανός	Letter: I.2; II.9
C	A	κατά	Letter: I.10; I.11; I.12; I.15; II.7; II.22; III.18
C2	A2	καταγράφω	Letter: I.23
C3	–	καταδουλόω	Letter: II.5
C	A	καταλείπω	Letter: I.28
C	A	κατάλληλος	Letter: I.21
C1	A21	καταψεύδομαι	Letter: II.11; II.20
C	A	κατηχούμενος	Letter: I.18
C	A	καυχάομαι	Letter: I.6
C1	A2	κῆπος	*SG: II.26*
C4	–	Κλήμης	**Heading: I.1**
C	A	κομίζω	Letter: I.19; II.6
C7	–	κρᾶμα	Letter: II.9
C	A	κρατέω	*SG: III.3*
C	A	Κύριος	Letter: I.16; I.24; II.18; II.18 (II Cor. 3.17)
C	A	λανθάνω	Letter: I.5
C	A	λέγω	Letter: I.5 (Apoc. 2.24); I.8; I.14; II.13 (Philo, *Q.G.* IV.67) *SG: II.24*
C	A	λέξις	Letter: II.8; II.20; II.22
C	A	λίθος	*SG: III.2*
C	A	λόγιον	Letter: I.25
C	A	μαθητής	*SG: II.25*
C	A	μάλα	Letter: II.1
C	A	Μᾶρκος	Letter: I.12; I.15; I.19; II.11
C	A	μαρτυρέω	Letter: I.18
C	A	μέγας	Letter: II.2 *SG: III.1*

C	A	μέν	Letter: I.12; III.11; III.18
C	A	μέντοι	Letter: I.16
C	A	μένω	*SG: III.9*
C	A	μετά	Letter: II.12; II.21; II.22 (Mk. 10.34); III.14
			SG: II.26; III.5; III.6
C	A	μεταφέρω	Letter: I.20
C	A	μή	Letter: II.16 (Mt. 25.29)
C	A	μήν	Letter: I.16
C	A	μήτηρ	*SG: III.16*
–	–	μηχανάω[7]	Letter: II.3
C	A	μιαίνω	Letter: II.8
C	A	μιαρός	Letter: II.2
C2	A11	μνημεῖον	*SG: II.26; III.1; III.2; III.6*
C	A	μόνος	Letter: II.1; III.14
C13	–	μυέω	Letter: II.2
C4	A2	μυσταγωγέω	Letter: I.25
C	A	μυστήριον	Letter: II.2
			SG: III.10
C	A	μυστικός	Letter: I.17; II.6; II.12
C4	A1	μωραίνω	Letter: I.15 (Lk. 14.34)
C1	A5	μωρία	Letter: II.14 (Prov. 26.5)
C	A	μωρός	Letter: II.14 (Prov. 26.5); II.16 (Eccles. 2.14)
C4	A2	νεανίσκος	*SG: III.3; III.4; III.6; III.8; III.15*
C	A	νομίζω	Letter: I.17
C	A	νοῦς	Letter: II.15
C	A	νῦν	Letter: II.1
C	A	νύξ	*SG: III.9*
C	A	ὁ, ἡ, τό	Not indexed
C	A	ὁδός	Letter: I.3; II.21 (Mk. 10.32)
C	A	οἰκία	*SG: III.6*
C	A	οἶμαι	Letter: I.27
C	A	ὀκνέω	Letter: II.19
C3	A8	ὄλεθρος	Letter: II.3
C	A	ὅμως	Letter: I.22
C	A	ὅπου	Letter: II.1
			SG: II.26; III.2
C	A	ὀργίζω	*SG: II.25*
C	A	ὅρκος	Letter: II.12
C	A	ὅς, ἥ, ὅ	Letter: I.17; I.20; I.25; II.6; III.13; III.17
			SG: II.23; III.15

7. C and A both have the middle.

C	A	οὐ	Letter: I.16; I.27; II.12 (Philo, *Q.G.* IV.67); II.19; III.13 *SG: III.16*
C	A	οὖ[8]	Letter: II.18 (II Cor. 3.17)
C	A	οὐδέ	Letter: I.8; I.9 (bis); I.13; I.16; I.23; I.27; II.10
C	A	οὐδέποτε	Letter: II.10
C	A	οὐδέπω	Letter: I.22
C	A	οὖν	Letter: I.7; I.26; II.10; III.18
C	A	οὗτος	Letter: I.3; I.7; I.14; II.9; II.10; II.13; III.11
C	A	οὕτως	Letter: I.8; I.13; I.26; II.5
–	–	ὀψία	*SG: III.7*
C	A	παντελῶς	Letter: I.12
C15+	A3	πάντῃ	Letter: I.8
C6+	A3	πάντοτε	Letter: II.3
C	A	πάντως	Letter: I.8
C	A	παρά	Letter: II.6
C	A	παραγγέλλω	Letter: II.13
C	A	παραδίδωμι	Letter: I.13
C	A	παρακαλέω	*SG: III.5*
C9	–	παραχαράσσω	Letter: I.14
C	A	παρέρχομαι	Letter: I.18
C	A	πᾶς	Letter: I.9; I.16; II.12 (Philo, *Q.G.* IV.67); II.18 (Titus 1.15); III.12
C	A	πέραν	*SG: III.11*
C	A	περί	Letter: I.11; I.21; III.13
C	A	περιβάλλω	*SG: III.8*
C	A	περιέχω	Letter: I.13
C	A	περικοπή	Letter: III.12
C	A	Πέτρος	Letter: I.15; I.18; I.19
C	A	πίστις	Letter: I.11; I.18
C	A	πλανάω	Letter: I.4
C7	–	πλανήτης	Letter: I.3 (Jude 13)
C	A	πλάσμα	Letter: I.14
C	A	πλούσιος	*SG: II.6*
C	A	πνεῦμα	Letter: II.17; II.18 (II Cor. 3.17)
C1	–	πνευματικώτερος[9]	Letter: I.21
C	A	ποιέω	Letter: I.2
C	A	πολύς	Letter: III.17

8. No listing in Müller, *Lexicon*.
9. A has only the positive.

C	A	πορεύω	Letter: II.16 (Eccles. 2.14)
C	A	πρᾶξις	Letter: I.16; I.24
C	A	πρεσβύτερος	Letter: II.5
C2	A5	προγράφω	Letter: I.24
C	A	προερέω	Letter: II.10
C	A	προκόπτω	Letter: I.20
C	A	προκρίνω	Letter: I.10
C5	–	προπαρασκευάζω	Letter: I.27
C	A	πρός	Letter: I.17; II.2; II.14
			SG: III.8
C1	–	προσεπάγω	Letter: I.24
C	A	προσέρχομαι	SG: III.1
C	A	προσκυνέω	SG: II.24
–	–	προσπορεύομαι	Letter: III.12 (Mk. 10.35)
C	A	προτείνω	Letter: II.11
C	A	προφητεύω	Letter: I.3
C	A	πρῶτος	Letter: I.20
C	A	Ῥώμη	Letter: I.15
C6	–	Σαλώμη	SG: III.16
C	A	σαρκικός	Letter: I.4; II.7
C1	A7	Σατανᾶς	Letter: I.5 (Apoc. 2.24)
C1	A1	σινδών	SG: III.8
C	A	σκότος	Letter: I.6 (Jude 13); II.16 (Eccles. 2.14)
C	A	Σολομῶν	Letter: II.13
C	A	σοφία	Letter: II.13
C1	A10	στενός	Letter: I.3
C24	–	στρωματεύς	**Heading: I.1**
C	A	σύ	Letter: II.19
C	A	σύγγραμμα	Letter: I.28
C2	A3	συγκεράννυμι	Letter: I.13
C	A	συγχωρέω	Letter: II.11
C3	A8	συμφωνέω	Letter: I.8
C	A	σύν	SG: III.9
C	A	συντάσσω	Letter: I.21
C	A	τέ	Letter: I.8; I.19
C	A	τελειόω	Letter: I.22
C	A	τέχνη	Letter: II.4
C	A	τηρέω	Letter: II.1
C	A	τις	Letter: I.8; I.12; I.25; II.5
C	A	τοίνυν	Letter: I.11; II.19
C	A	τρεῖς	Letter: II.22 (Mk. 10.34)
C	A	τυφλός	Letter: II.14
C	A	υἱός	Letter: II.17 (I Thess. 5.5)
			SG: II.24

C	A	ὑπό	Letter: II.4
C	A	ὑπόμνημα	Letter: I.19
C3	–	ὑποσημαίνω	Letter: I.17
C6+	A3	ὕψος	Letter: II.17
C	A	φαίνω	Letter: I.10; III.17
C	A	φημί	Letter: II.15; II.18
–	–	φθονερῶς[10]	Letter: I.27
C c. 300	–	φιλοσοφία	Letter: III.18
C3	A1	φυσιόω	Letter: I.5
C	A	φωνή	*SG: III.1*
C	A	φῶς	Letter: II.15; II.17 (I Thess. 5.5)
C	A	φωτίζω	Letter: II.17
C	A	χείρ	*SG: III.3; III.4*
C	A	χράω	Letter: II.4
C1	–	χρησιμώτατος[11]	Letter: I.17
C14+	A5	χρῆσις	Letter: I.22
C	A	ψεῦδος	Letter: I.6
C	A	ψεύδω	Letter: I.12
C2	A2	ψεῦσμα	Letter: II.9; III.17
C	A	ὧδε	Letter: II.22
C	A	ὡς	Letter: I.5 (Apoc. 2.24); I.27
C	A	ὥστε	Letter: I.14; II.6

10. A and C have the adjective.
11. A has only the positive.

Index II

QUOTATIONS AND REMINISCENCES IN THE LETTER

Asterisked items are quotations, the others reminiscences:

I.2	Titus I.11
*I.3	Jude 13
I.3	Wisdom 5.6
I.3	Mt. 7.13f
I.3	Prov. 2.13f
I.4	Enoch 21.2
I.5	I Cor. 8.1
*I.5	Apoc. 2.24
I.5	I Cor. 2.10
*I.6	Jude 13
I.7–8	I Pet. 5.9
I.9	Plato, *Republic* VI.501d
I.10	Plato, *Sophista* 229a
I.10–11	Plato, *Theaetetus* 162a
*I.14–15	Lk. 14.34 (parallel Mt. 5.13)
I.14–15	Jer. 28.17 (LXX)
II.3	*Odyssey* XVIII.143
II.9	John 2.8
*II.12–13	Philo, *Questions . . . on Genesis* IV.64
II.13	Lk. 11.49
*II.14	Prov. 26.5
II.14	Sophocles, *Oedipus tyrannus* 371
*II.16	Mt. 25.29 (parallel Lk. 19.26)
*II.16	Eccles. 2.14
*II.17	I Thess. 5.5
II.17	Lk. 1.78
II.18	Prov. 20.27
*II.18	II Cor. 3.17b
*II.18f	Titus 1.15
*II.21	Mk. 10.32
*II.22	Mk. 10.34

*II.23   Secret Gospel
*III.11f   Mk. 10.35
*III.13   Secret Gospel (Carpocratian version)
*III.14   Mk. 10.46
*III.14   Secret Gospel
 III.17   Plato, *Hippias Major* 294a–c

ANCIENT WORKS AND PASSAGES DISCUSSED

INDEX IV

GREEK WORDS AND PHRASES DISCUSSED*

* This list does not usually include words discussed in the commentaries on the letter and the Gospel fragment. For those, see Index I.

baptism (*continued*)

186; content of, 173; costume for, 116, 176f; difference from the Baptist's, 253; identifies with Jesus, 187; history in the Church, 183, 231, 240 n. 17, 259, 264; instruction for, 170, 171, 173; magical, 232; nocturnal, 175; nudity in, 65, 175f, 185, 216; origin, 219, 253; requirements for, 169, 172, 175, 185; a "seal", 183; substitutionary, 232; terminology, 171; "the mystery of the kingdom," 203, 244; underlies Mk. 10.13–45, 167–188

——, Jesus', 115, 237, 251, 253; difference from the Baptist's, 213; explains Christian practice, 253; explains the coming of the spirit, 252; involved ascent to the heavens, 237–247, 240 n. 17; magical, 220–236; "mystery of the kingdom of God" *see* mystery; origin of, 244; reinterpreted by his followers, 243; related to transfiguration, 243; source of libertinism, 259, 262; story of, 243

——, of fire, 269

——, Paul's, 179f, 213–219, 240 n. 17; elements derived from Jesus, 216–250; freed from Mosaic law, 248; led to possession, 215, 217; magical, 217, 220–236; rejected by second-century Christianity, 264f; secondary elements, 216–217; shamanistic, 242; united with Jesus, 215, 217

——, Qumran, 206 n. 3, 219

——, rabbinic, 207, 219

Baptist (the): achievement, 208; beginning of Christian tradition, 206; difference from Jesus, 205, 211, 213; expected response to, 205; importance of, 206; inferior to Jesus' followers, 213; libertine interpretation of, 207; rite peculiar, 207; polemic against, 174, 206, 209f, 219; role in relation to the Kingdom, 205–208; *see also* baptism, the Baptist's

Barnabas, 257, 267, 276

Barrett, C., 248; *Things Sacrificed*, 265

Bartimaeus, 188

Basilideans, 29

Basilides, 90, 272, 277

Bauer, W., 180; *Rechtgläubigkeit*, 252

Baumstark, A., *Lazarusakten*, 174

Beasley-Murray, G., *Baptism*, 209

Beelzebub, nickname of Jesus, 229

"beloved disciple," 119, 253

Ben Stada, 269; nickname of Jesus, 230

Benoit, A., *Baptême*, 264

Benoit, P., 113, 120, 141

Bethany, 99, 129, 152ff

Betz, O., *Proselytentaufe*, 206 n. 3

Bickerman, E., 6, 27, 55, 67, 142f, 230, 283

Bieler, L., θεῖος ἀνήρ, 228

Bieneck, J., *Sohn*, 228

binding by Satan, magical, 223

body of Messiah. *See* Church

Boismard, M., *Liturgie*, 170

Bonner, C., *Technique*, 223

Boobyer, G., *Redaction*, 178

book-burning, 283

books, preservation of, 283

Bornkamm, G., 180

Bousset, W.: *Antichrist*, 269; *Hauptprobleme*, 276; *Himmelsreise*, 239

boys, as mediums, 223; in early Christianity, 282; in magic, 223, 242

branding, ears, 268f, 270

Braude, W., 207

breathings, of MS., 2

Bultmann, R., 248; conjecture confirmed, 155; *Geschichte*, 211; *Johannes*, 209

Buonaiuti, E., *Fragments*, 277

Buri, E., *Clemens*, 265

burial, costume for, 177

Burkill, A., *Revelation*, 164

Burkitt, F., *Vestigia*, 206 n. 2

Burney, C., *Origin*, 244

Cadbury, H., 87, 111ff, 120, 123, 190; *Case*, 146

Calder, W. M. III, 6, 9, 14f, 39, 43, 46, 51, 56, 58, 67, 87, 99, 101, 103, 108, 114, 117, 118

Carpocrates: a primitive Christian, 276; and Carpocratians, 266–278; Clement's account of, 46f; commentaries on secret Mk., 90; connection with Alexandria, 82; connection with Jewish Christianity, 268 (Cerinthus), 278; corruption of the Gospel, 89; date, 90, 267f; Harpocrates, 90; name, 266f; position in lists of heretics, 267; practiced exorcism, 276; testimonia concerning, 295–350, these discussed, 268–276; the letter's account of, 46f; use of secret Mk., 90; use of a secret Gospel, 46; works on, 276–278

Carpocratianism: based on magic, 276f; diversification, 267, 277; Platonic traits, 268; primitive Christian traits, 271f; sources, 273; testimonia, 268–276

Carpocratians, 11, 13, 16, 79, 173, 185, 266–278; accused of magic, 47; appeal to Salome, 190f; attacks on, 47, 58, 273f; cause of scandal, 274; Clement's account of, 273; commentaries on secret Gospels, 90; communism, 274; connection with Ebionites, 276; decline of, 82, 287; denial of resurrection, 186; denial of virgin birth, 191; disappearance of, 275; diversification, 267, 277; doctrine of creation, 273; equalitarianism, 273; founder, 84; importance of, 82, 270, 272f, 275; in Irenaeus, 272; literature, 276; nicknamed "Harpocratians" (?), 65; practice of magic, 90; promiscuity, 273; relation to Salome, 121; reports of, 64, 274; secret books, 91; source of doctrine, 84, 273f, 277; testimonia concerning, 295–350; text of secret Gospel, 64, 91; their

ABBREVIATIONS AND WORKS CITED

A.D.N.: A. D. Nock

A.W.: A. Wifstrand

Aalen, *Reign*: S. Aalen, "'Reign' and 'House' in the Kingdom of God in the Gospels," *NTS* 8 (1962) 215ff

AANL: *Atti della Accademia Nazionale dei Lincei*

Account: M. Smith, "The Account of Simon Magus in Acts 8," in *Harry Austryn Wolfson Jubilee Volume*, Jerusalem, 1965, 3 vols., II.735ff

AJP: *American Journal of Philology*

Aland, *Säuglingstaufe*: K. Aland, *Die Säuglingstaufe im NT und in der alten Kirche*, Munich, 1961 (*Theologische Existenz heute*, N.F., 86)

Allo, *I Cor.*: E. Allo, *Saint Paul, Première Épître aux Corinthiens*, 2 ed., Paris, 1956 (*Études Bibliques*)

Altaner, *Patrologie*⁶: B. Altaner, *Patrologie*, 6 ed., Basel, 1960.

Amann, *Protévangile*: E. Amann, *Le Protévangile de Jacques*, Paris, 1910

AnBoll: *Analecta Bollandiana*

ANET: *Ancient Near Eastern Texts*, ed. J. Pritchard, 2 ed., Princeton, 1955

Annand, *He Was Seen*: R. Annand, "He Was Seen of Cephas," *SJT* 11 (1958) 180ff

Anrich, *Mysterienwesen*: G. Anrich, *Das antike Mysterienwesen in seinem Einfluss auf das Christentum*, Göttingen, 1894

Anz, *Frage*: W. Anz, *Zur Frage nach dem Ursprung des Gnosticismus*, Leipzig, 1897 (*TU* 15.4)

ARW: *Archiv für Religionswissenschaft*

Ast: F. Astius, *Lexicon Platonicum*, Leipzig, 1835–1838, 3 vols.

ATANT: *Abhandlungen zur Theologie des Alten und Neuen Testaments*

ATR: *Anglican Theological Review*

Audollent: A. Audollent, *Defixionum Tabellae*, Paris, 1904

B.: *Babylonian Talmud*

B.E.: Benedict Einarson, University of Chicago

Baarda: T. Baarda, *Mk. 9.49*, *NTS* 5 (1959) 318ff

Baedeker, *Palestine*: K. Baedeker, *Palestine and Syria*, 5 ed., Leipzig, 1912

Baer, *Seder*: I. Baer, *Seder 'Avodat Yisra'el*, Jerusalem, 1937

Baird, *Mature*: W. Baird, "Among the Mature," *Interpretation* 13 (1959) 425ff

Bardy, *Origènes*: G. Bardy, "Aux Origènes de l'école d'Alexandrie," *RechSR* 27 (1937) 65ff

Barnard: P. Barnard, *The Biblical Text of Clement of Alexandria*, Cambridge, Eng., 1899 (*Texts and Studies* 5.5)

Barnard, *Mark*: L. Barnard, "St. Mark and Alexandria," *HTR* 57 (1964) 145ff

Barnard, *Stephen*: L. Barnard, "St. Stephen and Early Alexandrian Christianity," *NTS* 7 (1960) 31ff

Barnes, *Origen*: T. Barnes, "Origen, Aquila, and Eusebius," *HSCP* 74 (1968) 313ff

Barrett: C. Barrett, *The Gospel According to St. John: An Introduction with Commentary and Notes*, London, 1960.

Barrett, *Things Sacrificed*: C. Barrett, "Things Sacrificed to Idols," *NTS* 11 (1965) 138ff

Bauer, *Ig.*: W. Bauer, *Die Briefe des Ignatios von Antiochia*, Tübingen, 1923 (*HNT, Ergänzungsband* 185ff)

Bauer, *Leben*: W. Bauer, *Das Leben Jesu im Zeitalter der neutestamentlichen Apokryphen*, Tübingen, 1909

Bauer, *Rechtgläubigkeit*: W. Bauer, *Rechtgläubigkeit und Ketzerei im ältesten Christentum*, Tübingen, 1934 (*Beiträge z. historischen Theologie* 10)

Bauer, *Sal*: J. Bauer, "Quod si sal infatuatum fuerit," *Verbum Domini* 29 (1951) 228ff

Bauer, *Wb.*: W. Bauer, *Griechisch-deutches Wörterbuch zu den Schriften des Neuen Testaments*, 5 ed., Berlin, 1958

Baumstark, *Lazarusakten*: A. Baumstark, "Verschollene Lazarusakten?" *Römische Quartalschrift* 14 (1900) 210ff

Baur: C. Baur, *Initia patrum graecorum*, Vatican City, 1955, 2 vols. (*Studi e Testi* 180, 181)

Beasley-Murray, *Baptism*: G. Beasley-Murray, *Baptism in the New Testament*, London, 1962

Beck: H. Beck, *Kirche u. theologische Literatur im byzantinischen Reich*, Munich, 1959 (*HdbAw* 12.2.1.)

BEHE: *Bibliothèque de l'École des hautes Études*

Bell, *Cults*: H. Bell, *Cults and Creeds in Graeco-Roman Egypt*, Liverpool, 1953

Benoit, *Baptême*: A. Benoit, *Le baptême chrétien au second siècle*, Paris, 1953 (*EHPR* 43)

Benoit, *Qumran*: P. Benoit, "Qumran et le Nouveau Testament," *NTS* 7 (1961) 276–296

Benoit, review of Mayeda: P. Benoit, review of G. Mayeda, *Das Leben-Jesu-Fragment Papyrus Egerton 2* in *RB* 55 (1948) 472ff

Bernard, *Study*: J. Bernard, "A Study of St. Mk. 10.38,39," *JTS* 28 (1927) 262ff

Bertinoro: O. di Bertinoro, *Commentary on the Mishnah*, in the fourth Horeb ed. of the *Mishnah*, New York, 1935

Best, *Spirit*: E. Best, "Spirit Baptism," *NovTes* 4 (1960) 236ff

Betz, *Proselytentaufe*: O. Betz, "Die Proselytentaufe der Qumransekte und die Taufe im Neuen Testament," *RdQ* 1 (1958) 213ff

BiblZ: *Biblische Zeitschrift*

Bickerman, *Esther*: E. Bickerman, "Notes on the Greek Book of Esther," *Proceedings of the American Academy for Jewish Research*, 20 (1951) 101ff

Bickerman, *Kaiserapotheose*: E. Bickerman, "Die römische Kaiserapotheose," *ARW* 27 (1929) 1ff

Bickerman, *Warning*: E. Bickerman, "The Warning Inscription of Herod's Temple," *JQR* NS 37 (1947) 387ff

Bidez, *Écoles*: J. Bidez, "Les Écoles chaldéennes sous Alexandre et les Sélucides," Université de Bruxelles, *Annuaire de l'Institut de Philologie et d'Histoire orientales* 3 (1935) 41ff

Bidez-Cumont, *Mages*: J. Bidez and F. Cumont, *Les Mages hellénisés*, Paris, 1938, 2 vols.

Bieler: L. Bieler, "Totenerweckung durch *ΣΥΝΑΝΑΧΡΩΣΙΣ*," *ARW* 32 (1935) 228ff

Bieler, Θεῖος ἀνήρ: L. Bieler, Θεῖος ἀνήρ Vienna, 1935–1936, 2 vols.

Bieneck, *Sohn*: J. Bieneck, *Sohn Gottes als Christusbezeichnung der Synoptiker*, Zürich, 1951 (*ATANT* 21)

Billerbeck: H. Strack and P. Billerbeck, *Kommentar zum Neuen Testament aus Talmud und Midrasch*, Munich, 1922–1928, 4 vols. in 5

Bird, γάρ: C. Bird, "Some γάρ Clauses in St. Mark's Gospel," *JTS* NS 4 (1953) 171ff

BJRL: *Bulletin of the John Rylands Library*

Black, *Aramaic*: M. Black, *An Aramaic Approach to the Gospels and Acts*, Oxford, 1946

Blass, *Acta*: F. Blass, *Acta apostolorum . . . editio philologica*, Göttingen, 1895

Blass-Debrunner-Funk: F. Blass and A. Debrunner, *A Greek Grammar of the New Testament*, tr. R. Funk, Chicago, 1961

Bludau, *Schriftfälschungen*: A. Bludau, *Die Schriftfälschungen der Häretiker*, Münster i. W., 1925 (*Neutestamentliche Abhandlungen* 11.5)

BM: British Museum

BN: Bibliothèque Nationale

Böhlig-Labib, *KGA*: A. Böhlig and P. Labib, *Koptisch-gnostische Apokalypsen aus Codex V von Nag Hammadi*, Halle-Wittenberg, 1963 (Wissenschaftliche Zeitschrift der Martin-Luther-Universität, Sonderband)

Boismard, *Liturgie*: M. Boismard, "Une Liturgie Baptismale dans le Prima Petri," *RB* 63 (1956) 182ff; 64 (1957) 161ff

Bolgiani, *Polemica*: F. Bolgiani, "La Polemica di Clemente Alessandrino contro gli gnostici libertini nel III libro degli 'Stromati,'" *Studi e Materiali di Storia delle Religioni* 38 (1967) 86ff

Bonitz, *Index*: H. Bonitz, "Index Aristotelicus," in *Aristotelis Opera*, ed. Academia Regia Borussica, vol. V, Berlin, 1870

Bonner, *Technique*: C. Bonner, "Traces of Thaumaturgic Technique in the Miracles," *HTR* 20 (1927) 171ff

Bonsirven, *Textes*: J. Bonsirven, *Textes rabbiniques des deux premiers siècles chrétiens*, Rome, 1955

Boobyer, *Redaction*: G. Boobyer, "The Redaction of Mk. IV.1–34," *NTS* 8 (1961) 59ff

Boobyer, *Secrecy*: G. Boobyer, "The Secrecy Motif in St. Mark's Gospel," *NTS* 6 (1960) 225ff

Bornkamm, μυέω: G. Bornkamm, "μυέω," *ThWb* IV.809ff

Botte: B. Botte, ed., *Hippolyte de Rome, La Tradition Apostolique*, Paris, n.d. (*Sources Chrétiennes* 11)

Bousset, *Antichrist*: W. Bousset, *The Antichrist Legend*, tr. A. Keane, London, 1896

Bousset, *Hauptprobleme*: W. Bousset, *Hauptprobleme der Gnosis*, Göttingen, 1907

Bousset, *Himmelsreise*: W. Bousset, "Die Himmelsreise der Seele," *ARW* 4 (1901) 136ff; 229ff

Bowman, *Calendar*: J. Bowman, "Is the Samaritan Calendar an Old Zadokite One?" *PEQ* 91 (1959) 23ff

Brandon, *Date*: S. Brandon, "The Date of the Markan Gospel," *NTS* 7 (1961) 126ff

Brandon, *Fall*: S. Brandon, *The Fall of Jerusalem and the Christian Church*, 2 ed., London, 1957

Brandon, *Personification*: S. Brandon, "The Personification of Death in Some Ancient Religions," *BJRL* 43 (1961) 317ff

Braumann, *Taufverkündigung*: G. Braumann, *Vorpaulinische christliche Taufverkündigung bei Paulus*, Stuttgart, 1962 (*BWANT* 82)

Brown, *Revision*: J. Brown, "An Early Revision of the Gospel of Mark," *JBL* 78 (1959) 215ff

Brown, *Scrolls*: R. Brown, "The Qumran Scrolls and the Johannine Gospel and Epistles," in *The Scrolls and the New Testament*, ed. K. Stendahl, New York, 1957, 183ff

Bruder: C. Bruder, *Concordantiae omnium vocum NT graeci*, 2 ed., Leipzig, 1853

Buber: S. Buber, *Midrasch Tanchuma*, Wilna, 1885, 2 vols.

Budge, *Texts*: E. Budge, *Miscellaneous Coptic Texts*, London, 1915

Bultmann, ἀλήθεια: R. Bultmann, "ἀλήθεια," *ThWb* I (1933) 233ff

Bultmann, *Geschichte*: R. Bultmann, *Die Geschichte der synoptischen Tradition*, 4 ed., and *Ergänzungsheft*, Göttingen, 1958 (*FRLANT* 29)

Bultmann, *Johannes*: R. Bultmann, *Das Evangelium des Johannes*, 16 ed., Göttingen, 1959 (*Meyers Kommentar*)

Bultmann, *Verhältnis*: R. Bultmann, *Das Verhältnis der urchristlichen Christusbotschaft zum historischen Jesus*, 2 ed., Heidelberg, 1961

Buonaiuti, *Fragments*: E. Buonaiuti, *Gnostic Fragments*, tr. E. Cowell, London, 1924

Burch, *Gospel*: V. Burch, "The Gospel According to the Hebrews," *JTS* 21 (1920) 310ff

Buri, *Clemens*: F. Buri, *Clemens Alexandrinus und der paulinische Freiheitsbegriff*, Zürich, n.d. (1939)

Burkert, *ΓΟΗΣ*: W. Burkert, "*ΓΟΗΣ*: Zum griechischen 'Schamanismus'," *Rheinisches Museum für Philologie*, NS 105 (1962) 36ff

Burkill, *Revelation*: T. Burkill, *Mysterious Revelation*, Ithaca, N.Y., 1963

Burkitt: F. Burkitt, "Introduction," in P. Barnard, *The Biblical Text of Clement of Alexandria*, Cambridge, Eng., 1899 (*Texts and Studies* 5.5)

Burkitt, *Vestigia*: F. Burkitt, "Vestigia Christi," in *Beginnings of Christianity*, ed. K. Lake *et al.*, I.ii, 1922, 485ff

Burney, *Origin*: C. Burney, *The Aramaic Origin of the Fourth Gospel*, Oxford, 1922

Buse: I. Buse, "The Cleansing of the Temple in the Synoptics and John," *ET* 70 (1958) 22ff

—— "John 5.8 and Johannine-Marcan Relationships," *NTS* 1 (1954) 134ff

—— "St. John and 'the First Synoptic Pericope'," *NovTes* 3 (1959) 57ff

—— "St. John and the Marcan Passion Narrative," *NTS* 4 (1958) 215ff

Butterworth: G. Butterworth, "The Deification of Man in Clement of Alexandria," *JTS* 17 (1916) 157ff, and "The Deification of Man in Clement of Alexandria: Some Further Notes," *JTS* 17 (1916) 257ff

BWANT: *Beiträge zur Wissenschaft vom Alten und Neuen Testament*

C.F.D.M.: C.F.D. Moule, Cambridge University

C.H.R.: C. H. Roberts, Oxford University

C. M.: C. Mondésert, University of Lyons

C. R.: Cyril Richardson, Union Theological Seminary, New York.

Cadbury, *Case*: H. Cadbury, "A Possible Case of Lukan Authorship," *HTR* 10 (1917) 237ff

Cadbury, *Dilemma*: H. Cadbury, "The Dilemma of Ephesians," *NTS* 5 (1959) 1ff

Cadbury, *Making*: H. Cadbury, *The Making of Luke-Acts*, 2 ed., London, 1958

Caird, *Chronology*: G. Caird, "Chronology of the NT," *IDB* I.599ff

Camelot, *Foi*: T. Camelot, *Foi et gnose*, Paris, 1945 (*Études de théologie et d'histoire de la spiritualité* 3)

Carlston, *Transfiguration*: C. Carlston, "Transfiguration and Resurrection," *JBL* 80 (1961) 233ff

Carrington, *Mark*: P. Carrington, *According to Mark*, Cambridge, Eng., 1960

Casey, *Clement*: R. Casey, "Clement and the Two Divine Logoi," *JTS* 25 (1923) 43ff

CBQ: *Catholic Biblical Quarterly*

CC: *Corpus Christianorum*

Cerfaux, *Gnose*: L. Cerfaux, "La Gnose Simonienne: I," *RechSR* 15 (1925) 488ff

CH: *Corpus Hermeticum*, ed. A. D. Nock and A.-J. Festugière, Paris, 1945–1954, 4 vols.

Chadwick, *Alexandrian Christianity*: H. Chadwick, "General Introduction" in *Alexandrian Christianity*, ed. H. Chadwick and J. Oulton, London, 1954 (Library of Christian Classics 2)

Chadwick, *Contra Celsum*: Origen, *Contra Celsum*, tr. with intro. and notes by H. Chadwick, Cambridge, Eng., 1953

Chadwick, *St. Paul and Philo*: H. Chadwick, *St. Paul and Philo of Alexandria*, Manchester, 1966 (*BJRL* 48 [1966] 286ff)

Chadwick, *Sextus*: H. Chadwick, ed., *The Sentences of Sextus*, Cambridge, Eng., 1959 (*Texts and Studies* NS 5)

ChH: *Church History*

Clasen, *Arkandiziplin*: U. Clasen, "Die Arkandiziplin in der alten Kirche" (unpub. diss.), Heidelberg, 1958 (microfilm)

Cloud: F. Cloud, *The Use of the Perfect Tense in the Attic Orators*, Philadelphia, 1910

Comments: M. Smith, "Comments on Taylor's Commentary on Mark," *HTR* 48 (1955) 21ff

Connolly: R. Connolly, *Didascalia Apostolorum*, Oxford, 1929

Const. Apos.: *Didascalia et Constitutiones Apostolorum*, ed. F. Funk, Paderborn, 1905, 2 vols.

Conzelmann, *Apostelgeschichte*: H. Conzelmann, *Die Apostelgeschichte*, Tübingen, 1963 (*HNT* 7)

Couchoud, *L'Évangile*: P. Couchoud, "L'Évangile de Marc a-t-il été écrit en latin," *RHR* 94 (1926) 161ff

Couchoud, *Marc latin*: P. Couchoud, "Marc latin et Marc grec," *RHR* 95 (1927) 287ff

CPJ: *Corpus Papyrorum Judaicarum*, ed. V. Tcherikover *et al.*, Cambridge, Mass., 1957–1964, 3 vols.

CR: *Classical Review*

Cramer: J. Cramer, *Catenae Graecorum Patrum in Novum Testamentum*, Oxford, 1844, 8 vols.

Cranfield: C. Cranfield, *The Gospel According to St. Mark*, Cambridge, Eng., 1959 (*Cambridge Greek Testament Commentary*)

Creed: J. Creed, *The Gospel According to St. Luke*, London, 1930

CSCO: *Corpus scriptorum christianorum orientalium*

CSEL: *Corpus scriptorum ecclesiasticorum latinorum*

Cullmann, *Baptism*: O. Cullmann, *Baptism in the NT*, London, 1950 (*Studies in Biblical Theology* 1)

Cullmann, *Significance*: O. Cullmann, "The Significance of the Qumran Texts for Research into the Beginnings of Christianity," in *The Scrolls and the New Testament*, ed. K. Stendahl, New York, 1957, 18ff

Cumont, *Égypte*: F. Cumont, *L'Égypte des Astrologues*, Brussels, 1937

Cumont, *Lux*: F. Cumont, *Lux Perpetua*, Paris, 1949

Cumont, *Religions*: F. Cumont, *Les Religions orientales dans le paganisme romain*, 4 ed., Paris, 1929

Cureton, *ASD*: W. Cureton, *Ancient Syriac Documents*, London, 1864

Curzon, *Visits*: R. Curzon, *Visits to Monasteries in the Levant*, ed. S. Dearden, Ithaca, N.Y., 1955

DACL: *Dictionnaire d'archéologie chrétienne et de liturgie*

Daehne: A. Daehne, *De ΓΝΩΣΕΙ Clementis Alexandrini*, Halae, 1831

Daiches: S. Daiches, "Zu II. Kg. 4, 34," *OLZ* 2 (1908) 492f

Dalman, *Orte*: G. Dalman, *Orte und Wege Jesu*, 3 ed., Gütersloh, 1924 (*Schriften des Deutschen Palästina-Instituts* 1)

Daniélou, *Étoile*: J. Daniélou, "L'Étoile de Jacob et la mission chrétienne à Damas," *VC* 11 (1957) 121ff

Daniélou, *Théologie*: J. Daniélou, *Théologie du Judéo-Christianisme*, Tournai, 1958 (*Bibliothèque de Théologie, Histoire des doctrines chrétiennes avant Nicée* 1)

Daniélou, *Traditions*: J. Daniélou, "Les Traditions secrètes des Apôtres," *Eranos Jahrbuch* 31 (1962) 199ff

Danker, *Lk. 16.16*: F. Danker, "Lk. 16.16—An Opposition Logion," *JBL* 77 (1958) 231ff

Daube, *NTRJ*: D. Daube, *The New Testament and Rabbinic Judaism*, London, 1956

Daube, *Reflections*: D. Daube, "Greek and Roman Reflections on Impossible Laws," *Natural Law Forum* 12 (1967) 50ff

Davies *Paul*: W. Davies, *Paul and Rabbinic Judaism*, 2 ed., London, 1955

DCB: W. Smith and H. Wace, *Dictionary of Christian Biography*, London, 1877

Delling, *Baptisma*: G. Delling, "*Baptisma baptisthenai*," *NovTes* 2 (1957) 92ff

Description: M. Smith, "The Description of the Essenes in Josephus and the Philosophumena," *HUCA* 29 (1958) 273ff

DHGE: *Dictionnaire d'histoire et de géographie ecclésiastiques*, Paris, 1912——

Dibelius, *Kolosser*: M. Dibelius, *An die Kolosser, Epheser, an Philemon*, 2 ed., Tübingen, 1927 (*HNT* 12)

427

Dibelius, *Structure*: M. Dibelius, "The Structure and Literary Character of the Gospels," *HTR* 20 (1927) 151ff

Dibelius-Kümmel, *Jesus*: M. Dibelius, *Jesus*, 3 ed. with postscript by W. Kümmel, Berlin, 1960 (*Sammlung Göschen* 1130)

Diels: H. Diels, *Die Fragmente der Vorsokratiker*, 7 ed., ed. W. Kranz, Berlin, 1954, 3 vols.

Dieterich, *Mithrasliturgie*: A. Dieterich, *Eine Mithrasliturgie*, 3 ed., ed. O. Weinriech, Leipzig, 1923

Dietzel, *Beten*: A. Dietzel, "Beten im Geist," *ThZ* 13 (1957) 12ff

Dionysius Hal., Usener–Raderm.: *Dionysii Halicarnasei Opuscula*, ed. H. Usener and L. Radermacher, Leipzig, 1899–1904, 2 vols. in 3

Dirlmeier: F. Dirlmeier, *Aristoteles, Magna Moralia*, Berlin, 1958 (*Aristoteles Werke*, ed. E. Grumbach, 8)

Discoveries: *Discoveries in the Judean Desert*, ed. D. Barthélemy, J. Milik *et al.*, Oxford, 1955——

Dix: G. Dix, *The Treatise on the Apostolic Tradition of St. Hippolytus*, London, 1937

DMP: *The Demotic Magical Papyrus of London and Leiden*, ed. F. Griffith and H. Thompson, Oxford, 1921 (text and translation)

Dodd, *Appearances*: C. Dodd, "The Appearances of the Risen Christ," in Nineham, *Studies*, 9ff

Dodd, *Close*: C. Dodd, "The Close of the Galilean Ministry," *The Expositor*, 8 Ser. 22 (1921) 273ff

Dodd, *Fourth Gospel*: C. Dodd, *The Interpretation of the Fourth Gospel*, Cambridge, Eng., 1953

Dodd, *Framework*: C. Dodd, "The Framework of the Gospel Narrative," in *New Testament Studies*, Manchester, 1954, 1ff

Dodd, *Herrnworte*: C. Dodd, "Some Johannine 'Herrnworte' with Parallels in the Synoptic Gospels," *NTS* 2 (1955) 75ff

Dodd, *Historical Tradition*: C. Dodd, *Historical Tradition in the Fourth Gospel*, Cambridge, Eng., 1963

Dodd, *New Gospel*: C. Dodd, "A New Gospel," in *New Testament Studies*, Manchester, 1954

Dodd, *Parables*: C. Dodd, *The Parables of the Kingdom*, 2 ed., London, 1961

Doeve, *Doop*: J. Doeve, "De Doop van Johannes en de Proselytendoop," *NTT* 9 (1954) 137ff

Dölger, *Sphragis*: F. Dölger, "Die Sphragis als religiöse Brandmarkung," *Antike und Christentum* 1 (1929) 73ff

Doudna, *Greek*: J. Doudna, *The Greek of the Gospel of Mark*, Philadelphia, 1961 (*JBL Monograph Series* 12)

DTC: *Dictionnaire de théologie catholique*

Dudley, *Cynicism*: D. Dudley, *A History of Cynicism*, London, 1937

Duensing: H. Duensing, tr., *Epistula apostolorum*, Bonn, 1925 (*Kleine Texte* 152)

Duplacy, *Où en est*: J. Duplacy, *Où en est la critique textuelle du Nouveau Testament?* Paris, 1959 (reprint of three articles from *RechSR* 45, 46 (1957–1958))

Düring, *Chion*: I. Düring, *Chion of Heraclea*, Göteborg, 1951 (*Acta Universitatis Gotoburgensis* 57)

E. B.: Elias Bickerman, Jewish Theological Seminary

Ebeling, *Messiasgeheimnis*: H. Ebeling, *Das Messiasgeheimnis und die Botschaft des Marcus-Evangelisten*, Berlin, 1939 (*ZNW Beiheft* 19)

Echle, *Baptism*: H. Echle, "The Baptism of the Apostles," *Traditio* 3 (1945) 365ff

Eckhardt, *Tod*: K. Eckhardt, *Der Tod des Johannes als Schlüssel zum Verständnis der johanneischen Schriften*, Berlin, 1961

EHPR: *Études d'histoire et de philosophie religieuses . . . de l'Université de Strasbourg*

Ehrhard, *Bibliothek*: A. Ehrhard, "Die griechische Patriarchal-Bibliothek von Jerusalem," *Römische Quartalschrift* 5 (1891) 217ff; 329ff; 383f

Ehrhard, *Kloster*: A. Ehrhard, "Das griechische Kloster Mar-Saba in Palaestina," *Römische Quartalschrift* 7 (1893) 32ff

Eisler, *Messiah*: R. Eisler, *The Messiah Jesus and John the Baptist*, tr. A. Krappe, London, 1931

Eitrem, *Demonology*: S. Eitrem, *Some Notes on the Demonology in the New Testament*, Oslo, 1950 (*Symbolae Osloenses*, suppl. 12; 2 ed. 1966, suppl. 20)

Elements: M. Smith, "The Jewish Elements in the Gospels," *JBR* 24 (1956) 90ff

Eliade, *Shamanism*: M. Eliade, *Shamanism*, tr. W. Trask, New York, 1964 (Bollingen Series 76)

Ephraem, *Commentaire*: Saint Ephrem, *Commentaire de l'Évangile concordant*, tr. L. Leloir, Louvain, 1954 (*CSCO* 145)

Epistula Apostolorum: *Epistula Apostolorum*, ed. H. Duensing, Berlin, 1925 (*Kleine Texte* 152). Now revised in Hennecke-Schneemelcher I.126ff

Eppel, *Piétisme*: R. Eppel, *Le Piétisme juif dans les Testaments des douze Patriarches*, Strasbourg, 1930 (*EHPR* 22)

ET: *Expository Times*

ETL: *Ephemerides Theologicae Lovanienses*

Eus., *HE*: Eusebius, *Historia Ecclesiastica*, ed. E. Schwartz, 5 ed., Berlin, 1952

Farmer, *Maccabees*: W. Farmer, *Maccabees, Zealots and Josephus*, New York, 1956

Farrer, *St. Mt.*: A. Farrer, *St. Matthew and St. Mark*, Westminster, 1954 (*Edward Cadbury Lectures* 1953–1954)

de Faye, *Gnostiques*: E. de Faye, *Gnostiques et gnosticisme*, 2 ed., Paris, 1925 (1 ed., 1913)

Feldman, *Josephus*: L. Feldman, *Josephus, Jewish Antiquities, Books XVIII–XX*, London, 1965 (*Loeb Josephus* 9)

Fendt: L. Fendt, *Gnostische Mysterien*, Munich, 1922

Fenton, *Destruction*: J. Fenton, "Destruction and Salvation in the Gospel According to St. Mark," *JTS* NS 3 (1952) 56ff

Festugière, *Révélation*: A. Festugière, *La Révélation d'Hermès Trismégiste*, III: *Les Doctrines de l'âme*, Paris, 1953

Feuillet, *Perspectives*: A. Feuillet, "Les Perspectives propres à chaque Évangéliste dans les récits de la transfiguration," *Biblica* 39 (1958) 281ff

FGrHist: F. Jacoby, *Die Fragmente der griechischen Historiker*, Berlin and Leiden, 1926——

Field: F. Field, *Origenis Hexaplorum*, Oxford, 1875, 2 vols.

Flemington, *Doctrine*: W. Flemington, *The New Testament Doctrine of Baptism*, London, 1948

Flusser, *Sect*: D. Flusser, "The Dead Sea Sect and Pre-Pauline Christianity," in *Aspects of the Dead Sea Scrolls*, ed. C. Rabin and Y. Yadin, Jerusalem, 1958 (*Scripta Hierosolymitana* 4), 215ff

Frangoulis: J. Frangoulis, *Die Begriff des Geistes "Πνεῦμα" bei Clemens Alexandrinus*, Borna-Leipzig, 1936

Freudenberger, *Verhalten*: R. Freudenberger, *Das Verhalten der römischen Behörden gegen die Christen im 2. Jahrhundert*, Munich, 1967 (*Münchener Beiträge zur Papyrusforschung und antiken Rechtsgeschichte* 52)

Fridrichsen, *Problème*: A. Fridrichsen, *La Problème du miracle dans le Christianisme primitif*, Paris, 1925 (*EHPR* 12)

von Fritz, *Present*: K. von Fritz, "The So-Called Historical Present in Early Greek," *Word* 5 (1949) 186ff

von Fritz and Knapp: K. von Fritz and E. Knapp, *Aristotle's Constitution of Athens*, New York, 1950

FRLANT: *Forschungen zur Religion u. Literatur des Alten und Neuen Testaments*

G.L.: G. W. H. Lampe, Cambridge University

Gärtner, *Temple*: B. Gärtner, *The Temple and the Community in Qumran and in the New Testament*, Cambridge, 1965 (*SNTS* Monograph Series 1)

GCS: *Die griechischen christlichen Schriftsteller der ersten Jahrhunderte*

Geiger, *Texts*: B. Geiger, "The Middle Iranian Texts," in Kraeling, *Dura*, 283ff

Gesenius-Buhl: W. Gesenius, *Handwörterbuch über das Alte Testament*, ed. F. Buhl, 16 ed., 1921

Glasson, *Mt.*: T. Glasson, "Did Mt. and Lk. Use a 'Western Text' of Mk.?" *ET* 55 (1943) 180ff

Gnilka, *Verstockung*: J. Gnilka, *Die Verstockung Israels*, Munich, 1961 (*SANT* 3)

Goguel, *Persécutions*: M. Goguel, "Avec des Persécutions," *RHPR* 8 (1928) 264ff

Goguel, review of Bauer: M. Goguel, review of W. Bauer, *Rechtgläubigkeit und Ketzerei im ältesten Christentum RHPR* 15 (1935) 163ff

Goldammer, *Schamanismus*: K. Goldammer, "Der Schamanismus in der Vorwelt und Umwelt des Christentums," *Theologische Literaturzeitung* 81 (1956) 393ff

Goodenough: E. Goodenough, *Jewish Symbols in the Greco-Roman Period*, New York, 1953–1968, 13 vols., (Bollingen Series 37)

Goodspeed, *Introduction*: E. Goodspeed, *An Introduction to the New Testament*, Chicago, 1943

Gospel of Thomas (Leipoldt): J. Leipoldt, *Das Evangelium nach Thomas*, Berlin, 1967 (*TU* 101)

Gottstein, *Traits*: M. Gottstein, "Anti-Essene Traits in the Dead Sea Scrolls," *VT* 4 (1954) 141ff

Grant, *Appeal*: R. Grant, "The Appeal to the Early Fathers," *JTS* NS 11 (1960) 13ff

Grant, *Children*: R. Grant, "Like Children," *HTR* 39 (1946) 71ff

Grant, *Decalogue*: R. Grant, "The Decalogue in Early Christianity," *HTR* 40 (1947) 1ff

Grant, *Gnosis*: R. Grant, "Gnosis Revisited," *ChH* 23 (1954) 3ff

Grant, *Gnosticism*: R. Grant, *Gnosticism and Early Christianity*, New York, 1959

Grant, *Idea*: F. Grant, "The Idea of the Kingdom of God in the New Testament," in *The Sacral Kingship*, ed. R. Pettazzoni, Leiden, 1958 (*Numen*, suppl. 4), 437ff

Grant, *Pliny*: R. Grant, "Pliny and the Christians," *HTR* 41 (1948) 273

Grant-Freedman: R. Grant and D. Freedman, *The Secret Sayings of Jesus*, New York, 1960

Grégoire, *Persécutions*: H. Grégoire et al., *Les Persécutions dans l'Empire Romain*, 2 ed., Brussels, 1964 (Académie royale de Belgique, *Mémoires in 8°*, 56.5)

Gressmann, *Aufgaben*: H. Gressmann, *Die Aufgaben der Wissenschaft des nachbiblischen Judentums*, Giessen, 1925

Griffiths, *Within*: J. Griffiths, "'Within You' Lk. 17.21," *The Bible Translator* 4 (1953) 7f

Grundmann: W. Grundmann, *Das Evangelium nach Markus*, Berlin, 1959 (*Th.Hdk.z.NT.* II²)

Guy, *Origin*: H. Guy, *The Origin of the Gospel of Mark*, New York, 1955

Guy, *Sayings*: H. Guy, "A Sayings-Collection in Mark's Gospel?" *JTS* 42 (1941) 173ff

H.C.: Henry Chadwick, Oxford University

H.J.C.: Henry Joel Cadbury

H.K.: Helmut Köster, Harvard University

Hadas: M. Hadas, ed., *Aristeas to Philocrates*, New York, 1951

Haenchen, *Apostelgeschichte*: E. Haenchen, *Die Apostelgeschichte*, Göttingen, 1959 (Meyer's *Kommentar*)

Haenchen, *Probleme*: E. Haenchen, "Johanneische Probleme," *ZTK* 56 (1959) 19ff

Harden: J. Harden, tr., *The Ethiopic Didascalia*, New York, 1920

Harnack, *Fragment*: A. von Harnack, "Ein neues Fragment aus den Hypotyposen des Clemens," *Sitzungsberichte*, Berlin, 1904, 901ff

Harnack, *Geschichte*: A. von Harnack, *Geschichte der altchristlichen Literatur bis Eusebius*, 2 ed., Leipzig, 1958, 2 vols. in 4

Harnack, *Gwynn'schen*: A. von Harnack, *Die Gwynn'schen Cajus-und-Hippolytus-Fragmente*, Leipzig, 1890 (*TU* 6.3)

Harnack, *Origin*: A. von Harnack, *The Origin of the New Testament*, tr. J. Wilkinson, New York, 1925

Harnack, *Pfaff'schen*: A. von Harnack, *Die Pfaff'schen Irenäus-Fragmente als Fälschungen Pfaffs nachgewiesen*, Leipzig, 1900 (*TU* 20.3)

Harnack, *Pistis-Sophia*: A. von Harnack, *Über das gnostische Buch Pistis-Sophia*, Leipzig, 1891 *TU* 7.2)

Harnack, *Pseudopapianisches*: A. von Harnack, "Pseudopapianisches," *ZNW* 3 (1902) 159ff

Harnack, *Quellenkritik*: A. von Harnack, *Zur Quellenkritik der Geschichte des Gnosticismus*, Leipzig, n.d. (1873)

Harvey: W. Harvey, *Sancti Irenaei Episcopi Lugdunensis Libros Quinque Adversus Haereses*, Cambridge, Eng., 1857, 2 vols.

Hatch, *Text*: W. Hatch, *The "Western" Text of the Gospels*, Evanston, 1937

Hatch-Redpath: E. Hatch and H. Redpath, *A Concordance to the Septuagint*, Oxford, 1897 (repr. Graz, 1954), 2 vols.

Hauschildt: H. Hauschildt, "πρεσβύτεροι in Ägypten im I–III Jhdt. n. Chr.," *ZNW* 4 (1903) 235ff

Hawkins, *Horae*: J. Hawkins, *Horae Synopticae*, 2 ed., Oxford, 1909

HdbAw: *Handbuch der Altertumswissenschaft*

Heckenbach, *De nuditate*: J. Heckenbach, *De nuditate sacra sacrisque vinculis*, Giessen, 1911 (*RgVV* 9.3)

Heim, *Incantamenta*: R. Heim, *Incantamenta magica*, Leipzig, 1892

Ἑλληνικὰ χειρόγραφα: M. Smith, "Ἑλληνικὰ χειρόγραφα ἐν τῇ Μονῇ τοῦ ἁγίου Σάββα," tr. K. Michaelides, *Νέα Σιών* 55 (1960) 110ff, 245ff

Heller: Yom Tov Lipman Heller, *Tosafot Yom Tov*, abr. by J. Katz, in the fourth Horeb ed. of the *Mishnah*, New York, 1935

Hennecke-Schneemelcher: E. Hennecke, *Neutestamentliche Apokryphen*, 3 ed., ed. W. Schneemelcher, 2 vols., Tübingen, 1959–1964

Heroes and Gods: M. Hadas and M. Smith, *Heroes and Gods*, New York, 1965 (*Religious Perspectives* 13)

Hilgenfeld, *Evangeliorum*: A. Hilgenfeld, *Evangeliorum secundum Hebraeos ... quae supersunt*, Leipzig, 1884

Hilgenfeld, *Ketzergeschichte*: A. Hilgenfeld, *Die Ketzergeschichte des Urchristentums*, Leipzig, 1884

Hilgenfeld, *Markus*: A. Hilgenfeld, *Das Markus-Evangelium*, Leipzig, 1850

Hills, *Caesarean Text*: E. Hills, "Harmonizations in the Caesarean Text of Mark," *JBL* 66 (1947) 135ff

HNT: *Handbuch zum Neuen Testament*

Hodayot: in *'Ozar Hamegillot Hagenuzot*, ed. E. Sukenik, Jerusalem, 1956

Holl: K. Holl, "Ein Bruchstück aus einem bisher ubekannten Brief des Epiphanius," in *Festgabe für A. Jülicher*, Tübingen, 1927, 159ff

Hooke, *Religion*: S. Hooke, *Babylonian and Assyrian Religion*, London, 1953

Hornschuh, *Anfänge*: A. Hornschuh, "Die Anfänge des Christentums in Ägypten" (unpub. diss.), Bonn, 1958 (microfilm)

Hornschuh, *Studien*: M. Hornschuh, *Studien zur Epistula Apostolorum*, Berlin, 1965 (*PTS* 5)

Hort and Mayor: F. Hort and J. Mayor, ed., *Clement of Alexandria Miscellanies Book VII*, London, 1902

HSCP: Harvard Studies in Classical Philology

HTR: Harvard Theological Review

HUCA: Hebrew Union College Annual

Huffmann, *Sources*: N. Huffmann, "The Sources of Mark," in *Quantulacumque* (Lake *Festschrift*), ed. R. Casey *et al.*, London, 1937, 123ff

Hunkin, ἄρχομαι: J. Hunkin, "'Pleonastic' ἄρχομαι in the New Testament," *JTS* 25 (1924) 390ff

Hyldahl: N. Hyldahl, "Hegesipps Hypomnemata," *StTh* 14 (1960) 70ff

ICC: International Critical Commentary

IDB: Interpreter's Dictionary of the Bible

Ignatius: "Ignatii Epistulae," in *PAO* (*Eph.* = ad Ephesios; *Mag.* = ad Magnesios; *Trall.* = ad Trallianos; *Rom.* = ad Romanos; *Phil.* = ad Philadelphenos; *Smyr.* = ad Smyrnaeos; *Poly.* = ad Polycarpum)

Image: M. Smith, "The Image of God," *BJRL* 40 (1958) 473ff

J.: Talmud Yerushalmi, ed. B. Behrend, Krotoshin, 1866

J.M.: Johannes Munck

J.R.: John Reumann, Lutheran Theological Seminary, Philadelphia

Jaeger, *Christianity*: W. Jaeger, *Early Christianity and Greek Paideia*, Cambridge, Mass., 1961

Jaeger, *Studien*: W. Jaeger, *Studien zur Entstehungsgeschichte der Metaphysik des Aristoteles*, Berlin, 1912

Jaeger, *Theology*: W. Jaeger, *The Theology of the Early Greek Philosophers*, Oxford, 1947 (Gifford Lectures, 1936)

James, *ANT*: M. James, *The Apocryphal New Testament*, Oxford, 1924

James, *Lost Apocrypha*: M. James, *The Lost Apocrypha of the Old Testament*, London, 1920

James, review of Hennecke[2]: M. James, review of E. Hennecke, *Neutestamentliche Apokryphen*, 2 ed., in *JTS* 25 (1924) 184ff, 422ff

JBL: Journal of Biblical Literature

JBR: Journal of Bible and Religion

JEA: Journal of Egyptian Archaeology

Jeremias, *Gleichnisse*: J. Jeremias, *Die Gleichnisse Jesu*, 2 ed., Zürich, 1952 (*ATANT* 11)

Jeremias, *Hg.*: J. Jeremias, *Heiligengräber in Jesu Umwelt*, Göttingen, 1958

Jeremias, *Jerusalem*: J. Jeremias, *Jerusalem zur Zeit Jesu*, 2 ed., Göttingen, 1958

Jeremias, *Kindertaufe*: J. Jeremias, *Die Kindertaufe in den ersten vier Jahrhunderten*, Göttingen, 1958

Jervell, *Imago*: J. Jervell, *Imago Dei*, Göttingen, 1960 (*FRLANT* 76)

Jesus' Attitude: M. Smith, "Jesus' Attitude Towards the Law," *Papers of the Fourth World Congress of Jewish Studies*, I, Jerusalem, 1967, Engl. sect. 241ff

Johnson, *Mark*: S. Johnson, *A Commentary on the Gospel According to St. Mark*, London, 1960

Jonas, *Religion*: H. Jonas, *The Gnostic Religion*, Boston, 2 ed., 1962

Josephus: *Flavii Josephi Opera Omnia*, ed. S. Naber, Leipzig, 1888–1896, 6 vols. (*AJ* = Antiquitates Iudaeorum; *BJ* = Bellum Iudaicum; *V* = Vita; *CA* = Contra Apionem)

JQR: Jewish Quarterly Review

JTS: Journal of Theological Studies

Jülicher-Fascher: A. Jülicher and E. Fascher, *Einleitung in das Neue Testament*, 7 ed., Tübingen, 1931

K.S.: Krister Stendahl, Harvard University

Kamerbeek, *Ajax*: Sophocles, *The Ajax*, ed. J. Kamerbeek, Leiden, 1954

Käsemann, *Analyse*: E. Käsemann, "Kritische Analyse von Phil. 2.5–11," *ZTK* 47 (1950) 313ff

Käsemann, *Ketzer*: E. Käsemann, "Ketzer u. Zeuge," *ZTK* 48 (1951) 292ff

Kees, *Himmelsreise*: H. Kees, "Die Himmelsreise im ägyptischen Totenglauben," *VBW* 1928–1929, 1ff

Kenny, *Transfiguration*: A. Kenny, "The Transfiguration and the Agony in the Garden," *CBQ* 4 (1957) 444ff

Kerényi: K. Kerényi, *Die griechisch-orientalische Romanliteratur*, Tübingen, 1927

Khitrowo, *Itinéraires*: B. de Khitrowo, *Itinéraires russes en orient*, Geneva, I, 1889

Kilpatrick, *Atticism*: G. Kilpatrick, "Atticism in the Text of the Greek New Testament," in *Neutestamentliche Aufsätze*, ed. J. Blinzler *et al.*, Regensburg, 1963, 125ff

Kilpatrick, *Disappearance*: G. Kilpatrick, "The Disappearance of Q," *JTS* 42 (1941) 182ff

Kilpatrick, ἐκεῖνος: G. Kilpatrick, "ἐκεῖνος in the Gospels and Acts," manuscript sent me by the author

Kilpatrick, *Mission*: G. Kilpatrick, "The Gentile Mission in Mark and Mark 13.9–11," in Nineham, *Studies*, 145ff

Kilpatrick, *Notes*: G. Kilpatrick, "Some Notes on Marcan Usage," *The Bible Translator* 7 (1956) 2ff, 51ff

Klijn, *P. Bodmer II*: A. Klijn, "Papyrus Bodmer II and the Text of Egypt," *NTS* 3 (1956) 327ff

Klijn, *Question*: A. Klijn, "The Question of the Rich Young Man in a Jewish-Christian Gospel," *NovTes* 8 (1966) 149ff

Klijn, *Survey*: A. Klijn, "A Survey of the Researches into the Western Text of the Gospels and Acts," *NovTes* 3 (1959) 1ff, 161ff

Klostermann: E. Klostermann, *Das Markusevangelium*, 4 ed., Tübingen, 1950 (*HNT*)

Knapp: see von Fritz

Knox, *Marcion*: J. Knox, *Marcion and The New Testament*, Chicago, 1942

Knox, *Note*: J. Knox, "A Note on Mark 14.51–52," in *The Joy of Study*, ed. S. Johnson, New York, 1951, 27ff

Koch, *Origenes*: H. Koch, "Origenes 5," *PW* 18.1 (1939) 1036ff

Koerte-Thierfelder: A. Koerte, *Menandri quae supersunt*, ed. A. Thierfelder, 2 ed., Leipzig, 1957–1959, 2 vols.

Köster, *ΓΝΩΜΑΙ*: H. Köster, "ΓΝΩΜΑΙ ΔΙΑΦΟΡΟΙ," *HTR* 58 (1965) 279ff

Köster, *Häretiker*: H. Köster, "Häretiker im Urchristentum," *RGG* 3 (1959) 17ff

Köster, *Herrenworte*: H. Köster, "Die ausserkanonischen Herrenworte," *ZNW* 48 (1957) 220ff

Köster, *Überlieferung*: H. Köster, *Synoptische Überlieferung bei den Apostolischen Vätern*, Berlin, 1957 (*TU* 65)

Kraeling, *Dura*: C. Kraeling, *The Synagogue*, New Haven, 1956 (*The Excavations at Dura-Europos: Final Report* 8.1)

Kraeling, *Necromancy*: C. Kraeling, "Was Jesus Accused of Necromancy?" *JBL* 59 (1940) 147ff

Kraft, *Anfänge*: H. Kraft, "Die Anfänge der Christlichen Taufe," *ThZ* 17 (1961) 399ff

Kraft, *Gab*: H. Kraft, "Gab es einem Gnostiker Karpokrates?" *ThZ* 5 (1952) 434ff

433

Kraft, *Oxyrhynchus*: R. Kraft, "Oxyrhynchus Papyrus 655 Reconsidered," *HTR* 54 (1961) 253ff

Kragerüd, *Lieblingsjünger*: A. Kragerüd, *Der Lieblingsjünger im Johannesevangelium*, Oslo, 1959

Kramer, *Christos*: W. Kramer, *Christos Kyrios, Gottessohn*, Zürich, 1963 (*ATANT* 44)

Krauss, *Leben*: S. Krauss, *Das Leben Jesu nach Jüdischen Quellen*, Berlin, 1902

Krauss, *Lehnwörter*: S. Krauss, *Griechische und lateinische Lehnwörter im Talmud, Midrasch und Targum*, Berlin, 1898–1899, 2 vols.

Kretschmar: G. Kretschmar, "Karpokrates," *RGG*³ 3 (1959) 1159

Kropp, *AKZ*: A. Kropp, *Ausgewählte koptische Zaubertexte*, Brussels, 1930–1931, 3 vols.

Kuhn, *Epheserbrief*: K. Kuhn, "Die Epheserbrief im Lichte der Qumrantexte," *NTS* 7 (1961) 334ff

Kuhn, *Phylakterien*: K. Kuhn, *Phylakterien aus Höhle 4 von Qumran*, Heidelberg, 1957 (*Abhandlungen*, Heidelberg, 1957, 1)

Kühner-Gerth: R. Kühner and B. Gerth, *Ausführliche Grammatik der griechischen Sprache*, 4 ed., Leverkusen, 1955, 2 vols.

Kümmel, *Eschatologie*: W. Kümmel, "Futurische und Präsentische Eschatologie im Ältesten Urchristentum," *NTS* 5 (1959) 113ff

Kutter: H. Kutter, *Clemens Alexandrinus und das NT*, Giessen, 1897

L.F.: Ludwig Früchtel

Ladd, *Reign*: G. Ladd, "The Kingdom of God: Reign or Realm," *JBL* 81 (1962) 230ff

Lagrange: M. Lagrange, *Évangile selon Saint Marc*, Paris, 1911

Lazzati: G. Lazzati, *Introduzione allo Studio di Clemente Alessandrino*, Milan, 1939 (*Pubb. dell' Univ. Cat. del S. Cuore*, ser. 4, vol. 2)

Lebon: J. Lebon, "Sur Quelques Fragments de lettres attribuées á Saint Epiphane de Salamine," in *Micellanea Giovanni Mercati*, Vatican City, 1946 (*Studi e Testi* 121)

Lebreton: J. Lebreton, "Le Désaccord de la foi populaire et de la théologie savante," *RHE* 19 (1923) 481ff; 20 (1924) 5ff

van Leeuwen: J. van Leeuwen, ed., *Aristophanis Aves*, Leiden, 1902

Legg, *Mk.*: *Novum Testamentum Graece secundum textum Westcotto-Hortianum, Evangelium secundum Marcum*, ed. S. Legg, Oxford, 1935

Legg, *Mt.*: idem., *Evangelium secundum Matthaeum*, Oxford, 1940

Leipoldt, *Geschichte*: J. Leipoldt, *Geschichte des neutestamentlichen Kanons*, *I: Die Entstehung*, Leipzig, 1907

Leisegang: J. Leisegang, *Indices ad Philonis Alexandrini Opera*, Berlin, 1926–1930, 2 v. (*Philonis Alex. Opera quae supersunt*, ed. L. Cohn and P. Wendland, 7)

Leisegang, *Gnosis*: H. Leisegang, *Die Gnosis*, Leipzig, 1924 (4 ed., Stuttgart, 1955)

Leutsch-Schneidewin, *Corpus*: E. von Leutsch and F. Schneidewin, *Corpus paroemiographorum graecorum*, Hildesheim, 1958 (repr. of Göttingen ed., 1839–1851), 2 vols.

Lévy, *Légende*: I. Lévy, *La Légende de Pythagore*, Paris, 1927 (*BEHE* 250)

Lewy, *Oracles*: H. Lewy, *Chaldaean Oracles and Theurgy*, Cairo, 1956 (Institut français d'archéologie orientale, *Recherches d'archéologie* 13)

Liboron: H. Liboron, *Die karpokratianische Gnosis*, Leipzig, 1938

Lieberman, *Greek*: S. Lieberman, *Greek in Jewish Palestine*, New York, 1942

Lieberman, *Hellenism*: S. Lieberman, *Hellenism in Jewish Palestine*, 2 ed., New York, 1962 (*Texts and Studies of the Jewish Theological Seminary of America*, 18)

Lieberman, *Tosefeth*: S. Lieberman, *Tosefeth Rishonim*, Jerusalem, 1938–1939, 4 vols.

Lieberman, *Tosefta*: S. Lieberman, *Tosefta Ki-fshutah*, pt. 5, New York, 1962

Lietzmann, *Korinther*: H. Lietzmann, *An die Korinther I/II*, 4 ed., ed. W. Kümmel, Tübingen (*HNT* 9)

Lightfoot, *Colossians*: J. Lightfoot, *St. Paul's Epistles to the Colossians and to Philemon*, Grand Rapids, N.D. (repr. of ed. of 1879)

Lightfoot, *Galatians*: J. Lightfoot, *The Epistle of St. Paul to the Galatians*, Grand Rapids, N.D., 1957 (repr., date of reprinted ed. not given)

Lightfoot, *Jn.*: R. Lightfoot, *St. John's Gospel: A Commentary*, Oxford, 1956

Lindeskog, *Logiastudien*: G. Lindeskog, "Logiastudien," *Studia Theologica* 4 (1952) 129ff

Lipsius, *Apostelgeschichten*: R. Lipsius, *Die apokryphen Apostelgeschichten und Apostellegenden*, Braunschweig, 1883–1890, 3 vols. in 4

Lohmeyer: E. Lohmeyer, *Das Evangelium des Markus*, Göttingen, 1957 (*Meyers Kommentar*, I.2)

Lohmeyer, *Galiläa*: E. Lohmeyer, *Galiläa und Jerusalem*, Göttingen, 1936

Lord, *Singer*: A. Lord, *The Singer of Tales*, Cambridge, Mass., 1960

LSJ: H. Liddell and R. Scott, *A Greek-English Lexicon*, ed. H. Jones, Oxford, n.d., 2 vols.

LTK: M. Buchberger, *Lexikon für Theologie und Kirche*

Luce: H. Luce, *The Gospel According to St. Luke*, Cambridge, Eng., 1933 (*Cambridge Greek Testament*)

Lundström, *Kingdom*: G. Lundström, *The Kingdom of God in the Teaching of Jesus*, tr. J. Bulman, Edinburgh, 1963

LXX: *Septuaginta*, ed. A. Rahlfs, Stuttgart, n.d., 2 vols.

M.: *The Mishnah*

M.H.: Moses Hadas

M.R.: M. Richard, Institut de Recherche et d'Histoire des Textes, Paris

Macgregor, *Principalities*: G. Macgregor, "Principalities and Powers," *NTS* 1 (1954) 17ff

Machen, *Origin*: J. Machen, *The Origin of Paul's Religion*, New York, 1921

MacMullen, *Enemies*: R. MacMullen, *Enemies of the Roman Order*, Cambridge, Mass., 1966

McNeile: A. McNeile, *The Gospel According to St. Matthew*, London, 1957

Manichaean Psalm Book: *A Manichaean Psalm Book*, pt. 2, ed. C. Allberry, Stuttgart, 1938 (Manichaean MSS in the C. Beatty Collection 2)

Manson, *Sayings*: T. Manson, *The Sayings of Jesus*, London, n.d. (repr. of 1949 ed.)

Manson, *Teaching*: T. Manson, *The Teaching of Jesus*, 2 ed., Cambridge, Eng., 1959

Manual: *The Dead Sea Scrolls of St. Mark's Monastery*, II: *Plates and Transcription of the Manual of Discipline*, ed. M. Burrows, New Haven, 1951

Margalioth, *Sepher ha-Razim*: M. Margalioth, *Sepher ha-Razim*, Jerusalem, 1966

Margulies: M. Margulies, *Midrash Wayyikra' Rabbah*, Jerusalem, 1953–1960, 5 vols.

Marrou, *Humanisme*: H. Marrou, "Humanisme et christianisme chez Clément d'Alexandrie," in *Recherches sur la tradition platonicienne*, Geneva, 1957 (Entretiens sur l'antiquité classique 3)

Marsh: H. Marsh, "The Use of μυστήριον in the Writings of Clement of Alexandria," *JTS* 37 (1936) 64ff

Martin, review of Köster: C. Martin, review of H. Köster, *Synoptische Überlieferung bei den apostolischen Vätern*, in *NRT* 81 (1959) 759ff

Marxsen, *Evangelist*: W. Marxsen, *Der Evangelist Markus*, 2 ed., Göttingen, 1959 (*FRLANT* 67)

Massaux, *État*: E. Massaux, "État actuel de la critique textuelle du NT," *NTR* 75 (1953) 702ff

Mayeda, *Leben-Jesu-Fragment*: G. Mayeda, *Das Leben-Jesu-Fragment Papyrus Egerton 2*, Bern, 1946

Méhat, *Étude*: A. Méhat, *Étude sur les "Stromates" de Clément d'Alexandrie*, Paris, 1966 (*Patristica Sorbonensia* 7)

Méhat, *Ordres*: A. Méhat, "Les Ordres de l'enseignement chez Célment d'Alexandrie et Sénèque," in *Studia Patristica*, Berlin, 1957 (*TU* 64). II, 351ff

Melamed, *Leshe'elat*: E. Melamed, "Leshe'elat bate hassefer hayyehudiim ba'arez," *Tarbiz* 22 (1951) 117ff

Metzger, *Reconsideration*: B. Metzger, "A Reconsideration of Certain Arguments against the Pauline Authorship of the Pastoral Epistles," *ET* 70 (1958) 91ff

Metzger, *Survey*: B. Metzger, "A Survey of Recent Research on the Ancient Versions of the New Testament," *NTS* 2 (1955–1956) 1ff

Michaelis, *Hintergrund*: W. Michaelis, "Zum jüdischen Hintergrund der Johannestaufe," *Judaica* 7 (1951) 81ff

Migne, *PG*: J. P. Migne, *Patrologiae cursus completus, series graeca*, Paris, 1857–1866, 161 vols.

Milik, *Inscription*: J. Milik, "Une Inscription et une lettre en Araméen christo-palestinien," *RB* 60 (1953) 526ff

Millet, *Recherches*: G. Millet, *Recherches sur l'iconographie de l'évangile*, Paris, 1916

Moingt: J. Moingt, "La Gnose de Clément d'Alexandrie," *RechSR* 37 (1950) 195ff, 398ff, 537ff; 38 (1951) 82ff

Molland: E. Molland, *The Conception of the Gospel in the Alexandrian Theology*, Oslo, 1938 (Norse Ak., Skrifter, HPK 1938, 2)

Monasteries: M. Smith, "Monasteries and Their Manuscripts," *Archaeology*, 13 (1960) 172ff

Mondésert, *Clément*: C. Mondésert, *Clément d'Alexandrie*, Paris, 1944 (*Théologie* 4)

Mondésert, *Stromateis*: C. Mondésert, ed., *Clément d'Alexandrie: Les Stromates*, I, Paris, 1951; II, Paris, 1954 (Sources Chrétiennes 30, 38)

Mondésert, *Symbolisme*: C. Mondésert, "Le Symbolisme chez Clément d'Alexandrie," *RechSR* 26 (1936) 158ff

Montgomery, *Incantation Texts*: J. Montgomery, *Aramaic Incantation Texts from Nippur*, Philadelphia, 1913 (University of Pennsylvania Museum, *Publications of the Babylonian Section* 3)

Moore, *Judaism*: G. Moore, *Judaism in the First Centuries of the Christian Era*, Cambridge, Mass., 1927–1930, 3 vols.

Morgenthaler: R. Morgenthaler, *Statistik des neutestamentlichen Wortschatzes*, Frankfurt am M., n.d. (1958)

Mossbacher: H. Mossbacher, *Präpositionen und Präpositionsadverbien ... bei Clemens von Alexandrien*, Erlangen, 1931

Moule, *Idiom-Book*: C. Moule, *An Idiom-Book of New Testament Greek*, 2 ed., Cambridge, Eng., 1960

Moule, *Intention*: C. Moule, "The Intention of the Evangelists," in *N.T. Essays*, ed. A. Higgins, Manchester, 1959, 165ff

Moule, review of Köster: C. Moule, review of H. Köster, *Synoptische Überlieferung bei den apostolischen Vätern*, in *JTS* 9 (1958) 368ff

Moulton-Geden: W. Moulton and A. Geden, *A Concordance to the Greek Testament*, 3 ed., Edinburgh, 1926 (repr. 1953)

Müller, *Lexicon*: G. Müller, *Lexicon Athanasianum*, Berlin, 1952

Müller, *Verklärung*: H. Müller, "Die Verklärung Jesu," *ZNW* 51 (1960) 56ff

Munck, *Presbyters*: J. Munck, "Presbyters and Disciples of the Lord in Papias," *HTR* 52 (1959) 223ff

Munck, *Untersuchungen*: J. Munck, *Untersuchungen über Klemens von Alexandria*, Stuttgart, 1933

Murphy: M. Murphy, *Nature Allusions in the Works of Clement of Alexandria*, Washington, D.C., 1941 (Catholic University of America, *Patristic Studies* 65)

Münderlein, *Erwählung*: G. Münderlein, "Die Erwählung durch das Pleroma," *NTS* 8 (1962) 264ff

MWVZ: *Monatsschrift des wissenschaftlichen Vereins in Zürich*

Nauck, *Salt*: W. Nauck, "Salt as a Metaphor," *Studia Theologica* 6 (1952) 163ff

Nautin, *Lettres*: P. Nautin, *Lettres et écrivains chrétiens*, Paris, 1961 (*Patristica* II)

Nesbitt: C. Nesbitt, "The Bethany Traditions in the Gospel Narratives," *JBR* 29 (1961) 119ff

Nestle-Kilpatrick: E. Nestle and G. Kilpatrick, ed., *H ΚΑΙΝΗ ΔΙΑΘΗΚΗ*, 2 ed., London, 1958

Neusner, *Life*: J. Neusner, *A Life of Rabban Yohanan ben Zakkai*, Leiden, 1962 (*Studia Post-Biblica* 6)

Nilsson: M. Nilsson, *Geschichte der griechischen Religion*, Munich, I² 1955, II 1950, II² 1961 (*HdbAw* V.2.1, 2)

Nilsson, *Zauberpapyri*: M. Nilsson, *Die Religion in den griechischen Zauberpapyri*, Lund, 1948 (*Bulletin de la Société Royale des Lettres de Lund* 1947–1948, 2)

Nineham, *Eyewitness*: D. Nineham, "Eyewitness Testimony and the Gospel Tradition," *JTS* NS 9 (1958) 12ff, 243ff; NS 11 (1960) 253ff

Nineham, *Order*: D. Nineham, "The Order of Events in St. Mark's Gospel" in Nineham, *Studies*, 223ff

Nineham, *Studies*: D. Nineham, ed., *Studies in the Gospels*, Oxford, 1955 (R. H. Lightfoot *Festschrift*)

Nock, *Alexander*: A. Nock, "Alexander of Abonuteichos," *Classical Quarterly* 22 (1928) 162ff

Nock, *EGC*: A. Nock, "Early Gentile Christianity," in *Essays on the Trinity and the Incarnation*, ed. A. Rawlinson, London, 1928

Nock, *Magus*: A. Nock, "Paul and the Magus," in *The Beginnings of Christianity*, ed. K. Lake *et al.*, London, pt. 1, V, 1933, 164ff

Nock, *Mysteries*: A. Nock, "Hellenistic Mysteries and Christian Sacraments," *Mnemosyne*, ser. 4, vol. 5 (1952) 177ff

Nock, *Mysterion*: A. Nock, "Mysterion," *Harvard Studies in Classical Philology* 60 (1951) 201ff

Nock, review of Goodenough V–VI: A. Nock, review of E. Goodenough, *Jewish Symbols in the Greco-Roman Period*, V–VI, in *Gnomon* 29 (1957) 527ff

Nock, review of Harder: A. Nock, review of R. Harder, *Karpokrates von Chalkis*, in *Gnomon* 21 (1949) 221ff

Nock, review of Schoeps: A. Nock, review of H. J. Schoeps, *Paulus*, in *Gnomon* 33 (1961) 581ff

Nock, review of Scholem: A. Nock, review of G. Scholem, *Jewish Gnosticism, Merkabah Mysticism and Talmudic Tradition*, in *Harvard Divinity School Bulletin*, April 1962, 27

Nock, *Sacramentum*: A. Nock, "The Christian Sacramentum in Pliny and a Pagan Counterpart," *CR* 38 (1924) 58f

Noth, *Fünf*: M. Noth, "Die fünf syrisch überlieferten apokryphen Psalmen," *ZAW* 48 (1930) 1ff

Notopoulos, *Homer*: J. Notopoulos, "Homer, Hesiod and the Achaean Heritage of Oral Poetry," *Hesperia* 29 (1960) 177ff

Notopoulos, *Hymns*: J. Notopoulos, "The Homeric Hymns as Oral Poetry," *AJP* 83 (1962) 337ff

NovTes: *Novum Testamentum*

NRT: *Nouvelle Revue théologique*

NT: *New Testament*

NTS: *New Testament Studies*

NTT: *Nederlands Theologisch Tidsskrift*

NTTS: *New Testament Tools and Studies*

Observations: M. Smith, "Observations on Hekhalot Rabbati," in *Biblical and Other Studies*, ed. A. Altmann, Cambridge, Mass., 1963 (Philip W. Lown Institute, *Studies and Texts*, 1), 142ff

Oehler, *Haeresiologici*: F. Oehler, *Corporis haeresiologici tomus primus*, Berlin, 1856

Oksala: P. Oksala, *Die griechischen Lehnwörter in den Prosaschriften Ciceros*, Helsinki, 1953

OLZ: *Orientalistische Literaturzeitung*

Oppenheim, *Interpretation*: A. Oppenheim, *The Interpretation of Dreams in the Ancient Near East*, Philadelphia, 1956 (*Transactions of the American Philosophical Society*, NS 46.3)

Osborn, *Philosophy*: E. Osborn, *The Philosophy of Clement of Alexandria*, Cambridge, Eng., 1957 (*Texts and Studies*, NS 3)

Osborn, *Teaching*: E. Osborn, "Teaching and Writing in the First Chapter of the Stromateis of Clement of Alexandria," *JTS*, NS 10 (1959) 335ff

OT: Old Testament

P.: Papyrus

P.B.: Pierre Benoit, O.P., École Biblique de Jérusalem

P. Egerton 2: *The New Gospel Fragments* (no editor named), London, 1935 (for the Trustees of the British Museum)

P. Erlangen: W. Schubart, *Die Papyri der Universitätsbibliothek Erlangen*, Leipzig, 1942

P. Oxy.: *The Oxyrhynchus Papyri*, ed. B. Grenfell, A Hunt, *et al.*, London, 1898——

P. Teb.: B. Grenfell, A Hunt, J. Smyly, C. Edgar, ed., *The Tebtunis Papyri*, London, 1902–1938, 3 vols.

Palladius, *HL*: *The Lausiac History of Palladius*, ed. C. Butler, Cambridge, 1898, 2 vols. (*Texts and Studies*, 6)

Palm, *Funktion*: J. Palm, "Zur Funktion und Stellung des attributiven Demonstrativums im Griechischen," *Scripta Minora Reg. Soc. Hum. Lit. Lund.*, 1959–1960, 2

PAO: *Patrum Apostolicorum Opera*, ed. O. Gebhardt, A. Harnack, T. Zahn, 6 ed., Leipzig, 1920

Papadopoulos-Kerameus: A. Papadopoulos-Kerameus, Ἱεροσολυμιτικὴ Βιβλιοθήκη, St. Petersburg, 1891–1915, 5 vols.

Parker, *Gospel*: P. Parker, *The Gospel before Mark*, Chicago, 1953

Parker, *John*: P. Parker, "John and John Mark," *JBL* 79 (1960) 97ff

Parker, *Two Editions*: P. Parker, "Two Editions of John," *JBL* 75 (1956) 303ff

Parry, *Studies*: M. Parry, "Studies in the Epic Technique of Oral Verse-Making, I: Homer and Homeric Style," *HSCP* 41 (1930) 73–147

PBA: *Proceedings of the British Academy*

PEQ: *Palestine Exploration Quarterly*

Pericoli-Ridolfini, *Origini*: F. Pericoli-Ridolfini, "Le Origini della Chiesa di Alessandria," *Atti della Accademia Nazionale dei Lincei*, ser. 8, vol. 17, *Rendiconti* (Classe di scienze morali), 1962, 317ff

Pernot, *Prétendu*: H. Pernot, "Un Prétendu original latin de l'Évangile de Marc," *RHR* 95 (1927) 43ff

Perrin, *Kingdom*: N. Perrin, *The Kingdom of God in the Teaching of Jesus*, Philadelphia, 1963

Perry: B. Perry, *Aesopica*, *I*, Urbana, 1952

Peterson, *Εἷς*: E. Peterson, *Εἷς Θεός*, Göttingen, 1926

PG: *Patrologia graeca*

PGM: *Papyri graecae magicae*, ed. K. Preisendanz, Leipzig, 1928–1931, 2 vols.

Phokylides, *Laura*: J. Phokylides, Η ΙΕΡΑ ΛΑΥΡΑ ΣΑΒΑ ΤΟΥ ΗΓΙΑΣΜΕΝΟΥ, Alexandria, 1927

Photius: Photius, *Bibliothèque*, ed. R. Henry, Paris, 1959—— for codices 1–185, otherwise Migne, *PG* 103–104

Pippidi, *Recherches*: D. Pippidi, *Recherches sur le culte impérial*, Paris, n.d. (Institut Roumain d'Études Latines, collection scientifique 2)

438

Plumley, Christianity: J. Plumley, "Early Christianity in Egypt," *PEQ* 89 (1957) 70ff

Preisigke, *Papyruswörterbuch*: F. Preisigke *et al.*, *Wörterbuch der griechischen Papyrusurkunden*, Berlin, 1925——

Preuschen, *Hymnen*: E. Preuschen, *Zwei gnostische Hymnen*, Giessen, 1904

Problems: M. Smith, "Pauline Problems," *HTR* 50 (1957) 116ff

PTS: *Patristische Texte und Studien*

Puech, *Où*: H. Puech, "Où en est le problème du gnosticisme," *Revue de l'Université de Bruxelles* 39 (1933) 137ff, 295ff

PW: *Paulys Realencyclopädie der classischen Altertumswissenschaft*

QDS: *Quis dives saluetur* (Stählin III.159–191)

Quispel, *Hebräerevangelium*: G. Quispel, "Das Hebräerevangelium im gnostischen Evangelium nach Maria," *VC* 11 (1957) 139ff

Quispel, *Syrian Thomas*: G. Quispel, "The Syrian Thomas and the Syrian Macarius," *VC* 18 (1964) 226ff

Quispel, *Thomas*: G. Quispel, "The Gospel of Thomas and the New Testament," *VC* 11 (1957) 189ff

R.G.: Robert Grant, University of Chicago

R.S.: R. Schippers, University of Amsterdam

Radermacher: L. Radermacher, *Neutestamentliche Grammatik*, 2 ed., Tübingen, 1925

Rauer: M. Rauer, *Origenes Werke 9*, Berlin, 1959 (*GCS*)

RB: *Revue biblique*

RdQ: *Revue de Qumran*

Reason: M. Smith, "The Reason for the Persecution of Paul and the Obscurity of Acts," in *Studies in Mysticism and Religion Presented to Gershom G. Scholem*, Jerusalem, 1967, 261ff

Réau, *Iconographie*: L. Réau, *Iconographie de l'art chrétien*, Paris, II, pt. 2, 1957

RechSR: *Recherches de science religieuse*

Reg. Soc. Hum. Lit. Lund.: *Regia Societas Humaniorum Litterarum Lundens*

Rengstorf: K. Rengstorf, *Das Evangelium nach Lukas*, 8 ed., Göttingen, 1958

Resch[1]: A. Resch, *Agrapha*, 1 ed., Leipzig, 1889 (*TU* 5.4)

Resch[2]: A. Resch, *Agrapha*, 2 ed., Leipzig, 1906 (*TU* 30.3/4)

Reumann, Οἰκονομία: J. Reumann, "Οἰκονομία as 'Ethical Accommodation' in the Fathers, and its Pagan Backgrounds, in *Studia Patristica* III, ed. F. Cross, Berlin, 1961 (*TU* 78)

RGG: *Religion in Geschichte und Gegenwart*

RgVV: *Religionsgeschichtliche Versuche und Vorarbeiten*

RHE: *Revue d'histoire ecclésiastique*

RHR: *Revue de l'histoire des religions*

Riedinger: U. Riedinger, "Neue Hypotyposen-Fragmente bei Pseudo-Caesarius und Isidor von Pelusium," *ZNW* 51 (1960) 154ff

Riesenfeld, ΠΑΡΑ: H. Riesenfeld, "ΠΑΡΑ ΑΝΘΡΩΠΟΙΣ - ΠΑΡΑ ΘΕΩΙ," *Nuntius Sodalicii Neotestamentici* 7 (1952) 51ff

Riesenfeld, *Tradition*: H. Riesenfeld, "Tradition und Redaktion im Markusevangelium," in *Neutestamentliche Studien für R. Bultmann*, Berlin, 1954, 157ff

Rigaux, *Thess.*: B. Rigaux, *Saint Paul: Les Épitres aux Thessaloniciens*, Paris, 1956 (*Études Bibliques*)

Roberts, *Christianity*: C. Roberts, "Early Christianity in Egypt," *JEA* 40 (1954) 92ff

Roberts, *Codex*: C. Roberts, "The Codex," *PBA* 40 (1956) 187ff

Robinson, *Gospels*: F. Robinson, *Coptic Apocryphal Gospels*, Cambridge, Eng., 1896 (*TS* 4.2)

Robinson, *Hymn*: J. Robinson, *The Hymn of The Soul*, Cambridge, Eng., 1897 (*TS* 5.3)

Robinson, *ΛΟΓΟΙ ΣΟΦΩΝ*: J. M. Robinson, "*ΛΟΓΟΙ ΣΟΦΩΝ*," in *Zeit und Geschichte*, ed. E. Dinkler, Tübingen, 1964, 77ff

Robinson, *Problem . . . Reconsidered*: J. M. Robinson, "The Problem of History in Mark, Reconsidered," *Union Seminary Quarterly Review*, 20 (1965) 131ff

Robinson, *Quest*: J. M. Robinson, *A New Quest of the Historical Jesus*, Naperville, 1959 (*SBT* 25)

Robinson, *Survey*: W. Robinson, "Historical Survey of the Church's Treatment of New Converts with Reference to Pre- and Post-Baptismal Instruction," *JTS* 42 (1941) 42ff

Robinson, *Text*: D. Robinson, "A Magical Text from Beroea in Macedonia," in *Classical and Medieval Studies*, ed. L. Jones, New York, 1938, 245ff

Ropes, *Sprüche*: J. Ropes, *Die Sprüche Jesu die in den kanonischen Evangelien nicht überliefert sind*, Leipzig, 1896 (*TU* 14.2)

Roscher, *Lexikon*: W. Roscher, *Ausführliches Lexikon der griechischen und römischen Mythologie*, Leipzig, 7 vols., 1884–1921 (Repr. Hildesheim, 1965)

Routh: M. Routh, *Reliquiae Sacrae*, 2 ed., Oxford, 1846–1848, 5 vols.

Rowley, *Baptism*: H. Rowley, "The Baptism of John and the Qumran Sect," in *New Testament Essays*, ed. A. Higgins, Manchester, 1959, 218ff

RQ: *Römische Quartalschrift*

RTK: *Realencyklopädie für protestantische Theologie und Kirche*

Russell, *Apocalyptic*: D. Russell, *The Method and Message of Jewish Apocalyptic*, Philadelphia, 1964

Rüther, *Kirche*: T. Rüther, "Die *eine* Kirche und die Haeresie bei Klemens von Alexandrien," *Catholica* 12 (1958) 37ff

Ruwet, *Clement*: J. Ruwet, "Clément d'Alexandrie: Canon d'Écritures et apocryphes," *Biblica* 29 (1948) 77ff, 240ff, 391ff

Samain, *Magie*: J. Samain, "L'Accusation de magie contre le Christ dans les Évangiles," *ETL* 15 (1938) 449ff

Sanday, *Gospels*: W. Sanday, *The Gospels in the Second Century*, London, 1876

Sanday-Headlam, *Romans*: W. Sanday and A. Headlam, *A Critical and Exegetical Commentary on the Epistle to the Romans*, 9 ed., New York, 1904 (*ICC*)

SANT: *Studien zum Alten u. Neuen Testament*

SBT: *Studies in Biblical Theology*

Scham: J. Scham, *Der Optativgebrauch bei Klemens von Alexandrien*, Paderborn, 1913

Schenke: H. Schenke, "Das Evangelium nach Philippus," in J. Leipoldt and H. Schenke, *Koptisch-gnostische Schriften aus den Papyrus-Codices von Nag-Hamadi*, Hamburg-Bergstedt, 1960 (*Theologische Forschung*, 20)

Schille, *Formgeschichte*: G. Schille, "Bemerkungen zur Formgeschichte des Evangeliums: Rahmen und Aufbau des Markus-Evangeliums," *NTS* 4 (1957) 1ff

Schille, *Tauflehre*: G. Schille, "Zur urchristlicher Tauflehre," *ZNW* 49 (1958) 31ff

Schlatter, *Sprache*: A. Schlatter, *Die Sprache und Heimat des vierten Evangelisten*, Gütersloh, 1902

Schmid: W. Schmid, *Der Atticismus*, Stuttgart, 1887–1897, 5 vols.

Schmidt, *Rahmen*: K. Schmidt, *Die Rahmen der Geschichte Jesu*, Berlin, 1919

Schmidt-Till: C. Schmidt and W. Till, ed., *Koptisch-Gnostische Schriften I*, 2 ed., Berlin, 1954 (*GCS*)

Schmithals, *Gnosis*: W. Schmithals, *Die Gnosis in Korinth*, Göttingen, 1956 (*FRLANT* 66)

Schoeps, *AFZ*: H. Schoeps, *Aus frühchristlicher Zeit*, Tübingen, 1950

Schoeps, *Judenchristentum*: H. Schoeps, *Das Judenchristentum*, Bern, 1964

Scholem, *Gnosticism*: Gershom Scholem, *Jewish Gnosticism, Merkabah Mysticism, and Talmudic Tradition*, 2 ed., New York, 1965

Schrade, *Ikonographie*: H. Schrade, "Zur Ikonographie der Himmelfahrt Christi," *VBW* 1928–1929, Berlin, 1930, 66 ff

Schürer, *Geschichte*: E. Schürer, *Geschichte des jüdischen Volkes im Zeitalter Jesu Christi*, 3–4 ed., Leipzig, 1901–1911, 4 vols.

Schweitzer, *Leben-Jesu-Forschung*: A. Schweitzer, *Geschichte der Leben-Jesu-Forschung*, 6 ed., Tübingen, 1951

Sect: M. Smith, "The Dead Sea Sect in Relation to Ancient Judaism," *NTS* 7 (1961) 347ff

SEG: *Supplementum Epigraphicum Graecum*

Seitz, *Criteria*: O. Seitz, "Criteria for the Esoteric Logia in Mk.," *ATR* 31 (1949) 218ff

Sextus Emp.: *Sextus Empiricus*, ed. R. Bury, London, 1939–1949, 4 vols. (*Pyrroneion Hypotyposeon* = *Outlines of Pyrrhonism*)

SH: *Subsidia Hagiographica*

Sherwin-White, *Letters*: A. Sherwin-White, *The Letters of Pliny: A Historical and Social Commentary*, Oxford, 1966

Sidebottom: E. Sidebottom, "The Ascent and Descent of the Son of Man," *ATR* 39 (1957) 115ff

SIG: G. Dittenberger, *Sylloge Inscriptionum Graecarum*, 4 ed., Hildesheim, 1960

Simon, *Stephen*: M. Simon, *St. Stephen and the Hellenists*, New York, 1958 (*Haskell Lectures*, 1956)

SJT: *Scottish Journal of Theology*

Smith, *Jn. 12.12*: D. Smith, "Jn. 12.12f. and the Question of John's Use of the Synoptics," *JBL* 82 (1963) 58ff

SNTS: Society for New Testament Studies

Soden, *Tatianos*: E. von Soden, "Tatianos," in *RGG*

Sophia J.C.: *Die Sophia Jesu Christi*, in *Die gnostischen Schriften des koptischen Papyrus Berolinensis 8502*, ed. W. Till, Berlin, 1955 (*TU* 60)

SP: *Select Papyri*, ed. A. Hunt, C. Edgar, D. Page, London, 1950——

Speyer, *Vorwürfen*: W. Speyer, "Zu den Vorwürfen der Heiden gegen die Christen," *Jahrbuch für Antike und Christentum* 6 (1963) 129ff

Spicq: C. Spicq, *L'Épitre aux Hébreux*, Paris, 1952–1953, 2 vols.

Stählin: O. Stählin, ed., *Clemens Alexandrinus*, Leipzig, I, 2 ed., 1936; II, 3 ed., ed. L. Früchtel, 1960; III and IV, 1909–1936 (*GCS* 12, 15, 17, 39)

Stählin, *Quellen*: H. Stählin, *Die gnostischen Quellen Hippolyts*, Leipzig, 1890 (*TU* 6.3)

Stanley, *Kingdom*: D. Stanley, "Kingdom to Church," *Theological Studies* 16 (1955) 1ff

Stauffer, *Kalifat*: E. Stauffer, "Zum Kalifat des Jacobus," *ZRGG* 4 (1952) 213 ff

Stendahl, *School*: K. Stendahl, *The School of St. Matthew*, Uppsala, 1954 (*Acta Seminarii Neotestamentici Upsaliensis* 20)

Stieren: A. Stieren, *Sancti Irenaei Episcopi Lugdunensis Quae Supersunt Omnia*, Leipzig, 1848–1853, 2 vols. in 4

Strack, *Jesus*: H. Strack, *Jesus, die Häretiker und die Christen*, Leipzig, 1910

Strack-Billerbeck: H. Strack and P. Billerbeck, *Kommentar zum Neuen Testament aus Talmud und Midrasch*, Munich, 1922–1928, 4 vols.

Strömberg, *Proberbs*: R. Strömberg, *Greek Proverbs*, Göteborg, 1954

Strömsholm, *Examination:* D. Strömsholm, "A Literary Examination of Mark," *Hibbert Journal* 26 (1927) 252ff

Strugnell, *Angelic Liturgy*: J. Strugnell, "The Angelic Liturgy at Qumran—4 Q Serek Širôt 'Ôlat Haššabbat," in *VT Supplements VII*, Leiden, 1960 (Congress Volume, Oxford, 1959)

Strycker: É. de Strycker, *La Forme la plus ancienne du Protévangile de Jacques*, Brussels, 1961 (*SH* 33)

Strzygowski, *Kloster*: J. Strzygowski, "Das griechische Kloster Mar Saba in Palästina," *Repertorium für Kunstwissenschaft* 19 (1896) 1ff

StTh: *Studia Theologica*

Swanson, *Text*: R. Swanson, "The Gospel Text of Clement of Alexandria" (unpub. diss.), Yale University, 1956

Swete: H. Swete, *The Gospel According to St. Mark*, 3 ed., London, 1909

T.: *Tosephta*, ed. M. Zuckermandel, 2 ed., Jerusalem, 1937, 2 vols.

T.B.: T. Baarda, University of Amsterdam

Tamborino, *Daemonismo*: J. Tamborino, *De antiquorum daemonismo*, Giessen, 1909 (*RgVV* 7.3)

Taylor: V. Taylor, *The Gospel According to Mark*, London, 1952

Taylor, *Beginning*: T. Taylor, "The Beginning of Jewish Proselyte Baptism," *NTS* 2 (1955) 193ff

Taylor, *Origin*: V. Taylor, "The Origin of the Markan Passion Sayings," *NTS* 1 (1954) 159ff

Tengblad: E. Tengblad, *Syntaktisch-Stilistische Beiträge zur Kritik und Exegese des Clemens von Alexandrien*, Lund, 1932

Testuz: M. Testuz, *Papyrus Bodmer V: Nativité de Marie*, Bibliotheca Bodmeriana, 1958

Theodor: J. Theodor and C. Albeck, *Bereschit Rabba*, Berlin, 1927–1931, 3 vols.

Theophylact: *Theophylacti Archiepiscopi Bulgariae Commentarii in Quatuor Evangelia*, ed. C. Morell, Paris, 1635

Th.Hdk.z.NT: *Theologischer Handkommentar zum Neuen Testament*

Thomas, *Mouvement*: J. Thomas, *Le Mouvement baptiste en Palestine et Syrie*, Gembloux, 1935, (*U. Cat. Louvan. Dissertationes* [theological], ser. 2.28)

ThWb: *Theologisches Wörterbuch zum Neuen Testament*

ThZ: *Theologische Zeitschrift*

Till, *Gnosis*: W. Till, "Die Gnosis in Aegypten," *La Parola del Passato* 4 (1949) 230ff

TS: *Texts and Studies*

Tollington: R. Tollington, *Clement of Alexandria*, London, 1914, 2 vols.

Torrey, *Four Gospels*: C. C. Torrey, *The Four Gospels*, New York, 1933

Torrey, *Translated*: C. C. Torrey, *Our Translated Gospels*, New York, 1936

Trocmé, *Formation*: E. Trocmé, *La Formation de l'Évangile selon Marc*, Paris, 1963 (*EHPR* 57)

Tsermoulas: J. Tsermoulas, *Die Bildersprache des Klemens von Alexandrien*, Cairo, 1934

TU: *Texte und Untersuchungen*

Turner, *Commentary*: C. Turner, "A Textual Commentary on Mk. 1," *JTS* 28 (1927) 145ff

Turner, *Readings*: C. Turner, "Western Readings in the Second Half of St. Mark's Gospel," *JTS* 29 (1928) 1ff

Turner, *Usage*: C. Turner, "Marcan Usage: Notes, Critical and Exegetical, on the Second Gospel," *JTS* 25 (1924) 377ff; 26 (1925) 12ff, 145ff, 225ff, 337ff; 27 (1926) 58ff; 28 (1927) 9ff, 349ff; 29 (1928) 275ff, 346ff

Usener, *Weihnachtsfest*: H. Usener, *Das Weihnachtsfest*, I–III, 2 ed., Bonn, 1911

Vaganay, *Absence*: L. Vaganay, "L'Absence du sermon sur la montagne chez Marc," *RB* 58 (1951) 5ff

Vaganay, *Évangile*: L. Vaganay, *L'Évangile de Pierre*, Paris, 1930

Vaganay, *Problème*: L. Vaganay, *Le Problème synoptique*, Paris, 1954

Vailhé, *Écrivains*: S. Vailhé, "Les Écrivains de Mar Saba," *Échos d'Orient* 2 (1898) 1ff, 33ff

Vallarsi: D. Vallarsi, ed., *Sancti Eusebii Hieronymi . . . opera*, 2 ed., Venice, 1766–1772, 11 vols.

de Vaux, *Fouille*: R. de Vaux, "Fouille au Khirbet Qumran," *RB* 60 (1953) 83ff

VBW: *Vorträge der Bibliothek Warburg*

VC: *Vigiliae Christianae*

Vielhauer, *Evangelien*: P. Vielhauer, "Judenchristliche Evangelien," in Hennecke-Schnee-melcher 75ff

Viereck, *Ostraka*: P. Viereck, *Griechische und griechisch-demotische Ostraka . . . zu Strassburg, I: Texte*, Berlin, 1923

Völker: W. Völker, *Der wahre Gnostiker nach Clemens Alexandrinus*, Berlin, 1952 (*TU* 57)

Volkmar: G. Volkmar, "Über die Häretiker Epiphanes und Adrianus," *MWVZ* 1 (1856) 276ff

Voss: Voss, Isaac, ed., *Epistulae genuinae S. Ignatii Martyris*, Amsterdam, 1646

Vouaux: L. Vouaux, ed., *Les Actes de Paul*, Paris, 1913

VT: *Vetus Testamentum*

W.J.: Werner Jaeger

W.M.C.: William M. Calder III, Columbia University

W.V.: W. Völker, University of Mainz

Wagner, *Problem*: G. Wagner, *Das religionsgeschichtliche Problem von Römer 6, 1–11*, Stuttgart, 1962 (*ATANT* 39)

Waitz, *Evangelien*: A. Waitz, "Die judenchristlichen Evangelien in der altkirchlichen Literatur," in E. Hennecke, *Neutestamentliche Apokryphen*, 2 ed., Tübingen, 1924, 10ff

Walter, *Analyse*: N. Walter, "Zur Analyse von Mk. 10.17–31," *ZNW* 53 (1962) 206ff

Warnach, *Tauflehre*: V. Warnach, "Die Tauflehre des Römerbriefes in der neueren theologischen Diskussion," *Archiv für Liturgiewissenschaft* 5 (1958) 274

Weichert: V. Weichert, ed., *Demetrii et Libanii . . . τύποι ἐπιστολικοί*, Leipzig, 1910

Weinreich: O. Weinreich, "Zum Wundertypus der ΣΥΝΑΝΑΧΡΩΣΙΣ," *ARW* 32 (1935) 246ff

Weiss, *Christianity*: J. Weiss, *Earliest Christianity*, New York, 1959, 2 vols. (pagination continuous)

Wellhausen, *EM*: J. Wellhausen, *Das Evangelium Marci*, Berlin, 1903

Wendling, *Ur-Marcus*: E. Wendling, *Ur-Marcus*, Tübingen, 1905

Werblowsky, *Rite*: R. Werblowsky, "On the Baptismal Rite according to St. Hippolytus," in *Studia Patristica*, ed. K. Aland and F. Cross, Berlin, 1957, 93ff (*TU* 64)

Werner, *Einfluss*: M. Werner, *Der Einfluss paulinischer Theologie im Markusevangelium*, Giessen, 1923 (Beihefte *ZNW* 1)

Westcott and Hort: B. Westcott and F. Hort, ed., *The New Testament in the Original Greek*, London, 1881, 2 vols. (I: Text, II: Introduction, Appendix, app. paginated separately)

Wetstein: J. Wetstein, ed., *Novum Testamentum graecum*, Amsterdam, 1751–1752, 2 vols.

Wetter, *Sohn*: G. Wetter, *Der Sohn Gottes*, Göttingen, 1916

Wey: H. Wey, *Die Funktionen der bösen Geister bei den griechischen Apologeten*, Winterthur, 1957

Wikgren, *APXH*: A. Wikgren, "*APXH TOY EYAΓΓEΛIOY*," *JBL* 61 (1942) 11ff

Wilkens, *Erweckung*: W. Wilkens, "Die Erweckung des Lazarus," *ThZ* 15 (1959) 22ff

Williams, *Alterations*: C. Williams, *Alterations to the Text of the Synoptic Gospels and Acts*, Oxford, 1951

Williger: E. Williger, *Hagios*, Giessen, 1922 (*RGVV* 19.1)

Wilson, *Problem*: R. Wilson, *The Gnostic Problem*, London, 1958

Windisch-Preisker, *Briefe*: H. Windisch, *Die Katholischen Briefe*, 3 ed., ed. H. Preisker, Tübingen, 1951 (*HNT* 15)

Wohleb, *Beobachtungen*: L. Wohleb, "Beobachtungen zum Erzählungsstil des Markusevangeliums," *RQ* 36 (1928) 185ff

Wolfson: H. Wolfson, *Philo*, Cambridge, 1947, 2 vols.

Wordsworth and White: J. Wordsworth and H. White, *Novum Testamentum latine: Editio Maior*, I, Oxford, 1889

Wrede, *Messiasgeheimnis*: W. Wrede, *Das Messiasgeheimnis in den Evangelien*, Göttingen, 1901

Wytzes: J. Wytzes, "The Twofold Way (1)," *VC* 11 (1957) 226ff

Yates, *Form*: J. Yates, "The Form of Mk. 1.8b," *NTS* 4 (1958) 334ff

Yoder: J. Yoder, *Concordance to the Distinctive Greek Text of the Codex Bezae*, Leiden, 1961 (*NTTS* 2)

Yom Tov: see Heller

Zahn: T. Zahn, *Forschungen zur Geschichte des neutestamentlichen Kanons III: Supplementum Clementinum*, Erlangen, 1884

ZAW: *Zeitschrift für die alttestamentliche Wissenschaft*

ZDPV: *Zeitschrift des Deutschen Palästina-Vereins*

Zerwick, *Untersuchungen*: M. Zerwick, *Untersuchungen zum Markus-Stil*, Rome, 1937 (*Scripta Pontificii Instituti Biblici*)

ZKathTh: *Zeitschrift für katholische Theologie*

ZNW: *Zeitschrift für die neutestamentliche Wissenschaft*

ZRGG: *Zeitschrift für Religions-und Geistesgeschichte*

ZTK: *Zeitschrift für Theologie und Kirche*

THE FRAGMENT

TRANSLATION, TRANSCRIPTION, AND PHOTOGRAPHS

TRANSLATION OF THE TEXT

Folio 1, recto
From the letters of the most holy Clement, the author of the Stromateis. To Theodore.

You did well in silencing the unspeakable teachings of the Carpocratians. For these are the "wandering stars" referred to in the prophecy, who wander from the narrow road of the commandments into a boundless abyss of the carnal and bodily sins. |[1] For, priding themselves in knowledge, as they say, "of the deep things of Satan," they do not know that they are casting themselves away into "the nether world of the darkness" of falsity, and, boasting that they are free, they have become slaves of servile desires. Such men are to be opposed in all ways and altogether. For, even if they should say something true, one who loves the truth should not, even so, agree with them. For not all true things are the truth, nor should | that truth which merely seems true according to human opinions be preferred to the true truth, that according to the faith.

Now of the things they keep saying about the divinely inspired Gospel according to Mark, some are altogether falsifications, and others, even if they do contain some true elements, nevertheless are not reported truly. For the true things being mixed with inventions, are falsified, so that, as the saying goes, even the salt | loses its savor.

As for Mark, then, during Peter's stay in Rome he wrote an account of the Lord's doings, not, however, declaring all of them, nor yet hinting at the secret ones, but selecting what he thought most useful for increasing the faith of those who were being instructed. But when Peter died a martyr, Mark came over to Alexandria, bringing both his own notes and those of Peter, | from which he transferred to his former book the things suitable to whatever makes for progress toward knowledge. Thus he composed a more spiritual Gospel for the use of those who were being perfected. Nevertheless, he yet did not divulge the things not to be uttered, nor did he write down the hierophantic teaching of the Lord, but to the stories already written he added yet others and, moreover, brought in certain | sayings of which he knew the interpretation would, as a mystagogue, lead the hearers into the innermost sanctuary of that truth hidden by seven veils. Thus, in sum, he prepared matters, neither grudgingly nor incautiously, in my

1 verso
opinion, and, dying, he left his composition to the church in | Alexandria, where it even yet is most carefully guarded, being read only to those who are being initiated into the great mysteries.

But since the foul demons are always devising destruction for the race of men, Carpocrates, instructed by them and using deceitful arts, | so enslaved a certain presbyter of the church in Alexandria that he got from him a copy of the secret Gospel, which he both interpreted according to his blasphemous and carnal doctrine and, moreover, polluted, mixing with the spotless and holy words

---

1. These lines indicate as closely as possible the beginning of each fifth line of the Greek text.

446

10 utterly shameless lies. From this mixture is drawn off | the teaching of the Carpocratians.

To them, therefore, as I said above, one must never give way; nor, when they put forward their falsifications, should one concede that the secret Gospel is by Mark, but should even deny it on oath. For, "Not all true things are to be said to all men." For this reason the Wisdom of God, through Solomon, advises,

15 "Answer the fool from his folly," | teaching that the light of the truth should be hidden from those who are mentally blind. Again it says, "From him who has not shall be taken away," and, "Let the fool walk in darkness." But we are "children of light," having been illuminated by "the dayspring" of the spirit of the Lord "from on high," and "Where the Spirit of the Lord is," it says, "there is liberty," for "All things are pure to the pure."

20 To you, therefore, I shall not hesitate to answer the questions you have asked, | refuting the falsifications by the very words of the Gospel. For example, after "And they were in the road going up to Jerusalem," and what follows, until "After three days he shall arise," the secret Gospel brings the following material word for word: "And they come into Bethany. And a certain woman whose brother had died was there. And, coming, she prostrated herself before Jesus

25 and says to him, 'Son of David, | have mercy on me.' But the disciples rebuked her. And Jesus, being angered, went off with her into the garden where

2 recto the tomb was, and | straightway a great cry was heard from the tomb. And going near Jesus rolled away the stone from the door of the tomb. And straightway, going in where the youth was, he stretched forth his hand and raised him, seizing his hand. But the youth, looking upon him, loved him and | began to beseech

5 him that he might be with him. And going out of the tomb they came into the house of the youth, for he was rich. And after six days Jesus told him what to do and in the evening the youth comes to him, wearing a linen cloth over his naked body. And he remained with him that night, for | Jesus taught him the mystery

10 of the kingdom of God. And thence, arising, he returned to the other side of the Jordan."

After these words follows the text, "And James and John come to him," and all that section. But "naked man with naked man," and the other things about which you wrote, are not found.

And after the words, "And he comes into Jericho," the secret Gospel adds only,

15 "And | the sister of the youth whom Jesus loved and his mother and Salome were there, and Jesus did not receive them." But the many other things about which you wrote both seem to be and are falsifications.

Now the true explanation and that which accords with the true philosophy

[Here the fragment ends.]

+ ἐκ τῶν ἐπιστολῶν τοῦ ἁγιωτάτου κλήμεντος τοῦ στρωματέως· θεοδώρῳ·

καλῶς ἐποίησας ἐπιστομίσας τὰς ἀρρήτους διδασκαλίας τῶν καρποκρατιανῶν·

οὗτοι γὰρ οἱ προφητευθέντες ἀστέρες πλανῆται· οἱ ἀπὸ τῆς στενῆς τῶν ἐντολῶν ὁ

δοῦ εἰς ἀπέρατον ἄβυσσον πλανώμενοι τῶν σαρκικῶν καὶ ἐνσωμάτων ἁμαρτιῶν·

5 πεφυσιωμένοι γὰρ εἰς γνῶσιν· ὡς λέγουσι· τῶν βαθέων τοῦ σατανᾶ· λανθάνουσιν εἰς

τὸν ζόφον τοῦ σκότους τοῦ ψεύδους ἑαυτοὺς ἀπορρίπτοντες· καὶ καυχώμενοι

ἐλευθέρους εἶναι· δοῦλοι γεγόνασιν ἀνδραποδώδων ἐπιθυμιῶν· τούτοις οὖν ἀν

τιστατέον πάντη τε καὶ πάντως· εἰ γὰρ καί τι ἀληθὲς λέγοιεν· οὐδ' οὕτω συμ

φωνοίη ἂν αὐτοῖς ὁ τῆς ἀληθείας ἐραστής· οὐδὲ γὰρ πάντα τἀληθῆ ἀλήθεια· οὐδὲ

10 τὴν κατὰ τὰς ἀνθρωπίνας δόξας φαινομένην ἀλήθειαν προκριτέον τῆς ἀλη

θοῦς ἀληθείας τῆς κατὰ τὴν πίστιν· τῶν τοίνυν θρυλουμένων περὶ τοῦ θεοπνεύστου κα

τὰ μάρκον εὐαγγελίου· τὰ μὲν ψεύδεται παντελῶς· τὰ δὲ· εἰ καὶ ἀληθῆ τινα :

περιέχει· οὐδ' οὕτως ἀληθῶς παραδίδοται· συγκεκραμένα γὰρ τἀληθῆ

τοῖς πλάσμασι παραχαράσσεται ὥστε· τοῦτο δὴ τὸ λεγόμενον· καὶ τὸ ἅ

15 λας μωρανθῆναι· ὁ γοῦν μάρκος· κατὰ τὴν τοῦ πέτρου ἐν ῥώμῃ διατριβὴν·

ἀνέγραψε τὰς πράξεις τοῦ κυρίου· οὐ μέντοι πάσας ἐξαγγέλλων· οὐδὲ μὴν τὰς

μυστικὰς ὑποσημαίνων· ἀλλ' ἐκλεγόμενος ἃς χρησιμωτάτας ἐνόμισε πρὸς αὔ

ξησιν τῆς τῶν κατηχουμένων πίστεως· τοῦ δὲ πέτρου μαρτυρήσαντος· παρῆλθεν

εἰς ἀλεξάνδρειαν ὁ μάρκος· κομίζων καὶ ταταυτοῦ καὶ τὰ τοῦ πέτρου ὑπο

20 μνήματα· ἐξ ὧν μεταφέρων εἰς τὸ πρῶτον αὐτοῦ βιβλίον τὰ τοῖς προκόπ

τουσι περὶ τὴν γνῶσιν κατάλληλα· συνέταξε πνευματικώτερον εὐ :

αγγέλιον εἰς τὴν τῶν τελειουμένων χρῆσιν· οὐδέπω ὅμως αὐτὰ τὰ ἀπόρρη :

τα ἐξωρχήσατο· οὐδὲ κατέγραψε τὴν ἱεροφαντικὴν διδασκαλίαν τοῦ

κυρίου· ἀλλὰ ταῖς προγεγραμμέναις πράξεσιν ἐπιθεὶς καὶ ἄλλας· ἔτι προσε

25 πήγαγε λόγιά τινα ὧν ἠπίστατο τὴν ἐξήγησιν μυσταγωγήσειν τοὺς ἀκροα

τὰς εἰς τὸ ἄδυτον τῆς ἑπτάκις κεκαλυμμένης ἀληθείας· οὕτως οὖν :

προπαρεσκεύασεν· οὐ φθονερῶς οὐδ' ἀποφυλάκτως· ὡς ἐγὼ οἶμαι· καὶ

ἀποθνήσκων κατέλιπε τὸ αὐτοῦ σύγγραμμα τῇ ἐκκλησίᾳ τῇ ἐν :

16 κυρίου: MS κ̄ο̄ῡ, so again in 24 and II.18 (bis)   19 ταταυτοῦ: sic   23 ἱεροφαντικήν: MS perhap

26 ἑπτάκις: sic   27 και: sic (without accent)   27 ἀποθνήσκων: νησκ written over other letters now illegi

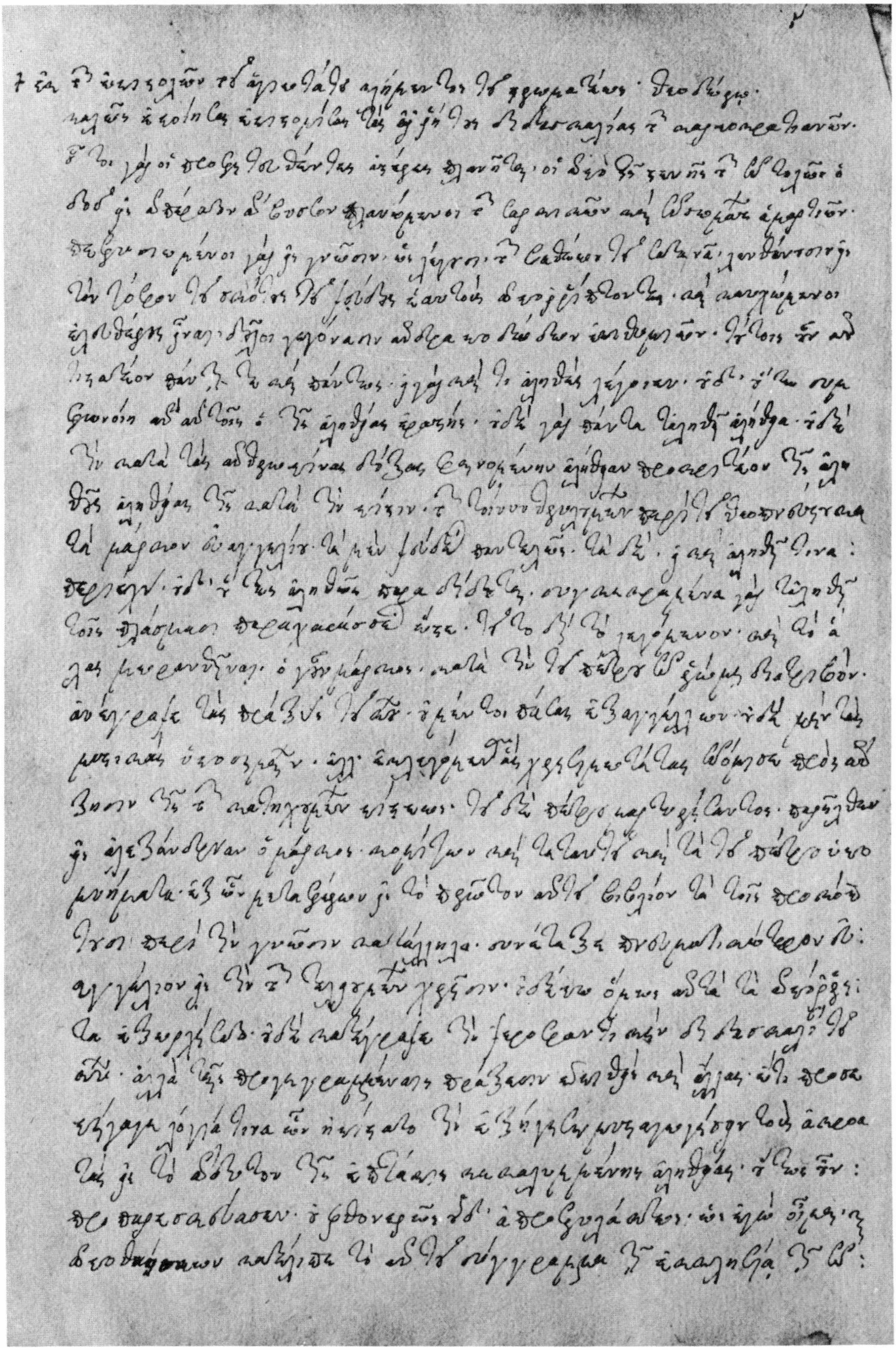

ἀλεξανδρείᾳ· ὅπου εἰσέτι νῦν ἀσφαλῶς εὖ μάλα τηρεῖται· ἀναγινωσ

κόμενον πρὸς αὐτοὺς μόνους τοὺς μυουμένους τὰ μεγάλα μυστήρια· τῶν δὲ μι

αρῶν δαιμόνων ὄλεθρον τῷ τῶν ἀνθρώπων γένει πάντοτε μηχανώντων· ὁ καρ

ποκράτης· ὑπ' αὐτῶν διδαχθείς· καὶ ἀπατηλοῖς τέχναις χρησάμενος·

5 οὕτω πρεσβύτερόν τινα τῆς ἐν ἀλεξανδρείᾳ ἐκκλησίας κατεδούλωσεν

ὥστε παρ' αὐτοῦ ἐκόμισεν ἀπόγραφον τοῦ μυστικοῦ εὐαγγελίου· ὁ καὶ

ἐξηγήσατο κατὰ τὴν βλασφημὸν καὶ σαρκικὴν αὐτοῦ δόξαν· ἔτι:

δὲ καὶ ἐμίανε· ταῖς ἀχράντοις καὶ ἁγίαις λέξεσιν ἀναμιγνὺς ἀναιδέ

στατα ψεύσματα· τοῦ δὲ κράματος τούτου ἐξαντλῆται τὸ τῶν καρποκρατι

10 ανῶν δόγμα· τούτοις οὖν· καθὼς καὶ προείρηκα· οὐδέποτε εἰκτέον· οὐ

δὲ προτείνουσιν αὐτοῖς τὰ κατεψευσμένα συγχωρητέον τοῦ μάρκου εἶ

ναι τὸ μυστικὸν εὐαγγέλιον· ἀλλὰ καὶ μεθ' ὅρκου ἀρνητέον· οὐ γὰρ ἅπασι πάν

τα ἀληθῆ λεκτέον· διὰ τοῦτο ἡ σοφία τοῦ θεοῦ διὰ ϲολομῶντος παραγ

γέλλει· ἀποκρίνου τῷ μωρῷ ἐκ τῆς μωρίας αὐτοῦ· πρὸς τοὺς τυφλοὺς τὸν

15 νοῦν τὸ φῶς τῆς ἀληθείας δεῖν ἐπικρύπτεσθαι διδάσκουσα· αὐτίκα φη

σί· τοῦ δὲ μὴ ἔχοντος ἀρθήσεται· καὶ· ὁ μωρὸς ἐν σκότει πορευέσθω· ἡμεῖς

δὲ υἱοὶ φωτός ἐσμεν· πεφωτισμένοι τῇ ἐξ ὕψους ἀνατολῇ τοῦ πνεύματος

τοῦ κυρίου· οὗ δὲ τὸ πνεῦμα τοῦ κυρίου· φησίν· ἐκεῖ ἐλευθερία· πάντα γὰρ κα

θαρὰ τοῖς καθαροῖς· σοὶ τοίνυν οὐκ ὀκνήσω τὰ ἠρωτημένα ἀποκρί:

20 νασθαι· δι' αὐτῶν τοῦ εὐαγγελίου λέξεων τὰ κατεψευσμένα ἐλέγχων· ἀ:

μέλει μετὰ τὸ· ἦσαν δὲ ἐν τῇ ὁδῷ ἀναβαίνοντες εἰς ἱεροσόλυμα· καὶ τὰ

ἑξῆς ἕως· μετὰ τρεῖς ἡμέρας ἀναστήσεται· ὧδε ἐπιφέρει κατὰ λέξιν·

καὶ ἔρχονται εἰς βηθανίαν καὶ ἦν ἐκεῖ μία γυνὴ ἧς ὁ ἀδελφὸς αὐτῆς ἀπέ:

θανεν· καὶ ἐλθοῦσα προσεκύνησε τὸν ἰησοῦν καὶ λέγει αὐτῷ· υἱὲ δα

25 βὶδ ἐλέησόν με· οἱ δὲ μαθηταὶ ἐπετίμησαν αὐτῇ· καὶ ὀργισθεὶς ὁ

ἰησοῦς ἀπῆλθεν μετ' αὐτῆς εἰς τὸν κῆπον ὅπου ἦν τὸ μνημεῖον· καὶ

3 ἀνθρώπων; MS ἀνῶν   6 ὁ: sic   7 βλασφημὸν: sic   9 ἐξαντλῆται: almost certainly, but ἐξηντλῆται is possi
21 ἱεροσόλυμα: sic   22 ἑξῆς: sic

εὐθὺς ἠκούσθη ἐκ τοῦ μνημείου φωνὴ μεγάλη· καὶ προσελθὼν ὁ ἰησοῦς ἀπ

εκύλισε τὸν λίθον ἀπὸ τῆς θύρας τοῦ μνημείου· καὶ εἰσελθὼν εὐθὺς ὅπου

ἦν ὁ νεανίσκος ἐξέτεινεν τὴν χεῖρα καὶ ἤγειρεν αὐτόν· κρατήσας :

τῆς χειρός· ὁ δὲ νεανίσκος ἐμβλέψας αὐτῷ ἠγάπησεν αὐτὸν καὶ :

5 ἤρξατο παρακαλεῖν αὐτὸν ἵνα μετ᾽ αὐτοῦ ᾖ· καὶ ἐξελθόντες ἐκ

τοῦ μνημείου ἦλθον εἰς τὴν οἰκίαν τοῦ νεανίσκου· ἦν γὰρ πλούσιος· καὶ μεθ᾽

ἡμέρας ἓξ ἐπέταξεν αὐτῷ ὁ ἰησοῦς· καὶ ὀψίας γενομένης ἔρχεται ὁ

νεανίσκος πρὸς αὐτόν· περιβεβλημένος σινδόνα ἐπὶ γυμνοῦ· καὶ

ἔμεινε σὺν αὐτῷ τὴν νύκτα ἐκείνην· ἐδίδασκε γὰρ αὐτὸν ὁ

10 ἰησοῦς τὸ μυστήριον τῆς βασιλείας τοῦ θεοῦ· ἐκεῖθεν δὲ ἀναστὰς :

ἐπέστρεψεν εἰς τὸ πέραν τοῦ ἰορδάνου· ἐπὶ μὲν τούτοις ἔπεται τὸ· καὶ

προσπορεύονται αὐτῷ ἰάκωβος καὶ ἰωάννης· καὶ πᾶσα ἡ περι

κοπή· τὸ δὲ γυμνὸς γυμνῷ καὶ τἆλλα περὶ ὧν ἔγραψας οὐκ εὑ :

ρίσκεται· μετὰ δὲ τό· καὶ ἔρχεται εἰς ἰεριχὼ ἐπάγει μόνον· καὶ ἦ

15 σαν ἐκεῖ ἡ ἀδελφὴ τοῦ νεανίσκου ὃν ἠγάπα αὐτὸν ὁ ἰησοῦς· καὶ

ἡ μήτηρ αὐτοῦ καὶ σαλώμη· καὶ οὐκ ἀπεδέξατο αὐτὰς ὁ ἰησοῦς·

τὰ δὲ ἄλλα τὰ πολλὰ ἃ ἔγραψας ψεύσματα καὶ φαίνεται καὶ ἔστιν· ἡ

μὲν οὖν ἀληθὴς καὶ κατὰ τὴν ἀληθῆ φιλοσοφίαν ἐξήγησις

11 και: sic (without accent)   13 ουκ: sic (before a rough breathing)
17 ἔστιν the ς was miswritten but corrected by the original hand

Autograph of the Oecumenical Patriarch
Callinicus III, about 1760. See p. 2.
(Reproduced by permission of Professor V. Scouvaras)